Worldwide Distributor:
Ruşen MEYLANİ and Mustafa Atak
RUSH Publications and Educatio
1901 60th Place, L7432, Bradenton
FL 34203
United States

(Ruşen MEYLANİ and Mustafa Atakan ARIBURNU are founders of *RUSH* Publications and Educational Consultancy, LLC; each of whom owns 50% of this company.)

All inquiries, suggestions and comments should be addressed to:

Ruşen MEYLANİ
ARMA Publishing and Trade Ltd.
Akatlar Yildirim Oguz Goker C. 8. Gazeteciler Sitesi A1 Blok No: 2
Levent, Istanbul
80630, TURKEY

url	:	http://www.rushsociety.com
e-mail	:	rushco@superonline.com
phone	:	+90 212 278 4954
fax	:	+90 212 278 4953

Printed in Istanbul, Turkey; by Seçil Ofset; **phone:** +90 212 629 0615

ISBN: 0-9748222-1-3

Author: Ruşen MEYLANİ
Co – Authors: Emel UYSAL, Ebru Acuner MEYLANİ
Figures by: Fatih KAYA
Edited by: Emel UYSAL
Answers to Exercises: Emel UYSAL and Ruşen MEYLANİ
Solutions to Model Tests: Ahmet ARDUÇ
Cover design by: Pınar ERKORKMAZ; **e-mail:** mail@pinare.com

All graphics and text based on TI 83 – 84 have been used with the permission granted by Texas Instruments.

From: Bassuk, Larry <l-bassuk@ti.com>
Sent: Thursday, February 27, 2002 16:23 PM
To: Meylani, Rusen <meylani@superonline.com>; Foster, Herbert <h-foster@ti.com>; Vidori, Erdel <e-vidori@ti.com>
RE: USAGE OF TI 83+ FACILITIES IN MY SAT II MATH BOOKS
Rusen Meylani,
Again we thank you for your interest in the calculators made by Texas Instruments.
Texas Instruments is pleased to grant you permission to copy graphical representations of our calculators and to copy graphics and text that describes the use of our calculators for use in the two books you mention in your e-mail below.
We ask that you provide the following credit for each representation of our calculators and the same credit, in a way that does not interrupt the flow of the book, for the copied graphics and text:
Courtesy Texas Instruments
Regards,
Larry Bassuk
Copyright Counsel
972-917-5458

-----Original Message-----
From: Bassuk, Larry
Sent: Thursday, February 21, 2002 9:14 AM
To: 'Rusen Meylani'; Foster, Herbert
Subject: RE: USAGE OF TI 83+ FACILITIES IN MY SAT II MATH BOOKS
We thank you for your interest in TI calculators.
I am copying this message to Herb Foster, Marketing Communications Manager for our calculator group. With Herb's agreement, Texas Instruments grants you permission to copy the materials you describe below for the limited purposes you describe below.
Regards,
Larry Bassuk
Copyright Counsel
972-917-5458

-----Original Message-----
From: Rusen Meylani [mailto:meylani@superonline.com]
Sent: Wednesday, February 20, 2002 5:57 PM
To: copyrightcounsel@list.ti.com - Copyright Legal Counsel
Subject: USAGE OF TI 83+ FACILITIES IN MY SAT II MATH BOOKS
Dear Sir,
I am an educational consultant in Istanbul Turkey and I am working with Turkish students who would like to go to the USA for college education. I am writing SAT II Mathematics books where I make use of TI 83+ facilities, screen shots, etc. heavily.
Will you please indicate the copyright issues that I will need while publishing my book?
Thanks very much in advance. I am looking forward to hearing from you soon.
Rusen Meylani.

ACKNOWLEDGMENTS

I would like to thank TEXAS INSTRUMENTS for providing scientists and mathematicians such powerful hand - held computers, the TI family of graphing calculators. With these wonderful machines, teachers of mathematics can go beyond horizons without the need to reinvent the wheel all the time. I would also like to thank TEXAS INSTRUMENTS for providing me with a limited copyright to use the graphs that have been produced by the TI 83 / 84 Family of graphing calculators throughout this book.

I would like to thank Zeynel Abidin ERDEM, the chairman of the Turkish – American Businessmen Association (TABA) for his valuable support and contributions on our projects.

I would like to thank Pınar ERKORKMAZ for her excellent work on the cover design and Fatih KAYA for his valuable contributions on the graphics.

I would like to thank Selahi ÇİLOĞLU on behalf of Seçil OFSET for the superb printing of this book.

I would like to thank the editors, Emel UYSAL, and my wife Ebru Acuner MEYLANİ, who have helped me in editing and proofreading this book. Without their efforts this book would have never been completed.

I would like to thank Emel UYSAL, and Ahmet ARDUÇ, for solving the exercises and model tests.

I would like to thank Nuran TUNCALI; for showing me the right path to follow and everything else that she has done and has been doing since the day I had the chance to become her student.

I would like to thank Yorgo İSTEFANOPULOS, Ayşın ERTÜZÜN, Bayram SEVGEN and Zeki ÖZDEMİR, for whatever I know of analytical thinking and mathematics.

I would like to thank my mother and father for being who I am.

I would like to thank my wife who has continuously encouraged and supported me throughout every stage of preparing this book.

Last but not the least, I would like to thank my former student and current partner Mustafa Atakan ARIBURNU, who has supported me all the way, believing in this project and the others since the day we first met. Therefore I dedicate this book specifically to Atakan with a special indication that I am proud of him.

To Atakan,

the one person who believed in me right from the very first moment we met

"**Without your support, none of our projects would have become real. We love you.**"

Mustafa Atakan ARIBURNU

Atakan is a young entrepreneur who has the skills and talent for establishing a multinational company. After graduating from the Koç School* with high honors, he got his Bachelor of Arts degree in Economics from the Johns Hopkins University in Baltimore, Maryland, USA. Atakan and the author had a student – tutor relationship at first, that extended to a long term friendship, finally becoming a lifetime partnership. Atakan is an expert in management strategies and he is not only a real genius but also a pride to his parents and the *RUSH* crew especially to the author.

*The Koç School is a distinguished and internationally recognized educational institution located in İstanbul, TURKEY.

If you give yourself to mathematics, mathematics will give you the world.

TABLE OF CONTENTS

LEGEND

1-2	Covered in both Level 1 and Level 2
1	Covered in Level 1 only
2	Covered in Level 2 only
O	Optional topics (likely to appear in the future)

For easier usage, the Table of Contents can be downloaded from:

w w w . r u s h s o c i e t y . c o m

	ACKNOWLEDGMENTS	iii
	TABLE OF CONTENTS	v
	PREFACE	xv
1-2	**CHAPTER 1 – FUNCTIONS**	1
1-2	**1.1 ALGEBRA AND BASICS**	3
1-2	Interval notation	3
1-2	Number sets	3
1-2	Properties of the real numbers	3
1-2	Fractions	4
1-2	Inequalities	4
1-2	Letters in the English alphabet	4
1-2	Unit conversions	4
1-2	Rules of divisibility	5
1-2	Absolute values	5
2	Means	8
1-2	**1.2 MOST COMMON GRAPHING CALCULATOR TECHNIQUES**	13
1-2	Solving equations with TI 83 – 84	13
1-2	Solving inequalities with TI 83 – 84	13
1-2	**1.3 FUNCTIONS**	16
1-2	Definition	16
1-2	Vertical line test	17
1-2	Horizontal line test	17
O	Types of functions	19
O	Into function	19
O	Onto function	19
O	One to one function	19
O	Many to one function	19
1-2	Constant function	20
1-2	Identity function	20
1-2	Multivariable function	20
1-2	Polynomial function	20
1-2	Domains of specific functions	22
1-2	Operations on functions	26
1-2	How to find the inverse of a function	27
1-2	Function compositions and inverses	28
1-2	Finding other function when the composition and one function are given	28
1-2	Inverses of specific functions	31
1-2	Completing the square	33
1-2	Reflections	35
2	Periodic functions	36
1-2	Evenness and oddness	45

1-2	Algebraically	45
1-2	Graphically	45
1-2	Polynomial functions	45
O	Relations given as sets	45
O	Relations given algebraically	45
1-2	Tests for symmetry	46
1-2	Basic functions	52
1-2	Line passing through the origin	52
1-2	Identity function	52
1-2	Absolute value function	52
1-2	Square function	52
1-2	Cube function	52
1-2	Square root function	52
2	Cube – root function	52
2	Reciprocal function	53
2	Chimney function	53
2	Greatest integer function	53
2	Sine function	54
2	Cosine function	54
1-2	Exponential growth function	54
1-2	Exponential decay function	54
2	Logarithmic function (increasing)	54
2	Logarithmic function (decreasing)	54
2	Hyperbolic rational function (increasing)	55
2	Hyperbolic rational function (decreasing)	55
1-2	1.4 GEOMETRIC TRANSFORMATIONS	56
1-2	Types of transformations	56
O	Isometry	56
1-2	Rotation	56
1-2	Stretch	57
1-2	Reflection	57
O	Enlargement	58
1-2	Translation	58
O	Shear	58
2	Inverse transformations	59
O	Composition of transformations	60
1-2	1.5 SYMMETRY AND ROTATIONS	63
1-2	Types of symmetry	63
1-2	Line symmetry	63
1-2	Point symmetry	64
1-2	1.6 ADVANCED GRAPHING OF TRANSFORMATIONS ON FUNCTIONS	68
1-2	Horizontal shifts	68
1-2	Horizontal shrink – stretch	69
1-2	Reflections in the y – axis	69
1-2	Vertical shifts	70
1-2	Vertical shrink – stretch	70
1-2	Reflections in the x – axis	71
1-2	Absolute values	71
1-2	Inverse of a function	72
1-2	Reciprocal of a function	73
1-2	Table of transformations	74
1-2	1.7 LINEAR FUNCTIONS	79
1-2	Distance between two points	79
1-2	Midpoint of a line segment	79
1-2	Parallelogram	80
1-2	Slope of a line segment	81

1-2	General form of a line	81
1-2	Slope – intercept form of a line	81
1-2	Two lines (slope-intercept form)	82
1-2	Two lines (general form)	82
1-2	Distance from a point to a line	83
1-2	Angle between two lines	83
1-2	Area of a closed convex figure	84
1-2	Line equations	85
1-2	Perpendicular bisector of a line segment	87
1-2	Reflections	87
1-2	Linear models	88
1-2	Finding the equation of a line using regression	88
2	Linear interpolation	88
1-2	**1.8 QUADRATIC FUNCTIONS**	93
1-2	Roots of a quadratic equation	93
1-2	Sum and product of the roots of a quadratic equation	94
1-2	Given the roots, construct the equation	94
1-2	Completing the square	97
2	A parabola and a line	97
2	Quadratic Models	98
1-2	**1.9 POLYNOMIAL FUNCTIONS**	102
1-2	Coefficients	102
1-2	Constant term	102
1-2	Linear term	102
1-2	Quadratic term	102
1-2	Cubic term	102
1-2	Quartic term	102
1-2	Quintic term	102
1-2	Leading term	102
1-2	Degree of the polynomial	102
1-2	Leading coefficient	102
1-2	Zero polynomial	102
1-2	Constant polynomial	102
1-2	Linear polynomial	102
1-2	Quadratic polynomial	102
2	Cubic polynomial	102
2	Quartic polynomial	102
2	Quintic polynomial	102
1-2	Real polynomial	102
1-2	Rational polynomial	102
1-2	Integral polynomial	102
1-2	Monomial	102
1-2	Binomial	102
1-2	Trinomial	102
1-2	Identities	103
1-2	Properties of higher degree polynomial functions	103
1-2	Remainder theorem	104
1-2	Factor theorem	104
1-2	Rational root theorem	105
2	Relation between zeros and coefficients	106
2	Descartes' rule of signs	106
1-2	Synthetic division	107
1-2	**1.10 TRIGONOMETRY**	115
1-2	Definition of an angle	115
1-2	Angle in standard position	115
1-2	Circle equation	115

1-2	Trigonometric ratios in the right triangle	116
1-2	SOH – CAH – TOA	116
1-2	Angle of elevation and angle of depression	116
2	Unit circle	121
2	Signs of trigonometric functions	121
2	All Silver Tea Cups	121
1-2	Special angles	121
1-2	45°	121
1-2	30°, 60°	122
1-2	0°, 90°, 180°, 270°, 360°	122
2	Radian and degree	123
1-2	Arc length and area of a sector	124
1-2	α in degrees	124
2	α in radians	124
1-2	Trigonometric identities	125
1-2	Easy	125
2	Hard	125
2	Functions and cofunctions	125
2	Reference angle	125
2	Common transformations on trigonometric functions	127
2	Special cases	127
1-2	Trigonometric equations	128
1-2	Solving trigonometric equations with the TI	128
2	Solving trigonometric inequalities with TI	131
2	Sum and difference formulas	134
2	Double angle formulas	134
2	Sine rule	135
2	Cosine rule	136
2	Area of a triangle	136
2	Domains and ranges of trigonometric functions	139
2	Even and odd trigonometric functions	139
2	Graphs of trigonometric functions	140
2	Sinx	140
2	Cosx	140
2	Tanx	140
2	Cotx	140
2	Secx	140
2	Cscx	140
2	Periodicity	141
2	Odd powers of sine and cosine	141
2	Even powers of sine and cosine	141
2	All powers of tangent and cotangent	141
2	Finding a trigonometric model	142
2	Amplitude	142
2	Period	142
2	Frequency	142
2	Phase shift	142
2	Offset	142
2	Axis of wave	142
2	Range	144
2	Inverse trigonometric functions	144
2	$Sin^{-1}x$	144
2	$Cos^{-1}x$	144
2	$Tan^{-1}x$	144
2	$Cot^{-1}x$	144
2	$Sec^{-1}x$	144

2	$Csc^{-1}x$	144
2	Domains and ranges inverse trigonometric functions	145
2	Solving inverse trigonometric equations with TI	145
2	Built in trigonometric functions in TI	147
2	Additional trigonometric functions with TI	147
1-2	**1.11 EXPONENTIAL AND LOGARITHMIC FUNCTIONS**	166
1-2	Exponents	166
1-2	Exponential growth	166
1-2	Exponential decay	166
1-2	Logarithms	169
2	Logarithmic inequalities	170
2	Domain of logarithms	170
2	**1.12 RATIONAL FUNCTIONS**	180
2	Zero	180
2	Hole	180
2	Vertical asymptote	180
2	Horizontal asymptote	180
2	Existence of limit	180
2	Continuity	180
2	Limits at infinity	180
2	Hyperbolic rational functions	180
2	Exploring limits with TI	182
2	**1.13 GREATEST INTEGER FUNCTION**	188
2	TI usage	188
1-2	**CHAPTER 2 – COMBINATORICS**	193
1-2	**2.1 PERMUTATIONS AND COMBINATIONS**	195
1-2	Factorial notation	195
1-2	Counting by multiplication	195
1-2	Definition of permutation	195
1-2	Definition of combination	195
1-2	Round table problem	196
1-2	Necklace – bracelet problem	196
1-2	Repeated permutations	197
1-2	Difference between permutation and combination	198
1-2	Properties of combinations	199
2	**2.2 BINOMIAL THEOREM**	209
2	Pascal's triangle	210
2	Negative and fractional powers of binomials	211
1-2	**2.3 PROBABILITY**	213
1-2	Set theory in brief	213
1-2	The universal set	213
1-2	Intersection	213
1-2	Union	213
1-2	Difference	213
1-2	Complement	214
1-2	Sample space	214
1-2	Event	214
1-2	Probability of an event	214
1-2	Odds in favor of an event	215
1-2	Odds against an event	215
1-2	Combined events	215
1-2	Mutually exclusive events	215
1-2	Independent events	215
1-2	Conditional probability	216
1-2	Venn diagrams	216
1-2	Lists and charts	217

1-2	Lists	217
1-2	Possibility space charts	217
1-2	Tables of outcomes	218
1-2	Tree diagrams	220
1-2	Binomial probabilities	221
1-2	2.4 STATISTICS	229
O	Population	229
O	Sample	229
O	Discrete data	229
2	Frequency	229
1-2	Mean	229
1-2	Median	229
1-2	Mode	229
1-2	Range	229
2	Variance and standard deviation	229
2	Quartiles	229
1-2	TI calculator usage	230
1-2	**CHAPTER 3 – GEOMETRY**	237
1-2	3.1 BASICS	239
1-2	3.2 LOCUS	245
1-2	Two dimensional loci	245
1-2	Conic sections in two dimensions	246
1-2	Three dimensional loci	246
1-2	3.3 ANGLES	248
1-2	3.4 POLYGONS	252
1	3.5 TRIANGLES	254
1	3.7 CONGRUENCE	263
1-2	3.8 SIMILARITY	265
1	3.9 QUADRILATERALS	269
1	3.10 CIRCLES	273
1	3.11 THREE-DIMENSIONAL GEOMETRY	284
1	3.12 INSCRIBED FIGURES IN TWO DIMENSIONS	291
1	Quadrilateral inscribed in a circle	291
1	Circle inscribed in a quadrilateral	291
1	Circle inscribed in a square	291
1	Square inscribed in a circle	292
1	Rectangle inscribed in a circle	292
1	Circle inscribed in a triangle	292
1	Triangle inscribed in a circle	292
1	Equilateral triangle inscribed in a circle	292
1	Circle inscribed in an equilateral triangle	293
1	Isosceles triangle inscribed in a circle	293
1	Circle inscribed in an isosceles triangle	293
1-2	3.13 INSCRIBED FIGURES IN THREE DIMENSIONS	294
1-2	Sphere inscribed in a cube	294
1-2	Cube inscribed in a sphere	294
1-2	Rectangular box inscribed in a sphere	294
1-2	Cylinder inscribed in a sphere	295
1-2	Cone inscribed in a sphere	295
1-2	Sphere inscribed in a cone	295
1-2	Cylinder inscribed in a cone	296
1-2	3.14 COMMON ROTATIONS	298
1-2	**CHAPTER 4 – MISCELLANEOUS**	305
1-2	4.1 COMPLEX NUMBERS, POLAR COORDINATES AND GRAPHING	307
1	Rectangular coordinates	307
2	Polar coordinates	307

2	Rectangular to polar conversion	307
2	Polar to rectangular conversion	307
O	Euler's identity	307
1-2	De Moivre's identities	307
1-2	TI usage	308
1-2	Properties of complex numbers	308
2	Polar graphing with TI	309
1-2	**4.2 VECTORS AND THREE DIMENSIONAL COORDINATE GEOMETRY**	313
1-2	Vector	313
1-2	Scalar	313
1-2	Position vector	313
1-2	Negative of a vector	313
1-2	Magnitude of a vector	313
1-2	Resultant vector	313
1-2	Linear combination of two vectors	314
1-2	Unit vector	315
1-2	Basis vectors	315
1-2	Scalar product, dot product or inner product	315
1-2	Two vectors being parallel	315
1-2	Two vectors being perpendicular	315
2	Plane equation	316
2	x, y, z intercepts	316
2	xy, xz, yz traces	316
2	3 – D line equation	317
2	Direction vector of a line	317
2	Direction cosines of a line	317
2	Cartesian (rectangular) form of a line	317
2	Parametric form of a line	317
2	Vector form of a line	317
2	Distance from a point to a plane	318
2	Distance between two points	319
2	Reflections in three dimensions	319
2	Sphere equation	319
1-2	**4.3 PARAMETRIC EQUATIONS AND PARAMETRIC GRAPHING**	319
2	**4.4 CONIC SECTIONS**	321
2	Circle	324
2	The unit circle	325
2	Semicircles centered at the origin	325
2	Ellipse	326
2	Ellipses in standard position (x – ellipse and y – ellipse)	326 – 327
2	Coordinates of the center of the ellipse	326 – 327
2	Foci of the ellipse	326 – 327
2	Vertices of the ellipse	326 – 327
2	Length of major axis of the ellipse	326 – 327
2	Length of minor axis of the ellipse	326 – 327
2	Eccentricity of the ellipse	326 – 327
2	Directrices of the ellipse	326 – 327
2	Length of latus rectum of the ellipse	326 – 327
2	Area of the ellipse	326 – 327
2	When coordinates of center is (h,k)	327
2	Hyperbola	330
2	Hyperbolas in standard position (x – hyperbola and y – hyperbola)	330
2	Coordinates of the center of the hyperbola	330
2	Vertices of the hyperbola	330
2	Foci of the hyperbola	330
2	Transverse axis of the hyperbola	330

2	Conjugate axis of the hyperbola	330
2	Eccentricity of the hyperbola	330
2	Directrices of the hyperbola	330
2	Length of latus rectum of the hyperbola	330
2	Asymptotes of the hyperbola	330
2	When coordinates of center is (h,k)	331
2	Hyperbolas in the form xy = k	334
2	Hyperbolic rational functions	334
2	Domain of a hyperbolic rational function	334
2	Range of a hyperbolic rational function	334
2	Horizontal asymptote of a hyperbolic rational function	334
2	Vertical asymptote of a hyperbolic rational function	334
2	Parabola	335
2	Parabolas in standard position	335
2	Vertex of the parabola	335
2	Directrix of the parabola	335
2	Focus of the parabola	335
2	Eccentricity of the parabola	335
2	Axis of symmetry of the parabola	335
2	Eccentricity of the parabola	335
2	Length of the latus rectum of the parabola	335
2	When coordinates of the vertex is (h,k)	336
1-2	**4.5 SEQUENCES AND SERIES**	343
1-2	Sequences	343
1-2	Series	343
1-2	Infinite sequence	343
1-2	Finite sequence	343
1-2	Infinite series	343
1-2	Finite series	343
1-2	Arithmetic sequences and series	343
1-2	Explicit definition of an arithmetic sequence	343
1-2	Recursive definition of an arithmetic sequence	343
1-2	Sum of the first n terms of an arithmetic series	343
1-2	Geometric sequences and series	343
1-2	Explicit definition of a geometric sequence	343
1-2	Recursive definition of a geometric sequence	344
1-2	Sum of the first n terms of a geometric series	344
1-2	Infinite geometric series	344
1-2	Sigma notation	346
O	Commonly used formulas	346
1-2	**4.6 VARIATION**	349
1-2	Direct variation	349
1-2	Inverse variation	349
1-2	**4.7 BINARY OPERATIONS**	351
1-2	Closure property	351
1-2	Associative property	351
1-2	Identity element	351
1-2	Inverse element	351
1-2	Commutative property	351
1-2	**4.8 COMPUTER PROGRAMS**	353
2	**4.9 LOGIC**	355
2	Conjunction	355
2	Disjunction	355
2	Negation of conjunction	355
2	Negation of disjunction	355
2	Implication	355

2	Sufficient condition	355
2	Necessary condition	355
2	Double implication	355
2	Statement	355
2	Equivalent statement	355
2	Negation of a statement	355
2	Converse of a statement	355
2	Inverse of a statement	355
2	Contrapositive of a statement	355
2	Tautology	355
2	Contradiction	355
2	Indirect proof	355
2	Negations	355
2	Truth tables	356
2	Or	356
2	And	356
2	Implication	356
2	4.10 MATRICES AND DETERMINANTS	358
2	Matrices	358
2	Matrix arithmetic	358
2	Matrix multiplication	358
2	2 by 2 matrices	360
2	Identity matrix	360
2	Zero matrix	360
2	Diagonal matrix	360
2	Triangular matrices	360
2	Inverse	360
2	Matrix transposition	361
2	Determinants	361
2	Two by two determinant	361
2	Three by three determinant	361
2	Properties of determinants	361
2	Cramer's rule for 2 unknowns	362
2	Cramer's rule for 3 unknowns	362
1-2	4.11 WORD PROBLEMS	364
1-2	Rate problems	367
1-2	Mixture problems	368
1-2	Work – pool problems	369
1-2	Age problems	370
1-2	Investment problems	370
1-2	Fraction word problems	371
1-2	Miscellaneous word problems	371
	CHAPTER 5 – MODEL TESTS	377
	Level 1 – Model Tests 1	379
	Level 1 – Model Tests 2	397
	Level 1 – Model Tests 3	409
	Level 1 – Model Tests 4	425
	Level 1 – Model Tests 5	441
	Level 2 – Model Tests 1	455
	Level 2 – Model Tests 2	467
	Level 2 – Model Tests 3	479
	Level 2 – Model Tests 4	491
	Level 2 – Model Tests 5	503
	Answers to Level 1 – Model Tests	515
	Answers to Level 2 – Model Tests	516
	Level 1 – Model Tests 1 Solutions	517

Level 1 – Model Tests 2 Solutions	522
Level 1 – Model Tests 3 Solutions	526
Level 1 – Model Tests 4 Solutions	531
Level 1 – Model Tests 5 Solutions	536
Level 2 – Model Tests 1 Solutions	540
Level 2 – Model Tests 2 Solutions	545
Level 2 – Model Tests 3 Solutions	550
Level 2 – Model Tests 4 Solutions	555
Level 2 – Model Tests 5 Solutions	559
ANSWERS TO EXERCISES	563
INDEX	575

PREFACE

Mathematics Level 1 and Mathematics Level 2 are the two subject tests that the College Board offers. Both tests require at least a scientific, preferably a graphing, calculator. Each test is one hour long. These subject tests were formerly known as the Math Level IC and Math Level IIC subject tests.

Mathematics Level 1 Subject Test

Structure: A Mathematics Level 1 test is made of 50 multiple choice questions from the following topics:

- Algebra and algebraic functions
- Geometry (plane Euclidean, coordinate and three-dimensional)
- Elementary statistics and probability, data interpretation, counting problems, including measures of mean, median and mode (central tendency.)
- Miscellaneous questions of logic, elementary number theory, arithmetic and geometric sequences.

Calculators in the Test

Approximately 60 percent of the questions in the test should be solved without the use of the calculator. For the remaining 40 percent, the calculator will be useful if not necessary.

Mathematics Level 2 Subject Test

Structure: A Mathematics Level 2 test also is made of 50 multiple choice questions. The topics included are as follows:

- Algebra
- Geometry (coordinate geometry and three-dimensional geometry)
- Trigonometry
- Functions
- Statistics, probability, permutations, and combinations
- Miscellaneous questions of logic and proof, elementary number theory, limits and sequences

Calculators in the Test

In Math Level 2, 40 percent of the questions should be solved the without the use of the calculator. In the remaining 60 percent, the calculator will be useful if not necessary.

Which calculator is allowed and which is not

The simplest reference to this question is this: No device with a QWERTY keyboard is allowed. Besides that any hand held organizers, mini or pocket computers, laptops, pen input devices or writing pads, devices making sounds (Such as "talking" computers) and devices requiring electricity from an outlet will not be allowed. It would be the wisest to stick with TI

84 or TI 89. Both of these calculators are easy to use and are the choices of millions of students around the world who take SAT exams and also university students in their math courses. It is very important to be familiar with the calculator that you're going to use in the test. You will lose valuable time if you try to figure it out during the test time.

Be sure to learn to solve each and every question in this book. They are carefully chosen to give you handiness and speed with your calculator. You will probably gain an extra 150 to 200 points in a very short period of time.

IMPORTANT: Always take the exam with fresh batteries. Bring fresh batteries and a backup calculator to the test center. You may not share calculators. You certainly will not be provided with a backup calculator or batteries. No one can or will assist you in the case of a calculator malfunction. In such case, you have the option of notifying the supervisor to cancel your scores for that test. Therefore, always be prepared for the worst case scenario (Don't forget Murphy's Rules.)

Number of questions per topics covered

The following chart shows the approximate number of questions per topic for both tests.

Topics	Approximate Number of Questions	
	Level 1	Level 2
Algebra	15	9
Plane Euclidean Geometry	10	0
Coordinate Geometry	6	6
Three-dimensional Geometry	3	4
Trigonometry	4	10
Functions	6	12
Statistics	3	3
Miscellaneous	3	6

Similarities and Differences

Some topics are covered in both tests, such as elementary algebra, three-dimensional geometry, coordinate geometry, statistics and basic trigonometry. But the tests differ greatly in the following areas.

Differences between the tests

Although some questions may be appropriate for both tests, the emphasis for Level 2 is on more advanced content. The tests differ significantly in the following areas:

Geometry

Euclidian geometry makes up the significant portion of the geometry questions in the Math Level 1 test. Though in Level 2, questions are of the topics of coordinate geometry, transformations, and three-dimensional geometry and there are no direct questions of Euclidian geometry.

Trigonometry

The trigonometry questions on Level 1 are primarily limited to right triangle trigonometry and the fundamental relationships among the trigonometric ratios. Level 2 places more emphasis on the properties and graphs of the trigonometric functions, the inverse trigonometric functions, trigonometric equations and identities, and the laws of sines and cosines. The trigonometry questions in Level 2 exam are primarily on graphs and properties of the trigonometric functions, trigonometric equations, trigonometric identities, the inverse trigonometric functions, laws of sines and cosines. On the other hand, the trigonometry in Level 1 is limited to basic trigonometric ratios and right triangle trigonometry.

Functions

Functions in Level 1 are mostly algebraic, while there are more advanced functions (exponential and logarithmic) in Level 2.

Statistics

Probability, mean median, mode counting, and data interpretation are included in both exams. In addition, Level 2 requires permutations, combinations, and standard deviation.

In all SAT Math exams, you must choose the best answer which is not necessarily the exact answer. The decision of whether or not to use a calculator on a particular question is your choice. In some questions the use of a calculator is necessary and in some it is redundant or time consuming. Generally, the angle mode in Level 1 is degree. Be sure to set your calculator in degree mode by pressing "Mode" and then selecting "Degree." However, in Level 2 you must decide when to use the "Degree" mode or the "Radian" mode. There are figures in some questions intended to provide useful information for solving the question. They are accurate unless the question states that the figure is not drawn to scale. In other words, figures are correct unless otherwise specified. All figures lie in a plane unless otherwise indicated. The figures must NOT be assumed to be three-dimensional unless they are indicated to be. The domain of any function is assumed to be set of all real numbers x for which f(x) is a real number, unless otherwise specified.

Important Notice on the Scores

In Level 1 questions the topics covered are relatively less than those covered in the Level 2 test. However, the questions in the Level 1 exam are more tricky compared to the ones in Level 2. This is why if students want to score 800 in the Level 1 test, they have to answer all the 50 questions correctly. But in the Level 2 test, 43 correct answers (the rest must be omitted) are sufficient to get the full score of 800.

Scaled Score	Raw Score in Level 1 Test	Raw Score in Level 2 Test
800	50	43
750	45	38
700	38	33
650	33	28
600	29	22
550	24	16
500	19	10
450	13	3
400	7	0
350	1	-3

How to make the most of this book

This book is designed for all college bound students who have to take either or both of the Math Level 1 and Math Level 2 subject tests. Topics are classified in accordance with their relevance to the specific test, Level 1, Level 2 or both. Please follow the guideline shown at the legend on top of the Table of Contents. Each chapter contains the key concepts that must be learnt as well as many fully solved examples and tons of fully answered exercises. The model tests are up to date reflecting the trends in standardized testing in the last three years and the solutions to the model tests have been produced in a very detailed fashion.

We hope you get as much pleasure using this book as we got while producing it and we are sure that this book will be of great help to students worldwide creating many perfect scorers in the SAT Math subject tests.

Best of luck,

Ruşen MEYLANİ.

Those who are not bound to get any rest never get tired.

Mustafa Kemal Atatürk

CHAPTER 1 – *Functions*

Algebra and Basics

Most Common Graphing Calculator Techniques

Functions

Geometric Transformations

Symmetry and Rotations

Advanced Graphing of Transformations

Linear Functions

Quadratic Functions

Polynomial Functions

Trigonometry

Exponential and Logarithmic Functions

Rational Functions

Greatest Integer Function

1.1 ALGEBRA AND BASICS

Interval Notation

$(a,b) = \{x \mid a < x < b\}$ 　　　$[a,b] = \{x \mid a \le x \le b\}$

$(a,b] = \{x \mid a < x \le b\}$ 　　　$[a,b] = \{x \mid a \le x \le b\}$

$(-\infty, a) = \{x \mid x < a\}$ 　　　$(a, \infty) = \{x \mid x > a\}$

$(-\infty, a] = \{x \mid x \le a\}$ 　　　$[a, \infty) = \{x \mid x \ge a\}$

Number Sets

Complex Numbers $= \left\{a + bi : a \text{ and } b \text{ are real numbers and } b = \sqrt{-1}\right\}$

Subsets of the Real Numbers:

Natural Numbers $= \{1, 2, 3, ...\}$

Whole Numbers $= \{0, 1, 2, 3, ...\}$

Digits $= \{0, 1, 2, 3, 4, 5, 6, 7, 8, 9\}$

Integers $= \{...-3, -2, -1, 0, 1, 2, 3, ...\}$

Rational Numbers $= \left\{\dfrac{a}{b} : a \text{ and } b \text{ are integers with } b \ne 0\right\}$

Irrational Numbers $= \{x \mid x \text{ is not rational}\}$. Irrational numbers include all n'th roots that cannot be written as a fraction. All non-repeating decimals as well as the numbers e and π are irrational.

Prime Numbers: $\{2,3,5,7,11,13,17,19,23,29,31,...\}$ A number is called prime if it has exactly two distinct positive divisors.

Properties of the Real Numbers

For all real numbers a, b, and c:

Commutative Properties: 　　$a+b = b+a$; $a \cdot b = b \cdot a$

Associative Properties: 　　$(a+b)+c=a+(b+c)=a+b+c$; $(ab)c=a(bc)=abc$

Distributive Properties: 　　$a(b+c)=ab+ac$; $(b+c)a=ba+ca$; $a(b-c)=ab-ac$; $(b-c)a=ba-ca$

Identity Elements: 　　$a+0=0+a=a$; $1 \cdot a=a \cdot 1=a$

Inverse Elements: 　　$a + (-a) = (-a) + a = 0$; $a \cdot \dfrac{1}{a} = \dfrac{1}{a} \cdot a = 1$ where $a \ne 0$

Null Element: 　　$a \cdot 0=0 \cdot a=0$; $\dfrac{0}{a} = 0$ where $a \ne 0$:

Important Concepts

Division by zero is not defined

If $a \ne 0$: $a^0=1$; 0^0 is undefined.

0 is even, not prime, not positive, not negative.

1 is odd, not prime and positive.

Fractions

$$\frac{a}{b} + \frac{c}{d} = \frac{ad + bc}{bd}$$

$$\frac{a}{b} \cdot \frac{c}{d} = \frac{ac}{bd}$$

$$\frac{\frac{a}{b}}{\frac{c}{d}} = \frac{a}{b} : \frac{c}{d} = \frac{a}{b} \cdot \frac{d}{c}$$

$$\frac{-a}{b} = \frac{a}{-b} = -\frac{a}{b}$$

$$a : b : c = d : e : f \Rightarrow \frac{a}{d} = \frac{b}{e} = \frac{c}{f}$$

Inequalities

If u<v and v<w, then u<w.

If u<v, then u±w < v±w.

If u<v and c>0, then uc < vc.

If u<v and c<0, then uc > vc.

If 0<u<v or u<v<0 then $\dfrac{1}{u} > \dfrac{1}{v}$.

Letters in the English Alphabet

The English alphabet has 26 letters:

ABCDEFGHIJKLMNOQRSTUVWXYZ are the **capital** letters.

abcdefghijklmnopqrstuvwxyz are the **small** letters.

A – a, E – e, I – i, O – o, U – u, are the **vowels** and the rest of the letters are **consonants**.

Unit Conversions

Length

1 mile (mi) = 1760 yards (yd)   1 yard = 3 feet (ft)   1 foot (ft) = 12 inches (in)

Volume

1 gallon (ga) = 4 quarts (qt)   1 quart (qt) = 2 pints (pt)

Weight

1 pound (lb) = 16 ounces (oz)

Money

1 penny = 1 cent (¢)   1 nickel = 5 cents

1 dime = 10 cents   1 quarter = 25 cents

1 dollar ($) = 100 cents

Rules of Divisibility

- By 2 = 2^1: Last digit must be 0 or divisible by 2.
- By 4 = 2^2: Last 2 digits must be 00 or divisible by 4.
- By 8 = 2^3: Last 3 digits must be 000 or divisible by 8.
- By 5 = 5^1: Last digit must be 0 or divisible by 5.
- By 25 = 5^2: Last 2 digits must be 00 or divisible by 25.
- By 125 = 5^3: Last 3 digits must be 000 or divisible by 125.
- By 3: The sum of the digits must be an integer multiple of 3.
- By 9: The sum of the digits must be an integer multiple of 9.
- By 11: The difference between the sum of the even digits (2nd, 4th, 6th, 8th, etc.) and the sum of the odd digits (1st, 3rd, 5th, 7th, etc.) must be an integer multiple of 11.
- By 10 = 10^1: Last digit must be 0.
- By 100 = 10^2: Last 2 digits must be 00.
- By 1000 = 10^3: Last 3 digits must be 000.
- If an integer N is divisible by A and B, then N is divisible by the LCM (least common multiple) of A and B as well. For example, if N is divisible by 6 and 10, it is also divisible by 30 which is the LCM of 6 and 10.
- If an integer N is divisible by AB given that A and B are relatively prime (meaning that their greatest common divisor is 1) then N is also divisible by A and by B. For example, if an integer is divisible by 15, it is divisible by 3 and 5.
- If an integer N is divisible by A then it is also divisible by every integer divisor of A.

Example:

234AB is divisible by 15. What is the maximum possible value of A + B?

Solution:

The number is divisible by 15 therefore it must be divisible by both 5 and 3. Therefore B is either 0 or 5. The maximum value of B is 5. The number is divisible by 3 therefore the sum of the digits that is 14+A must be a multiple of 3. A can be 1, 4 or 7. The maximum value of A + B is 7 + 5 = 12.

Absolute Values

1. $\sqrt[n]{x^n} = \begin{cases} x & \text{if n is odd} \\ |x| & \text{if n is even} \end{cases}$

   $\sqrt{x^2} = |x|$
   $\sqrt[3]{x^3} = x$

2. $|x| \geq 0$

3. Given that A > 0

$|x| = A \Rightarrow x = \pm A$

$x^2 = A^2 \Rightarrow x = \pm A$

$|x| = |A|$

4. $|x| < A \Rightarrow -A < x < A$

$x^2 < A^2 \Rightarrow -A < x < A$

5. $|x| > A \Rightarrow x > A$ or $x < -A$

$x^2 < A^2 \Rightarrow x > A$ or $x < -A$

6. $B \leq |x| < A \Rightarrow B \leq x < A$ or $-A < x \leq -B$

$B^2 \leq |x| \leq A^2 \Rightarrow B \leq x \leq A$ or $-A \leq x \leq -B$

7. $y = |x| = abs(x)$

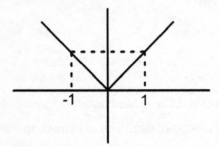

8.   Graph of f(x)

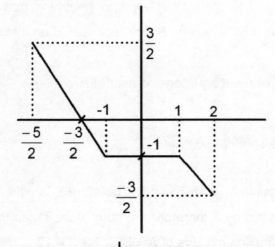

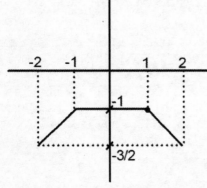

Graph of f (|x|)

Duplicate RHS (+ve x portion of f(x))

by reflecting across the y axis.

Suppress LHS (- ve x portion of f (x))

LHS: Left Hand Side

RHS: Right Hand Side

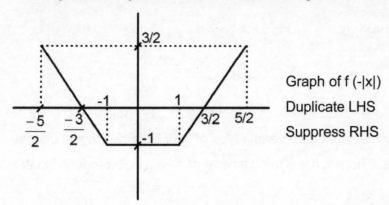

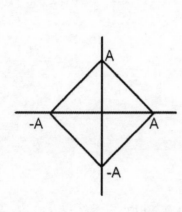

Graph of f (-|x|)

Duplicate LHS

Suppress RHS

9. If f(x)= f(|x|) or f(x)= f(-|x|) then f (x) must be even and therefore symmetric in the y-axis.

10. |x| + |y|=A |x| - |y|=A |y| - |x|=A

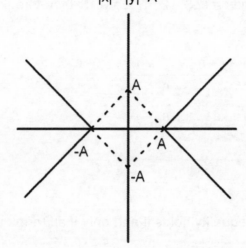
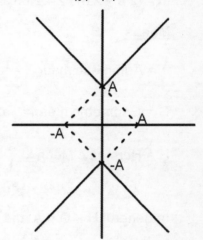

11. |-a|=|a|

12. | ab| = |a|.|b|

13. $\dfrac{|a|}{|b|} = \dfrac{|a|}{|b|}$

14. For all numbers a and b, the triangle inequality holds: $\left\| a \right| - \left| b \right\| \le \left| a + b \right| \le | a | + | b |$

15.   For all a the following inequality holds: $- | a | \le a \le | a |$

16. Graph of |x-a| < b

17. Graph of |x-a| ≤ b:

18. Graph of |x-a| > b:

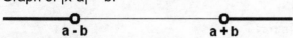

19. Graph of |x-a| ≥ b:

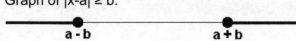

20. If $a < x < b$ then $|x - m| < r$ where $m = \dfrac{b + a}{2}$ and $r = \dfrac{b - a}{2}$

21. If $x < a$ or $x > b$ then $|x - m| > r$ where $m = \dfrac{b + a}{2}$ and $r = \dfrac{b - a}{2}$

Example:

The standards in a light bulb factory state that for a certain type of light bulb the longest diameter must be at least 2.5 inches and at most 2.8 inches. If x is the diameter of a light bulb produced in this factor then $|x - m| \le r$. Find m and r.

Solution:

$m = (2.8 + 2.5) / 2 = 2.65$ and $r = (2.8 - 2.5) / 2 = 0.15$; therefore $|x - 2.65| < 0.15$.

Means

$A = \text{Arithmetic mean} = \dfrac{a_1 + a_2 + a_3 + \ldots\ldots\ldots\ldots + a_n}{n}$

$G = \text{Geometric mean} = \sqrt[n]{a_1 . a_2 . a_3 \ldots\ldots . a_n}$

$H = \text{Harmonic Mean} = \dfrac{n}{\dfrac{1}{a_1} + \dfrac{1}{a_2} + \dfrac{1}{a_3} + \ldots\ldots\ldots + \dfrac{1}{a_n}}$

In general $H \le G \le A$ and equality holds if and only if all terms are equal.

$H = G = A \Leftrightarrow a_1 = a_2 = a_3 = \ldots\ldots\ldots\ldots = a_n$

Exercises

1. $A = \dfrac{2}{\dfrac{1}{x} + \dfrac{1}{y}}$, $B = \sqrt{xy}$, $C = \dfrac{x + y}{2}$.

   For any two given numbers x and y such that x·y is nonnegative:

   a. If A=B=C, what is the relation between x and y?

   b. If $A \le B \le C$, what is the relation between x and y?

   c. If $A \ge B \ge C$, what is the relation between x and y?

2. Average of five distinct numbers is N. Which one(s) of the following are correct?

   a. At least one number is grater than N.

   b. At least one number is less than N.

   c. At least two numbers are greater than N.

3. $\dfrac{a + b + c}{3} = \sqrt[3]{abc} = 3 \div \left(\dfrac{1}{a} + \dfrac{1}{b} + \dfrac{1}{c} \right)$

   What does the above equality imply?

4. $-3<x<5$ and $-4<y<7$ are given. Find greatest value of a; and the least value of b in each case:

   a. $a<x+y<b$

   b. $a<x-y<b$

   c. $a<x \cdot y<b$

   d. $a<\dfrac{x}{y}<b$

5. $-3<x<5$ and $3<y<7$ are given. Find greatest value of a and the least value of b in each case:

   a. $a<\dfrac{x}{y}<b$

   b. $a<\dfrac{y}{x}<b$

6. Find the solution sets of the following:

   a. $x^2-8x+7<0$

   b. $\dfrac{x}{x-3}>4$

   c. $f(x)=x+\sqrt{2x+1}$ and $f(x)\le 4$.

   d. $x(x-1)(x+2)(x-3)<0$

   e. $x(x-2)(x+1)>0$

   f. $x^2(x-2)(x+1)\ge 0$

   g. $\dfrac{x+2}{x}<4$

   h. $4x^2-x<3$

   i. $\dfrac{(x+1)^2}{x^3}>0$

   j. $x^2+12<7x$

7. Find solution set of the equation given by

$$\sqrt{x-\frac{1}{2}}+\sqrt{x-\frac{2}{3}}+\sqrt{x-0.75}=\sqrt{x-2}+\sqrt{x-1.5}+\sqrt{x-\frac{4}{3}}.$$

8. $(x-1)^2+(y+3)^2=0 \Rightarrow x+y=?$

9. $\sqrt{x-1}+\sqrt{y-3}=0 \Rightarrow x+y=?$

10. $3x-7<2x+5<3x+2 \Rightarrow$ What is the solution set for x?

11. $\dfrac{1}{x}+\dfrac{1}{y}=1$; If x and y are positive integers, $x+y=?$

12. $\dfrac{1}{x}+\dfrac{1}{y}+\dfrac{1}{z}=1$; If x,y,z are positive integers then find all possible values of x+y+z.

13. $(x^2-4)(y^2-9)=0$ is given. Which one(s) of the following can be true?

    a. $|x| + 1= |y|$

    b. $|x| + 2=|y|$

    c. x and y are both zero

    d. x and y are both nonnegative

    e. At least one of x and y is nonzero

14. $x=\dfrac{a+by}{c-dy}$; find y in terms of x.

15. Solve for x:

    a. $|2x-3|<3x-6$

    b. $\dfrac{1}{x}<1$

    c. $\dfrac{1}{x}>1$

    d. $\dfrac{1}{x^2}<1$

    e. $\dfrac{1}{x^2}>1$

16. Calculate the following

    a. $\begin{array}{l}\sqrt[3]{y}=2.6\\ \sqrt[4]{10y}=?\end{array}$

    b. $\left(\dfrac{28}{34}\right)^{\frac{-5}{6}}=?$

    c. $\sqrt{3}.\sqrt[3]{4}.\sqrt[4]{5}=?$

    d. $\left(-\dfrac{2}{9}\right)^{3/5}=?$

    e. $3^{4/3}+4^{5/4}=?$

17. What are all values of x for which $|x-1|<2$?

18. How many integers are in the solution set of $|2x-8|>3$?

19. $f(x)=|x+3|$ is given. If $f(x-a)$ is symmetric about the y-axis, $a=?$

20. If $1-y=-x$, then what is the value of $|x-y|+|y-x|$?

21. How many numbers n in the set {-5, - 3, -1, 0, 1, 3, 5} satisfy the conditions $|n-1|\leq5$ and $|n+2|<5$?

22. $|3x-1| = 4x+6$. How many numbers are there in the solution set of the above equation?

23. $|x-3| + |2x+1| = 6 \Rightarrow x = ?$

24. $|3x-5| = 4 \Rightarrow x = ?$

25. $|4x+6| = 3x+4 \Rightarrow x = ?$

26. $\dfrac{|x-3|}{x} = 4 \Rightarrow x = ?$

27. Find solution set of the following inequality: $\dfrac{|x-2|}{x} > 3$

28. Find solution set of the following inequality: $|2x+5| \geq 3$

29. Find solution set of the following inequality: $|x-2| \leq 1$

30. Solve for x:

   (a) |x|<1

   (b) |x-1|+1<0

   (c) -3|x|>-6

   (d) |x|>1

   (e) |x+3|<0

   (f) -3|x|<-6

   (g) |x+1|>2

   (h) |x+3|+|2x-6|<0

   (i) |x-1|+1>0

   (j) |x-3|+|3-x|<0

31. x is within L units of ε; ε>0. Find the solution set of x if L=2 and ε=0.1.

32. Find the solution set:

   (a) |x-3|=x-3

   (b) |x-1|=x-1

   (c) |x-1|=1-x

   (d) |x-1|+|y+3|=0

   (e) |x-1|+3=0

33. OPTIONAL EXERCISE

    Plot the relation in each case

    (a) $|x|+|y|=1$

    (b) $|x|-|y|=1$

    (c) $|y|-|x|=1$

    (d) $|xy|=1$

    (e) $|x|=|y-1|$

    (f) $|x-2|\cdot|y+3|=0$

    (g) $|xy|=1$

    (h) $|xy| < 0$

34. x is in a neighborhood of L with radius ε, $\varepsilon>0$. find solution set of x if L=1 and $\varepsilon=0.2$

35.

    (A) $L-\varepsilon$ ——○—— L ——○—— $L+\varepsilon$ ○

    (B) $L-\varepsilon$ ——○—— L ——●—— $L+\varepsilon$ ○

    (C) ——●— $L-\varepsilon$ —— L —— $L+\varepsilon$ ●——

    1. $|X-L| < \varepsilon$

    2. $|X-L| > \varepsilon$

    3. $0<|X-L|<\varepsilon$

    Match A,B,C with 1,2,3 given that $\varepsilon>0$.

1.2 MOST COMMON GRAPHING CALCULATOR TECHNIQUES

Solving Equations with TI 83 - 84

When solving a polynomial or algebraic equation in the form **f(x)=g(x),** perform the following steps:

- Write the equation in the form: **f(x)-g(x)=0.**

- Plot the graph of **y=f(x)-g(x)**.

- Find the x-intercepts using the **Calc Zero** of TI-84 Plus. However when the graph seems to be tangent to the x-axis at a certain point, you may use the **Calc Min** or **Calc Max** facilities but you should make sure that the y-coordinate of the minimum or maximum point is zero.

Solving Inequalities with TI 83 - 84

When solving an inequality in the form **f(x)<g(x),** or **f(x)≤g(x),** or **f(x)>g(x),** or **f(x)≥g(x)** perform the following steps:

- Write the inequality in the form: **f(x)-g(x)<0 or f(x)-g(x)≤0 or f(x)-g(x) >0 or f(x)-g(x)≥0.**

- Plot the graph of **y=f(x)-g(x)**.

- Find the x-intercepts using the **Calc Zero** of TI-84 Plus. However when the graph seems to be tangent to the x-axis at a certain point, you may use the **Calc Min** or **Calc Max** facilities but you should make sure that the y-coordinate of the minimum or maximum point is zero.

- Any value like **-6.61E -10** or **7.2E -11** can be interpreted as 0 as they mean **-6.6x10^{-10}** and **7.2x10^{-11}** respectively.

- The solution of the inequality will be the set of values of x for which the graph of f(x)-g(x) lies below the x axis if the inequality is in one of the forms **f(x)-g(x)<0** or **f(x)-g(x)≤0.** The solution of the inequality will be the set of values of x for which the graph of f(x)-g(x) lies above the x axis if the inequality is in one of the forms **f(x)-g(x)>0** or **f(x)-g(x)≥0.** If ≤ or ≥ symbols are involved, then the x-intercepts are also in the solution set.

- Please note that the x-values that correspond to asymptotes are never included in the solution set.

Example:

$P(x)= 2x^2+3x+1$; $P(a)= 7 \Rightarrow a=?$

Solution:

$2a^2+3a+1=7 \Rightarrow 2a^2+3a-6=0$

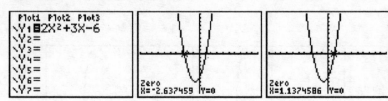

Answer: -2.637 or 1.137

Example:

$f(x) = \sqrt{3x+4}$

$g(x) = x^3$

If is given what (fog)(x)=(gof)(x), then what is x?

Solution:

$(fog)(x) = \sqrt{3x^3 + 4}$

$(gof)(x) = (\sqrt{3x+4})^3$

$\sqrt{3x^3 + 4} = (\sqrt{3x+4})^3$

$\sqrt{3x^3 + 4} - (\sqrt{3x+4})^3 = 0$

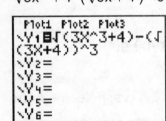 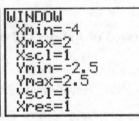 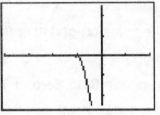

Answer: -1

Example:

$|x-3| + |2x+1| = 6 \Rightarrow x = ?$

Solution:

$|x-3| + |2x+1| - 6 = 0$

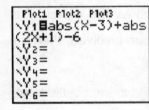 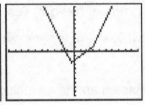 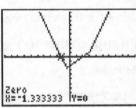 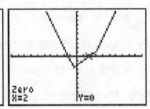

Answer: x= -1.33 or 2

Example:

$2^{x+3} = 3^x \Rightarrow x = ?$

Solution:

$2^{x+3} - 3^x = 0$

 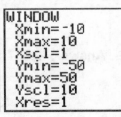 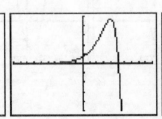 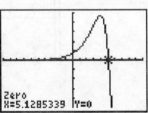

Answer: 5.129

Example:

$\log_x 3 = \log_4 x \Rightarrow$ What is the sum of the roots of this equation?

Solution:

$\log_x 3 - \log_4 x = 0$

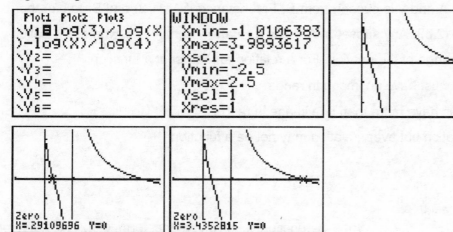

Answer: 0.291+3.435=3.726

Example:

Solve for x: $\dfrac{|x-2|}{x} > 3$

Solution:

$\dfrac{|x-2|}{x} - 3 > 0$

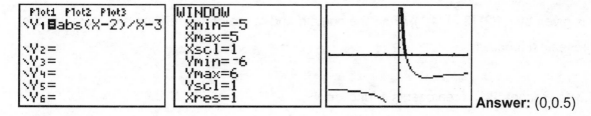

Answer: (0,0.5)

Example:

$x^2(x-2)(x+1) \geq 0$

Solution:

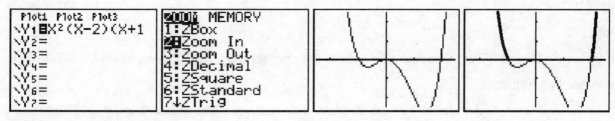

Answer: $(-\infty, -1]$ or $\{0\}$ or $[2, \infty)$

1.3 FUNCTIONS

Definition

Cartesian product of the sets A and B denoted as A × B is the set that contains the ordered pairs (x,y) such that x is chosen from A and y is chosen from B. For instance if A={1,2} and B={a,b,c} then A×B={(1,a),(1,b),(1,c),(2,a),(2,b),(2,c)}. Any subset of A × B is a **relation** from A to B where A is called the **domain** and B is called the **range** of the relation. For a relation to represent a function:

- Each element in the domain must have an image in range.

- No element in the domain can have more than one image in range.

Therefore every function is a relation but every relation may not be a function.

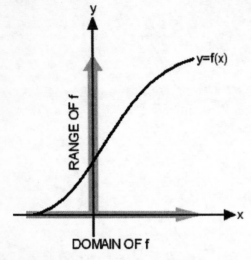

When a function is given in the form y=f(x), the set of all possible values of x constitute the domain of f(x) and the set of all possible values of y constitute the range of f(x). A function can also be defined as a mapping between the elements in the domain and the elements in the range.

Example:

A relation f is given by {(1,2),(3,2),(4,1)}. Find the domain and range of this relation and state whether or not it represents a function.

Solution:

Domain={1,3,4}; Range={2,1}; f represents a function.

Example:

Find the domain and range of each relation and state whether or not it represents a function.

1. $\beta=\{(x,y)|x^2=y^3; x,y\in R\}$.
2. $\beta=\{(x,y)|x^3=y^2; x,y\in R\}$.

Solution:

1. Let $y=1 \Rightarrow x^2=1 \Rightarrow x=\pm1$: Two different elements in the domain may have the same image. Therefore f represents a function.

2. Let $x=1 \Rightarrow y^2=1 \Rightarrow y=\pm1$: An element in the domain may not have two different images. Therefore f does not represent a function.

Vertical Line Test

This test gives whether or not a given graph represents a function; if a vertical line cuts the graph of a function at more than one point, the graph does not represent a function and the function fails this test.

Horizontal Line Test

This test gives whether or not the inverse of a given graph represents a function; if a horizontal line cuts a graph at more than one point, the inverse does not represent a function.

Example:

State which of the following functions represents a function of x.

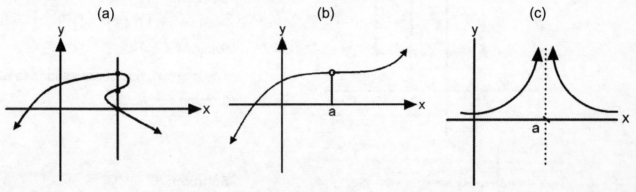

Solution:

(a) The given relation does not pass the vertical line test therefore it does not represent a function.

(b) and (c) The relation given is undefined at x=a. Therefore if the domain is R then the graph does not represent a function. However if the domain is R-{a} then the graph represents a function.

Example:

Find the domain and range each time, state if the graph may correspond to a function or not.

a)

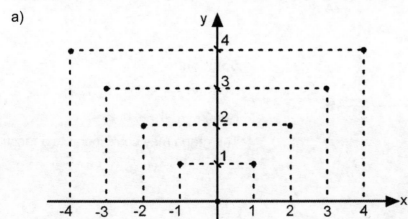

Solution:

Domain = {-4,-3,-2,-1,0,1,2,3,4}

Range = {0,1,2,3,4}

The graph may correspond to a function.

b)

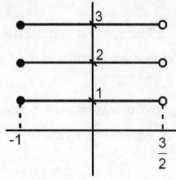

Solution:

Domain = $-1 \leq x < \dfrac{3}{2}$

Range = {1,2,3}

The graph does not correspond to a function.

c)

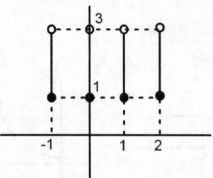

Solution:

Domain = {-1,0,1,2}

Range = $1 \leq y < 3$

The graph does not correspond to a function.

d)

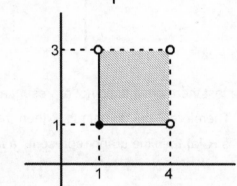

Solution:

Domain = $1 \leq x < 4$

Range = $1 \leq y < 3$

The graph does not correspond to a function.

e)

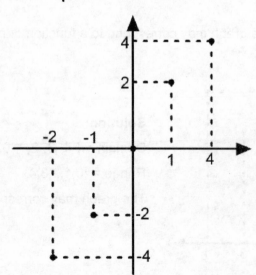

Solution:

Domain = { -2, -1, 0, 1, 2}

Range = { -4, -2, 0, 2, 4}

The graph may correspond to a function.

f)

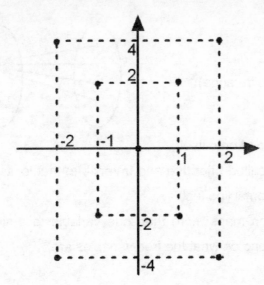

Solution:

Domain = { -2, -1, 0, 1, 2}

Range = { -4, -2, 0, 2, 4}

The graph does not correspond to a function.

Types of functions

Into function

(range is not completely covered)

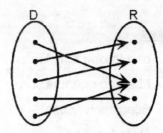

Onto function

(range is completely covered)

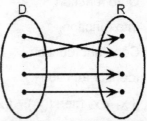

One to one function

(no two elements in the domain have the same image in range)

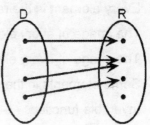

Many to one function

(some elements in the domain do have the same image in range)

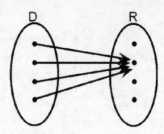

Constant function: f(x)=C

(all elements in the domain have the same image in range)

Identity function: $I(x)=x$; (every element is mapped onto itself).

When a function is **one to one and onto**, it is called **bijective** and **invertible**; that is, its inverse will also be a function; such functions pass the horizontal line test.

Multivariable Function: A multivariable function maps more than one variable to a single value. They are often written as $f(x,y)$ or $f(x,y,z)$ depending on what the free variables are.

Examples:

$f(x,y)= 2x^2 - y^2$, $g(x)= 5^x \Rightarrow g(f(4,3)) = g(2 \cdot 4^2 - 3^2) = g(23) = 5^{23} = 1.2 \cdot 10^{16}$

$f(x,y)= \sqrt{3x^2 - 4y}$ and $g(x)= 3^x \Rightarrow g(f(2,1))=g(\sqrt{3.2^2 - 4.1})=3^{\sqrt{8}}=22.4$

Polynomial Function:

$P(x) = a_n x^n + a_{n-1}x^{n-1} + a_{n-2}x^{n-2} + \ldots + a_5 x^5 + a_4 x^4 + a_3 x^3 + a_2 x^2 + a_1 x + a_0$

For $P(x)$ to be a polynomial function a_n values must be complex numbers (in SAT II context they will all be real numbers) and n values must be nonnegative integers.

Exercises

1. A. one to one function

   B. Many to one function

   C. Bijective function

   D. Onto function

   E. Into function

   F. Constant function

   G. Identity function

   1. If $x_1 \neq x_2$ then $f(x_1) \neq f(x_2)$

   2. Every element in the range is an image of at least one element in the domain.

   3. The image of every element in the domain is the same.

   4. The image of every element in the domain is itself.

   5. Some elements in the range are not images.

   6. Invertible function.

   7. Some elements in the domain have the same image in range.

   Match the letters A through G with the numbers 1 through 7.

2. State whether each of the following graphs represents a function or not.

(A)   (B)   (C)   (D)

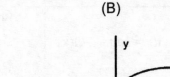
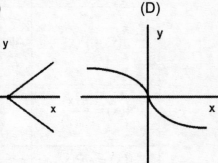

(E)

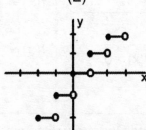

3. Find range of the function defined by f(x)= $\dfrac{1}{x}-2$?

4. Find the range of the function defined by:

$$f(x)= \begin{cases} x^{\frac{1}{3}} & ,\ x > 1 \\ 3x-1 & ,\ x \le 1 \end{cases}$$

5. A= {a, b, c, d}; B= {1, 2, 3}

Which one(s) of the following is a function from A to B?

a. {(a,1), (b,1), (c,2), (d,3)}

b. {(a,1), (a,2), (b,1), (c,3), (d,3)}

c. {(a,1), (b,2), (c,3)}

Domains of Specific Functions

Type of Function	Domain	Type of Function	Domain
$f(x) = P(x)$	All real numbers	$f(x) = \log_{P(x)} Q(x)$	$Q(x) > 0$ $P(x) > 0$ $P(x) \neq 1$
$f(x) = \dfrac{P(x)}{Q(x)}$	$Q(x) \neq 0$	$f(x) = \sqrt[3]{P(x)}$ $f(x) = \sqrt[2n+1]{P(x)}$	All real numbers
$f(x) = \sqrt{P(x)}$ $f(x) = \sqrt[2n]{P(x)}$	$P(x) \geq 0$	$f(x) = \dfrac{1}{\sqrt[3]{P(x)}}$ $f(x) = \dfrac{1}{\sqrt[2n+1]{P(x)}}$	$P(x) \neq 0$
$f(x) = \dfrac{1}{\sqrt{P(x)}}$ $f(x) = \dfrac{1}{\sqrt[2n]{P(x)}}$	$P(x) > 0$		

P(x) and Q(x) are polynomial functions

Example:

Find the domain of each of the following functions:

(1) $f(x) = \dfrac{x+1}{x^2 - 4}$ (2) $f(x) = \sqrt{x - 1}$ (3) $f(x) = \dfrac{1}{\sqrt{x+1}}$ (4) $f(x) = \sqrt{x^2 - 1}$

(5) $f(x) = \dfrac{1}{\sqrt[3]{x^2 - 1}}$ (6) $f(x) = \sqrt[3]{x^2 - 1}$ (7) $f(x) = \log_2(x - 3)$ (8) $f(x) = \log_{(5-x)}(x-1)$

Solution:

(1) $x^2 - 4 = 0 \Rightarrow x^2 = 4 \Rightarrow x = \pm 2$; therefore domain is R - { -2 , 2 }.

(2) $x - 1 \geq 0 \Rightarrow$ Domain: $x \geq 1$.

(3) $x + 1 > 0 \Rightarrow$ Domain: $x > -1$.

(4) $x^2 - 1 \geq 0 \Rightarrow x^2 \geq 1$; domain is $x > 1$ or $x < -1$

(5) $x^2 - 1 = 0 \Rightarrow x^2 = 1 \Rightarrow x = \pm 1$; therefore domain is R - { -1 , 1 }.

(6)   Domain is R.

(7) $x - 3 > 0 \Rightarrow$ Domain: $x > 3$.

(8)   The following conditions have to be satisfied at the same time:

   (i) $x - 1 > 0$

   (ii) $5 - x > 0$

   (iii) $5 - x \neq 1 \Rightarrow$ Therefore the domain is $1 < x < 5$ and $x \neq 4$.

Exercises

1. If $f(x) = \sqrt{5-x}$, find domain of f(x)?

2. The function f, where $f(x) = (2+x)^2$, is defined for $-3 \le x \le 3$. What is the range of f?

3. If $f(x) = x^2 - x - 6$, find the set of all values of c that satisfy the equation $f(-c) = f(c)$.

4. If $f(x) = 4x - 3$ and $0 < x < 2$, then f(x) is between which two numbers?

5. If $-\dfrac{1}{y} = \dfrac{1}{\frac{1}{x}}$, then $2 < x < 6$ if and only if y is between a and b. What are the values of a and b?

6. What is the domain and range of $f(x) = \sqrt[3]{-x^2 + 17}$?

7. $y = \sqrt[3]{9 - x^2}$. Find maximum value of y.

8. Find the domain of $f(x) = \log \sqrt{2x^2 - 15}$.

9. Find domain and range of the function $y = x^{-4/3}$

10. Find the domain and range of the function $f(x) = 4 - \sqrt{2x^3 - 16}$

11. $f(x) = 2x^2 + 5x + 2$ and $g(x) = 4x^2 - 4$. In order that $\left(\dfrac{f}{g}\right)(x)$ be a function what values must be excluded from the domain?

12. Find domain and range of $y = \sqrt{x^2 - 9}$.

13. Find domain and range of $y = \sqrt{9 - x^2}$.

14. Find largest possible domain for each function:

    (a) $f(x) = \dfrac{x^2 - 1}{x^2 - 4}$

    (b) $f(x) = \sqrt{x+4} + \dfrac{1}{x - 3}$

    (c) $f(x) = \log_{(x-3)}(9-x)$

15. Which one(s) of the following functions has an inverse that also represents a function?

a.

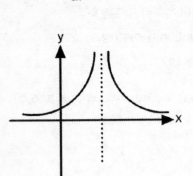

b.

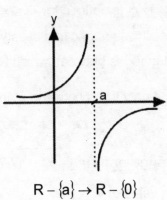

$R - \{a\} \rightarrow R - \{0\}$

c.

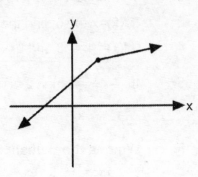

d.

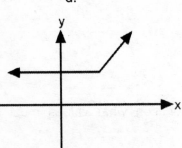

e.

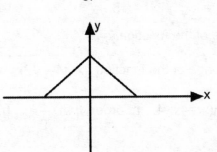

f.

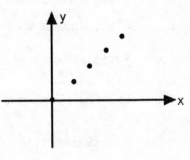

g.

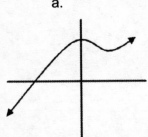

16. Which one(s) of the following graphs represent(s) functions?

a.

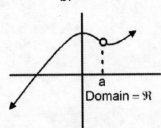

b.

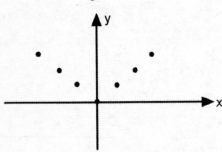

Domain = ℜ

c.

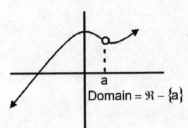

Domain = ℜ − {a}

d.

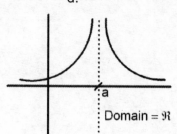

Domain = ℜ

e.

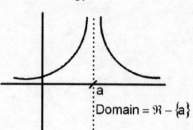

Domain = ℜ – {a}

f.

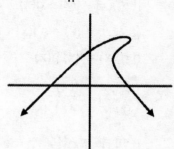

g.

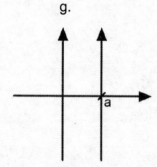

h.

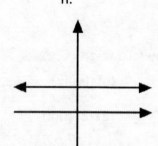

i.

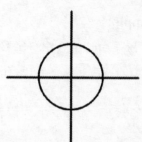

j.

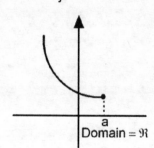

Domain = ℜ

k.

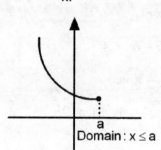

Domain : x ≤ a

l.

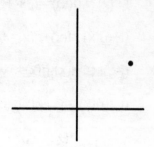

m.

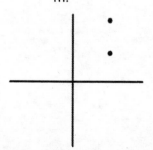

n.

Empty Set

Operations on Functions

1. $(f \pm g)(x) = f(x) \pm g(x)$

2. $(a.f \pm b.g)(x) = a.f(x) \pm b.g(x)$

3. $(f.g)(x) = f(x).g(x)$

4. $\left(\dfrac{f}{g}\right)(x) = \dfrac{f(x)}{g(x)}$

5. $(f^n)(x) = [f(x)]^n$

Example:

$f(x) = 3x-1$ and $g(x) = 2x+5$. Compute the following:

(a) $f^2(x)$ (b) $(f+g)(x)$ (c) $(f-g)(x)$ (d) $(f.g)(x)$

(e) $(\frac{f}{g})(x)$ (f) $(\frac{1}{f})(x)$ (g) $(2f-g)(x)$

Solution:

(a) $f^2(x) = (f(x))^2 = (3x-1)^2 = 9x^2 - 6x+1$

(b) $(f+g)(x) = f(x)+g(x) = 3x-1+2x+5 = 5x + 4$

(c) $(f-g)(x) = f(x)-g(x) = 3x-1-(2x+5) = x - 6$

(d) $(f.g)(x) = f(x).g(x) = (3x-1).(2x+5) = 6x^2+13x-5$

(e) $(\frac{f}{g})(x) = \dfrac{f(x)}{g(x)} = \dfrac{3x-1}{2x+5}$

(f) $(\frac{1}{f})(x) = \dfrac{1}{f(x)} = \dfrac{1}{3x-1}$

(g) $(2f-g)(x) = 2f(x)-g(x) = 2.(3x-1)-(2x+5) = 4x-7$

Exercises

1.   If $f(x) = \dfrac{-2}{x}$ for $x<0$, then $f(-3.5) = ?$

2.   Given that $f(x) = 3x-4$ and $g(x) = 7x+9$, find the value of p such that $f(p) = g(p)$.

3.   Solution set of $f(x) = 0$ is $\{-7,12\}$. What is the solution set of $f(x+2) = 0$?

4.   If f and g are functions such that $f(x) = 3x-5$ and $f(g(x)) = x$, then $g(x) =$

5.   If $f(x) = \sqrt{0.7x^2 - x + 2}$ and $g(x) = \dfrac{x-2}{x+3}$, then $g(f(4)) = ?$

6. If x represents the depth in meters of a dam and f(x) represents the thickness, in tenths of a meter of the concrete, then $f(x)=\frac{1}{8}(x^2-3x+5)$. What is the thickness, in meters, of the concrete at a depth of 1.5 meters?

7. If $h(x)=\frac{3-x}{x-3}$, which one(s) of the following statements must be true?

    a. h(1)=h(4)

    b. h(0)=h(2)

    c. h(0)=h(5)

    d. h(3)=h(-3)

8. If $f(x)=-x^2+5x+m$ and if f(-2)= 0, then m=?

9. If functions f, g, and h are defined by f(x)= - 4x, g(x)=2x+1, and $h(x)=-x^2$, then f(g(h(4)))=?

10. If $f(x)=3x^2-x$, then f(a+1)=?

11. If $f(x)=x^3+4$, what is $f^{-1}(2)$?

12. If $f(x)=\sqrt[3]{x^5+1}$, what is $f^{-1}(2.5)$?

13. Determine which of the following functions has an inverse that is also a function.

    a. $y=x^2-3x+5$ b. $y=|x+2|-1$ c. $y=\sqrt{16-9x^2}$ d. $y=x^3+5x-2$

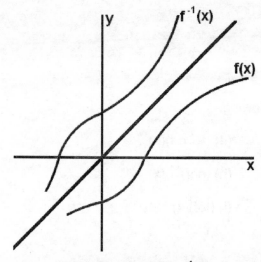

Graph of f(x) and $f^{-1}(x)$

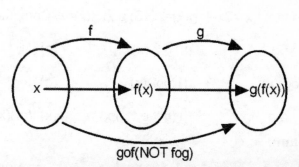

The composition (gof) of two functions f and g

How to Find the Inverse of a Function

In order to find the inverse of y=f(x) carry out the following procedure:

(i)   replace f(x) with y.

(ii) switch x and y in y=f(x) $\Rightarrow$ x=f(y).

(iii) solve for y; express y as a function of x only.

(iv) replace y with $f^{-1}(x)$.

Example:

Find the inverse of the function f(x)=3x -1.

Solution:

$$f(x) = 3x - 1$$

$$y = 3x - 1$$

$$x = 3y - 1$$

$$y = \frac{x+1}{3}$$

$$f^{-1}(x) = \frac{x+1}{3}$$

Function Compositions and Inverses

1. (fog)(x)=f(g(x)) and (gof)(x)=g(f(x))

2. f o I = I o f = f where I(x)=x is the identity function.

3. f o f $^{-1}$ = f $^{-1}$ o f = I

4. (fog) $^{-1}$= g $^{-1}$ o f $^{-1}$

   (gof) $^{-1}$= f $^{-1}$ o g $^{-1}$

5. (fogoh) $^{-1}$ = h $^{-1}$ o g $^{-1}$ o f $^{-1}$

6. In general (fog)(x) ≠ (gof)(x). If (fog)(x) = (gof)(x) then one of the following cases must hold:

   - f(x) = g(x)

   - f(x) = g $^{-1}$(x) or g(x)=f $^{-1}$(x)

   - f(x) or g(x) or both are identity.

Example:

Given that f(x)=3x-1; g(x)=2x+5; and I(x)=x. Compute the following:

(a) f $^{-1}$ (x)　　　　(b) g $^{-1}$ (x)　　　　(c) (f o f $^{-1}$)(x)　　　　(d) (f $^{-1}$ o f)(x)

(e) (fog)(x)　　　　(f) (gof)(x)　　　　(g) (fog) $^{-1}$ (x)　　　　(h) (gof) $^{-1}$ (x)

(i) (f $^{-1}$ o g $^{-1}$)(x)　　　　(j) (g $^{-1}$ o f $^{-1}$)(x)　　　　(k) (foI)(x)　　　　(l) (Iof)(x)

Solution:

(a) $f(x) = 3x - 1 \Rightarrow f^{-1}(x) = \frac{x+1}{3}$

(b) $g(x) = 2x + 5$

$$y = 2x + 5$$

$$x = 2y + 5$$

$$y = \frac{x-5}{2} \Rightarrow g^{-1}(x) = \frac{x-5}{2}$$

(c) (f o f $^{-1}$)(x)=$(3x - 1)o(\frac{x+1}{3}) = 3.\frac{x+1}{3} - 1 = x = I(x)$

(d) $(f^{-1} \circ f)(x) = (\dfrac{x+1}{3}) \circ (3x-1) = \dfrac{3x-1+1}{3} = x = I(x)$

From parts (c) and (d) please notice that f o f $^{-1}$ = f $^{-1}$ o f = I (rule number 3).

(e) $(fog)(x) = (3x-1) \circ (2x+5) = 3.(2x+5)-1 = 6x+15-1 = 6x+14$

(f) $(gof)(x) = (2x+5) \circ (3x-1) = 2.(3x-1)+5 = 6x-2+5 = 6x+3$

From parts (e) and (f) please notice that fog ≠ gof (rule number 6).

(g) $(fog)(x) = 6x + 14$

$y = 6x + 14$

$x = 6y + 14$

$y = \dfrac{x-14}{6} \Rightarrow (fog)^{-1}(x) = \dfrac{x-14}{6}$

(h) $(gof)(x) = 6x + 3$

$y = 6x + 3$

$x = 6y + 3$

$y = \dfrac{x-3}{6} \Rightarrow (gof)^{-1}(x) = \dfrac{x-3}{6}$

(i)

$(f^{-1} \circ g^{-1})(x) = (\dfrac{x+1}{3}) \circ (\dfrac{x-5}{2}) = \dfrac{\dfrac{x-5}{2}+1}{3} = \dfrac{\dfrac{x-5+2}{2}}{3} = \dfrac{x-3}{6}$

(j)

$(g^{-1} \circ f^{-1})(x) = (\dfrac{x-5}{2}) \circ (\dfrac{x+1}{3}) = \dfrac{\dfrac{x+1}{3}-5}{2} = \dfrac{\dfrac{x+1-15}{3}}{2} = \dfrac{x-14}{6}$

Please notice from parts (h) – (i) and (g) – (j) that (fog) $^{-1}$ = g $^{-1}$ o f $^{-1}$ and (gof) $^{-1}$ = f $^{-1}$ o g $^{-1}$
(rule number 4).

(k) $(foI)(x) = (3x-1) \circ (x) = 3x-1 = f(x)$

(l) $(Iof)(x) = (x) \circ (3x-1) = 3x-1 = f(x)$

Please notice from parts (k) and (l) that foI=Iof=f (rule number 2).

<u>**Finding other function when the composition and one function are given**</u>

Case 1: (fog)(x) is given, g(x) is given, f(x) = ?

   i. Find g $^{-1}$(x)   **ii.** (fog)og $^{-1}$=f

Case 2: (fog)(x) is given, f(x) is given, g(x) = ?

   i. Find f $^{-1}$(x)   **ii.** f $^{-1}$o(fog)=g

Example:

(fog)(x)=2x+3; g(x)=4x-5; f(x)=?

Solution:

$g(x)=4x-5 \Rightarrow g^{-1}(x) = \dfrac{x+5}{4}$

$f = (fog)og^{-1} = (2x+3)o\left(\dfrac{x+5}{4}\right) = 2.\dfrac{x+5}{4}+3 = \dfrac{2x+22}{4} \Rightarrow f(x) = \dfrac{2x+22}{4}$

Example:

$f(4x-5)=2x+3 \Rightarrow f(x)=?$

Solution:

(take the inverse of the inside of f; plug in x)

$y=4x-5 \Rightarrow x = 4y-5 \Rightarrow y = \dfrac{x+5}{4}$

$f(4\dfrac{x+5}{4}-5) = f(x) = 2.\dfrac{x+5}{4}+3 = \dfrac{2x+22}{4}$

(Please notice that the previous two examples are identical but they are given differently.)

Example:

(fog)(x)=2x+3; f(x)=4x-5; g(x)=?

Solution:

$f(x)=4x-5 \Rightarrow f^{-1}(x) = \dfrac{x+5}{4}$

$g = f^{-1}o(fog) = \left(\dfrac{x+5}{4}\right)o(2x+3) = \dfrac{2x+3+5}{4} = \dfrac{x}{2}+2$

Example:

(fog)(x)=x; f(x)=4x-5 $\Rightarrow$ g(x)=?

Solution:

$g(x) = f^{-1}(x) = \dfrac{x+5}{4}$

Exercises

1. If f(x) = 2x+1 and g(x) = 3x–1, then f(g(x))=

2. If f(x)=3x+7 and f(g(1))=13, which of the following could be g(x)?

    i. x+1   ii. 3x-1   iii. 2x+1

3. If f(g(x))=6x+4 and g(x)=2x+3, then find f(x).

4. If $f(x) = \dfrac{2x - 4}{3x}$ and $g(x) = \dfrac{4}{x}$, then $f(g(3)) = ?$

5. If $f(x) = 4x$ and $f(g(x)) = -x$, then $g(x) = ?$

6. If $f(5x + 2) = 5x - 2$ then $f(x) = ?$

7. $f(x) = \dfrac{x + 3}{x + 4}$; $g(x) = -x^2$; $g(f(3)) = ?$

Inverses of Specific Functions

1. $f(x) = a^x \Leftrightarrow f^{-1}(x) = \log_a x$

   $f(x) = 10^x \Leftrightarrow f^{-1}(x) = \log_{10} x = \log x$

   $f(x) = e^x \Leftrightarrow f^{-1}(x) = \log_e x = \ln(x)$

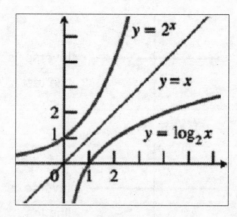

$f(x) = 2^x$ and $f(x) = \log_2 x$ are inverses of each other.

2. $f(x) = a(x - h)^2 + k$

If domain of f is: $R \Rightarrow f^{-1}(x) = h \pm \sqrt{\dfrac{x - k}{a}}$ (f^{-1} is not a function)

If domain of f is: $x \geq h \Rightarrow f^{-1}(x) = h + \sqrt{\dfrac{x - k}{a}}$ (f^{-1} is a function)

Right hand side of vertex corresponds to ($+\sqrt{}$): Right Hand Side $\Leftrightarrow + \sqrt{}$

If domain of f is: $x \leq h \Rightarrow f^{-1}(x) = h - \sqrt{\dfrac{x - k}{a}}$ (f^{-1} is a function)

Left hand side of vertex corresponds to ($-\sqrt{}$): Left Hand Side $\Leftrightarrow -\sqrt{}$

Examples:

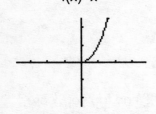 $\Rightarrow$ 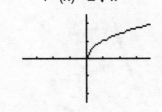 Inverse is not a function as it fails the vertical line test.

$f(x)=x^2$ $f^{-1}(x)= \pm\sqrt{x}$

$\Rightarrow$ Inverse is a function as it passes the vertical line test.

$f(x)=x^2$ and $x \geq 0$ $f^{-1}(x)= +\sqrt{x}$

$\Rightarrow$ Inverse is a function as it passes the vertical line test.

$f(x)=x^2$ and $x \leq 0$ $f^{-1}(x)= -\sqrt{x}$

3. $\quad f(x) = \dfrac{ax+b}{cx+d} \Rightarrow f^{-1}(x) = \dfrac{-dx+b}{cx-a}$ (a and d change places and are multiplied by -1)

Derivation:

$f(x) = \dfrac{ax+b}{cx+d}$

$\Rightarrow y = \dfrac{ax+b}{cx+d} \Rightarrow x = \dfrac{ay+b}{cy+d}$

$\Rightarrow x(cy+d) = ay+b$

$\Rightarrow cxy+dx = ay+b$

$\Rightarrow cxy-ay = -dx+b$

$\Rightarrow y(cx-a) = -dx+b$

$\Rightarrow y = \dfrac{-dx+b}{cx-a} \Rightarrow f^{-1}(x) = \dfrac{-dx+b}{cx-a}$

Procedure for Completing the Square

$y = ax^2 + bx + c$

i.   write the x terms in the parenthesis of the leading coefficient a.

$$y = ax^2 + bx + c = a(x^2 + \frac{b}{a}x) + c$$

ii.   add the square of half of the coefficient of x to the inside of the parenthesis; that is add

$(\frac{b}{2a})^2 = \frac{b^2}{4a^2}$ to the inside; and subtract $(a. \frac{b^2}{4a^2}) = \frac{b^2}{4a}$ from the outside of the parenthesis.

$$y = ax^2 + bx + c = a(x^2 + \frac{b}{a}x) + c = a(x^2 + \frac{b}{a}x + \frac{b^2}{4a^2}) - \frac{b^2}{4a} + c$$

iii.   the parenthesis becomes a perfect square.

$$y = ax^2 + bx + c = a(x^2 + \frac{b}{a}x) + c = a(x^2 + \frac{b}{a}x + \frac{b^2}{4a^2}) - \frac{b^2}{4a} + c = a(x + \frac{b}{2a})^2 + (c - \frac{b^2}{4a})$$

$$y = a(x - h)^2 + k; \text{ where } h = \frac{b}{2a} \text{ and } k = c - \frac{b^2}{4a}$$

Examples:

Apply completing the square procedure to each of the following functions:

(i) $f(x) = 2x^2 - 12x + 3$

(ii) $f(x) = -3x^2 - 6x + 1$

Solution:

(a) $f(x) = 2x^2 - 12x + 3 = 2(x^2 - 6x) + 3 = 2(x^2 - 6x + 9) - 18 + 3 = 2(x-3)^2 - 15$

(b) $-3x^2 - 6x + 1 = -3(x^2 + 2x) + 1 = -3(x^2 + 2x + 1) + 3 + 1 = -3(x+1)^2 + 4$

Example:

Find the inverse of each of the following functions:

(a) $f(x) = \frac{2x - 3}{4x + 7}$

(b) $f(x) = \frac{2}{3x + 5}$

(c) $f(x) = \frac{2x + 3}{4}$

(d) $f(x) = 3^x$

(e) $f(x) = \frac{2}{3} \cdot 4^{5x-6} + 8$

(f) $f(x) = 3.10^{2x} + 4$

(g) $f(x) = 3.\ln \frac{2x + 1}{4} + 5$

(h) $f(x) = 2\log_3(3x - 5) + 6$

(i) $f(x) = 3\log(2x - 1) + 4$

(j) $f(x) = x^2 - 12$

(k) $f(x) = -3x^2 - 6x + 1$

(l) $f(x) = 2x^2 - 12x + 3$

Solution:

(a) $f(x) = \frac{2x - 3}{4x + 7} \Rightarrow f^{-1}(x) = \frac{-7x - 3}{4x - 2}$

(b) $f(x) = \frac{2}{3x + 5} = \frac{0x + 2}{3x + 5} \Rightarrow f^{-1}(x) = \frac{-5x + 2}{3x}$

(c) $f(x) = \dfrac{2x+3}{4} = \dfrac{2x+3}{0x+4} \Rightarrow f^{-1}(x) = \dfrac{-4x+3}{-2}$

(d) $f(x) = 3^x \Rightarrow f^{-1}(x) = \log_3 x$

(e) $f(x) = \dfrac{2}{3} \cdot 4^{5x-6} + 8$

$y = \dfrac{2}{3} \cdot 4^{5x-6} + 8$

$x = \dfrac{2}{3} \cdot 4^{5y-6} + 8$

$\dfrac{3}{2}(x-8) = 4^{5y-6} \Rightarrow 5y - 6 = \log_4[\dfrac{3}{2}(x-8)]$

$y = \dfrac{6 + \log_4[\dfrac{3}{2}(x-8)]}{5} \Rightarrow f^{-1}(x) = \dfrac{6}{5} + \dfrac{1}{5} \cdot \log_4[\dfrac{3}{2}(x-8)]$

(f) $f(x) = 3 \cdot 10^{2x} + 4$

$y = 3 \cdot 10^{2x} + 4$

$x = 3 \cdot 10^{2y} + 4$

$\dfrac{x-4}{3} = 10^{2y} \Rightarrow 2y = \log\dfrac{x-4}{3} \Rightarrow y = \dfrac{1}{2}\log\dfrac{x-4}{3} \Rightarrow f^{-1}(x) = \dfrac{1}{2}\log\dfrac{x-4}{3}$

(g) $f(x) = 3 \cdot \ln\dfrac{2x+1}{4} + 5$

$y = 3 \cdot \ln\dfrac{2x+1}{4} + 5 \Rightarrow x = 3\ln\dfrac{2y+1}{4} + 5 \Rightarrow \dfrac{x-5}{3} = \ln\dfrac{2y+1}{4}$

$\dfrac{2y+1}{4} = e^{\frac{x-5}{3}} \Rightarrow y = \dfrac{4 \cdot e^{\frac{x-5}{3}} - 1}{2} \Rightarrow f^{-1}(x) = \dfrac{4 \cdot e^{\frac{x-5}{3}} - 1}{2}$

(h) $f(x) = 2\log_3(3x-5) + 6 \Rightarrow y = 2\log_3(3x-5) + 6 \Rightarrow x = 2\log_3(3y-5) + 6$

$\dfrac{x-6}{2} = \log_3(3y-5) \Rightarrow 3y - 5 = 3^{\frac{x-6}{2}} \Rightarrow y = \dfrac{5 + 3^{\frac{x-6}{2}}}{3} \Rightarrow f^{-1}(x) = \dfrac{5 + 3^{\frac{x-6}{2}}}{3}$

(i) $f(x) = 3\log(2x-1) + 4 \Rightarrow y = 3\log(2x-1) + 4 \Rightarrow x = 3\log(2y-1) + 4$

$\dfrac{x-4}{3} = \log(2y-1) \Rightarrow 2y - 1 = 10^{\frac{x-4}{3}} \Rightarrow y = \dfrac{1 + 10^{\frac{x-4}{3}}}{2} \Rightarrow f^{-1}(x) = \dfrac{1 + 10^{\frac{x-4}{3}}}{2}$

(j) $f(x) = x^2 - 12 \Rightarrow y = x^2 - 12 \Rightarrow x = y^2 - 12 \Rightarrow y = \pm\sqrt{x+12}$

If Domain of $f(x)$ is R then $f^{-1}(x) = \pm\sqrt{x+12}$ and $f^{-1}(x)$ is not a function.

If Domain of $f(x)$ is $x \geq 0$ (or a subset of $x \geq 0$) then $f^{-1}(x) = \sqrt{x+12}$ and $f^{-1}(x)$ is a function.

If Domain of f(x) is x ≤ 0 (or a subset of x ≤ 0) then $f^{-1}(x) = -\sqrt{x+12}$ and $f^{-1}(x)$ is a function.

(k) $f(x) = -3x^2 - 6x + 1 = -3(x+1)^2 + 4$

$y = -3(x+1)^2 + 4 \Rightarrow x = -3(y+1)^2 + 4 \Rightarrow \dfrac{x-4}{-3} = (y+1)^2$

$(y+1) = \pm\sqrt{\dfrac{x-4}{-3}} \Rightarrow y = -1 \pm \sqrt{\dfrac{x-4}{-3}}$

If Domain of f(x) is R then $f^{-1}(x) = -1 \pm \sqrt{\dfrac{x-4}{-3}}$ and $f^{-1}(x)$ is not a function.

If Domain of f(x) is x ≥ -1 then $f^{-1}(x) = -1 + \sqrt{\dfrac{x-4}{-3}}$.

If Domain of f(x) is x ≤ -1 then $f^{-1}(x) = -1 - \sqrt{\dfrac{x-4}{-3}}$.

(l) $f(x) = 2x^2 - 12x + 3 = 2(x-3)^2 - 15$

$y = 2(x-3)^2 - 15 \Rightarrow x = 2(y-3)^2 - 15 \Rightarrow \dfrac{x+15}{2} = (y-3)^2 \Rightarrow (y-3) = \pm\sqrt{\dfrac{x+15}{2}} \Rightarrow y = 3 \pm \sqrt{\dfrac{x+15}{2}}$

If Domain of f(x) is R then $f^{-1}(x) = 3 \pm \sqrt{\dfrac{x+15}{2}}$ and $f^{-1}(x)$ is not a function.

If Domain of f(x) is x ≥ 3 then $f^{-1}(x) = 3 + \sqrt{\dfrac{x+15}{2}}$.

If Domain of f(x) is x ≤ 3 then $f^{-1}(x) = 3 - \sqrt{\dfrac{x+15}{2}}$.

Reflections

When you reflect a function y = f(x)

- in the **x – axis** : replace (x, y) by **(x, -y)**

- in the **y – axis** : replace (x, y) by **(-x, y)**

- in the **origin** : replace (x, y) by **(-x, -y)**

- in the line **x = a** : replace (x, y) by **(2a-x, y)**

- in the line **y = b** : replace (x, y) by **(x, 2b-y)**

- in the point **(a, b)** : replace (x, y) by **(2a-x, 2b-y)**

- in the line **y = x** : replace (x, y) by **(y, x)**

- in the line **y = - x** : replace (x, y) by **(-y, -x)**

Example:

The function given by f(x) = 2x² + 3 is reflected in the line x = 3. What is the resulting function?

Solution:

replace (x, y) by (6-x,y) ; the function becomes y = 2(6-x)² + 3

Periodic Functions

For a function f(x) if there exists a positive real number P such that f(x)=f(x+P) then f(x) is called a periodic function and the minimum value of P is called the period of the function f(x). Please note the following definitions for periodic functions as well:

$$\text{Frequency} = \frac{1}{\text{Period}} = \frac{1}{P} \qquad \text{Offset} = \frac{y_{max} + y_{min}}{2}$$

$$\text{Amplitude} = \frac{y_{max} - y_{min}}{2} \qquad \text{Axis of wave is the line given by } \mathbf{y = offset}$$

Example:

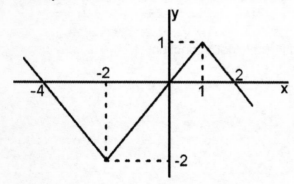

Graph of a periodic function is given above such that one period is plotted and the period is 6. Find the x-coordinates of the first 6 maxima, minima and zeros whose x coordinates are positive. Find the domain, range, amplitude, offset, axis of wave, and frequency.

Solution :

Maxima → 1, 7, 13, 19, 25, 31; Minima → 4, 10, 16, 22, 28, 34; Zeros → 2, 6, 8, 12, 14, 18

Domain: R, Range: $-2 \leq y \leq 1$; Amplitude = $\frac{1--2}{2} = 1.5$, Offset = $\frac{1+(-2)}{2} = -0.5$

Axis of wave: the line given by y = - 0.5; Frequency = $\frac{1}{6}$.

Exercises

1.

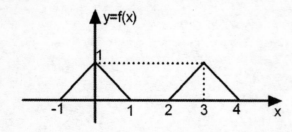

Find domain, range, period and frequency of the functions given.

2.

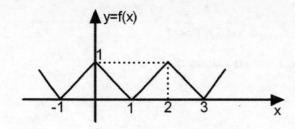

Find domain, range, amplitude, offset, axis of wave, period and frequency of the function given.

3.   If $f(x)=10^x$, then what is $\dfrac{f^{-1}(m)}{f^{-1}(n)}$ where m>0 and n>0?

4.   If $f(x)=2^x$, then what is $\dfrac{f^{-1}(m)}{f^{-1}(n)}$ where m>0 and n>0?

5.   If $f(x) = \log_2 x$ for x>0, then $f^{-1}(x)=$?

6.   If $f(x) = \log x$ for x>0, then $f^{-1}(x)=$?

7.   If $f(x) = \ln x$ for x>0, then $f^{-1}(x)=$?

8. $f(x)=\sqrt{x+3}$ where $x \geq -3$. Find $f^{-1}(x)$ and the domain of $f^{-1}(x)$.

9.   If $f(x,y)=x^2-xy+y^2$ for all real numbers x and y, which of the following are true?

a. $f(x,y)=f(x,-y)$ b. $f(x,y)=f(-x,y)$ c. $f(x,y)=f(-x,-y)$

10.

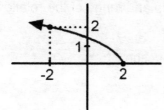

$f(x)=\sqrt{ax+b}$

a=?

b=?

11. $f(x)=\dfrac{x+1}{x-3}$; domain of f(x)=?

12.

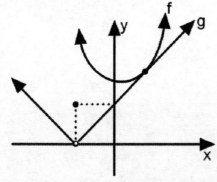

Which one(s) of the following are correct?

a.   (f+g)(x) is always positive.

b.   (f-g)(x) is always positive.

c.   (f.g)(x) is always nonzero.

d. $\left(\dfrac{f}{g}\right)(x)$ is always defined.

e.   g(x) is a strictly positive function.

13. $y=\dfrac{1}{x^2+1}$; If $\left(A,\dfrac{1}{2}\right)$ is a point on the curve, what are the possible values for A?

14. $\dfrac{x-4}{(x-1)^2}$ is not defined for x=A. A=?

15. $f(x)=x^2+1$; g(x)=x+1; (fog)(x)=(gof)(x) $\Rightarrow$ x=?

16.   f(a+b)=f(a)·f(b) such that f(x)>0.

a) f(x)=?   b) f(0)=?

17.   f(ab)=f(a)+f(b), such that f(x) is defined for all positive values of x.

a) f(x)=?   b) f(1)=?

18. $f(x)=x^3+x^5-1$. If f(a)=10 then find f(-a)=?

19.   Given that f is odd and g is even and that f(a)=b=g(c) and f(a)=b=g(c).

$$\frac{f(-a)}{g(-c)} + f(-a) - g(-c) = ?$$

20.   f(a)>0 and f(c)<0 given. A is the point (a,f(a)) and B is the point (c,f(c)) on the continuous function f(x) where a<c<0. Which one(s) of the following are correct?

1. f(x) has at least one negative real zero

2. f(x) has at least one positive real zero.

3. f(x) has a zero between a and c.

4. f(x) has a zero either less than a or greater than c.

5. Slope of AB is negative

6. f(x) has at least one point such that the slope of the tangent to f(x) at this point is negative.

21.

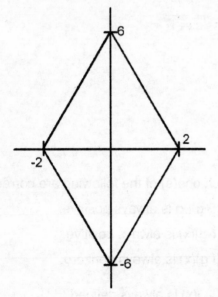

a. What is the domain and range of the relation given?

b. Is the relation a function?

22.

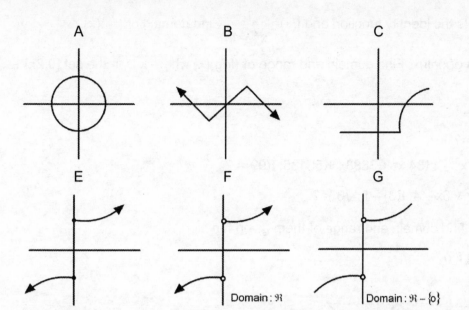

Determine whether or not each relation given above represents a function

23.

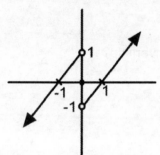

$f(f(-2) + f(2)) = ?$

24.

$$f(x) = \begin{cases} 2x & x \geq 3 \\ 1 & -2 < x < 0 \\ x - 4 & x \leq -2 \end{cases}$$

Domain of f is [-4,4]; range of f=?

25.

$$f(x) = \begin{cases} x + 3 & x > 0 \\ x - 3 & x < 0 \end{cases}$$

Find domain and range of f.

26. $f(x) = \sqrt{9 - x}$ and $g(x) = \sqrt[3]{x}$. Calculate $(f+g)(8)$, $(f\text{-}g)(8)$, $(f.g)(8)$, $(\frac{f}{g})(8)$.

27.   f(x)=3x; g(x)= -x²; h(x)=1

w(x)=(fogoh)(x)

What is the range of w(x)?

28. $f(x) = \sqrt{9 - x}$ and g(x)=x². Find domain and range of f(x), g(x), (fog)(x) and (gof)(x).

29. I(x) represents the identity function and f(x)= $\dfrac{1}{x^2-1}$. Find domain of $(\dfrac{f}{I})(x)$.

30. f(x)=sinx and g(x)=lnx. Find domain and range of (fog)(x) where x is in the set $[0,2\pi]$.

31. f(x)=x³+x+1

   a. $(f^{-1}of)(x)$=?

   b. $(fof^{-1})(2)$=?

32. f(x)= $x^4 - 88 x^3 - 1134 x^2 + 3888x + 56135$; f(99)= ?

33. f(x)= $x^3 - 4x^2 + 6x - 4$; $f(3) - f(\sqrt{3})$=?

34. f(x)= $\sqrt{x+4}$; find domain and range of them given function.

35.

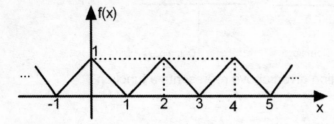

In which of the following intervals f(x) is one to one, therefore invertible?

i) [-3,-5]

ii) [1,2]

iii) [2,3]

iv) [3,4]

v) [-1,1]

36. Which one(s) of the following graphs represents one to one functions?

A   B   C   D

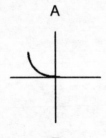 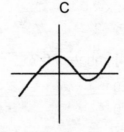 

E   F   G   H

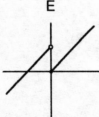 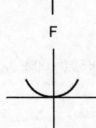 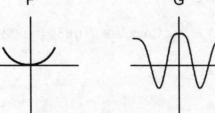 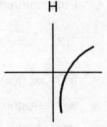

37.   The functions g and h are each periodic with period 5 such that g(3)=4 and h(-2)=8 calculate the following:

   a. g(23)+h(8)

   b. (g-2h)(18)=?

   c. $(\frac{g}{h})(23)$=?

   d. g(h(3)-5)=?

   e. g(h(28))=?

38.   f(x)= e^x; g(x)=cos x.

   (fog)($\sqrt{3}$)=

39.   Find inverse of each function or relation.

   a. f={(3,4),(2,1),(2,3),(0,-1),(0,0)}

   b. g(x)=x²+1; x>0

   c. h(x)=x²+1; x<0

   d. f(x)=$\sqrt{x+3}$; x>-3

   e. g(x)=-x³

   f.   h(x)=$\dfrac{2}{x+3}$

40.   What is one possible expression for y in terms of x?

   a. $\dfrac{f(x)}{f(y)}$=f(x-y).

   b. f(x).f(y)=f(x+y).

   c. f(xy)=f(x)+f(y)

   d. f($\dfrac{x}{y}$)=f(x)-f(y)

   e. f(xy)=f(x).f(y)

   f.   f($\dfrac{x}{y}$)=$\dfrac{f(x)}{f(y)}$

41.   f(x,y)= $2x^2 - y^2$

   g(x)= 5^x

   g(f(4,3))= ?

42.   f(x,y)= $\sqrt{3x^2 - 4y}$

   g(x)= 3^x

   g(f(2,1)) = ?

43. $f(x)= \sqrt{3x-4}$; $g(x)= x^3 + x + 1$; $f(g(2))= ?$

44. $f(x)= \sqrt{2x-2}$; $g(x)= \cos x$

    $g^{-1}(f(\sqrt{2}))=?$

45. $f(x)=3x$; $f(\log_7 4)=?$

46. $f(x)= x^2 + 5x -7$; $g(x)= x - 5$; $f(g(\ln 9))= ?$

47. $f(x)= \sqrt{x}$; $g(x)= \sqrt[3]{(x+2)^2}$; $h(x)= \sqrt[5]{x-4}$; $h(g(f(2)))= ?$

48. $f(x)= x \ln x$; $g(x)= 10^{x+1}$

    $g(f(3))=?$

49. $f(x)= 3x^2 + 8x - 6$; Find the negative value of $f^{-1}(0)$

50.
    f(x) is given as follows: $f(x) = \begin{cases} \dfrac{1}{x^2 - 1} & x < 2 \\ \\ x + 2 & x > 3 \end{cases}$

    a. Find domain of f(x)

    b. For what values of x is f(x-1) not defined?

51. $f(x)= x\sqrt[3]{x}$; $f(\sqrt{2})= ?$

52. Determine the domains of the following functions

    a. $f(x)= \dfrac{|x|}{x}$

    b. $f(x)= \dfrac{x^2}{x^3 - 27}$

    c. $f(x)= \sqrt{x^3 - 27}$

    d. $f(x)= \sqrt{x^2 - 9}$

    e. $f(x)= \dfrac{x^2 - 1}{x - 1}$

53. Find domain and range of f(x) if $f(x) = \begin{cases} 3 & x \geq 1 \\ x-1 & x < -3 \end{cases}$

54.   Determine the period in each case:

a)

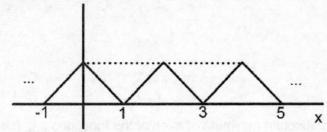

b)

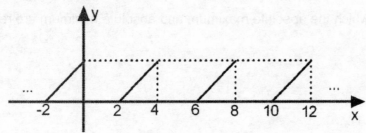

c)

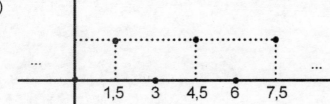

d) f(x)=|cosx|

e) f(x)=|tanx|

f) f(x)= $\begin{cases} 0 & \text{if x is even} \\ 3 & \text{if x is odd} \end{cases}$

g) f(x)=|cscx|

h) f(x)=The remainder when [x] is divided by 3, where [x] represents the greatest integer less than or equal to x.

55.   OPTIONAL QUESTION

f(x) is given as follows: f(x)= $\begin{cases} 0 & \text{if x < 0} \\ 1 & \text{otherwise} \end{cases}$. Sketch the graph of

a. f(x)

b. f(x+1)

c. f(1-x)

56. Let

i. $f(x)=x^2, -2<x<2$

ii. $g(x)=x^3, -2<x<2$

iii. $h(x)=\sqrt{x}, 0<x<4$

iv. $p(x)=x^{1/3}, -8<x<8$

Find the absolute maximum and absolute minimum of each of the functions f, g, h and p.

Determine the points at which the absolute maximum and absolute minimum are reached.

Evenness and Oddness

E V E N	O D D
A l g e b r a i c a l l y	
f(-x)= f(x)	f(-x)= - f(x)
G r a p h i c a l l y	
f(x) = f(-x) = A ⇒ (x,A) and (-x,A) are on the same graph 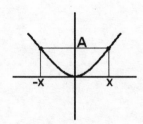 Graph is symmetric with respect to the y - axis.	f(x) = A and f(-x)= -A ⇒ (x,A) and (-x, -A) are on the same graph 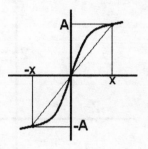 Graph is symmetric with respect to the origin.
P o l y n o m i a l F u n c t i o n s	
If a polynomial function contains only even powers of x with or without a constant term, then it is even.	If a polynomial function contains only odd powers of x and no constant term, then it is odd.
R e l a t i o n s G i v e n a s S e t s	
If a relation contains (x,A) and (-x,A) pairs with or without (0, B), then the relation is even.	If a relation contains (x,A), (-x,-A) pairs with or without (0, 0), then the relations is odd.
R e l a t i o n s G i v e n A l g e b r a i c a l l y	
When x is replaced by –x, if no change occurs in relation then the relation is even. (Replace x by –x; if no change then even).	When x is replaced by –x and y is replaced by –y, if no change occurs in the relation, then the relation is odd. (Replace x by –x and y by –y, if no change then odd.)

Tests for Symmetry

A relation is symmetric

- across the **x axis** if its equation undergoes no change when (x, y) is replaced by **(x, -y)**.

- across the **y axis** if its equation undergoes no change when (x, y) is replaced by **(-x, y)**.

- across the **origin** if its equation undergoes no change when (x, y) is replaced by **(-x, -y)**.

- across the line **y = x** if its equation undergoes no change when (x, y) is replaced by **(y, x)**.

- across the line **y = -x** if its equation undergoes no change when (x, y) is replaced by **(-y, -x)**.

Exercises

1.   State whether each of the following relation or function is even, odd, both odd and even, or neither odd nor even.

a.

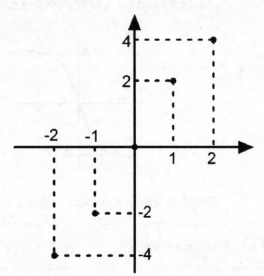

b.

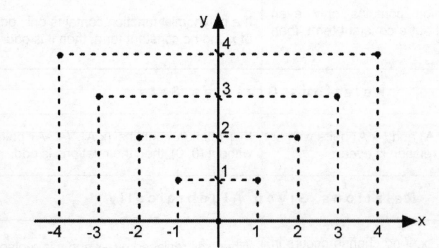

c. $x^2+y^3=4y+5$

d. $x^2+y^2+xy+3=0$

e. $x^2+y^2=9$

f. $x^5+y^3=9$

g. $f(x) = -3x^6 - 4x^4 + 5x^2 + 7$

h. $f(x) = 2x^5 - 4x^3 - 6x$

i. $f(x) = x^4 + x^3$

j. $f(x) = 3x^4 - 2x^2$

k. $f(x) = 3x^4 + 2x^2 + 5$

l. $f(x) = -7x^3 + x$

m. $f(x) = 2x^3 + x - 5$

n. $f(x) = 1$

o. $f(x) = \dfrac{1}{\sec x}$

p. $f(x) = \cos x$

q. $f(x) = \dfrac{1}{\csc(x)}$

r. $f(x) = \sin x$

s. $f(x) = \sin x + 1$

t. $f(x) = \dfrac{1}{x}$

u. $f(x) = |x|$

v. $f(x) = \log(x^2)$

w. $f(x) = -x^2 + \sin x$

x. $f(x) = x^4 - 3x^2 + 5$

2.   State whether each of the following relation or function is even, odd, both odd and even, or neither odd nor even.

a. $f(x) = 3x^3 + 5$

b. $f(x) = 12x^6 + 4x^4 - 13x^2$

c. $f(x) = -x^5 - 8x^3 + 12x$

d. $f(x) = x^3$

e. $f(x) = 3x^4 + 2x^2 - 8$

f. $y = 2$

g. $y = 0$

h. $y = x$

i. $f(x) = x^3 - 1$

j. $f(x) = x^2 - 1$

k. $f(x) = -x + \sin x$

l. $f(x) = -x$

m. $f(x) = x^2$

n. $f(x) = \dfrac{1}{x^2}$

o. $f(x) = 2x^4$

p. $f(x) = x^3 + 1$

q. $f(x) = \dfrac{x}{x-2}$

r. $f(x) = x^3 + x$

s. $x = 2$

t. $x = 0$

u. $f(x) = \sin(x)$

v. $f(x) = \sqrt{x^2} + 1$

3. Given that (x,A) and (-x,A) are both on the graph of an odd relation then find all possible values of x and A.

4. Given that (x,A) and (-x,-A) are both on the graph of an even relation then find all possible values of x and A.

5. If a point (a,b) is on the graph of a function and its inverse then find all possible values for a and b.

6. $f(x) = \cos x$ and $g(x) = 2x+1$.

    i. $f(x) \cdot g(x)$

    ii. $f(g(x))$

    iii. $g(f(x))$

7. Determine if each of the following functions is even, odd, both odd and even, or, neither odd nor even.

    i. $f(x) = 2^x$

    ii. $f(x) = \ln(x)$

    iii. the product of two even functions.

    iv. the quotient of two even functions

    v. the product of two odd functions.

    vi. the quotient of two odd functions.

    vii. the composition of two odd functions

    viii. the composition of two even functions.

8.   Given that a function satisfies only one of the conditions A, B, C; match the cases A, B, C with 1,2,3.

A: For every point (x,y) on the graph, (x,-y) is also on the same graph.

B: For every point (x,y) on the graph (-x,-y) is also on the same graph.

C: For every point (x,y) on the graph (-x,y) is also on the same graph.

1: The graph is symmetric about the origin and is odd.

2: The graph is symmetric about the y axis and is even.

3: The graph is symmetric about the x axis and it is neither odd nor even.

9.   Match each relation given in i. through ix. with the following cases:

a) Odd symmetry

b) Even symmetry

c) Symmetry in the x axis

d) Symmetry in the line y=x.

e) Symmetry in the line y=-x

f) Symmetry in the point (1,1).

i) $y=x^2+1$

ii) $y=x^3$

iii) $y=\dfrac{1}{x}$

iv) $x^2+y^2=1$

v) $(x-1)^2+(y-1)^2=1$

vi) $x^2-y^2=1$

vii) $\dfrac{x^2}{25}-\dfrac{y^2}{144}=1$

viii) $xy=6$

ix) $xy=-1$

10.   Discuss the symmetry of the graph of each function and determine whether the function is even, odd, or neither.

a. $f(x)=x^6+1$

b. $f(x)=x^4-3x^2+4$

c. $f(x)=x^3-x^2$

d. $f(x)=2x^3+3x$

e. $f(x)=(x-1)^3$

f. $f(x)=(x+1)^4$

g. $f(x) = \sqrt{x^2 + 4}$

h. $f(x) = 4|x| + 2$

i. $f(x) = (x^2 + 1)^3$

j. $f(x) = \dfrac{x^2 - 1}{x^2 + 1}$

k. $f(x) = \sqrt{4 - x^2}$

l. $f(x) = x^{\frac{1}{3}}$

11. Determine whether each of the following functions is even, odd or one-to-one. If it is one-to-one, compute its inverse.

   a. $f(x) = x^2 - 1$

   b. $g(x) = x^3 - 1$

   c. $h(x) = \sqrt{9 - x}, x \geq 9$

   d. $k(x) = x^{2/3}$

12. For a function $f(x)$ the following new functions $g(x)$ and $h(x)$ are defined:

   $g(x) = \dfrac{f(x) + f(-x)}{2}$ and $h(x) = \dfrac{f(x) - f(-x)}{2}$

   Which one(s) of the following are correct?

   a. $f = g + h$

   b. g is even and h is odd

   c. it cannot be determined whether or not g or h is odd

13. For each of the following relations given in a through e, state which of the following is correct:

   1. Relation is even only.   a. {(1,3), (1, -3), (-1, 3), (-1, -3), (0,0)}

   2. Relation is odd only.   b. {(1,3), (-1,3), (2,-4), (-2,-4), (0,-2)}

   3. Relation is both odd and even. c. {(1,3), (-1,3), (0,2), (0,-2)}

   4. Relation is neither odd nor even. d. {1,3), (-1,3), (0,0), (0,4)}

                                      e. {1,3), (-1,-3), (2,-4), (-2, 4), (0,2), (0,-2)}

14.   Which one(s) of the following are correct?

1. Even functions are never invertible.

2. Odd functions are always invertible.

3. Only nonzero even functions are invertible.

4. Only nonzero odd functions are invertible.

Basic Functions

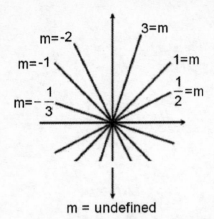

m = undefined

Line Passing Through the Origin

f(x)=mx; odd

Domain=R; Range=R

Inverse is a function.

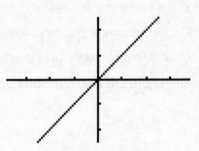

Identity Function

f(x)=x; odd

Domain=R; Range=R

Inverse is a function.

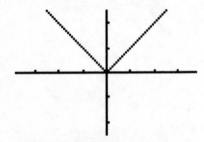

Absolute Value Function

f(x)=|x|=abs(x); even

Domain=R; Range=[0,∞)

Inverse is not a function.

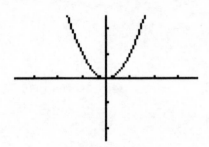

Square Function

f(x)=x²; even

Domain=R; Range=[0, ∞)

Inverse is not a function.

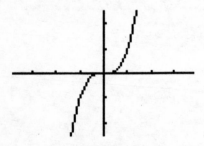

Cube Function

f(x)=x³; odd

Domain=R; Range=R

Inverse is a function.

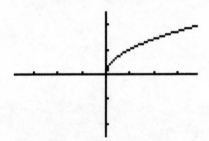

Square Root Function

f(x)= $\sqrt{x}$; neither odd nor even

Domain=[0,∞); Range=[0,∞)

Inverse is a function.

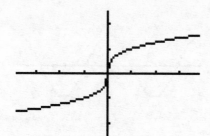

Cube – Root Function

$f(x)=\sqrt[3]{x}$: odd

Domain=R; Range=R

Inverse is a function.

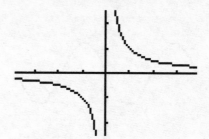

Reciprocal Function

$f(x)=\dfrac{1}{x}$; odd

Domain=R-{0}; Range= R-{0}

Inverse is a function.

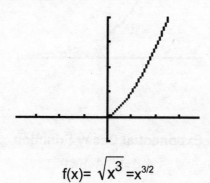

$f(x)=\sqrt{x^3}=x^{3/2}$

neither odd nor even

Domain=[0,∞); Range=[0,∞)

Inverse is a function.

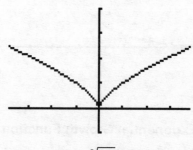

$f(x)=\sqrt[3]{x^2}=x^{2/3}$

even

Domain=R; Range=[0,∞)

Inverse is not a function.

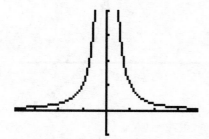

Chimney Function

$f(x)=\dfrac{1}{x^2}$; even

Domain=R-{0}; Range=(0, ∞)

Inverse is not a function.

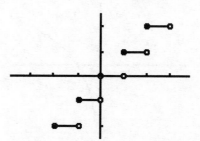

Greatest Integer Function

$f(x)=[[x]]=[x]=int(x)$

neither odd nor even

Domain=R; Range=all integers

Inverse is not a function.

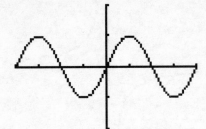

Sine Function

f(x)=sin(x); odd

Domain=R; Range=[-1, 1]

Inverse is not a function.

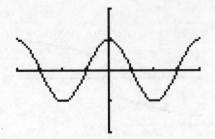

Cosine Function

f(x)=cos(x); even

Domain=R; Range=[-1,1]

Inverse is not a function.

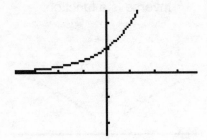

Exponential Growth Function

f(x)=b^x, b>1

neither odd nor even

Domain=R; Range=(0,∞)

Inverse is a function.

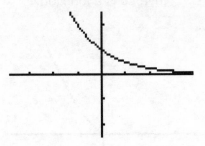

Exponential Decay Function

f(x)=b^x, 0<b<1

neither odd nor even

Domain=R; Range=(0, ∞)

Inverse is a function.

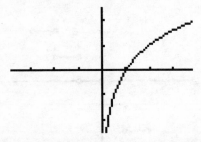

Logarithmic Function (Increasing)

f(x)=log$_b$(x), b > 1

neither odd nor even

Domain=(0,∞); Range=R

Inverse is a function.

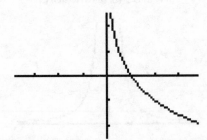

Logarithmic Function (Decreasing)

f(x)=log$_b$(x), 0 < b < 1

neither odd nor even

Domain=(0,∞); Range=R

Inverse is a function.

Hyperbolic Rational Function (Increasing)   **Hyperbolic Rational Function (Decreasing)**

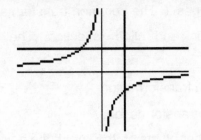 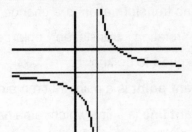

$$f(x) = \frac{ax + b}{cx + d}$$

$$\text{Domain} = R - \left\{\frac{-d}{c}\right\} \text{ and Range} = R - \left\{\frac{a}{c}\right\}$$

It is odd provided that –d/c = a/c = 0; otherwise neither odd nor even.

Inverse is a function.

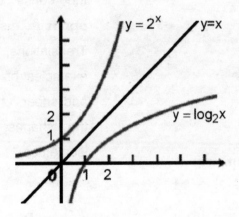

$f(x)=2^x$ and $f(x)=\log_2 x$ are inverses of each other.

1.4 GEOMETRIC TRANSFORMATIONS

A geometric transformation is a change to a shape that changes it. The common transformations are reflection, rotation, translation, enlargement, stretch, shear, and glide reflection. The following definitions need to be known:

- **Invariant point** is a point that remains unchanged during a transformation.

- **Invariant line** is a line which remains unchanged during a transformation.

Please note that points on the line may have moved, but to other points on the line. If the points on the line are also invariant then we have an invariant line of invariant points.

Types of Transformations

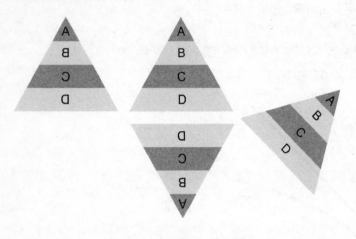

Examples of Isometry

Isometry is a transformation that leaves shape and size unchanged. A **direct isometry** leaves the "sense" of the shape unaffected and an **opposite isometry** reverses the sense. Translations, reflections and rotations are examples of isometries. Enlargement, stretch and shear, change the lengths of the sides of the shapes they transform and are not isometries.

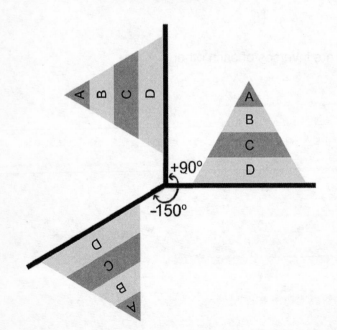

Example of Rotation

Rotation is defined by a center and an angle (including direction); and points are rotated about the center through the same angle; rotation is a direct isometry and center is the only invariant point.

Stretch is defined by an invariant line and a scale factor; points move perpendicular to the invariant line and their distances are multiplied away by the scale factor; neither shape nor size is preserved, but area is multiplied by the scale factor; the invariant line is a line of invariant points.

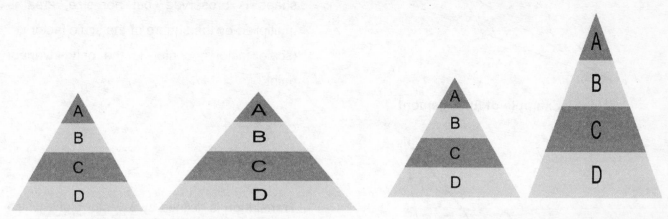

Example of Horizontal Stretch   **Example of Vertical Stretch**

Reflection is defined by a line (the mirror line) or a point; the mirror becomes the perpendicular bisector of every point and its image; it is an opposite isometry and mirror line is a line of invariant points. In point reflection, the point becomes the midpoint of every line segment that connects the point and its image.

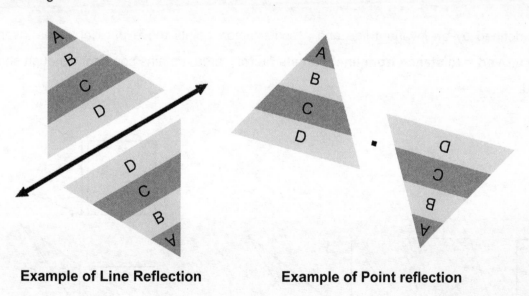

Example of Line Reflection   **Example of Point reflection**

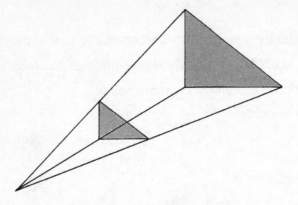

Example of Enlargement

Enlargement is defined by a center and a scale factor; the distance of the points from the center are multiplied by the scale factor; shape is preserved, but not size, area is multiplied by the square of the scale factor i.e. (scale factor)^2; center is the only invariant point.

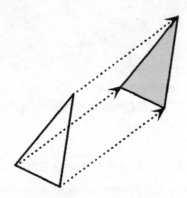

Example of Translation

Translation is defined by a vector along which all points slide; it is a direct isometry with no invariant points.

Shear is defined by an invariant line and a scale factor; points move parallel to the invariant line; **distance moved = (distance from line) · (scale factor)**; area remains constant although shape is not preserved.

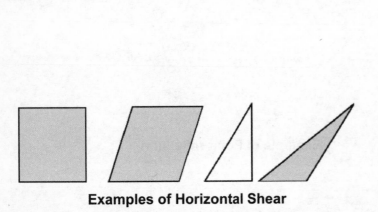

Examples of Horizontal Shear

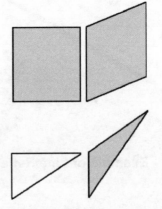

Examples of Vertical Shear

Inverse Transformations

It is sometimes desirable to undo a transformation being sometimes as simple as reversing what has been done. The inverse of a translation is the translation that is of the same length but in the opposite direction (Figure A). The inverse of a reflection is the same reflection; for example, the inverse of reflection in the y-axis is also reflection in the y-axis (Figure B). There may be sometimes more than one inverse for a given transformation. For example, the inverse of a 90° counterclockwise rotation about the origin is a 90° clockwise rotation about the origin; or another counterclockwise rotation of 270° could shape it back to its original position (Figure C).

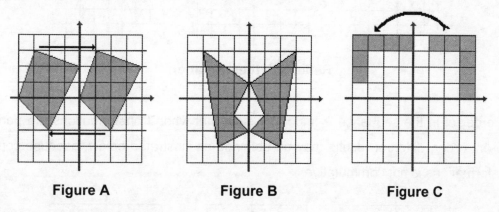

| Figure A | Figure B | Figure C |

Transformation	Inverse Transformation
Translation along vector **(a, b)**	Translation along vector **(– a, – b)**
Rotation about **(a, b)**, by angle α°	Rotation about **(a, b)**, by angle α° in the opposite direction
Reflection in any line	Reflection in the same line
Stretch by a factor of **a**, with respect to any invariant line	Stretch by a factor of **(1/a)** with respect to the same invariant line
Shear by a factor of **a**, with respect to any invariant line	Shear by a factor of **(1/a)**, with respect to the same invariant line

Composition of Transformations

- The following figure shows the result of first reflecting a shape in the y-axis and then rotating it by 90° counterclockwise about the origin. This type of sequence of transformations is known as a composition or a composite.

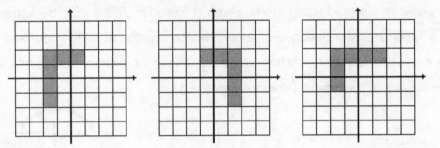

Reflection then Rotation

- The order of in the sequence is important such that when transformations are performed in a different order, different results may be obtained as illustrated below, because composition of transformations is not commutative.

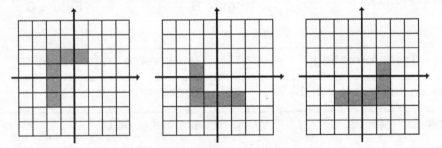

Rotation then Reflection

- Sometimes a single transformation may replace a composition of transformations. For example rotation by 50° followed by another 100° can be replaced by a single rotation of one 150° all being counterclockwise. In this example the order of the transformation does not matter. Please note that this is not generally the case.

- One last thing to note is the fact that the inverse of a 45° clockwise rotation followed by a reflection in the origin is a reflection in the origin followed by a 45° counterclockwise rotation. In the inverse of a composition of transformations, not only the transformations but also the order of transformations is reversed.

Example:

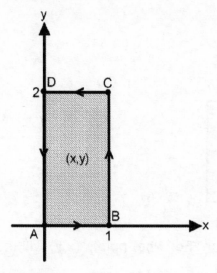

The points shown in the shaded region above are (x,y). Plot the region that would be represented by (-2x, x+y)

Solution:

(x.y)	(-2x,x+y)
(0,0)	(0,0)
(1, 0)	(-2, 1)
(1, 2)	(-2,3)
(0,2)	(0,2)
(0,0)	(0,0)

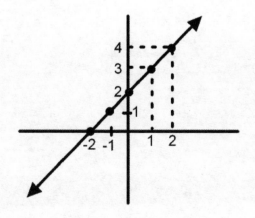

Example:

The points on the graph of y= x+2 are denoted as (x,y). Plot the graph of the points (x+2, $\sqrt{y}$)

Solution:

Method 1:

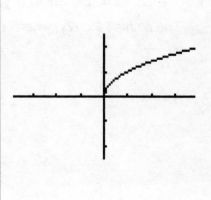

(x ,y)	(x+2, $\sqrt{y}$)
(-2,0)	(0,0)
(-1,1)	(1, 1)
(0,2)	(2, $\sqrt{2}$)
(1,3)	(3, $\sqrt{3}$)
(2,4)	(4, 2)

Method 2:

x'=x+2

$y' = \sqrt{y} = \sqrt{x+2}$

Mode: Parametric; $x_{1T}=x'=t+2$; $y_{1T}=y'=\sqrt{t+2}$; $t_{min}= -2\pi$

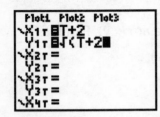 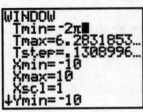 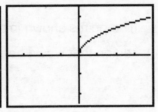

Exercises

1.   f:(x,y) → (x,y+2x) is given for every pair (x,y) in the plane. For what points (x,y) will it be true that (x,y)→(x,y)?

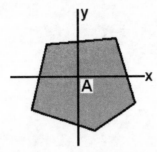

2.   In the figure above, shaded region A has an area of 7. Identify the type of transformation and state whether or not each transformation is an isometry. Find area of the specified region in each case. Find the inverse transformation for each one as well.

a.   The points (x+1,y–2) where (x,y) is in A.

b.   The points (x,-y) where (x,y) is in A.

c.   The points (-x,y) where (x,y) is in A.

d.   The points (-x,-y) where (x,y) is in A.

e.   The points (y,x) where (x,y) is in A.

f.   The points (x, 2y) where (x,y) is in A.

g.   The points (-2x, -2y) where (x,y) is in A.

1.5 SYMMETRY AND ROTATIONS

Types of Symmetry

Line Symmetry: A figure has line symmetry if a line can be drawn that divides the figure into two parts that are mirror images. The line of symmetry may be a horizontal line, a vertical line, or neither.

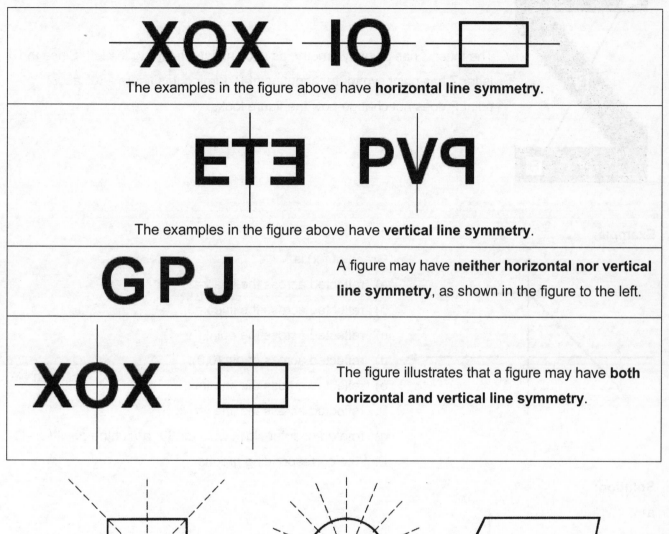

The examples in the figure above have **horizontal line symmetry**.

The examples in the figure above have **vertical line symmetry**.

A figure may have **neither horizontal nor vertical line symmetry**, as shown in the figure to the left.

The figure illustrates that a figure may have **both horizontal and vertical line symmetry**.

Four lines of symmetry

An infinite number of lines of symmetry

No line of symmetry

As shown in the figure above, a figure may have more than one line of symmetry or may have no line of symmetry.

Point Symmetry: A figure has point symmetry if it is possible to locate a point, P, such that, if any line is drawn through point P and intersects the figure in another point, A, it will also intersect the figure in a different point, call it B, so that AP = BP.

The letter Z has point symmetry, as shown in the figure to the left. Since the letter Z has point symmetry about point P, turning this figure 180° about point P does not change how the figure looks.

Example:

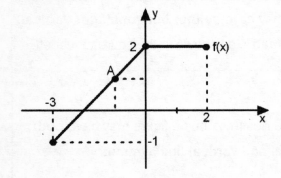

Graph of f(x) is

a) reflected across the line y=3;

b) reflected across the line x=3;

c) reflected across the point (3, -1);

d) reflected across origin (0,0);

e) reflected across the line y=x;

f) reflected across the line y= -x;

g) rotated counter clock wise for 90° about the point (2, -1)

Plot the corresponding graphs

Solution:

a)

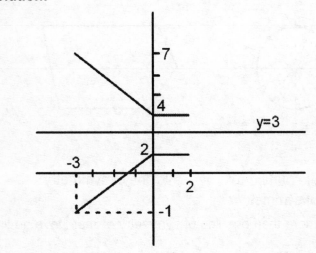

b)

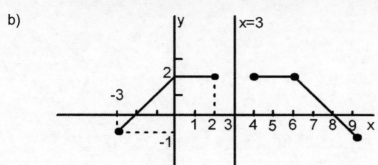

c)

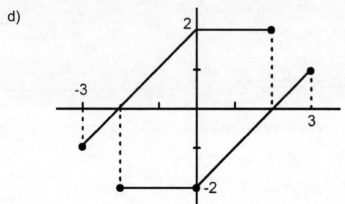

d)

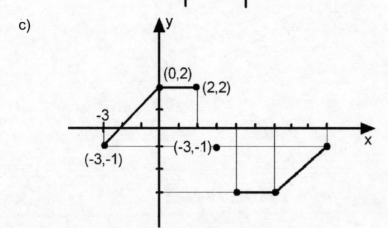

e)

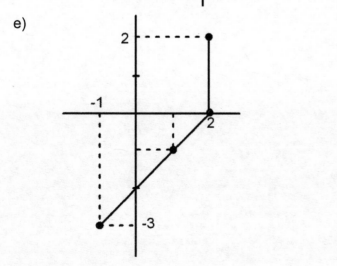

f)

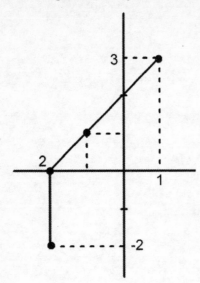

g)

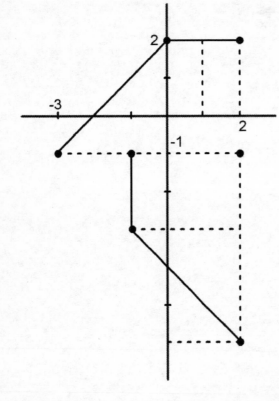

Exercises

1. If the point A(1,-1) is reflected across the line y=x+1 to get point B what are the coordinates of B?

2.

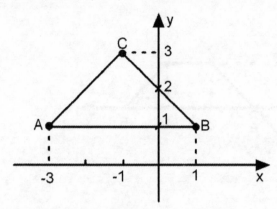

What will be the new coordinates of point A, B, and C, if the point A (a, b) is reflected across?

   a. the line x= 5
   b. the line x= -5
   c. the line y=4
   d. the line y= -4
   e. the point (2, -1)

3. The line y=x+1 is reflected across the point A(1, -1) to get the line l. What is the equation of line l?

4. The parabola $y=(x-2)^2$ is reflected across the point A(1,-2) to get the parabola given by y=g(x). g(x)=?

5.

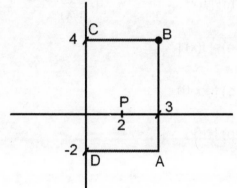

If the rectangle ABCD given above is rotated clockwise for 90° about point P, what will be the new coordinates of points A, B, C, and D?

1.6 ADVANCED GRAPHING OF TRANSFORMATIONS ON FUNCTIONS

Example:

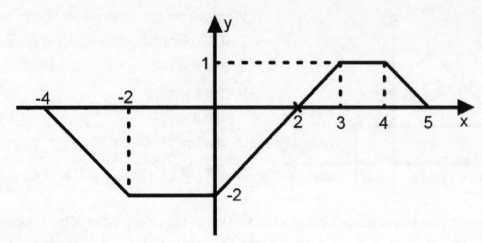

Graph of f(x) is given above, plot the graphs of the following:

a) f(x-2)	e) f(-x)	l) f(x) + 2	m) | f(x) |	q) $\dfrac{1}{f(x)}$
b) f(x+2)	f) f(|x|)	j) 2f(x)	n) -| f(x) |	
c) f(2x)	g) f(-|x|)	k) $\dfrac{f(x)}{2}$	o) f(2x-6)	
d) f($\dfrac{x}{2}$)	h) f(x) -1	l) – f(x)	p) f $^{-1}$(x)	

Solution:

(Horizontal Shifts)

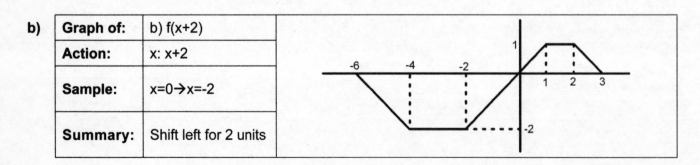

a)

Graph of:	b) f(x-2)
Action:	x: x-2
Sample:	x=0→x=2
Summary:	Shift right for 2 units

b)

Graph of:	b) f(x+2)
Action:	x: x+2
Sample:	x=0→x=-2
Summary:	Shift left for 2 units

(Horizontal Shrink - Stretch)

c)

Graph of:	b) f(2x)
Action:	x: 2x
Sample:	x=0→x=0 $x=1→x=\dfrac{1}{2}$
Summary:	Shrink horizontally by a factor of $\dfrac{1}{2}$

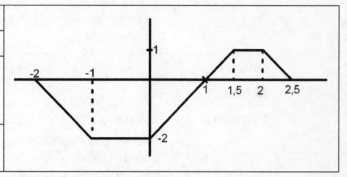

d)

Graph of:	$f(\dfrac{x}{2})$
Action:	x: $\dfrac{x}{2}$
Sample:	x=0→x=0 x=1→x=2
Summary:	Stretch horizontally by a factor of 2

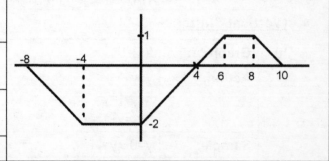

(Reflections in the y - axis)

e)

Graph of:	f(-x)
Action:	x: -x
Sample:	x=0→x=0 x=1→x=-1 x=-1→x=1
Summary:	Reflect in the y – axis

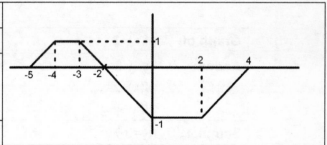

f)

$$f(|x|) = \begin{cases} f(x) & x \geq 0 \\ f(-x) & x < 0 \end{cases}$$

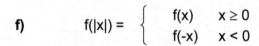

Graph of:	f(|x|)
Action:	x: |x|
Summary:	• Suppress negative x portion of f(x). • Reflect and duplicate positive x portion of f(x). Resulting function becomes even (i.e. symmetric in the y-axis) **Even: f(-x)=f(x);** **symmetry in the y – axis**

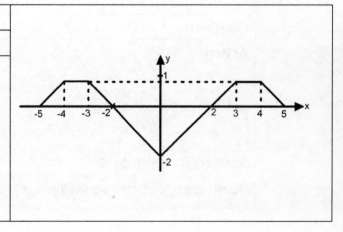

g) $f(-|x|) = \begin{cases} f(-x) & x \geq 0 \\ f(x) & x < 0 \end{cases}$

Graph of:	f(-|x|)
Action:	x: -|x|
Summary:	• Suppress positive x portion of f(x). • Reflect and duplicate negative x portion of f(x). Resulting function becomes even (i.e. symmetric in the y-axis)

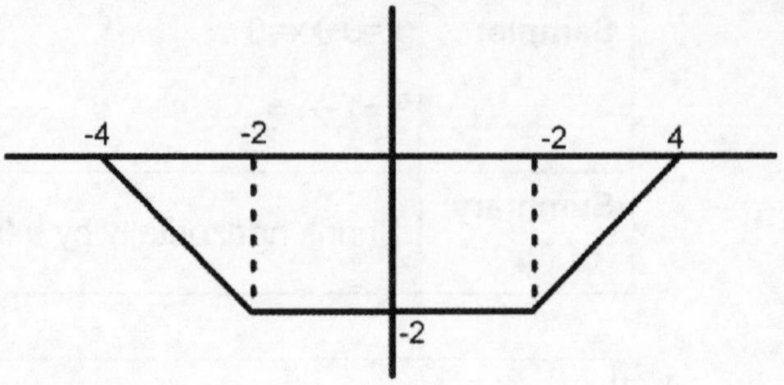

(Vertical Shifts)

h)

Graph of:	f(x)-1
Action:	y: y+1 f(x)–1=y f(x)=y+1
Sample:	y=0➔y=-1
Summary:	Shift down for 1 unit.

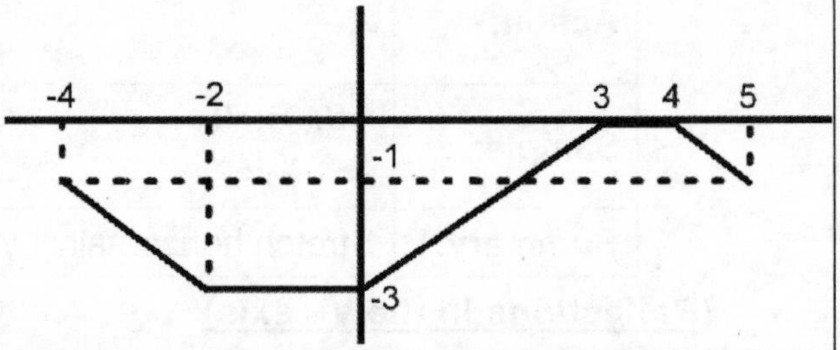

i)

Graph of:	f(x)+2
Action:	y: y-2 f(x)+2=y f(x)=y-2
Sample:	y=0➔y=2
Summary:	Shift up for 2 units.

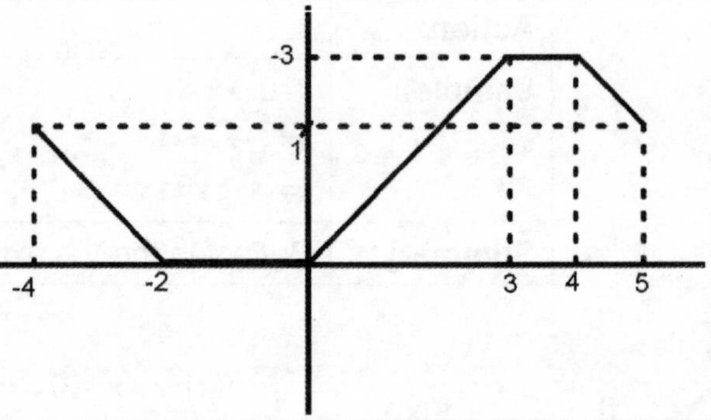

(Vertical Shrink - Stretch)

j)

Graph of:	2f(x)
Action:	$y: \dfrac{y}{2}$ 2f(x)=y $f(x)=\dfrac{y}{2}$
Sample:	y=0➔y=2
Summary:	Stretch vertically by a factor of 2

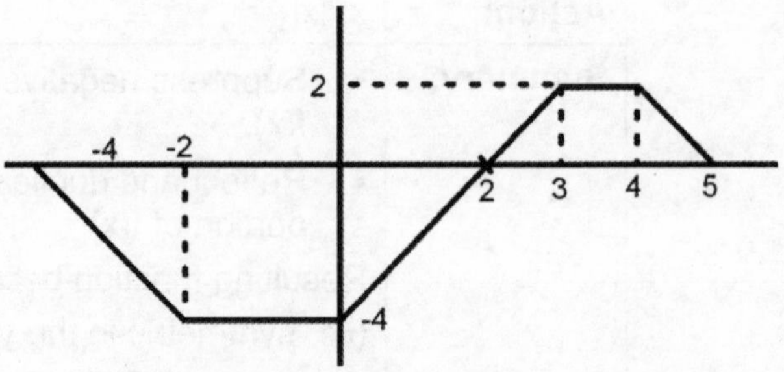

k)

Graph of:	$\dfrac{f(x)}{2}$
Action:	y:2y $\dfrac{f(x)}{2} = y$ f(x)= 2y
Sample:	y=0→y=0 y=1→y=1/2
Summary:	Shrink vertically by a factor of $\dfrac{1}{2}$

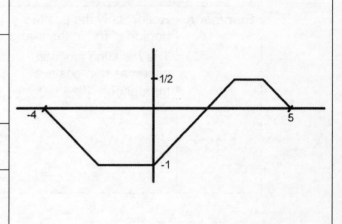

(Reflections in the x - axis)

l)

Graph of:	–f(x)
Action:	y:-y –f(x)=y f(x)= -y
Sample:	y=0→y=0 y=1→y= -1 y=-1→y=1
Summary:	Reflect in the x-axis

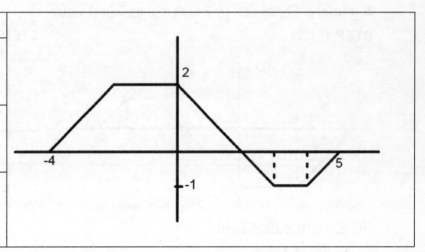

(Absolute Values)

m)

Graph of:	|f(x)|
Summary:	Reflect only the negative y portion of f(x) in the x-axis The resulting function becomes non-negative throughout: |f(x)| ≥ 0

n)

Graph of:	-|f(x)|
Summary:	Reflect only the positive y portion of f(x) in the x-axis The resulting function becomes non-positive throughout: -|f(x)| $\leq$ 0

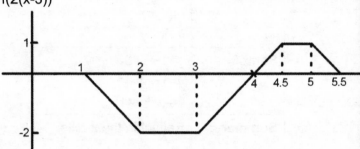

o) Graph of: f(2x – 6)=f(2(x – 3)):

$f(x) \rightarrow f(2x) \rightarrow f(2x - 6)$

Summary: Shrink in x by 2 shift in x by 3 (not by 6)

STEP 1: x:2x

f(2x)

STEP 2: x:x-3

f(2(x-3))

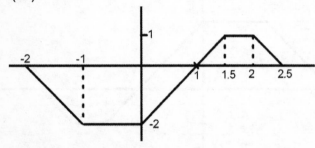

(Inverse of a function)

p) Graph of: f $^{-1}$(x)

Summary: Reflect in the line y=x

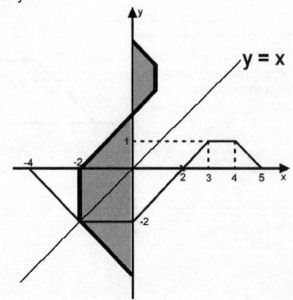

Resulting graph may not correspond to a function

(Reciprocal of a function)

q) Graph of: $\dfrac{1}{f(x)}$

Domain of f: $-4 \le x \le 5$ Range f: $-2 \le y \le 1$

Domain of $\dfrac{1}{f}$: $-4 < x < 2$ or $2 < x < 5$ Range of $\dfrac{1}{f}$: $y \ge 1$ or $y \le -1/2$

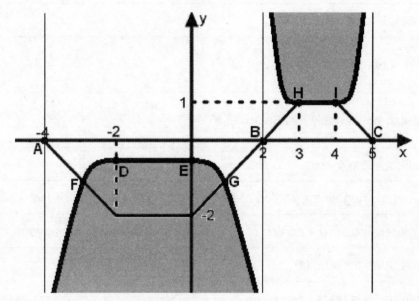

1. $f(x) = 0 \Rightarrow \dfrac{1}{f(x)} = \dfrac{1}{0} =$ undefined $\Rightarrow$ vertical asymptotes (A,B,C) x=-4, 2, 5

2. $f(x) = -2 \Rightarrow \dfrac{1}{f(x)} = \dfrac{1}{-2} = -0,5$ (D $\leftrightarrow$ E) $-2 \le x \le 0$

3. $f(x) = -1 \Rightarrow \dfrac{1}{f(x)} = \dfrac{1}{-1} = -1$ (F,G)

4. $f(x) = 1 \Rightarrow \dfrac{1}{f(x)} = \dfrac{1}{1} = 1$ (H $\leftrightarrow$ I) $3 \le x \le 4$

5. $f(x) \to 0^{+} \Rightarrow \dfrac{1}{f(x)} \to +\infty$ RHS of x=2 & LHS of x=5

       $f(x) \to 0^{-} \Rightarrow \dfrac{1}{f(x)} \to -\infty$ RHS of x=-4 & LHS of x=2

(RHS: Right Hand Side; LHS: Left Hand Side)

Please note that the graph of a function can never intersect with the vertical asymptotes.

A variety of transformations can be applied on a function given by y = f(x). A partial list of the most common transformations is given in the following table.

Table of Transformations

a and **b** are positive real numbers greater than 1

f(x–**a**)	Shift right for **a** units
f(x+**a**)	Shift left for **a** units
f(**a**x)	Shrink horizontally by a factor of $\dfrac{1}{a}$
$f(\dfrac{x}{a})$	Stretch horizontally by a factor of **a**
f(–x)	Reflect in the y–axis
f(|x|)	Suppress negative x portion of f(x), reflect and duplicate positive x portion of f(x)
f(–|x|)	Suppress positive x portion of f(x), reflect and duplicate negative x portion of f(x)
f(x)–**a**	Shift down for **a** units
f(x)+**a**	Shift up for **a** units
a f(x)	Stretch vertically by a factor of **a**
$\dfrac{f(x)}{a}$	Shrink vertically by a factor of $\dfrac{1}{a}$
–f(x)	Reflect in the x–axis
|f(x)|	Reflect only the negative y portion of f(x) in the x–axis
–|f(x)|	Reflect only the positive y portion of f(x) in the x–axis
f(**a**x ± **b**)	Shrink in x by **a**; shift in x by $\dfrac{b}{a}$ (not by b)
f $^{-1}$(x)	Reflect in the line y=x

Example:

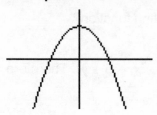

Graph of f(x) is given above. Plot the graph of the slopes of tangents to f(x) at each point.

Solution:

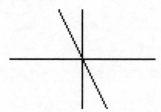

Example:

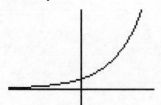

Graph of f(x) is given. Plot the graph of $\dfrac{1}{f(x)}$

Solution:

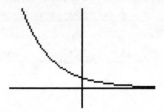

Example:

f(x)=x^2

1. Shift right for 3 units

2. Shift down for 1 unit

3. Reflect in the x axis

4. Reflect in the y axis

If steps 1 through 4 are applied to f(x) successively, what will be the resulting function?

Solution:

$x^2 \rightarrow (x-3)^2 \rightarrow (x-3)^2-1 \rightarrow -(x-3)^2 + 1 \rightarrow -(-x-3)^2 + 1 = -(x^2+6x+9) +1 = -x^2 -6x-8$

Example:

If the function $f(x)=x^2+3x-6$ is reflected across the point $(2,-3)$ what will be resulting function?

Solution:

Each point (x, y) on the curve when reflected across $(2, -3)$ gives the point $(4 - x, -6 - y)$. Therefore the resulting curve is obtained by replacing x with $(4 - x)$ and y with $(-6 - y)$ in

$y=x^2+3x-6.$ $\Rightarrow -6 - y = (4 - x)^2 + 3(4 - x) - 6 \Rightarrow y = -x^2 + 11x - 28.$

Example:

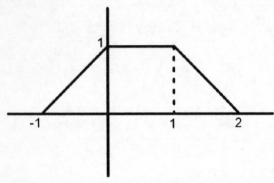

f(x) whose graph is given is reflected across the point $(3, -1/2)$ to get $a.f(x+b)+c$. Find a, b, and c.

Solution:

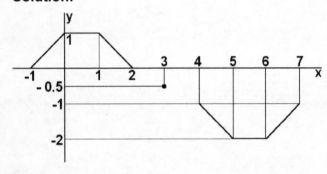

Shift right for 5 units; reflect across the x-axis and shift down for one unit .

$\Rightarrow -f(x-5)-1= a.f(x+b)+c \Rightarrow$ a= -1; b= -5; c= -1

Exercises

1.

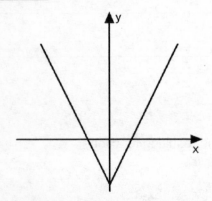

Given the graph of y=f(x). Plot the graph of:

i. $y=|f(x)|$ ii. $y=\dfrac{f(x)+|f(x)|}{2}$ iii. $y=\dfrac{f(x)-|f(x)|}{2}$

2. The solution set of $f(x)=A$ is $\{2,-3\}$. What is the solution set of $f(x-3)=A$?

3. The graph of $f(x)= -x^2$ is translated 2 units left and 1 unit up to represent $g(x)$. What is the value of $g(3.2)$?

4.

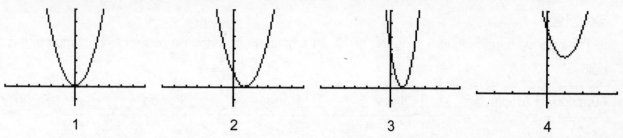

1   2   3   4

The diagrams show how the graph of y=x² is transformed to the graph of y=f(x) in three steps. For each diagram, write down the equation of the curve.

5.

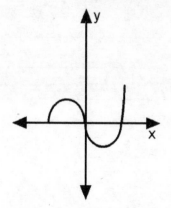

In the given figure, the area of the shaded region bounded by the graph of the parabola y=f(x) and the x-axis is 6. Find the area of the region bounded by the graph of y=f(x-4) and the x-axis.

6.

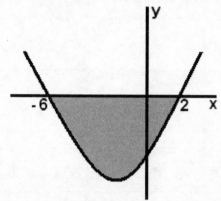

The graph of y=f(x) is given. Plot the graphs of the following.

a. y=|f(x)|

b. y=-|f(x)|

c. y=f(|x|)

d. y=f(-|x|)

7.   f: (x,y) → (x²+1, y²+4)

g: (x,y) → (2x, 4y)

Find the points on the coordinate plane that are mapped to the same location using any of the above transformations.

Exercises

f(x) is a periodic function with a period of 10; an amplitude of 4 and an offset of -1. Complete the chart below:

Function	Amplitude	Offset	Range	Period	Frequency
f(x–2)					
f(x+2)					
f(2x)					
$f(\frac{x}{2})$					
f(–x)					
f(x)–2					
f(x)+2					
2.f(x)					
$\dfrac{f(x)}{2}$					
–f(x)					
f(2x ± 6)					

1.7 LINEAR FUNCTIONS

A function is called **linear** if it is in the form **f(x)=mx+b** where m and b are constants; and **y=mx+b** is the equation of a **line**.

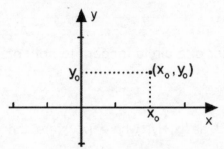

$(x_o , y_o) \Rightarrow x_o = x$ - coordinate or abscissa; $y_o = y$ - coordinate or ordinate

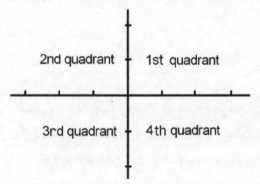

Distance between two points

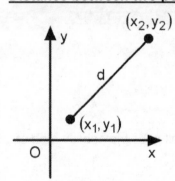

Distance d between the points (x_1, y_1) and (x_2, y_2) is found by:

$$d = \sqrt{(x_1 - x_2)^2 + (y_1 - y_2)^2}$$

Midpoint of a line segment

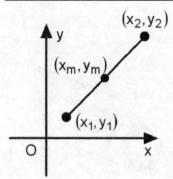

Midpoint (x_m , y_m) of the line segment whose endpoints are (x_1, y_1) and

(x_2, y_2) is found by: $(x_m, y_m) = \left(\dfrac{x_1 + x_2}{2}, \dfrac{y_1 + y_2}{2} \right)$

Exercises

1. The following points O(0,0), A(6,0), B(7,5), and C(1,1) are given in the xy coordinate plane. Which two segments have the same length?

   i. OA   ii. OB   iii. OC   iv. AB   v. AC

2. What is the distance between the points (5, 0) and (-12,0)?

3. Which of the following could be the coordinates of the center of a circle tangent to both of the x- and the y- axes?

   i. (3,-3)   ii. (0,3)   iii. (-3,0)   iv. (-3,-3)

4. The "reach" of a point in the xy coordinate plane is defined as $|x|+|y|$ where (x,y) are the coordinates of the point. Which of the following points has the same reach as $\left(\dfrac{-3}{2},\dfrac{1}{2}\right)$?

   i. (-1, 1)   ii. (0, -2)   iii. (2,1)

5. What is the midpoint of the line segment joining the points (-5,3) and (3,9)?

Parallelogram

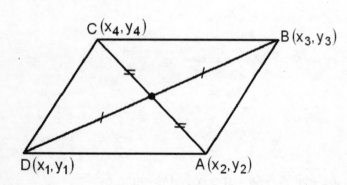

In a parallelogram, the diagonals bisect each other. Therefore the midpoint of line segment AC and the line segment BD is the same point P. Therefore

$$\left(\frac{x_4+x_2}{2},\frac{y_4+y_2}{2}\right)=\left(\frac{x_1+x_3}{2},\frac{y_1+y_3}{2}\right)$$

which implies the following:

$x_4+x_2=x_1+x_3$ and $y_4+y_2=y_1+y_3$

Example:

Three vertices of a parallelogram are given by (2,3), (5,6) and (-1, -7). Find all possible coordinates of the fourth vertex.

Solution:

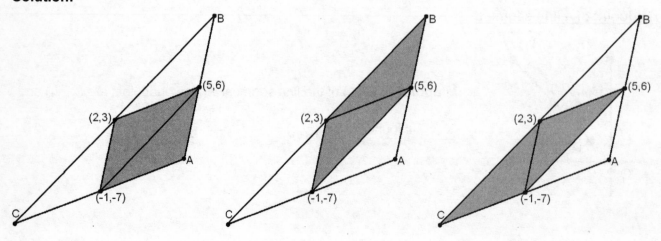

The third vertex can be any of the points A, B, and C given above. Please notice that each shaded region is a parallelogram in the figures given above.

Coordinates of A are (5-3, 6-10) = (2, -4).

Coordinates of B are (5+3, 6+10) = (8, 16).

Coordinates of C are (-1-3, -7-3) = (-4, -10).

Slope of a line segment

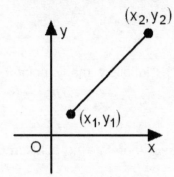

Slope m of the line segment whose endpoints are (x_1,y_1) and (x_2,y_2) is found by the following formula.

$$m = \frac{rise}{run} = \frac{\Delta y}{\Delta x} = \frac{y_2 - y_1}{x_2 - x_1}$$

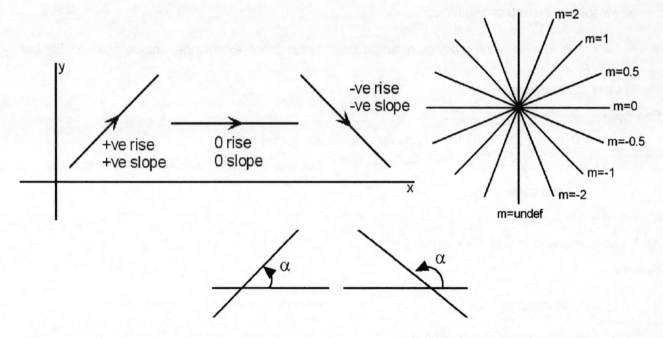

General Form of a Line: Ax + By + C = 0

Slope – Intercept Form of a Line: y= mx + b where m=slope and b=y-intercept

$$Ax+By+C=0 \Rightarrow By= -Ax-C \Rightarrow y=\frac{-A}{B}x - \frac{C}{B}$$

$$y=\frac{-A}{B}x - \frac{C}{B} = mx+b \Rightarrow m=\frac{-A}{B} \text{ and } b=-\frac{C}{B}$$

If B=0 (if there is no y term) $\Rightarrow$ the line cannot be expressed in slope – intercept form. Therefore Ax+By+C=0 is more general than y=mx+b.

Two Lines (Slope-Intercept Form)

l_1: $y = m_1 x + b_1$

l_2: $y = m_2 x + b_2$

- $l_1 = l_2 \Rightarrow m_1 = m_2$ and $b_1 = b_2$
- $l_1 \parallel l_2 \Rightarrow m_1 = m_2$ and $b_1 \neq b_2$
- l_1 and l_2 intersect at a single point $\Rightarrow m_1 \neq m_2$

l_1 and l_2 intersect at right angles $\Rightarrow m_1 . m_2 = -1$

Two Lines (General Form)

l_1: $a_1 x + b_1 y + c_1 = 0$

l_2: $a_2 x + b_2 y + c_2 = 0$

- $\dfrac{a_1}{a_2} = \dfrac{b_1}{b_2} = \dfrac{c_1}{c_2} \Rightarrow l_1 = l_2$; since lines are the same then they intersect at infinitely many points therefore infinitely many solutions exist for the system of equations.

- $\dfrac{a_1}{a_2} = \dfrac{b_1}{b_2} \neq \dfrac{c_1}{c_2} \Rightarrow l_1 \parallel l_2$; since lines are parallel then they do not intersect therefore no solution exists for the system of equations.

- $\dfrac{a_1}{a_2} \neq \dfrac{b_1}{b_2} \Rightarrow l_1$ and l_2 intersect at a single point; then there exists one unique solution for the system of equations.

Example:

l_1: $2x - my + 3 = 0$; l_2: $3x + 2y + n = 0$. Find all possible values for m and n if:

a. l_1 and l_2 are // lines.

b. l_1 and l_2 are the same lines.

c. l_1 and l_2 are $\perp$.

d. l_1 and l_2 intersect at a single point.

Solution:

a. The following condition must hold: $\dfrac{2}{3} = \dfrac{-m}{2} \neq \dfrac{3}{n}$; therefore m = -4/3 and n ≠ 9/2

b. The following condition must hold: $\dfrac{2}{3} = \dfrac{-m}{2} = \dfrac{3}{n}$; therefore m = -4/3 and n = 9/2

c. The following condition must hold: $\dfrac{2}{m} \cdot \dfrac{-3}{2} = -1$; therefore m = 3

d. The following condition must hold: $\dfrac{2}{3} \neq \dfrac{-m}{2}$ therefore m ≠ - 4/3

Exercises

1. Find the coordinates of the point of intersection of the lines whose equations are $\sqrt{3}x + 3y = 1$ and
    $x - \sqrt{3}y = \sqrt{3}$.

2. The solution to the pair of equations $\begin{cases} ax + by = 1 \\ bx + ay = 2 \end{cases}$ is x=3, y=2. What are a and b?

3. If the straight lines whose equations are $\begin{cases} -2x + my = 3 \\ 3x - 6y = -4 \end{cases}$ are parallel, then m=?

4. If f(x)=6x – 3 then what is the slope of the line given by y=f(-2x+1)?

Distance from a point to a line

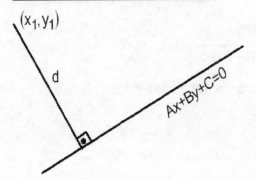

Distance **d** from the point (x_1, y_1) to the line Ax+By+C=0 is found

by: $d = \dfrac{|Ax_1 + By_1 + C|}{\sqrt{A^2 + B^2}}$

Example:

What is the distance from the point (2, -3) to the line 5x – 12y + 3 = 0?

Solution:

$d = \dfrac{|5 \cdot 2 - 12 \cdot -3 + 3|}{\sqrt{5^2 + (-12)^2}} = 3.769$

Angle between two lines

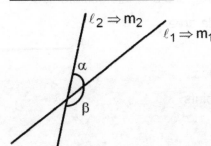

The tangent of the **acute angle** α between the lines l_1 and l_2 whose slopes

respectively are m_1 and m_2 is found by: $\tan\alpha = \left| \dfrac{m_1 - m_2}{1 + m_1 m_2} \right|$

There are three cases about the angle between two lines l_1 and l_2 whose slopes are m_1 and m_2
respectively:

Case 1: $\tan \alpha = 0$

         $\Rightarrow \alpha = 0 \Rightarrow m_1 = m_2 \Rightarrow$ lines are the same or ||

Case 2: $\tan \alpha > 0 \Rightarrow \alpha$ is the acute angle between the lines

         If β is the obtuse angle between the lines then $\beta = 180° - \alpha$

Case 3: $\tan \alpha =$ undefined

         $\Rightarrow \alpha = 90°$ or the lines are perpendicular to each other.

         $\Rightarrow 1 + m_1 m_2 = 0$

         $\Rightarrow m_1 \cdot m_2 = -1$

Example:

What is the obtuse angle between the lines given by $y = 2x - 4$ and $y = -3x + 5$?

Solution:

If α is the acute angle between the lines then $\tan\alpha = \left| \dfrac{m_1 - m_2}{1 + m_1 m_2} \right| = \left| \dfrac{2 - -3}{1 + 2 \cdot -3} \right| = 1$.

Therefore $\alpha = \tan^{-1}(1) = 45°$ and the obtuse angle between the lines is $180° - 45° = 135°$.

Area of a closed convex figure

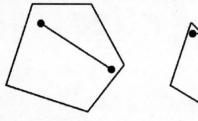

    Convex   **Not Convex**

When any two points in a region are connected to give a line segment that lies entirely within that region, the region is called convex. The following method can be used to calculate the area of any closed convex region regardless of the number of sides that it has. When the region is not convex, it is possible to partition the region to two or more non-overlapping convex regions and use this method for each of the convex regions that result and sum them up to get the whole area.

Rules

1. The region must be convex; however it can have any number of sides.

2. Counter-clockwise direction must be followed when selecting the points.

3. First point must be used twice.

4. The numbers on the same line are multiplied

5. Left Hand Side → -

    Right Hand Side → +

6. $\dfrac{1}{2}$ must not be forgotten.

Example:

Find the area of the quadrilateral given below:

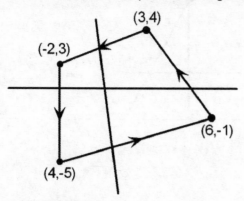

Solution:

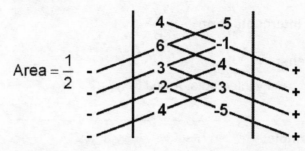

$$\text{Area} = \frac{1}{2}$$

$$\text{Area} = \frac{1}{2}(30+3+8-12-4+24+9+10)=\frac{1}{2}(68)=34$$

Line Equations

line equation 1:

slope-intercept form: $y = mx + b$

givens:

slope = m = $\tan \alpha$ and y - intercept = b

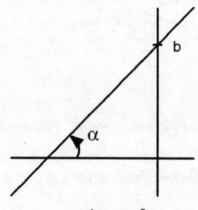

m = tan α > 0   m = tan α < 0

line equation 2:

slope point form: $y - y_1 = m(x - x_1)$

givens:

slope = m = $\tan \alpha$ and point = (x_1, y_1)

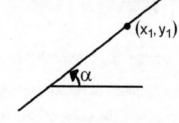

m = tan α

line equation 3:

two point form: $\dfrac{y - y_1}{y_1 - y_2} = \dfrac{x - x_1}{x_1 - x_2}$

givens:

the points (x_1, y_1) and (x_2, y_2) that are

both on the line

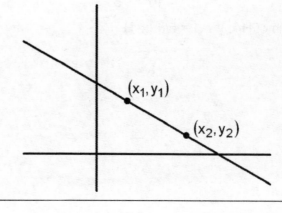

line equation 4:

x-y intercepts form $\dfrac{x}{A} + \dfrac{y}{B} = 1$

givens:

the x and y intercepts, **A** and **B**

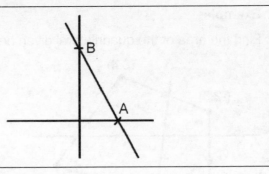

Example:

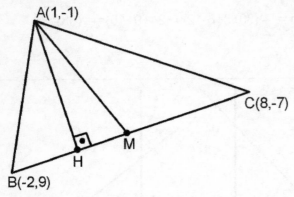

$AH \perp BC$ and M is the midpoint of line segment BC. Find the equation of each of the lines HA and MA.

Solution:

In order to find the equation of MA we first find point M by the midpoint formula, then use line equation 3 given above.

$$M\left(\dfrac{-2+8}{2}, \dfrac{9-7}{2}\right) = M(3,1)$$

Equation of MA: $\dfrac{y-1}{1--1} = \dfrac{x-3}{3-1} \Rightarrow y = x - 2$

In order to find the equation of HA we first find the slope of segment CB then the slope of HA, which is the negative reciprocal of the slope of CB. Then we use line equation 2.

Slope of BC = $\dfrac{9--7}{-2-8} = \dfrac{16}{-10} = -\dfrac{8}{5}$; therefore slope of HA = 5/8.

Equation of HA: y - -1 = 5/8 ·(x-1)

Perpendicular Bisector of a Line Segment

The locus of points equidistant from two given points in a plane is the line that perpendicularly bisects the line segment that joins those points.

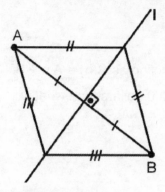

In order to find the equation of line l,

i.   Find the slope m_{AB} of line AB and the slope m_l of line l using the relation $m_{AB} \cdot m_l = -1$

ii. Find the midpoint of line AB.

iii. Use line equation 2 to find the equation of line l.

Example:

What is the equation of the perpendicular bisector of segment AB whose endpoints are given by A(1,5) and B(7,-3)?

Solution:

Midpoint of AB: $\left(\dfrac{1+7}{2}, \dfrac{5-3}{2} \right) = (4,1)$; Slope of AB: $\dfrac{5--3}{1-7} = -\dfrac{8}{6} = -\dfrac{4}{3}$;

Slope of the perpendicular bisector = 3/4

Equation of the perpendicular bisector is $y - 1 = 3/4 \cdot (x - 4)$

Reflections

Reflection of the point **(x,y)** in the **x – axis: (x, -y)**

Reflection of the point **(x,y)** in the **y – axis: (-x, y)**

Reflection of the point **(x,y)** in the **origin: (-x, -y)**

Reflection of the point **(x,y)** in the line **x = a: (2a-x, y)**

Reflection of the point **(x,y)** in the line **y = b: (x, 2b-y)**

Reflection of the point **(x,y)** in the point **(a, b): (2a-x, 2b-y)**

Reflection of the point **(x,y)** in the line **y = x: (y, x)**

Reflection of the point **(x,y)** in the line **y = - x: (-y, -x)**

Please note that when a line **y = mx + b** is reflected across

- **the x axis** it becomes: **y = – mx – b.**
- **the y axis** it becomes: **y = – mx + b.**
- **the origin** it becomes: **y = mx – b.**
- **the line y = x** it becomes: **x = my + b.**
- **the line y = - x** it becomes: **– x = – my + b.**

Linear Models

A mathematical model is a set of equations, inequalities, functions, graphs, tables, etc. used to describe a real world problem. **A linear model** is an input output model of the form **f(x) = a·x + b** where **x** is the input and **f(x)** is the output.

Example:

In a production plant the cost C of producing n items is defined by a linear function as C(n) = A·n + B. If the cost of producing 800 items is 2,000 dollars and that of 1400 items is 3,200 dollars then what will be the cost of producing

(a) 500 items

(b) no items

Solution:

2000 = 800 A + B

3200 = 1400 A + B

$\Rightarrow$ 1200 = 600 A; A = 2 and B = 400

Therefore C(n) = 2n + 400

(a) C(500) = 2 · 500 + 400 = 1400

(b) C(0) = 400

Finding the Equation of a Line Using Regression

Example:

Find the equation of the line through the points (1, 3) and (2, -4)?

Solution:

Linear Interpolation

Suppose that **(a,f(a))** and **(b,f(b))** are two points on a continuous function. We are given that f(x) contnuously increases or decreases when **a < x < b** and we would like to calculate $f\left(\dfrac{a+b}{2}\right)$. In order

to accomplish such a task, we can find the midpoint of the points **(a,f(a))** and **(b,f(b))** in order to get an

estimate of $f\left(\dfrac{a+b}{2}\right)$ which is $f\left(\dfrac{a+b}{2}\right) = \dfrac{f(a)+f(b)}{2}$. We have assumed that **f(x)** is a linear function of

x when **a < x < b**. This is called linear interpolation.

Example:

(0.5, 0.479) and (0.9, 0.783) are two points on y = sin(x). The midpoint will be calculated as (0.7, 0.631). The actual value of sin(0.7) is 0.644. The error that we have done is 2%.

Exercises

1. In the xy plane, what is the area of a triangle whose vertices are ($\sqrt{3}$,0), (2, $-\sqrt{5}$), and (5,0)?

2. If the points A(4,0), B(0,-1.1), C(1.8,0) and D(0,3.2) are connected in that order to form a quadrilateral with sites AB, BC, CD, and DA, What will be the area of the quadrilateral?

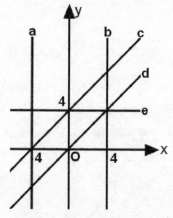

3. Find the equation of each of the lines a, b, c, d, and e given in the figure above.

4. Which quadrants of the plane contain points of the graph of 2x–3y>6?

5. If a line contains the points (-1, 3) and (3, 9), then its x-intercept is

6. The points A and B have coordinates A(4,0) and B(-3,7). Find the equation of the line which is perpendicular to AB and passes through the point B. Give your answer in slope-intercept form i.e. y=mx+b.

7. Line l has a negative slope and a positive y-intercept. Line m is parallel to l and has a negative y-intercept. Compare the x-intercepts of l and m giving their signs also.

8. Find the equation of the line passing through (4,-5) which is perpendicular to -2y+4x=3.

9. If line m is the perpendicular bisector of the line segment with endpoints (4,0) and (0,-4), what is the slope and equation of line m?

10. Find the coordinates of the point that is the image of W (4, -3), after a reflection in the:

    a. x - axis

    b. y - axis

    c. the line y = x

    d. the line y = -x

    e. origin

    f. the point (7,-5)

    g. the line x=1

    h. the line y=1

11.

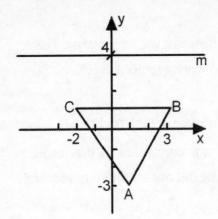

In the above figure, if ΔABC is reflected across line m, what will be the coordinates of the reflection of point A?

12.

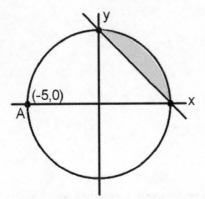

What is the area of the shaded region in the above figure if the center of the circle is the origin and point A has the coordinates of (-5,0)?

13.

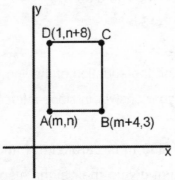

In the rectangle ABCD given above, what are the coordinates of vertex C?

14.   Find slope and y intercept of the line given by x=5t+4 and y=-2t-3

15.   If one vertex of a square coincides with the origin of the xy-plane, how many other vertices of the square must lie on the x- and y- coordinate axes.

16.   What are the x- and y-intercepts of the line 6x-3y=12?

17.   Find equation of the line that

   i.   has the slope of 3 and passes through (1, -2).

   ii. makes 135° with the x axis and passes through (-2, -3).

   iii. passes through the points (1,2) & (3,6).

   iv. intersects the y axis at (0, -2) and x axis at (3,0).

   v.   is equidistant from the points (1,2) and (3,6).

   vi. has the x and y intercepts of 5 and -3.

18. Given the circle $x^2-4x+y^2+6y-23=0$ and the line $y=-x-15$. If A is a point on the circle, what are the maximum and minimum distances from A to the given line.

19. If the circle $x^2-2x+y^2=0$ is tangent to the line $y=mx+3$ then find all possible values for m?

20. Find the obtuse angle between the lines $y=x+3$ and $y=-\sqrt{3}x+2$.

21. If the point $(3,b)$ is on the line passing through $(1,-1)$ and $(4,5)$ then b=?

22. The line $y=3x-5$ is reflected across the point $(1,-3)$; what will be the resulting line?

23. The point $A(3,5)$ and $B(m,n)$ are symmetric in the line $3x-4y+1=0$. Distance AB=?

24. G is the centroid of $\triangle ABC$ whose vertices are $A(3,9)$, $B(1,2)$ and $C(8,1)$. Find area of $\triangle AGB$.

25. Find the distance between the two parallel lines $3x+2y+2=0$ and $6x+4y+10=0$

26. $\left.\begin{array}{l} x+3y=7 \\ 12x-2y=8 \end{array}\right\} \dfrac{x}{y}=?$

27. $\left.\begin{array}{l} x+y+z=6 \\ 2x-y+3z=9 \\ 3x+y-4z=-7 \end{array}\right\} x^2+y^2+z^2=?$

28. Express the equations of the lines satisfying the given information in the form $y=mx+b$.

    a. line passing through $(2,4)$ and $(5,-2)$

    b. Line passing through $(1,1)$ and $(3,4)$

    c. Line with slope 3 which passes through $(2,1)$

    d. Line with slope 3 and y-intercept 4

    e. Line with slope 2 and x-intercept 3

    f. Line with x-intercept 2 and y-intercept 4.

29. Find the equation of a line that passes through $(1,1)$ and is

    a. parallel to the line with equation $2x-3y=6$

    b. perpendicular to the line with equation $3x+2y=6$

30. Find the equation of a line that is parallel to the line $y=3x-2$ passing through $(1,4)$.

31. Find the equation of a line that is perpendicular to the line with equation $y=3x-2$ which passes through $(1,4)$.

32. Find the equation of a line with y-intercept 4 which is parallel to $y=-3x+1$.

33. Find the equation of a line with y-intercept 4 which is perpendicular to $y=-3x+1$.

34. $(a-1)x+3y-4=0$; $5x-2y+c=0$

    If the system of equations above has infinitely many solutions then a+c=?

35. Find all possible coordinates of the fourth vertex of the parallelogram if there of the vertices are $(-1,-2)$, $(1,4)$ and $(7,-1)$.

36. Find the coordinates of the center of gravity of the triangle with vertices $(1,4)$ $(7,-1)$ and $(3,9)$.

37. Two pegs A and B nailed on a rectangular wall 30ft in length and 10ft in height in the following way: Peg A is nailed 3 ft down from the upper edge and 5ft left from the right edge of the wall. Peg B is nailed 2 ft up from the bottom edge and 7ft right from the left edge of the wall. What is shortest distance between these pegs?

1.8 QUADRATIC FUNCTIONS

$y = f(x) = ax^2 + bx + c$; $a \neq 0$; $a, b, c \in \mathbb{R}$

$y = ax^2 + bx + c \Rightarrow y = a(x-h)^2 + k$ where (h,k) is the vertex and it can be found using one of the following ways:

1. Completing the square

2. $h = \dfrac{-b}{2a}$ and $k = \dfrac{4ac - b^2}{4a}$

3. $h = \dfrac{-b}{2a}$ and $k = f(h)$

4. $f'(x) = 2ax + b = 0$

   $x = \dfrac{-b}{2a} = h$ and $k = f(h)$

   (by using derivatives)

5. By using a graphing calculator to find the max or the min point by graphing the function, which will be the point (h,k)

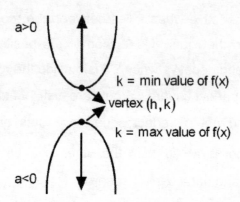

a>0

k = min value of f(x)

vertex (h, k)

k = max value of f(x)

a<0

The larger the value of |a|, the narrower the parabola will be.

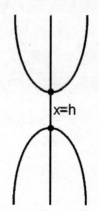

x=h

x=h: axis of symmetry

Roots of a quadratic equation

$f(x) = ax^2 + bx + c = 0$

$\Delta = b^2 - 4ac$: discriminant

$$x_1 = \frac{-b + \sqrt{\Delta}}{2a} \quad \text{and} \quad x_2 = \frac{-b - \sqrt{\Delta}}{2a}$$

Case 1: Δ<0

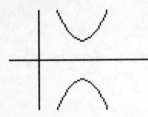

two complex conjugate zeros

- If one root is **a+bi** then the other is **a-bi**, or vice versa.
- f(x) is always positive or always negative.

Case 2: Δ=0

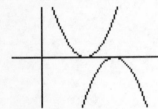

two real equal zeros, one double root

$\Rightarrow$ f(x) is always non-negative or always non-positive.

Case 3: Δ>0

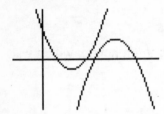

two real unequal (distinct, different) roots

$$x_1 = \frac{-b + \sqrt{\Delta}}{2a} \text{ and } x_2 = \frac{-b - \sqrt{\Delta}}{2a}$$

- f(x) is not always positive or negative.
- If a>0 then f(x) is negative when x lies between the roots and positive when x lies outside the roots. If a<0 then f(x) is positive when x lies between the roots and negative when x lies outside the roots.
- If Δ is nonzero and perfect square $\Rightarrow$ roots are distinct and rational.
- If Δ is positive and not a perfect square $\Rightarrow$ roots are distinct and irrational. If one root is **a+ $\sqrt{b}$** then the other is **a- $\sqrt{b}$** or vice versa, where b is positive and not a perfect square.

Please note that if Δ≥0 then the roots are real (they may be equal or distinct).

Sum and product of the roots of a quadratic equation

$ax^2+bx+c=0$

- sum of the roots = S = $\dfrac{-b}{a}$ = $x_1 + x_2$

- product of the roots = P = $\dfrac{c}{a}$ = $x_1 . x_2$

Given the roots, construct the equation

S= x_1+x_2 and P= $x_1 . x_2$ $\Rightarrow$ x²-Sx+P=0

Example:

For the function $f(x)=x^2 - 4x - 5$; find the vertex, the x and y intercepts, the axis of symmetry, the max or min value of the function, the domain and range of the function.

Solution:

$y = x^2 - 4x - 5 = x^2 - 4x + 4 - 9 = (x - 2)^2 - 9$

vertex is (2, -9)

$x = 0 \Rightarrow y = -5$ therefore y intercept is -5 (the point whose coordinates are (0, -5))

$y = 0 \Rightarrow (x-5)(x+1)=0 \Rightarrow x = 5$ or $x = -1$ therefore x intercepts are 5 and -1; (the points (5,0) and (-1,0))

axis of symmetry is the line given by $x = 2$

minimum value of the function is -9

domain is all real numbers; range is $y \geq -9$.

Example:

Domain of f(x) is given by $x^2+3x-4<0$ and $f(x)=x^2+4x+5$. Find range of f(x).

Solution:

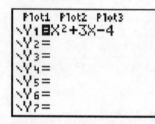 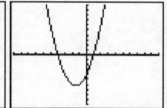 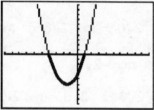

Domain: $-4 < x < 1$

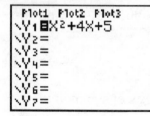 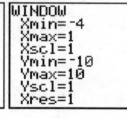 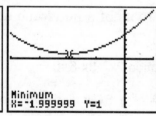 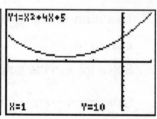

Answer: $1 \leq y < 10$

Example:

Construct a quadratic equation that has

a. two roots -3 and 5.

b. two roots 0 and 2.

c. two roots $3+\sqrt{5}$ and $3 - \sqrt{5}$.

d. two roots $3 - i$ and $3 + i$.

e. the only root of $\dfrac{4}{3}$.

Solution:

a. $S = -3+5 = 2$; $P = -3 \cdot 5 = -15$; $x^2 - 2x - 15 = 0$

b. $S = 0+2 = 2$; $P = 0 \cdot 2 = 0$; $x^2 - 2x = 0$

c. $S = 3+\sqrt{5} + 3 - \sqrt{5} = 6$; $P = (3+\sqrt{5})(3-\sqrt{5}) = 9 - 5 = 4$; $x^2 - 6x + 4 = 0$

d. $S = 3 - i + 3 + i = 6$; $P = (3-i)(3+i) = 9 + 1 = 10$; $x^2 - 6x + 10 = 0$

e. $S = \dfrac{4}{3} + \dfrac{4}{3} = \dfrac{8}{3}$; $P = \dfrac{4}{3} \cdot \dfrac{4}{3} = \dfrac{16}{9}$; $x^2 - \dfrac{8}{3}x + \dfrac{16}{9} = 0 \Rightarrow 9x^2 - 24x + 16 = 0$

Example:

$f(x) = 2x^2 - mx + 3$. Find all possible values for m if

a. $f(x)$ intersects the x axis at two distinct points.

b. $f(x)$ is tangent to the x axis.

c. $f(x)$ does not intersect the x axis.

Solution:

$\Delta = b^2 - 4ac = m^2 - 4 \cdot 2 \cdot 3 = m^2 - 24$

a. $m^2 - 24 > 0 \Rightarrow |m| > \sqrt{24} = 2\sqrt{6} \Rightarrow m > 2\sqrt{6}$ or $m < -2\sqrt{6}$

b. $m^2 - 24 = 0 \Rightarrow m = 2\sqrt{6}$ or $m = -2\sqrt{6}$

c. $m^2 - 24 < 0 \Rightarrow |m| < \sqrt{24} = 2\sqrt{6} \Rightarrow -2\sqrt{6} < m < 2\sqrt{6}$

<u>Exercises</u>

1. The sum of the two roots of a quadratic equation is 5 and their product is -6. Find the equation.

2. Solve for x in the equation $2x^2 + 3x - 6 = 0$

3. Sketch the graph of $y = -x^2 + 6x$, indicate the vertex, x and y intercept(s), axis of symmetry, domain and range.

4. If -3 and 2 are both zeros of the polynomial $P(x)$, then $P(x)$ definitely has a quadratic factor. Find this factor.

5. If $P(x) = ax^2 + bx + c$ for all real numbers x and if $P(0) = 3$ and $P(-1) = 5$, then $a - b =$

6. Match the graphs given in (A) through (F) of the equation $y = ax^2 + bx + c$ with the following cases:

   i. $\Delta = b^2 - 4ac > 0$

   ii. $\Delta = b^2 - 4ac = 0$

   iii. $\Delta = b^2 - 4ac < 0$

   For each graph give the sign of a also.

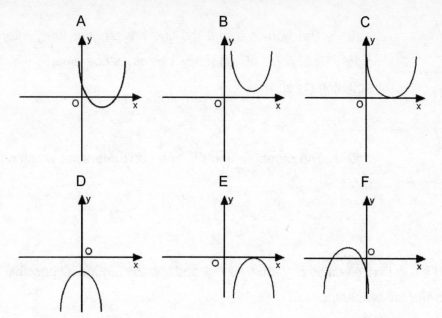

Completing the square (revisited)

$y = ax^2+bx+c$

$\quad = a(x^2+\dfrac{b}{a}x)+c$

$\quad = a(x^2+\dfrac{b}{a}x+\dfrac{b^2}{4a^2})-\dfrac{b^2}{4a}+c$

$\quad = a(x+\dfrac{b}{2a})^2+(c-\dfrac{b^2}{4a})$

$y = a(x-h)^2+k$

where $h=\dfrac{b}{2a}$ and $k=c-\dfrac{b^2}{4a}$

A parabola and a line:

$y=f_1(x)=ax^2+bx+c$

$y=f_2(x)=mx+p$

$f_1(x)=f_2(x) \Rightarrow mx+p=ax^2+bx+c \Rightarrow ax^2+(b-m)x+(c-p)=0$

A quadratic equation is obtained and depending on the roots of this equation there will be three cases:

$Ax^2+Bx+C=0$ where $A=a$; $B=b-m$; $C=c-p$ \qquad\qquad (1)

$\Delta=(B)^2 - 4(A)(C)$

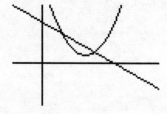

$\Delta>0 \Rightarrow$ The parabola and the line intersect at two points whose x-coordinates are the roots of equation (1) above.

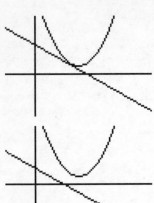

$\Delta=0 \Rightarrow$ The parabola and the line are tangent (they intersect at a single point). The point of tangency has an x-coordinate, which is the root of equation (1) above.

$\Delta<0 \Rightarrow$ The parabola and the line don't intersect; equation (1) has no real roots.

Example:

A parabola p and a line l are given by p: $y=mx^2 + x + 1$ and l: $y=2x+3$. Find all possible values for m if

a. parabola and line are tangent;

b. parabola and line don't intersect;

c. parabola and line intersect;

d. line cuts the parabola at two distinct points.

Solution:

$mx^2 + x + 1 = 2x+3$

$mx^2 - x - 2 = 0$

$\Delta = 1 - 4 \cdot m \cdot (-2) = 1 + 8m$

a. $1 + 8m = 0 \Rightarrow m = -1/8$

b. $1 + 8m \neq 0 \Rightarrow m \neq -1/8$

c. $1 + 8m \geq 0 \Rightarrow m \geq -1/8$

d. $1 + 8m > 0 \Rightarrow m > -1/8$

Quadratic Models

A quadratic model is an input output model of the form $f(x) = ax^2 + bx + c$ where **x** is the input and **f(x)** is the output.

Example:

The cost of production in a certain factory is a quadratic function of the production. The fixed costs, i.e. the cost of producing no items is $500; the cost of producing 100 items is $30,500 and the cost of producing 150 items is $38,000. What is the cost of producing 180 items in this factory?

Solution:

$f(x) = ax^2 + bx + c$

$f(0) = 500 = c$

$f(100) = 30,500 = 10,000a + 100b + c$

$f(150) = 38,000 = 22,500a + 150b + c$

10,000a + 100b = 30,000

22,500a + 150b = 37,500

Solving the above system yields a = -1 and b = 400.

Therefore f(x) = $-x^2$ + 400x + 500

f(180) = -180^2+400·180+500=40,100

Example:

Find the equation of the parabola through the points (1, 4), (0, 3), and (-1, 6)?

Solution:

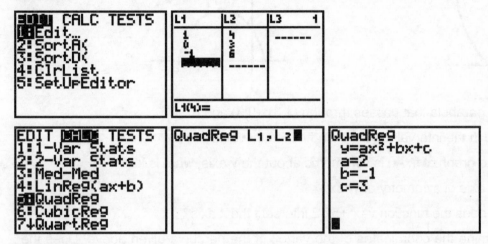

Exercises

1. If ax^2+6x+4=0 has -3/2 as its only solution, what is the value of a?

2. A parabola that opens downward has the vertex of (2,-1) and the y-intercept of -5. Find the equation of this parabola and the points on the parabola at which y= -2x.

3. If 6x–4y+7=0 and $2y-x^2$=0 for x ≥ 0, then x=?

4. Given that f(x)=$(x+5)^2$+2, find the minimum value of the function f(x).

5. The graph of a quadratic function with equation y=x^2+ax+b cuts the x–axis at 2 and -3. Find a and b and coordinates of the point where the graph cuts the y-axis.

6. The quadratic equation $2x^2$+2px+5=0, p>0, has exactly one solution for x. Find p.

7. Express f(x)=x^2 – 4x + 9 in the form f(x)=$(x-h)^2$+k. Hence, or otherwise, write down the coordinates of the vertex of the parabola with equation y= x^2 – 4x + 9.

8. Solve for x and y in the following simultaneous equations: $\begin{cases} y = x^2 - 4x + 3 \\ y = -x^2 + 6x - 9 \end{cases}$

9. Find equation of the parabola for each of the following graphs:

a.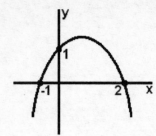

b.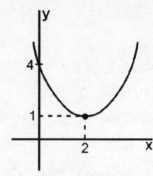

c.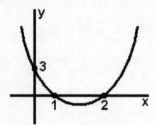

d.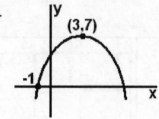

10. Find equation of the parabola that passes through (1,3); (9;3) and (0,-2)

11. $f(x)=2x^2+1$ is defined in the interval $-3\leq x \leq 3$. find minimum value of f(x).

12. $f(x)=2x^2+12x+3$. If the graph of f(x-k) is symmetric about the y axis, what is k?

13. Find equation of the axis of symmetry of $y=3x^2-x+2$.

14. At how many points does the function $y=x^2+5x-2$ intersect the x axis?

15. $y= -2x^2+4x-7$. Determine the coordinates of the vertex of the parabola given above. Does the above function have a maximum or minimum? What is this value? Find the equation of the axis of symmetry also.

16. Find range of $y=8-2x-x^2$.

17. $s(t)=3t^2-9t+2$

   a. s(0) - s(-1)=?

   b. What is the t value that makes s a minimum? What is this minimum value

18. What is the condition that must be satisfied so that the roots of the quadratic equation $ax^2+bx+c= 0$ are

   a. real

   b. real and equal

   c. real and unequal

   d. complex

   e. rational numbers.

19. $f(x)= ax^2+bx+c$; $a, b, c \in R$

Given that the zeros of a quadratic polynomial are non-real and the graph is a parabola that opens upward. Which one(s) of the following must be correct?

i. discriminant is negative.

ii. a is positive

iii. $f(x) \geq 0$ for all x

iv. $f(x)$ is strictly positive.

20.   The function $f(x)=x^2+4x+5$ is defined for those values of x that satisfy the inequality given by $x^2+3x-4<0$. Find range of $f(x)$.

21. $x^2+x+4=0$. The quadratic equation given has the roots x_1 and x_2. Compute the following:

   a. $x_1 + x_2$

   b. $x_1 \cdot x_2$

   c. $\dfrac{1}{x_1} + \dfrac{1}{x_2}$

   d. $x_1^2 + x_2^2$

22.   Find the range of each of the following quadratic functions for the given domains.

   a.   domain=[1,5]; $f(x)= x^2 - 3x+4$

   b.   domain= [2,4]; $f(x)= x^2 - 2x$

   c.   domain= [-2,2]; $f(x)= x^2 + 3$

   d. $y= -x^2 + 3$; domain [-4,2]

23.   The maximum number of non-overlapping regions that n distinct lines can separate a plane is a quadratic function of n. Find this function.

1.9 POLYNOMIAL FUNCTIONS

$P(x) = a_nx^n + a_{n-1}x^{n-1} + a_{n-2}x^{n-2} + \ldots + a_5x^5 + a_4x^4 + a_3x^3 + a_2x^2 + a_1x + a_0$

for P(x) to be a polynomial function:

- a_n values must be complex numbers (in SAT II context they will all be real numbers) and

- n values must be nonnegative integers.

a_n 's are called **coefficients**.

a_0 is called the **constant** term

a_1x is called the **linear** term

a_2x^2 is called the **quadratic** term

a_3x^3 is called the **cubic** term

a_4x^4 is called the **quartic** term

a_5x^5 is called the **quintic** term

a_nx^n is called the **leading** term (the term with the greatest exponent).

The **greatest exponent** is called the **degree of the polynomial**.

Coefficient of the leading term is called the **leading coefficient**.

Two terms of a polynomial are like terms if they have the same variables and each variable has the same exponent.

$P(x)=0$: **zero polynomial**.

$P(x)=a_0$: **constant polynomial**.

$P(x)=a_1x+a_0$: **linear polynomial**, $a_1 \neq 0$

$P(x)=a_2x^2+a_1x+a_0$: **quadratic polynomial**, $a_2 \neq 0$

$P(x)=a_3x^3+a_2x^2+a_1x+a_0$: **cubic polynomial**, $a_3 \neq 0$

$P(x)= a_4x^4+a_3x^3+a_2x^2+a_1x+a_0$: **quartic polynomial**, $a_4 \neq 0$

$P(x)= a_5x^5+a_4x^4+a_3x^3+a_2x^2+a_1x+a_0$: **quintic polynomial**, $a_5 \neq 0$

If all **coefficients** are **real**, then the polynomial is a **real polynomial**.

If all **coefficients** are **rational**, then the polynomial is a **rational polynomial**.

If all **coefficients** are **integers**, then the polynomial is an **integral polynomial**.

A **monomial** has only **one term**: $2x^4$; $5x^3y^2$; $-8x^4yz^3$

A **binomial** has only **two terms**: $2x-4y$; $1-5x$; $9x^2yz-st^3$

A **trinomial** has only **three terms**: $3x+y-z$, $2x^2+15y^3-z^5$

Identities

$(A+B)^2=A^2+2AB+B^2$

$(A-B)^2=A^2-2AB+B^2$

$(A+B)^3=A^3+3A^2B+3AB^2+B^3$

$(A-B)^3=A^3-3A^2B+3AB^2-B^3$

$A^2-B^2=(A-B)(A+B)$

$A^3+B^3=(A+B)(A^2-AB+B^2)$

$A^3-B^3=(A-B)(A^2+AB+B^2)$

$(A+B+C)^2=A^2+B^2+C^2+2AB+2AC+2BC$

$A^n-B^n=(A-B)(A^{n-1}+A^{n-2}B+A^{n-3}B^2+....+AB^{n-2}+B^{n-1})$ where $n>1$

$A^n+B^n=(A+B)(A^{n-1}-A^{n-2}B+A^{n-3}B^2-....)$ where $n>1$ and n is odd.

Please note that the coefficients of the terms in $(x+y)^n$ are the same as the numbers in Pascal's Triangle.

$(x+y)^0=1$ **1**

$(x+y)^1=x+y$ **$1x+1y$**

$(x+y)^2=x^2+2xy+y^2$ **$1x^2+2xy+1y^2$**

$(x+y)^3=x^3+3x^2y+3xy^2+y^3$ **$1x^3+3x^2y+3xy^2+1y^3$**

$(x+y)^4=x^4+4x^3y+6x^2y^2+4xy^3+y^4$ **$1x^4+4x^3y+6x^2y^2+4xy^3+1y^4$**

$(x+y)^5=x^5+5x^4y+10x^3y^2+10x^2y^3+5xy^4+y^5$ **$1x^5+5x^4y+10X^3y^2+10x^2y^3+5xy^4+1y^5$**

Examples:

$(x+y)^3 = x^3 + 3x^2y + 3xy^2 + y^3$

$(x+y)^4 = x^4 + 4x^3y + 6x^2y^2 + 4xy^3 + y^4$

Please also note that when expanding $(x-y)^n$ the signs of terms should alternate.

$(x-y)^3 = x^3 - 3x^2y + 3xy^2 - y^3$

$(x-y)^4 = x^4 - 4x^3y + 6x^2y^2 - 4xy^3 + y^4$

Properties of Higher Degree Polynomial Functions

1.   Polynomial functions are always continuous curves whose graphs can be drawn without your hand leaving the paper.

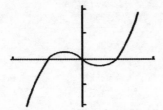 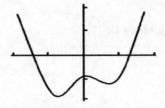

2. If the largest exponent is even (polynomial has an even degree), the both ends leave from top or from bottom.

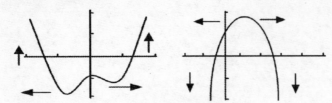

When x increases or decreases without bound, y increases without bound.

OR:

When x increases or decreases without bound, y decreases without bound.

⇒ End behavior is the same at both ends

$$\lim_{x \to \pm\infty} f(x) = +\infty \quad \text{or} \quad \lim_{x \to \pm\infty} f(x) = -\infty$$

3. If the largest exponent is odd (polynomial has an odd degree), then the ends leave from opposite sides.

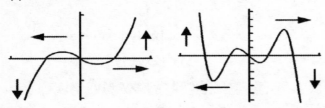

When x increases or decreases without bound, y decreases or increases without bound.

OR:

When x decreases or increases without bound, y increases or decreases without bound.

⇒ End behavior is opposite at the ends (two opposite behaviors.)

$$\lim_{x \to \pm\infty} f(x) = \pm\infty \quad \text{or} \quad \lim_{x \to \pm\infty} f(x) = \mp\infty$$

4. If all exponents are even, with or without a constant term ⇒ polynomial is even.

5. If all exponents are odd and there is no constant term ⇒ polynomial is odd.

6. **Remainder theorem**

$$\begin{array}{r|l} P(x) & x-a \\ \hline & Q(x) \end{array} \qquad P(x)=(x-a)Q(x)+P(a)$$

$P(a)$

When P(x) is divided by (x-a), remainder is P(a).

7. **Factor theorem:**

$P(a)=0 \iff P(x) = (x-a)\,Q(x)$

If P(x) has a root which is equal to **a**, it has a factor of **(x-a)** or vice-versa.

8. Every polynomial with a degree of n has exactly n zeros.

    Some can be real, some can be complex, some can be positive, some can be negative, some can be integers or rational or irrational, some can be the same and some can be different. However the total number of zeros is always n.

9. **Rational root theorem:** If $\dfrac{p}{q}$ is a rational zero of the polynomial $P(x)=a_nx^n+a_{n-1}x^{n-1}+\ldots+a_1x+a_0$, reduced

    to its lowest terms, then p is a factor of a_0 and q is a factor of a_n. However; $\dfrac{p}{q}$ may be a zero or may not

    be a zero at all.

    Example:

    $P(x)= 2x^3+13x^2-15kx+6 \Rightarrow$ The possible rational zeros are: $\dfrac{p}{q}$ where p is a factor of 6 :

    $\pm1,\pm2,\pm3,\pm6$ and q is a factor of 2: $\pm1, \pm2$. Therefore $\dfrac{p}{q} \Rightarrow \pm1, \pm2, \pm3, \pm6, \pm\dfrac{1}{2}, \pm\dfrac{3}{2}$, are all of the

    possible zeros. However it is also possible that none of the above appear as zeros.

10. If P(x) is a rational polynomial (a polynomial with rational coefficients) then irrational zeros

    appear in conjugate pairs. $\Rightarrow$ If $p+\sqrt{q}$ is a zero of P(x) so is $p-\sqrt{q}$ or vice versa.

    Therefore a rational polynomial has definitely an even number of irrational zeros.

11. If P(x) is a real polynomial (a polynomial with real coefficient) then complex (non-real) zeros

    appear in conjugate pairs. $\Rightarrow$ If p+qi is a root so is p-qi or vice versa where $i=\sqrt{-1}$

    Therefore a real polynomial has definitely an even number of complex zeros.

Degree of polynomial with real coefficients	Number of real zeros	Number of complex zeros
1	1	0
2	2	0
	0	2
3	3	0
	1	2
4	4	0
	2	2
	0	4
5	5	0
	3	2
	1	4

Observations:

-   A polynomial with real coefficients and odd degree has at least one real root definitely.
-   A polynomial with real coefficients but no real zeros must have even degree.

12. **Relation between zeros & coefficients**

$P(x) = ax+b$ $\qquad$ $x_1 = \dfrac{-b}{a}$ $\qquad\qquad$ (-)

$P(x) = ax^2+bx+c$ $\qquad$ $x_1 + x_2 = \dfrac{-b}{a}$ $\qquad\qquad$ (-)

$\qquad\qquad\qquad\qquad\qquad$ $x_1 . x_2 = \dfrac{c}{a}$ $\qquad\qquad$ (+)

$P(x) = ax^3+bx^2+cx+d$ $\qquad$ $x_1 + x_2 + x_3 = \dfrac{-b}{a}$ $\qquad$ (-)

$\qquad\qquad\qquad\qquad\qquad$ $x_1x_2 + x_1x_3 + x_2x_3 = \dfrac{c}{a}$ $\qquad$ (+)

$\qquad\qquad\qquad\qquad\qquad$ $x_1x_2x_3 = \dfrac{-d}{a}$ $\qquad\qquad$ (-)

$P(x) = ax^4+bx^3+cx^2+dx+e$ $\qquad$ $x_1 + x_2 + x_3 + x_4 = \dfrac{-b}{a}$ $\qquad$ (-)

$\qquad\qquad\qquad\qquad\qquad$ $x_1x_2 + ... + x_3x_4 = \dfrac{c}{a}$ $\qquad$ (+)

$\qquad\qquad\qquad\qquad\qquad$ $x_1x_2x_3 + ... + x_2x_3x_4 = \dfrac{-d}{a}$ $\qquad$ (-)

$\qquad\qquad\qquad\qquad\qquad$ $x_1x_2x_3x_4 = \dfrac{e}{a}$ $\qquad\qquad$ (+)

Example:

$3x^3+5x^2-7x+6=0$; $\dfrac{1}{x_1} + \dfrac{1}{x_2} + \dfrac{1}{x_3} = ?$

Solution:

$$\dfrac{1}{x_1} + \dfrac{1}{x_2} + \dfrac{1}{x_3} = \dfrac{x_2x_3 + x_1x_3 + x_1x_2}{x_1x_2x_3} = \dfrac{\dfrac{-7}{3}}{\dfrac{-6}{3}} = \dfrac{7}{6}$$

13. $P(x) = ax^2+bx+c=0 \Rightarrow x^2+\dfrac{b}{a}x+\dfrac{c}{a}=0$

$(x-x_1)(x-x_2) = x^2-x_1x-x_2x+x_1x_2 = x^2-(x_1+x_2)x+x_1x_2$

$\Rightarrow x^2-(x_1+x_2)x+x_1x_2=x^2+\dfrac{b}{a}x+\dfrac{c}{a}$

$S = x_1+x_2=\dfrac{-b}{a}$ = sum of the roots

$P = x_1 . x_2 =\dfrac{c}{a}$ = product of the roots

14. **Descartes' Rule of Signs:**

Number of the positive real zeros of a real polynomial P(x)

= Number of sign changes in P(x) – (an even number less)

Number of the negative real zeros of a real polynomial P(x)

= Number of sign changes in P(-x) –(an even number less)

Example:

How many positive or negative real zeros does the polynomial $P(x)=18x^4-bx^3+7x^2+8x-5$ have where b>0?

Solution:

First order the terms in decreasing powers of x:

$P(x) = +18x^4 \quad -bx^3 \quad +7x^2 \quad +8x \quad -5$

3 sign changes exist in P(x) therefore P(x) has 3 or 1 positive real zeros

$P(-x) = +18x^4 \quad +bx^3 \quad +7x^2 \quad +8x \quad -5$

1 sign change exists in P(-x) therefore P(x) has 1 negative real zero.

15. **Synthetic Division:**

Example: Divide $P(x)=3x^5+2x^4-13x^2-90x-10$ by x+3. Find quotient and remainder.

$x+3=0 \Rightarrow x=-3$

$$P(x) \mid x+3$$
$$\overline{\quad\quad \mid Q(x)}$$
$$R(x)$$

	3	2	0	-13	- 90	-10
- 3		- 9	21	- 63	228	- 414
	3	- 7	21	- 76	138	- 424 = P(-3) = Remainder of the division

Coefficients of Q(x) are 3, -7, 21, -76, and 138.

Q(x) is a polynomial with a degree 1 less than P(x) as the degree of (x+3) is 1.

R(x) = - 424

$Q(x)= 3x^4 - 7x^3 + 21x^2 - 76x + 138$

Example: Divide P(x) by 2x+6

Quotient changes; it is divided by the 2 of 2x+6 $\Rightarrow$ Q(x)=$\dfrac{3x^4 - 7x^3 + 21x^2 - 76x + 138}{2}$

Remainder does not change $\Rightarrow$ R(x) = - 424

16. When roots are given and equation is required; find the sum and the product of the roots, then construct the following equation:

$x_1 + x_2 = S$; $x_1. x_2 = P$; and $x^2 - Sx + P = 0$

17.　　Sum of the coefficients of $P(x)=P(1)$

(When there are more variables than one variable, replace all variables by 1 to find the sum of the coefficients.)

18.　　Constant term of $P(x)=P(0)$

(When there are more variables than one variable, replace all variables by 0 to find the constant term)

20.

$$\begin{array}{c|c} P(x) & D(x) \\ \hline & \overline{Q(x)} \\ R(x) & \end{array}$$

degree of $D(x)$ > degree of $R(x) \geq 0$

degree of $P(x)$ = degree of $D(x)$ + degree of $Q(x)$

21.　　If two polynomials, $P(x)$ and $Q(x)$ are equal, then the coefficients of the same degree terms are equal on both polynomials.

Exercises

1.　　Simplify $\left(\dfrac{x^2 - 3x + 2}{x + 3} \right)\left(\dfrac{x^2 + 2x - 3}{x - 2} \right)$

2.　　$y=(x+1)^2(x-4)$

a) Sum of the zeros=?

b) Product of the zeros=?

3.　　Solve for x: $3x^3 - 4x = 4x^2$

4.　　If $x + 2$ is a factor of $x^3 + kx^2 + 14x - 6$, then k=

5.　　Which of the following are equivalent to $(a-b+2).(a-b+2)$?

i.　　$(a-b)^2+4(a-b)+4$

ii.　　$(a-b)^2+4$

iii.　　a^2+b^2+4

iv.　　$a^2+b^2-2ab+4a - 4b+4$

6.　　$P(x)= 3x^3-5x^2+6x-3$

The zero of the above polynomial lies between two consecutive integers. What are these integers?

7.　　$y= 3x^2-4x-5$

What is the positive zero of the above function correct to the nearest hundredth?

8.　　Is $x-99$ a factor of the following polynomial?

$P(x)= 2x^4-200x^3+194x^2+400x-394$

9.　　Find all real zeros of the following polynomial:

$P(x)=2x^6-2x^5-8x^4-2x^3+10x^2+16x+8$

10. What is the least positive integer greater than the zero of the following polynomial?

$$P(x) = -\frac{3}{2}x^3 - x^2 - 2x + 3$$

11. $P(x) = 3x^4 - x^3 + 2x^2 + 5x - 1$

How many positive and negative real zeros does the above polynomial have?

12. $x^2 + x + 2 = 0$

What is the nature of the roots of the above equation?

13. Given that $P(x) = 2x^3 + x^2 + 3x - 5$, calculate:

a. The remainder when P(x) is divided by x+1.

b. The remainder when P(x) is divided by x-2.

c. The remainder when P(x) is divided by x.

d. The remainder when P(x+2) is divided by x+1.

e. The remainder when P(x+2) is divided by x-2.

f. The remainder when P(x+2) is divided by x.

g. The remainder when P(x-2) is divided by x+1.

h. The remainder when P(x-2) is divided by x-2.

i. The remainder when P(x-2) is divided by x.

j. The sum of the coefficients of P(x).

k. The sum of the coefficients of P(x+2).

l. The sum of the coefficients of P(x-2).

m. The constant term of P(x).

n. The constant term of P(x+2).

o. The constant term of P(x-2).

14. Find the positive rational root of the following equation: $2x^3 - 5x^2 + 14 x = 35$

15. What is the absolute difference between the zeros of the following polynomial?

$P(x) = 7x^2 + 11.5 x - 25$

16. $P(x) = 6x^2 + 12 x - 3$: $P(q) = 2 \Rightarrow$ What are the possible values for q?

17. Find the sum of the roots of $6x^3 + 8x^2 - 8x = 0$.

18. $P(x) = 2x^2 + 3x + 1$; $P(a) = 7 \Rightarrow a = ?$

19. What is the product of the roots of the following equation $(x - \sqrt{3}).(x^2 - ex - \pi) = 0$?

20. $\dfrac{2x - 1}{x^2 - 2x - 3} = \dfrac{A}{x - 3} + \dfrac{B}{x + 1}$

Find A and B if the above equality holds for all values for x other than 3 and -1.

21. $\dfrac{2x-1}{(x+1)(x-3)^2} = \dfrac{A}{x-3} + \dfrac{B}{(x-3)^2} + \dfrac{C}{(x+1)}$

    Find A, B and C if the above equality holds for all values for x other than 3 and -1.

22. $P(x)= x^3 + 6x - 14$ has a zero between which two consecutive integers?

23. $2x^4 + 3x^3 + 2x -1= 0$, Find nature of the roots.

24. Is $3x+1$ a factor of $2x^3 + 4x^2 - 4x - 3$?

25. What is the sum of the coefficients in the expansion of $(5x-4y)^{40}$?

26. What is the sum of the coefficients in the expansion of $(3x^2 - 2x+1)^5 (5x-4)^7$?

27. Find the number of the positive real zeros of the following equation:

    $x^4 + 2x^3 - 4x^2 - 5x = 0$

28. Find product of the real roots of the following equation: $x^4 - 3x^3 - 72x^2 - 3x -18 =0$.

29. $y= ax^4 - 2bx^3 + 11cx^2 - 4x - 3$

    Given that (x,y) is a point on the graph of P(x); as x increases without bound, y decreases without bound. What happens when x decreases without bound?

30. $y= ax^5 - 2bx^4 + 11cx^3 - 4x - 3$

    Given that (x,y) is a point on the graph of P(x); as x increases without bound, y decreases without bound. What happens when x decreases without bound?

31. Find the polynomial of lowest degree that gives each graph.

    A

    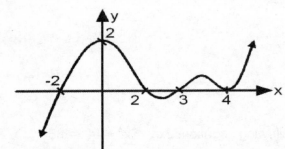

    B

    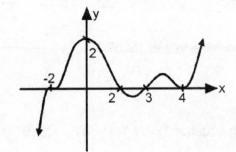

C

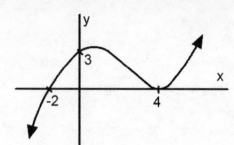

D

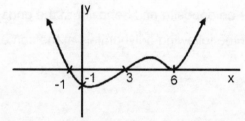

E

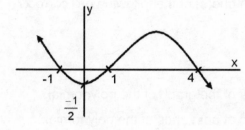

32.   P(x) gives the remainders of 3 and -2 respectively when divided by x+4 and x–1. Find the remainder when P(x) is divided by x^2+3x-4.

33. $P(x)=(3x^2-2x+1)^{12}$.

After P(x) is expanded and all terms are ordered in the decreasing powers of x, compute:

i.   Sum of the coefficients of P(x).

ii.   Constant term of P(x).

34.   What is the least degree of the polynomials whose graphs are given below?

(A)   (B)   (C)

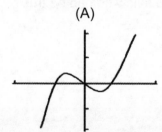   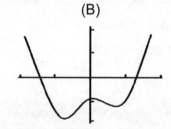   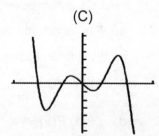

35.   If $P(x)=(2+i)x^2-x^3+4x+7$ then P(i)+P(1)+P(0)=?

36.   Find the sum and product of all roots of $x(x-1)^2(x+2)(x^2+1)=0$

37. $P(x)=(x+1)^2.(-2x^2+3x+9)$. When P(x) is expanded, find the coefficient of x^2 in the resulting polynomial.

38. Determine which one(s) of the following are polynomials.

    1. $P(x)= (1+2i)x^3-2ix^2+3x+4$

    2. $P(x)= 3$

    3. $P(x)= 0$

    4. $P(x)= x^{\frac{1}{2}} +3x-4$

    5. $P(x)= x^{-3}+2x^2+3x-1$

    6. $P(x)=\dfrac{1}{x}$

    7. $P(x)= 2x^3-\sqrt{3}\,x^2+ex+\pi$

39. For the polynomial $P(x)= -2x^4-3x^3-7x+4$ which one(s) of the following are correct?

    1. $P(x)$ is a continuous function of x

    2. $\lim\limits_{x\to\mp\infty} P(x)=-\infty$

    3. The end behavior is the same at both ends of the graph of the polynomial.

    4. The graph of the polynomial opens upward at both ends of the polynomial.

    5. The graph of the polynomial demonstrates an opposite end behavior at the ends.

40. A real polynomial can satisfy which one(s) of the following polynomials at the same time?

    1. Its graphs cuts the x axis exactly once.

    2. $\lim\limits_{x\to\mp\infty} P(x)=\pm\infty$

    3. The degree of $P(x)$ is even.

    4. The graph of $P(x)$ is symmetric about the origin.

41. Factorize completely:

    a) x^6-1

    b) x^7-y^7

    c) x^3-64y^6

    d) x^5+1

42. If $P(x)$ is a decreasing function of x then which one(s) of the following can be true?

    a. $P(x)$ is an odd degree polynomial

    b. $P(x)$ is an even degree polynomial

    c. $\lim\limits_{x\to-\infty} P(x)=\infty$

    d. $\lim\limits_{x\to-\infty} P(x)=-\infty$

    e. $P(x)$ has no real roots

    f. $P(x)$ has at least one real root.

43. $P(x)$ is a 5th degree polynomial with a leading coefficient of 4 and a constant term of 6. List all possible rational roots of $P(x)$.

44. Which one(s) of the following cannot be the roots of the integral polynomial given below?

    $P(x)=-4x^5+ax^4+bx^3-x+5$

    (i) $\dfrac{1}{2}$ (ii) 1   (iii) $\dfrac{3}{2}$ (iv) 2   (v) $\dfrac{5}{2}$

45. Identify which one(s) of the following are factors of $P(x) = 6x^6-4x^2+4x+2$

    a. x-1

    b. x+1

    c. x

46. State whether each statement given as follows is true or false:

    a. x+1 is a factor of $x^{17}+1$?

    b. x-2 is a factor of x^4-16?

    c. x+2 is a factor of x^4-16?

    d. x-1 is a factor of $x^{17}-1$?

47. Construct the real polynomial of the least degree whose roots include

    a) -2 and 3i

    b) 1 and i

    c) -1 and 3-i

48. Indicate whether each statement is true or false:

    a. x^4+ax^2+bx-5 can have an irrational root between 0 and 1, where a and b are positive integers .

    b. x^4+ax^2+bx-5 can have a rational root between 0 and 1, where a and b are positive integers.

    c. x^4+ax^2+bx-5 has four zeros two of which are real, one positive and one negative.

    d. As x increases or decreases without bound, x^2-x^4-1 decreases without bound.

49. $x^6-x^4+ax^3+bx^2-x+1=0$ where a and b are positive real numbers is given. Find maximum number of positive and negative real roots the given polynomial may have.

50. $P(x)=6x^6-ax^5+bx^4+cx^3-15$. Which of the following cannot be a zero of $P(x)$?

    i. -1.5   ii. 0.75   iii. 1/6   iv. 5/3   v. -15

51. $P(x)=ax^2+bx+c$; P(1)=2; P(2)=4; P(3)=7. Find a,b, and c.

52. $P(x)=4x^5-ax^4+bx^3-cx-6$ is given where a, b, c are positive integers. If P(x) has a negative rational root between -2 and -1, what is this rational root?

53. What is the remainder when $3x^4 + 8x^3 + 9x^2 - 3x - 4$ is divided by x + 1?

54. $P(x)=6x^3+ax^2+bx+17$

    If the integral polynomial given above has a rational zero between 5 and 6;

    i. What is this zero?   ii. What is the relation between a and b?

55. If a, b, c are the roots of the equation $2x^3-6x^2+8x-3=0$, what is the sum of the numbers a, b, c, and their reciprocals?

56. A quadratic equation with integral coefficients has a root of $-2+\sqrt{3}$. Find this equation.

57. A quadratic equation with real coefficients has a root of -2+3i. Find this equation.

58. $y=2x^3+x+1$.

     Find the distance between the x and y intercepts of the above function.

59. A polynomial gives the remainder of 4 when it is divided by (x-2) and the remainder of 3 when it is divided by (x+1). What is the remainder when this polynomial is divided by (x^2-x-2)?

60. A polynomial gives the remainder of 4 when it is divided by (x-1) and the remainder of 3x+2 when it is divided by (x^2+x+1). What is the remainder when this polynomial is divided by (x^3-1)?

1.10 TRIGONOMETRY

Definition of an Angle

Two rays emerging from the same point.

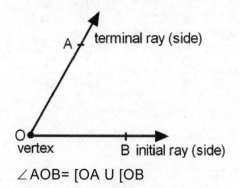

$\angle$AOB= [OA U [OB

Angle in standard position

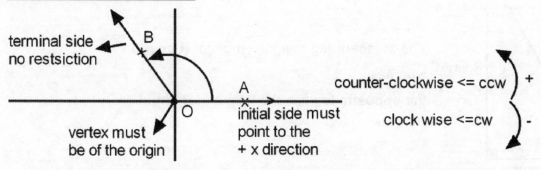

Point B is on the terminal side of angle AOB that is in standard position.

Circle Equation

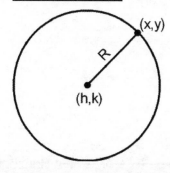

Circle is the locus of points that are equidistant (distance=radius=R) from a fixed point (center = (h,k)) in a plane.

$$R = \sqrt{(x-h)^2 + (y-k)^2} \Rightarrow (x-h)^2 + (y-k)^2 = R^2$$

If equation of the circle is given by $x^2+y^2+Dx+Ey+F=0$ then the center and radius can be found by completing squares or by the following formulas: center=$(-\dfrac{D}{2}, -\dfrac{E}{2})$; radius=$\dfrac{1}{2}\sqrt{D^2 + E^2 - 4F}$

Example:

Find center and radius of the following circle: $x^2-6x+y^2+4y=1$.

Solution:

$x^2-6x+9+y^2+4y+4=1+9+4$

$(x-3)^2+(y+2)^2=14 \Rightarrow$ Center C(3, -2); Radius= $\sqrt{14}$

Trigonometric Ratios in the Right Triangle

SOH-CAH-TOA

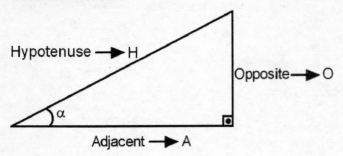

$$SOH : \sin\alpha = \frac{O}{H} \qquad \cot\alpha = \frac{1}{\tan\alpha} = \frac{A}{O}$$

$$CAH : \cos\alpha = \frac{A}{H} \qquad \sec\alpha = \frac{1}{\cos\alpha} = \frac{H}{A}$$

$$TOA : \tan\alpha = \frac{O}{A} \qquad \csc\alpha = \frac{1}{\sin\alpha} = \frac{H}{O}$$

Reminders

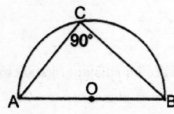

The **adjacent leg** has the length of **R·cos(θ)**

whereas

the **opposite leg** has the length of **R·sin(θ)**.

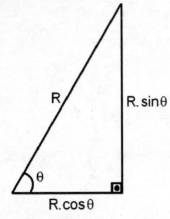

The angle ∠C that "sees" the diameter is 90°.

Angle of Elevation and Angle of Depression

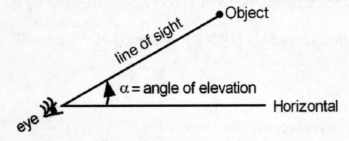

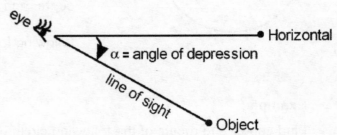

Example:

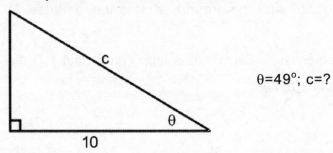

$\theta=49°$; c=?

Solution:

$$\cos 49° = \frac{10}{c} \Rightarrow c = \frac{10}{\cos 49°} = 15.24$$

Example:

From a plane flying at a height of 4000 feet, the angle of depression to a landmark on the ground is 55°. What is the horizontal distance the plane has to fly to be directly over the mark?

Solution:

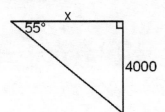

$$\tan 55° = \frac{4000}{x} \Rightarrow x = \frac{4000}{\tan 55°} = 2800.8$$

<u>Exercises</u>

1. In △ABC, the measure of ∠A is 70° and the length of side AB is 18. What is the length of the height from vertex B to side AC?

2. If x is the measure of an acute angle such that tan(x)=a/4 then calculate sin(x) and cos(x).

3. If x is the measure of an obtuse angle such that sin(x)=a/4 then calculate cos(x) and tan(x).

4. If the measure of one angle of a rhombus is 120°, then what is the ratio of the length of its shorter diagonal to the length of its longer diagonal?

5. If θ is an acute angle and sinθ=a/b, where 0<a<b then cosθ=?

6. If θ is an obtuse angle and sinθ=a/b, where 0<a<b then cosθ=?

7. What is the area of a right triangle with an angle of 38° and shorter leg of length 17?

8.   A kite string is attached to the ground. If 200 meters of kite string are played out on the kite and the string makes an angle of 50° with the ground, what is the distance, in meters, from the kite to the ground?

9.   In a right triangle, ratio of a leg to the hypotenuse is 3/4. What is tan(x) given that x is the degree measure of the larger acute angle in this triangle?

10.

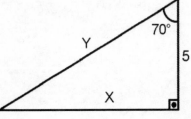

In right triangle ACB given in the figure, cos ∠BAC=?

11.

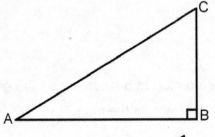

In the △ABC given above, AC is 16 and the measure of ∠CAB is 37°, what is the length of side BC?

12.

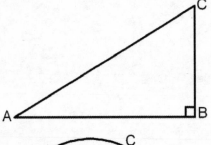

Find X and Y:

13.

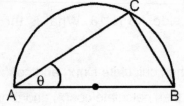

AC=20; sinA=0.8.

i.   BC=?

ii. AB=?

14.

If AB=2, what is the area of △ABC in terms of θ?

15.

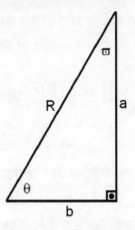

a. Which one(s) of the following are equal to sinθ in the given triangle?

    i. cosω ii. a/R iii. b/R

b. In the given triangle calculate the following:

    i. R.cosθ=? ii. R.sinθ=? iii. a.tanω=?

16.

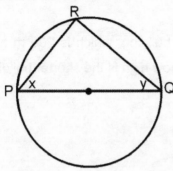

cosx=3/5 ⇒ cosy=?

17.

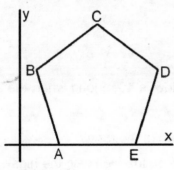

ABCDE is a regular pentagon with a side length of 4. If the x coordinate of point A is 3, find the coordinates of points B, C and D.

18.

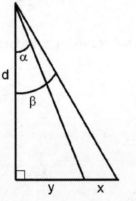

Find an equation for y and d in terms of x, β, and α.

19. The angle of depression of a boat is 33° from the top of a lighthouse that is 200 feet high, Find the distance from the boat to the bottom of the lighthouse.

20. A 25-foot pole is attached at a 57° angle to the ground with a cable. What is the length of this cable to the nearest hundredth of a foot?

21. A ladder leans against a wall making an angle of 31° with the ground. The length of the ladder

is 24 feet. Find the distance in feet from the foot of the ladder to the lowee end of the wall.

22. A road that is 2200 feet long climbs up to a mountain with an angle of elevation of 26°. How high is the mountain?

23. A kite, whose string is 240 meters, is flying at an angle of elevation of about 42°. What is the height of the kite to the nearest meter?

24. An aircraft flying at 33,000 ft, starts descending at a 3.9° angle of depression. What is the ground distance from the airport to the point directly below the aircraft to the nearest 1000 feet?

25. Ebru is 174 cm tall and her nephew Deniz is just 90 cm tall. Whose shadow is longer by how much when the sun is: i. 20°; ii. 70°, above the horizon?

26. Two buildings are 50 meters apart. From the top of a tall building, which is 200 m high, the angle of depression to the top of a shorter building, is 15°. How high is the shorter building?

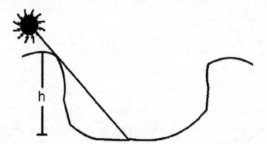

27. Calculate the depth h of the trough given above if the shadow is 40 m long when the angle of elevation of the sun is 40°.

28. A road 1.6 km long rises 600 m. What is the angle of elevation of the road?

29. A highway is sloping up such that for every 1000 m distance on the highway, the highway rises by 75 m. What is the angle of elevation of the highway?

30. A road 2000m is declining with an angle of depression 10° form a hill of height h meters. h=?

Unit Circle

$$x^2 + y^2 = 1 \Rightarrow \text{center} = (0,0) \text{ and } \text{radius} = R = 1$$

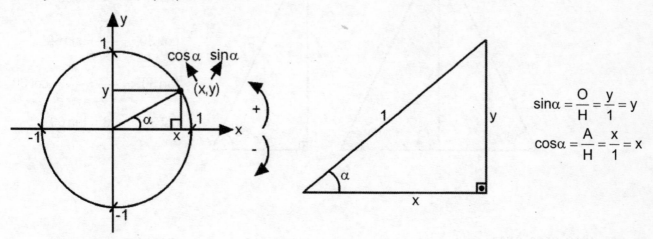

For every angle α on the unit circle, **x = cos α** and **y = sin α**, therefore:

$$x^2 + y^2 = 1 \Rightarrow \cos^2 \alpha + \sin^2 \alpha = 1$$
$$-1 \le x \le 1 \Rightarrow -1 \le \cos \alpha \le 1$$
$$-1 \le y \le 1 \Rightarrow -1 \le \sin \alpha \le 1$$

Signs of Trigonometric Functions

SILVER	Sinx +			Sinx +	**ALL**
	Cosx -			Cosx +	
	Tanx -	II	I	Tanx +	
	Sinx -	III	IV	Sinx -	
	Cosx -			Cosx +	
TEA	Tanx +			Tanx -	**C**UPS

Please note that **cotx** and **tanx** always have the **same sign**.

Special Angles

45°

$$\sin 45^\circ = \frac{1}{\sqrt{2}} = \frac{\sqrt{2}}{2} = \cos 45^\circ$$

$$\tan 45^\circ = 1 = \cot 45^\circ$$

30° and 60°

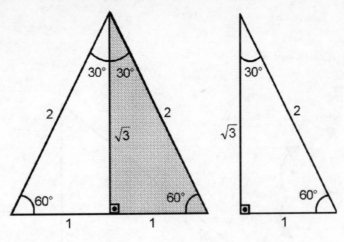

$$\sin 30° = \frac{1}{2} = \cos 60°$$

$$\cos 30° = \frac{\sqrt{3}}{2} = \sin 60°$$

$$\tan 30° = \frac{1}{\sqrt{3}} = \frac{\sqrt{3}}{3} = \cot 60°$$

$$\cot 30° = \sqrt{3} = \tan 60°$$

0°, 90°, 180°, 270°, 360°

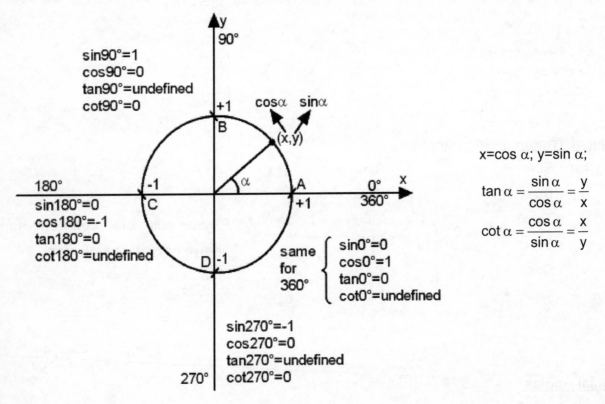

sin90°=1
cos90°=0
tan90°=undefined
cot90°=0

sin180°=0
cos180°=-1
tan180°=0
cot180°=undefined

same for 360°
{ sin0°=0
cos0°=1
tan0°=0
cot0°=undefined

sin270°=-1
cos270°=0
tan270°=undefined
cot270°=0

x=cos α; y=sin α;

$$\tan \alpha = \frac{\sin \alpha}{\cos \alpha} = \frac{y}{x}$$

$$\cot \alpha = \frac{\cos \alpha}{\sin \alpha} = \frac{x}{y}$$

	0°	30°	45°	60°	90°
sin	$\dfrac{\sqrt{0}}{2}=0$	$\dfrac{\sqrt{1}}{2}=\dfrac{1}{2}$	$\dfrac{\sqrt{2}}{2}$	$\dfrac{\sqrt{3}}{2}$	$\dfrac{\sqrt{4}}{2}=1$
cos	1	$\dfrac{\sqrt{3}}{2}$	$\dfrac{\sqrt{2}}{2}$	$\dfrac{1}{2}$	0
tan	0	$\dfrac{1}{\sqrt{3}}=\dfrac{\sqrt{3}}{3}$	1	$\sqrt{3}$	undefined
cot	undefined	$\sqrt{3}$	1	$\dfrac{\sqrt{3}}{3}$	0

Radian and Degree

O   R $\pi=3.141592...$

$$\Rightarrow \frac{R}{\pi}=\frac{D}{180°}$$

O°   D   180°

Degree to Radian Conversion: $D \cdot \dfrac{\pi}{180°}=R$

Radian to Degree Conversion: $R \cdot \dfrac{180°}{\pi}=D$

Example:

It is given that $\sin x=\dfrac{5}{13}$ where $90° \le x \le 180°$ and $\cos y=\dfrac{4}{9}$ where y is in 4'th quadrant.

$\sin (x+y)= ?$

Solution:

Angle Mode: Degrees

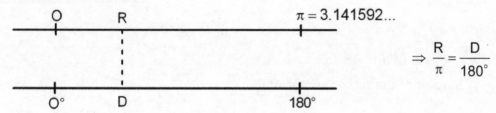

```
sin⁻¹(5/13
          22.61986495
180-Ans
          157.3801351
Ans→X
          157.3801351
```
```
cos⁻¹(4/9
          63.61220004
360-Ans
          296.3878
Ans→Y
          296.3878
```
```
sin(X+Y
          .9978384015
```

Answer: 0.9978

Example:

$f(x) = e^x$; $g(x) = \cos x$; $(f \circ g)(\sqrt{3}) = ?$

Solution:

Angle Mode: Radians

```
e^(cos(√(3
        .85166967
```

Answer: 0.85

Arc Length and Area of a Sector

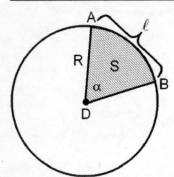

l: length of arc $\overset{\frown}{AB}$

S: area of the minor sector AOB

α in degrees:	α in radians:
$l = 2\pi R \cdot \dfrac{\alpha}{360°}$	$l = 2\pi R \cdot \dfrac{\alpha}{2\pi} = R \cdot \alpha \implies \boxed{l = R\,\alpha}$
$S = \pi R^2 \cdot \dfrac{\alpha}{360°}$	$S = \pi R^2 \cdot \dfrac{\alpha}{2\pi} = \dfrac{1}{2} \cdot R^2 \cdot \alpha = \dfrac{1}{2} \cdot R\alpha \cdot R = \dfrac{1}{2} l \cdot R \implies \boxed{S = \dfrac{l \cdot R}{2} = \dfrac{1}{2} \cdot R^2 \alpha}$

Identities

EASY	HARD
$\tan x = \dfrac{\sin x}{\cos x}$	$\sin^2 x + \cos^2 x = 1$
$\cot x = \dfrac{\cos x}{\sin x}$	$1 + \tan^2 x = \sec^2 x$
$\tan x \cdot \cot x = 1$	$1 + \cot^2 x = \csc^2 x$
$\tan x = \dfrac{1}{\cot x}$	
$\cot x = \dfrac{1}{\tan x}$	
$\sec x = \dfrac{1}{\cos x}$	
$\csc x = \dfrac{1}{\sin x}$	

Functions and Cofunctions

$\sin x \Leftrightarrow \cos x$

$\tan x \Leftrightarrow \cot x$

$\sec x \Leftrightarrow \csc x$

Reference Angle

The acute angle that the given angle makes with the x axis:

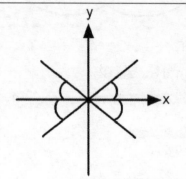

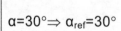
$\alpha = 30° \Rightarrow \alpha_{ref} = 30°$
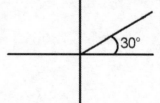

$\alpha = 155° \Rightarrow \alpha_{ref} = 25°$
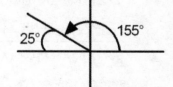

$\alpha = 215° \Rightarrow \alpha_{ref} = 35°$
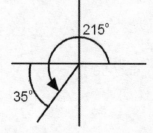

$\alpha = 340° \Rightarrow \alpha_{ref} = 20°$
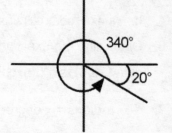

Exercises

1. Given that $f(x)=x^2$ and $g(x)=\cos(x)$; find

   i. An expression for $(f \circ g)(x)$ and $(g \circ f)(x)$ each;

   ii. The exact value of $(f \circ g)(2\pi)$.

2. Convert the following angle measures that are in radians to degrees:

   $\dfrac{\pi}{2}, \dfrac{\pi}{3}, \dfrac{\pi}{4}, \dfrac{\pi}{6}, \pi, \dfrac{2\pi}{3}, \dfrac{3\pi}{2}, \dfrac{5\pi}{6}, 2\pi, 1, 1.5708.$

3. Convert the following angle measures that are in degrees to radians:

   $15°, 18°, 30°, 36°, 45°, 60°, 90°, 120°, 135°, 150°, 180°, 225°, 270°, 315°, 360°$

4.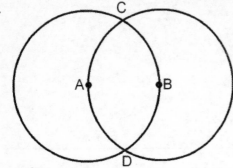
   In the given figure, circles with center A and B intersect at points C and D. Arc CBD has length 4π. Calculate area of the circle with center A and area of the quadrilateral ADBC.

5. Simplify

   a. $(\sin^2\theta + \cos^2\theta + 2)^4 =$

   b. $\csc(2\theta)\sin(2\theta) + 1 + \cos^2\theta + \sin^2\theta = ?$

   c. $\dfrac{\sec x}{\csc x} = ?$

   d. $\dfrac{\tan^2(x)\csc^2(x) - 1}{\csc(x)\tan^2(x)\sin(x)} = ?$

   e. $\dfrac{\cot^2(x)\sec^2(x) - 1}{\sec(x)\cot^2(x)\cos(x)} = ?$

   f. $\sec^2 x - \tan^2 x + \csc^2 x - \cot^2 x = ?$

   g. $\sin^2 x + \cos^2 x + \dfrac{\sec x}{\csc x} \cdot \cot x = ?$

   h. $(\sin x + \cos x)^2 + (\sin x - \cos x)^2 = ?$

6. Determine the exact values of each of the following:

   $\cot(-17\pi/3), \sin(5\pi), \cos(420°), \tan(9\pi/4), \csc(-9\pi/2), \sec(-30°).$

7. $\dfrac{3\pi}{2}$ radians = x degrees; x=?

Common Transformations on Trigonometric Functions

Function	→ Function if π, 2π	
$\sin(\mp x \mp \pi)$	→ **?** sinx	
$\mp x \mp 2\pi$		
$\cos(\mp x \mp 2\pi)\rightarrow$	→ **?** cosx	
$\tan(\mp x \mp 2\pi)$	→ **?** tanx	
$\cot(\mp x \mp 2\pi)$	→ **?** cotx	**?:** Means the sign, **+** or **−**.
Function	→ **Cofunction if $\pi/2$, $3\pi/2$**	While determining sign:
$\sin(\mp x \mp \dfrac{\pi}{2})$	→ **?** cosx	• x must be assumed as an acute angle
$\mp x \mp \dfrac{3\pi}{2}$		• the given function (not the function that it is transformed to) and its region must be used in determining the sign.
$\cos(\mp x \mp \dfrac{\pi}{2})$	→ **?** sinx	
$\tan(\mp x \mp \dfrac{\pi}{2})$	→ **?** cotx	
$\cot(\mp x \mp \dfrac{\pi}{2})$	→ **?** tanx	

Special Cases

$\sin(-x) = -\sin x$

$\cos(-x) = \cos x$

$\tan(-x) = -\tan x$

$\cot(-x) = -\cot x$

$\cos(\pi - x) = -\cos x$

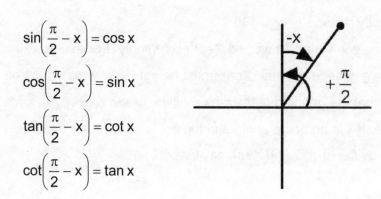

$\sin\left(\dfrac{\pi}{2} - x\right) = \cos x$

$\cos\left(\dfrac{\pi}{2} - x\right) = \sin x$

$\tan\left(\dfrac{\pi}{2} - x\right) = \cot x$

$\cot\left(\dfrac{\pi}{2} - x\right) = \tan x$

This means when $\alpha + \beta = 90°$

$\sin\alpha = \cos\beta$

$\tan\alpha = \cot\beta$

$\sec\alpha = \csc\beta$

Examples:

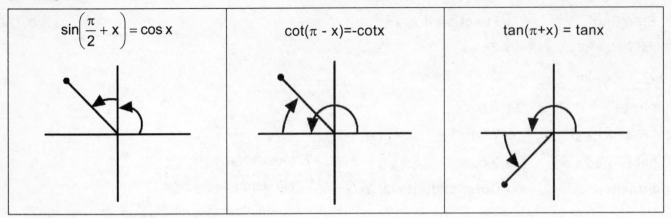

| $\sin\left(\dfrac{\pi}{2}+x\right)=\cos x$ | $\cot(\pi - x)=-\cot x$ | $\tan(\pi+x) = \tan x$ |

Trigonometric Equations

- $\sin x=\sin\alpha \Rightarrow x=\alpha+k.2\pi$ OR $x=\pi-\alpha+k.2\pi$ (a direct result of the fact that $\sin(x)=\sin(\pi\text{-}x)$)

- $\cos x=\cos\alpha \Rightarrow x=\mp\alpha+k.2\pi$ (a direct result of the fact that $\cos(x)=\cos(\text{-}x)$)

- $\tan x=\tan\alpha$ or $\cot x=\cot\alpha \Rightarrow x=\alpha+k.\pi$ (a direct result of the fact that period of the tangent and cotangent functions are each π)

Solving Trigonometric Equations with the TI

When solving a trigonometric equation in the form **f(x)=g(x),** perform the following steps:

i.   Write the equation in the form: **f(x)-g(x)=0**.

ii.   While writing the trigonometric expressions please observe the rules given in parts 1.17 and 1.18 that involve the trigonometric functions that are built in TI or otherwise.

iii.   Plot the graph of **y=f(x)-g(x)**.

iv.   Set the **angle mode to radians or degrees** depending on which angle measure is used in the question. If no degree signs (like in 90°) are used then the mode should be radians. However when exact values are required you may wish to solve the equation in degrees and convert the answer to radians using the following formula $\dfrac{R}{\pi}=\dfrac{D}{180°}$. In such a case finding the answer in radians and then trying to find which answer choice matches this answer can also be an option; while doing so you may directly replace π with 180°

v.   If x is limited to a certain interval then set **Xmin**; **Xmax** and **Xscl** accordingly. For example, if x is an acute angle and the angle mode is degrees, then **Xmin** must be set to 0°; **Xmax** must be set to 90° and **Xscl** must be set so that the grigding of the x-axis will be made properly In such a case **Xscl** being 30° would be fine. If x is an acute angle and the angle mode is radians, then **Xmin** must be set to 0; **Xmax** must be set to π/2 and **Xscl** may be set to 1.

vi. When only sines and cosines are involved, **ZoomFit** option may give a clearer graph. However, since only the x-intercepts are required, the window setting parameters **Ymin= -1** and **Ymax = 1** can give a clear view of the zeros.

vii. Find the x-intercepts using the **Calc Zero** of TI-84 Plus. However when the graph seems to be tangent to the x-axis at a certain point, you may use the **Calc Min** or **Calc Max** facilities but you should make sure that the y-coordinate of the minimum or maximum point is zero.

viii. Any value like **-6.61E -10** or **7.2E -11** can be interpreted as 0 as they mean **-6.6x10** $^{-10}$ and **7.2x10** $^{-11}$ respectively.

Example:

$\cos(2x) = 2\sin(90° - x)$. What are all possible values of x between 0° & 360°?

Solution:

Mode: Degrees

$\cos(2x) - 2\sin(90° - x) = 0$

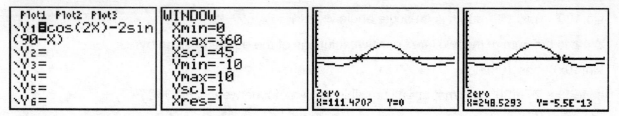

Answer: 111.47°, 248.53°

Example:

$2\sin x + \cos(2x) = 2\sin^2 x - 1$ and $0 \le x < 2\pi \Rightarrow x = ?$

Solution:

Mode: Radians

$2\sin x + \cos(2x) - 2\sin^2 x + 1 = 0$

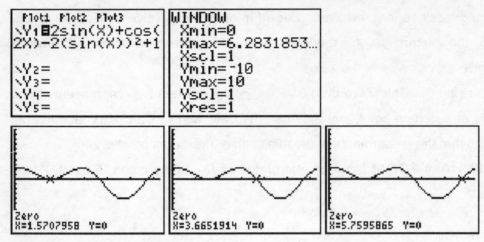

Answer: 1.57, 3.67, 5.76

Exercises

1. How many solutions does the following equation have between 0° and 360°?

    $$\sec^2 x - \frac{\sin x}{\cos x} = 1$$

2. $\cos(33°) = \tan x° \Rightarrow x = ?$ (x is an acute angle)

3. $0 < x < \frac{\pi}{4}$ and $\tan(4x) = 3$. What is x and what is tanx?

4. $\sin(120°-n) = \sin 50°$ and n is an acute angle $\Rightarrow$ n=?

5. What is the sum of the two least positive solutions of the equation given by:

    $\sin(10x) = -\cos(10x)$?

6. $\cos(2x) = 2\sin(90°-x)$. What are all possible values of x between 0° & 360°?

7. $\frac{1}{4}\sin^2(2x) + \sin^2(x) + \cos^4(x) = 1$ If x is positive and less than 2π, how many different values

    can x have?

8. $\frac{1}{\cot(5x)} = -2 \Rightarrow$ What is the smallest positive value for x?

9. $\frac{8\sin(2\theta)}{1 - \cos(2\theta)} = \frac{4}{3}$ and θ is between 0° and 180°. What is θ?

10. $\frac{\sin x + \cos 36°}{\cos \dfrac{4\pi}{3} - \sin(-90°)} = 0$ and x is between 90° and 270° $\Rightarrow$ x=?

11. $\frac{\sin\theta}{\cos\theta - 1} = -\sqrt{3} \Rightarrow$ If θ is an acute angle, θ=?

12. $2\sin x + \cos(2x) = 2\sin^2 x - 1$ and $0 \le x < 2\pi \Rightarrow$ x=?

13. $\cos(130°-2x) = \sin(70°-3x)$ and x is an acute angle. What is x?

14. x is in quadrant 3 and $\cot(120°-x)=\dfrac{1}{\tan x} \Rightarrow x=?$

15. $\left.\begin{array}{l} \dfrac{\sin(2\theta)}{2}=\dfrac{1}{4} \\[2mm] 0° \le \theta < 360° \end{array}\right\}$ What is θ?

16. $\left.\begin{array}{l} \sec\theta \cdot \csc\theta = 4 \\ 0° \le \theta < 360° \end{array}\right\}$ $\theta=?$

17. $\left.\begin{array}{l} 0° \le x < 90° \\ \tan(4x)=1 \end{array}\right\}$ $x=?$

18. $\tan(6x)=\sqrt{3}$ and x is an acute angle $\Rightarrow$ x=?

19. $\left.\begin{array}{l} \dfrac{\sqrt{3}}{2}\cos x + \dfrac{1}{2}\sin x = 1 \\[2mm] 0 \le x < 2\pi \end{array}\right\} \Rightarrow x=?$

20. $2\sin^2 x=3(1+\cos x)-\dfrac{1}{2}$ and x is in 3rd quadrant. What is x in radians?

21. $\cos x \cos 45° - \sin x \sin 45° = -1$ and x is an obtuse angle $\Rightarrow$ x=?

22. $\left.\begin{array}{l} \sin x \sec x = \sqrt{3} \\ 0 \le x < 2\pi \end{array}\right\} \Rightarrow x=?$

23. x is acute and $\cos x=\dfrac{3}{5} \Rightarrow \sin x + \tan x=?$

Solving Trigonometric Inequalities with TI

When solving a trigonometric inequality in the form **f(x)<g(x)**, or **f(x)≤g(x)**, or **f(x)>g(x)**, or **f(x)≥g(x)** perform the following steps:

i. Write the inequality in the form: **f(x)-g(x)<0 or f(x)-g(x)≤0 or f(x)-g(x) >0 or f(x)-g(x)≥0.**

ii. While writing the trigonometric expressions please observe the rules given in parts 1.17 and 1.18 that involve the trigonometric functions that are built in TI or otherwise.

iii. Plot the graph of **y=f(x)-g(x).**

iv. Set the **angle mode to radians or degrees** depending on which angle measure is used in the question. If no degree signs (like in 90°) are used then the mode should be radians. However when exact values are required you may wish to solve the equation in degrees and convert the answer to radians using the following formula $\dfrac{R}{\pi}=\dfrac{D}{180°}$. In such a case finding the answer in radians and then trying to find which answer choice matches this answer can also be an option; while doing so you may directly replace π with 180°

v.   If x is limited to a certain interval then set **Xmin**; **Xmax** and **Xscl** accordingly. For example, if x is an acute angle and the angle mode is degrees, then **Xmin** must be set to 0°; **Xmax** must be set to 90° and **Xscl** must be set so that the grigding of the x-axis will be made properly In such a case **Xscl** being 30° would be fine. If x is an acute angle and the angle mode is radians, then **Xmin** must be set to 0; **Xmax** must be set to $\pi/2$ and **Xscl** may be set to 1.

vi.   When only sines and cosines are involved, **ZoomFit** option may give a clearer graph. However, since only the x-intercepts are required, the window setting parameters **Ymin= -1** and **Ymax = 1** can give a clear view of the zeros.

vii. Find the x-intercepts using the **Calc Zero** of TI-84 Plus. However when the graph seems to be tangent to the x-axis at a certain point, you may use the **Calc Min** or **Calc Max** facilities but you should make sure that the y-coordinate of the minimum or maximum point is zero.

viii. Any value like **-6.61E -10** or **7.2E -11** can be interpreted as 0 as they mean **-6.6x10^{-10}** and **7.2x10^{-11}** respectively.

ix.   The solution of the inequality will be the set of values of x for which the graph of f(x)-g(x) lies below the x axis if the inequality is in one of the forms **f(x)-g(x)<0** or **f(x)-g(x)≤0.** The solution of the inequality will be the set of values of x for which the graph of f(x)-g(x) lies above the x axis if the inequality is in one of the forms **f(x)-g(x)>0** or **f(x)-g(x)≥0.** If ≤ or ≥ symbols are involved, then the x-intercepts are also in the solution set.

x.   Please note that the x-values that correspond to asymptotes are never included in the solution set.

Example:

sin(2x) > sinx

Find the set of values of x that satisfy the above inequality in the interval 0<x<2π.

Solution:

sin(2x) - sinx > 0

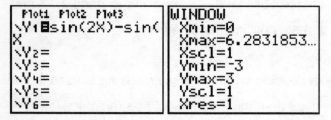

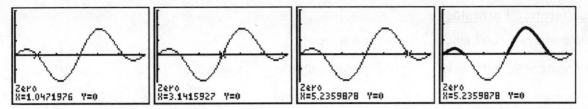

Answer: (0, 1.05) or (3.14, 5.24)

Example:

cos(2x) ≥ cosx

Find the set of values of x that satisfy the above inequality in the interval 0 ≤ x ≤ 360°.

Solution:

cos(2x) - cosx ≥ 0

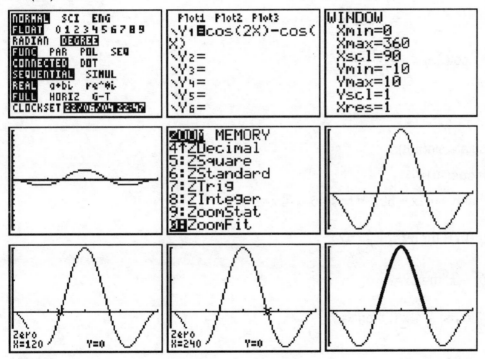

Answer: [120°, 240°] or {0°,360°}

<u>**Exercises**</u>

1.	x < cosx

	What is the solution set of the above inequality?

2.	If x is between 0 and 2π, what will be the set of x values for which sinx < cosx?

Sum and Difference Formulas

$\sin(x \mp y) = \sin x \cos y \mp \cos x \sin y$ (same sign)

$\cos(x \mp y) = \cos x \cos y \pm \sin x \sin y$ (opposite sign)

$$\tan(x + y) = \frac{\tan x + \tan y}{1 - \tan x \tan y} \qquad \tan(x - y) = \frac{\tan x - \tan y}{1 + \tan x \tan y}$$

$$\cot(x + y) = \frac{\cot x \cot y - 1}{\cot x + \cot y} \qquad \cot(x - y) = \frac{-\cot x \cot y - 1}{\cot x - \cot y}$$

Double Angle Formulas

$$\sin(2x) = 2 \cdot \sin x \cdot \cos x \qquad \cos(2x) = \cos^2 x - \sin^2 x$$
$$= 1 - 2 \cdot \sin^2 x$$
$$= 2 \cdot \cos^2 x - 1$$

$$\tan(2x) = \frac{2 \tan x}{1 - \tan^2 x} \qquad \cot(2x) = \frac{\cot^2 x - 1}{2 \cot x}$$

Exercises

1. If $\sin\theta = 0.7$ then calculate $\sin(\pi - \theta)$.

2. $\sin\theta + \sin(-\theta) + \cos\theta + \cos(-\theta) = ?$

3. Given that $0° < x < 90°$ and $\sin(2x + 60)° = \cos(45 - x)°$. $x = ?$

4. If $0 < x < \pi$ and $\cos x = 0.76$ then $\tan\left(\dfrac{x}{2}\right) = ?$

5. If $\sin x = -\cos x$ and $0 \leq x \leq \pi$, then $x = ?$

6. If $0 < x < \dfrac{3\pi}{2}$ and $\sin\dfrac{\pi}{2} = \cos\left(\dfrac{\pi}{2} + x\right)$, then $x = ?$

7. If $\sin(\sin x) = 0$ and $0 \leq x \leq \dfrac{\pi}{2}$, then $x = ?$

8. Each vertex of a 9 sided polygon is 10 in from the center of the polygon.

   i. what is the length of one side of the polygon?

   ii. What is the area of the polygon?

9. If x and y are both acute angles and y is less than x then which one(s) of the following must be true?

   a. $\sin y < \sin x$

   b. $\cos y < \cos x$

   c. $\tan y < \tan x$

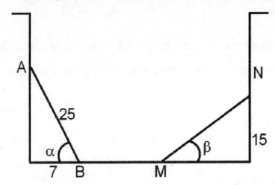

10. The figure shows the side views of two identical ladders that lean against two walls that are directly opposite each other. Ladder MN is stationary while ladder AB is sliding down. How many feet must the A end of ladder AB fall down so that tanα=tanβ will be valid?

11. $\cos^2 x = \cos x + 2$ and x is in the interval $[0, 2\pi]$.

12. $\sin^2 x = \sin x + 2$ and x is in the interval $[0, 360°]$.

13. What is the smallest positive value of x for which $\sin(3x)° = -\dfrac{\sqrt{3}}{2}$?

14. If $\sin x = \tan x$, what is the smallest positive radian value of x?

15. If $\cos x = \dfrac{\sqrt{3}}{2}$ and $0 \le x \le \dfrac{\pi}{2}$, then $\sin(2x) =$

Sine Rule

When

(i)   two sides and an angle opposite one of them are given or

(ii)   two angles and a side opposite one of them are given;

use the sine rule to find the other sides and angles. Please note that due to the identity **sin(180°-x)=sin(x)** there may be degenerate cases when there are two triangles that satisfy the given conditions. Moreover, the triangle inequality that requires that opposite a large angle lies the opposite side or vice versa has to hold in every case.

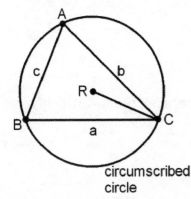

$$\frac{a}{\sin \hat{A}} = \frac{b}{\sin \hat{B}} = \frac{c}{\sin \hat{C}} = 2R$$

circumscribed circle

Cosine Rule

(i)   When three sides are given and an angle opposite one of them is to be calculated, or

(ii)   when two sides and the angle between them are given and the side opposite the given angle is to be calculated; use the cosine rule.

It may be necessary to note that: **cos(180°-x)= - cos(x)**

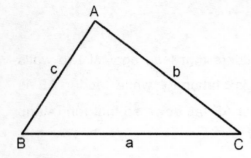

$$a^2=b^2+c^2 - 2bc \cdot \cos \hat{A}$$

$$b^2=a^2+c^2 - 2ac \cdot \cos \hat{B}$$

$$c^2=a^2+b^2 - 2ab \cdot \cos \hat{C}$$

Example

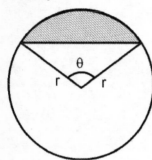

Area of the shaded part $= \dfrac{1}{2}r^2(\theta - \sin\theta)$

Area of a Triangle

$\text{Area} = \dfrac{1}{2}bc \sin \hat{A} = \dfrac{1}{2}ac \sin \hat{B} = \dfrac{1}{2}ab \sin \hat{C}$: Use when two sides and the angle between them are given in a triangle.

$\text{Area} = \sqrt{u(u-a)(u-b)(u-c)}$ where $u = \dfrac{a+b+c}{2}$ is the semi-perimeter: Use when all three sides of a triangle are given.

Example:

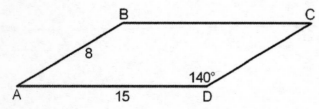

Find area of the parallelogram ABCD given in figure

Solution:

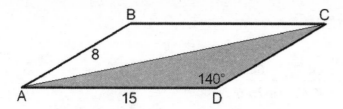

Area of parallelogram is twice the area of the shaded region and it is given by

$$2 \cdot \frac{1}{2} \cdot 8 \cdot 15 \cdot \sin 140° = 77.13$$

Example:

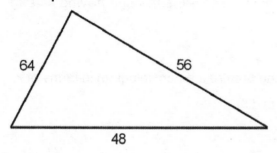

Largest angle=?

Area of the triangle=?

Radius of the circumscribed circle=?

Solution:

Largest angle is opposite 64 and it is denoted by x as it is given in the following figure: You should use cosine rule to find this angle.

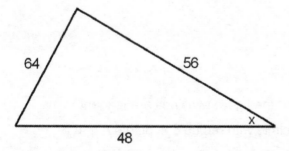

However, if two triangles are similar, then the corresponding angle measures are the same. So for simplicity you can reduce each side by the greatest common factor and find the angle in the simplified triangle that will give smaller numbers easier to manipulate.

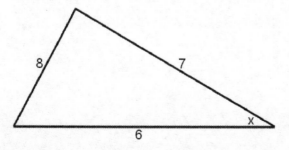

$8^2 = 7^2 + 6^2 - 2 \cdot 7 \cdot 6 \cdot \cos x \Rightarrow \cos x = 0.25 \Rightarrow x = 75.5°$

Area of the triangle is: $\dfrac{1}{2} \cdot 56 \cdot 48 \cdot \sin 75.5 = 1301.32$

If R = radius of the circumscribed triangle then $\dfrac{64}{\sin x} = \dfrac{64}{\sin 75.5°} = 2R$ and R = 33.05.

Exercises

1. What is the area of a triangle whose sides are 26, 26, and 20?

2. In triangle ABC, side BC is 8 and the angle A opposite this side is 45°. What is the radius of the circle that passes through the vertices of this triangle?

3. What is the degree measure of the vertex angle of the isosceles triangle having sides of lengths 25, 25, and 40 respectively?

4.

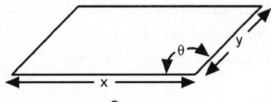

Find area of the parallelogram in terms of x, y and θ.

5.

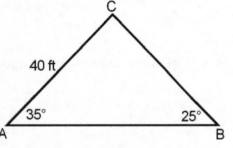

In the triangle ∠A=35° and ∠B=25°. If AC=40 ft, find length of AB in inches.

6.

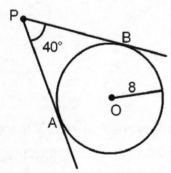

In the figure two lines are tangent to the circle with radius 8 at points A and B. Calculate the length of AB (not shown).

Domains and Ranges of Trigonometric Functions

Function	Domain	Range	Period
sinx cosx	R	$-1 \leq y \leq 1$	2π
tanx	$R - \left\{ \mp \dfrac{\pi}{2}, \mp \dfrac{3\pi}{2}, \mp \dfrac{5\pi}{2}, \ldots \right\} = R - \left\{ \mp (2k+1)\dfrac{\pi}{2} \mid k = \text{integer} \right\}$ All real numbers except for the odd multiples of $\dfrac{\pi}{2}$.	R	π
cotx	$R - \left\{ 0, \mp\pi, \mp2\pi, \mp3\pi, \ldots \right\} = R - \left\{ \pi k \mid k = \text{integer} \right\}$ All real numbers except for the integer multiples of π.	R	π
secx	Same as tanx	$y \leq -1$ or $y \geq 1$	2π
cscx	Same as cotx	$y \leq -1$ or $y \geq 1$	2π

Even and Odd Trigonometric Functions

$f(-x) = f(x)$:   even

cos (-x) = cosx   even

sec (-x) = secx   even

$f(-x) = -f(x)$:   odd

sin (-x) = -sinx   odd

tan (-x) = -tanx   odd

cot (-x) = -cotx   odd

csc (-x) = -cscx   odd

Graphs of Trigonometric Functions

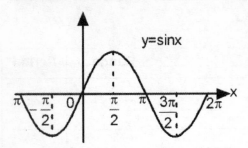

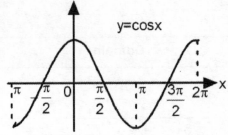

Domain: $-\infty < x < \infty$

Range: $-1 \le y \le 1$

Period: 2π

Domain: $-\infty < x < \infty$

Range: $-1 \le y \le 1$

Period: 2π

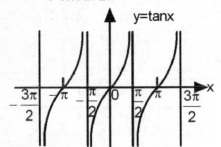

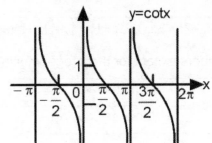

Domain: $x \ne \pm\dfrac{\pi}{2}, \pm\dfrac{3\pi}{2}, \ldots$

Range: $-\infty < y < \infty$

Period: π

Domain: $x \ne 0, \pm\pi, \pm2\pi, \ldots$

Range: $-\infty < y < \infty$

Period: π

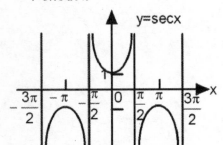

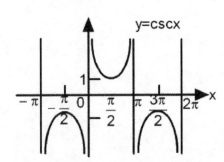

Domain: $x \ne \pm\dfrac{\pi}{2}, \pm\dfrac{3\pi}{2}, \ldots$

Range: $y \le -1$ or $y \ge 1$

Period: 2π

Domain: $x \ne 0, \pm\pi, \pm3\pi, \ldots$

Range: $y \le -1$ or $y \ge 1$

Period: 2π

Exercises

1.

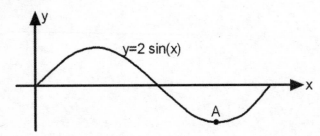

Figure shows one cycle of the graph of the function y=2sinx. If the minimum value of the function is at point A, then find the coordinates of A.

2.

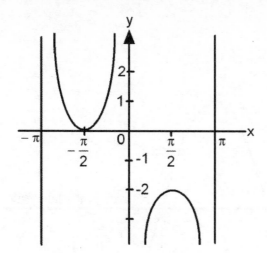

Which one(s) of the following functions has the graph shown?

y= -1/sinx -1

y= -sin $^{-1}$(x) -1

y= -csc(x) -1

3.

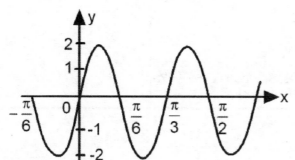

Which of the following functions has the graph shown?

2sin(6x)

2cos(6x)

2cos(6x- $\frac{\pi}{2}$)

4.   The graph of y=3+cos(2x) intersects the y-axis at point B. Find coordinates of B.

Periodicity

If there exists a positive real number P such that f(x+P)=f(x); then f(x) is called a periodic function and the smallest possible value of P is called the period of f(x).

sin (x+2π) = sinx	tan (x+π) = tanx	sec (x+2π) = secx
cos (x+2π) = cosx	cot (x+π) = cotx	csc (x+2π) = cscx

sin(x), cos(x), sec(x) and csc(x) are periodic with P=2π; tan(x) and cot(x) are periodic with P=π.

Odd powers of sine and cosine: $\sin^{2n+1}(Ax+B)$ or $\cos^{2n+1}(Ax+B) \Rightarrow P = \dfrac{2\pi}{|A|}$

Even powers of sine and cosine: $\sin^{2n}(Ax+B)$ or $\cos^{2n}(Ax+B) \Rightarrow P = \dfrac{\pi}{|A|}$

All powers of tangent and cotangent: $\tan^{n}(Ax+B)$ or $\cot^{n}(Ax+B) \Rightarrow P = \dfrac{\pi}{|A|}$

If there are more than one periodic functions that are added up, the common period is found by taking the LCM (Least Common Multiple) of the individual periods. If some of the individual periods are fractions then, their LCM is found by first reducing each of them into its lowest terms and then by taking the LCM of only the numerators of the individual periods.

Finding a Trigonometric Model

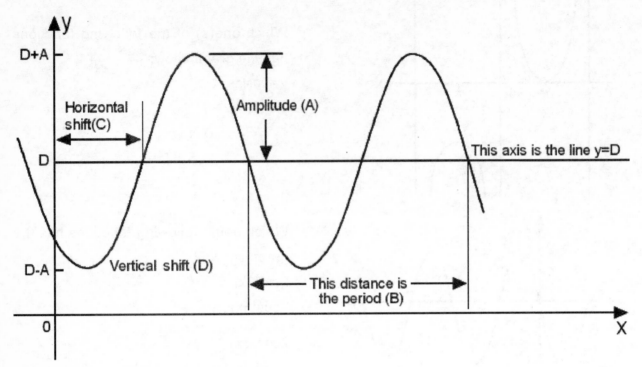

$$f(x) = A\sin\left[\frac{2\pi}{|B|}(x - C)\right] + D \text{ where}$$

- $|A|$ = Amplitude = $\frac{y_{max} - y_{min}}{2}$. If the function is upside down then A will be negative.

- $|B|$ = Period

- Frequency = $\frac{1}{\text{Period}}$

- C = Phase Shift (horizontal shift)

  If positive, indicates rightward shift for $|C|$ units.

  If negative indicates leftward shift for $|C|$ units

  For a function f(BX+C) where f is a trigonometric function, phase shift= $-\frac{C}{B}$

  (if positive, indicates rightward shift and if negative indicates leftward shift).

- D = Offset = $\frac{y_{max} + y_{min}}{2}$, offset is the vertical shift.

- Axis of wave is the line given by y=D.

- Range: $y_{min} \le y \le y_{max}$

Example:

$y = 2\cos^3(3x-5) + 4$

Offset is 4 units up

Axis of wave is y=4

Amplitude = $|2| = 2$

Phase shift= $\dfrac{--5}{3} = \dfrac{5}{3} \Rightarrow$ Rightward shift for $\dfrac{5}{3}$ units.

Period= $\dfrac{2\pi}{|3|} = \dfrac{2\pi}{3}$

Frequency= $\dfrac{3}{2\pi}$

Exercises

1. As x increases from 0 to π, what happens to $2\sin\dfrac{x}{2}$?

2. What is the amplitude, Axis of wave and offset of y=5sin(x)+12cos(x)-2?

3. What is the maximum value of $y = \sqrt{4 + \cos^2 x}$ in the interval $\left[\dfrac{-\pi}{2}, \dfrac{\pi}{2}\right]$

4. Find y intercept of the function $y = \left|\sqrt{3}\sec\left[3(x + \dfrac{\pi}{4})\right]\right|$

5. Find amplitude of the function $f(x) = -\dfrac{1}{2}\sin(x)\cos(x) + 1$

6. Find the primary period of $f(x) = \dfrac{\cos(2x)}{1 + \sin(2x)}$

7. Find primary period of $f(x) = 3\sin^2(2x)$

8. Find y intercept of $y = \sqrt{3}\sin(x + \dfrac{\pi}{3})$

9. What is the amplitude of the function y=3sinx+4cosx+1

10. Find maximum value of the function $f(x) = \sin(\dfrac{x}{4})$ over the interval $0 \le x \le \dfrac{\pi}{3}$

11. Find maximum value of 4 sinx cosx

12. What happens to sinx as x increases from $-\dfrac{\pi}{4}$ to $\dfrac{3\pi}{4}$?

13. What is the smallest positive x intercept of $y = 2\sin\left[3(x + \dfrac{3\pi}{4})\right]$?

14. What is the smallest positive angle that will make $y = 3 + \sin\left[3(x + \frac{\pi}{3})\right]$ a minimum?

15. Find amplitude of the graph of the function $y = \cos^4 x - \sin^4 x + 1$

16. Find amplitude, period and frequency of the following:

   i. $y = 2\sin(\pi x + \pi)$

   ii. $y = \frac{3}{4}\cos(\frac{x}{2} - \frac{\pi}{2})$

   iii. Find the coordinates of the first maximum point in the graph of $y = \sin(\frac{x}{2})$ that has a positive x-coordinate.

Inverse Trigonometric Functions

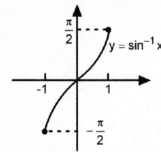

Domain : $-1 \le x \le 1$

Range : $-\frac{\pi}{2} \le y \le \frac{\pi}{2}$

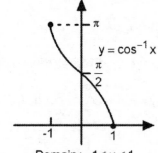

Domain : $-1 \le x \le 1$

Range : $0 \le y \le \pi$

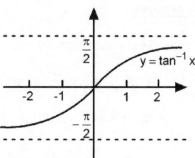

Domain : $-\infty < x < \infty$

Range : $-\frac{\pi}{2} < y < \frac{\pi}{2}$

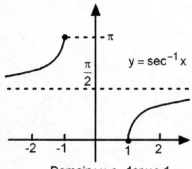

Domain : $x \le -1 \text{ or } x \ge 1$

Range : $0 \le y \le \pi, y \ne \frac{\pi}{2}$

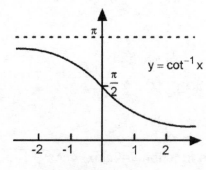

Domain : $-\infty < x < \infty$

Range : $0 < y < \pi$

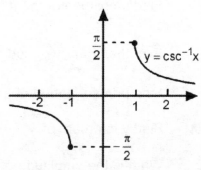

Domain : $x \le -1 \text{ or } x \ge 1$

Range : $-\frac{\pi}{2} \le y \le \frac{\pi}{2}, y \ne 0$

Domains and Ranges of Inverse Trigonometric Functions

Function	Domain	Range
$\sin^{-1}(x)=\text{Arcsin}(x)$	$-1 \le x \le 1$ $\lvert x \rvert \le 1$	$-\dfrac{\pi}{2} \le y \le \dfrac{\pi}{2}$ $\lvert y \rvert \le \dfrac{\pi}{2}$
$\cos^{-1}(x)=\text{Arccos}x$	$-1 \le x \le 1$	$0 \le y \le \pi$
$\tan^{-1}(x)=\text{Arctan}(x)$	R	$-\dfrac{\pi}{2} < y < \dfrac{\pi}{2}$ $\lvert y \rvert < \dfrac{\pi}{2}$
$\cot^{-1}(x)=\text{Arccot}(x)$	R	$0 < y < \pi$
$\sec^{-1}(x)=\text{Arcsec}(x)$	$x \le -1$ or $x \ge 1$ $\lvert x \rvert \ge 1$	$0 \le y \le \pi,\ y \ne \dfrac{\pi}{2}$
$\csc^{-1}(x)=\text{Arccsc}(x)$	$x \le -1$ or $x \ge 1$ $\lvert x \rvert \ge 1$	$\dfrac{-\pi}{2} \le y \le \dfrac{\pi}{2}, y \ne 0$

$\cot^{-1}(x) = \dfrac{\pi}{2} - \tan^{-1}(x)$ $\qquad$ (in radians)

$\cot^{-1}(x) = 90° - \tan^{-1}(x)$ $\qquad$ (in degrees)

$\sec^{-1}(x) = \cos^{-1}\left(\dfrac{1}{x}\right)$

$\csc^{-1}(x) = \sin^{-1}\left(\dfrac{1}{x}\right)$

Please note the following:

$\sec x = \dfrac{1}{\cos x}$ **however** $\sec^{-1}(x)=\cos^{-1}\left(\dfrac{1}{x}\right)$; **and** $\sec^{-1}(x) \ne \dfrac{1}{\cos^{-1}(x)}$.

$\csc x = \dfrac{1}{\sin x}$ **however** $\csc^{-1}(x)=\sin^{-1}\left(\dfrac{1}{x}\right)$; **and** $\csc^{-1}(x) \ne \dfrac{1}{\cos^{-1}(x)}$.

$\cot^{-1}(x) = \tan^{-1}(\dfrac{1}{x})$ is correct if and only if x is positive and **$\cot^{-1}(x) \ne \dfrac{1}{\tan^{-1}(x)}$.**

Solving Inverse Trigonometric Equations with TI

When solving an inverse trigonometric equation in the form **f(x)=g(x),** perform the following steps:

i. $\qquad$ Write the equation in the form: **f(x)-g(x)=0.**

ii. $\qquad$ While writing the trigonometric expressions please observe the rules given in parts 1.17 and 1.18 that involve the trigonometric functions that are built in TI or otherwise.

iii. $\qquad$ Plot the graph of **y=f(x)-g(x).**

iv.   Set the **angle mode to radians or degrees** depending on which angle measure is used in the question. If no degree signs (like in 90°) are used then the mode should be radians. However when exact values are required you may wish to solve the equation in degrees and convert the answer to radians using the following formula $\dfrac{R}{\pi} = \dfrac{D}{180°}$. In such a case finding the answer in radians and then trying to find which answer choice matches this answer can also be an option; while doing so you may directly replace π with 180°

v.   Find the x-intercepts using the **Calc Zero** of TI-84 Plus. However when the graph seems to be tangent to the x-axis at a certain point, you may use the **Calc Min** or **Calc Max** facilities but you should make sure that the y-coordinate of the minimum or maximum point is zero.

vi.   Any value like **-6.61E -10** or **7.2E -11** can be interpreted as 0 as they mean **-6.6x10 -10** and **7.2x10 -11** respectively.

Example:

Solve for x: $\cos^{-1}(2x - 2x^2) = \dfrac{2\pi}{3}$

Solution:

Mode: Radians

$$\cos^{-1}(2x - 2x^2) - \dfrac{2\pi}{3} = 0$$

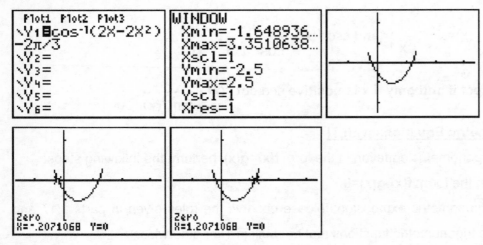

Answer: -0.207 or 1.207

Example:

cos (Arcsin $\frac{-4}{5}$ + Arccos $\frac{12}{13}$)= ?

Solution:

```
cos(sin⁻¹(-4/5)+c
os⁻¹(12/13
        .8615384615
```

Answer: 0.86

Built in Trigonometric Functions in TI

FUNCTION	DESCRIPTION	ABBREVIATION
sin(	Sine function	
cos(	Cosine function	
tan(	Tangent function	
sin⁻¹(	Arcsine or sine inverse function	Arcsin
cos⁻¹(	Arccosine or cosine inverse function	Arccos
tan⁻¹(	Arctangent or tangent inverse function	Arctan

Additional Trigonometric Functions with TI

WHEN YOU NEED	USE THE FOLLOWING DEFINITION	WARNING
sec(x)	1 / cos(x)	
csc(x)	1 / sin(x)	
cot(x)	cos(x) / sin(x)	Although mathematically correct, still DO NOT USE 1 / tan(x) for cot(x) because when tan(x) is undefined, TI will interpret 1 / tan(x) as undefined, too, which is not correct.
sec⁻¹(x)	cos⁻¹(1/x)	Do NOT use 1 / cos⁻¹(x), mathematically incorrect.
csc⁻¹(x)	sin⁻¹(1/x)	Do NOT use 1 / sin⁻¹(x), mathematically incorrect.
cot⁻¹(x)	$\pi/2$ – tan⁻¹(x) if in radians 90°– tan⁻¹(x) if in degrees	Do NOT use 1 / tan⁻¹(x), mathematically incorrect.

Exercises

1. Determine the exact values of each of the following:

   i. $\sin^{-1}(\tan(\frac{5\pi}{4}))$

   ii. $\text{arccsc}(-2)$

   iii. $\tan(\sin^{-1}(\frac{7}{25}))$

2.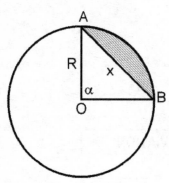

   i. x can be written as a function of R and α like the following: x=aR sin(bα). Find a, and b.

   ii. α can be written as a function of R and x as follows: $\alpha = 2\sin^{-1}(a \cdot \frac{x}{R})$. Find a.

   iii. Find area and perimeter of the shaded region in terms of R and α given that α is in radians.

3. $\cos^{-1}(\cos x)=0$ and $0 \leq x \leq \frac{\pi}{2} \Rightarrow x=?$

4.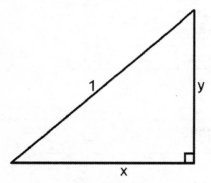

   $\sin^{-1}x = \cos^{-1}x \Rightarrow$ find y in terms of x.

5.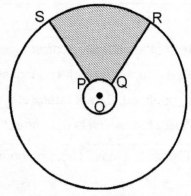

   Given two concentric circles with radii 2 and 7. If $\angle POQ=30°$, find

   Area of the shaded region.

   Perimeter of the shaded region.

6. If A is an obtuse angle and $\sin A=\frac{3}{5}$, calculate the exact value of sin(2A).

7. If A is an acute angle and $\sin A=\frac{3}{5}$, calculate the exact value of sin(2A).

8. Solve the following equations for x; find exact solutions.

    i. $\sin^2 x = \cos^2 x$ and $0° \le x \le 180°$

    ii. $\sin^2 x = 3\cos^2 x$ and $0° \le x \le 360°$

    iii. $\sin(2x) = \cos x$ and $0 \le x \le 2\pi$

    iv. $\sin(2x) = 2\sin x$ and $0 \le x \le 2\pi$

9. At a certain seaport, The depth d meters of water at time t hours after midnight is modeled

    by $d(t) = A + B \cdot \sin\left(\dfrac{\pi}{2} - \dfrac{\pi t}{6}\right)$, $0 \le t \le 24$, where A, and B are positive constants. M(6,9.5) and

    N(12,15.5) are minimum and maximum points on the graph of d(t) respectively.

    i.   Find the values of A and B.

    ii. Find the first time in the 24 hour period when the depth of water is 11m.

    iii. Find the time intervals during which the water is less than 10m deep.

10.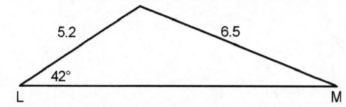

    Find measure of $\angle K$ correct to the nearest degree.

11. AB=54 km; AC=36 km; BC=63 km; calculate measure of $\angle BAC$ to the nearest degree.

12. When a car travels for 10 km on a road whose angle of elevation is 7.3°, how high up does it climb?

13.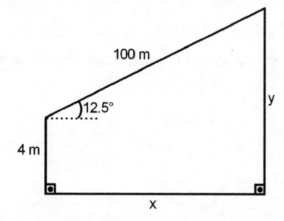

    x = ?

14. $(\sin x + \cos x)^2 = a + b\sin(2x) \Rightarrow a+b=?$

15. $\sin 315° = -\sin x = -\cos y$ where x and y are acute angles. (x,y)=?

16. $\tan 110° = -\cot y$ where y is an acute angle y=?

17. Solve for x: $\cos^{-1}(2x - 2x^2) = \dfrac{2\pi}{3}$

18. $\sin^{-1}(\cos 200°) = ?$

19. $\sin^{-1}(x) = 3 \cdot \text{Arccos} x \Rightarrow x=?$

20. sin 400° = sinx = cosy where x and y are both acute. x−y=?

21. Point A(-3,4) is on the terminal side of angle ∠AOB which is in standard position. Calculate
    sin∠AOB + tan∠AOB=?

22. Point A(5,-12) is on the terminal side of angle ∠AOB which is in standard position. cot∠AOB=?

23.

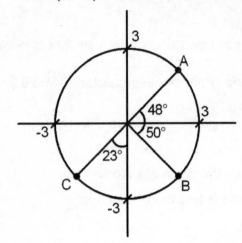

Find the coordinates of the points A, B and C

24.

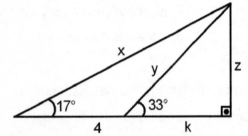

x= ?

y= ?

z= ?

k= ?

25. sin10°·sin10 − cos20°·cos20= ?

26. ln(sinx)=0 ⇒ what is the smallest positive value of x?

27. When a pendulum swings through 10°, it sweeps out on arc of length 20 cm. What is the length
    of the pendulum?

28. $\sin^{-1}(\sin 270°)$=?

29. $\cos^{-1}\left(\dfrac{\tan 45°}{\cot 30°}\right) = ?$

30. $\sin(\cos^{-1}\dfrac{3}{4} - \tan^{-1}\dfrac{1}{2})$=?

31. What is the angle that the diagonal of a cube makes with the vertical?

32. tan24°= x ⇒ tan 132°= ? in terms of x.

33. sinx + sin (-x) + cos x + cos (-x)=?

34. Sketch the graph of $y=2\sin\left(2x - \dfrac{\pi}{3}\right)$ over [-π, π]. Indicate amplitude, period, frequency, phase

    shift and all intercepts.

35. $\sin(2\tan^{-1}\frac{3}{4})=?$

36. Calculate the answers for the following questions both in degrees and radians.

   a) $\sin^{-1}\frac{1}{2} = ?$

   b) $\sin^{-1}\frac{-\sqrt{3}}{2} = ?$

   c) $\cos^{-1}\frac{\sqrt{3}}{2} = ?$

   d) $\arccos\frac{-\sqrt{3}}{2} = ?$

   e) $\tan^{-1}(1)=?$

   f) $\arctan(-1)= ?$

   g) $\cot^{-1}(\frac{1}{\sqrt{3}})=?$

   h) $\cot^{-1}(\frac{-1}{\sqrt{3}})=?$

   i) $\sec^{-1}(\sqrt{2})=?$

   j) $\sec^{-1}(-\sqrt{2})=?$

   k) $\csc^{-1}(2)= ?$

   l) $\csc^{-1}(-2)=?$

37. $\sin(\arccos\frac{4}{5})= ?$

38. $\cos(\arcsin\frac{-4}{5} + \arccos\frac{12}{13})= ?$

39. $\cos(\sin^{-1}(\frac{-1}{2}))=?$

40. $f(x)= \sin x \Rightarrow f^{-1}(\frac{3\pi}{14})=?$

41. $\sin(2\arctan(\frac{-15}{8}))=?$

42. $\tan(\arccos\frac{-3}{5})= ?$

43. $\arccos(\cos\frac{7\pi}{6})= ?$

44.   arctan(tan $\frac{\pi}{4}$)= ?

45.   arctan(tan $\frac{5\pi}{4}$)= ?

46.   sin(cos315°)= ?

47.

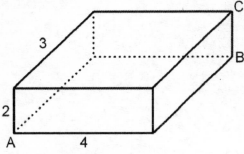

Measure of ∠ACB=?

48.

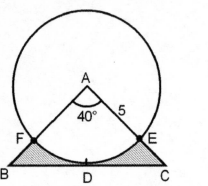

∠ABC is isosceles; AE=5 and point A is the center of the circle. Area of the shaded region=?

49.

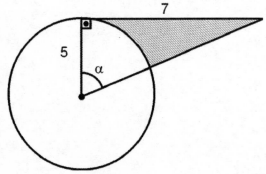

α=?

Area of the shaded region=?

50.

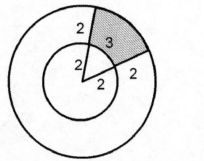

Concentric circles are given.

Shaded area=?

51.   In a triangle ABC AB=15, AC=9 and angle ∠B=30°

    a.   Measure of ∠C=?

    b.   radius of the circumscribed circle=?

c.   Area of the triangle ABC=?

d.   How many such Δ's are possible?

52.

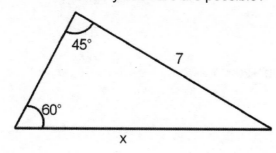

a.   x=?

b.   How many such Δ's are possible

53. $\sin(\pi-x)+\sin(\pi+x)+\cos(\frac{\pi}{2}+x)-\cos(\frac{3\pi}{2}-x)$=?

54. $\tan 14° = a \Rightarrow \cos 28°$= ?

55. $\sin x=\sin\alpha$ and $\cos x= -\cos\alpha$ are given. What is x in terms of α?

    a. $\pi-\alpha$

    b. $\pi+\alpha$

    c. $\pi/2+\alpha$

    d. $\pi/2-\alpha$

    e. α

56. $\sin x= -\sin\alpha$ and $\cos x=\cos\alpha$ are given. What is x in terms of α?

    a. $2\pi - \alpha$

    b. $2\pi + \alpha$

    c. $\alpha- \pi/2$

    d. $\alpha+\pi/2$

    e. $-\alpha$

57. $(\sin x+\cos y)^2 + (\sin y+\cos x)^2=a+b\sin(x+y) \Rightarrow (a,b)$=?

58. $\sin 12=a \Rightarrow$ What is $\sin 78°$ in terms of a?

59. $\cos 23°= b \Rightarrow$ What is $\sin 67° + \cos 67°$ in terms of b?

60.   If $\cos 143°= x$ than $\sin 16°$=?

61. $y= 3 \sin^2 \left(\frac{2x}{3}+\pi\right)+1 \Rightarrow$ period=?

62. $y= 2 \cos^3 \left(\frac{3x}{4}-\pi\right) \Rightarrow$ period=?

63. $y= - \tan^2 (2x) + 1 \Rightarrow$ period=?

64. $\left.\begin{array}{l} A = \text{Arctan}\left(\dfrac{-5}{12}\right) \\ \\ A + B = 300° \end{array}\right\} \Rightarrow B=?$

65. $\tan\theta = \dfrac{-4}{5}$ and $\sin\theta$ is positive. $\cos(3\theta) - \sin(90°+2\theta)= ?$

66. $\text{Sin}\theta= a$ and θ is acute

    a. $\cos \theta=?$

    b. $\tan \theta= ?$

67. $\tan\theta= a$ and θ is acute

    a. $\text{Sin}\theta=?$

    b. $\text{Cos}\theta=?$

68. $\text{Cos}\theta=a$ and θ is acute.

    a. $\text{Sin}\theta=?$

    b. $\tan\theta=?$

69. $\text{Sin}\theta=a$ and θ is obtuse.

    a. $\text{Cos}\theta=?$

    b. $\tan\theta=?$

70. $\tan\theta=a$ and θ is obtuse.

    a. $\text{Sin}\theta=?$

    b. $\text{Cos}\theta=?$

71. $\text{Cos}\theta=a$ and θ is obtuse

    a. $\text{Sin}\theta=?$

    b. $\tan\theta=?$

72. $\text{Cos}33°=a$. Calculate the following in terms of a.

    a. $\text{Cos}66°=?$

    b. $\text{Sin}66°=?$

73. $\text{Sin}33°=a$. Calculate the following in terms of a.

    a. $\text{Cos}66°=?$

    b. $\text{Sin}66°=?$

74. $\text{Sec } \theta = \dfrac{-13}{5}$ and $\tan\theta$ is positive.

    a. $\sin\theta = ?$

    b. $\cos\theta = ?$

    c. $\tan\theta = ?$

75. $y = \sin\dfrac{2x}{3} + \cos^2\dfrac{3x}{4} - \tan x + 1 \Rightarrow \text{period} = ?$

76. $\tan^2\theta = 4\tan\theta - 4$ and θ is on acute angle greater than $45°$. $\theta = ?$

77. A triangular field has two sides of length 200 and 240 ft and the angle between these sides is $40°$. What is the area of this field in square feet and square yards?

78. Express the angle that the diagonal of a cube makes with the diagonal of a face of this cube in terms of inverse trigonometric functions.

79. Express the angle that the diagonal of a cube makes with an adjacent side of the cube in terms of inverse trigonometric functions.

80. A ship sailing directly toward a light house is seeing the lighthouse at an angle of elevation of $2°$. When the ship approaches the lighthouse 20 km, it starts seeing the lighthouse at an angle of $3°$.

    a.   Originally how many km's away was the ship from the lighthouse?

    b.   How high is the lighthouse in meters?

81.

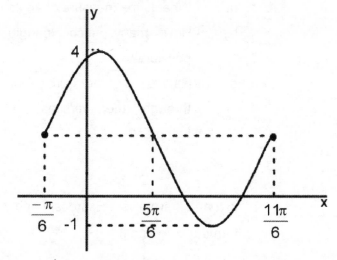

$f(x) = a\sin(bx+c) + d$

and a, b, c, d are positive

        a = ?

        b = ?

        c = ?

        d = ?

82.

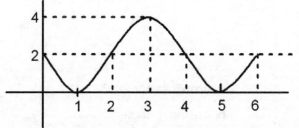

$f(x) = a\cos(bx+c) + d$

$a < 0;\ b > 0;\ c < 0;\ d > 0$

Determine the values of a, b, c, and d.

83.

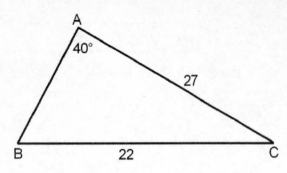

How many such triangles are possible?

84.

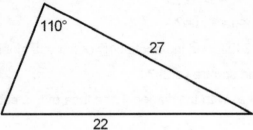

How many such triangles are possible?

85.

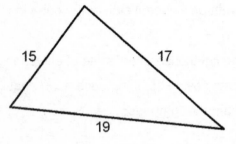

What is the measure of the largest angle in this triangle?

86.

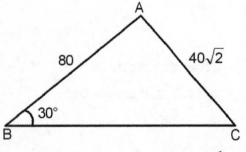

a.   What is the measure of angle C?

b.   How many such triangle are possible?

c.   Radius of the circle passing through the vertices of this triangle=?

87.

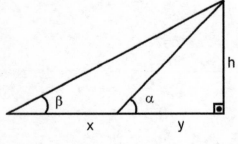

x, α and β are given. Express h and y in terms of x, α and β.

88.

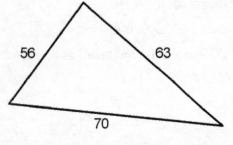

a. smallest angle=?

b. greatest angle=?

89.

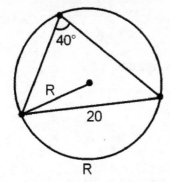

R=?

90.   sinx=cosx and 0<x<2π ⟹ x=?

91.   A man 1.8 m tall is holding a wire that runs to the top of a vertical pole. If the wire is 100 m and the angle of elevation is 40°, how high is the pole?

92.
$$\sin(3x)=\frac{\sqrt{3}}{2}.$$ Which one(s) of the following are possible solutions of the above equation?

   i.   20°

   ii.   40°

   iii. $\frac{1}{3}Sin^{-1}\frac{\sqrt{3}}{2}$

93.   Sin1470°=Sinx°=Cosy°. If x and y are acute angles then what is the degree value of x°-y°=?

94.   Sin²15°+Cos²15°+tan$\frac{\pi}{3}$-sin120°=?

95.   Cosx=$\frac{-1}{2}$ and x is an obtuse angle x=?

96.   Order from least to greatest:

   a. Cos0°, Cos30°, cos60°, Cos90°

   b. Sin0°, Sin30°, Sin60°, Sin90°

   c. tan1°, tan29°, tan60°, tan89°

   d. Sin91°, Sin120°, Sin143°, Sin169°

   e. Cos 91°, Cos 120°, Cos 143°, Cos 169°

   f. tan91°, tan120°, tan143°, tan 169°

97.

$$\sin(3x)=\frac{\sqrt{3}}{2}$$

Which one(s) of the following are possible solutions of the above equation?

a. $20°$

b. $40°$

c. $\frac{1}{3}\sin^{-1}\frac{\sqrt{3}}{2}$

d. $\frac{7\pi}{9}$

e. $\frac{8\pi}{9}$

f. $\frac{1}{3}\arcsin\frac{\sqrt{3}}{2}$

g. $\frac{1}{3}\arccos\frac{1}{2}$

98. The point A(-3,-1) is on the terminal side of angle $\angle AOB$ which is in standard position. $\tan\theta=?$

99. $\left.\begin{array}{l}f(x,y)=\tan(x)+\tan(y)\\g(x,y)=1-\tan(x)\tan(y)\end{array}\right\}\frac{f(10°,20°)}{g(10°,20°)}=?$

100. $\sin A=\frac{5}{13}$ $90°\le A\le 180°$; $\cos B=\frac{4}{9}$, B is in 4'th quadrant; $\sin(A+B)=?$

101.

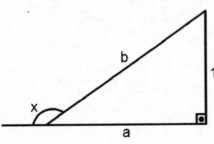

A) $\sin x=?$

B) $\cos x=?$

102.

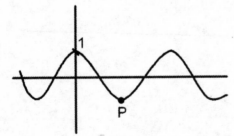

Portion of the graph of the function $y=\cos(3x)$ is shown in the figure. Find coordinates of P.

103. Simplify

    a. $\dfrac{\sin^2 x}{\cos x} + \cos x + \dfrac{\cos^2 x}{\sin x} + \sin x = ?$

    b. $(1+\tan^2\theta)\cdot\cos^2\theta = ?$

    c. $\sin^2 x \cdot (1+\tan^2 x) - 1 = ?$

    d. $\sin^4 x - \sin^2 x - \cos^4 x + \cos^2 x = ?$

    e. $\tan^2 x - \dfrac{1}{\cos^2 x} + 2 \cdot \dfrac{\sin x}{\cos x} = ?$

104. $f(x) = \sin(\cos(x))$. $f(320°) = ?$

105. $f(r,\theta) = r\cos\theta$. $f(12,13) = ?$

106. $\csc\left(\tan^{-1}\dfrac{1}{\sqrt{2}}\right) = ?$

107. $\cos x = \dfrac{1}{3}$; $\sqrt{\sec x} = ?$

108. $f(x) = 14x^2$; $g(x) = f(\cos x) + f(\tan x)$; $g(12°) = ?$

109. $\cos 30 . \cos 30° - \sin 45 . \sin 45° = ?$

110. $\cos A = 0.6631$; $\tan A = -1.12884 \Rightarrow A = ?$ (in degrees)

111. Find amplitude, period, phase shift and offset (OPTIONAL).

    a. $y = -3\sin(-3x) + 1$

    b. $y = -2\cos\left(\pi x + \dfrac{\pi}{2}\right) - 1$

    c. $y = \dfrac{1}{4}\cos(2x+3)$

    d. $y = \dfrac{13}{2}\sin\left(\dfrac{-x}{2} + 3\right)$

112. $\cos\left(2\sin^{-1}\left(\dfrac{-5}{13}\right)\right) = ?$

113. Calculate the exact values of:

    a. $\cos 15°$

    b. $\sin 75°$

    c. $\tan \dfrac{\pi°}{12}$

    d. $\cos 165°$

    e. $\sin 105°$

    f. $\tan \dfrac{3\pi}{4}$

114. $\arcsin 0.6 + \cos^{-1} 0.6 = ?$

115. $\sec 4.1 = x$; $\csc(3 \arctan x) = ?$

116. $A \# B = \sqrt{\cos A + \sec B}$; $4 \# 5 = ?$

117. In which quadrant is the angle represented by $\arcsin\left(\dfrac{-3}{5}\right) + \arccos\left(\dfrac{-12}{13}\right)$?

118. $\dfrac{\cos 15^{o}}{\sin 75^{o}} = ?$

119. $\dfrac{\tan 25^{o}}{\cos 65^{o}} = ?$

120. $\cos(\tan^{-1}(1/3)) = ?$

121. $\dfrac{\sin 135^{o} \cdot \cos \dfrac{5\pi}{6}}{\tan 225^{o}} = ?$

122. $\csc\theta = \dfrac{4}{3}$. $\cos\theta < 0$. $\tan\theta = ?$

123. $\cos 310^{o} + \sin 140^{o} = 2x$. $\Rightarrow x = ?$

124. $\cos \pi - \sin 930^{o} - \csc\left(\dfrac{-5\pi}{2}\right) + \sec(0^{o}) = ?$

125. $\tan(-135^{o}) + \cot\left(\dfrac{-7\pi}{8}\right) = ?$

126. $\tan(-30^{o}) = -\cot x \Rightarrow x = ?$ (x is in 3rd quadrant)

127. $\cos 210^{o} + \sin 330^{o} = ?$

128. $\sec\dfrac{7\pi}{6}$. $\tan\dfrac{3\pi}{4}$. $\sin\dfrac{2\pi}{3} = ?$

129. A is in 3rd quadrant and $\tan A = \dfrac{8}{15}$. B is in 2nd quadrant and $\tan B = \dfrac{-3}{4}$

   In which quadrant does (A+B) lie?

130. Given that $\tan\theta = \dfrac{-5}{12}$ and $\sin\theta$ is positive. $\cos(2\theta) - \sin(180^{o} - \theta) = ?$

131. A and B are acute angles and $\tan(A) = \dfrac{12}{5}$ and $\sin(B) = \dfrac{4}{5} \Rightarrow \cos(2A + B) = ?$

132. $\cos\theta = \dfrac{4}{5}$. $\sin(2\theta) = ?$ $\tan(2\theta) = ?$

133. $\dfrac{\tan 100^{o} + \tan 35^{o}}{1 - \tan 100^{o} \cdot \tan 35^{o}} = ?$

134. $\tan \theta = \dfrac{3}{4} \Rightarrow \sin \theta = ?$

135. $\cos^2 20° - \sin^2 20° = ?$

136. $\sin A = \dfrac{3}{5}$ and $\cos A < 0$ $\tan (2A) = ?$

137. If $y = \tan\left(\dfrac{x}{2}\right)$, then

     a.   Cosx = ?

     b.   Sinx = ?

138. Sketch the graphs of the following functions (OPTIONAL) and compute the amplitude, period, frequency and phase shift, as applicable.

     a. $y = 3\sin x$

     b. $y = 4\cos x$

     c. $y = 2\sin(3x)$

     d. $y = -4\cos(2x)$

     e. $y = -3\sin(4x)$

     f. $y = 2\sin(x + \dfrac{\pi}{6})$

     g. $y = -2\sin(x - \dfrac{\pi}{6})$

     h. $y = 3\cos(2x + \pi)$

     i. $y = -3\cos(2x - \pi)$

     j. $y = 2\sin(4x + \pi)$

     k. $y = -2\cos(6x - \pi)$

     l. $y = 3\sin(6x - \pi)$

139. Show that each of the following equations is valid (OPTIONAL).

     a. $\arcsin x + \arccos x = \dfrac{\pi}{2}$

     b. $\arctan x + \text{arccot} x = \dfrac{\pi}{2}$

     c. $\text{arcsec} x + \text{arccsc} x = \dfrac{\pi}{2}$

140. If $\theta = \arcsin x$, then compute $\cos\theta$, $\tan\theta$, $\cot\theta$, $\sec\theta$ and $\csc\theta$.

141. Make the given substitutions to simplify the given radical expression and compute all trigonometric functions of θ.

   a. $\sqrt{4-x^2}, x = 2\sin\theta$

   b. $\sqrt{x^2 - 9}, x = 3\sec\theta$

   c. $(4+x^2)^{\frac{1}{2}}, x = 2\tan\theta$

142. Find the exact value of y in each of the following.

   a. $y=\arccos\left(-\dfrac{1}{2}\right)$

   b. $y=\arcsin\left(\dfrac{\sqrt{3}}{2}\right)$

   c. $y=\arctan\left(-\sqrt{3}\right)$

   d. $y=\text{arccot}\left(-\dfrac{\sqrt{3}}{3}\right)$

   e. $y=\text{arcsec}\left(-\sqrt{2}\right)$

   f. $y=\text{arccsc}\left(-\sqrt{2}\right)$

   g. $y=\text{arcsec}\left(-\dfrac{2}{\sqrt{3}}\right)$

   h. $y=\text{arccsc}\left(-\dfrac{2}{\sqrt{3}}\right)$

   i. $y=\text{arcsec}(-2)$

   j. $y=\text{arccsc}(-2)$

   k. $y=\arctan\left(\dfrac{-1}{\sqrt{3}}\right)$

   l. $y=\text{arccot}(-\sqrt{3})$

143. Solve the following equations for x in radians (all possible answers) (OPTIONAL).

   a. $2\sin^4 x = \sin^2 x$

   b. $2\cos^2 x - \cos x - 1 = 0$

   c. $\sin^2 x + 2\sin x + 1 = 0$

   d. $4\sin^2 x + 4\sin x + 1 = 0$

144. If arcsint=x, compute sinx, cosx, tanx, cotx, secx and cscx in terms of t.

145. If arccost=x, compute sinx, cosx, tanx, cotx, secx and scsx in terms of t.

146. If arctant=x, compute sinx, cosx, tanx, cotx, secx, and cscx in terms of t.

147. If arccott=x, compute sinx, cosx, tanx, cotx, secx, and cscx in terms of t.

148. If arcsect=x, compute sinx, cosx, tanx, cotx, secx and cscx in terms of t.

149. If arccsct=x, compute sinx, cosx, tanx, cotx, secx and cscx in terms of t.

150. Simplify $\dfrac{2}{3+3Cosx}+\dfrac{2}{3-3Cosx}$.

151. Simplify $\dfrac{2}{3+3Sinx}+\dfrac{2}{3-3Sinx}$

152. Determine the amplitude frequency, period and phase shift for each of the following functions. Sketch their graphs.

    a.   y=2sin(3x-π)

    b.   y=-2cos(2x-1)

    c.   y=3sin(2x)+4cos(2x)

    d.   y= 5sin(2x)-12cos(2x)

153. Evaluate each of the following

    a. $3\arcsin\left(\dfrac{1}{2}\right)+2\arccos\left(\dfrac{\sqrt{3}}{2}\right)$

    b. $4\arctan\left(\dfrac{1}{\sqrt{3}}\right)+5\,\mathrm{arc\,cot}\left(\dfrac{1}{\sqrt{3}}\right)$

    c. $2\,\mathrm{arc\,sec}(-2)+3\,\mathrm{arc\,csc}\left(-\dfrac{2}{\sqrt{3}}\right)$

    d.   cos(2arccos(x))

    e.   sin(2arccos(x)

154. What is the acute angle between two diagonals of a cube?

155. $A=\dfrac{\sin x \cos y + \cos x \sin y}{\cos x \cos y - \sin x \sin y}$; $B=\dfrac{\tan x + \tan y}{1- \tan x \tan y}$. In order to obtain B from A, every term of A must be divided by which of the following?

    a.   sinx·cosy

    b.   cosx·siny

    c.   cosx·cosy

    d.   sinx·siny

    e.   none of the above

156. $A = \dfrac{\cos x \cos y - \sin x \sin y}{\sin x \cos y + \cos x \sin y}$; $B = \dfrac{\cot x . \cot y - 1}{\cot x - \cot y}$. In order to be able to obtain B from A, each term

of A must be divided by which of the following?

   a.   sinx·siny

   b.   cosx·cosy

   c.   sinx·cosy

   d.   cosx·siny

   e.   none of the above

157. Match a, b, c, d with i, ii, iii, iv.

   a.   Obtain sin(2x)=2sinxcosy from sin(x+y)=sinxcosy+cosx.siny

   b.   Obtain sin(x-y)=sinxcosy-cosxsiny from sin(x+y)=sinxcosy+cosxsiny

   c.   Obtain cos(x+y)=cosxcosy-sinxsiny from sin(x+y)=sinxcosy+cosxsiny

   d.   Obtain sinx+siny=2sin$\dfrac{x+y}{2}$·cos$\dfrac{x-y}{2}$ from sin(x+y)+sin(x-y)=2sinxcosy

   i.   Replace y with x

   ii.   Replace x with ($\dfrac{\pi}{2}$-x) and y with –y

   iii.   Replace x with $\dfrac{x+y}{2}$ and y with $\dfrac{x-y}{2}$

   iv.   Replace y with –y

158. Find amplitude, offset, axis of wave, period, frequency, domain, range, max and min values of.

   a.   f(x)=3sin(2x)-4cos(2x)

   b.   f(x)=-2cos(2x-π)

   c.   f(x)=sin(2x).cos(2x)

159.   Find range of the functions:

    a. $f(x)=\sin(3x) \cdot \cos(5x)$

    b. $f(x)=\sin(4x) \cdot \cos(4x)$

    c. $f(x)=\cos(5x)+\cos(3x)$

    d. $f(x)=\sin(\cos^{-1}(x))$

    e. $f(x)=\cos(\sin^{-1}(x))$

1.11 EXPONENTIAL AND LOGARITHMIC FUNCTIONS

Exponents

1. $x^a \cdot x^b = x^{a+b}$ and $\dfrac{x^a}{x^b} = x^{a-b}$

2. $(x^a)^b = x^{ab}$

3. $x^a \cdot y^a = (xy)^a$ and $\dfrac{x^a}{y^a} = \left(\dfrac{x}{y}\right)^a$

4. $x^0 = 1$ where $x \neq 0$; $x^1 = x$; $x^{-1} = \dfrac{1}{x}$

5. $x^{\frac{a}{b}} = \sqrt[b]{x^a}$

6. $\sqrt{x^2} = |x|$ and $\sqrt[2n]{x^{2n}} = |x|$

7. $\sqrt[3]{x^3} = x$ and $\sqrt[2n+1]{x^{2n+1}} = x$

8. $f(a)\,f(b) = f(a+b)$

    $\dfrac{f(a)}{f(b)} = f(a-b)$

    $f(a)^n = f(an)$

9. If $a^x = a^y$ then one of the following conditions holds:
    - $a = 1 \Rightarrow x$ and y are any real numbers.
    - $a = -1 \Rightarrow x$ and y are both odd or both even.
    - $a = 0 \Rightarrow x$ and y are both positive.
    - $a \notin \{1, -1, 0\} \Rightarrow x = y$

10. If $a^x = b^x$ and x is an integer then one of the following conditions holds:
    - $x = 0 \Rightarrow a$ and b are any nonzero real numbers
    - $x = \text{even} \Rightarrow |a| = |b|$
    - $x = \text{odd} \Rightarrow a = b$

Exponential Growth

$A = B \cdot (1 + r)^t$ or $A = B \cdot e^{rt}$

Exponential Decay

$A = B \cdot (1 - r)^t$ or $A = B \cdot e^{-rt}$

where

B: Initial amount

A: Final amount

r: Growth or Decay rate as a decimal

t: number of periods of Growth or Decay

Example:

At the beginning of 2000, the population of a certain city was 1,096,250. If the population increases at the rate 2.5 percent each year, what will the population of the city be at the end of 2005?

Solution:

$$A = 1,096,250 \cdot \left(1 + \frac{2.5}{100}\right)^5 = 1,240,306$$

Example:

1000$ is invested for 2 years in a bank that pays 8% interest each year. Find the total interest earned if the investment is compounded

a. yearly.

b. semi-annually.

c. quarterly.

d. monthly.

e. weekly (1 year= 52 weeks).

f. daily (1 year= 365 days).

g. continuously.

Solution:

a. $1000 \cdot (1 + 0.08)^2 = 1,166.4$

b. $1000 \cdot \left(1 + \frac{0.08}{2}\right)^4 = 1,169.9$

c. $1000 \cdot \left(1 + \frac{0.08}{4}\right)^8 = 1,171.7$

d. $1000 \cdot \left(1 + \frac{0.08}{12}\right)^{24} = 1,172.9$

e. $1000 \cdot \left(1 + \frac{0.08}{52}\right)^{104} = 1,173.4$

f. $1000 \cdot \left(1 + \frac{0.08}{365}\right)^{730} = 1,173.5$

g. $1000 \cdot e^{0.08 \cdot 2} = 1,173.5$

Example:

If a certain car now worth $45,000 decreases in value at the rate of 8 percent per year, how much will it be worth 3 years from now?

Solution:

$45,000 \cdot (1 - 0.08)^3 = 35,041$

<u>Exercises</u>

1. $21^m = 3^4 \cdot 7^4$; m?

2. Determine the least and the greatest value of the following:

    i. 20^{200}

    ii. 200^{20}

    iii. $(20 \cdot 20^{20})^{20}$

    iv. $200 \cdot (20^{20})^{20}$

    v. $20,000,000,000$

3. $f(x) = a^x$ and $f(x+4) = 16 \cdot f(x)$; a=?

4. If $27^{2x} = 9$, then x=

5. Simplify $(27^{3a})(3^{27a})$

6. Find the solution set of $3^{-x} < 0$.

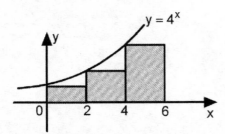

7. Figure shows a portion of the graph of $y = 4^x$. What is the sum of the shaded areas?

8. $4^x + 4^x + 4^x + 4^x = k4^{x+1}$; k=?

9. Cihan invested $3000 for 4 years at 6% compound interest per year. Calculate the amount at the end of 4 years.

10. Solve for x:

    i. $2^x - 4 \cdot 16^x = 0$.

    ii. $8^x = 0.25^{3x-1}$.

    iii. $\dfrac{1}{6^x} = \sqrt[3]{36}$

11. In January 1995 the world's population was 6 billion. Assuming a growth rate of 3 percent per year, what will be the population growth from January 2000 to January 2001?

12. A group of twenty baboons is introduced to a zoo. After t years the number of baboons, N, is modeled by $N = 20 \cdot e^{0.3t}$.

   i. How many baboons are there after 3 years?

   ii. How long will it take for the number of baboons to exceed 100?

13. A population of bacteria is growing at the rate of 3.1% per hour. How long, to the nearest hour, will it take the population to double?

14. In a radioactive decay process, the amount of the radioactive element that exists at any time t can be calculated by the function $E(t) = A \cdot e^{\frac{-t}{1,000}}$, where A is the initial amount and t is the time elapsed in days. How many years would it take for an initial amount of 10 grams of this element to decay to 3 grams?

Logarithms

1. $\log_a b = x \Rightarrow a^x = b$

2. $\log_{10} x = \log x; \; \log_e x = \ln x$

3. $\log_a a = 1; \; \log 10 = 1; \; \ln(e) = 1$

   $\log_a 1 = 0; \; \log 1 = 0; \; \ln(1) = 0$

4. $\log_a (xy) = \log_a x + \log_a y$

5. $\log_a \left(\dfrac{x}{y} \right) = \log_a x - \log_a y$

6. $\log_{a^x} (b^y) = \dfrac{y}{x} \log_a b$

7. $e = \lim\limits_{n \to \infty} \left(1 + \dfrac{1}{n} \right)^n$

8. $\log_a b = \dfrac{\log_x b}{\log_x a} = \dfrac{\log b}{\log a} = \dfrac{\log_{10} b}{\log_{10} a} = \dfrac{\ln b}{\ln a} = \dfrac{\log_e b}{\log_e a}$

   $\log_3 7 = \dfrac{\ln 7}{\ln 3} = \dfrac{\log(7)}{\log(3)}$

9. $a^{\log_a b} = b; \; 10^{\log b} = b; \; e^{\ln(b)} = b$

   $3^{\log_3 9} = 9$

10. $f(ab) = f(a) + f(b)$

   $f\left(\dfrac{a}{b} \right) = f(a) - f(b)$

   $f(a^n) = n \cdot f(a)$

11. The logarithm (base 10) of a positive number can be expressed as the sum of an integer (called the characteristic) and the log of a number (called the mantissa) between 1 and 0. The characteristic, when it is positive, is 1 less than the number of digits before the decimal point of the given number.

12. $f(x) = a^x \Leftrightarrow f^{-1}(x) = \log_a x$

$f(x) = 10^x \Leftrightarrow f^{-1}(x) = \log_{10} x = \log x$

$f(x) = e^x \Leftrightarrow f^{-1}(x) = \log_a x = \ln x$

Logarithmic Inequalities

$\log_a x < \log_a y$ implies that

Case 1: If $a>1$ $\Rightarrow$ $0<x<y$

Case 2: If $0<a<1$ $\Rightarrow$ $x>y>0$

Domain of Logarithms

$Y = \log_{A(x)} B(x)$

Domain: $A(x) > 0$, $A(x) \neq 1$, $B(x) > 0$

Example:

$\log_{36} 6 - \log_3 27 + \log_2 (0.25)^{1/3} = ?$

Solution:

$$\log_{36} 6 - \log_3 27 + \log_2 (0.25)^{1/3} = \log_{6^2} 6 - \log_3 3^3 + \log_2 \left(2^{-2}\right)^{\frac{1}{3}} = \log_{6^2} 6 - \log_3 3^3 + \log_2 \left(2^{-\frac{2}{3}}\right)$$

$$= \frac{1}{2} + 3 - \frac{2}{3} = \frac{17}{6}$$

Example:

$2^{x+3} = 3^x \Rightarrow x = ?$

Solution:

$2^{x+3} - 3^x = 0$

We would like to find the zero of the function $y = 2^{x+3} - 3^x$

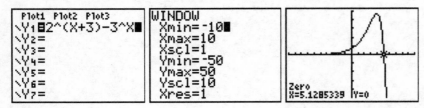

Answer: 5.13

Example:

$e^{-x} - e^x = 2 \Rightarrow x = ?$

Solution:

$e^{-x} - e^x - 2 = 0$

We would like to find the zero of the function $y = e^{-x} - e^x - 2$

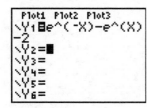 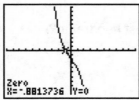 Answer: -0.88

Example:

log(sin2)+ log(sin20)+ log(sin20°)=?

Solution:

The following calculation is carried out in the radian mode of TI 84.

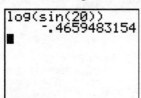

The following calculation is carried out in the degree mode of TI 84.

```
log(sin(20))
     -.4659483154
■
```

Answer: -0.808493-0.4659483 ≈ -0.547

Example:

Find the inverse of f(x)=3·2^{x+1}

Solution:

$f(x) = 3 \cdot 2^{x+1} \Rightarrow y = 3 \cdot 2^{x+1}$

$x = 3 \cdot 2^{y+1} \Rightarrow \dfrac{x}{3} = 2^{y+1} \Rightarrow \log\dfrac{x}{3} = (y+1)\log 2$

$y + 1 = \dfrac{\log\dfrac{x}{3}}{\log 2} = \log_2\left(\dfrac{x}{3}\right) \Rightarrow y = \log_2\left(\dfrac{x}{3}\right) - 1$

$f^{-1}(x) = \log_2\left(\dfrac{x}{3}\right) - 1$

Example:

Find the inverse of f(x)=4ln(x+2)

Solution:

$f(x) = 4\ln(x+2) \Rightarrow y = 4\ln(x+2)$

$x = 4\ln(y+2) \Rightarrow \dfrac{x}{4} = \ln(y+2)$

$y+2 = e^{\frac{x}{4}} \Rightarrow y = e^{\frac{x}{4}} - 2 \Rightarrow f^{-1}(x) = e^{\frac{x}{4}} - 2$

Example:

What is the approximate value of $\log_3 8$ correct to the nearest hundredth?

Solution:

$\log_3 8 = \dfrac{\log 8}{\log 3} = 1.89$

Example:

How many digits does the number 777^{777} have?

Solution:

$\log 777^{777} = 777 \cdot \log 777 = 2245.85$

Therefore 777^{777} has 2246 digits.

Example:

log2=A and log3=B. In terms of A and B calculate the following:

a. $\log\left(\dfrac{20}{9}\right)$

b. $\log(3.6)$

Solution:

a. $\log\left(\dfrac{20}{9}\right) = \log\left(\dfrac{10 \cdot 2}{3^2}\right) = \log 10 + \log 2 - \log 3^2 = \log 10 + \log 2 - 2\log 3 = 1 + A - 2B$

c. $\log(3.6) = \log\dfrac{36}{10} = \log\dfrac{2^2 \cdot 3^2}{10} = \log 2^2 + \log 3^2 - \log 10 = 2\log 2 + 2\log 3 - \log 10 = 2A + 2B - 1$

Exercises

1. Solve the equation $5^x - 5 \cdot 8^x = 0$.

2. If $\log_7 3 = r$ and $\log_7 5 = s$, Express each logarithm in terms of r and s.

    i) $\log_7 75$

    ii) $\log_7 225$

    iii) $\log_7 0.12$

    iv) $\log_7 \dfrac{1}{15}$

3. Simplify $\log_8\left(\dfrac{1}{32}\right)$

4. $2.7^a = 3.29^b \Rightarrow$ find a/b.

5. Find the solution set of each of the following equations:

   i) $\log x^2 = 2\log x$

   ii) $\log x^3 = 3\log x$

   iii) $\log_7(x+3) - \log_7(x-4) = 1$

6. Express the equation given by $\log_a b = c$ in exponential form.

7. $\log_3 100$ is between which two consecutive integers?

8. If $3^x = 5$, what does 2^x equal?

9. $\log_{10} A = x$, $\log_{10} B = y$, $\log_{10} C = z$. Express $\log_{10}\left(\dfrac{A}{BC^3}\right)^4$ in terms of x, y and z.

10. If $\log_a 3 = x$ and $\log_a 5 = y$, find in terms of x and y expressions for $\log_3 5$ and $\log_a 75$.

11. If $f(x) = 5^x$, then $\dfrac{f^{-1}(a)}{f^{-1}(b)} = ?$

12. $\log_4 x \cdot \log_5 6 = 7 \Rightarrow x = ?$

13. $A = e^{Bt}$; $A = 1000$, $T = 4$, $B = ?$

14. $f(x) = e^x$ and $h(x) = f(-x) + f^{-1}(-x)$ then $h(-2) = ?$

15. If $\log x = \dfrac{3}{4}$ then $\log(1000x^2) = ?$

16. $\log_3 2 = x \cdot \log_6 5 \Rightarrow x = ?$

17. $\log_x 3 = \log_4 x \Rightarrow$ What is the sum of the roots of this equation?

18. $f(x) = 3.5^x + 1$; $f^{-1}(10) = ?$

19. $3^{x+2} = 27 \Rightarrow x = ?$

20. Which of the following statements are correct?

   i) $\log\dfrac{t+1}{t-1} = \log(t+1) - \log(t-1)$; $t > 1$

   ii) $\log((t+1)\cdot(t-1)) = \log(t+1) + \log(t-1)$; $t > 1$

   iii) $\log((t+1) - (t-1)) = \dfrac{\log(t+1)}{\log(t-1)}$; $t > 1$

   iv) $\log((t+1) + (t-1)) = \log(t+1)\cdot\log(t-1)$; $t > 1$

21. Which of the following statements are correct?

   i) $\log x^2 = 2\log x$ for all x.

   ii) $\log(xy) = \log x + \log y$ for all positive values of x and y

   iii) $\log\dfrac{x}{y} = \log x - \log y$ for all nonzero values of x and y.

   iv) $\log \dfrac{1}{x} = -\log x$, for all positive values of x.

22. Solve the following inequalities for x:

    i) $\log_2(1-x) < \log_2 4$

    ii) $\log_{0.5}(1-x) < \log_{0.5} 4$

23. $f(x) = \log(\sin x)$. Find domain of f(x).

24. Find the point of intersection of the graphs $y = \log x$ and $y = \ln \dfrac{x}{2}$

25. Find x and y intercept(s) of the graph of equation $y = (x^2-4)\ln(x^2+9)$.

26. $\log_4(\cos 290°) = ?$

27. $\displaystyle\sum_{i=9}^{12} \ln i = ?$

28. $\log_6 3 + \log_4 \sqrt{32} = ?$

29. $F(x,y) = \log_y x$. $F(e, \pi^2) = ?$

30. $\log_4(\sin x) = -1$; Find smallest positive value of x.

31. $\log_{\sqrt{5}} 4 - \log_{16} \sqrt{125} = ?$

32. Order the numbers A, B, C, D and E from least to greatest.

   $A = 99999 \cdot 10^{2007}$

   $B = 9999 \cdot 11^{2006}$

   $C = 999 \cdot 12^{2005}$

   $D = 99 \cdot 13^{2004}$

   $E = 9 \cdot 14^{2003}$

33. If $\log_8 5 = x$ and $\log_8 4 = y$, Express each logarithm in terms of x and y.

    i) $\log_8 100$

    ii) $\log_8\left(6\dfrac{1}{4}\right)$

34. Write each expression in terms of logA and logB.

    i) $\log(AB)^3$

    ii) $\log \dfrac{A}{B^3}$

    iii) $\log \sqrt[5]{\dfrac{A}{B}}$

    iv) $\log(A\sqrt[3]{B})$

    v) $\log(A^3\sqrt{B})$

35. Solve for x.

    i) $3^x = 15$

    ii) $4^x = 1000$

    iii) $3.14^x = 9$

    iv) $\pi^x = 9$

    v) $0.95^x = 0.76$

    vi) $e^x = 28$

    vii) $e^{-x} = 0.08$

    viii) $\sqrt{e^x} = 70$

    ix) $(e^x)^4 = 350$

    x) $3^{2x} - 3^x - 12 = 0$

    xi) $e^{2x} - 7e^x + 12 = 0$

    xii) $5^{2x+1} - 7.5^x + 2 = 0$

36. Evaluate the following:

    i) $\log_3 5 \cdot \log_5 3$

    ii) $\log_3 7 \cdot \log_7 27$

    iii) $\log_{25} 4 \cdot \log_4 5$

    iv) $\dfrac{1}{\log_5 20} + \dfrac{1}{\log_4 20}$

    v) $\dfrac{1}{\log_4 10} + \dfrac{1}{\log_{25} 10}$

    vi) $\log_3 5 \cdot \log_5 9$

37. Solve for x.

    i) $\log_3(4x+1) - 7 = \log_3(0.2)$

    ii) $\log_9(2x-5) + \dfrac{1}{2} = \log_9 x$

    iii) $2\log_9(x-1) + 2 = \log_3(3x+13)$

    iv) $(\ln x)^2 - 13 \ln x = -40$

    v) $3^{2x-1} = 4^x$

    vi) $\log_3(x+5) - \log_3(x-5) = 2$

38. Write as a single logarithm.

    i) $\log_2 4 - 2\log_2 6 + \log_2 12$

    ii) $\log_3 x + 1.5\log_3 \sqrt{x} - \log_3 x^2$

39. Find the domain and the inverse of the given function.

    i) $f(x) = 4e^{2x+3}$

      ii) $f(x) = \log \sqrt{3x - 7}$

40. Solve for x and y if

      i) $xy = 48$ and $\log x - 2\log y = 1$

      ii) $\log_2(x^2 - y^2) = 3$ and $\log_4(x - y) = 1$

      iii) $\ln x^2 + \ln y^3 = 5$ and $\ln x - \ln y = 1$

41. Simplify $\log_5 100 - \log_5 4$.

42. Find $\log_3 13$ to four significant digits.

43. Find x in terms of e where e is the base of the natural logarithm in: $\ln(3x-4) + 2 = 0$

44. $\log_5 45$ is between which two consecutive integers?

45. $2.3^{3x} = 3.4^{\frac{y}{2}} \Rightarrow \dfrac{x}{y} = ?$

46. Evaluate the following:

      i) $\log_{16} 32 - \log_4 0.125 + \log_8 256 - \log_{\frac{1}{5}} 625$

      ii) $\log_6 5 \cdot \log_2 4 \cdot \log_{16} 216 \cdot \log_5 8$

      iii) $\log 1000 + \log_{\sqrt{2}} \sqrt[3]{64} - \log_8 4 + \log_9\left(\dfrac{81}{27}\right)$

      iv) $\log 25 + \log 400$

      v) $\dfrac{\log 256}{\log 64}$

      vi) $\log_3\left(\dfrac{1}{28}\right) - \log_{125} 5 + \log_{a^2} a^4 - 2^{\log_2 6} - 6^{-\log_6 2} + 10^{\log 3 - \ln 2} - e$

47. Solve for x

      i) $\log_3 x < 0$

      ii) $\log_{(2-x)}(x - 5) < 0$

      iii) $\log_2(x^2) > 0$

48. Given that $\log_x y = 4$; $\log_y z = 5$; calculate the following:

      i) $\log_x z = ?$

      ii) $\log_x(yz) = ?$

      iii) $\log_x\left(\dfrac{y}{z}\right) = ?$

      iv) $\log_y(yz) = ?$

      v) $\log_y(xy) = ?$

49. $f^{-1}(x) = ?$ If

      i) $f(x) = 2^x$

- ii) $f(x)=e^x$
- iii) $f(x)=10^x$
- iv) $f(x)=\log_3 x$
- v) $f(x)=\ln x$
- vi) $f(x)=\log x$
- vii) $f(x)=2e^x-1$
- viii) $f(x)=10^{2x+4}$
- ix) $f(x)=2\ln(4-x)$

50. $2^{x-1}=A$. Find x if

- i) $A=16$
- ii) $A=1$
- iii) $A=-4$
- iv) $A=\dfrac{1}{4}$
- v) $A=3$

51. The points (x,y) on the graph of y=f(x) satisfy the relation $\log_3 y;=-x$

    a. f(x)=?

    b. range of f(x)=?

52. $f(x)=\left(\dfrac{1}{3}\right)^{2x+1}$; range of f(x)=?

53. $\log_6 120$ is between which two consecutive integers?

54. $\log(4x)=3 \Rightarrow x=?$

55. $2^x=5 \Rightarrow 3^{-x}=?$

56. If $2^x=x$ then x=?

57. If $2^x=x^2$ then x=?

58. $f(x)=3.\log(x^2)$; Find domain and range of f(x).

59. What are all possible (x,y) values for which the points described by $\log x=\log y^2$ and $\log x=2\log y$ are the same?

60. Which one(s) of the following are definitely correct?

- i)   x and y are both positive
- ii)   x is positive only.
- iii)   Each equation gives the points on the line $y=\mp\sqrt{x}$
- iv)   Only the points on the curve $y=\sqrt{x}$ can satisfy both equations.
- v) $x=y^2$ is the solution set.

vi)   x=y² where y>0 is the solution set.

61. Eliminate quotients and exponents in the following equation by taking the natural logarithm of both

sides. $y = \dfrac{(x+1)^3(2x-3)^{\frac{3}{4}}}{(1+7x)^{\frac{1}{3}}(2x+3)^{\frac{3}{2}}}$

62. Evaluate each of the following

i) $\log_{10}(0.001)$

ii) $\log_2(1/64)$

iii) $\ln(e^{0.001})$

iv) $\log_{10}\left(\dfrac{(100)^{\frac{1}{3}}(0.01)^2}{(.0001)^{\frac{2}{3}}}\right)^{0.1}$

v) $e^{\ln(e^{-2})}$

63. Solve the following equation for x: $\log_3(x^4)+\log_3 x^3-2\log_3 x^{\frac{1}{2}}=5$

64. Solve the following equation for x: $\dfrac{e^x}{1+e^x}=\dfrac{1}{3}$

65. log2=A and log3=B. In terms of A and B calculate the following:

a. log536

b. $\log\left(\dfrac{27}{16}\right)$

c. log6000

d. $\log\left(\dfrac{6^{12}}{20^{20}}\right)$

66. Solve for x:

i)   lnx=ln(x+1)+ln4

ii)   log(x-3)²=log(x+5)+2log2

iii)   log(x²)=(logx)²

iv) $e^{2x}-6e^x+5=0$

v) $6e^x+e^{-x}=5$

67. Match a through d with 1 through 4 assuming that a is greater than 1.

a. $f(x)=a^x$

b. $f(x)=-a^{-x}$

c. $f(x)= -a^x$

d. f(x)= a^{-x}

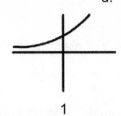 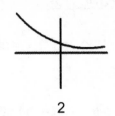 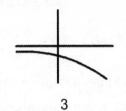 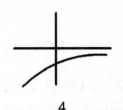

| 1 | 2 | 3 | 4 |

68. Match a through f with 1 through 4.

   a. f(x)=log$_a$x; a>1

   b. f(x)=log$_a$x; 0<a<1

   c. f(x)=log$_a$(-x); a>1

   d. f(x)=log$_a$(-x); 0<a<1

   e. f(x)= -log$_a$x; a>1

   f. f(x)= -log$_a$x; 0<a<1

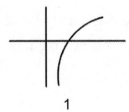 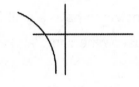 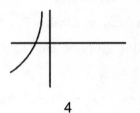

| 1 | 2 | 3 | 4 |

1.12 RATIONAL FUNCTIONS

A rational function f(x) is defined as $f(x) = \dfrac{P(x)}{Q(x)}$ where P(x) and Q(x) are both polynomial functions.

Zero: If $P(x_o)=0$ and $Q(x_o)\neq 0$ then f(x) has a zero at $x=x_o$.

Hole: If $P(x_o)=0$ and $Q(x_o)=0$, and the multiplicity of x_o is the same in both polynomials, then f (x) has a hole at $x=x_o$

Vertical asymptote: If $P(x_o) \neq 0$ but $Q(x_o)=0$, then f (x) has a vertical asymptote at $x=x_o$

Horizontal asymptote: If the limit of $\dfrac{P(x)}{Q(x)}$ equals b as x goes to $\pm\infty$ then y=b is the horizontal asymptote.

Remark: The graph of a function can intersect the horizontal asymptote; but it can not intersect the vertical asymptote.

Existence of Limit: For a function to have a limit for a given value of x=a, the right hand limit at a^+ and the left hand limit at a^- must be the same and each limit must be equal to a real number L other than infinity:

If $\lim\limits_{x \to a^+} f(x) = \lim\limits_{x \to a^-} f(x) = L$ and $L \in R$ then $\lim\limits_{x \to a} f(x) = L$.

Continuity: If $\lim\limits_{x \to a^+} f(x) = \lim\limits_{x \to a^-} f(x) = f(a) \in R$ then f(x) is continuous at x=a.

Limits at infinity:

$$\lim_{x \to \pm\infty} \frac{P(x)}{Q(x)} = \begin{cases} 0 & \text{if } d(P(x)) < d(Q(x)) \\ \pm\infty & \text{if } d(P(x)) > d(Q(x)) \\ \text{ratio of leading coefficient of P(x) to that of Q(x)} & \text{if } d(P(x)) = d(Q(x)) \end{cases}$$

where d(P(x)) = degree of P(x) and d(Q(x)) = degree of Q(x).

Hyperbolic Rational Functions

$f(x) = \dfrac{ax + b}{cx + d}$

Domain $= R - \left\{\dfrac{-d}{c}\right\}$; Range $= R - \left\{\dfrac{a}{c}\right\}$

Horizontal asymptote: y = a/c

Vertical asymptote: x = -d/c

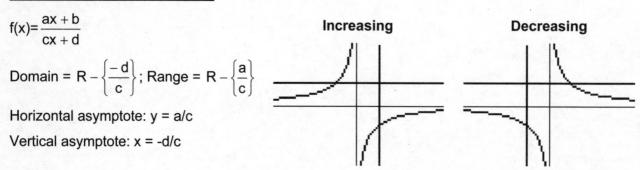

Increasing   **Decreasing**

Examples:

$$\lim_{x \to -\infty} \frac{3x^3 - 5x^2 + 2}{2x^2 - 4x + 2} = \frac{3x^3}{2x^2} = \frac{3x}{2} = -\infty$$

$$\lim_{x \to +\infty} \frac{3x^3 - 5x^2 + 2}{-2x^3 - 4x + 7} = \frac{3}{-2}$$

$$\lim_{x \to +\infty} \frac{2x^2 - 5x - 7}{-3x^3 + 1} = 0$$

Example:

Find all asymptotes of the function given by $y = \dfrac{2x^2 - 18}{x^2 - 4}$.

Solution:

$$y = \frac{2x^2 - 18}{x^2 - 4} = \frac{2x^2 - 18}{(x - 2) \cdot (x + 2)}$$

Vertical asymptotes are x = 2 and x = -2.

$\lim_{x \to \infty} \dfrac{2x^2 - 18}{x^2 - 4} = 2$; therefore y = 2 is the horizontal asymptote.

Example:

$$f(x) = \begin{cases} \dfrac{4x^2 + 3x}{x} & \text{if } x \neq 0 \\ m & \text{if } x = 0 \end{cases}$$

If f(x) is a continuous function then m = ?

Solution:

$$m = \lim_{x \to 0} \frac{4x^2 + 3x}{x} = \lim_{x \to 0} \frac{x \cdot (4x + 3)}{x} = \lim_{x \to 0} (4x + 3) = 3$$

Example:

$$f(x) = \begin{cases} x + 4 & x > 3 \\ 6 & x = 3 \\ x + 2 & x < 3 \end{cases}$$

a. $\lim_{x \to 3^+} f(x) = ?$

b. $\lim_{x \to 3^-} f(x) = ?$

c. f(3)=?

Solution:

$$\lim_{x \to 3^+} f(x) = 3 + 4 = 7$$

$$\lim_{x \to 3^-} f(x) = 3 + 2 = 5$$

f(3) = 6

Example:

At which point does the graph of $f(x) = \dfrac{x^2 - 1}{x - 1}$ have a hole?

Solution:

$$f(x) = \frac{x^2 - 1}{x - 1} = \frac{(x - 1) \cdot (x + 1)}{x - 1}$$

The function $f(x) = \dfrac{x^2 - 1}{x - 1}$ has a hole at x = 1.

$$\lim_{x \to 1} \frac{x^2 - 1}{x - 1} = \frac{(x - 1) \cdot (x + 1)}{x - 1} = \lim_{x \to 1} x + 1 = 2$$. Therefore the hole is at (1, 2).

Exploring Limits with TI

- Limit for a certain value of x or limit at infinity can be calculated by using the **STO**re facility of TI. What must be done is simply to store a value in x and calculate the value of the expression for this x-value.

- ∞ can be replaced by 100,000,000,000; and -∞ can be replaced by -100,000,000,000.

- Limit at a value of x other than $\pm \infty$ must be calculated as follows: If for example the limit at x=3 will be calculated, 3.000000001 (which means the right hand limit at 3⁺) must be stored in x and the expression must be evaluated; then 2.999999999 (which means the left hand limit at 3⁻) must be stored in x and the expression must be evaluated again. If both limits are the same, say L, then the limit is equal to L, otherwise there is no limit.

Example:

$$\lim_{x \to 3} \frac{x^3 - 27}{x^4 - 81} = ?$$

Solution:

```
3.0000001→X              2.999999→X
          3.0000001                2.999999
(X^3-27)/(X^4-81         (X^3-27)/(X^4-81
)                        )
               .25                 .2500000417
```

Limit at x = 3 is 0.25.

Complete Prep for the SAT Math Subject Tests – Level 1 and Level 2

Exercises

1. For every $\varepsilon>0$, there exists an n_ε such that if $n>n_\varepsilon$ then $|f(n)-L|<\varepsilon$. When n gets infinitely large, to what value does f(n) approach?

2. If for $\forall \varepsilon>0$ there exists a positive δ such that if $o<|x-a|<\delta$ then $|f(x)-L|<\varepsilon$; to what value does f(x) approach when x approaches to a?

3. If $f(x) = x + 3$ and $g(x) = \dfrac{x^2 - 9}{x - 3}$ how are the graphs of f and g related?

4. Sketch the graph of $f(x) = \dfrac{x}{4 - x}$, indicate all intercepts, and asymptotes.

5. $\lim \dfrac{x^3 + x^2 - 6x}{x - 2} = ?$

6. Find the vertical asymptotes of $y = \dfrac{x}{x^2 - 4}$.

7. If $f(x) = \dfrac{x^2 - 16}{x - 4}$, what value does f(x) approach as x approaches 4?

8. If $f(x) = \dfrac{3x + 12}{2x - 12}$, what value does f(x) approach as x gets infinitely large?

9. Which of the following lines are asymptotes of the graph of $y = \dfrac{1 + x}{x}$?

10. If $f(x) = \dfrac{x + 4}{(x - 4)(x^2 + 4)}$, for what value of x is f(x) undefined?

11. Evaluate the following limits:

    a. $\lim\limits_{x \to 2} \dfrac{-x^2 + 4}{x^3 + 8} = ?$

    b. $\lim\limits_{x \to -\infty} \dfrac{x^3 - 27}{x^4 - 81} = ?$

    c. $\lim\limits_{x \to 3} \dfrac{x^3 - 27}{x^4 - 81} = ?$

    d. $\lim\limits_{x \to 2^+} \dfrac{3x + 5}{x - 2} = ?$

    e. $\lim\limits_{x \to 2} \dfrac{3x + 5}{x - 2} = ?$

    f. $\lim\limits_{n \to \infty} \dfrac{(-1)^n + 1}{n} = 0$

g. $\lim_{n\to\infty}\left\{\dfrac{n^2}{n+3}-\dfrac{n^2}{n+4}\right\}=$

h. $\lim_{n\to\infty}(\sqrt{n+4}-n)$

i. $\lim_{n\to\infty}(\sqrt{n^2+4n}-n)$

j. $\lim_{n\to1}\dfrac{\ln x-1}{x^2}$

k. $\lim_{n\to1}\dfrac{\ln x}{x^2-1}$

l. $\lim_{n\to1}\dfrac{\ln x}{x-1}$

m. $\lim_{x\to-\infty}\dfrac{x^2+4x-7}{x^3+5x^2+2}$

n. $\lim_{x\to-\infty}\dfrac{x^3+4x-7}{x^3+5x^2+2}$

o. $\lim_{x\to-\infty}\dfrac{3x^3+4x-7}{2x^2+5x+2}$

p. $\lim_{x\to-\infty}\dfrac{-x^4+3x-10}{2x^2+3x-5}$

q. $\lim_{x\to1}\dfrac{x^2-1}{x^3-1}$

r. $\lim_{x\to2^+}\dfrac{1}{x^2-4}$

s. $\lim_{x\to2^-}\dfrac{1}{x^2-4}$

t. $\lim_{x\to2}\dfrac{x-2}{x^2-4}$

u. $\lim_{x\to2^+}\dfrac{x-2}{|x-2|}$

v. $\lim_{x\to2^-}\dfrac{x-2}{|x-2|}$

w. $\lim_{x\to2}\dfrac{x-2}{|x-2|}$

x. $\lim\limits_{x \to 3} \dfrac{x^2 - 9}{x - 3}$

y. $\lim\limits_{x \to 3} \dfrac{x^2 - 9}{x + 3}$

z. $\lim\limits_{x \to 4^+} \dfrac{\sqrt{x} - 2}{x - 4}$

aa. $\lim\limits_{x \to 4} \dfrac{\sqrt{x} - 2}{x - 4}$

bb. $\lim\limits_{x \to 3} \dfrac{x^4 - 81}{x^2 - 9}$

cc. $\lim\limits_{x \to 1} \dfrac{x^2 - 1}{x^2 - 2x + 1} = ?$

12. In order to be continuous at x=2 what must $f(x) = \dfrac{x^4 - 16}{x^3 - 8}$ be defined to be equal to?

13. $f(x) = \begin{cases} \dfrac{6x^2 - 6}{x - 1} & x \neq 1 \\ A & x = 1 \end{cases}$

What must be A if f(x) is a continuous function?

14. Find the horizontal and vertical asymptotes as well as the domain and range of:

a. $y = \dfrac{x + 2}{x^2 - 4}$

b. $y = \dfrac{x^2 - 4x - 5}{x^2 - 1}$

c. $y = \dfrac{x + 3}{(x - 3)(x^2 - 9)}$

15. $f(x) = \dfrac{3x + 4}{x + 2}$. Find domain and range of f(x)

16. $f(x) = \dfrac{x + 1}{2x - 2}$. What value(s) must be excluded from the domain of f(x) and what is the range of f(x)?

17. What is the domain and range of $y = \dfrac{x^2 - 4}{x^2 - 2x}$?

18. $f(x) = \begin{cases} x + 3 & x \neq 2 \\ 4 & x = 2 \end{cases}$

a. $\lim\limits_{x \to 2} f(x) = ?$

b. $f(2) = ?$

19.

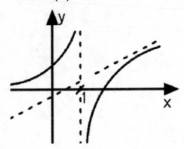

a. $\lim\limits_{x \to 1^+} f(x) = ?$

b. $\lim\limits_{x \to 1^-} f(x) = ?$

c. $\lim\limits_{x \to \infty} f(x) = ?$

d. $\lim\limits_{x \to -\infty} f(x) = ?$

e. Is f(x) continuous at x=1? if not, identity the type of the discontinuity.

20.

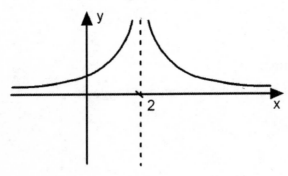

a. $\lim\limits_{x \to 2^+} f(x) = ?$

b. $\lim\limits_{x \to 2^-} f(x) = ?$

c. $\lim\limits_{x \to 2} f(x) = ?$

d. Does the function have a limit at x=2?

e. $\lim\limits_{x \to \mp\infty} f(x) = ?$

f. $f(2) = ?$

g. Is f(x) continuous at x=2? if not, identity the type of the discontinuity.

21.

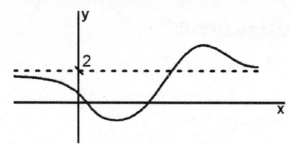

$$\lim_{x\to\mp\infty} f(x) = ?$$

22.

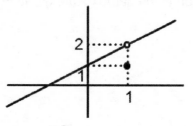

(a) $\lim_{x\to 1} f(x) = ?$

(b) f(1)=?

(c) Is f(x) continuous at x=1? If not identify the type of the discontinuity

23.

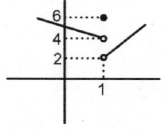

(a) $\lim_{x\to 1^-} f(x) = ?$

(b) $\lim_{x\to 1^+} f(x) = ?$

(c) f(1)=?

(d) Is f(x) continuous at x=1? If not identify the type of the discontinuity.

24. For the function given by f(x) = $5^{\frac{4}{2x-6}}$, indicate domain, range and the horizontal asymptote.

25. Identify the horizontal and vertical asymptotes for each of the following functions. If the function has a hole, indicate the x coordinate of the hole.

a. f(x)= $\dfrac{x}{x-2}$

b. g(x)= $\dfrac{x^2-1}{x^2-3x+2}$

c. f(x)= $\dfrac{3}{x+1}$

d. g(x)= $\dfrac{2x^2}{x^2+1}$

e. f(x)= $\dfrac{3x^2}{4x^2-1}$

1.13 GREATEST INTEGER FUNCTION

[x] = [|x|] = The greatest integer less than or equal to x.

f(x) = k if k ≤ x<k+1 and k=integer ⇒ f(x) = [x]

⌈x⌉ = The least integer greater than or equal to x: The ceiling function.

⌊x⌋ = The greatest integer less than or equal to x: The floor function is the same as the greatest integer function.

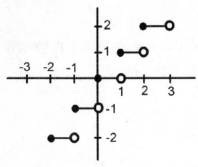

[4] = 4   [0.5]= 0   [9.76]= 9   [-3]= -3[-8.67]= -9   [-0.32]= -1

TI Usage:

y=int(x) and style must be set to dot

Properties:

If [x+k]= [x] + k then k must be integer

y= [x]: {Domain = All real numbers} and {Range= Set of integers}

Example:

f(x)=k where k is an integer for which k ≤ x < k+1 and g(x) = |f(x)|-f(x)+1. What is the minimum value for g(x)?

Solution:

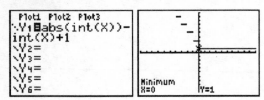

Answer: 1

Example:

f(x)=|1-2x+2[x]|

What is the period and frequency of the above function if [x] represents the greatest integer less than or equal to x? What are the maximum and the minimum values of f(x)? What is the amplitude, offset, and equation of the Axis of wave? What is the domain and range?

Solution:

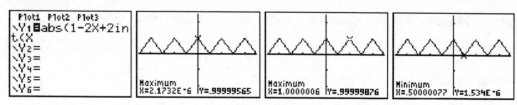

Min = 0; Max = 1

Period = | 1 – 0 | = 1 → (The distance between two adjacent maxima or minima)

Frequency = 1 → (Frequency = 1 / Period)

Amplitude = (1 – 0) / 2 = 1/2 → (Amplitude = (Ymax – Ymin) / 2)

Offset: (1 + 0) / 2 = 1/2 → (Offset = (Ymax + Ymin) / 2)

Axis of wave: y = 1/2 → (Axis of wave equation is y = Offset)

Domain: R, Range: 0 ≤ y ≤ 1.

Example:

f(x)=[x] where [x] represents the greatest integer function. What is the range of f(x)?

Solution:

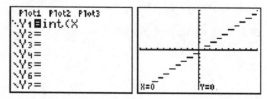

Answer: The range is all integers. The domain is all real numbers.

Example:

 [4.6]- [-5.4]+2[0.3]+ [4]- [0]=?

Solution:

```
int(4.6)-int(-5.
4)+2int(0.3)+int
(4)-int(0
              14
```

Answer: 14

Exercises

1.   The total cost, in dollars, of a telephone call that is m minutes in length from City R to City T is given by the function f(m)=1.06 (0.75 ⌈m⌉+1), where m>0 and ⌈m⌉ is the least integer greater than or equal to m. What is the total cost of a 5.5 – minute telephone call from City R to City T?

2.   f(x)=k where k is an integer for which k ≤ x < k+1 and g(x) = |f(x)|-f(x)+1. What is the minimum value for g(x)?

3.   g(x)=[x]-2x+1 what is the period of g(x)?

4.   f(x)=| [2x] | where [x] represents the greatest integer less than or equal to x. What is the range of f(x)?

5. $\lceil x \rceil$ = The least integer greater than or equal to x.

$\lfloor x \rfloor$ = The greatest integer less than or equal to x. Which one(s) of the following are correct?

a. $\lceil x \rceil = \lfloor x \rfloor$ is valid for all integer values of x.

b. $\lceil x+k \rceil = \lceil x \rceil + k$ is valid for all x if and only if k is 0.

c. $\lfloor x+k \rfloor = \lfloor x \rfloor + k$ is valid for all x if and only if k is an integer.

6.   f(x)=$\lfloor x \rfloor$ = The greatest integer less then or equal to x. g(x) = $\lceil x \rceil$= The least integer greater than or equal to x.

a. Calculate f(e), f(π), f($\sqrt{2}$), f($\frac{1}{3}$), f(-5.44), f(-0.73), f(0.21)

b. Calculate g(e), g(π), g($\sqrt{2}$), g($\frac{1}{3}$), g(-5.44), g(-0.73), g(0.21)

c. Given that the domain of f(x) is positive real numbers, find range of f(x)

d. Given that the domain of g(x) is negative real numbers, find range of g(x)

7.   f(x)=|x|+[x]; f(1.5)-f(-4.5)=?

If at first an idea is not absurd, then there is no hope for it.

Albert Einstein

CHAPTER 2 – *Combinatorics*

Permutations and Combinations

Binomial Theorem

Probability

Statistics

2.1 PERMUTATIONS AND COMBINATIONS

Factorial Notation

$n! = n\,(n-1)\,(n-2)\,(n-3)\ldots\ldots 3.2.1$

$1! = 1$

$0! = 1$

Counting by Multiplication

Example:

T-shirts at the school store are sold at 15 different models, 8 different colors and 4 different sizes. How many unique types of T-shirts does the school store sell?

Solution:

$\left.\begin{array}{l} 15 \text{ models} \\ 8 \text{ colors} \\ 4 \text{ sizes} \end{array}\right\} 15 \cdot 8 \cdot 4 = 480$

Definition of Permutation

$P(n,r) = {}^{n}Pr = nPr = P_{r}^{n} = \dfrac{n!}{(n-r)!}$

Definition of Combination

$C(n,r) = \dfrac{n!}{(n-r)!.r!} = \dfrac{P(n,r)}{r!} = \dbinom{n}{r} = C_{r}^{n} = {}^{n}C_{r} = {}_{n}C_{r}$

Examples:

$P(9,4) = 9.8.7.6$: (Write 4 consecutive integers in decreasing order starting with 9)

$C(9,4) = \dfrac{9.8.7.6}{4.3.2.1}$: (Write 4 consecutive integers in decreasing order, starting with 9; and divide by a sequence of 4 consecutive integers in decreasing order starting with 4)

$\dfrac{(5+3)!}{5!+3!} = 320$

$C(9,3) = \dbinom{9}{3} = 9\,nCr\,3 = nCr(9,3) = 84$

$P(9,3) = 9\,nPr\,3 = nPr(9,3) = 504$

Round Table Problem

If **n** people will sit at a round table and rotations do not make a difference then there are **(n-1)!** different seating schemes.

Example:

In how many ways can 4 people be seated at a round table?

Solution:

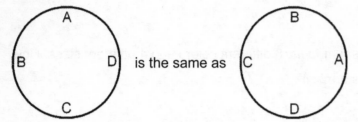

is the same as

Rotations do not make any difference in round tables as the relative positions of the people do not change. The seating scheme changes only if the relative positions change. Therefore we choose1 person and keep that person's position fixed; the remaining 3 people can be seated in 3! ways.

Necklace – Bracelet Problem

If a necklace or a bracelet will be made using **n** different beads the number of different necklaces is:

$$\frac{(n-1)!}{2}$$

Example:

4 seashells will be used to make bracelets, how many different bracelets can be made?

Solution:

This is similar to the round table problem however when the bracelet is turned upside down, a different arrangement is not obtained, so every arrangement is actually counted twice so the round table approach must be divided by two.

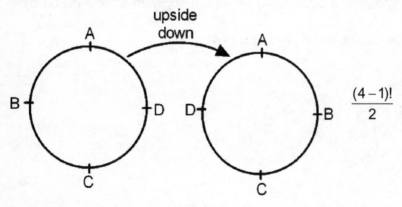

$$\frac{(4-1)!}{2}$$

Example:

With 6 stones each having different colors, how many different necklaces can be made?

Solution:

$$\frac{(6-1)!}{2}$$

Repeated Permutations

Example:

MASSACHUSETTS

Using all letters of the above word, how many different words can be obtained?

Solution:

$$\frac{13!}{2!\cdot4!\cdot2!}$$

Example:

UUURR

Using all letters of the above word, how many different words can be obtained?

Solution:

$$\frac{5!}{3!\,2!}=\binom{5}{3}=\binom{5}{2}$$

Example:

HHHHTT

Using all letters of the above word, how many different words can be obtained?

Solution:

$$\frac{6!}{4!\cdot2!}$$

Example:

In how many ways can 9 apples be distributed to 3 friends?

Solution:

AAAASAASAAA: This notation symbolizes that the 1st person gets 4 apples; 2nd one gets 2 apples and the 3rd one gets 3 apples. Each S letter stands for a separator.

$$\frac{11!}{9!\,2!}$$

Example:

How many different paths are there from A to B going one unit upward or one unit rightward in a single move?

Solution:

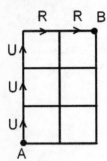

$$UUURR \Rightarrow \frac{5!}{3!.2!} = 10 \text{ paths}$$

Difference between Permutation and Combination

P(n,r) = There are n people and r different seats available where n≥r. In how many ways can these people be seated leaving no empty space?

Example:

4 of 9 people will be seated at 4 seats available; in how many ways can they be seated?

Solution:

$\underline{9}\ \underline{8}\ \underline{7}\ \underline{6}$ = P(9,4)

C(n,r) = $\binom{n}{r}$ = There are n different people. In how many ways can a team of r people be made?

Example:

From 9 people how many different teams with 4 members can be made?

Solution:

$$\binom{9}{4} = \frac{9.8.7.6}{4.3.2.1}$$

Example:

A, B, C, D

If three of the letters above are chosen to make words how many different words can be made?

Solution:

ABC	ABD	ACD	BCD
ACB	ADB	ADC	BDC
BAC	BAD	CAD	CBD
BCA	BDA	CDA	CDB
CAB	DAB	DAC	DBC
CBA	DBA	DCA	DCB

$\Rightarrow$ 24 different words are possible

Example:

Ali, Berk, Cem, Deniz

Among the 4 people given above, how many three member teams can be made?

Solution:

$\left. \begin{array}{l} A,B,C \\ A,B,D \\ A,C,D \\ B,C,D \end{array} \right\}$ 4 teams $C(4,3) = \dfrac{4!}{1!.3!} = 4$ different teams are possible

ABC is a word; switch places of B and C	Ali, Berk, Cem is a team; switch places of Berk & Cem
ACB is different from the word ABC.	Ali, Cem, Berk is the SAME team as Ali, Berk, Cem
Different orders are considered to be different.	Different orders are NOT considered to be different.
$\Rightarrow$ PERMUTATION	$\Rightarrow$ COMBINATION

Properties of Combinations

1) $C(0,0) = 1$

2) $C(n,0) = 1$

3) $C(n,n) = 1$

4) $C(n,r) = C(n,n-r)$

5) $C(n,0) + C(n,1) + C(n,2) + \ldots\ldots + C(n,n) = 2^n$

   The total number of subsets of a set having n elements is 2^n.

6) The total number of combinations of a set of n elements is the total number of those subsets that contain at least one element, and this number is $2^n - 1$.

7) $C(n,r) + C(n,r+1) = C(n+1, r+1)$

Examples:

$$\binom{9}{3} = \binom{9}{6}$$

$$\binom{16}{x} = \binom{12}{x} \Rightarrow x = 0$$

$$\binom{x}{6} = \binom{x}{9} \Rightarrow x = 15$$

$$\binom{9}{2} + \binom{9}{3} = \binom{10}{3}$$

Example:

$$\left.\begin{array}{l} \text{1 penny} \\ \text{1 nickel} \\ \text{1 dime} \\ \text{1 querter} \\ \text{1 \$} \end{array}\right\} \text{How many different sums of money can be made?}$$

Solution:

$$\binom{5}{1} + \binom{5}{2} + \binom{5}{3} + \binom{5}{4} + \binom{5}{5} = 2^5 - 1 = 31$$

Ace, King, Queen, Jack, 10, ..., 2: Totally 13 cards		**Black cards: Spades** and **Clubs**
Spades ♠ **Clubs ♣**	**Diamonds ♦** **Hearts ♥**	**Red cards: Diamonds** and **Hearts**
Face cards: King, Queen, Jack		

Example:

40 cards will be selected from a standard deck of 52 cards. How many selections can be made?

Solution:

52 Cards, Choose 40 Cards; $\binom{52}{40}$

Example:

From a standard deck of 52 cards; we would like to choose 10 cards so that 3 of them will be spades and 7 of them will be diamonds. In how many ways can this be done?

Solution:

$$\binom{13}{3}\cdot\binom{13}{7}$$

Example:

5 cards will be selected from 52 cards and order is not considered to be important. How many different selections are possible?

Solution:

$$\binom{52}{5}$$

Example:

There are 10 points no 3 of which are collinear. How many lines do they determine such that each line passes through exactly 2 of the points?

Solution:

$$\binom{10}{2}$$

Example:

10 people will shake hands so that each person shakes hands with every other person exactly once. How many different handshakes are possible?

Solution:

$$\binom{10}{2}$$

Example:

How many unique diagonals does a regular octagon have?

Solution:

$$\binom{8}{2}-8$$

Exercises

1. $_5P_2 + {}^6P_3 + P(5,3) = ?$

2. $\dfrac{(n-1)!}{n!} + \dfrac{(n+1)!}{n!}$.

3. $\dfrac{[(n-1)!]^2}{[n!]^2}$.

4. $\dbinom{5}{3} + C_2^8 + {}_6C_3 = ?$

5. $\dfrac{(6+3)!}{6! + 3!}$

6. Solve for n:

   a. $P(n,2) - C(n,2) = 36$

   b. $\dfrac{P(n,2)}{3} = C(n-1,3)$

7. In how many ways can 15 people be partitioned into two groups, one with 5 and the other with 10 people?

8. In how many ways can 15 people be partitioned into two groups A and B, one with 5 and the other with 10 people?

9. The license plates in a certain state used to be written with 3 letters followed by 3 digits. A new regulation changed the license plates to 4 letters and 2 digits. Approximately how many more license plates can be issued now?

10. There are 5 points on a line l_1 and 3 points on a line l_2 where $l_1 \parallel l_2$.

    a. If three of these points will be used at a time to make up the vertices of a triangle, how many different triangles can be constructed?

    b. How many lines pass through two or more of these 8 points?

11. The telephone area codes in the country Phonia are three-digit numbers of the form abc. Shown below are sets A, B, and C from which the digits a, b, and, c are chosen respectively. How many possible area codes are there?

    A= {4, 5, 6, 7, 8, 9}

    B= {0, 1, 2}

    C= {0, 1, 2, 3, 4, 5, 6, 7, 8, 9}

12. A group of 4 English, 5 French, and 6 German people will be seated in a row. In how many ways

    a. can they be seated with no restriction?

    b. can they be seated so that the people from the same country must sit together?

13. A group of 4 English, 5 French, and 6 German people will be seated at a round table. In how many ways

    a. can they be seated with no restriction?

    b. can they be seated so that the people from the same country must sit together?

14. 7 men and 7 women will be seated in a row. In how many ways can they sit if:

    a. there is no restriction?

    b. three particular men must sit together?

    c. two particular women must sit together?

    d. two particular women must not sit together?

    e. the women must sit together?

    f. the men and women must alternate?

15. 7 men and 7 women will be seated at a round table. In how many ways can they sit if:

    a. there is no restriction?

    b. three particular men must sit together?

    c. two particular women must sit together?

    d. two particular women must not sit together?

    e. the women must sit together?

    f. the men and women must alternate?

16. A group of 5 will be chosen from a crowd of 6 men and 7 women that includes Neva and Dilara. How many different groups can be made if:

    a. exactly 3 women must be in the group?

    b. exactly 3 men must be in the group?

    c. at least 3 women must be in the group?

    d. at most 3 women must be in the group?

    e. Neva and Dilara must be in the group?

    f. Neva and Dilara must not be in the group?

17. Ali wants that in his party there are totally 5 girls and 6 boys from his class that consists of 10 girls that include Emine and 11 boys that include Hilmi. She wants to invite Emine but not Hilmi to her party. In how many different ways can she choose her guests?

18. A club has 18 members, consisting of 10 men and 8 women.

    a. In how many ways can a president, a vice-president, and a secretary be elected?

    b. In how many ways can a president, a vice-president, and a secretary be elected if the president must be a man and the secretary must be a woman?

    c. In how many ways can a board consisting of a president, a vice-president, a secretary and three board members be formed?

19. A student .has to answer exactly 10 of the 15 questions in an exam.

    a. In how many ways can he answer the questions?

    b. In how many ways can he answer the questions if he must answer exactly 5 of the first 7 questions?

    c. In how many ways can he answer the questions if he must answer at least 5 of the first 7 questions?

20. A={a, b, c, d, e, f, g, h}

    a. How many subsets does set A have?

    b. How many of the subsets of set A have exactly 5 elements?

    c. How many of the subsets of set A have at least 5 elements?

    d. How many of the subsets of set A have at most 5 elements?

    e. How many of the subsets of set A have contain the element a?

    f. How many of the subsets of set A have contain the element a, but not b?

    g. How many of the subsets of set A have contain the elements a and b, but not c?

    h. How many subsets of set A contain 5 elements that include a, but not b?

    i. How many subsets of set A contain 5 elements that include both a and b?

    j. How many subsets of set A contain 5 elements that include both a and b but not c?

    k. How many subsets of set A contain 5 elements that include neither a nor b?

21. Using the letters of the word UNIFORM

    a. how many different words can be formed if each word must contain 2 vowels and 2 consonants?

    b. how many different words can be formed if each word must contain 2 vowels and 2 consonants if vowels must be together?

    c. how many different words can be formed if each word must contain 2 vowels and 2 consonants if vowels and consonants must be together?

    d. how many different words can be formed if each word must contain 2 vowels and 2 consonants if vowels and consonants must alternate?

22. Using all letters of the word ABRAKADABRA how many words can be constructed?

23. In how many ways can 10 apples be distributed to 3 people if apples are considered to be identical?

24. How many 4-digit positive odd integers do not contain the digit 4?

25. How many 4-digit positive odd integers do not contain the digit 5?

26. How many 4-digit positive even integers do not contain the digit 4?

27. How many 4-digit positive even integers do not contain the digit 5?

28. Using the digits in the set {0, 1, 2, 3, 4, 5, 6, 7, 8} how many

    a. four digit numbers can be made?

    b. four digit odd numbers can be made?

    c. four digit even numbers can be made?

    d. four digit numbers can be made if digits are not repeated?

    e. four digit odd numbers can be made if digits are not repeated?

    f. four digit even numbers can be made if digits are not repeated?

    g. four digit numbers divisible by 5 can be made if digits are not repeated?

29.   How many distinct

    a. three digit numbers are there?

    b. three digit odd numbers are there?

    c. three digit even numbers are there?

    d. three digit numbers are there if digits are not repeated?

    e. three digit odd numbers are there if digits are not repeated?

    f. three digit even numbers are there if digits are not repeated?

    g. three digit numbers divisible by 5 are there if digits are not repeated?

30.   A video store has 50 action movies and 70 sci-fi movies. How many different selections can a person make if

    a. he wishes to choose 1 movie?

    b. he wishes to choose 2 movies?

    c. he wishes to choose one movie of each kind?

    d. he wishes to choose 2 action and 3 sci-fi movies?

31.   Cherries, strawberries, vanilla, chocolate, tutti-frutti.

    A person wishes to select one or more of the given toppings for his ice-cream. How many different combinations are possible assuming that order of toppings is not important?

32.   A palindrome is a number that reads the same forward as it does backward. How many distinct

    a. 2 digit

    b. 3 digit

    c. 4 digit

    d. 5 digit palindromes are there?

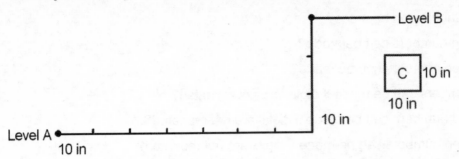

33. Stairs will be built that will enable a person to go up from level A to B in totally 3 rising steps. If the stairs is to be built of cubic blocks of shape and size C, then how many different stairs are possible?

34. In how many ways can 5 married couples
    a. line up in a row?
    b. line up in a row so that ladies sit together?
    c. line up in a row so that ladies sit together and so do the gentlemen?
    d. line up in a row so that each married couple sits together?
    e. sit at a round table?
    f. sit at a round table so that ladies sit together?
    g. sit at a round table so that ladies sit together and so do the gentlemen?
    h. sit at a round table so that each married couple sit together?

35. A text editing program can select 16 of the available 32 colors for the font and one other color for the background. How many color combinations are possible?

36. A= {1, 2, 3, 4, 5, 6} and B={a, b, c, d, e, f, g}
    a. How many elements does A×B have if A×B denotes the cartesian product?
    b. How many different relations can be defined from A to B?
    c. How many different functions can be defined from A to B?
    d. How many different one to one functions can be defined from A to B?
    e. How many different constant functions can be defined from A to B?

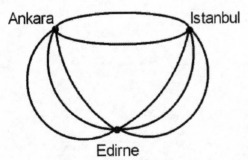

37. Erela starts at Ankara, makes a round trip; does not take any road and does not pass through any city more then once. How many different routes are possible for the round trip?

38. There are three roads from Ankara to Istanbul and four roads from Istanbul to Kırklareli.

    a. A person would like to go from Ankara to Kırklareli passing through Istanbul taking any road only once. How many different routes are possible?

    b. The person would like to go from Ankara to Kırklareli and come back, passing through Istanbul in both directions. How many different routes are possible?

    c. The person would like to go from Ankara to Kırklareli and come back, passing through Istanbul in both directions and not taking any road more than once. How many different routes are possible?

39. How many diagonals does a regular polygon with n sides have?

40. From 20 people, how many different committees can be selected if each committee should contain.

    a. A president, a vice president and a secretary.

    b. A president, a vice president, a secretary and three members.

41. In how many ways can 6 people line up in a row?

42. In low many ways can 6 people line up in a row if Estreya and Eli must be next to each other?

43. In how many ways can 6 people sit at a round table?

44. In how many ways can 6 people sit at a round table if Selen and Ferhan must sit next to each other?

45. In how many ways can 5 letters be mailed through 8 mailboxes?

46. In how many ways can 5 letters be mailed through 8 mailboxes if each letter must be mailed through a different mailbox?

47. In how many ways can a board with a president, a vice president and four board members be selected from 30 people?

48. From 10 experts and 20 trainees, how many different teams are there if each team must consist of 2 experts and 4 trainees?

49. How many different words can be made using all letters of the word AAABBBBCCCCC?

50. 5 girls and 10 boys will sit at a circular table. In how many ways can they sit if every two boys must sit between two girls?

51. How many 5 digit numbers can be written by rearranging the digits of the number 42524?

52. How many 5 digit numbers can be written by rearranging the digits of the number 42524 if each number must start with 4 and end with 2?

53. How many 6 digit numbers can be written by rearranging the digits of the number 425524 if each number must start with 4 and end with 2?

54. After a meeting everyone shakes hands with one another and altogether 55 handshakes take place. How many people attend the meeting?

55. Dila remembers the first five digits of a seven digit code number but she knows that neither of the last two digits was zero. In order to find the correct code number, at least how many trials does she need?

56. There are 4 pairs of black, 6 pairs of gray and 8 pairs of white socks in a bag. Assuming that all socks are identical except their color

    a. how many socks must he withdraw from the bag to make sure that he has at least one pair of black socks?

    b. how many socks must he withdraw from the bag to make sure that he has at least one pair of socks with the same color?

57. 9 people attend a competition and first, second, and third places will be awarded.

    a. In how many different ways can the prizes be given?

    b. How many different groups of 3 people will be awarded?

58. There are 5 points on a line l_1 and 7 points on a line l_2 parallel to l_1.

    a. How many distinct triangles can be formed if the vertices of each triangle must be selected among these 14 points?

    b. How many distinct lines pass through exactly two of these 12 points?

    c. How many distinct lines pass through two or more of these 12 points?

2.2 BINOMIAL THEOREM

$$(x+y)^n = \binom{n}{0} x^n$$

$$+ \binom{n}{1} x^{n-1} y^1$$

$$+ \binom{n}{2} x^{n-2} y^2$$

$$+ \binom{n}{3} x^{n-3} y^3 \qquad \rightarrow \qquad \text{4 th term.}$$

$$+ \dots$$

$$+ \binom{n}{n-1} x\, y^{n-1}$$

$$+ \binom{n}{n} y^n$$

(r+1)'th term in the expansion of $(x+y)^n = \binom{n}{r} x^{n-r} y^r$ where $r \le n$

$$\binom{9}{4} = \frac{9.8.7.6}{4.3.2.1}$$

Observation:

$(x+y)^n$:

- Number of terms = (n+1) if n is a positive integer.

- If n is even; there is a middle term and $r = \dfrac{n}{2}$ for the middle term.

- If n is not a positive integer meaning that if
    i)   n is not positive
    ii) n is not an integer
    iii) n is neither positive nor an integer
    then there are infinitely many terms!

Pascal's Triangle

Please note that the coefficients of the terms in $(x+y)^n$ are the same as the numbers in Pascal's Triangle.

$(x+y)^0 =$ $\qquad$ **1**

$(x+y)^1 =$ $\qquad$ **1x+1y**

$(x+y)^2 =$ $\qquad$ **1x²+2xy+1y²**

$(x+y)^3 =$ $\qquad$ $\mathbf{1x^3+3x^2y+3xy^2+1y^3}$

$(x+y)^4 =$ $\qquad$ $\mathbf{1x^4+4x^3y+6x^2y^2+4xy^3+1y^4}$

$(x+y)^5 =$ $\qquad$ $\mathbf{1x^5+5x^4y+10X^3y^2+10x^2y^3+5xy^4+1y^5}$

$$1$$
$$1 \quad 1$$
$$1 \quad 2 \quad 1$$
$$1 \quad 3 \quad 3 \quad 1$$
$$1 \quad 4 \quad 6 \quad 4 \quad 1$$
$$1 \quad 5 \quad 10 \quad 10 \quad 5 \quad 1$$

$(x+y)^3 = x^3 + 3x^2y + 3xy^2 + y^3$

$(x+y)^4 = x^4 + 4x^3y + 6x^2y^2 + 4xy^3 + y^4$

Please also note that when expanding $(x-y)^n$ the signs of terms should alternate.

$(x-y)^3 = x^3 - 3x^2y + 3xy^2 - y^3$

$(x+y)^4 = x^4 - 4x^3y + 6x^2y^2 - 4xy^3 + y^4$

Negative and Fractional Powers of Binomials

Example:

$(x-2y)^{1/4}$; give the first 4 terms.

Solution:

$$\binom{1/4}{0}x^{\frac{1}{4}} + \binom{1/4}{1}x^{\frac{1}{4}-1}(-2y)^1 + \binom{1/4}{2}x^{\frac{1}{4}-2}(-2y)^2 + \binom{1/4}{3}x^{\frac{1}{4}-3}(-2y)^3$$

$$= 1 \cdot x^{\frac{1}{4}} + \frac{1}{4}x^{-\frac{3}{4}}(-2y) + \frac{\frac{1}{4}\cdot\left(\frac{1}{4}-1\right)}{2\cdot 1}x^{-\frac{7}{4}}\left(4y^2\right) + \frac{\frac{1}{4}\cdot\left(\frac{1}{4}-1\right)\cdot\left(\frac{1}{4}-2\right)}{3\cdot 2\cdot 1}x^{-\frac{11}{4}}\left(-8y^3\right)$$

$$= x^{\frac{1}{4}} - \frac{1}{2}x^{-\frac{3}{4}}y - \frac{3}{8}x^{-\frac{7}{4}}y^2 - \frac{7}{16}x^{-\frac{11}{4}}y^3$$

Example:

$(x-y)^{-5}$; give the first 4 terms.

Solution:

$$\binom{-5}{0}x^{-5} + \binom{-5}{1}x^{-5-1}(-y)^1 + \binom{-5}{2}x^{-5-2}(-y)^2 + \binom{-5}{3}x^{-5-3}(-y)^3$$

$$= 1 \cdot x^{-5} + (-5)x^{-6}(-y) + \frac{-5\cdot(-5-1)}{2\cdot 1}x^{-7}y^2 + \frac{-5\cdot(-5-1)\cdot(-5-2)}{3\cdot 2\cdot 1}x^{-8}\left(-y^3\right)$$

$$= x^{-5} + 5x^{-6}y + 15x^{-7}y^2 + 35x^{-8}y^3$$

Exercises

1. If $(1-\sqrt{2})^3$ is expanded to get $a+b\sqrt{2}$ then $a+b=?$

2. If $(2x-3)^5 = 32x^5 + Px^4 + Qx^3 + Rx^2 + Sx - 243$ find the value of $P - Q$.

3. Give the first 4 terms, in simplified form, in the expansion of $(x^2-3y)^{10}$ when the terms are ordered in the decreasing powers of x.

4. If the sum of the coefficients in the expansion $(ax-3y)^{12}$ is 1 then find all possible values of a.

5. $\left(x^2 - \dfrac{5}{x}\right)^9$

   a. Find constant term.

   b. Find coefficient of x^6.

   c. Find the 3rd term when all terms are ordered in the decreasing powers of x.

6. $\left(x - \dfrac{3}{x^2}\right)^{10}$; find middle term.

7. $(x-2y)^{12}$; find middle term.

8. $(x+2y)^{-5}$; give the first 4 terms (OPTIONAL).

9. $(x-3y)^{1/3}$; give the first 4 terms (OPTIONAL).

10. $(x-2y+3z)^9$; find coefficient of $x^2y^3z^4$.

2.3 PROBABILITY

Set Theory in Brief

The term **set** represents a group of objects named so as to provide a check that indicates whether or not some particular object belongs to (symbolized as " $\in$ ") the set. Objects that belong to a set are called **elements** or **members** of that set. The Universal set denoted by U consists of all elements A and B and possibly the elements other than those of A and B

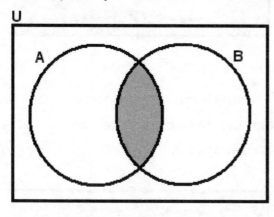

$A \cap B$

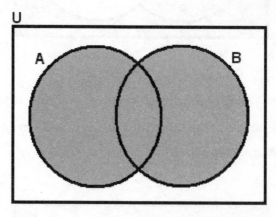

$A \cup B$

A **intersection** B consists of the elements that belong to both sets.

A **union** B consists of the elements that belong to either or both sets.

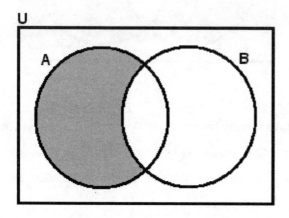

$A - B = A / B = A \setminus B$

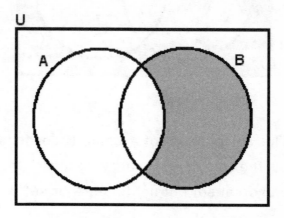

$B - A = B / A = B \setminus A$

A **difference** B consists of the elements that belong to A but not to B

B **difference** A consists of the elements that belong to B but not to A

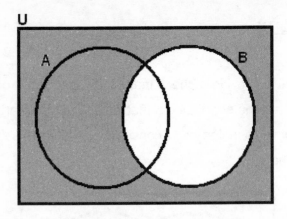

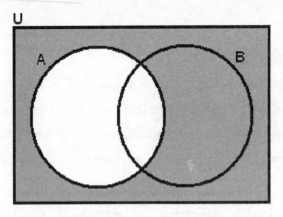

$$B' = U - B$$

B **complement** consists of the elements that belong to the universal set but not to B

$$A' = U - A$$

A **complement** consists of the elements that belong to the universal set but not to A

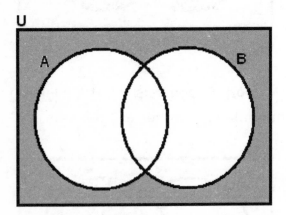

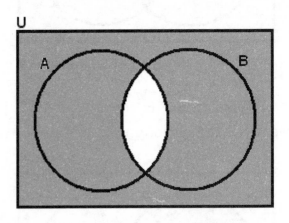

$$(A \cup B)' = A' \cap B'$$

The complement of A union B consists of the elements that belong to the universal set but not to set A or set B.

$$(A \cap B)' = A' \cup B'$$

The complement of A union B consists of the elements that belong to the universal set or set A or set B but not to both sets.

The **sample space** is the set of everything that can happen and is defined by the letter U (the universal set in set theory).

An **event** is one particular thing that can happen and is given any other capital letter, such as A.

P stands for **probability**, and **P(A)** stands for the **probability of event A**.

The number of ways an event A can happen is denoted by **n(A)**. To find the probability of event A we divide the number of ways event A can happen by the total number of possibilities in the sample space: $P(A) = \dfrac{n(A)}{n(U)}$.

Since A is a subset of U then n(A) ≤ n(U) which implies that probabilities are always nonnegative real numbers that cannot be greater than 1: $0 \le P(A) \le 1$. P(A) is between **0 (the event definitely will not happen)** and **1 (the event will definitely happen)** inclusive.

The probability that **event A does not happen** is denoted by **P(A')**. It follows that P(A)+P(A')=1

Odds in favor of an event A = $\dfrac{P(\text{event A happens})}{P(\text{event A does not happen})}$

Odds against an event A = $\dfrac{P(\text{event A does not happen})}{P(\text{event A happens})}$

Example:

What are the odds in favor of getting a number greater than 1 when one die is thrown?

Solution:

$$\frac{P(\text{event happens})}{P(\text{event does not happen})} = \frac{P(\text{number is greater than 1})}{P(\text{number is not greater than 1})} = \frac{\frac{5}{6}}{\frac{1}{6}} = \frac{5}{1}$$

Example:

What are the odds against getting a number greater than 1 when one die is thrown?

Solution:

$$\frac{P(\text{event does not happen})}{P(\text{event happens})} = \frac{1}{5}$$

The symbols ∩ and ∪ in the set theory are used for the words "and" and "or" in probability theory respectively.

Combined Events: The probability of event A or B or both happening.

If the events A and B are **mutually exclusive** then they cannot happen at the same time. This implies the following:

P(A∪B) = P(A) + P(B)

P(A∩B)=0

If two events A and B are mutually exclusive and A can happen in a ways while B can happen in b ways, then one or the other event can occur in a+b ways.

If the events A and B are not mutually exclusive then the following holds:

P(A∪B) = P(A) + P(B) – P(A∩B)

If A and B are **independent events** then the probability of the events A and B both happening is calculated by multiplication

$$P(A \cap B) = P(A) \cdot P(B)$$

Please note that multiplying simple fractions gives a smaller result and thus it is less likely that both events will happen than just one. If A and B are independent then one of them happening does not affect the probability of the other happening.

If the events are not independent we have to deal with **conditional probability** – i.e. the probability of one event happening given that the other has already happened. This is written as P(A|B), and read as "the probability of A given B." The related formula is $P(A \mid B) = \dfrac{P(A \cap B)}{P(B)}$.

Note that the definition of independence is P(A) = P(A|B) = P(A|B'). In other words, the probability of A is the same whether or not B has happened. But if you are asked to test whether events are independent, just investigate if P(A∩B) = P(A) · P(B) holds or not.

- Suppose that a bag contains balls of two different colors. One is taken out, then another. The color of the second is independent of the first if the first has been put back.

- If the first is not replaced in the bag then the color of the second depends on the color of the first.

Venn Diagrams

Venn Diagrams can be used to simulate an event. In such a case the symbols ∩ and ∪ in the set theory are used for the words "and" and "or" in probability theory respectively.

Example:

Among the 107 seniors in **RUSH** academy 68 take math classes and 45 take history classes. If 20 take both classes then what is the probability that a randomly selected student

- a) takes math only?
- b) takes history only?
- c) takes both math and history?
- d) takes math or history or both?
- e) does not take math?
- f) does not take history?
- g) takes neither math nor history?
- h) takes math given that he takes history?
- i) takes history given that he takes math?

Solution:

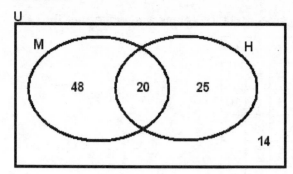

a) $P(M) = \dfrac{68}{107}$ b) $P(H) = \dfrac{45}{107}$

c) $P(M \cap H) = \dfrac{20}{107}$ d) $P(M \cup H) = \dfrac{93}{107}$

e) $P(M') = \dfrac{39}{107}$ f) $P(H') = \dfrac{62}{107}$

g) $P(H') = \dfrac{14}{107}$ h) $P(M|H) = \dfrac{20}{45}$

i) $P(H|M) = \dfrac{20}{68}$

Example:

For the events A and B, P(A) = 0.5, P(B) = 0.4.

a) Find P(A∪B) if A and B are independent.

b) Find P(A'∩B') if A and B are mutually exclusive.

Solution:

a) $P(A \cap B) = 0.5 \cdot 0.4 = 0.2$

   $P(A \cup B) = P(A) + P(B) - P(A \cap B) = 0.5 + 0.4 - 0.2 = 0.7$

b) $P(A' \cap B') = P((A \cup B)') = 1 - P(A \cup B) = 1 - (P(A) + P(B)) = 1 - (0.5 + 0.4) = 0.1$.

Lists and Charts

Lists: A list of possible outcomes is useful if there aren't too many of them. And it is important to be sure that each outcome in the list is equally likely. For example, when three coins are thrown, the possible combinations of heads and tails are HHH, HHT, HTH, HTT, THH, THT, TTH, and TTT. If we would like to find the probability of getting exactly two heads, we can see that there are three possible ways that are HHT, HTH and THH so the probability is 3/8. As another example, when four coins are thrown, the possible combinations of heads and tails are TTTT, TTTH, TTHT, TTHH, THTT, THTH, THHT, THHH, HTTT, HTTH, HTHT, HTHH, HHTT, HHTH, HHHT, and HHHH.

Possibility Space Chart: This is a way of showing a list of outcomes on a diagram, but can only be used for two events.

Example:

The diagram below shows all the possible totals when two six-sided dice (black and white) are thrown:

	6	7	8	9	10	11	12
	5	6	7	8	9	10	11
	4	5	6	7	8	9	10
Black	**3**	4	5	6	7	8	9
	2	3	4	5	6	7	8
	1	2	3	4	5	6	7
		1	**2**	**3**	**4**	**5**	**6**
				White			

Note that there is only one way a double 2, say, can happen - a 2 on the black and a 2 on the white.

But a 1 and a 3 can happen in two ways: 1 on the black and 3 on the white, or the other way around.

Thus there are 36 possibilities.

Some examples of probabilities are:

P(Total of 9) = 4/36

P(Total of 9 or 7) = 10/36

P(Total of 10 or a double) = 8/36

P(Double | Total ≥ 9) = 2/10

Tables of Outcomes: Tables of outcomes show how many ways two events can, or cannot, happen.

Example:

In a survey of 400 people, 170 of whom were female, it was found that 120 people were unemployed, including 30 males. If a person is selected at random from the 400, find the probability that this person is

a) An unemployed female.

b) A male, given that the person is employed.

Solution:

	Males	**Females**	**Totals**
Unemployed	**30**	90	**120**
Employed	200	80	280
Totals	230	**170**	**400**

a) There are 90 unemployed females cut of 200, so P(unemployed female) = 90/400

b) This is a conditional probability. There are 280 employed people. Of these, 200 are males.

So P(male | employed) = 200/280

Example:

In a survey, 100 students were asked "do you prefer to watch television or play sport?" Of the 46 boys in the survey, 33 said they preferred sport, while 29 girls made this choice. Complete the table and find the probability that:

a) A student selected at random prefers to watch television.

b) A student selected at random is a boy.

c) A student selected at random is a boy who prefers to watch television i.e. the student is a boy **and** he prefers to watch television.

d) A student selected at random is a boy **or** he prefers to watch television.

e) A student prefers to watch television, given that the student is a boy.

f) A student is a boy, given that he prefers to watch television.

g) Are the events of being a boy and preferring to watch the television mutually exclusive or not?

h) Are the events of being a boy and preferring to watch the television statistically dependent or independent?

Solution:

	Boys	Girls	Total
Television	13	25	38
Sport	33	29	62
Total	46	54	100

B: The event that a randomly selected person is a boy

T: The event that a randomly selected person prefers to watch television

a) $P(T) = \dfrac{38}{100}$

b) $P(B) = \dfrac{46}{100}$

c) $P(B \cap T) = \dfrac{13}{100}$

d) $P(B \cup T) = \dfrac{33+13+25}{100} = \dfrac{71}{100}$

e) $P(T \mid B) = \dfrac{13}{46}$

f) $P(B \mid T) = \dfrac{13}{38}$

g) $P(B \cap T) = \dfrac{13}{100} \neq 0 \Rightarrow$ not mutually exclusive.

h) $P(B \cap T) = \dfrac{13}{100} = 0.13; P(B) \cdot P(T) = \dfrac{38}{100} \cdot \dfrac{46}{100} = 0.1748$

$P(B \cap T) \neq P(B) \cdot P(T) \Rightarrow$ not independent.

Tree Diagrams

Tree diagrams are used to work out the probabilities for a sequence of events. To find the probability of a set of consecutive branches, each individual probability is multiplied. To find the probability of one of several branches that may take place, probabilities of each outcome are added.

Example:

The probability that it may be foggy today is 0.8. If it is foggy today, the probability that it will be foggy tomorrow is 0.6. If it is not foggy today, the probability that it will not be foggy tomorrow is 0.7.

Calculate the following probabilities:

a) The probability that both today and tomorrow will be foggy

b) The probability that neither today nor tomorrow is foggy

c) The probability that exactly one of today and tomorrow is foggy

d) The probability that it is foggy today given that it is foggy tomorrow

Solution:

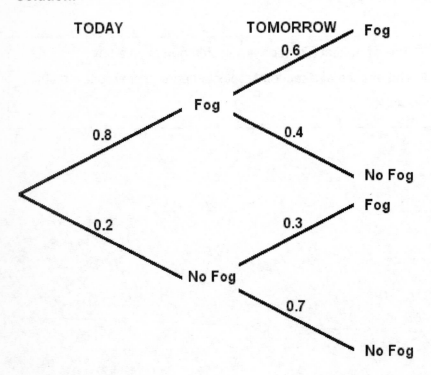

a) $0.8 \cdot 0.6 = 0.48$

b) $0.2 \cdot 0.7 = 0.14$

c) $0.8 \cdot 0.4 + 0.2 \cdot 0.3 = 0.38$

d) $\dfrac{0.8 \cdot 0.6}{0.8 \cdot 0.6 + 0.2 \cdot 0.3} = \dfrac{0.48}{0.54}$

Please note the following:

- Probabilities of branches coming out of one point add up to 1 since they generate all possibilities.
- The overall probabilities also add up to 1.
- The fact that it is foggy tomorrow is not independent of the fact that it is foggy today.

Example:

A bag contains 4 red, 6 green and 7 blue balls. Two balls are drawn at random from the bag without replacement. What is the probability that the balls

a) are both blue?

b) are same in color?

c) are different in color?

Solution:

There are two events (1st ball, 2nd ball) with three outcomes each time. So one should end up with nine branches. Please note that drawing two balls at the same time from the bag is the same as drawing two balls from the bag one at a time without replacement.

a) $\dfrac{7}{17} \cdot \dfrac{6}{16}$ b) $\dfrac{7 \cdot 6 + 6 \cdot 5 + 4 \cdot 3}{17 \cdot 16}$ c) $1 - \dfrac{7 \cdot 6 + 6 \cdot 5 + 4 \cdot 3}{17 \cdot 16}$

Binomial Probabilities

Example:

In a bag there are 9 red and 7 blue balls. If 5 balls are drawn from the bag one after another **without replacement**, what will be the probability that

a) all will be red

b) all will be blue

c) 3 of them will be red and 2 of them will be blue

Solution:

a) $\dfrac{9}{16} \cdot \dfrac{8}{15} \cdot \dfrac{7}{14} \cdot \dfrac{6}{13} \cdot \dfrac{5}{12}$ or alternatively $\dfrac{\binom{9}{5}}{\binom{16}{5}}$

b) $\dfrac{7}{16} \cdot \dfrac{6}{15} \cdot \dfrac{5}{14} \cdot \dfrac{4}{13} \cdot \dfrac{3}{12}$ or alternatively $\dfrac{\binom{7}{5}}{\binom{16}{5}}$

c) $\dfrac{9}{16} \cdot \dfrac{8}{15} \cdot \dfrac{7}{14} \cdot \dfrac{7}{13} \cdot \dfrac{6}{12} \cdot \dfrac{5!}{3!.2!}$ or alternatively $\dfrac{\dbinom{9}{3} \cdot \dbinom{7}{2}}{\dbinom{16}{5}}$

Example:

In a bag there are 9 red and 7 blue balls. If 5 balls are drawn from the bag one after another **with replacement**, what will be the probability that

a) all will be red

b) all will be blue

c) 3 of them will be red and 2 of them will be blue

Solution:

a) $\left(\dfrac{9}{16}\right)^5$ b) $\left(\dfrac{7}{16}\right)^5$ c) $\left(\dfrac{9}{16}\right)^3 \left(\dfrac{7}{16}\right)^2 \dfrac{5!}{3!.2!}$

Example:

A bag contains a large number of balls of whose 70% are red and 30% are blue. If 5 balls are drawn from the bag one after another (with or without replacement), what will be the probability that

a) all will be red

b) all will be blue

c) 3 of them will be red and 2 of them will be blue

Solution:

a) $(0.7)^5$ b) $(0.3)^5$ c) $(0.7)^3 (0.3)^2 \dfrac{5!}{3!.2!}$

Exercises

1. When a coin is tossed three times

    a. what is the probability of getting exactly 1 head?

    b. what is the probability of getting exactly 2 heads?

    c. what is the probability of getting exactly 3 heads?

    d. what is the probability of getting at least 1 head?

    e. what is the probability of getting at least 2 heads?

2. When a coin is tossed five times

    a. what is the probability of getting exactly 2 heads?

    b. what is the probability of getting at least 2 heads?

3. A die is rolled and a coin is tossed. What is the probability of getting a number greater than 2 on the die and a head on the coin?

4.   A card is drawn from a standard deck of cards. What is the probability that it is

   a. a king?

   b. a diamond?

   c. a red card?

   d. a face card?

   e. a red face card?

   f.   a diamond face card?

   g. a face card or a diamond

   h. a 2 or a king?

   i.   a 2 or a diamond

5.   Each of the seven identical cards in a bag is labeled with a different letter selected from the set {A, B, C, D, E, F, G}. Two cards are selected at random from this bag without replacement.

   a.   What is the probability that the cards are both vowels?

   b.   What is the probability that the cards are both consonants?

   c.   What is the probability that one of the cards is a vowel and the other one is a consonant?

6.   Two cards are drawn at random from a standard deck of cards one after another with replacement. What is the probability that

   a.   both of the cards are aces?

   b.   none of the cards is an ace?

   c.   one card is an ace and one is not?

7.   Two cards are drawn at random from a standard deck of cards one after another without replacement. What is the probability that

   a.   both of the cards are aces?

   b.   none of the cards is an ace?

   c.   one card is an ace and one is not?

8.   In a game, cards are dealt from standard well shuffled deck of 52 cards one at a time until a king comes up. What is the probability that

   a.   king appears on the first trial?

   b.   king appears on the second trial?

   c.   king appears on the third trial?

   d.   king appears on the first, second or the third trial?

9.   All distinct 4 – digit numbers are written on cards and placed in a bag and a card is drawn at random. What is the probability that the number on the card has

   a.   no repeating digit?

   b.   no successive digits that are the same?

10. If two fair dice are tossed, what is the probability that the sum of the numbers on the top faces will be 9?

11. If two fair dice are tossed. what is the probability of getting a sum of 6 given that both numbers are even?

12. A die is rolled. What is-the probability that the outcome is:

    a. an even number?

    b. a prime number?

    c. a 2?

13. A die is rolled. What is the probability of getting a number

    a. divisible by 2 or by 3?

    b. divisible by 2 and by 3?

14. A white and a black die are rolled. What is the probability that the sum of the numbers on the top faces of the dice is 7 or 8?

15. A pair of dice is rolled .What is the probability that the sum of the numbers on the top faces is 8 if it is already known that

    a. each number is an odd number?

    b. each number is an even number?

    c. the numbers are the same?

    d. the numbers are different?

16. Two fair dice are rolled. What is the probability that each of the numbers on the top faces are even given that their sum is 8?

17. A pair of dice is biased so that for each die the probability of getting a 6 is 1/4 and each of the other numbers is equally likely. (OPTIONAL)

    a. What is the probability of getting a sum of 12 when the dice are rolled?

    b. What is the probability of getting a sum of 10 when the dice are rolled?

18. Two marbles are drawn from a box containing 3 red, 4 green and 5 white marbles. What is the probability that they

    a. are both red?

    b. are both green?

    c. are both white?

    d. both have a color other than white?

    e. have different colors?

19. Two marbles are drawn one at a time without replacement from a box containing 3 red, 4 green and 5 white marbles.

    a. What is the probability that both are white?

b. What is the probability that both marbles are white given that the marbles are not red?

c. What is the probability that one marble is red and one marble is green?

d. What is the probability that one marble is red and one marble is green given that the first marble is green?

20. Three marbles are drawn at once from a box containing 7 white and 8 red marbles. What is the probability of getting

a. 3 red marbles?

b. 3 white marbles?

c. marbles of the same color?

d. a red marble followed by two white marbles?

e. one red and two white marbles?

21. Three marbles are drawn one after another without replacement from a box containing 7 white and 8 red marbles. What is the probability of getting

a. 3 red marbles?

b. 3 white marbles?

c. marbles of the same color?

d. a red marble followed by two white marbles?

e. one red and two white marbles?

22. Three marbles are drawn one after another with replacement from a box containing 7 white and 8 red marbles. What is the probability of getting

a. 3 red marbles?

b. 3 white marbles?

c. marbles of the same color?

d. a red marble followed by two white marbles?

e. one red and two white marbles?

23. There are n blue and 35 red marbles in a bag. If the probability of taking a blue marble from the bag is that sack is 5/12 then what is n?

24. A bag contains 4 red and 8 white marbles, and a second bag contains 5 red and 10 white marbles. If a marble is drawn from each bag what is the probability that

a. both are red?

b. both are white?

c. one is red and one is white?

25. 6 marbles are drawn at random from a bag containing 7 red, 6 blue, 5 green marbles. What is the probability of getting

a. exactly 3 red marbles?

    b. 2 red, 3 blue, 1 green marble in the given order?

    c. 2 red, 3 blue, 1 green marble in any order?

26.   A box contains 300 batteries of which 20 are defective. If a random sample of 5 batteries selected, what is the probability that at least one of them is defective?

27.   Three light bulbs are selected from a box that contains 20 bulbs of which 20% are defective. What is the probability that:

    a. none of them are defective?

    b. exactly one of them is defective?

    c. exactly two of them are defective?

    d. at least one of them is defective?

28.   Three light bulbs are selected from a box that contains a large number of bulbs of which 20% are defective. What is the probability that:

    a. none of them are defective?

    b. exactly one of them is defective?

    c. exactly two of them are defective?

    d. at least one of them is defective?

29.   Box A contains 10 items of which 4 are defective. Box B contains 9 items of which 2 are defective. An item is drawn at random from each box. What is the probability that

    a. both of the items are non-defective?

    b. exactly one of the items is defective?

    c. exactly one of the items are defective given that the defective one comes from box A?

    d. exactly one of the items are defective given that the defective one comes from box B?

30.   The table shows a group of high school students by gender and class.

	Freshmen	Sophomores	Juniors	Seniors
Males	9	7	13	4
Females	12	10	8	6

If a student is selected at random from this group, what is the probability that the student is

    a. a freshman or a junior

    b. a male or a senior

    c. a male sophomore or a female junior

31. Each of the 80 students in the senior class of **RUSH** Academy studies one foreign language and one branch of science. The students' choices are shown in the partially completed table given below:

	Physics	Chemistry	Biology	Total
French	12			52
Spanish		10		
Total	16		24	

   a. Find the probability that a randomly chosen student

      i. studies Physics.

      ii. studies Spanish.

      iii. studies Physics and Spanish

      iv. studies Physics or Spanish

      v. studies Physics given that he studies Spanish

      vi. studies Spanish given that he studies Physics

   b. Are the events of studying Physics and studying Spanish independent?

   c. Are the events of studying Physics and studying Spanish mutually exclusive?

32. Set A contains all four digit numbers written by interchanging the digits of the number 3210. If a number selected at random from this set, what is the probability that the number selected is even?

33. Set A contains all distinct three digit integers. If an integer is randomly selected from set A what is the probability that

   a.   its hundreds digit is 5

   b.   at least one of its digits is 5

   c.   none of its digits is 5

   d.   it is divisible by 5

34. During a flu outbreak, 40% of the students in a school have the flu. Of the students with the flu, 80% of the students have high fever. However, 12% of the students without the flu have a high fever.

   a.   What is the probability that a randomly selected student has the flu?

   b.   What is the probability that a randomly selected student has high fever?

   c.   If a student selected at random is given to have high fever, what is the probability he has the flu?

   d.   If a student selected at random is given to have the flu, what is the probability he has high fever?

35. A single player game is played in such a way that the player tosses a coin until it comes up heads. What is the probability that the game will be over at an even numbered trial; that is at the 2nd, 4th, 6th trial, etc?

36. A single player game is played in such a way that the player tosses a coin until it comes up heads. What is the probability that the game will be over at an odd numbered trial; that is at the 1st, 3rd, 5th trial, etc?

2.4 STATISTICS

A **population** is a group of data for which statistics are calculated.

A **sample** is a subgroup drawn from the population. Sample statistics (such as the mean) can be used to estimate the statistics of the population.

Discrete data are restricted to certain values that are often integers whereas **continuous data** can take any values.

Frequency is the number of times a particular value occurs.

Mean, Median and Mode

These measures can be used as a representative of the entire group of numbers. The most commonly used measures are as follows:

- The **mean** or the **average** of n numbers is the sum of the numbers divided by n:

Mean = $\bar{x} = \dfrac{x_1 + x_2 + ... + x_n}{n}$

- The **median** of n numbers is the middle number when the numbers are written in increasing or decreasing order. If n is even, the median is the average of the two middle numbers.

- The **mode** of n numbers is the number that is most frequent. If two numbers tie for the most frequent occurance, the group has two modes and it is called **bimodal**.

- The **range** of a group of data is the difference between the maximum and the minimum values in this group.

Variance and Standard Deviation

These quantities are the **measures of dispersion**, that are different from the mean of the set. These two measures are called the **variance** (σ^2) of the set and the **standard deviation** (σ) of the set. If the data is closely packed about the mean then σ will be small and if the data is loosely packed about the mean then σ will be large. Consider a group of numbers x_1, x_2,...., x_n with a mean of $\bar{x}$. The **variance** of the set is given by $\sigma^2 = \dfrac{(x_1 - \bar{x})^2 + (x_2 - \bar{x})^2 + ... + (x_n - \bar{x})^2}{n}$ where the **standard deviation** of the set is σ.

Quartiles

The **lower quartile** is the median of the numbers that occur before the median and the **upper quartile** is the median of the numbers that occur after the median. A cruder measure of dispersion is the interquartile range which is calculated by subtracting the lower quartile from the upper quartile.

TI Calculator Usage

The TI 83 – 84 family of graphing calculators is very useful in studying the statistics of the group of data. However before performing any statistical calculations, it may be essential to clear any previous list entries. **MEMory ClrAllLists** option will accomplish this task. The data may be given in two ways, in raw format or in data-frequency format. When data is given in raw format, all data is entered in the list named L_1 using the **STAT EDIT** option. When data is given in data-frequency format, the data is entered in the list named L_1 and the individual frequencies are entered in the list named L_2, again using the **STAT EDIT** option. When data is in raw format, the command of **1-Var Stats** or **1-Var Stats** L_1 will calculate the statistics of the data, these commands can be accessed through the **STAT CALC** option. When data is in data-frequency format, the command of **1-Var Stats** L_1, L_2 must be used to calculate the statistics of the data. The calculated statistics and their meanings are as follows:

$\bar{x}$: The arithmetic mean of the data.

$\sum x$: Sum of all individual entries in the data set.

$\sum x^2$: Sum of the squares of all individual entries in the data set.

Sx: The sample standard deviation.

σx: The population standard deviation.

n: number of data

minX: Minimum entry in the data set.

Q_1: Lower Quartile

Med: Median

Q_3: Upper Quartile

MaxX: Maximum entry in the data set.

Example:

Find the statistics of the following data:1, 3, 5, 6, 3, 6, 6.

Solution:

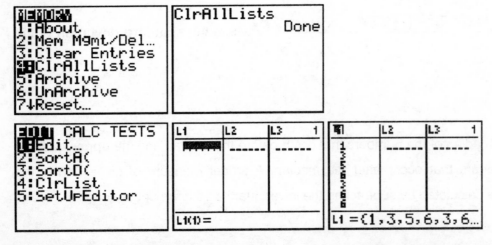

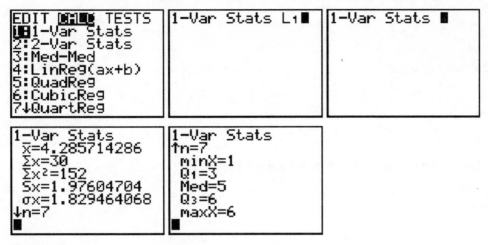

Example:

Find the statistics of the following data:

Data	1	3	5	6
Frequency	1	2	1	3

Solution:

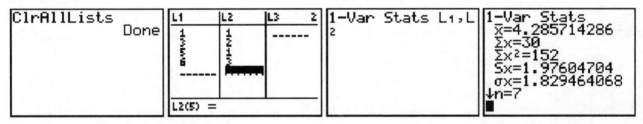

Example:

100 people are staying at a hotel: 56 are men and 44 women. The mean have a mean height of 1.78 meters and the women have a mean height of 1.65 meters. Find the mean height of the 100 people correct to the nearest tenth of a meter.

Solution:

Mean Height = $\dfrac{56 \cdot 1.78 + 44 \cdot 1.65}{100} = 172.3$

Example:

Score	10	15	20	25	30
Number of studentse	2	3	5	m	4

The table shows the scores of students in a competition. The mean score is 21.75; find the value of m.

Solution:

$$\frac{10 \cdot 2 + 15 \cdot 3 + 20 \cdot 5 + 25 \cdot m + 30 \cdot 4}{2 + 3 + 5 + m + 4} = 21.75 \Rightarrow m = 6$$

Example:

1, 1, 2, 3, 3

Find mean, variance and standard deviation

Solution:

Step 1: find mean = $\dfrac{1+1+2+3+3}{5} = \dfrac{10}{5} = 2$

Step 2: Find deviation from the mean (subtract mean from each data)

1	1	2	3	3
-2	-2	-2	-2	-2
-1	-1	0	+1	+1

Step 3. Square the differences and sum them up: 1+1+0+1+1= 4

Step 4: Divide the sum by the number of terms and you get **variance**: $\dfrac{4}{5} = 0.8 = \sigma^2$

Step 5: Find the square root of the result and you get the standard deviation= $\sqrt{0.8} = 0.89 = \sigma$

Example:

Data	Frequency
0	2
1	3
2	5
3	8
4	2

Find mode, median, mean, range, frequency of each data for the group of data given above.

Solution:

mode = 3

median = $\dfrac{2+3}{2} = 2.5$

mean = $\dfrac{0 \cdot 2 + 1 \cdot 3 + 2 \cdot 5 + 3 \cdot 8 + 4 \cdot 2}{20} = \dfrac{45}{20} = 2.25$

range = max – min = 4 – 0=4

frequency of 0 = 2; frequency of 1 = 3; frequency of 2 = 5; frequency of 3 = 8; frequency of 4 = 2

Exercises

1. Find all statistics of the following groups of data

   a. 1, 1, 2, 4, 6, 6, 6, 7, 7, 8, 9, 10, 10, 12, 15, 18

   b. 24, 26, 27, 27, 28, 32, 30, 33

Waiting time (min)	Number of clients
0 – 10	7
10 – 20	12
20 – 30	18
30 – 40	15
40 – 50	8

2. A survey is conducted to explore the waiting times for 60 clients in a post office whose results are given in the table above. Estimate the mode, median, mean, range, standard deviation, lower and upper quartiles, and the interquartile range (Hint: use the mid interval values to represent the data in each interval.)

3. Given that a is a positive number greater than 1, how will the quantities, mode, median, mean, range, standard deviation, and variance be altered when the followings are applied to each term of a group of data separately?

   a. Each term is increased by a positive number a.

   b. Each term is decreased by a positive number a.

   c. Each term is multiplied by a positive number a.

   d. Each term is divided by a positive number a.

4. The mean μ of a group of data is calculated and turns out to be nonzero. If μ is subtracted from each term, what will be the new mean?

5. The standard deviation σ of a group of data is calculated and turns out to be a nonzero number other than 1. If each term in the group is divided by σ, what will be the new standard deviation?

6. In order to convert a certain group of data to a standard normal distribution whose mean and standard deviation are 0 and 1 respectively, what procedure must be followed?

7. The daily temperatures, in degrees Fahrenheit, for 10 days in July were 61, 64, 62, 63, 63, 75, 68, 63, 75, and 79.

   a. Find the mean, median, and mode for the temperatures.

   b. If each day had been 7 degrees cooler, what would be the mean, median, and mode for those 10 data?

8. The ages, in years, of the workers in a small company are 21, 38, 21, 28, 27, 31, 43, and 24.

   a. Find the mean, median, mode, range and standard deviation for the 8 ages.

   b. If each of the employees had been 5 years older, what would have been the range and standard deviation of their ages?

Data (x)	Frequency (f)
0	2
1	6
2	3
3	2
4	4

9. Find the mean, median, mode, range, and standard deviation for x, given the frequency distribution above.

10. Which of the following sets of numbers has the least and the greatest standard deviation?

    a. 1005, 1007, 1009

    b. 100, 101, 102

    c. 0.01, 0.02, 0.03

    d. 10000, 10000, 10000

    e. 5, 9, 17

Let no one enter who does not know geometry.

Inscription on Plato's door at the Academy in Athens.

CHAPTER 3 – Geometry

Basics

Locus

Angles

Polygons

Triangles

Right Triangles

Congruence

Similarity

Quadrilaterals

Circles

Three-Dimensional Geometry

Inscribed Figures Two Dimensions

Inscribed Figures In Three Dimensions

Rotations

3.1 BASICS

Points, Lines, Rays, Half Lines, Line Segments, Angles, Planes And Space

Line *l* or AB

Half line]AB

Ray [AB

Line segment]AB[or (AB)

Line segment [AB]

Line segment [AB[or [AB)

Line segment]AB] or (AB]

1. A point has neither width nor thickness, only position.

2. A line is a set of points that straightly continues in both directions, with no thickness.

3. A plane is a set of points that continues infinitely in all directions and has no thickness or depth.

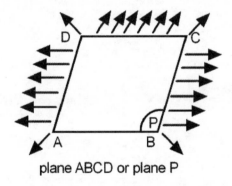

plane ABCD or plane P

4. Two lines are parallel if they lie in the same plane and do not intersect.

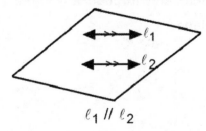

$\ell_1 \; // \; \ell_2$

5.   The distance between two parallel lines is always constant.

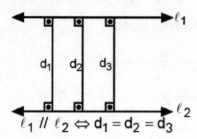

6.   A line contains at least two points; a plane contains at least three points which are not all in one line; space contains at least four points which are not all in one plane. Two distinct points determine a line; three distinct non collinear points determine a plane and four distinct non coplanar points determine a space.

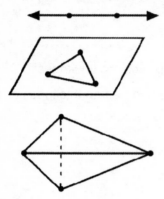

7.   Through any two points there is exactly one line.

8.   Through any three points there is at least one plane, and through any three points which are not in the same line, there is exactly one plane.

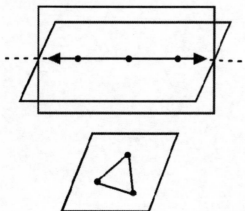

9.   If two points are in a plane, then the line that contains those points is in the same plane as well.

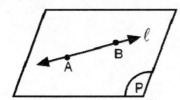

If $A \in P$ and $B \in P$ then $AB = \ell \in P$

10.   The intersection of two distinct non parallel planes is a line.

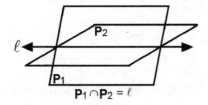

$P_1 \cap P_2 = \ell$

11.   The intersection of two distinct coplanar lines is a point.

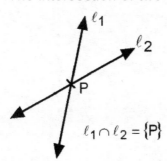

$\ell_1 \cap \ell_2 = \{P\}$

12.   Exactly one plane contains both of a line and a point which is not on that line.

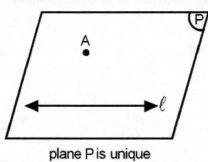

plane P is unique

13.   Exactly one plane contains both of two intersecting lines.

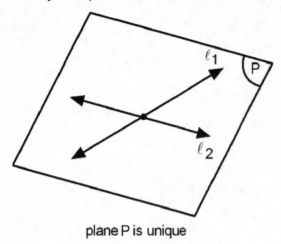

plane P is unique

14.   If two parallel planes are intersected by a third plane, then the resulting lines of intersection are parallel.

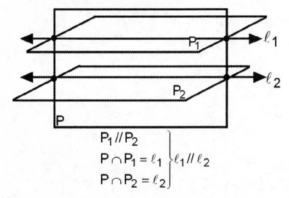

$$\left.\begin{array}{l} P_1 \mathbin{/\mkern-5mu/} P_2 \\ P \cap P_1 = \ell_1 \\ P \cap P_2 = \ell_2 \end{array}\right\} \ell_1 \mathbin{/\mkern-5mu/} \ell_2$$

15.   If a transversal is perpendicular to a line, then the transversal is perpendicular to any line contained within the same plane and parallel to the given line. In a plane two or more lines perpendicular to the same line are parallel.

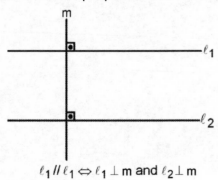

$$\ell_1 \mathbin{/\mkern-5mu/} \ell_1 \Leftrightarrow \ell_1 \perp m \text{ and } \ell_2 \perp m$$

16. There is exactly one line parallel to a given line through a point outside the line.

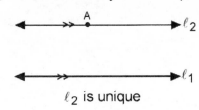

ℓ_2 is unique

17. There is exactly one line perpendicular to a given line through a point outside the line,

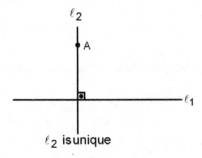

ℓ_2 is unique

18. Two lines parallel to a third line are parallel to each other.

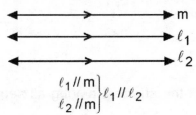

$\left.\begin{array}{c} \ell_1 /\!/ m \\ \ell_2 /\!/ m \end{array}\right\} \ell_1 /\!/ \ell_2$

19. If a point lies on the perpendicular bisector of a line segment, then the distances from the point to the endpoints of the segment are equal. If a point is equidistant from the endpoints of a line segment, then the point lies on the perpendicular bisector of this segment.

20. If three parallel lines generate equal segments on one transversal, then they generate equal segments on every transversal.

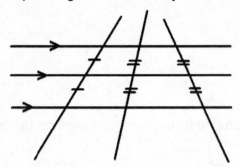

21. The perpendicular segment from a point to a line is the shortest among all segments from the point to the line.

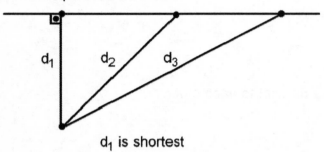

d_1 is shortest

22. The perpendicular segment from a point to a plane is the shortest among all segments from the point to the plane.

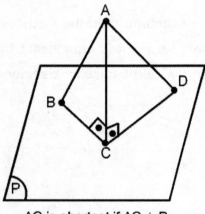

AC is shortest if AC $\perp$ P

3.2 LOCUS

Locus is the geometric figure that results when all points that satisfy a certain condition are joined. The phrases of "locus of points" and "set of points" can be used interchangeably (locus: singular, loci: plural).

Two Dimensional Loci

- The locus of points equidistant from a given point in a plane is the circle whose center is the given point.

- The locus of points equidistant from a given line in a plane consists of two parallel lines that have the given line in between.

_____

_____

_____

- The locus of points equidistant from two parallel lines in a plane is the line that is equally spaced between these two lines.

_____

_____

_____

- The locus of points equidistant from two intersecting lines in a plane consists of the bisectors of the vertical angles formed by these lines.

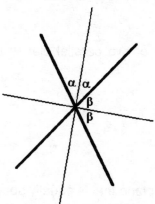

- The locus of points equidistant from two given points in a plane is the perpendicular bisector of the segment that joins these two points.

Conic Sections in Two Dimensions

- The locus of points at a distance r from a given point P in a plane is the circle whose center is at P and whose radius is r.

- The locus of points in a plane, whose distances from two fixed points F1 and F2 sums up to 2A is the ellipse whose foci are at F1 and F2 having a major axis of length 2A.

- The locus of points in a plane, whose distances from two fixed points F1 and F2 have a constant difference of 2A is the hyperbola whose foci are at F1 and F2 having a transverse axis of length 2A.

- The locus of points in a plane, equidistant from a given point P and a line d is the parabola whose focus is at P and whose directrix is d.

Three Dimensional Loci

- The locus of points equidistant from a given point in space is the sphere whose center is the given point.

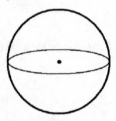

- The locus of points equidistant from a given plane in space consists of two parallel planes that have the given plane in between.

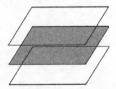

- The locus of points equidistant from two parallel planes in space is the plane that is equally spaced between these two planes.

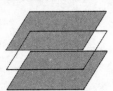

- The locus of points equidistant from two given points in space is the plane that perpendicularly bisects the segment that joins these two points.

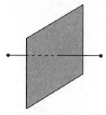

- The locus of points equidistant from a given line in space consists of a hollow cylinedrical surface (a cylindrical tube) whose axis of symmetry is the given line.

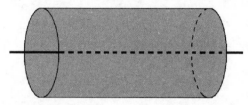

Exercises

1. What is the locus of points at a distance of 8 inches from a plane and at a distance of 10 inches from a point on this plane?

2. What is the locus of points at a distance of 3 inches from a plane and at a distance of 4 inches from a point 5 feet above this plane?

3. What is the locus of points at a distance of 5 inches from each of two points that 6 inches apart in space?

4. What is the locus of points equidistant from two points that are 6 inches apart in space?

5. What is the locus of points at a distance of 8 inches from a line and at a distance of 10 inches from a point on this line?

6. What is the locus of points in space at a distance of 5 inches from a line segment that is 5 inches long?

3.3 ANGLES

1.   A right angle has the degree measure of 90°.

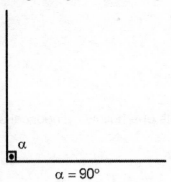

$$\alpha = 90°$$

2.   An obtuse angle has a measure that is greater than 90° and less than 90°.

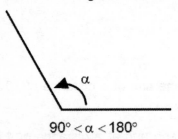

$$90° < \alpha < 180°$$

3.   An acute angle has a measure less than 90°.

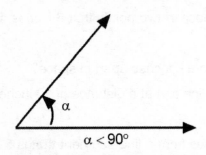

$$\alpha < 90°$$

4.   If two parallel lines are cut by a transversal, then the resulting corresponding angles are congruent.

5.   Two angles are complementary if their measures add up to 90°.

6.   Two angles are supplementary if their measures add up to 180°.

7.   The supplements of congruent angles (or of the same angle) are also congruent.

$$\left.\begin{array}{r}\hat{x}+\hat{y}=180°\\ \hat{x}+\hat{z}=180°\end{array}\right\}\ \hat{y}=\hat{z}$$

The complements of congruent angles (or of the same angle) are also congruent.

$$\left.\begin{array}{r}\hat{x}+\hat{y}=90°\\ \hat{x}+z=90°\end{array}\right\}\ \hat{y}=\hat{z}$$

8.   Vertical angles are congruent.

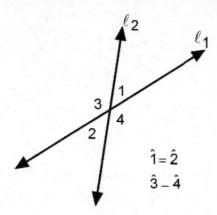

$$\hat{1} = \hat{2}$$
$$\hat{3} = \hat{4}$$

9. If two lines are perpendicular, then they generate congruent adjacent angles. If two lines generate congruent adjacent angles, then the lines are perpendicular.

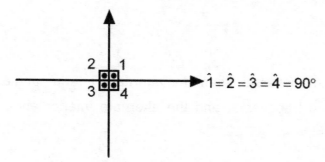

$$\hat{1} = \hat{2} = \hat{3} = \hat{4} = 90°$$

10. If the exterior sides of two adjacent acute angles are perpendicular to each other, then the angles are complementary.

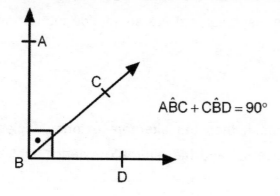

$$A\hat{B}C + C\hat{B}D = 90°$$

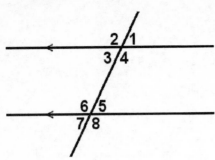

11. If two parallel lines are cut by a transversal, then the corresponding angles are congruent. If two lines are cut by a transversal and the corresponding angles are congruent, then the lines are parallel.

$$\hat{1} = \hat{5}$$
$$\hat{2} = \hat{6}$$
$$\hat{3} = \hat{7}$$
$$\hat{4} = \hat{8}$$

12. If two parallel lines are cut by a transversal, then the alternate interior angles are congruent. If two lines are cut by a transversal and the alternate interior angles are congruent, then the lines are parallel.

$$\hat{3} = \hat{5}$$
$$\hat{4} = \hat{6}$$

13. If two parallel lines are cut by a transversal, then the same-side interior angles are supplementary. If two lines are cut by a transversal and the same-side interior angles are supplementary, then the lines are parallel.

$$\hat{4} + \hat{5} = 180°$$
$$\hat{3} + \hat{6} = 180°$$

14. If two parallel lines are cut by a transversal, then the alternate exterior angles are congruent. If two lines are cut by a transversal and the alternate exterior angles are congruent, then the lines are parallel.

$$\hat{1} = \hat{7}$$
$$\hat{2} = \hat{8}$$

15. If two parallel lines are cut by a transversal, then the same-side exterior angles are supplementary. If two lines are cut by a transversal and the same-side exterior angles are supplementary, then the lines are parallel.

$$\hat{1} + \hat{8} = 180°$$
$$\hat{2} + \hat{7} = 180°$$

16.   If a point lies on the bisector of an angle, then the point is equidistant from the sides of the angle. If a point is equidistant from the sides of an angle, then the point lies on the bisector of the angle.

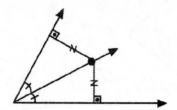

3.4 POLYGONS

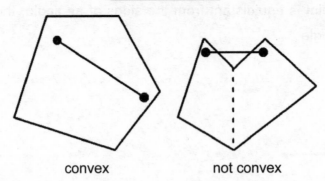

convex   not convex

1. Sum of the measures of the interior angles of a convex polygon is $(n-2) \cdot 180°$, where n is the number of sides.

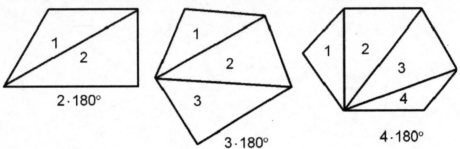

$2 \cdot 180°$ $3 \cdot 180°$ $4 \cdot 180°$

2. Sum of the measures of the exterior angles of a convex polygon is $360°$.

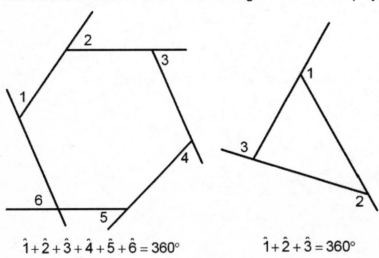

$\hat{1} + \hat{2} + \hat{3} + \hat{4} + \hat{5} + \hat{6} = 360°$ $\hat{1} + \hat{2} + \hat{3} = 360°$

3. Area of a regular polygon equals half the product of length of the apothem and the perimeter. ($A = \dfrac{1}{2} aP$; a is length of the apothem and P is the perimeter of the polygon)

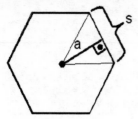

Area $= \dfrac{1}{2} \cdot a \cdot (6s)$

Where $6s =$ perimeter

3.5 TRIANGLES

1. Sum of the measures of the angles of a triangle is 180°.

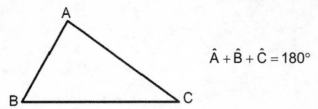

$$\hat{A} + \hat{B} + \hat{C} = 180°$$

2. Measure of an exterior angle of a triangle is equal to the sum of the measures of its remote interior angles.

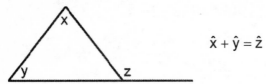

$$\hat{x} + \hat{y} = \hat{z}$$

3. The area A of any triangle is related to the length, a, of any base and the altitude, h_a, to that base by A= $\frac{1}{2}$ a h_a.

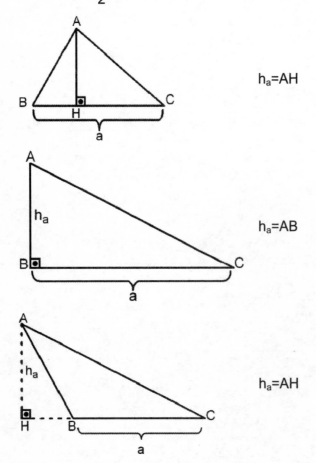

$h_a = AH$

$h_a = AB$

$h_a = AH$

4. If A and B are the midpoints of the sides of a triangle, then AB = $\frac{1}{2}$ CD and AB || CD. AB is also

    called the midbase.

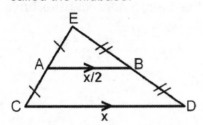

If A & B are midpoints of EC and ED respectively then

AB || CD and

$|CD| = x$

$|AB| = \dfrac{x}{2}$

5. A line containing the midpoint of one side of a triangle being parallel to another side
    passes through the midpoint of the third side.

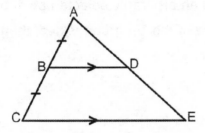

AB = BC and BD // CE $\Rightarrow$ AD = DE

6. If two sides of a triangle are congruent, then the angles opposite those sides are
    congruent or if two angles of a triangle are congruent, then the sides opposite those
    angles are congruent.

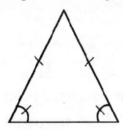

7. The bisector of the vertex angle of an isosceles triangle is perpendicular to the base at
    its midpoint.

8.   If the bisector of the vertex angle of a triangle is perpendicular to the base, the triangle is isosceles. If the bisector of the vertex angle of a triangle intersects the base at its midpoint, the triangle is isosceles. If the altitude to the base intersects the base at its midpoint, the triangle is isosceles.

9.   In an isosceles triangle ABC, C is the vertex and P is an arbitrarily selected point on the base. If segments PQ and PR are each parallel to one of the congruent sides, then their lengths sum up to the length of a congruent side.

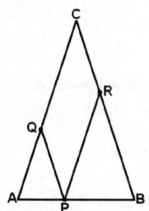

PQ + PR = CA = CB

10.   In an isosceles triangle ABC, C is the vertex and P is an arbitrarily selected point on the base. If segments PQ and PR are each perpendicular to one of the congruent sides, then their lengths sum up to the length of an altitude to a congruent side.

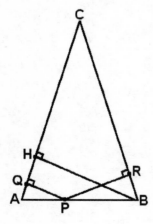

$PQ + PR = h_a = h_b$

11. An equiangular triangle is equilateral and an equilateral triangle is equiangular. Each angle of an equiangular triangle has measures 60°. Each angle of an equilateral triangle measures 60°.

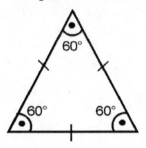

12. If s is the length of one side of an equilateral triangle and h is the length of the length of each side then the following equalities hold:

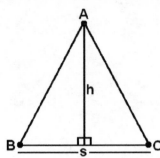

$$\text{Area of } \overset{\Delta}{ABC} = \frac{s^2\sqrt{3}}{4}$$

$$h = \frac{s\sqrt{3}}{2}$$

13. In an equilateral triangle ABC, P is an arbitrarily selected point inside the triangle. If segments PD, PE and PF are each parallel to one side of the triangle, then their lengths sum up to the length one of the sides.

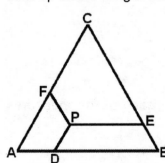

$$PD + PE + PF = a = b = c$$

14. In an equilateral triangle ABC, P is an arbitrarily selected point inside the triangle. If segments PD, PE and PF are each perpendicular to one side of the triangle, then their lengths sum up to the length an altitude.

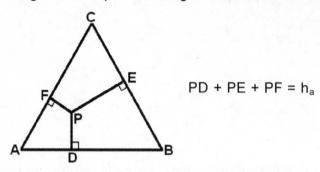

$PD + PE + PF = h_a$

15. If two angles of one triangle are congruent to two angles of another triangle, then the third angles are congruent.

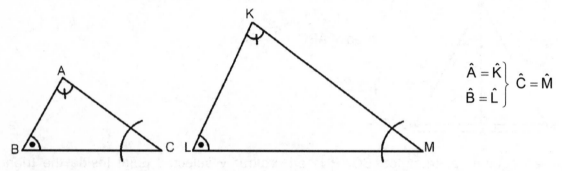

$$\left. \begin{array}{c} \hat{A} = \hat{K} \\ \hat{B} = \hat{L} \end{array} \right\} \hat{C} = \hat{M}$$

16. In a triangle, there can be at most one right angle or obtuse angle.

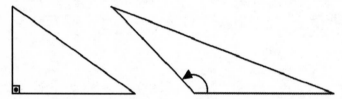

17. Measure of an exterior angle of a triangle is greater than each of the measures of the remote interior angles.

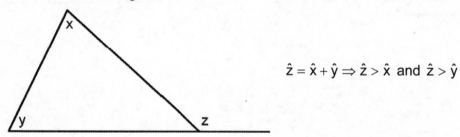

$$\hat{z} = \hat{x} + \hat{y} \Rightarrow \hat{z} > \hat{x} \text{ and } \hat{z} > \hat{y}$$

18.   If one side of a triangle is longer than a second side, then the angle opposite the first side is greater than the angle opposite the second side; if one angle of a triangle is greater than a second angle, then the side opposite the first angle is longer than the side opposite the second angle.

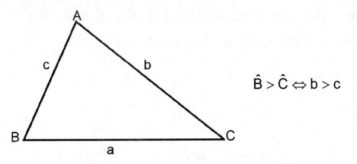

$$\hat{B} > \hat{C} \Leftrightarrow b > c$$

19.   The same relation exists between the sides and the angles of a triangle.

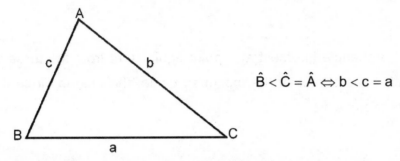

$$\hat{B} < \hat{C} = \hat{A} \Leftrightarrow b < c = a$$

20.   Sum of the lengths of any two sides of a triangle is greater than the length of the third side. Difference of the lengths of any two sides of a triangle is less than the lengths of the third side. Sum of the lengths of the two shortest sides of a triangle must exceed the longest side for the triangle to be realized.

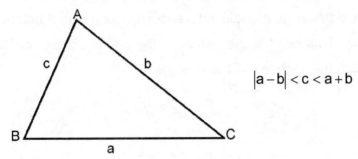

$$\left| a - b \right| < c < a + b$$

21.   If two sides of one triangle are congruent to two sides of another triangle, but the included angle in the first triangle is larger than the included angle in the second one, then the third side of the first triangle is longer than the third side of the second triangle. If two sides of one triangle are congruent to two sides of another triangle, but the third side of the first triangle is longer than the third side of the second; then the included angle in the first triangle is larger than the included angle in the second.

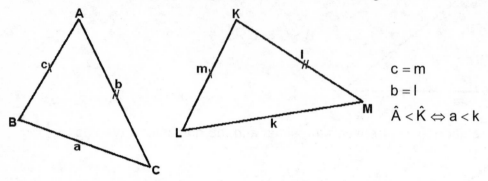

$$c = m$$
$$b = l$$
$$\hat{A} < \hat{K} \Leftrightarrow a < k$$

22.   Bisectors of the angles of a triangle intersect at a point equidistant from the three sides of the triangle. This point is the center of the inscribed circle, the unique circle that is tangent to all sides of this triangle.

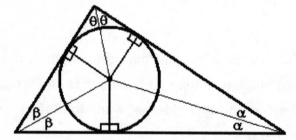

23.   Perpendicular bisectors of the sides of a triangle intersect at a point equidistant from the three vertices of the triangle. This point is the center of the circumscribed circle, the unique circle that passes through the vertices of the triangle.

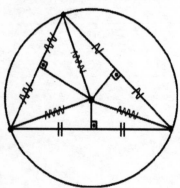

24. Altitudes of a triangle intersect at a unique point.

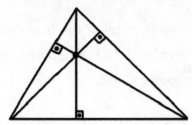

25. Medians of a triangle intersect at a unique point called the center of gravity or the centroid. The distance from the centroid to a vertex is two thirds of the length of the corresponding median length.

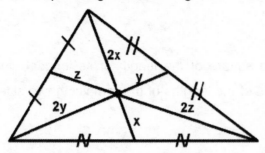

3.6 RIGHT TRIANGLES

1.   Midpoint of the hypotenuse of a right triangle is equidistant from all of the three vertices of this triangle (the rule of the "magnificent three"). The median to the hypotenuse of a right triangle has a length that is half the length of the hypotenuse.

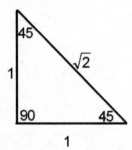

2.   A triangle is a right triangle if and only if the square of the length of its longest side (the hypotenuse) is equal to the sum of the squares of the lengths of the remaining two sides (the legs). This is called the Pythagorean theorem.

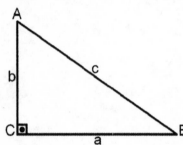

$$\hat{C} = 90° \Leftrightarrow a^2 + b^2 = c^2$$

3.   The $45° - 45° - 90°$ triangle.

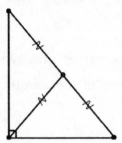

4.   The 30° - 60° - 90° triangle.

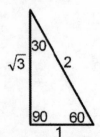

5.   Triangles with sides having the lengths of 3-4-5, 5-12-13, 8-15-17 and 7-24-25 are right triangles and so are triangles with sides that are enlarged in the same proportion.

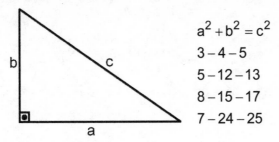

$$a^2 + b^2 = c^2$$
$$3 - 4 - 5$$
$$5 - 12 - 13$$
$$8 - 15 - 17$$
$$7 - 24 - 25$$

6.   Euclid's Relations:

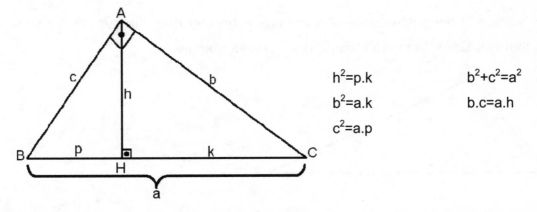

$h^2 = p \cdot k$ $b^2 + c^2 = a^2$

$b^2 = a \cdot k$ $b \cdot c = a \cdot h$

$c^2 = a \cdot p$

7.   Acute angles of a right triangle are complementary.

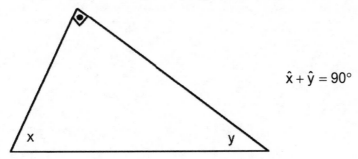

$$\hat{x} + \hat{y} = 90°$$

8.   If the altitude is drawn to the hypotenuse of a right triangle, then the two triangles generated are similar to the original triangle and to each other.

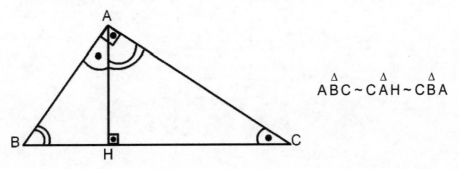

$$\overset{\Delta}{ABC} \sim \overset{\Delta}{CAH} \sim \overset{\Delta}{CBA}$$

9.   If the square of the longest side of a triangle is less than the sum of the squares of the other two sides, then the triangle is an acute triangle.

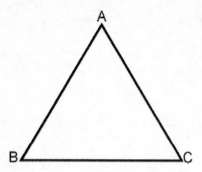

$$\hat{A} < 90° \Leftrightarrow a^2 < b^2 + c^2$$

10.   If the square of the longest side of a triangle is greater than the sum of the squares of the other two sides, then the triangle is an obtuse triangle.

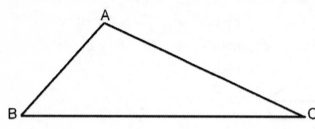

$$\hat{A} > 90° \Leftrightarrow a^2 > b^2 + c^2$$

3.7 CONGRUENCE

1. If two triangles are congruent then all pairs of corresponding parts of the triangles are also congruent. Congruent triangles are identical in every aspect (CPCT: **C**orresponding **P**arts of **C**ongruent **T**riangles).

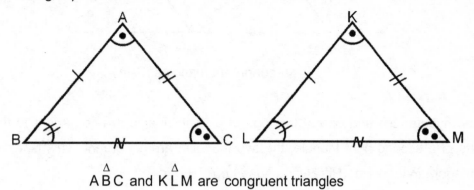

$\overset{\Delta}{ABC}$ and $\overset{\Delta}{KLM}$ are congruent triangles

2. If two sides and the angle included in one triangle are each congruent to the corresponding parts of a second triangle, the triangles are congruent. (SAS: **S**ide **A**ngle **S**ide)

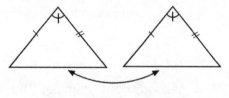

congruent triangles (SAS)

3. If two angles and the included side in one triangle are each congruent to the corresponding parts of a second triangle, the triangles are congruent. (ASA: **A**ngle **S**ide **A**ngle)

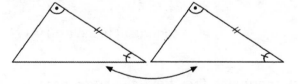

congruent triangles (ASA)

4. If the three sides of one triangle are each congruent to the corresponding sides of a second triangle, then the triangles are congruent. (SSS: **S**ide **S**ide **S**ide)

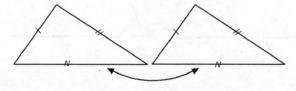

congruent triangles (SSS)

5. If two angles and a side opposite one of the angles are each congruent to the corresponding parts of a second triangle, the triangles are congruent. This is a direct result of the ASA postulate. (SAA: **S**ide **A**ngle **A**ngle)

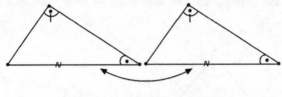

congruent triangles (SAA)

6. If the hypotenuse and one of the legs of a right triangle are congruent to the corresponding parts of a second right triangle, the two triangles are congruent. This is a direct result of the Pythagorean theorem. (HL: **H**ypotenuse **L**eg)

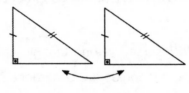

congruent triangles (HL)

7. If the hypotenuse and one of the acute angles of a right triangle are congruent to the corresponding parts of a second right triangle, the two triangles are congruent. (HA: **H**ypotenuse **A**ngle)

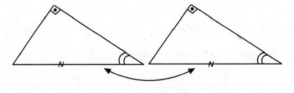

congruent triangles (HA)

8. If two figures are congruent, they have the same area.

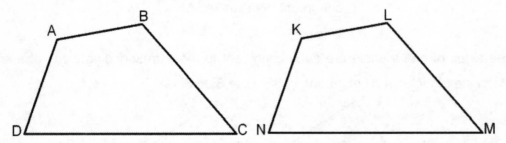

3.8 SIMILARITY

1. If the lengths of all three pairs of corresponding sides are proportional then the triangles are similar (**SSS**: **S**ide **S**ide **S**ide).

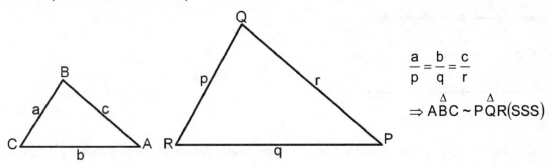

$$\frac{a}{p} = \frac{b}{q} = \frac{c}{r}$$

$$\Rightarrow \overset{\triangle}{ABC} \sim \overset{\triangle}{PQR}(SSS)$$

2. If any two pairs of corresponding angles are congruent then the triangles are similar (**AA**: **A**ngle **A**ngle or **AAA**: **A**ngle **A**ngle **A**ngle).

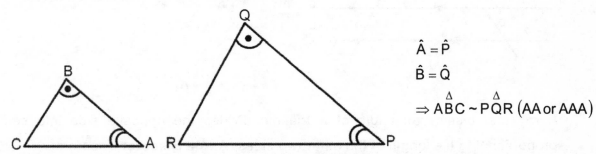

$$\hat{A} = \hat{P}$$
$$\hat{B} = \hat{Q}$$

$$\Rightarrow \overset{\triangle}{ABC} \sim \overset{\triangle}{PQR} \left(AA\, or\, AAA\right)$$

3. If two pairs of corresponding sides are proportional and their included angles are congruent then the triangles are similar (**SAS**: **S**ide **A**ngle **S**ide).

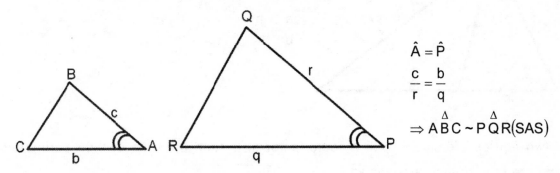

$$\hat{A} = \hat{P}$$
$$\frac{c}{r} = \frac{b}{q}$$

$$\Rightarrow \overset{\triangle}{ABC} \sim \overset{\triangle}{PQR}(SAS)$$

4. If two triangles are similar, then the pairs of corresponding sides, altitudes, medians, angle bisectors, radii of inscribed circles, radii of circumscribed circles, and the sine of the corresponding angles are proportional with the same scale factor.

5. A line parallel to one side of a triangle intersecting the other two sides divides those sides proportionally (**Thales** theorem).

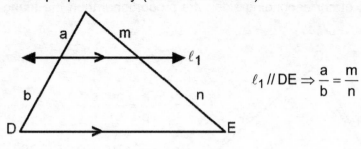

$$\ell_1 \text{ // } DE \Rightarrow \frac{a}{b} = \frac{m}{n}$$

Three parallel lines that intersect two transversals divide the transversals proportionally.

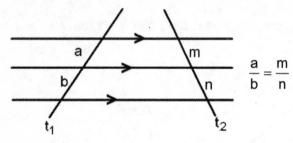

$$\frac{a}{b} = \frac{m}{n}$$

6. A ray that bisects an angle of a triangle divides the opposite side into segments proportional to the length of the other two sides (**Angle Bisector** Theorem).

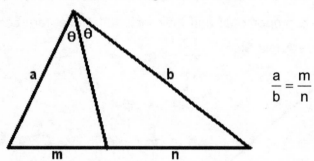

$$\frac{a}{b} = \frac{m}{n}$$

7. If two figures are similar with a scale factor of k, then the ratio of their perimeters is k and the ratio of their areas is k^2.

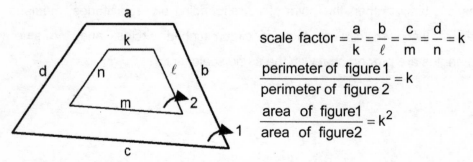

$$\text{scale factor} = \frac{a}{k} = \frac{b}{\ell} = \frac{c}{m} = \frac{d}{n} = k$$

$$\frac{\text{perimeter of figure 1}}{\text{perimeter of figure 2}} = k$$

$$\frac{\text{area of figure 1}}{\text{area of figure 2}} = k^2$$

3.9 QUADRILATERALS

1. If both pairs of opposite sides or opposite angles of a quadrilateral are congruent, then the quadrilateral is a parallelogram.

    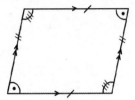

2. If diagonals of a quadrilateral bisect each other, then the quadrilateral is a parallelogram.

    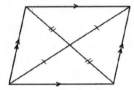

3. If a pair of opposite sides of a quadrilateral are both parallel and congruent, then the quadrilateral is a parallelogram.

    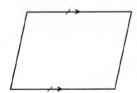

4. If both pairs of opposite angles of a quadrilateral are congruent, then the quadrilateral is a parallelogram.

    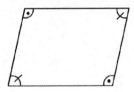

5. If two lines are parallel, then the perpendicular distance between the lines is always the same.

    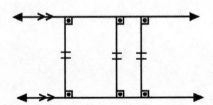

6.   Diagonals of a rectangle are equal in length.

7.   Diagonals of a rhombus are perpendicular.

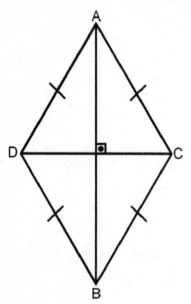

8.   Each diagonal of a rhombus bisects two opposite angles of the rhombus.

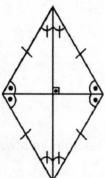

9.   If one angle of a parallelogram measures 90 degrees, then the parallelogram is a rectangle.

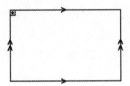

10.   If two consecutive sides of a parallelogram are congruent; then it is a rhombus.

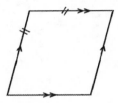

11.   Base angles of an isosceles trapezoid are congruent.

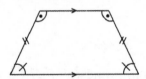

12.   Midbase of a trapezoid is parallel to the bases and has a length is equal to the average of the base lengths. Area of a trapezoid equals half the product of the altitude and the sum of the bases.

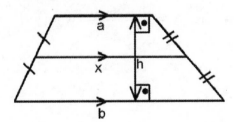

$$x = \frac{a+b}{2}$$

$$\text{Area} = \frac{a+b}{2}h$$

13.   If A is the area of a square and s is the length of one side, then A=s². The perimeter, P, is 4s.

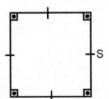

14. If A is the area of a rectangle, l is its length and w its width, then A=lw. Perimeter, P, equals 2l+2w.

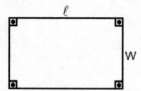

15. Area of a parallelogram equals the product of one of the bases and the altitude to that base. ($A = b.h_b = a.h_a$)

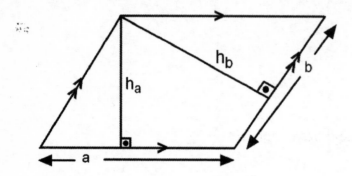

16. Area of a rhombus equals half the product of length of its diagonals ($A = \dfrac{d_1.d_2}{2}$). In a quadrilateral, if diagonals d_1 and d_2 are perpendicular to each other, area of the quadrilateral (deltoid for instance) equals half the product of its diagonals ($A = \dfrac{d_1.d_2}{2}$).

If diagonals are not perpendicular, area A is given as: $A = \dfrac{d_1.d_2 \sin(\alpha)}{2}$ where α equals the measure of the angle between the diagonals.

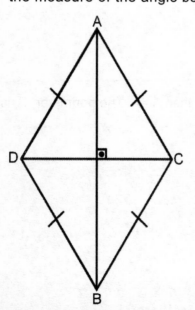

3.10 CIRCLES

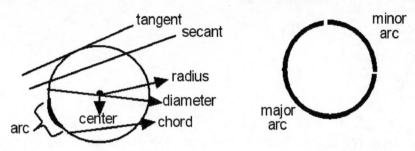

1. Central angle measures as much as its intercepted arc.

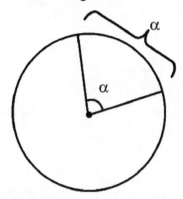

2. Inscribed angle measures half as much as its intercepted arc.

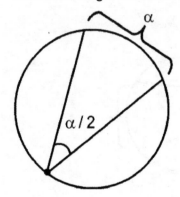

3. Tangent-chord angle measures half as much as its intercepted arc.

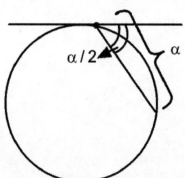

4. An angle inscribed in a semicircle is a right angle and measures 90°.

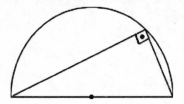

5. An interior angle in a circle measures half as much as the average of its intercepted arcs.

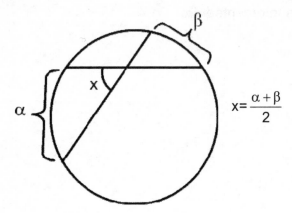

$$x = \frac{\alpha + \beta}{2}$$

6. An exterior angle measures half as much as the difference of its intercepted arcs.

$$x = \frac{\alpha - \beta}{2}$$

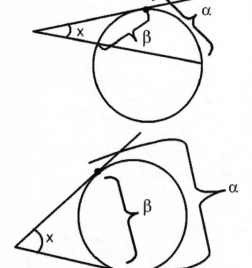

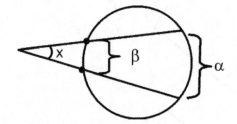

Special case: α+β=360°   x+β=180°

7.   If a line is tangent to a circle, then the line is perpendicular to the radius at the point of tangency. If a line in the plane of a circle is perpendicular to a radius, then the line is tangent to the circle.

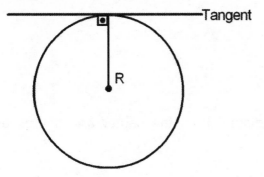

8.   Tangents to a circle from a point outside the circle are congruent.

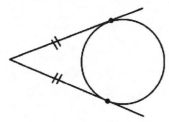

9.   Two minor arcs in a circle are congruent if and only if their central angles have equal measures.

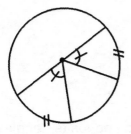

10.   Congruent arcs in a circle contain congruent chords and congruent chords in a circle contain congruent arcs.

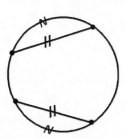

11.   A diameter perpendicular to a chord bisects the chord and its two arcs.

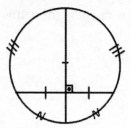

12.   In a circle, congruent chords are equally distant from the center and chords equally distant from the center are congruent.

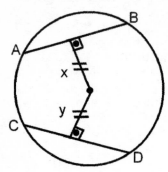

13.   If two inscribed angles intercept the same arc, then their measures are equal.

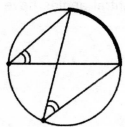

14.   If a quadrilateral can be inscribed in a circle, then its opposite angles are supplementary.

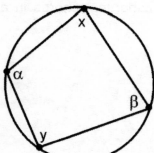

$x+y=\alpha+\beta=180°$

15.   If a circle can be inscribed in a quadrilateral, then the following equality holds: x+y=a+b.

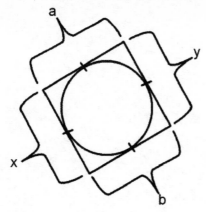

16.   The following relations are present concerning the lengths of the tangent and secant lines originating from the same point outside a circle:

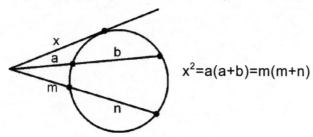

$$x^2=a(a+b)=m(m+n)$$

17.   The following relations are present concerning the lengths of the chords intersecting inside a circle:

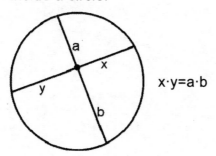

$$x \cdot y = a \cdot b$$

18.   Area and perimeter of a circle are given by the following formulas, where r and d represent the radius and the diameter of the circle:

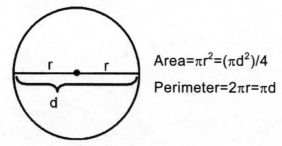

$$\text{Area} = \pi r^2 = (\pi d^2)/4$$
$$\text{Perimeter} = 2\pi r = \pi d$$

19.   Area of a circular ring is given as follows:

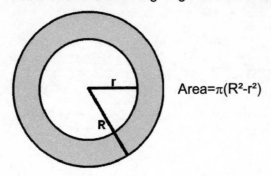

Area=$\pi(R^2-r^2)$

Exercises

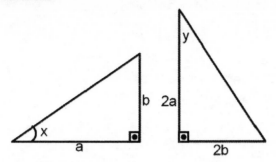

1. Which one(s) of the following are correct?

    a. x is less than y.

    b. x is greater than y.

    c. x and y are equal.

    d. x and y are acute angles.

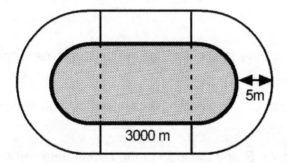

2. The shaded region given above represents a baseball field, constructed from two semicircles and a square in between, with a perimeter of 3000 m represented by the solid line. The walk around the field is 5m wide and its outer edge is constructed from two semicircles and two line segments each of which is as long as the side length of the inner square. What is the area occupied by the walk?

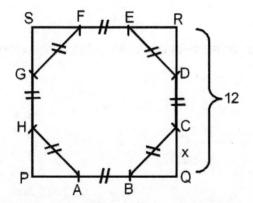

3. Regular octagon and square are given above ⇒ x=?

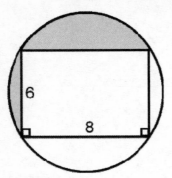

4. Find the shaded area in the figure above.

5. The length of a rectangle is 70 feet longer than the width. If the diagonal is 130 feet, what are the sides of the rectangle?

6. Find the lengths of the sides of a right triangle if its sides are

   a. consecutive numbers.

   b. consecutive even numbers.

   c. consecutive multiples of 4 Find the sides.

   d. are consecutive multiples of 5 Find the sides.

7. If the area of the rectangle is 160 square inches and the length and the width of this rectangle differ by 10 inches, what is the perimeter of the rectangle?

8. When each side of a square is shortened by 10 inches, the area is decreased by 500 square inches. Find the area of the original square.

9. The radii of two concentric circles are r and R where r < R and the area of the region between the circles is 20π. If the radii differ by 5 then what is R?

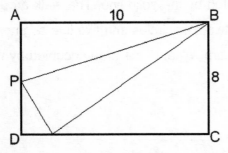

10. Where must P be chosen on AD so that when the rectangular piece of paper ABCD is folded along the line BP, point A will coincide with line CD?

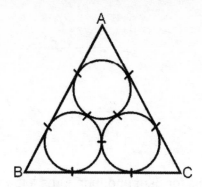

11. The identical circles are inscribed in the equilateral triangle so that each circle is tangent to the other circles and two sides of the equilateral triangle. If radius of each of the circles is R and the side length of the equilateral triangle is X, find R in terms of x.

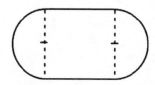

12. A hockey field is constructed from two semicircles and a square. If the perimeter of the field is 3000 m, what is its area?

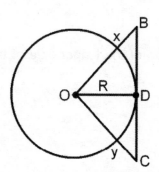

13. OB=OC and BC is tangent to the circle with center O at the point D. Find BX in terms of α and R if $\alpha=\angle BOC$.

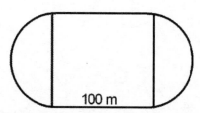

14. The field is constructed from two semicircles and a rectangle. If perimeter of the field is 357 m, what is it's area correct to the nearest m^2?

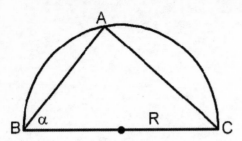

15. Find length of the altitude from A to BC in terms of R and α.

16. A man travels 10 km heading towards north, turns right and travels for 5km and then turns left and travels for a further 2 km. How far is the men from his starting position?

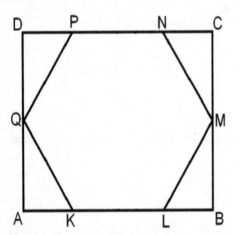

17. KLMNPQ is a regular hexagon and ABCD is a rectangle. Find the ratio of the longer side of the rectangle to its shorter side.

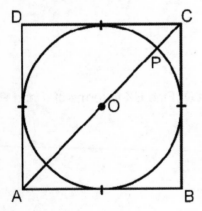

18. ABCD is a square.

   a. OP=R

   b. PC=x

   c. Find R in terms of x.

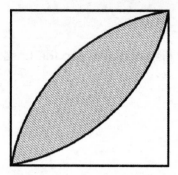

19. Two quarter circles and a square with a side of length R are given. Find shaded are in terms of R.

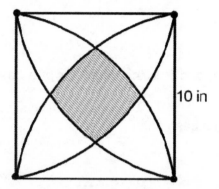

20. 4 quarter circles and a square with side length of 10 are given. Shaded area=?

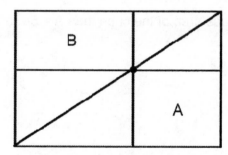

21. A is square with a side length of 10. Area of rectangle B=?

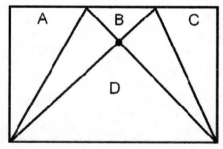

22. Area of region D=100 in². Total area of A,B and C=?

3.11 THREE-DIMENSIONAL GEOMETRY

1. If V is the volume of a prism, h is the altitude (the perpendicular distance between the bases), and B is the area of a base, then $V = B \cdot h$.

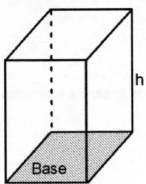

2. If S_L is the lateral surface area of a prism, h is its altitude, and P is the perimeter of a base, then $S_L = P \cdot h$.

3. If S_T is the total surface area of a prism and B is the area of a base, then
$S_T = h \cdot (\text{perimeter of base}) + 2B$

4. Every rectangular prism has 8 vertices, 6 faces, 12 sides.

5. Given that number of vertices of a geometric object is V, the number of faces it has is F and the number of sides it has is S then $V + F = S + 2$.

6. If e is the length of a side of a cube and A is the total surface area of the cube then $A = 6e^2$ and if V is the volume of the cube then $V = e^3$.

Diagonal of a face of the cube = $x = e\sqrt{2}$

Diagonal of the cube = $y = e\sqrt{3}$

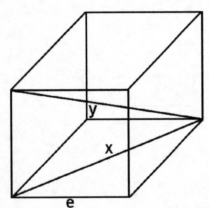

7. If V is the volume of a pyramid or a cone, h its altitude, and B is the area of a base, then

    $V = \frac{1}{3} hB$. The lateral area of a regular pyramid equals half the perimeter of the base

    times the slant height. (L.A. = $\frac{1}{2}$ perimeter of base.h_1)

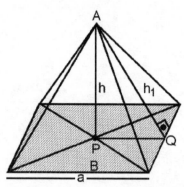

In order to find h_1, Pythagorean theorem may be used since APQ is a right triangle.

8. If V is the volume of a sphere, S is its surface area, and r is its radius, then $V = \frac{4}{3}\pi r^3$ and

    $S = 4\pi r^2$.

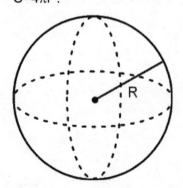

9. Lateral area of a cylinder equals perimeter of the base times the altitude of the cylinder; (L.A. = $2\pi rh$). Volume of a cylinder equals the area of a base times the altitude of the cylinder ($V = \pi r^2 h$).

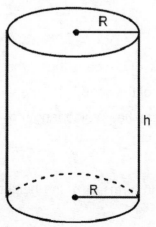

10. Lateral area of a cone equals half the perimeter of the base times the slant height; (L.A. = πrl). Volume of a cone equals one third the area of the base times the height of the cone (V = $\frac{1}{3}$ πr²h).

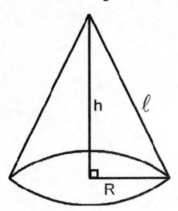

$h^2+R^2=l^2$ (l: slant height)

Total surface area= $\pi r^2+\pi rl$

11. If the scale factor of two similar solids is k, then the ratio of corresponding sides is k and the ratio of corresponding areas is k^2 and the ratio of corresponding volumes is k^3.

Exercises

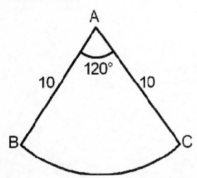

1. If the given sector of a circle is bent to form a cone so that AB and AC will coincide, what will be the dimensions (radius and height) and the volume of the cone that results?

2. What is the volume of the sphere

   (a) whose surface area is 100?

   (b) whose surface area and volume are numerically equal.

3. If the lateral area of a cone is twice as much as the base area of a cone, then what is the expression for h (the height of the cone) in terms of R (the base radius) of the cone?

4. A parallel cross-section to the base of a square pyramid, whose base has a side length of x, cuts the pyramid into two parts that are in a ratio of $\frac{8}{19}$ by volume.

   (a) What is the distance between the base and the cross-section in terms of h, the height of the pyramid?

(b) What is the area of the cross-section in terms of x?

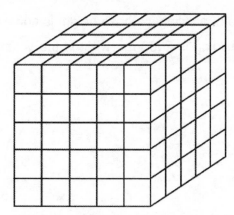

5. The big white cube given above has a side of length 5 and it is painted red on all of its faces. It is then cut into smaller cubes each having a side of length 1 in.

    (a) How many smaller cubes are there?

    (b) How many smaller cubes have 1 red faces?

    (c) How many smaller cubes have 2 red faces?

    (d) How many smaller cubes have 3 red faces?

    (e) How many smaller cubes have no red faces?

    (f) At least how many cuts are needed?

    (g) If the corner cubes are removed, what will be the surface area in square inches and volume in cubic inches of the resulting solid?

    (h) If the corner cubes are removed what will be the ratio of the area of the red to white surface on the resulting solid?

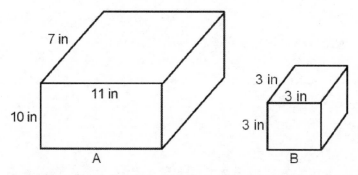

6. Answer the following questions based on the figure above.

    (a) How many boxes of B can be put in container A?

    (b) How many B's can be filled completely with the liquid that fills A to capacity?

    (c) How many times must B be used to fill A to capacity?

7. If the base radius of a cone is increased by 10 %, how must the height of the cone be changed so that the volume of the cone will be

(a) the same?

(b) decreased by 20%?

8. A building is built in the shape of a hemisphere placed on top of a cylinder whose height is equal to its diameters. If the surface area of the outer surface of the building is 2000 m², what is the volume that it occupies (OPTIONAL)?

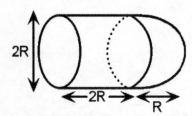

9. If the surface area of the bullet above is 3cm², what is R (OPTIONAL)?

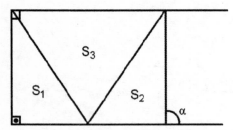

10. Which one(s) of the following are correct for the figure given above?

(a) If $\alpha = 90°$ then $S_1 + S_2 = S_3$

(b) If $\alpha > 90°$ then $S_1 + S_2 > S_3$

(c) If $\alpha < 90°$ then $S_1 + S_2 > S_3$

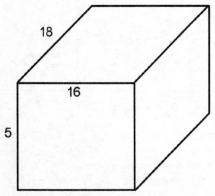

11. At most how many identical spheres of maximum volume can be placed in the box given?

12. A cylinder whose height is 1.5 times its radius is inscribed in a sphere whose radius is 10 in. What is the ratio of the volume of the sphere to that of the cylinder?

13. Which one(s) of the following cannot be obtained by taking cross-sections from a cube with a single plane?

(a) Triangle

(b) Parallelogram

(c) Trapezoid

(d) Pentagon

(e) Hexagon

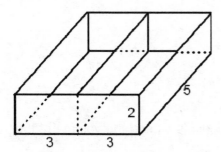

14. Figure above shows a box produced for a special purpose. 125 such boxes have been built and they will be painted to white inside-out. If 1 gallon of paint can cover 4000 cm^2 of surface and is sold at the rate of $36 per gallon at whole gallons, what is the amount of money needed to complete this task?

15. A and B are two different points on the surface of a cylinder with base radius 5 and height 24. What is the greatest possible value of AB?

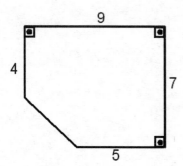

16. Figure shows the base of a right prism with altitude of length 10 in. Find volume and surface area of the prism.

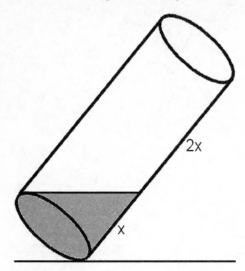

17. A cylindrical can containing some liquid is tilted. If volume of the liquid is V_1 and the volume of the can not occupied by the liquid is V2 then $\dfrac{V_1}{V_2}$ =?

18. A right square pyramid has a height of 12 cm and its base has a side length of 10 cm. find the volume and the surface area of the pyramid.

19. A sphere A is inscribed in a cube B which is inscribed in a sphere C. What is the ratio of the radius of the outer sphere C to that of the inner sphere A?

20. Five identical tennis balls can just be placed in a cylindrical can that has a radius of 4 cm. Find

    (a) the ratio of the volume of the balls to the volume of the can

    (b) the volume inside the can and outside the balls.

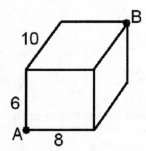

21. If only up, right, front directions will be used then how many different paths can there be from A to B?

3.12 INSCRIBED FIGURES IN TWO DIMENSIONS

Quadrilateral inscribed in a circle

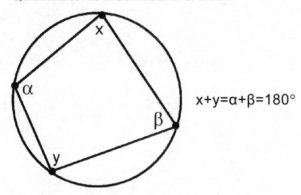

$x+y=\alpha+\beta=180°$

Circle inscribed in a quadrilateral

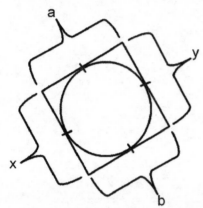

Sum of the pairs of opposite sides are equal:

$x+y=a+b$

Circle inscribed in a square

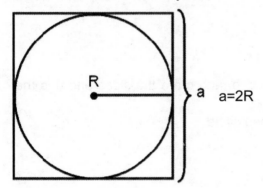

$a=2R$

Square inscribed in a circle

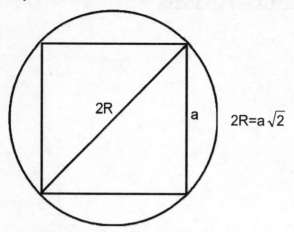

$2R = a\sqrt{2}$

Rectangle inscribed in a circle

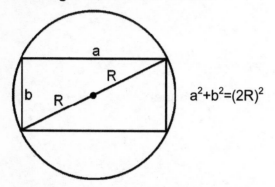

$a^2 + b^2 = (2R)^2$

Circle inscribed in a triangle

The area of the triangle = $ur = \sqrt{u(u-a)(u-b)(u-c)}$ where a, b, and c are the sides and u is the semi-perimeter of the triangle; r is the radius of the inscribed circle.

Triangle inscribed in a circle

The area of the triangle = $\sqrt{u(u-a)(u-b)(u-c)} = \dfrac{abc}{4R}$ where a, b, and c are the sides and u is the semi-perimeter of the triangle; R is the radius of the circumscribed circle.

Equilateral triangle inscribed in a circle

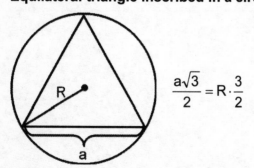

$\dfrac{a\sqrt{3}}{2} = R \cdot \dfrac{3}{2}$

Circle inscribed in an equilateral triangle

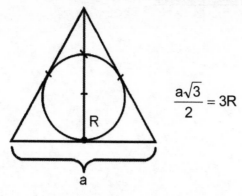

$$\frac{a\sqrt{3}}{2} = 3R$$

Isosceles triangle inscribed in a circle

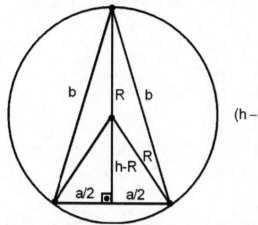

$$(h-R)^2 + (\frac{a}{2})^2 = R^2 \quad \text{and} \quad b^2 = h^2 + (\frac{a}{2})^2$$

Circle inscribed in an isosceles triangle

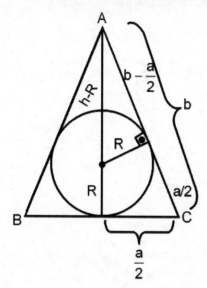

$$(h-R)^2 = R^2 + (b-\frac{a}{2})^2 \quad \text{and} \quad h^2 = b^2 - (\frac{a}{2})^2$$

3.13 INSCRIBED FIGURES IN THREE DIMENSIONS

Sphere inscribed in a cube

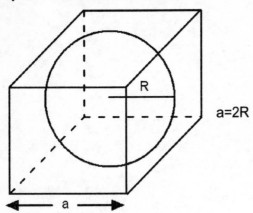

$a=2R$

Cube inscribed in a sphere

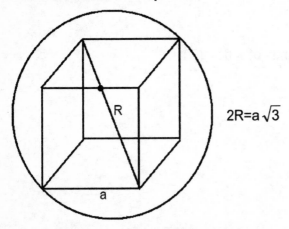

$2R=a\sqrt{3}$

Rectangular box inscribed in a sphere

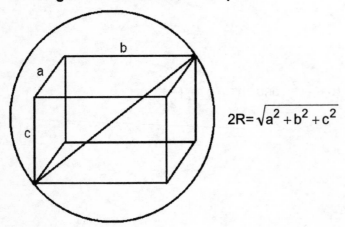

$2R=\sqrt{a^2+b^2+c^2}$

Cylinder inscribed in a sphere

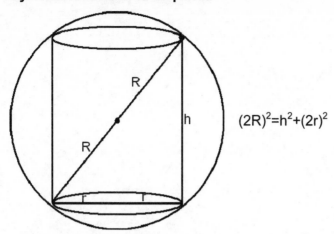

$$(2R)^2=h^2+(2r)^2$$

Cone inscribed in a sphere

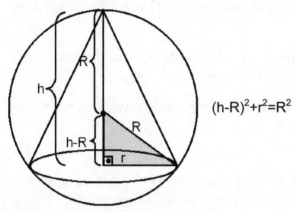

$$(h-R)^2+r^2=R^2$$

Sphere inscribed in a cone

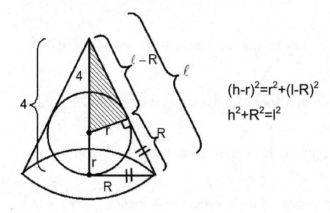

$$(h-r)^2=r^2+(l-R)^2$$
$$h^2+R^2=l^2$$

Cylinder inscribed in a cone

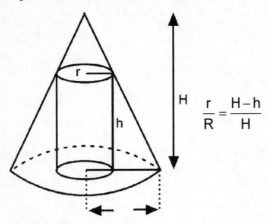

$$\frac{r}{R} = \frac{H-h}{H}$$

Exercises

1. Find ratio of the radius of the inscribed circle to that of the circumscribed circle of an equilateral triangle.

2. A rectangle having an area of 48 square units and a perimeter of 28 units, is inscribed in a circle. What will be the area of a square inscribed in the same circle?

3. R and r are the radii of the circumscribed and the inscribed circles of a triangle with side lengths of 5,12 and 13. $\frac{r}{R} = ?$

4. What is the ratio of the radius of the inscribed to that of the circumscribed circle of an isosceles triangle with a base length of 10 and a side of length 13?

5. Identical spheres of maximum radii are placed in a rectangular box with dimensions 3,7 and 11 in . Find volume of the box not occupied by the spheres.

6. How many identical cubes with edge lengths of 1 in can be placed inside a sphere with radius of $\sqrt{3}$ inches?

7. A cylinder with a base radius of 12 inches is inscribed in a sphere with diameter of length 26 inches. Find volume of the sphere not occupied by the cylinder.

8. A cone with a base radius of 15 inches and a height of 25 inches is inscribed in a sphere with diameter d; d=?

9. A sphere is with radius of 3 inches is inscribed in a cone of base radius of 4 inches. What is the volume of the cone?

10. Identical spheres of maximum size are placed in a cylinder with a base radius of 3 inches and a height of 10 inches. What is the volume of the cylinder not occupied by the spheres?

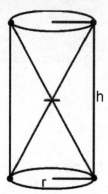

11. Find ratio of the total volume occupied by the identical cones to that of the cylinder.

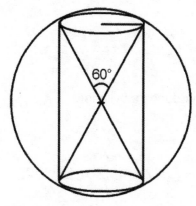

12. If the radius of the sphere is R then find the volume inside the sphere and outside the cylinder.

13. A sphere x is inscribed in a cube y which is inscribed in a sphere z; find ratio of the radius of x to that of z.

14. A sphere is inscribed in a cone; the set of the points of intersection of the sphere and the cone contains which elements?

3.14 ROTATIONS

Given below is a summary of the common rotations in the context of SAT math subject tests.

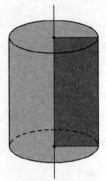

A rectangle rotated about its edge for 360° produces a cylinder.

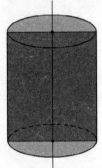

A rectangle rotated about its central axis for 180° produces a cylinder.

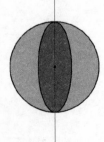

A semicircle rotated about its diameter for 360° produces a sphere.

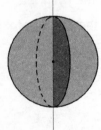

A circle rotated about its diameter for 180° produces a sphere.

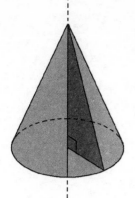

A right triangle rotated about one of its legs (for 360°) produces a cone.

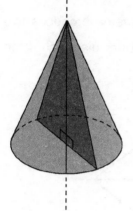

An isosceles triangle rotated about its axis of symmetry, (for 180°) produces a cone.

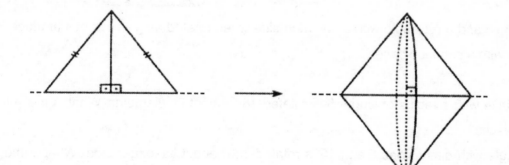

An isosceles triangle rotated (for 360°) about its base produces two cones that have a common base, with their radii each equal to the altitude to the base of the triangle, and, with their altitudes each equal to half of the base length of the triangle.

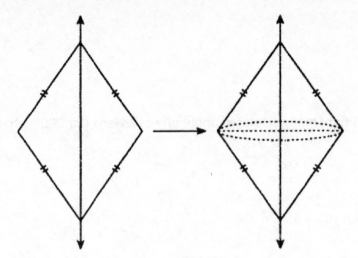

A rhombus rotated (for 180°) about its longer diagonal (one of its axes of symmetry) produces two cones that have a common base with their radii equal half the length of the shorter diagonal of the rhombus and their altitudes equal to the half the length of the longer diagonal.

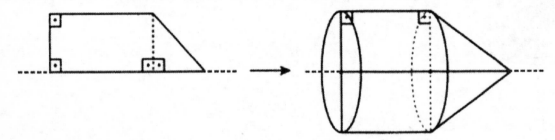

A right triangle and a rectangle with a common side when rotated as given above produces a cylinder and a cone with a common base.

Exercises

1. A semicircle with a radius of length 5 is rotated 180° about its diameter. What is the volume of the solid that results?

2. A rectangle with dimensions 5 and 10 is rotated 180° about its longer side. What is the volume of the solid that results?

3. The portion of the line y=2x-6 that is in quadrant 4 is revolved around the y axis to get a cone of volume V_1 and around the x axis to get a cone of volume V_2. $\dfrac{V_1}{V_2}$=?

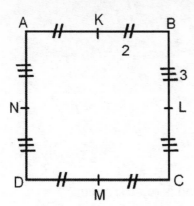

4. ABCD is a rectangle and K, L, M and N are midpoints of AB, BC, CD, and AD respectively. KB=2 and BL=3. Find the volume of the solid generated when rectangle ABCD is rotated

    (a) about BC for 360°.

    (b) about CD for 270°.

    (c) about KM for 180°.

    (d) about LN for 180°.

5. A circle with radius of length 2 is rotated about its its diameter for 180°. Find volume of the resulting solid.

6. An isosceles right triangle with a hypotenuse of length $2\sqrt{2}$ is rotated for 360° about its hypotheses. Find volume of the solid that results.

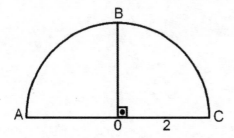

7. A semicircle with center O and radius 2 is given. Find volume of the solid generated when the semicircle is rotated about.

    (a) AC for 360°

    (b) AC for 180°

    (c) OB for 180°

8. An isosceles right triangle with a hypotheses of length $2\sqrt{2}$ is rotated about one of its legs

    (a) for 180°

    (b) for 360°.

Find volume of the solid that results in each case.

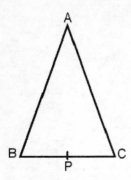

9. AB=AC=13; P is the midpoint of BC. BC=10. The isosceles triangle given is rotated about

    (a) BC for 360°

    (b) BC for 180°

    (c) BC for 90°

    (d) AP for 180°

10. A rhombus with a side of length 2 and an interior angle of 60° is rotated about

    (a) its longer diagonal for 180°

    (b) its shorter diagonal for 180°.

Find volume of the resulting one in each case.

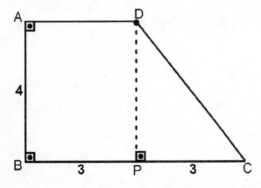

11. The trapezoid given above is rotated about

    (a) BC for 360°

    (b) AB for 360°

Find the volume of the resulting solid in each case.

Some men see things as they are and say "Why?"

I see the things that never were and say "Why not!"

Robert F. Kennedy

CHAPTER 4 – Miscellaneous

Complex Numbers, Polar Coordinates and Graphing

Vectors and Three Dimensional Coordinate Geometry

Parametric Equations and Graphing

Conic Sections

Sequences and Series

Variations

Binary Operations

Computer Programs

Logic

Matrices and Determinants

Word Problems

4.1 COMPLEX NUMBERS, POLAR COORDINATES AND GRAPHING

z=x+yi where $i = \sqrt{-1}$ or $i^2 = -1$

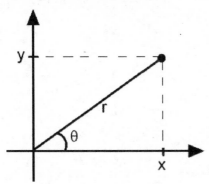

$r \cdot \cos\theta = x$ and $r \cdot \sin\theta = y$

$x+yi = r \cdot \cos\theta + i \cdot r \cdot \sin\theta = r(\cos\theta + i \cdot \sin\theta) = r \cdot \text{cis}\theta = r \cdot e^{i\theta}$

$e=2.71828\ldots= \lim_{n \to \infty} \left(1+\dfrac{1}{n}\right)^n$

Set of complex numbers= $C = \left\{ x + yi : x, y \in R, i = \sqrt{-1} \right\}$

Rectangular to Polar Conversion

Replace

- x by $r \cdot \cos\theta$
- y by $r \cdot \sin\theta$

Polar to Rectangular Conversion

Replace

- $r \cdot \cos\theta$ by x
- $r \cdot \sin\theta$ by y
- r by $\sqrt{x^2 + y^2}$

Euler's Identity

$e^{i\theta}=\cos\theta + i \cdot \sin\theta = \text{cis}\theta$

De Moivre's Identities

$z_1 = r_1 \cdot \text{cis}\theta_1 = r_1 \cdot e^{i\theta_1}$; $z_2 = r_2 \cdot \text{cis}\theta_2 = r_2 \cdot e^{i\theta_2}$

Identity 1:

$z_1 \cdot z_2 = r_1 \cdot r_2 \cdot e^{i\theta_1} e^{i\theta_2}$

$= r_1 r_2 \cdot e^{i\theta_1 + i\theta_2} = r_1 r_2 \cdot e^{i(\theta_1 + \theta_2)} = r_1 r_2 \cdot \text{cis}(\theta_1 + \theta_2)$

$= r_1 r_2 (\cos(\theta_1 + \theta_2) + i \sin(\theta_1 + \theta_2))$

Identity 2:

$$\frac{z_1}{z_2} = \frac{r_1 e^{i\theta_2}}{r_2 e^{i\theta_2}} = \frac{r_1}{r_2} \cdot e^{i(\theta_1 - \theta_2)} = \frac{r_1}{r_2} \cdot cis(\theta_1 - \theta_2)$$

$$= \frac{r_1}{r_2} \cdot (\cos(\theta_1 - \theta_2) + i\sin(\theta_1 - \theta_2))$$

Identity 3:

$$(z_1)^n = (r_1 . e^{i\theta_1})^n = r_1^n . (e^{i\theta_1})^n = r_1^n . e^{i\theta_1 . n} = r_1^n . cis(n\theta_1)$$

$$= r_1^n . [\cos(n\theta_1) + i\sin(n\theta_1)]$$

Identity 4:

The n'th root of $z = r.cis\theta$

$r = |z|$; $z = r\,cis\theta$

$$z^{1/n} = r^{1/n} cis\left(\frac{\theta + k.2\pi}{n}\right) \text{ where } k = 0,1,2,.....,n-1$$

TI Usage

$z = x + yi$

$\bar{z} = x - yi = $ conjugate of $z = conj(z)$

$|z| = \sqrt{x^2 + y^2} = r = abs(z)$

$x = real(z)$

$y = image(z)$

Properties of Complex Numbers

1. $i^{4n} \equiv 1$; $i^{4n+1} \equiv i$; $i^{4n+2} \equiv i^2 \equiv -1$; $i^{4n+3} \equiv i^3 = -i$ given that n is a positive integer

2. $a + bi = c + di \Rightarrow a = c$ and $b = d$.

3. $z = a + bi \Rightarrow |z| = \sqrt{a^2 + b^2}$

4. $|z_1 . z_2| = |z| . |z_2|$

5. $\left|\frac{z_1}{z_2}\right| = \frac{|z_1|}{|z_2|}$

6. $|z^n| = |z|^n$

7. $conj(z) = a - bi$

   $|z| = |-z| = |conj(z)|$

8. $z \cdot \bar{z} = |z|^2 = a^2 + b^2$

Example:

What is the reciprocal of 3+4i

Solution:

```
1/(3+4i
          .12-.16i
```

Answer: 0.12 – 0.16i

Example:

$z = \dfrac{1+i\sqrt{3}}{-1+i\sqrt{3}}$, what is the value of z in trigonometric form?

Solution:

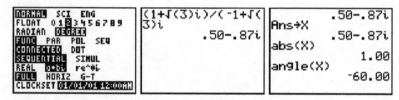

Answer: 1·(cos(-60°)+isin(-60°))

Polar Graphing with TI

Polar graphing allows the user to plot **r** versus **θ** where **r** denotes **radius**, **θ** denotes **angle** and **(r,θ)** represents the **polar coordinates**. Settings must be changed to the **Pol**ar mode so that the Y= Editor will enable that **r** be defined in terms of the parameter **θ**. In the **Pol**ar mode the variable **θ** will appear when the ⬡ˣ,ᵀ,θ,ⁿ key is pressed.

For example the input and output for the following relation

r=1-2cos(θ)

will be as follows:

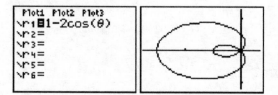

Example:

What is the polar representation of the curve given by the relation $x^2+3y^2-5x+3y=0$?

Solution:

$(r\cdot\cos\theta)^2+3(r\cdot\sin\theta)^2-5r\cdot\cos\theta+3r\cdot\sin\theta=0$

$r^2\cos^2\theta+3r^2\sin^2\theta-5r\cos\theta+3r\sin\theta=0$

$r\cos^2\theta+3r\sin^2\theta-5\cos\theta+3\sin\theta=0$

$$r=\frac{5\cos\theta-3\sin\theta}{\cos^2\theta+3\sin^2\theta}$$

Example:

What is the rectangular representation of the curve given by the relation $r=3\cos\theta+7\sin\theta$?

Solution:

$r=3\cos\theta+7\sin\theta$

$r^2=3r\cos\theta+7r\sin\theta$

$x^2+y^2=3x+7y$

Exercises

1. $4(\text{cis}70°)^4=?$

2. $f(x)=3x^5-2x^3+8x-2;\ f(i)=?$

3. $i^{4n+5}+i^{4n+6}+i^{4n+7}+i^{4n+8}=?$

4. $i^{192}+i^{193}+i^{194}+i^{195}=?$

5. What is the reciprocal of $3+4i$

6. $\dfrac{1+i}{6i+8}=?$

7. $z=3\text{cis}\dfrac{\pi}{8};z^3=?$

8. Find polar coordinates of the following points:

   a. $(1,\sqrt{3})$

   b. $(-1,1)$

   c. $(-2\sqrt{3},2)$

   d. $(1,-\sqrt{3})$

9. $z=\dfrac{1+\sqrt{3}i}{-1+\sqrt{3}i}$, what is the value of z in trigonometric form?

10. $A=3\text{cis}40°;\ B=4(\cos50°+i\sin50°);\ A\cdot B=?$

11. Regarding the polar coordinates of the points on a polar curve match 1, 2, 3 with the letters A, B, C if

    1. (r,θ) and $(r,-\theta)$ lie on the same curve.

    2. (r,θ) and $(r,\pi-\theta)$ lie on the same curve.

    3. (r,θ) and $(r,\theta+\pi)$ lie on the same curve.

    A. curve is symmetric about the x axis.

    B. curve is symmetric about the origin.

    C. curve is symmetric about the y axis.

12. Regarding the polar coordinates of each of the following polar curves match 1, 2, 3 with the letters A, B, C.

    1. $r=\dfrac{e}{1+e\cos\theta}, e = 0.5$ A. Ellipse

                                           B. Parabola

    2. $r=\dfrac{2e}{1-e\cos\theta}, e = 1$ C. Hyperbola

    3. $r=\dfrac{2e}{1+e\sin\theta}, e = 3$

13. Find Cartesian equation in each case.

    a. $r=3\sin\theta$

    b. $r= -2\cos\theta$

14. Find all cubic roots of

    a. $z=-i$

    b. $z=i$

    c. $z=-1$

    d. $z=1$

15. Find the rectangular (Cartesian) coordinates of the point whose polar coordinates are $(4,220°)$.

16. Find all polar representations of the point whose cartesian coordinates are $(2, 2\sqrt{3})$.

17. Find all polar representations of the point whose cartesian coordinates are $(1, -\sqrt{3})$.

18. Convert each of the polar equations given above to cartesian form.

    a. $r^2=\sec(2\theta)$

    b. $r^2=\csc(2\theta)$

    c. $r^2=\sin(2\theta)$

    d. $r^2=\cos(2\theta)$

19. Given that (r, θ) are the polar coordinates of a point on the polar curve $r=f(\theta)$ then indicate the symmetry the curve has in each of the following cases.

    a. (r, θ) and $(r,-\theta)$ are interchangeable.

b. (r, θ) and $(r, 180°-\theta)$ are interchangeable.

c. (r, θ) and $(-r, \theta)$ are interchangeable.

20. Convert to rectangular coordinates and indicate the symmetry in each case.

   a. $r=\sin\theta$

   b. $r=2$

   c. $r=-\cos\theta$

   d. $\theta=\dfrac{\pi}{3}$

   e. $r\sin\theta=1$

   f. $r=\theta$

   g. $r\cos\theta=1$

   h. $r=2+3\sin\theta$

   i. $r=2-3\sin\theta$

21. Identify each of the following graphs

   a. $r=2$

   b. $\theta=\dfrac{\pi}{3}$

   c. $r=\theta$

   d. $r^2=\sin(2\theta)$

   e. $r^2=\cos(2\theta)$

22. Write the polar equation

   a. $y=x$

   b. $y=-x$

   c. $y=-\dfrac{1}{\sqrt{3}}x$

   d. $x^2+y^2=1$

   e. $\dfrac{x^2}{9}+\dfrac{y^2}{16}=1$

23. Find points of intersection.

   a. $r=\cos\theta$ and $r=1-\cos\theta$

   b. $r=2+\sin\theta$ and $r=1+2\sin\theta$

4.2 VECTORS AND THREE DIMENSIONAL COORDINATE GEOMETRY

A **vector** is a number with magnitude, unit and direction whereas a **scalar** is a number with magnitude, unit and no direction.

- A **position vector** is one whose starting point is the origin. In the following figure the vector $\overrightarrow{OP} = \overrightarrow{P}$ is given.

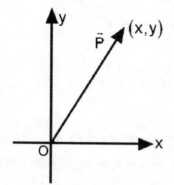

$$\overrightarrow{OP} = \overrightarrow{P} = \begin{pmatrix} x \\ y \end{pmatrix}$$

- The **negative** of a vector $\vec{A} = \begin{pmatrix} a_1 \\ a_2 \end{pmatrix}$ is the vector whose direction is exactly the opposite of vector $\vec{A} = \begin{pmatrix} a_1 \\ a_2 \end{pmatrix}$ and it is given by $-\vec{A} = \begin{pmatrix} -a_1 \\ -a_2 \end{pmatrix}$.

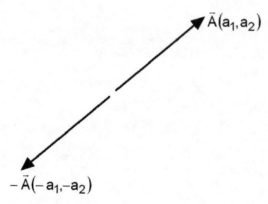

- The **magnitude** of a vector is its length given by $\left| \overrightarrow{OP} \right| = \left| \vec{P} \right| = \sqrt{x^2 + y^2}$

- The **resultant** of two vectors $\vec{A} = \begin{pmatrix} a_1 \\ a_2 \end{pmatrix}$ and $\vec{B} = \begin{pmatrix} b_1 \\ b_2 \end{pmatrix}$ is their vectorial sum and it is given by $\vec{A} + \vec{B} = \begin{pmatrix} a_1 + b_1 \\ a_2 + b_2 \end{pmatrix}$.

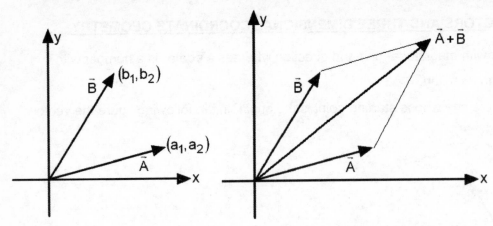

- The magnitude R of the resultant $\vec{A} + \vec{B}$ of two vectors $\vec{A}$ and $\vec{B}$ is given by

$$R^2 = A^2 + B^2 + 2AB \cdot \cos\alpha$$

where A and B are the magnitudes of the vectors $\vec{A}$ and $\vec{B}$ respectively and α is the angle between them. Please also notice that the formula resembles the cosine rule except that the sign of the $2AB \cdot \cos\alpha$ term is negative in the cosine rule, however it is positive the above formula.

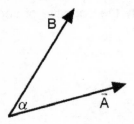

- The vector $\overrightarrow{AB}$ starts at point A and ends at point B and it is given by $\overrightarrow{AB} = \vec{B} - \vec{A}$

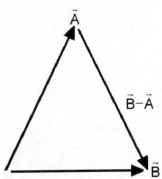

- **Linear combination** of vectors $\vec{A}$ and $\vec{B}$ is the sum given by $m\vec{A} + n\vec{B}$ where m and n are scalars.

- A **unit vector** has a length of 1. If $\hat{a}$ is the unit vector in the direction of $\vec{A}$ then it is given by $\dfrac{\vec{A}}{|\vec{A}|}$.

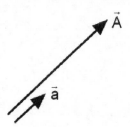

- **Basis vectors** are parallel to the coordinate axes and each of them has a length of 1.

$$\vec{A} = \begin{pmatrix} a_1 \\ a_2 \end{pmatrix} = a_1\,\vec{i} + a_2\,\vec{j} \text{ where } \vec{i} \text{ and } \vec{j} \text{ are the basis vectors.}$$

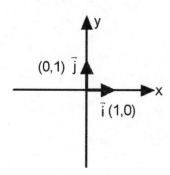

- The scalar product (dot product or inner product) of two vectors $\vec{A} \cdot \vec{B} = <\vec{A}, \vec{B}>$ is given by

$\vec{A} \cdot \vec{B} = a_1 b_1 + a_2 b_2 = |\vec{A}|.|\vec{B}|.\cos\alpha$ where α is the angle between these vectors and $|\vec{A}|$ and $|\vec{B}|$ are the lengths of the corresponding vectors.

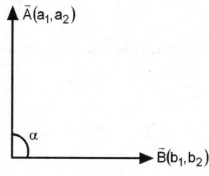

- Given that $\vec{A} = \begin{pmatrix} a_1 \\ a_2 \end{pmatrix}$ and $\vec{B} = \begin{pmatrix} b_1 \\ b_2 \end{pmatrix}$; if the two vectors are parallel then $\dfrac{a_2}{a_1} = \dfrac{b_2}{b_1}$.

- Given that $\vec{A} = \begin{pmatrix} a_1 \\ a_2 \end{pmatrix}$ and $\vec{B} = \begin{pmatrix} b_1 \\ b_2 \end{pmatrix}$; if the two vectors are perpendicular then: $\alpha = 90°$ which implies

that $\cos 90° = 0$ and $\vec{A} \cdot \vec{B} = |\vec{A}|.|\vec{B}|.\cos 90° = 0$.

Consequently if the vectors are perpendicular then $a_1 b_1 + a_2 b_2 = 0$

- For the scalar product the following properties also hold:

  a. $(\vec{A})^2 = \vec{A} \cdot \vec{A} = |\vec{A}|^2$

  b. $\vec{A} \cdot \vec{B} = \vec{B} \cdot \vec{A}$

  c. $\vec{A} \cdot (\vec{B} + \vec{C}) = \vec{A}\vec{B} + \vec{A}.\vec{C}$

- For the three dimensional vectors please note the following:

  a. $\overrightarrow{OA} = \vec{A} = \begin{pmatrix} a_1 \\ a_2 \\ a_3 \end{pmatrix} \Rightarrow |\vec{A}| = \sqrt{a_1^2 + a_2^2 + a_3^2}$

  b. If $\vec{A} = \begin{pmatrix} a_1 \\ a_2 \\ a_3 \end{pmatrix}$ and $\vec{B} = \begin{pmatrix} b_1 \\ b_2 \\ b_3 \end{pmatrix}$ then $\vec{A} \cdot \vec{B} = a_1 b_1 + a_2 b_2 + a_3 b_3$

     i. $\vec{A} \parallel \vec{B} \Rightarrow \dfrac{a_1}{b_1} = \dfrac{a_2}{b_2} = \dfrac{a_3}{b_3}$

     ii. $\vec{A} \perp \vec{B} \Rightarrow a_1 b_1 + a_2 b_2 + a_3 b_3 = 0$

Example:

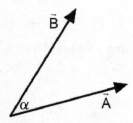

If the magnitudes of vectors $\vec{A}$ and $\vec{B}$ are 10 and 20 respectively and the angle between them is 35°
then what is the magnitude of $\vec{A} + \vec{B}$?

Solution:

$\vec{R} = \vec{A} + \vec{B}$

$R^2 = 10^2 + 20^2 + 2 \cdot 10 \cdot 20 \cdot \cos 35° \Rightarrow R = 28.77$

Plane Equation

$Ax + By + Cz + D = 0$

Example:

  $3x - 4y + 5z = 60$ is given.

  a) Find x,y,z intercepts.

  b) Find xy, xz, yz traces.

  c) Find the volume of the pyramid that forms with the coordinate axes and this plane.

Solution:

a) x intercept: y=z=0 ➔ 3x=60   (20,0,0)

    y intercept : (0,-15,0)

    z intercept : (0,0,12)

b) xy trace : z=0 ➔ 3x-4y=60

    yz trace : -4y+5z=60

    xz trace : 3x+4z=60

c)

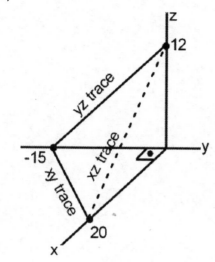

$$V = \frac{BA \cdot h}{3} \text{ (for cones \& pyramids)} = \frac{\frac{15 \cdot 20}{2} \cdot 12}{3} = 600$$

3 – D Line Equation

Example:

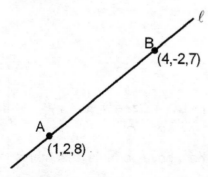

a) Find direction vector of line l

b) Find direction cosines of line l

c) Find cartesian & parametric forms of the line equation for line l.

d) Find distance AB

Solution:

a) direction vector= $\overrightarrow{AB} = \overrightarrow{B} - \overrightarrow{A} = (3,-4,-1)$

b)   direction cosines= $\dfrac{\vec{AB}}{\left|\vec{AB}\right|} = \dfrac{(3,-4,-1)}{\sqrt{9+16+1}} = \left(\dfrac{3}{\sqrt{26}}, \dfrac{-4}{\sqrt{26}}, \dfrac{-1}{\sqrt{26}}\right)$

c) $\vec{AB} = (3,-4,-1)$ and $\vec{AC} = (x-1, y-2, z-8)$

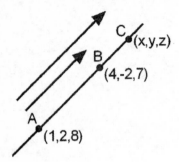

$\vec{AB} // \vec{AC} \Rightarrow \dfrac{x-1}{3} = \dfrac{y-2}{-4} = \dfrac{z-8}{-1} = t$

Cartesian (rectangular) form: $\dfrac{x-1}{3} = \dfrac{y-2}{-4} = \dfrac{z-8}{-1}$

Parametric form:

x=3t+1

y=-4t+2

z=-t+8

Vector form:

$\begin{pmatrix} x \\ y \\ z \end{pmatrix} = \begin{pmatrix} 1 \\ 2 \\ 8 \end{pmatrix} + t \begin{pmatrix} 3 \\ -4 \\ -1 \end{pmatrix}$

d) $\vec{AB} = (3,-4,-1) \Rightarrow AB = \sqrt{9+16+1} = \sqrt{26}$

Distance From a Point to a Plane

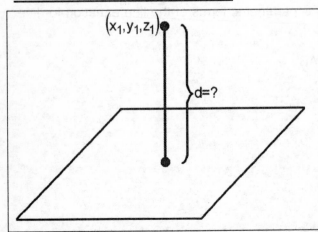

$d = \dfrac{\left|Ax_1 + By_1 + Cz_1 + D\right|}{\sqrt{A^2 + B^2 + C^2}}$

Please note that the above formula resembles the formula used for finding the distance from a point to a line.

Distance Between Two Points

Distance between two points with coordinates (x_1, y_1, z_1) and (x_2, y_2, z_2) is given by:

$$d = \sqrt{(x_1 - x_2)^2 + (y_1 - y_2)^2 + (z_1 - z_2)^2}.$$

Reflections in Three Dimensions

The reflection of a point (x, y, z) across

- the xy plane gives (x, y, -z).

- the xz plane gives (x, -y, z).

- the yz plane gives (-x, y, z).

Sphere equation

$(x-a)^2 + (y-b)^2 + (z-c)^2 = R^2$

center (a, b, c)

radius = R

Example:

$x^2 - 6x + y^2 + 8y + z^2 - 2z + 1 = 0$

Find volume of the above sphere.

Solution:

$x^2 - 6x + 9 + y^2 + 8y + 16 + z^2 - 2z + 1 = 9 + 16 + 1 - 1$

$(x-3)^3 + (y+4)^2 + (z-1)^2 = 25$

Center (3, -4, 1)

Radius = $\sqrt{25} = 5$

$V = \dfrac{4}{3} . \pi . r^3$

Exercises

1. If the magnitudes of vectors **a** and **b** are 8 and 14, respectively, then what can be the magnitude of vector (**b-a**)?

2. A line passes through (2, -3) and its direction is parallel to vector $\begin{pmatrix} -3 \\ 4 \end{pmatrix}$. What is the equation of this line in vector and Cartesian form?

3. What is the angle between the vectors $-4i - 3j$ and $2i - 8j$ to the nearest degree?

4. A line passes through (2, -3) and its direction is perpendicular to vector $\begin{pmatrix} -3 \\ 4 \end{pmatrix}$. What is the equation of this line in vector and Cartesian form?

5. A car moves in a straight line, and after t seconds its position (x,y) is given by the vector equation

$$\begin{pmatrix} x \\ y \end{pmatrix} = \begin{pmatrix} 3 \\ -1 \end{pmatrix} + t\begin{pmatrix} 0.4 \\ 2 \end{pmatrix}$$

    a. How far is the car from the point (0,0) after 2 seconds

    b. What is the speed of the car?

    c. What is the equation of the car's route in the form ax + by = c

6. Find parametric, vector and Cartesian equations for

    a. the line passing through (3,-2) and having the direction vector (1,2).

    b. the line that passes through (1,3) and (2,4).

    c. the line passing through (1,2,-3) and having the direction vector (3,-1,4).

    d. the line that passes through (1,3,4) and (2,-6,5).

7. The position of an object given in terms of the coordinates (x,y) satisfies the following relation:

    (x,y)=(1,2)+t(3,4) where t ≥ 0 is in seconds and the coordinates are in meters.

    a. How far will the object have traveled between t=3 and t=5?

    b. What is the speed of the object?

    c. What is the initial position of the object?

8. Find center and radius of the sphere $x^2 + y^2 + z^2 + 4x - 6y + 22 = 0$

9. If A is a point on the sphere given by $x^2 + y^2 + z^2 + 4x - 6y + 22 = 0$ and B is the point (7, 7, 9); find the least and the greatest length of the segment AB.

10. What is the minimum distance from the point (3, 4, -2) to the plane 2x+3y+5z=21?

11. In the three dimensional space which one(s) of the following are correct regarding the equations a given below?

    A: x+y+z=2

    B: −x−y−z=4

    C: x=y=z

    1. A and B are parallel planes

    2. C is a line parallel to the planes A and B.

    3. C is a line perpendicular to the planes A and B.

    4. C is a plane perpendicular to the lines A and B

12. Calculate the distance between (3,4,5) and (8,-2,-6).

13. Compute the shortest distance from the point (8,-2,6) to the plane 3x-4y+12z=4.

14. Two friends Efe and Zeynep start at the some position and travel in opposite directions for 800 meters each, then they turn left and each one travels for another 600 meters. What is the final distance between them?

4.3 PARAMETRIC EQUATIONS AND PARAMETRIC GRAPHING

Parametric graphing in TI allows its user to plot y versus x when the y- and x- variables are defined in terms of a **parameter "T"** which usually denotes the time variable (for example y and x can represent the y- and x-coordinates that define the position of an object at time t). Settings must be changed to the **Par**ametric mode so that the Y= Editor will enable that the relation between y- and x- be both defined in terms of the parameter **T**. In the **Par**ametric mode the variable T will appear when the $\boxed{X,T,\theta,n}$ key is pressed. Please note that in the **Func**tion mode the variable X used to appear when the $\boxed{X,T,\theta,n}$ key was pressed.

For example the following relation

x = 3cos(t)   y = 2sin(t)

must be input as follows (t will be replaced by T):

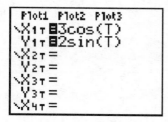

and the output will be an ellipse:

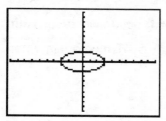

The important issue in the **Par**ametric mode is the fact that the **T** variable in TI is designed to represent the time variable **t** and therefore the default value for **Tmin** in the window settings is 0 (zero) as time is supposed to be always nonnegative.

```
WINDOW
 Tmin=0
 Tmax=6.2831853…
 Tstep=.1308996…
 Xmin=-10
 Xmax=10
 Xscl=1
↓Ymin=-10
```

However, **T** does not necessarily have to denote time. For example the parametric equation above could also be given as follows:

$x = 3\cos(\theta)$ $y = 2\sin(\theta)$

where **θ** is a parameter that does not represent time. On the other hand although the variable used may be t, it may still not represent time, either. In such cases where the free variable does not denote time, leaving **Tmin** as 0 will result in an incorrect and misleading graph that will represent only a portion of the actual graph. Therefore when **T** is not given to represent time, **Tmin** must be changed to **–Tmax**: The default settings for **Tmax** in **Radian** mode is 2π that appears as 6.28… and **Tmin** must be set to -2π that will also appear as -6.28… after enter key is pressed.

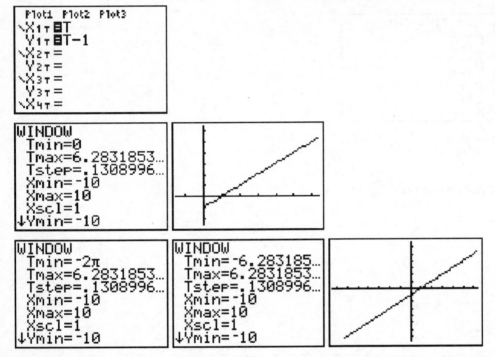

It is also essential to be aware of the fact that the **ZStandard (Zoom Standard)** action will reset **Tmin** back to 0. Therefore after **ZStandard** is performed **Tmin** must be changed to **–Tmax** again when needed.

Exercises

Perform the following operations for each of the parametric relations that will be given:

    a. Eliminate parameter

    b. Plot the graph of the points (x,y) as t changes.

    c. What does the graph represent?

    d. Does the graph represent a relation or a function?

    e. Find domain and range.

1. x=-2t and y=6t

2. x=2t-1 and y=4t+3

3. x=2t² and y=4t²+3

4. $x=t^2$ and $y=2t^4+1$

5. $x=t$ and $y=t^2$

6. $x=3Sint$ and $y=4Cost$

7. $x=3Sint+1$ and $y=4Cost-2$

8. $x=\dfrac{-1}{t}$ and $y=t$

9. $x=2t^2$ and $y=t$

10. $(x,y)=(2t,t-1)$

11. $(x,y)=(2t,t^2)$

12. $(x,y)=(1,-3+t)$

13. $(x,y)=(2,t^2)$

14. $(x,y)=(-3,t^3)$

15. $(x,y)=(t^2-1,1)$

4.4 CONIC SECTIONS

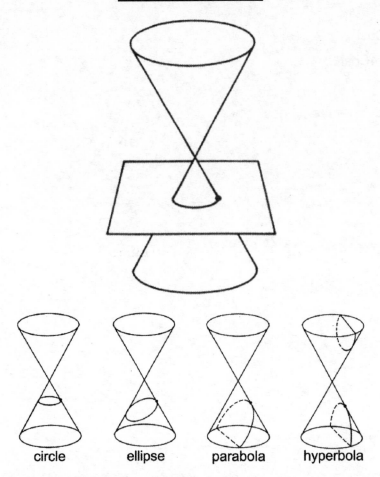

| circle | ellipse | parabola | hyperbola |

General equation of a conic is as follows: $Ax^2+Bxy+Cy^2+Dx+Ey+F=0$. One of the following cases hold in general:

i.   If $B^2 – 4AC<0$ and $A = C$, graph is a circle

ii. If $B^2 – 4AC<0$ and $A \neq C$, graph is an ellipse.

iii. If $B^2 – 4AC=0$, graph is a parabola.

iv. If $B^2 – 4AC>0$, graph is a hyperbola.

However in the SAT II context, B will be zero most of the time, i.e. there will usually be no xy term. The xy term accounts for the cases when the conic section is rotated by an angle which is not an integer multiple of 90 degrees. In such cases you should suspect that the graph is:

i.   a circle if A=C;

ii. an ellipse if A and C are unequal but they have the same sign;

iii. a hyperbola if A and C have different signs;

iv. a parabola if either A or C is zero but not both of them are zero, i.e. the case when one of A or C is missing.

Circle

A circle is the set of points in a plane whose distance a fixed point in the plane is constant. The fixed point is the center of circle; the constant distance is the radius.

$(x-h)^2+(y-k)^2=R^2$ with center at (h,k) and radius = R

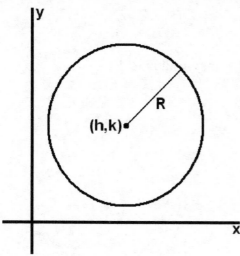

The unit circle

It is the circle centered at the origin having the radius of 1. Its equation is $x^2 + y^2 = 1$.

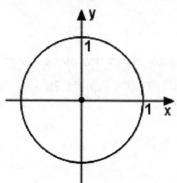

Semicircles centered at the origin:

$$y = \sqrt{R^2 - x^2}$$

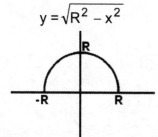

$$y = -\sqrt{R^2 - x^2}$$

$$x = \sqrt{R^2 - y^2}$$

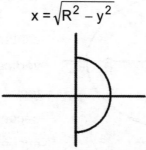

$$x = -\sqrt{R^2 - y^2}$$

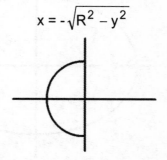

Example:

What does each of the following relations represent?

a. $4x^2 + 4y^2 - 8x + 16y + 16 = 0$

b. $4x^2 + 4y^2 - 8x + 16y + 20 = 0$

c. $4x^2 + 4y^2 - 8x + 16y + 24 = 0$

Solution:

a. $4x^2 + 4y^2 - 8x + 16y + 16 = 0$

$x^2 + y^2 - 2x + 4y + 4 = 0$

$x^2 - 2x + 1 + y^2 + 4y + 4 = 1$

$(x-1)^2 + (y+2)^2 = 1$

The relation represents a circle whose center is at (1, -2) and whose radius is 1.

b. $4x^2 + 4y^2 - 8x + 16y + 20 = 0$

$x^2 + y^2 - 2x + 4y + 5 = 0$

$x^2 - 2x + 1 + y^2 + 4y + 4 = 0$

$(x-1)^2 + (y+2)^2 = 0$

The relation represents the point (1, -2).

c. $4x^2 + 4y^2 - 8x + 16y + 24 = 0$

$x^2 + y^2 - 2x + 4y + 6 = 0$

$x^2 - 2x + 1 + y^2 + 4y + 4 + 1 = 0$

$(x-1)^2 + (y+2)^2 = -1$

The relation represents the empty set.

Ellipse

An ellipse is the set of points in a plane whose distances from two fixed points in the plane have a constant sum. The fixed points are the foci of the ellipse and the constant sum equals 2a.

Ellipses in Standard Position

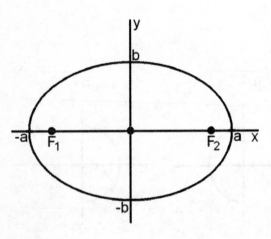

x - ellipse

a=semimajor axis length

b=semiminor axis length

$$\frac{x^2}{a^2} + \frac{y^2}{b^2} = 1 \quad (a>b>0)$$

center: (0,0)

vertices: ($\pm a$, 0); co-vertices: (0, $\pm b$)

foci: ($\pm c$, 0), where $c^2 = a^2 - b^2$

c=center to focus distance

eccentricity: e=c/a and 0<e<1

major axis: horizontal; minor axis: vertical

directrices: The lines defined by x = $\pm a/e$

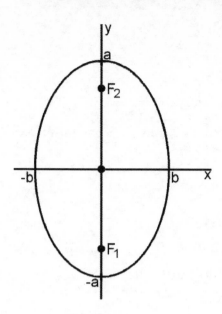

y - ellipse

a=semimajor axis length

b=semiminor axis length

$$\frac{x^2}{b^2} + \frac{y^2}{a^2} = 1 \quad (a>b>0)$$

center: (0,0)

vertices: (0, ±a); co-vertices: (±b, 0)

foci: (0, ±c), where $c^2 = a^2 - b^2$

c=center to focus distance

eccentricity: e=c/a and 0<e<1

major axis: vertical; minor axis: horizontal

directrices: The lines defined by y = ±a/e

When coordinates of center is (h,k):

$$\begin{cases} \dfrac{(x-h)^2}{a^2} + \dfrac{(y-k)^2}{b^2} = 1, \text{ major axis horizontal} \\ \dfrac{(x-h)^2}{b^2} + \dfrac{(y-k)^2}{a^2} = 1, \text{ major axis vertical} \end{cases} \text{ given that } a > b.$$

coordinates of center: (h,k)

foci: ±c units from center along major axis where $c^2 = a^2 - b^2$

vertices: ±a units from center along major axis

length of major axis: 2a

length of minor axis (perpendicular to the major axis at center): 2b

eccentricity = e = $\dfrac{c}{a}$

directrices: The lines perpendicular to the major axis ±a/e units from center. Please note that

$\dfrac{a}{e} > a$.

length of latus rectum (the chord passing through one of the foci and perpendicular to the major axis)

$= \dfrac{2b^2}{a}$

area of an ellipse: πab

Example:

Analyze each of the following conic sections:

a. $\dfrac{x^2}{25} + \dfrac{y^2}{9} = 1$

b. $\dfrac{x^2}{25} + \dfrac{y^2}{169} = 1$

c. $\dfrac{(x-2)^2}{100} + \dfrac{(y-1)^2}{36} = 1$

d. $\dfrac{(x+1)^2}{144} + \dfrac{(y-2)^2}{225} = 1$

Solution:

a.

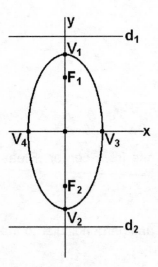

$$\dfrac{x^2}{25} + \dfrac{y^2}{9} = 1$$

x-ellipse

a = 5 and b = 3; therefore c = 4.

center: (0, 0)

foci: F_1(4, 0), F_2(-4, 0)

vertices: V_1(5, 0), V_2(-5, 0)

covertices: V_3(0, 3), V_4(0, -3)

eccentricity: e= 0.8

directrices: d_1: x = 6.25 and d_2: x = -6.25

major axis: x axis

length of the major axis: 10

minor axis: y axis

length of the minor axis: 6

latus rectum = 3.6

area = 15π

b.

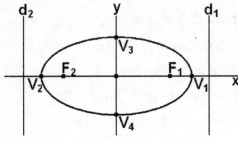

$$\dfrac{x^2}{25} + \dfrac{y^2}{169} = 1$$

y-ellipse

a = 13 and b = 5; therefore c = 12.

center: (0, 0)

foci: F_1(0, 12), F_2(0, -12)

vertices: V_1(0, 13), V_2(0, -13)

covertices: V_3(5, 0), V_4(-5, 0)

eccentricity: e= 12/13

directrices: d_1: y = 169/12 and d_2: x = -169/12

major axis: y axis

length of the major axis: 26

minor axis: x axis

length of the minor axis: 10

latus rectum = 50 /13

area = 65π

c.

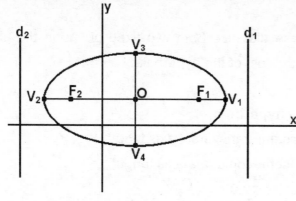

$$\frac{(x-2)^2}{100} + \frac{(y-1)^2}{36} = 1$$

x-ellipse

a = 10 and b = 6 therefore c = 8

center: O(2, 1)

foci: F_1(-6, 1), F_2(10, 1)

vertices: v_1(-8, 1), v_2(12, 1)

covertices: v_3(2, 7), v_4(2, -5)

eccentricity: e= 0.8

directrices:

d_1: x = -10.5 and d_2: x = 14.5

major axis: y = 1 line

length of the major axis: 20

minor axis: x = 2 line

length of the minor axis: 12

latus rectum = 7.2

area = 60π

d.

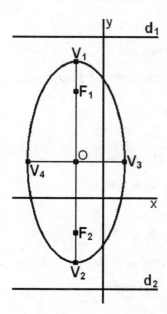

$$\frac{(x+1)^2}{144} + \frac{(y-2)^2}{225} = 1$$

y-ellipse

a = 15 and b = 12 therefore c = 9

center: O(-1, 2)

foci: F_1(-1, 11), F_2(-1, -7)

vertices: V_1(-1, 17), V_2(-1, -13)

covertices: V_4(-13, 2), V_3(11, 2)

eccentricity: e= 0.6

directrices:

d_1: y = 27 and d_2: y = -23

major axis: x = -1 line

length of the major axis: 30

minor axis: y = 2 line

length of the minor axis: 24

latus rectum = 19.2

area = 180π

Hyperbola

A hyperbola is the set of points in a plane whose distance from two fixed points in the plane have a constant difference. The fixed points are the foci of the hyperbola.

Hyperbolas in Standard Position

$$\frac{x^2}{a^2} - \frac{y^2}{b^2} = 1$$

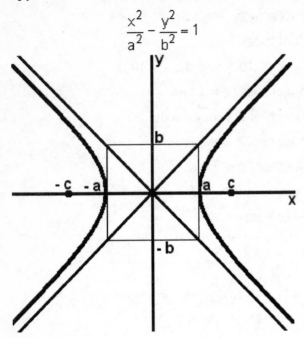

x - hyperbola

a=semi-transversal axis length

b=semi-conjugate axis length

center: (0,0)

vertices: ($\pm$a, 0)

foci: ($\pm$c, 0), where $c^2 = a^2 + b^2$

c=center to focus distance

asymptotes: $y = \pm \dfrac{b}{a}x$

eccentricity: e=c/a and e>1

transverse axis: horizontal

conjugate axis: vertical

directrices: The lines defined by x = $\pm$a/e

$$\frac{y^2}{a^2} - \frac{x^2}{b^2} = 1$$

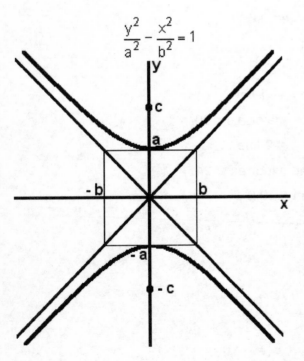

y - hyperbola

a=semi-transversal axis length

b=semi-conjugate axis length

center: (0,0)

vertices: (0, $\pm$a)

foci: (0, $\pm$c), where $c^2 = a^2 + b^2$

c=center to focus distance

asymptotes: $y = \pm \dfrac{a}{b}x$

eccentricity: e=c/a and e>1

transverse axis: vertical

conjugate axis: horizontal

directrices: The lines defined by y = $\pm$a/e

When coordinates of center is (h,k):

$$\frac{(x-h)^2}{a^2} - \frac{(y-k)^2}{b^2} = 1, \text{ transverse axis horizontal}$$

$$\frac{(y-k)^2}{a^2} - \frac{(x-h)^2}{b^2} = 1, \text{ transverse axis vertical}$$

where $c^2 = a^2 + b^2$.

coordinates of center: (h,k).

vertices: ±a units along the transverse axis from center

foci: ±c units along the transverse from center

conjugate axis: perpendicular to transverse axis at center

eccentricity = e = c/a and e>1

directrices: The lines perpendicular to the transverse axis ±a/e units from center. Please note that $\frac{a}{e} < a$.

length of latus rectum (the chord passing through one of the foci and perpendicular to the transverse axis) = $\frac{2b^2}{a}$

asymptotes slopes = $\pm\frac{b}{a}$ if transverse axis is horizontal or $\pm\frac{a}{b}$ if transverse axis is vertical

Example:

Analyze each of the following conic sections:

a. $\dfrac{x^2}{9} - \dfrac{y^2}{16} = 1$

b. $\dfrac{y^2}{144} - \dfrac{x^2}{25} = 1$

c. $\dfrac{(x+4)^2}{9} - \dfrac{(y-7)^2}{16} = 1$

d. $\dfrac{(y-6)^2}{9} - \dfrac{(x-5)^2}{16} = 1$

e. $16y^2 - 9x^2 + 64y + 18x + 55 = 0$

Solution:

a.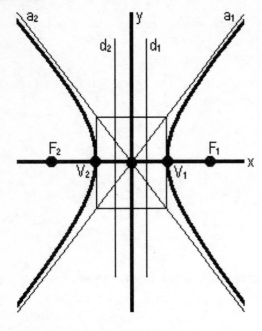

center: (0,0)

vertices: $V_1(3, 0)$ and $V_2(-3, 0)$

foci: $F_1(5, 0)$ and $F_2(-5, 0)$

asymptotes: a_1: $y = \dfrac{4}{3}x$ and a_2: $y = -\dfrac{4}{3}x$

eccentricity: $e = 5/3$

$a/e = 1.8$

directrices: d_1: $x = 1.8$ and d_2: $x = -1.8$

transverse axis: x axis

transverse axis length = 6

conjugate axis: y axis

conjugate axis length = 8

latus rectum = 32 / 3

$$\frac{x^2}{9} - \frac{y^2}{16} = 1$$

x-hyperbola

a = 3 and b = 4 therefore c = 5

b.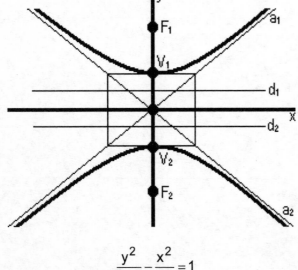

center: (0,0)

vertices: $V_1(0, 12)$ and $V_2(0, -12)$

foci: $F_1(0, 13)$ and $F_2(0, -13)$

asymptotes: a_1: $y = \dfrac{12}{5}x$ and a_2: $y = -\dfrac{12}{5}x$

eccentricity: $e = 13/12$

$a/e = 144/13$

directrices: d_1: $y = 144/13$ and d_2: $y = -144/13$

transverse axis: y axis

transverse axis length = 24

conjugate axis: x axis

conjugate axis length = 10

latus rectum = 50 /12

$$\frac{y^2}{144} - \frac{x^2}{25} = 1$$

y-hyperbola

a = 12 and b = 5 therefore c = 13

c.

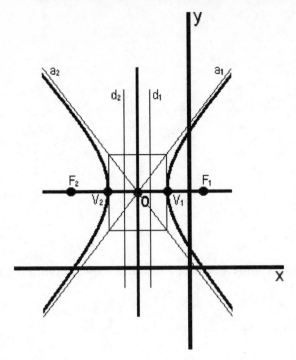

$$\frac{(x+4)^2}{9} - \frac{(y-7)^2}{16} = 1$$

x-hyperbola

a = 3 and b = 4 therefore c = 5

center: O(-4,7)

vertices: V_1(-7, 7) and V_2(-1, 7)

foci: F_1(1, 7) and F_2(-9, 7)

asymptotes:

a_1: $y - 7 = \frac{4}{3}(x+4)$ and a_2: $y - 7 = -\frac{4}{3}(x+4)$

eccentricity: e = 5/3

a/e = 1.8

directrices: d_1: x = -4 + 1.8 and d_2: x = -4 -1.8

transverse axis: y = 7 line

transverse axis length = 6

conjugate axis: x = -4 line

conjugate axis length = 8

latus rectum = 32 / 3

d.

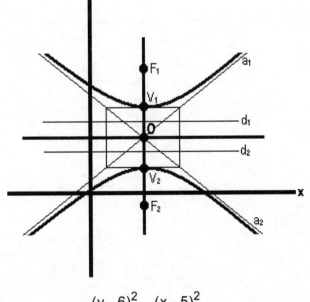

$$\frac{(y-6)^2}{9} - \frac{(x-5)^2}{16} = 1$$

y-hyperbola

a = 3 and b = 4 therefore c = 5

center: O(5,6)

vertices: V_1(5, 9) and V_2(5, 3)

foci: F_1(5, 11) and F_2(5, 1)

asymptotes:

a_1: $y - 6 = \frac{3}{4}(x-5)$ and a_2: $y - 6 = -\frac{3}{4}(x-5)$

eccentricity: e = 5/3

a/e = 1.8

directrices: d_1: y = 6 + 1.8 and d_2: y = 6 -1.8

transverse axis: x = 5 line

transverse axis length = 6

conjugate axis: y = 6 line

conjugate axis length = 8

latus rectum = 32 / 3

e. $16y^2 - 9x^2 + 64y + 18x + 55=0$

$16(y^2+4y)-9(x^2-2x)=-55$

$16(y^2+4y+4)-9(x^2-2x+1)=-55+64-9$

$16(y^2+4y+4)-9(x^2-2x+1)=0$

$16(y+2)^2-9(x-1)^2=0$

$16(y+2)^2=9(x-1)^2$

therefore

$4(y+2)=\pm3(x-1)$

$(y+2)=\pm\dfrac{3}{4}(x-1)^2$

The conic section represents two intersecting lines with slopes of 3/4 and -3/4 passing through the point (1,-2).

Hyperbolas in the form: xy = k

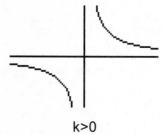

k>0   k<0

Example:

Analyze the hyperbola xy = 4

Solution:

Center: (0, 0)

Vertices (2, 2) and (-2, -2)

Transverse axis: the line defined by y = x

Conjugate axis: the line defined by y = -x

Transverse axis length = $2\sqrt{2}$

Conjugate axis length = $2\sqrt{2}$

Asymptotes: y = 0 (the x-axis) and x = 0 (the y-axis)

<u>**Hyperbolic Rational Functions**</u>

$f(x)=\dfrac{ax+b}{cx+d}$

Domain = $R-\left\{\dfrac{-d}{c}\right\}$; Range = $R-\left\{\dfrac{a}{c}\right\}$

Horizontal asymptote: y = a/c

Vertical asymptote: x = -d/c

Increasing   **Decreasing**

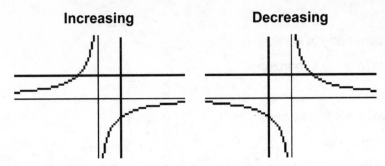

Parabola

A parabola is the set of points in a plane equidistant from a given fixed point and a given fixed line in the plane. The fixed point is the *focus* of the parabola; the line is the *directrix*.

Parabolas in Standard Position

$x^2 = 4py$

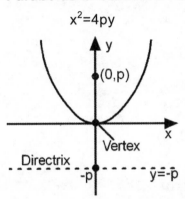

Vertex: (0, 0)

Directrix: y = -p

Focus: (0, p)

Eccentricity = e = 1 (for all parabolas)

$x^2 = -4py$

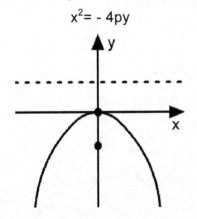

$y^2 = 4px$

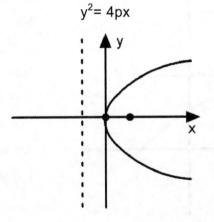

$y^2 = -4px$

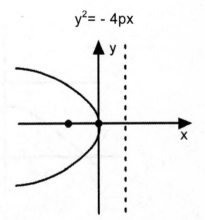

When coordinates of vertex is (h,k):

$(x-h)^2 = \pm 4p(y-k)$ opens up or down – axis of symmetry is vertical

$(y-k)^2 = \pm 4p(x-h)$, opens to the side – axis of symmetry is horizontal

Coordinates of vertex: (h, k)

Equation of axis of symmetry: x = h if vertical, y = k if horizontal

Focus: p units along the axis of symmetry from vertex

Equation of directrix: y = - p if axis of symmetry is vertical, x = - p if axis of symmetry is horizontal

Eccentricity = e = 1

Length of latus rectum = 4p

Example:

Analyze each of the following conic sections:

a. $y^2 = 8x$

b. $(x+2)^2 = - 4(y-3)$

a.

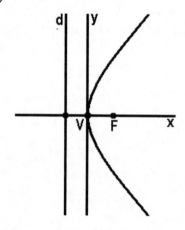

$y^2 = 8x$

Vertex (0,0)

p = 2

Vertex: V(0, 0)

Directrix: d: x = -2

Focus: F(2, 0)

Eccentricity: e = 1

Latus rectum = 8

b.

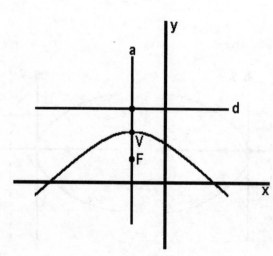

$(x+2)^2 = - 4(y-3)$

Vertex (-2,3)

p = 1

Vertex: V(-2, 3)

Directrix: d: y = 4

Focus: F(-2, 2)

Eccentricity: e = 1

Latus rectum = 4

Example:

Convert each of the following conic sections to its standard form and state what it represents.

a. $25x^2+16y^2+150x-32y+241=0$

b. $16y^2 - 9x^2 + 64y + 18x - 89=0$

c. $y^2 + 4y + 2 - 2x = 0$

d. $xy=0$

Solution:

a. $25x^2+16y^2+150x-32y+241=0$

$25(x^2+6x)+16(y^2-2y)= -241$

$25(x^2+6x+9)+16(y^2-2y+1)= -241+225+16$

$25(x+3)^2+16(y-1)^2=0$

The conic represents the point whose coordinates are (-3,1)

b. $16y^2 - 9x^2 + 64y + 18x - 89=0$

$16y^2 + 64y - 9x^2 + 18x = 89$

$16(y^2+4y)-9(x^2-2x)=89$

$16(y^2+4y+4)-9(x^2-2x+1)=89+64-9$

$16(y+2)^2-9(x-1)^2=144$

$$\frac{(y+2)^2}{9} - \frac{(x-1)^2}{16} = 1$$

The conic represents a hyperbola centered at (1, -2); a=3 and b=4.

c. $y^2 + 4y + 2 - 2x = 0$

$y^2 + 4y = 2x - 2$

$y^2 + 4y +4 = 2x - 2 + 4$

$y^2 + 4y +4 = 2x + 2$

$(y+2)^2 = 2(x+1)$

The conic represents a parabola whose vertex is at (-1, -2) and p = ½

d. xy=0 means x = 0 or y = 0; representing the x and y axes.

<u>Exercises</u>

1. What is the relation between x and y if (x,y) satisfies the condition that

   a. the sum of the distances from (x,y) to (3,7) and (3,-1) is 10?

   b. the distances from (x,y) to (3,7) and (3,-1) differ by 1?

   c. it is at a distance of 10 from (3,-1)?

   d. it is equidistant from the point (3,-1) and the line x=-7?

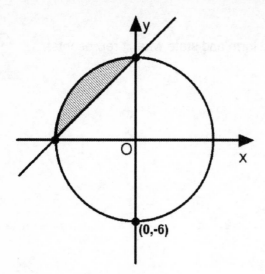

2. What is the area of the shaded region in the given figure above if the origin 0 is the center of the circle?

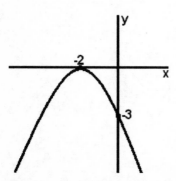

3. On the parabola given above, determine the points (x,y) for which y=2x.

4. What are the x-coordinates of the points of intersection of the line with equation y=6 and the circle with center (3,4) and radius 3?

5. Find the equation of the circle having its center at the origin and passing through the point (5, -12).

$$x = 8t - 4$$
$$y = -64t^2$$

6. The parametric representation above is the graph of which of the following?

   a. a circle

   b. a parabola

   c. an ellipse

   d. a hyperbola

   e. a straight line

7. The set of (x,y) that satisfy the equation $x+2iy=\dfrac{1}{x-2iy}$ are points on which of the following?

    a. a circle

    b. a parabola

    c. an ellipse

    d. a hyperbola

    e. a straight line

8. The set of (x,y) that satisfy the equation $x+2y=\dfrac{1}{x-2y}$ are points on which of the following?

    a. a circle

    b. a parabola

    c. an ellipse

    d. a hyperbola

    e. a straight line

9. Suppose the graph of $f(x)=-x^2$ is translated 2 units right and 4 units down to obtain the parabola g(x). Find the focus, directrix, latus rectum and eccentricity of g(x).

10. What is the length of the major axis of the ellipse whose equation is $5x^2+20y^2=100$?

11. If the line y = p is tangent to the circle $(x-2)^2 + y^2 = 9$, then p=?

12. What is the relation between x and y if equation of the set of all points (x,y) that are equidistant from the x-axis and the point (1, - 4)?

13. What does each of the following represent, a circle, a point or empty set? Find radius and center when appropriate.

    a. $x^2 + y^2 - 4x + 6y - 3 = 0$

    b. $x^2 + y^2 - 4x + 6y + 13 = 0$

    c. $x^2 + y^2 - 4x + 6y + 19 = 0$

14. Find area of the region enclosed by $y= -\sqrt{9-x^2}$ and the x axis.

15. Find area of the region enclosed by $x= \sqrt{16-y^2}$ and the y axis.

16. Find the vertex, focus and directrix of each of the following parabolas

    a. $x^2 + 4x + 2 + 2y = 0$

    b. $y^2 + 4y + 2 - 2x = 0$

    c. $y^2 + 4x + 4 = 0$

    d. $x^2 - 4y + 4 = 0$

17. What does each of the following represent; an ellipse, a point or empty set? Find; major and minor axis length, eccentricity, center, foci, directrices, latus rectum and the area enclosed when appropriate.

a. $9x^2 + 25y^2 = 225$

b. $25x^2 + 16y^2 = 400$

c. $9x^2 + 25y^2 - 18y + 100y - 116 = 0$

d. $9x^2 + 25y^2 - 18x + 100y + 109 = 0$

e. $9x^2 + 25y^2 - 18x + 100y + 110 = 0$

f. $25x^2 + 16y^2 + 150x - 32y - 159 = 0$

g. $25x^2 + 16y^2 + 150x - 32y + 241 = 0$

18. Find center, foci, vertices, transverse and conjugate axes, eccentricity, length of the latus rectum and asymptotes when appropriate.

a. $16y^2 - 9x^2 + 64y + 18x - 89 = 0$

b. $\dfrac{x^2}{16} - \dfrac{y^2}{9} = 1$

c. $\dfrac{y^2}{25} - \dfrac{x^2}{144} = 1$

19. It is given that xy = k. For each of the following values of k, state what the curve represents. When appropriate find the asymptotes, center, vertices & length of the transverse axis.

a.   k = 0

b.   k = 1

c.   k = - 4

a. $y = \dfrac{-1}{x}$	(i) Hyperbola
b. $y = x^2 + 1$	(ii) Parabola
c. $y = 2x - 1$	(iii) Line
d. $y = \sqrt{1 - x^2}$	(iv) Portion of a circle

20. Match the letters a through d with numbers (i) through (iv) for the givens above.

21. By taking cross-sections from an upright cone using one or two planes, which one(s) of the following figures can be obtained?

a. Circle   e. Angle

b. Ellipse   f. Parabola

c. Triangle   g. Hyperbola

d. Trapezoid   h. Point

22. By taking cross-sections from two upright cones with the same vertex using one or two planes, which one(s) of the following figures can be obtained?

    a. Circle

    b. Ellipse

    c. Triangle

    d. Trapezoid

    e. Angle

    f. Parabola

    g. Hyperbola

    h. Point

23. Find the asymptotes for each hyperbola:

    a. $\dfrac{x^2}{16} - \dfrac{y^2}{9} = 1$

    b. $x^2 - y^2 = 1$

    c. $y^2 - x^2 = 1$

    d. $y = \dfrac{x+3}{x+1}$

    e. $xy = 3$

    f. $(x-1)(y+2) = 1$

24. Plot the graphs of the following.

    a. $\dfrac{x}{y} < 1$

    b. $\dfrac{x}{y} \geq 1$

    c. $\dfrac{x^2}{9} + \dfrac{y^2}{16} \geq 1$

    d. $\dfrac{x^2}{16} - \dfrac{y^2}{25} < 1$

    e. $xy < 1$

25. What is the set of points equidistant from the point A(5,2) and the line y=-4?

26. Find the equation of the circle

    a. tangent to both axes, centered at (2, -2).

    b. tangent to both axes, passing through (8, -8).

    c. centered at the origin and passing through (5, -12).

    d. tangent to the y – axis and having ist center at (-5, 2).

    e. centered at (3, 4) and tangent to the line $5x – 12y = 32$.

4.5 SEQUENCES AND SERIES

In general, **sequence**s are functions that map positive integers to real numbers. For example for the

following sequence then **n'th term** is given by $t_n = f(n) = \dfrac{1}{n+5}$ where n is a positive integer:

$\dfrac{1}{6}, \dfrac{1}{7}, \dfrac{1}{8}, \ldots, t_n, \ldots$ The term **series** corresponds to the sum of the terms of a sequence.

Infinite Sequence: $\left\{ \dfrac{1}{6}, \dfrac{1}{7}, \dfrac{1}{8}, \dfrac{1}{9}, \ldots\ldots\ldots\ldots \right\}$

Finite Sequence: $\left\{ \dfrac{1}{6}, \dfrac{1}{7}, \dfrac{1}{8}, \ldots\ldots\ldots\ldots, \dfrac{1}{50} \right\}$

Infinite Series: $\dfrac{1}{6} + \dfrac{1}{7} + \dfrac{1}{8} + \ldots\ldots\ldots\ldots$

Finite Series : $\dfrac{1}{6} + \dfrac{1}{7} + \dfrac{1}{8} + \ldots\ldots\ldots\ldots + \dfrac{1}{50}$

Arithmetic Sequences (Sequence ≡ Progression) and Series

1. Explicit definition of an arithmetic sequence:

   $a_n = a + (n-1)d$

   a: first term

   d: common difference

2. Recursive definition of an arithmetic sequence:

   $a_{n+1} = a_n + d$

   $a_1 = a$

3. $a_n = a_p + (n-p)d$

   $a_{16} = a_{12} + 4d$

   $a_{12} = a_{16} - 4d$

4. $a_n = \dfrac{a_{n+1} + a_{n-1}}{2} = \dfrac{a_{n+p} + a_{n-p}}{2}$

5. S_n: Sum of the first n terms of an arithmetic series.

   1. If S_n is a quadratic function of n then S_n represents an arithmetic series: $S_n - S_{n-1} = a_n$

   2. $S_n = n\left(\dfrac{a_1 + a_n}{2} \right)$ or $S_n = \dfrac{n}{2}[2a_1 + (n-1)d]$

Geometric Sequences and Series

1. Explicit definition of a geometric sequence:

   $a_n = a \cdot r^{n-1}$

   a: first term

r: common ratio

2. Recursive definition of a geometric sequence:

$$a_{n+1} = a_n \cdot r$$

$$a_1 = a$$

3. $a_n = a_p \cdot r^{n-p}$

$$a_{16} = a_{12} \cdot r^4$$

$$a_{12} = a_{16}/r^4$$

4. $a_n^2 = a_{n+1} \cdot a_{n-1} = a_{n+p} \cdot a_{n-p}$

5. S_n: Sum of the first n terms of a geometric series;

$$S_n = a\frac{1-r^n}{1-r}$$

6. If S_n is an exponential function of n then S_n represents a geometric series: $S_n - S_{n-1} = a_n$

7. Infinite geometric series:

$$a + ar + ar^2 + ar^3 + \ldots = S = \frac{a}{1-r} \text{ if } (|r| < 1)$$

Example:

The 1st term of an arithmetic sequence is 3 and the 5th term is 17.

a. What is the 55th term of the sequence?

b. What is the sum of the first 55 terms of this sequence?

Solution:

a. $a_1 = a = 3$ and $a_5 = a + 4d = 3 + 4d = 17 \Rightarrow d = 3.5$

$a_{55} = 3 + 54 \cdot 3.5 = 192$

b. $S_{55} = \frac{55}{2}(a_1 + a_{55}) = \frac{55}{2}(3 + 192) = 5362.5$

Example:

Sum of the first n terms of a sequence is given by $3n^2 - 5n$. What is the nth term of the sequence?

Solution:

$a_n = S_n - S_{n-1} = 3n^2 - 5n - (3(n-1)^2 - 5(n-1)) = 6n - 8$

Example:

The 2nd term of a geometric sequence is 2 and the 6th term is 162.

What is the 16th term of the sequence?

What is the sum of the first 16 terms of this sequence?

Solution:

$a_2 = ar = 2$ and $a_6 = ar^5 = 162 \Rightarrow r^4 = 81 \Rightarrow r = \pm 3$ and $a = \pm 2 / 3$

Therefore $a_{16} = a_2 \cdot r^{14} = 2 \cdot (\pm 3)^{14} = 2 \cdot 3^{14}$

$$\text{Sum} = a \cdot \left(\frac{1 - r^{16}}{1 - r} \right) = \pm \frac{2}{3} \cdot \left(\frac{1 - (\pm 3)^{16}}{1 - (\pm 3)} \right) = 14348907 \text{ or } -7174454$$

Example:

The decimal given by 0.1232323... is expressed as a common fraction. What is the simplest form of this fraction?

Solution:

0.1232323...

$= 0.1 + 0.023 + 0.00023 + 0.0000023 + \ldots = 0.1 + 0.023 \,(1 + 0.01 + 0.01^2 + \ldots)$

$= 0.1 + 0.023 \cdot \dfrac{1}{1 - 0.01} = \dfrac{61}{495}$

Example:

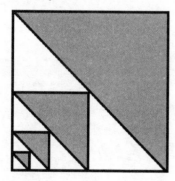

If one side of the outermost square is 4 then what is the total perimeter and the total area of all shaded triangles?

Solution:

Total area $= 16 / 2 + 4 / 2 + 1 / 2 + \ldots = \dfrac{8}{1 - \dfrac{2}{8}} = \dfrac{32}{3}$

Total Perimeter $= 8 + 4\sqrt{2} + \dfrac{1}{2}(8 + 4\sqrt{2}) + \dfrac{1}{4}(8 + 4\sqrt{2}) + \ldots = \dfrac{8 + 4\sqrt{2}}{1 - \dfrac{1}{2}} = 16 + 8\sqrt{2}$

Example:

Insert 4 arithmetic means between 1 and 10.

Solution:

$1 + 5d = 10$; therefore $d = 1.8$; the numbers are 2.8, 4.6, 6.4 and 8.2

Example:

Insert 4 geometric means between 1 and 10.

Solution:

$1 \cdot r^5 = 10 \Rightarrow r = \sqrt[5]{10}$

The numbers are $\sqrt[5]{10}$, $\sqrt[5]{100}$, $\sqrt[5]{100}$, $\sqrt[5]{1000}$

Sigma Notation

Examples:

a. $2 + 4 + 6 + \dots\dots\dots\dots + 20 = \sum_{i=1}^{10}(2i)$

b. $90 + 94 + 98 + \dots\dots\dots + 490 = \sum_{i=1}^{101}(4i + 86)$

c. $\ln(1) + \ln(2) + \ln(3) + \ln(4) + \ln(5) = \sum_{i=1}^{5}\ln(i)$

Commonly Used Formulas

$$\sum_{i=1}^{n} i = 1+2+3+\dots+n = \frac{n(n+1)}{2}$$

$$\sum_{i=1}^{n} i^2 = 1^2+2^2+3^2+\dots+n^2 = \frac{n(n+1)(2n+1)}{6}$$

$$\sum_{i=1}^{n} i^3 = 1^3+2^3+3^3+\dots+n^3 = \left[\frac{n(n+1)}{2}\right]^2$$

$$\sum_{i=1}^{n} r^{i-1} = 1+r+r^2+\dots+r^{n-1} = \frac{1-r^n}{1-r}$$

Exercises

1. If $x_1 = \dfrac{1}{2}$ and if $x_{n+1} = (x_n)^2$ for $n = 1, 2, 3,\dots$ What is the smallest n for which $x_n < 0.001$?

2. If $x_0 = 0$ and $x_{n+1} = \sqrt{6 + x_n}$, then $x_3 =$

3. For some real number the first three terms of an arithmetic sequence are t, $5t - 1$, and $6t + 2$. What is the numerical value of the fourth term?

4. If $\displaystyle\sum_{k=0}^{10}(3 + k) = X + \sum_{k=0}^{10}k$, then $X = ?$

5. What number should be added to each of the three numbers 3, 8, and 20 so that the resulting three numbers form a geometric sequence?

6. Find the number of terms and sum of all terms for the geometric series: $1 + 3 + 9 + 27 + \ldots + 59049$

7. Find the number of terms and sum of all terms for the arithmetic series: $31+33+35+37+\ldots+351$

8. Find the sum of the infinite geometric series: $\dfrac{1}{3} - \dfrac{2}{9} + \dfrac{4}{27} - \dfrac{8}{81} + \ldots$

9. The nth term of a sequence is given by: $t_n = 5n+7$, $n = 1, 2, 3\ldots$

   a. Find the value of t_{25}

   b. Find $t_{n+1} - t_n$; Why is the sequence arithmetic?

10. Mary invested $10000 for 5 years at 8% simple interest a year. Calculate the amount at the end of 5 years.

11. Arda invested $10000 for 5 years at 8% compound interest per year. Calculate the amount at the end of 5 years.

12. Each day a runner trains for a 10 km race. On the 1st day he runs 2000m, and then increases the distance by 200 m on each following day.

   a. On which day does she run a distance of 10 km?

   b. What is the total distance she will have run in training by the end of the day she runs a distance of 10 km?

13. $x_0 = \sqrt{5}$; $x_{n+1} = x_n \cdot \sqrt[3]{x_n + 5}$; $x_5 = ?$

14. $x_0 = 0$ and $x_{n+1} = \sqrt{x_n + 10}$

   a. $x_{10} = ?$

   b. $x_{100} = ?$

   c. $x_{1000} = ?$

15. A geometric sequence with the first term and the common ratio equal to 5 and $\dfrac{3}{4}$ respectively is gives. What is the first term less than 0.0001?

16. $35+38+41+44+\ldots+185 = ?$

17. Sum of the first n terms of a sequence is given by $S_n = 3n^2 - 4n$.

   a. Determine whether the sequence is arithmetic or geometric.

   b. Find the first term and the common difference or common ratio.

   c. Calculate the nth term of the sequence.

   d. Calculate the 10th term of the sequence.

18. $f(n) = \displaystyle\sum_{k=1}^{n} k^3$; $S = (n+1)^3 + (n+2)^3 + \ldots + (2n-1)^3 + (2n)^3$ where $n > 10$; What is S in terms of $f(n)$.

19. $\dfrac{1}{k(k+1)} = \dfrac{A}{k} - \dfrac{B}{k+1}$ for every positive integer k. $2A - 3B = ?$

20. $f(n) = \sum_{k=1}^{n} \dfrac{1}{k(k+1)} = ?$; $\lim_{n \to \infty} f(n) = ?$

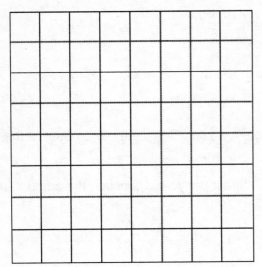

21. One wheat is placed on the top leftmost square. From left to right and from top to bottom to each successive square twice as many wheat are placed each time. According to this rule, how many wheat will be placed on the bottom rightmost square and on all squares totally?

22. $64, 16, 4, 1, \dfrac{1}{4}, ?$

23. $0, 2, 6, 14, 30, 62, ?$

4.6 VARIATION

y varies directly as x:

$y = k.x \Rightarrow \dfrac{y}{x} = k \Rightarrow$ the ratio of y to x is a constant

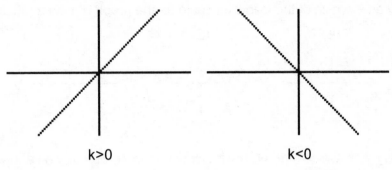

$$k>0 \qquad\qquad k<0$$

y varies inversely as x:

$y = k.\dfrac{1}{x} \Rightarrow x.y = k \Rightarrow$ the product of y and x is constant

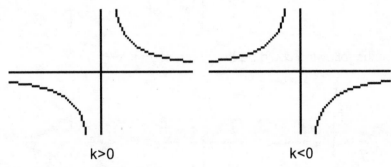

$$k>0 \qquad\qquad k<0$$

y varies directly as a and inversely as b:

$y = k \cdot \dfrac{a \rightarrow \text{Direct}}{b \rightarrow \text{Inverse}}$

k: constant of variation

Example:

It is given that y varies directly as the square of x and inversely as the square root of z.

a. If y = 3 when x = 2 and z = 9 then what will be x when y = 1 and z = 4?

b. What will happen to y when z is quadrupled and x is halved?

Solution:

a. $y = k \cdot \dfrac{x^2}{\sqrt{z}}$

$3 = k \cdot \dfrac{2^2}{\sqrt{9}}$; and k = $\dfrac{9}{4}$; therefore $y = \dfrac{9}{4} \cdot \dfrac{x^2}{\sqrt{z}}$.

$1 = \dfrac{9}{4} \cdot \dfrac{x^2}{\sqrt{4}}$ implies that $x^2 = \dfrac{8}{9}$ and $x = \pm \dfrac{2\sqrt{2}}{3}$

b. $y = \dfrac{\left(\dfrac{1}{2}\right)^2}{\sqrt{4}} = \dfrac{1}{8}$ meaning that y is reduced to one eight.

Exercises

1. If y varies directly as x, which of the following could be the graph of y as a function of x ?

(A)	(B)	(C)	(D)	(E)
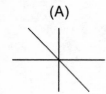	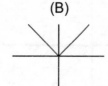		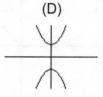	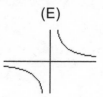

2. If y varies inversely as x, which of the following could be the graph of y as a function of x ?

(A)	(B)	(C)	(D)	(E)
	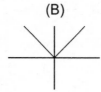			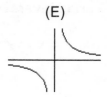

3. If $f(x) = \dfrac{1}{x}$, which of the following could be the graph of y= f(-x)?

(A)	(B)	(C)	(D)	(E)
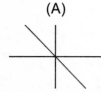	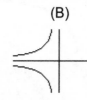	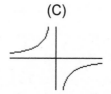	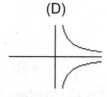	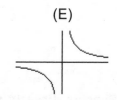

4. y varies directly as the square of x and the cube of z and inversely as the square root of b. How does y change if x and z are doubled and b is quadrupled?

5. y varies directly as the square of a and the square root of b. When a is 4 and b is 4, y is 5.

   a. find the proportionality constant

   b. find y when a is 4 and b is 3.

4.7 BINARY OPERATIONS

A binary operation Δ is a function $f(x, y)$ whose domain is a subset of R^2 i.e. the points in the Cartesian plane. Usually a binary operation is defined as $x \Delta y = f(x, y)$ by a rule given by f.

Closure property: If x and y are both elements of a set A and $x \Delta y$ is also an element of set A for all x, y; then the operation given by Δ is said to be closed over set A.

Associative property: $(x \Delta y) \Delta z = x \Delta (y \Delta z)$ implies that Δ is associative

Identity element: If there is an element e in set A such that $x \Delta e = e \Delta x = x$ then e is the identity element for the operation Δ.

Inverse element: If for each x in set A there exists an element x^{-1} such that $x \Delta x^{-1} = x^{-1} \Delta x = e$ then x^{-1} is the inverse of x with respect to the operation Δ.

Commutative property: $x \Delta y = y \Delta x$ implies that Δ is commutative.

Example:

For m > 0 and n > 0 it is given that $m^2 \Delta n^2 = \dfrac{1}{m} + \dfrac{1}{n}$. $9 \Delta 4 = ?$

Solution:

$9 \Delta 4 = 1/3 + 1/2 = 5/6$

Example:

If $(a, b) \# (c, d) = (a + c, b - d)$ and $(4, 3) \# (x, y) = (1, -2)$ then $x + y = ?$

Solution:

$(4, 3) \# (x, y) = (1, -2)$

$(4 + x, 3 - y) = (1, -2)$

$4 + x = 1$ and $3 - y = -2$

$x = -3$ and $y = 5$. Therefore $x + y = 2$.

Exercises

1. $a \Omega b = \dfrac{a}{e + \dfrac{\pi}{b}}$; $(2 \, \Omega \, 3) \, \Omega \, 4 = ?$

2. $a * b = \dfrac{\sqrt[3]{a} + \sqrt[3]{2b} - 1}{\sqrt{ab + 1}}$; $3 * \pi = ?$

3. On R_1 $a \Omega b = 2a + 3b + 4(b \Omega a)$ is given. Compute

   a) $0 \Omega 0$ b) $1 \Omega 2$ c) $5 \Omega 5$

4. On R^2 $a \Delta b = \begin{cases} ab & a > b \\ a+b & a < b \\ 1 & a = b \end{cases}$ is given. Find $(2\Delta2)\Delta(6\Delta2)$

5. It is given that $m \Delta n = \dfrac{1}{m} + \dfrac{1}{n} + 3$ where m and n are both nonzero. If $(x-1) \Delta 2 = -3\Delta4$ then x = ?

6. On R_1 the operation Ω is defined as : $a\Omega b = 4a + 4b + 3ab + 4$

    (a) Find the identity element

    (b) Find the inverse of x

    (c) Find the inverse of 5

    (d) Which element does not have an inverse?

    (e) Is Ω commutative?

    (f) Is Ω associative?

7. $a \# b = a^b - b^a$; If $3 \# k = k \# 2$ then k=?

4.8 COMPUTER PROGRAMS

A computer program is a sequence of instructions performed by the following rules:

1. The last value stored in a variable must be used in a computation.

2. When a certain instruction on a program line is performed, the instruction in the next program line will be performed unless specified by an instruction.

Example:

1. S = 0 and N = 1
2. If N ≤ 5 go to step 3 otherwise go to step 6
3. Increase S by N
4. Increase N by 1
5. Go to step 2
6. Write the final value of S.

What is the final value of S?

Solution:

S = 0; N = 1

N = 1 ≤ 5 ⇒ S = 0 + 1 = 1; N = 1 + 1 = 2

N = 2 ≤ 5 ⇒ S = 1 + 2 = 3; N = 2 + 1 = 3

N = 3 ≤ 5 ⇒ S = 3 + 3 = 6; N = 3 + 1 = 4

N = 4 ≤ 5 ⇒ S = 6 + 4 = 10; N = 4 + 1 = 5

N = 5 ≤ 5 ⇒ S = 10 + 5 = 15 N = 5 + 1 = 6

S = 15 is written

Exercises

1) If the instructions below are carried out, what will be the final value of S?

1. Let S = 0
2. Let N = 1
3. If $N^2 > 25$ go to step 6 otherwise go to step 4.
4. Increase S by 10 and decrease N by 1.
5. Go back to step 3.
6. Write the final value of S.

2) If the instructions below are carried out, what number will be printed first?

1. Let A=2.
2. Let B=2.

3. Go to step 5.

4. Replace B by A+3.

5. If A<8, replace A by B+1 and go to step 4, otherwise print B.

3) If the instructions below are carried out, what will be the final value of P?

1. P = 1

2. N = 1

3. Multiply P by N and save this product as P

4. Increase N by 1

5. If N ≤ 5 go to step 3 otherwise go to step 6

6. Write the value of P+N.

4.9 LOGIC

Conjunction: $A \wedge B$, A and B, $A \cap B$

Disjunction: $A \vee B$, A or B, $A \cup B$

Negation of Conjunction: $(A \wedge B)' \equiv A' \vee B'$

Negation of Disjunction: $(A \vee B)' \equiv A' \wedge B'$

Implication: $A \Rightarrow B$; if A, then B; A implies B; A only if B; B, if A;

$(A \Rightarrow B) \equiv (A' \vee B)$

In an implication **A** is the **sufficient** condition and **B** is the **necessary** condition.

Double implication: $A \Leftrightarrow B$; A if and only if B; A iff B

$A \Leftrightarrow B \equiv (A \Rightarrow B) \wedge (B \Rightarrow A)$

1. **Statement**   : $A \Rightarrow B$
2. **Equivalent statement** : $A' \vee B$
3. **Negation**   : $(A' \vee B)' \cong A \wedge B'$
4. **Converse**   : $B \Rightarrow A$
5. **Inverse**   : $A' \Rightarrow B'$
6. **Contrapositive**   : $B' \Rightarrow A'$

Please note that 1, 2 and 6 are all equivalent.

A statement which is **always correct** is a **TAUTOLOGY**.

A statement which is **always false** is a **CONTRADICTION**.

Indirect proof: Proving a statement $(A \Rightarrow B)$ is equivalent to proving its contrapositive $(B' \Rightarrow A')$ since $A \Rightarrow B$ and $B' \Rightarrow A'$ are equivalent statements. Proving the contrapositive of a statement instead of the statement itself is called indirect proof. The initial assumption to be made while making an indirect proof is B'.

Negations

(All $\equiv \forall$; Some $\equiv$ At least one $\equiv \exists$; T$\equiv$True; F$\equiv$False)

(All)' $\equiv$ Some $\equiv$ At least one

(Some)'$\equiv$All

$(\forall)' \equiv \exists$ $(\exists)' \equiv \forall$

$(>)' \equiv \leq$ $(\wedge)' \equiv \vee$

$(\geq)' \equiv <$ (and)' $\equiv$ or

$(<)' \equiv \geq$ $(V)' \equiv \wedge$

$(\leq)' \equiv >$ (or)' $\equiv$ and

$(=)' \equiv \neq$ (True)' $\equiv$ False

(≠)' ≡ =	(False)' ≡ True
(A)' ≡ not A	(1)' ≡ 0
(A')' ≡ A	(0)' ≡ 1

Examples:

(all men are mortal)' ≡ some men are not mortal

(for some x, x=z)' ≡ for all x, x ≠ z

(some boys play tennis)' ≡ all boys don't play tennis.

(All cats are not dogs)' ≡ some cats are dogs

Truth Tables

OR

A	B	A ∨ B
T	T	T
T	F	T
F	T	T
F	F	F

AND

A	B	A ∧ B
T	T	T
T	F	F
F	T	F
F	F	F

IMPLICATION

A	B	A'	A' ∨ B	A ⇒ B
T	T	F	T	T
T	F	F	F	F
F	T	T	T	T
F	F	T	T	T

Please note that A ⇒ B is false only if A is true and B is false.

Example:

Find the equivalent, negation, converse, inverse and contrapositive of the statement "If x=3, then x^2=9".

Solution:

Equivalent: $x \neq 3$ or x^2=9

Negation: x=3 and $x^2 \neq 9$

Converse: if x^2 = 9, then x=3 (not correct because x can be -3 as well)

Inverse: If $x \neq 3$, then $x^2 \neq 9$ (not correct because if x= -3 then x^2=9 still holds)

Contrapositive: If $x^2 \neq 9$, then $x \neq 3$; definitely correct.

Exercises

1. Statement: If $x \neq 6$ then $x^2 \neq 36$.

   Find inverse, converse, contrapositive and negation of the statement given above.

2. Find the negation of each statement.

   a. Some people never use umbrellas.

   b. All numbers are real.

   c. If x=-2 then x^2= 4

   d. All people will die one day.

   e. Some people are brunettes.

   f. Some men see things as they are.

   g. For some x, x^2= 1

   h. At least one lady is a blonde.

3. Statement: A real number has a positive cube root. In order to disprove the statement given, give an example of one number that can be used.

4. Statement: If x= 2 then x^2= 4.

   Find two statements equivalent to the one given above.

5. Statement: The equation x^2=5 has two irrational roots. What must be the initial assumption in order to prove the above statement indirectly?

4.10 MATRICES AND DETERMINANTS

Matrices are blocks of numbers used to store information (singular – matrix; plural – matrices). Following is a 3 by 5 matrix.

$$\begin{bmatrix} 2 & 0 & 2 & -4 & 7 \\ 5 & 6 & 8 & 0 & -9 \\ 2 & 0 & 7 & 10 & 0 \end{bmatrix}_{3 \times 5}$$

Matrix Arithmetic

Addition, subtraction and other linear combinations are carried out similarly. It should be noticed that matrices of different orders cannot be linearly combined.

Example:

Three matrices are defined as follows:

$$A = \begin{bmatrix} 2 & -5 & 4 \\ 1 & 4 & -2 \end{bmatrix}; B = \begin{bmatrix} 1 & 2 \\ -2 & 5 \end{bmatrix}; C = \begin{bmatrix} -1 & 3 & 0 \\ -3 & -2 & 6 \end{bmatrix}$$

Evaluate

(i) 2B   (ii) –3C(iii) A+C   (iv) A + B   (v) 2A – 3C

Solution:

(i) $2B = 2 \times \begin{bmatrix} 1 & 2 \\ -2 & 5 \end{bmatrix} = \begin{bmatrix} 2 & 4 \\ -4 & 10 \end{bmatrix}$

(ii) $-3C = -3 \times \begin{bmatrix} -1 & 3 & 0 \\ -3 & -2 & 6 \end{bmatrix} = \begin{bmatrix} 3 & -9 & 0 \\ 9 & 6 & -18 \end{bmatrix}$

(iii) $A + C = \begin{bmatrix} 2 & -5 & 4 \\ 1 & 4 & -2 \end{bmatrix} + \begin{bmatrix} -1 & 3 & 0 \\ -3 & -2 & 6 \end{bmatrix} = \begin{bmatrix} 1 & -2 & 4 \\ -2 & 2 & 4 \end{bmatrix}$

(iv) A + B cannot be calculated as the matrices do not match in dimensions.

(v) $2A - 3C = 2 \begin{bmatrix} 2 & -5 & 4 \\ 1 & 4 & -2 \end{bmatrix} - 3 \begin{bmatrix} -1 & 3 & 0 \\ -3 & -2 & 6 \end{bmatrix} = \begin{bmatrix} 7 & -19 & 8 \\ 11 & 14 & -22 \end{bmatrix}$

Matrix Multiplication

$$A = \begin{bmatrix} 2 & 4 & 7 \\ 5 & 0 & -3 \\ 1 & -3 & 4 \end{bmatrix}; B = \begin{bmatrix} 1 & 3 & -1 \\ 0 & 4 & 6 \\ 2 & -3 & 2 \end{bmatrix}; A \times B = ?$$

The definition involves taking the rows of the left hand matrix and pairing these with the columns of the second matrix.

$$\begin{bmatrix} 2 & 4 & 7 \\ 5 & 0 & -3 \\ 1 & -3 & 4 \end{bmatrix} \times \begin{bmatrix} 1 & 3 & -1 \\ 0 & 4 & 6 \\ 2 & -3 & 2 \end{bmatrix}$$

If the problem is to find the product, the first step is to take the first row of the left hand matrix [2 4 7]

and pair it up with the first column $\begin{bmatrix} 1 \\ 0 \\ 2 \end{bmatrix}$. The pairs are then multiplied and results are added to give a

single number: 2 x 1 + 4 x 0 + 7 x 2 = 16. This number is the result of combining the first row and the

first column. It becomes the number in the first row and first column of the resulting matrix. A similar

calculation must be carried out for each row and column combination. The resulting matrix is:

$$\begin{bmatrix} 16 & 1 & 36 \\ -1 & 24 & -11 \\ 9 & -21 & -11 \end{bmatrix}.$$

It should be noted that matrix multiplication is not commutative. This means that the order in which the

matrices are multiplied does matter. This is different from ordinary multiplication which is commutative.

In the above case B x A = $\begin{bmatrix} 16 & 7 & -6 \\ 26 & -18 & 12 \\ -9 & 2 & 31 \end{bmatrix}$ which is different from A x B.

Not only square matrices can be multiplied. The necessary condition is that the number of columns of

the first matrix must equal the number of rows of the second matrix.

Example:

For the following matrices: A = $\begin{bmatrix} 1 & 0 \\ 3 & -6 \end{bmatrix}$; B = $\begin{bmatrix} 2 & -4 & -1 \\ 1 & 0 & -3 \end{bmatrix}$; C = $\begin{bmatrix} -2 & -1 \\ -3 & 4 \\ 1 & -4 \end{bmatrix}$

Calculate where possible:

(i) AB

(ii) AC

(iii) BC

(iv) CB

(v) A²

Solution:

(i) AB = $\begin{bmatrix} 1 & 0 \\ 3 & -6 \end{bmatrix}\begin{bmatrix} 2 & -4 & -1 \\ 1 & 0 & -3 \end{bmatrix} = \begin{bmatrix} 2 & -4 & -1 \\ 0 & -12 & 15 \end{bmatrix}$

(ii) AC cannot be calculated.

(iii) $BC = \begin{bmatrix} 2 & -4 & -1 \\ 1 & 0 & -3 \end{bmatrix} \begin{bmatrix} -2 & -1 \\ -3 & 4 \\ 1 & -4 \end{bmatrix} = \begin{bmatrix} 7 & -14 \\ -5 & 11 \end{bmatrix}$

(iv) $CB = \begin{bmatrix} -2 & -1 \\ -3 & 4 \\ 1 & -4 \end{bmatrix} \begin{bmatrix} 2 & -4 & -1 \\ 1 & 0 & -3 \end{bmatrix} = \begin{bmatrix} -5 & 8 & 5 \\ -2 & 12 & -9 \\ -2 & -4 & 11 \end{bmatrix}$

(v) $A^2 = \begin{bmatrix} 1 & 0 \\ 3 & -6 \end{bmatrix} \begin{bmatrix} 1 & 0 \\ 3 & -6 \end{bmatrix} = \begin{bmatrix} 1 & 0 \\ -15 & 36 \end{bmatrix}$

2 by 2 Matrices

These are the matrices having two rows and two columns.

Identity Matrix

The identity matrix is defined as the matrix such that $AI = IA = A$ for all square matrices A. For 2 by 2

matrices, $I_2 = \begin{bmatrix} 1 & 0 \\ 0 & 1 \end{bmatrix}$. For 3 by 3 matrices, $I_3 = \begin{bmatrix} 1 & 0 & 0 \\ 0 & 1 & 0 \\ 0 & 0 & 1 \end{bmatrix}$. The identity matrix is the identity element

for matrix multiplication.

Zero Matrix

All elements of a zero matrix are zeros.

Diagonal Matrix

All elements other than the diagonal elements of a diagonal matrix are zeros. Following are examples of diagonal matrices:

$\begin{bmatrix} 4 & 0 & 0 \\ 0 & -5 & 0 \\ 0 & 0 & 7 \end{bmatrix}$; $\begin{bmatrix} 0 & 0 & 4 \\ 0 & -5 & 0 \\ -9 & 0 & 0 \end{bmatrix}$

Triangular Matrices

All elements other than the triangular elements are zeros. Following are examples of triangular matrices.

Upper triangular: $\begin{bmatrix} 4 & -2 & 3 \\ 0 & -5 & 0 \\ 0 & 0 & 7 \end{bmatrix}$; Lower triangular: $\begin{bmatrix} 4 & 0 & 0 \\ 9 & -5 & 0 \\ 1 & -2 & 7 \end{bmatrix}$

Inverse

The inverse of a square matrix A is written as A^{-1}. The product of a matrix and its inverse is the identity matrix, I, $A A^{-1} = A^{-1} A = I$. For 2 by 2 matrices, the inverse can be found as follows:

If $A = \begin{bmatrix} a & b \\ c & d \end{bmatrix}$, then, $A^{-1} = = \dfrac{1}{\det A}\begin{bmatrix} d & -b \\ -c & a \end{bmatrix} = \dfrac{1}{ad-bc}\begin{bmatrix} d & -b \\ -c & a \end{bmatrix}$ where detA is the determinant of

matrix A given by $ad - bc$.

Matrix Transposition

When a matrix is transposed, its rows and columns are interchanged. Therefore an m by n matrix when transposed gives an n by m matrix. Transpose of a matrix A is denoted as A^T.

For example if $A = \begin{bmatrix} 2 & -1 \\ -3 & 2 \\ 1 & 4 \end{bmatrix}$ then $A^T = \begin{bmatrix} 2 & -3 & 1 \\ -1 & 2 & 4 \end{bmatrix}$

Two by Two Determinant

$$\begin{vmatrix} a & b \\ c & d \end{vmatrix} = ad - bc$$

Three by Three Determinant

$$\begin{vmatrix} a & b & c \\ d & e & f \\ g & h & k \end{vmatrix} = \; = (aek + dhc + gbf) - (gec + fha + dbk)$$

Properties of Determinants

1. If a row or a column is multiplied by k, determinant is multiplied by k.
2. If all elements are multiplied by k in an n x n determinant, the determinant is multiplied by k^n.
3. If two rows are the same or two column are the same then determinant is 0.
4. If two rows are multiples of each other or if two columns are multiples of each other in a determinant then determinant is 0.

Example:

$$\begin{vmatrix} 19999 & 19998 \\ 20000 & 19999 \end{vmatrix} = ?$$

Solution:

$$\begin{vmatrix} x & x-1 \\ x+1 & x \end{vmatrix} = x^2 - (x+1)(x-1)$$

$$= x^2 - (x^2 - 1)$$

$$= x^2 - x^2 + 1 = 1$$

Example:

$$\begin{vmatrix} 1 & 2 & 3 \\ 0 & 2 & 4 \\ 8 & -1 & 0 \end{vmatrix} = ?$$

Solution:

Determinant = $0 + 0 + 64 - 48 + 4 - 0 = 68 - 48 = 20$

Cramer's Rule for 2 Unknowns

$a_1x + b_1y = c_1$

$a_2x + b_2y = c_2$

x=?, y=?

$$\Delta = \begin{vmatrix} a_1 & b_1 \\ a_2 & b_2 \end{vmatrix} \qquad \Delta_1 = \begin{vmatrix} c_1 & b_1 \\ c_2 & b_2 \end{vmatrix} \qquad \Delta_2 = \begin{vmatrix} a_1 & c_1 \\ a_2 & c_2 \end{vmatrix}$$

$$x = \frac{\Delta_1}{\Delta} \qquad y = \frac{\Delta_2}{\Delta}$$

Example:

x+2y=3

x+4y=5

x=? and y=?

Solution:

$$\Delta = \begin{vmatrix} 1 & 2 \\ 1 & 4 \end{vmatrix} = 2$$

$$\Delta_1 = \begin{vmatrix} 3 & 2 \\ 5 & 4 \end{vmatrix} = 2$$

$$\Delta_2 = \begin{vmatrix} 1 & 3 \\ 1 & 5 \end{vmatrix} = 2$$

$$x = \frac{\Delta_1}{\Delta} = \frac{\begin{vmatrix} 3 & 2 \\ 5 & 4 \end{vmatrix}}{\begin{vmatrix} 1 & 2 \\ 1 & 4 \end{vmatrix}} = \frac{2}{2} = 1 \text{ and } y = \frac{\Delta_2}{\Delta} = \frac{\begin{vmatrix} 1 & 3 \\ 1 & 5 \end{vmatrix}}{\begin{vmatrix} 1 & 2 \\ 1 & 4 \end{vmatrix}} = \frac{2}{2} = 1$$

Cramer's Rule for 3 Unknowns

$a_1 x + b_1 y + c_1 z = d_1$

$a_2 x + b_2 y + c_2 z = d_2$

$a_3 x + b_3 y + c_3 z = d_3$

$$\Delta = \begin{vmatrix} a_1 & b_1 & c_1 \\ a_2 & b_2 & c_2 \\ a_3 & b_3 & c_3 \end{vmatrix} \quad \Delta_1 = \begin{vmatrix} d_1 & b_1 & c_1 \\ d_2 & b_2 & c_2 \\ d_3 & b_3 & c_3 \end{vmatrix} \quad \Delta_2 = \begin{vmatrix} a_1 & d_1 & c_1 \\ a_2 & d_2 & c_2 \\ a_3 & d_3 & c_3 \end{vmatrix} \quad \Delta_3 = \begin{vmatrix} a_1 & b_1 & d_1 \\ a_2 & b_2 & d_2 \\ a_3 & b_3 & d_3 \end{vmatrix}$$

$$x = \frac{\Delta_1}{\Delta} \quad y = \frac{\Delta_2}{\Delta} \quad z = \frac{\Delta_3}{\Delta}$$

Exercises

1. $\begin{vmatrix} x-1 & 2 & 3 \\ 1 & x & 4 \\ 2 & 3 & x+1 \end{vmatrix} = 0 \Rightarrow x = ?$

2. The eigenvalues λ of an n×n square matrix A are those values that satisfy the relation $A - \lambda I = 0$, where I is the n×n identity matrix. What are the eigenvalues of the following matrices?

    a. $\begin{bmatrix} 1 & 3 \\ 4 & 2 \end{bmatrix}$

    b. $\begin{bmatrix} 1 & 0 & 0 \\ 0 & 2 & 0 \\ 0 & 0 & -1 \end{bmatrix}$

3. For the following matrices: $A = \begin{bmatrix} 1 & 2 \\ -1 & -6 \end{bmatrix}$; $B = \begin{bmatrix} 2 & -5 & -1 \\ 1 & 0 & -2 \end{bmatrix}$; $C = \begin{bmatrix} -4 & -1 \\ -3 & 5 \\ 1 & -6 \end{bmatrix}$; Calculate where possible:

    a. AB

    b. AC

    c. CB

    d. $A \cdot C^T$

    e. $B \cdot B^T$

    f. B^2

    g. A^3

    h. A^{-1}

4.11 WORD PROBLEMS

Example:

A man goes to the woods with the speed of 30 mph and returns the same route with the speed of 40 mph. If the total time it takes for the round trip is 3.5 hours, what is the total distance he has covered?

Solution:

If d is the distance to the woods then the time forward is $\dfrac{d}{30}$ and the time backward is $\dfrac{d}{40}$. Total time is 3.5 therefore $3.5 = \dfrac{d}{30} + \dfrac{d}{40}$. Solving for d we get d = 60 and the total distance covered is 120 miles.

Example:

A bus leaves Istanbul for Ankara averaging 56 miles per hour. Half an hour later a second bus leaves from the same station for Ankara averaging 60 miles per hour. How long will it take the second bus to overtake the first?

Solution:

If t is the time for the second bus, the time for the first one is (t + 0.5). At the instant when the second bus overtakes the first one, the distances covered by each of them are the same. Ü

Therefore 56(t + 0.5) = 60t and solving for t we get t = 7 hours.

Example:

A speed boat goes 100 miles downstream in 2.5 hours. Going upstream it traveled the same distance in 4 hours. What is the rate of the boat in still water, and what is the rate of the stream?

Solution:

If b is the rate of the boat and r is the rate of the stream then

b + r = 100 / 2.5 = 40 and b − r = 100 / 4 = 25.

Solving for b and r we get b = 32.5 and r = 7.5

Example:

How many quarts of pure water must be added to 60 quarts of a 15% acid solution in order to obtain a 12% acid solution?

Solution:

The quarts of pure acid remains the same for both solutions therefore if q is the quarts of pure acid then $60 \cdot \dfrac{15}{100} = (60 + q) \cdot \dfrac{12}{100}$. Solving for q we get q = 15 quarts.

Example:

If the sum of the consecutive integers from –28 to x, inclusive, is 90, what is the value of x?

Solution:

The integers are -28, -27, -26, …, -1, 0, 1, 2, …, 28, 29, 30, 31. Therefore x is 31. Please note that the sum of the integers from -28 to 28 is zero and 29 + 30 + 31 = 90.

Example:

An expert can do a job on the computer in 8 hours. His secretary can do the same job in 10 hours. After the expert works on the job for 4 hours, his secretary takes over and completes the job. How many hours did it take the secretary to complete the job?

Solution:

The expert does 1/8 of the job in an hour and his secretary can do 1/10 of the job in an hour. If h is the number of hours that the secretary works then $\frac{1}{8} \cdot 4 + \frac{1}{10} \cdot h = 1$ and solving for h we get h = 5 hours.

Example:

Tibet and Selen can do a job in 4 days. Selen and Cem can do the job in 5 days. Tibet and Cem can do the job in 6 days. In how many days will the job finish if Selen does half of the job; Cem does one third; and Tibet does the rest?

Solution:

$$\frac{1}{a} + \frac{1}{b} = \frac{1}{4}$$

$$\frac{1}{b} + \frac{1}{c} = \frac{1}{5}$$

$$\frac{1}{a} + \frac{1}{c} = \frac{1}{6}$$

Solving for a, b, and c we get $a = \frac{120}{13}$, $b = \frac{120}{17}$, and $c = \frac{120}{7}$

Berna has worked for $\frac{120}{17} \cdot \frac{1}{2} = \frac{60}{17}$ days; Cem has worked for $\frac{120}{7} \cdot \frac{1}{3} = \frac{40}{7}$ days and Ali has worked for $\frac{120}{13} \cdot \left(1 - \frac{1}{2} - \frac{1}{3}\right) = \frac{20}{13}$ days. The job will be completed in 60/17+40/7+20/13 = 10.78 days approximately.

Example:

If 5 men working 8 hours a day can complete 3 jobs in 10 days, 8 men working 6 hours a day can complete 2 jobs in how many days?

Solution:

Number of men and number of days are inversely proportional; number of hours per day and number of days are inversely proportional; number of jobs and number of days are directly proportional. Therefore:

5 men——8 h/day   3 jobs   10 days

8 men   6 h/day   2 jobs   x days

and $x = \dfrac{5 \cdot 8 \cdot 2 \cdot 10}{8 \cdot 6 \cdot 3} = \dfrac{50}{9}$ days.

Example:

Cana is 4 years older than Senem. When Cana was at Senem's age, Senem's age was one third of Cana's age at that time. What is the sum of their ages now?

Solution:

Now: Cana = x + 4 and Senem = x

In the past: Cana = x and Senem = x / 3.

The age difference between Cana and Senem remains the same therefore: $x - \dfrac{x}{3} = 4$ and x = 6.

Example:

In a group of 2,000 students, 900 are studying Spanish, 700 are studying French, and 500 are studying German. What is the greatest possible number of these students that might NOT be studying any of these languages?

Solution:

All of the students studying French or German may be a subset of the students studying Spanish, therefore 2000 – 900 = 1100 students is the maximum.

Example:

One number is 14 less than another number and the product of the two numbers is 204, what are the numbers?

Solution:

If one of the numbers is x, then the other one is x-14.

$x(x-14) = 72 \Rightarrow x^2 -14x - 72 = 0 \Rightarrow (x-18)(x+4) = 0$

x = 18 or x = -4; one is 18 and the other one is 4 or one is -4 and the other one is -18.

Example:

Mr. Acuner invested part of his $80,000 investment partially in bonds paying 10% and the remaining in stocks paying 7%. If his annual income from both investments is $6,500.00, how much did he invest in the bonds and in the stocks?

Solution:

Money invested in bonds: x and money invested in stocks: 80000 – x

$$x \cdot \frac{10}{100} + (80000 - x) \cdot \frac{7}{100} = 6500$$

Solving for x we get x = 30000.

He invested $30,000 in bonds and $50,000 in stocks.

Example:

N=360.

a. How many distinct positive factors does N have?

b. How many distinct negative factors does N have?

c. How many distinct factors does N have?

d. What is the sum of the distinct positive factors of N?

e. What is the sum of the distinct negative factors of N?

f. What is the sum of the distinct factors of N?

Solution:

$360 = 2^3 \cdot 3^2 \cdot 5^1$

a. Number of distinct positive factors is (3+1)(2+1)(1+1)=24.

b. Number of distinct negative factors is also 24.

c. Number of distinct factors is 48.

d. Sum of the distinct positive factors is $\left(1 + 2 + 2^2 + 2^3\right)\left(1 + 3 + 3^2\right)(1 + 5) = 1170.$

e. Sum of the distinct negative factors is -1170.

f. Sum of the distinct factors is 0.

<u>**Exercises**</u>

Rate Problems

1. A jet travels 500 kilometers in 40 minutes with a tail wind. Returning, the jet takes 50 minutes to cover the same distance. What is the rate of the plane and that of the wind?

2. On a beautiful Sunday, Mert drove his family to Marmaris that was 60 miles away from his house. While coming back he increased his average speed by 9 miles per hour covering the same distance in 20 minutes less time. What was his average speed going and returning?

3. Two routes to get from Bodrum to Fethiye differ by 20 miles. The time required is the same if a

car travels 50 miles per hour over the shorter route and 55 miles per hour over the longer route. How long is each route in miles?

4. Two motorcyclists start toward each other from towns 212 miles apart. If one motorcyclist travels 40 miles per hour and the other 66 miles per hour, in how many hours will they meet?

5. Two fishing boats leave the same port traveling in opposite directions along the north coast of Turkey, one boat traveling 5 miles per hour faster than the other. At the end of one day's travel they are 540 miles apart. What is the speed of each boat per hour?

6. A college student walks from his home to the beach at 8 mph, stays at the beach for 4 hours and then drives back home at the rate of 40 mph. If the student comes back home after 7 hours, what is the distance from his home to the beach?

7. A canoeist paddled down a river a distance of 2 miles in three fourths of an hour. Paddling upstream on his return, it took him an hour and a half. Find the rate of the canoe in still water.

8. Mr. Erdem, flew his jet plane from Ankara to Istanbul, a distance of 420 km, in 1.5 hours against the wind. On his return trip, it took 30 minutes less to cover the same distance. Assuming the same wind speed in both directions what was this speed?

9. Two cyclists leave the same place going in the same direction with speeds of 30 and 35 mph respectively. If the faster one starts 2 hours later in how many hours will the faster cyclist catch up the slower one?

10. Two motor-bicycles leave Istanbul at the same time, one traveling east at the speed of 40 miles per hour and the other west at the rate of 65 miles per hour. After how many hours will they be 840 miles apart?

11. A car leaves Izmir heading towards a famous resort in Turkey, Marmaris, traveling at the rate of 50 miles per hour. One hour later a faster car sets out from the same city to overtake the first. At what rate must the faster car travel in order to overtake the first in 5 hours?

12. Two men, 55 miles apart, start walking toward each other traveling at the respective rates of 5 miles and 6 miles in 2 hours. How many miles will each have traveled when they meet?

Mixture Problems

1. Zeynep has 490 coins in her bank made up of dimes and quarters making up a total value of $92.50. How many quarters does she have?

2. How many pounds of $3.20 per pound tea must be added to tea costing $3.60 per pound to make a mixture of 200 pounds costing $3.50 per pound?

3. How much water must be evaporated from a 5% salt solution weighing 60 liters to obtain a 10% salt solution?

4. The charge for admission to the natural history museum is $15 for adults and 10 dollar for children. If 1,000 people visited the museum in one day and the total receipts were $11,300; how

many of each kind of ticket was sold?

5. Ebru has 250 liters of milk testing 6% fat. How many liters of no fat milk must she add to reduce the fat content to 5%?

6. A salesman wishes to combine grade A coffee worth $2.50 per pound with grade B worth $1.50 per pound to obtain 400 pounds worth $2.00 per pound. How many pounds of each grade must he use?

7. A solution is made by mixing concentrate with water. How many liters of concentrate should be mixed with 3 liters of water so that 25 percent of the solution is concentrate?

8. Two mixtures A and B that are 40% and 20% alcohol by volume respectively are mixed to make C which is 35% alcohol by volume. What is the ratio of the volume of A to the volume of B in the mixture?

9. Two solutions a% and b% alcohol by volume are mixed to make an x lt solution which is c% alcohol by volume. If a<c<b then how many liters of the a% solution was used?

10. Serra checks her car radiator and finds that it contains 40% antifreeze. If the radiator holds 20 quarts and is full, how many quarts must be drained off and replaced by pure antifreeze in order to get a 50% antifreeze content?

11. How many liters of a 20%, alcohol solution must be mixed with a 50% alcohol solution to get a 40 liter solution which is %40 alcohol by volume?

Work – Pool Problems

1. It takes Ekin twice as long to harvest a cornfield as it does Emine. If both work together, they can harvest the field in 3 days. How many days would it take each alone to harvest the crop?

2. It takes Dilara 4 hours to do the house cleaning that Mina can do in 6 hours and Nancy can do in 8 hours. If all three work together, how many hours will it take them to do it?

3. It takes Seda 5 hours to do the house cleaning that Emel can do in 6 hours and Nancy can do in 7 hours. If all three work together, how many hours will it take them to clean two such houses?

4. Romeo can mow the lawn in 3 hours. When Juliet helps him, together they can complete the mowing in 2 hours. How long will it take Juliet to do the mowing alone?

5. Raif can paint a house in 4 days. His cousin Christina can paint the same house in 6 days. After working 2 days, Raif became ill and Christina finished the job. How long did it take Christina to finish the job?

6. A storage pipe can fill a tank in 10 days. Another smaller pipe can fill it in 15 days. After the larger pipe is on for 4 days, it breaks down. The smaller pipe is opened and completes the job of filling the tank. How long did it take for the smaller pipe to complete the job alone?

7. An expert can do a job in 4 hours. The expert and two trainees who work at the same rate can finish the job in 2 hours. How many hours would each trainee take to do the job alone?

8. Working together, an old pipe and a new pipe can fill a tank in 2 hours. If the new pipe can fill the tank in 3 hours less time than the old pipe, how many hours will it take each pipe to fill the tank?

9. An expert can complete a job in 6 hours and his helper can do the same job in 9 hours. If they both work together how many hours will it take them to complete three such jobs?

10. If 40 men working on a project can complete 2 jobs in 100 hours, how many men would be required to complete 3 jobs in 80 hours?

11. Two pipes can fill a tank in 12 hours and 15 hours respectively. A third pipe can empty the tank in 18 hours. How long will it take the tank to be filled if all three pipes are open?

12. Zeynep can type a legal brief in 6 hours. Her assistant Elif can type the same brief in 9 hours. If they both work together for 3 hours and then Zeynep works alone, how many hours will it take her to finish the job?

13. Trainee A can complete a job in 8 hours and trainee B can complete the same job in 10 hours. Expert C works 1.5 times as fast as both trainees together. In how many hours can C complete the job?

Age Problems

1. The sum of the ages of two men is 62 years. Two years ago, the age of the younger man was 2 years less than half of the older man's age at that time. How old is each man now?

2. Mukadder is now 5 times as old as his son. In 5 years he will be 3 times as old as his son will be then. How old will Mukadder be 5 years from now?

3. In 8 years, Nancy will be as old as Melissa is now. Three years later the sum of their ages will be 28. What are their ages?

Investment Problems

1. Ebru has 2 investments which yield an annual income of $1,992.00. One investment yields 6% and the other 9%. How much is invested in each if the total amount invested is $25,600?

2. A financial advisor invests $9,000 at a certain rate and $12,000 at a rate that is 1% less than twice the rate at $9,000. If the total income from both investments is $1,860.00, find the rate of each investment.

3. Mr. Meylani invested $3,000 more at 6% than at 4%. If his yearly income from both investments is $1,180.00, how much did he invest at each rate?

4. Two sums of money differing by $4,500 were invested, the larger amount at 5% and the smaller at 6%. If the difference in their yield is $138.00, how much was invested at each rate?

Fraction Word Problems

1. A certain energy saving device saves 30 million gallons of gas per company on the average in one year. If the number of companies were increased by one – fifth, the total number of companies would become 36.

   a. How many oil companies are there at present?

   b. How many gallons of gas will be saved if all companies use the same device at present?

2. The membership fee to a certain union will become $300 when it is $8 less than the current fee increased by one tenth. What is the current membership fee?

3. If the number of questions in a math test is increased by one half then decreased by one half, there will be 45 questions in the test. How many questions are there in the test currently?

4. A number is increased by 6; the result is increased by one third and the final result is halved to get the original number back again. What is the original number?

Miscellaneous

1. The rental cost of a certain video game is $4 per day for each of the first week and $3 per day for each succeeding day. Which of the following is an expression for the cost, in dollars, of renting this video game for n days, in n>7?

2. Ali and Aksel left for a week's vacation on the same day. Ali took $400 as spending money and spent $30 per day. Aksel took $350. He did not spend any money on the first 2 days, but thereafter he spent $35 per day. What is the expression for the difference between the amount they have after x days where $x \geq 2$?

3. If 9 red and 18 blue cubes that are identical in shape and dimensions are gathered together to make one big cube, what is the greatest ratio of the red surface to the blue surface the resulting cube can have?

4. 1024= A+B.3+C.9+D.27+E.81+F.243+G.729

   If each of the numbers A, B, C, D, E, F, and G is a member of the set {0,1,2} then what is the remainder when the seven digit number G,FED,CBA is divided by 9?

5. After Adnan gave $60 to Gizem and Gizem gave $52 to Ferhan, Adnan had $60 more than Gizem and $80 more than Ferhan. Originally, how much more did Adnan have than Gizem and Ferhan?

6. A man buys 3 eggs for $a and sells a eggs for $3. What is his rate of profit in terms of a given that a is a positive integer.

7. $A = 2^{2004}$; what is the remainder when A is divided by 10?

8. $A = 3^{1999}$; what is the remainder when A is divided by 5?

9. A cake in the shape of a square prism is partitioned into identical pieces with identical cuts.

   a. At least how many cuts are needed to obtain 16 pieces?

    b. If 16 pieces are obtained in 96 seconds, how many seconds are needed to obtain 25 pieces?

    c. In order to obtain k pieces, how many cuts are needed at least if k is a perfect square?

10. An electric sew can cut a long piece of wood into K pieces in x seconds. In how many seconds can the wood be cut into 2K pieces? Assume that cuts are identical and identical pieces are obtained.

11. A palindromic time is one that reads the same forward as it does backward, for example 12:21 and 4:04 are palindromic times: A 12 hour digital clock displays all times from 12.00 to 11.59. From 12.00 noon to 12.00 noon the next day, how many palindromic times are there?

12. A regulation states that the ramps to be built for the disabled must rise at most for 1 inch for every foot of horizontal distance. If the ramp has a width of 3.5 ft and it will rise to a height of three steps each 2.5 inches high and that the cost of the ramp is 10 $ for every square feet and that the ramp is sold in whole numbers of square feet, what is the minimum cost of the ramp?

13. The product of three positive integers is 72 and their sum is A. If one of the integers is greater than the other two, then what are the integers assuming that the value of A is known?

14. On a bookstore shelf there are 48 books of which is are hard cover, 20 are mathematics books and 18 are neither. How many hard cover mathematics books are there on the shelf?

15. What is the height in feet of a stack of 1000 papers each of which is x inches thick?

16. A man has 40 coins consisting of dimes and quarters only making up a total value of $5.5. What is the difference between the number of quarters and the number of dimes that the man has?

17. In a school there are x male and y female teachers. The number of female colleagues of each male teacher is 7 less than 3 times as many as his male colleagues. The number of male colleagues of each female teacher is 9 less than her female colleagues. How many teachers are there in this school?

18. It costs a cents for the first minute and b cents for each additional minute to make a phone call from city A to city B. Lara makes a phone call that is x minutes where x>1. Zeynep makes a phone call that is y minutes and pays c times as much as Lara did. What is the relation between x and y given a, b, c.

19. A store owner starts a promotion like: "Buy 3, pay for 2", on any 2 identical items. What is the rate of discount that he is making on an item?

Parking time	Total charge
0 to 1 hour	$4
1 to 2 hours	$6
2 to 4 hours	$9
4 to 8 hours	$12
8 to 12 hours	$15

20. Kaspar leaves his car on Thursday 5.00 PM and takes his car at 1.00 PM next Sunday. If the rates are decreased to 70% after midnight till noon and increased by 60% from Saturday 12.00 AM to Sunday 6.00 PM then what will be the amount in $ of the charge that he will have to pay? (A:$102.4)

21. The ratio of two numbers is 8:5. If the difference of the 2 numbers is 105, what are the numbers?

22. If one number is 10 less than another and the difference of their squares is 300, what are the numbers?

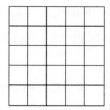

23. How many different squares are there in the given figure above?

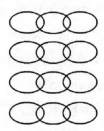

Cost of cutting a ring = $1

Cost of joining a ring = $3

24. If all given rings will be joined to make a bracelet chain, what is the minimum possible cost?

25. All candies are mandies. Some candies are tandies. Some mandies are neither candies nor tandies and there is a tandy which is not mandy. Which one(s) of the following must be true?

   a. A candy which is a tandy is a mandy.

   b. There is at least one tandy which is a mandy but not a candy

   c. At least one tandy is neither a candy nor a mandy.

26. In the sophomore class there are 200 people

   a. How many people are there between the best 50th and the worst 50th students?

    b. How many students are there between the students ranking 140th and 180th students?

27. The sum of two numbers is 50 and the difference of their squares is 300. What are the 2 numbers?

28. Divide 2 dollars into dimes and quarters so that there will be 6 more dimes than quarters.

29. A contractor needed to build a depot in 2 days. The first day he hired 4 experts and 2 trainees at a cost of $4,400 per day. The second day he hired 5 experts and 3 trainees at a cost of $5,800 per day. What did it cost him per day to pay each trainee and each expert?

30. Two boxers weighed a total of 540 pounds. After a month, one boxer gained 15% of his weight and the other lost 10% of his weight. If the sum of their weights is now 553.5 pounds, how many pounds did each weigh before the month?

31. Renan has twice as many dimes as quarters. If the dimes were quarters and the quarters were dimes, he would have $3.15 more than he has now. How many coins does he have totally?

32. If a triangle has exactly one of its vertices on a circle, What can be the number of points that the triangle and the circle have in common?

33. Ten different line segments are to be drawn so that each of the segments has an endpoint at point P. What is the greatest number of these line segments that could be intersected by some other line not drawn through P?

34. 48abc30 is a 7 digit number divisible by 19. How many ordered triples (a, b, c) are there?

35. A palindrome is a number that reads the same forward as it does backward.

    a. The next two palindromes greater than 41814 are x and y. What is x – y?

    b. The next two palindromes greater than 52925 are x and y. What is x – y?

36. A school supply cabinet stocks numerals to use for room numbers. If the stock consists of 20 each of the numerals 0, 1, 2, 3, 4, 5, 6, 7, 8, and 9, how many consecutive room numbers, beginning with room number 1, can be formed?

37. Kerem is writing the page number on the bottom of each page of a 60-page book report, starting with 1. How many digits will he have written altogether?

$$N = 1234567891011 \ldots 9899100$$

38. The integer N is formed by writing the positive integers in a row, starting with 1 and ending with 100, as shown above. Counting from the left, what is the 130th digit of N?

Yesterday's mistake is today's experience...

Roberto Baggio

CHAPTER 5 – 10 Model Tests

Level 1 - Model Tests 1 through 5

Level 2 - Model Tests 1 through 5

Answers to Model Tests

Solutions to Model Tests

P.S. Answer sheets can be downloaded from www.rushsociety.com.

Complete Prep for the SAT Math Subject Tests – Level 1 and Level 2

Level 1 – Model Test 1

Test Duration: 60 Minutes

Directions: For each of the following problems, decide which is the best of the choices given. If the exact numerical value is not one of the choices, select the choice that best approximates this value. Then fill in the corresponding oval on the answer sheet.

Notes:

- A calculator will be necessary for answering some (but not all) of the questions in this test. For each question you will have to decide whether or not you should use a calculator. The calculator you use must be at least a scientific calculator; programmable calculators and calculators that can display graphs are permitted.

- The only angle measure used on this test is degree measure. Make sure your calculator is in the degree mode.

- Figures that accompany problems in this test are intended to provide information useful in solving the problems. They are drawn as accurately as possible except when it is stated in a specific problem that its figure is not drawn to scale.

- All figures lie in a plane unless otherwise indicated.

- Unless otherwise specified, the domain of any function f is assumed to be the set of all real numbers x for which f(x) is a real number.

Reference Information: The following information is for your reference in answering some of the questions in this test.

- Volume of a right circular cone with radius r and height h: $V = \dfrac{1}{3}\pi r^2 h$

- Lateral area of a right circular cone with circumference of the base c and slant height l: $S = \dfrac{1}{2}cl$

- Volume of a sphere with radius r: $V = \dfrac{4}{3}\pi r^3$

- Surface area of sphere with radius r: $S = 4\pi r^2$

- Volume of a pyramid with base area B and height h: $V = \dfrac{1}{3}Bh$

1. $\dfrac{5^2-1}{5-1} + \dfrac{6^2-1}{6-1} + \dfrac{7^2-1}{7-1} = ?$

(A) 9   (B) 15   (C) 18   (D) 21   (E) 27

2. If $3x^2 - 2y^2 = -6x^2 + 14y^2$ then $\dfrac{x}{y}$ can be

(A) $\dfrac{16}{9}$ 　　　　(B) $\dfrac{9}{16}$ 　　　　(C) $\dfrac{3}{4}$ 　　　　(D) $-\dfrac{3}{4}$ 　　　　(E) $-\dfrac{4}{3}$

3. If $\dfrac{e}{r}$ is an integer, which of the following is also an integer?

(A) $e - r$ 　　　(B) $e + 4r$ 　　　(C) $e \cdot r$ 　　　(D) $\dfrac{r}{e}$ 　　　(E) $\dfrac{e^2}{r^2}$

4. If $E = x + xy$ where x and y are distinct prime numbers then which of the following is false?

(A) E is positive.

(B) E is an integer.

(C) E is always even.

(D) The minimum value of E is 8.

(E) E has at least four distinct positive divisors.

5. All of the following points line on the same line except

(A) $(0, -4)$ 　　　(B) $(1, -1)$ 　　　(C) $(2, 2)$ 　　　(D) $(3, 6)$ 　　　(E) $(4, 8)$

6. If $a^2 = 3^{4b}$, where a and b are positive integers, then in terms of b, $\dfrac{a}{27}$ equals?

(A) 3^{2b-3} 　　　(B) 3^{2b+27} 　　　(C) 3^{4b} 　　　(D) 3^{4b+1} 　　　(E) 3^{16b}

7. If $\dfrac{1}{e} < \dfrac{1}{r} < 0$, which of the following could be the value of $\dfrac{e}{r}$?

(A) -5　　　　　(B) $-\dfrac{2}{3}$　　　　　(C) $\dfrac{3}{7}$　　　　　(D) 4　　　　　(E) 9

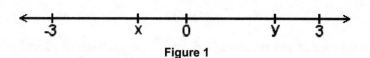

Figure 1

8. If x and y stand for real numbers on the number line given in figure 1 above, which of the following is correct?

I. x + y is a positive real number less than y.

II. $y - \dfrac{x}{2}$ is a positive real number between y and 3.

III. $x - \dfrac{y}{2}$ is a negative real number greater than x.

(A) I only　　　(B) II only　　　(C) I and II only　　　(D) I and III only　　　(E) I, II and III

9. How many positive 5 – digit integers can be made using only the digits 2, 3, and 4 if each of these digits must be used at least once in each 5 – digit integer?

(A) 15　　　　　(B) 25　　　　　(C) 125　　　　　(D) 243

(E) None of the above

Figure 2

10. In figure 2, if the length of BC = 2a + 4 and the length of AB is half the length of BC. What is the length of AC?

(A) a+2　　　(B) a+4　　　(C) 2a+2　　　(D) 3a+4　　　(E) 3a+6

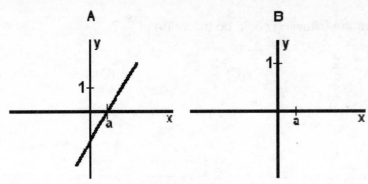

Figure 3

11. The line m given in figure 3.A will be sketched on the coordinate axes in figure 3.B where y axis is enlarged and x axis stays the same. Which of the following is correct regarding line m?

(A) It will be steeper.

(B) It will be less steep.

(C) It will stay the same.

(D) It will be reflected in the x axis.

(E) It will be reflected in the y axis.

12. Two planes start from the same point P and travel along separate straight routes that originate at P, forming an angle of 90°, how many miles apart are the two planes after each has traveled 2200 miles?

(A) 1859   (B) 1860   (C) 2344   (D) 2345   (E) 3111

13. If line m is given by $y - 3 = \frac{4}{3}(x + 5)$ then the slope of the line that is parallel to m can be

(A) -5   (B) $\frac{4}{3}$ (C) $-\frac{3}{4}$ (D) 3   (E) 12

14. What is the area of the shaded region given in figure 4?

(A) 16.0

(B) 16.5

(C) 17.0

(D) 17.5

(E) 18.0

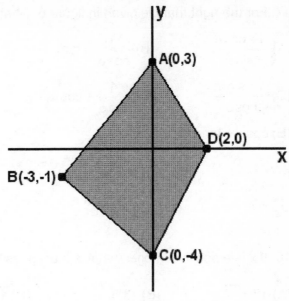

Figure 4

15. If in figure 5, the degree measures of arcs $\overset{\frown}{APB}$ and $\overset{\frown}{CQB}$ are 7x and 5x respectively, then x = ?

(A) 12° (B) 18°

(C) 24° (D) 36°

(E) None of the above

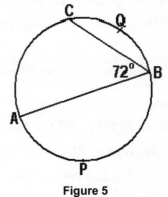

Figure 5

16. If $x^7 = 7$ then $\log_x 77 = ?$

(A) 15.4 (B) 15.5 (C) 15.6 (D) 15.7 (E) 15.8

17. For the right triangle given in figure 6, what is x + y in terms of α?

(A) $\dfrac{1+\cos\alpha}{\sin\alpha}$

(B) $\dfrac{1}{\cos\alpha} - \tan\alpha$

(C) $\dfrac{1+\sin\alpha}{\cos\alpha}$

(D) $\dfrac{1}{\tan\alpha} + \cos\alpha$

(E) $\cos\alpha + \tan\alpha$

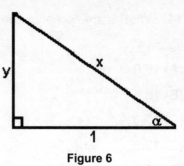

Figure 6

18. If x is a positive integer, what is least possible value of $15 - \dfrac{3}{x}$?

(A) 12   (B) 13.5   (C) 14   (D) 14.25   (E) 15

19. The graph of y = mx + 1 has points in the fourth quadrant if

(A) m = 0   (B) m < 0   (C) m > 0   (D) m < -1   (E) -1 < m < 0

20. In figure 7, AP is perpendicular to PD, and the degree measure of the angles APC and BPD are 40° and 70° respectively. What is half of the degree measure of angle BPC?

(A) 10°

(B) 20°

(C) 30°

(D) 40°

(E) 50°

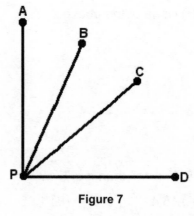

Figure 7

21. In figure 8, if x = 3z and $y = \dfrac{z}{3}$ then what is the volume of the rectangular box

in terms of y?

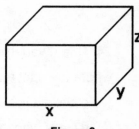

Figure 8

(A) $\dfrac{27}{y^3}$ (B) $\dfrac{y^3}{27}$ (C) y^3 (D) $27y^3$

(E) None of the above

22. If in figure 9, P is a variable point on BC then AP + PD can be at least

(A) 15

(B) 15.67

(C) 16.22

(D) 16.55

(E) 17.56

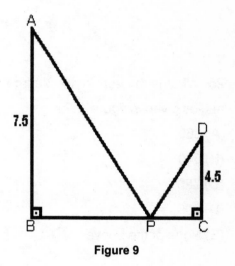

Figure 9

23. If the circle with the equation given by $(x + 2)^2 + (y - 3)^2 = 4$ is reflected across the line x = 1 then the resulting circle will be given by which of the following?

(A) $(x - 4)^2 + (y - 3)^2 = 4$ (B) $(x + 4)^2 + (y - 3)^2 = 4$ (C) $(x - 4)^2 + (y + 3)^2 = 4$

(D) $(x + 4)^2 + (y + 3)^2 = 4$ (E) $(x - 2)^2 + (y - 3)^2 = 4$

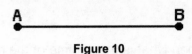

Figure 10

24. P is a variable point in the plane of segment AB given in figure 10 so that PAB is a right triangle where the right angle is at P. The locus of all such points P is

(A) a circle whose radius is AB.

(B) a circle whose diameter is AB.

(C) a semicircle whose diameter is AB.

(D) part of a circle whose diameter is AB.

(E) a circle whose diameter is greater than AB.

25. What is the sum of the degree measures of the ten marked angles given in figure 11?

(A) 360

(B) 540

(C) 720

(D) 900

(E) None of the above

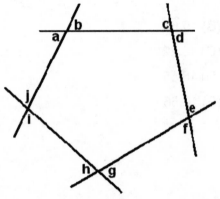

Figure 11

For questions 26 and 27 please refer to figure 12 given below.

26. A bug at point A is crawling along the darkened path toward B at a constant rate. Which of the following most correctly represents the bug's distance from point P as a function of time?

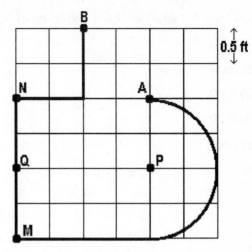

Figure 12

(A)

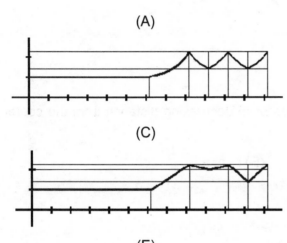

(B)

(C)

(D)

(E)

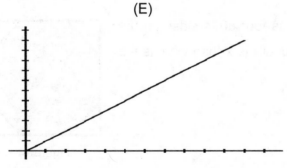

27. If the bug is at point M at 10.00 AM and moves toward point Q at the rate of 1 m/s, then which of the following gives the bug's distance from point P, t seconds after 10.00 AM?

(A) $2 + |1 - t|$ (B) $\sqrt{4 + (1 + t)^2}$ (C) $\sqrt{4 + (1 - t)^2}$ (D) $2 + |1 + t|$ (E) $\sqrt{4 - (1 - t)^2}$

28. If the right triangle given in figure 13 is rotated about the x axis for 180° what will be the volume of the resulting solid?

(A) 32.8

(B) 32.9

(C) 33.0

(D) 65.9

(E) 66.0

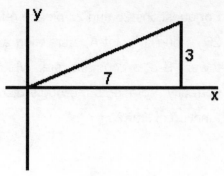

Figure 13

29. A circle has three chords with the following lengths:

chord a: 2.06 ft

chord b: $\dfrac{13}{5}$ ft

chord c: 2.006 ft

Which of the following is a list of these chords in the order of decreasing distance from the center of the circle?

(A) b, a, c　　(B) c, a, b　　(C) a, c, b　　(D) c, b, a　　(E) b, c, a

30. The shaded regular octagon given in figure 14 has four of its sides on the sides of the square. If the length of one side of the square is x then what is the length of one side of the octagon?

(A) $\dfrac{x}{2}$

(B) $\dfrac{x}{1+\sqrt{2}}$

(C) $x \cdot (\sqrt{2}+1)$

(D) $\dfrac{x}{\sqrt{2}}$

(E) $\dfrac{x\sqrt{2}}{1+\sqrt{2}}$

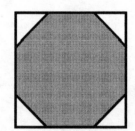

Figure 14

31. The distance between the centers of two circles with radii 5 and 9 is given as d. If d is a number between 6 and 12 then which of the following most accurately demonstrates the relative position of the two circles with respect to each other?

(A)   (B)   (C)   (D)   (E)

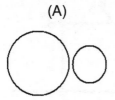 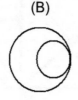 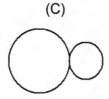 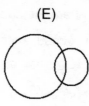

32. In order to win a game, Emel must toss two dice and the numbers on the top faces of the dice must sum up to a value greater than 8. What is the probability that Emel wins the game at her second trial?

(A) $\dfrac{5}{18} \cdot \dfrac{13}{18}$ (B) $\dfrac{5}{18} + \dfrac{13}{18}$ (C) 1   (D) 0

(E) None of the above

33. In figure 15, a different element of the set A = {1, 2, 3, 5, 6, 7, 8, 9} will be placed in each of the 8 remaining squares, so that in a row from left to right and in a column from top to bottom the numbers are in increasing order; then a – b – c + d = ?

(A) 2   (B) 3   (C) 5   (D) 7

(E) It cannot be determined from the information given.

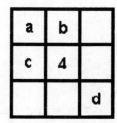

Figure 15

34. If i = $\sqrt{-1}$, then all of the following expressions are equal except

(A) $i^4 + i^6$ (B) $i^6 + i^8$ (C) $i^9 + i^{11}$ (D) $(2i)^2 - 4$ (E) $(-2i)^2 + 4$

35. In figure 16, rectangle OABC is rotated in the counterclockwise direction for θ degrees about point O, to get rectangle OA'B'C'. If the coordinates of B are (x,y) then what are the coordinates of point C'?

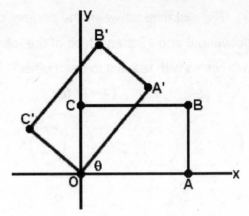

Figure 16

(A) (x·cosθ, x·sinθ)

(B) (– y·sinθ, y·cosθ)

(C) (y·sinθ, – y·cosθ)

(D) (x·cosθ – y·sinθ, x·sinθ + y·cosθ)

(E) (x·cosθ + y·sinθ, x·sinθ – y·cosθ)

36. The larger acute angle in a triangle with side lengths of 9, 12, and 15 is α whereas the smaller acute angle in a triangle with side lengths of 16, 30, and 34 is β. Which of the following statements must be incorrect?

I. sinα < sinβ

II. cosα < cosβ

III. tanα < tanβ

(A) All   (B) II only   (C) I and II only   (D) I and III only   (E) II and III only

37. If $f(x) = \dfrac{1}{x^2 - 1}$ and $g(x) = \sqrt{x - 1}$ then what is the domain of f(g(x))?

(A) All real numbers except 2

(B) All real numbers except -1 and 1

(C) All real numbers except -1, 1, and 2

(D) All real numbers greater than or equal to 1

(E) All real numbers greater than or equal to 1 except 2

38. What is the inverse of the function whose graph is given in figure 17?

(A) $f(x) = \dfrac{3x + 2}{4}$

(B) $f(x) = \dfrac{3x - 2}{4}$

(C) $f(x) = \dfrac{4x - 2}{3}$

(D) $f(x) = \dfrac{4x + 2}{3}$

(E) $f(x) = \dfrac{3x - 4}{2}$

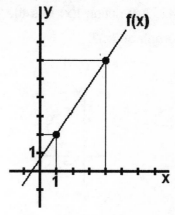

Figure 17

39. If the point with coordinates (5, 7) is on the graph of f(x,y) = 0 which is symmetric with respect to the origin, which of the following points is also on the same graph?

(A) (7, -5)　　　(B) (7, 5)　　　(C) (-5, -7)　　　(D) (-5, 7)　　　(E) (5, -7)

40. If x is an acute angle then $\dfrac{\sin x \cdot \cos x}{\tan x} = ?$

(A) $\sin^2 x$　　　(B) $\dfrac{1}{\sin^2 x}$　　　(C) $\cos^2 x$　　　(D) $\dfrac{1}{\cos^2 x}$　　　(E) $\tan x$

41. If $f(x) = \dfrac{2}{x - 2}$ and f(g(6))=2, then find g(x) can be

(A) $2 + \dfrac{2}{x}$　　　(B) $\dfrac{x}{x + 2}$　　　(C) $\dfrac{x}{x - 2}$　　　(D) $\dfrac{2x}{x - 2}$　　　(E) $\dfrac{x + 2}{2x}$

42. A function f(x) has the property that $f(x_2) \geq f(x_1)$ when $x_2 < x_1$; which of the following can be the graph of f(x)?

(A)

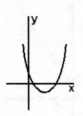

(B)

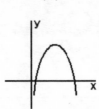

(C)

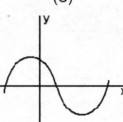

(D)

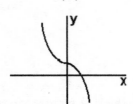

(E)

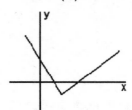

Figure 18

43. How many shaded squares are there in the n'th pattern given in figure 18 above?

(A) $\dfrac{n^2 + 3n + 2}{2}$

(B) $\dfrac{3n^2 + n + 2}{2}$

(C) $\dfrac{n^2 + 2n + 3}{2}$

(D) $\dfrac{2n^2 + 2n + 3}{2}$

(E) $\dfrac{2n^2 + 3n + 1}{2}$

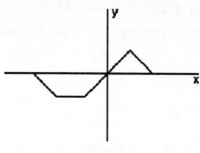

Figure 19

44. Graph of f(x) is given in figure 19 above. What will be the graph of |f(x)|?

(A)

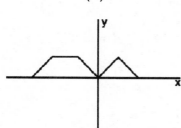

(B)

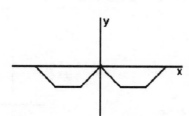

(C)

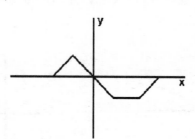

(D)

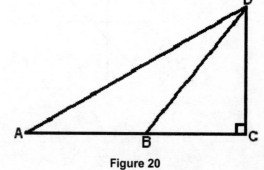

(E)

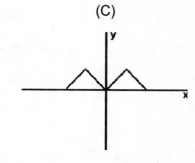

45. Given in figure 20, the lengths of AB, BD and AD are 9, 10, and 17 inches respectively. What is the length of CD?

(A) 6   (B) 8   (C) 10

(D) 12   (E) 14

Figure 20

Figure not drawn to scale

46. The price of a certain classical car grows at the rate of 5% each year. If the price of the car is $120,000 in 2004, what was its price in 1994 rounded to the nearest thousand dollars?

(A) 70,000   (B) 71,000   (C) 73,000   (D) 74,000   (E) 77,000

47. If $f(x) = x^2 - 1$ and $x \leq 0$ then $f^{-1}(x) = ?$

(A) $f(x) = \sqrt{x+1}$ (B) $f(x) = (x+1)^2$ (C) $f(x) = \pm\sqrt{x+1}$

(D) $f(x) = -\sqrt{x+1}$ (E) $f(x) = -(x+1)^2$

48. If $f(x) = \sqrt{x-1}$ and $g(x) = x^2$, which of the following is the graph of $y = f(g(x))$?

(A)

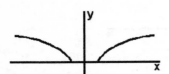

(B)

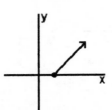

(C)

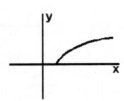

(D)

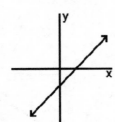

(E)

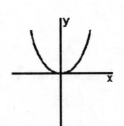

49. Which of the following figures best describes the region that represents the set of all points (x,y) for which $|y| \leq 1$?

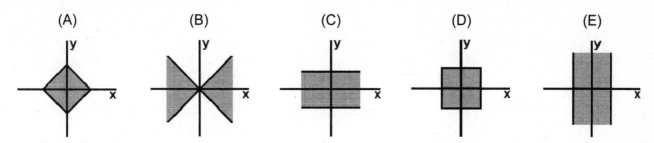

50. The hollow cube given in figure 21 is made by removing the front and back faces of a cube with the volume of 216 cubic feet. What is the perimeter in feet of the convex quadrilateral whose vertices are the centers of the remaining four faces of the hollow cube?

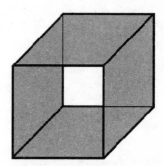

(A) 6   (B) 24   (C) $3\sqrt{2}$

(D) $2\sqrt{12}$ (E) $12\sqrt{2}$

Figure 21

S T O P

END OF TEST

Level 1 – Model Test 2

Test Duration: 60 Minutes

Directions: For each of the following problems, decide which is the best of the choices given. If the exact numerical value is not one of the choices, select the choice that best approximates this value. Then fill in the corresponding oval on the answer sheet.

Notes:

- A calculator will be necessary for answering some (but not all) of the questions in this test. For each question you will have to decide whether or not you should use a calculator. The calculator you use must be at least a scientific calculator; programmable calculators and calculators that can display graphs are permitted.

- The only angle measure used on this test is degree measure. Make sure your calculator is in the degree mode.

- Figures that accompany problems in this test are intended to provide information useful in solving the problems. They are drawn as accurately as possible except when it is stated in a specific problem that its figure is not drawn to scale.

- All figures lie in a plane unless otherwise indicated.

- Unless otherwise specified, the domain of any function f is assumed to be the set of all real numbers x for which f(x) is a real number.

Reference Information: The following information is for your reference in answering some of the questions in this test.

- Volume of a right circular cone with radius r and height h: $V = \frac{1}{3}\pi r^2 h$

- Lateral area of a right circular cone with circumference of the base c and slant height l: $S = \frac{1}{2}cl$

- Volume of a sphere with radius r: $V = \frac{4}{3}\pi r^3$

- Surface area of sphere with radius r: $S = 4\pi r^2$

- Volume of a pyramid with base area B and height h: $V = \frac{1}{3}Bh$

1. If 12a + 36 = b, then a + 3 =

(A) $\dfrac{b}{12}$ 　　　　(B) $\dfrac{12}{b}$ 　　　　(C) $\dfrac{1}{12b}$ 　　　　(D) $\dfrac{b-36}{12}$ 　　　　(E) 12b

2. A group of 300 delegates must vote to elect the leader of a campaign. If 50 delegates are undecided and 84% of the remaining delegates support Mr. Leadit how many delegates do not support Mr. Leadit?

(A) 40   (B) 48   (C) 90   (D) 210   (E) 260

3. The least positive integer greater than 200 that is divisible by 3, 9, and 8 is

(A) 72   (B) 216   (C) 252   (D) 288

(E) None of the above

4. If $\dfrac{3^{11}}{3^n} = 3^{11+n}$, then n = ?

(A) 3   (B) –1   (C) 0   (D) 1   (E) 2

5. In set X there are ten integers whose product is negative. Which of the following is a false statement?

(A) Each of the integers in set X is nonzero.

(B) At least one of the integers in set X is negative.

(C) There is an odd number of positive integers in set X.

(D) There is an even number of positive integers in set X.

(E) The product of any two numbers in set X is nonzero.

6. If $3x^2=11$ and $x > 0$, then x^3 = ?

(A) 1.91   (B) 3.66   (C) 3.67   (D) 7.02   (E) 24.65

7. Alihan traveled to Taksim. He took the metro $\dfrac{2}{5}$ of the way, then walked for 1.3 mile and then took

a taxi $\dfrac{1}{6}$ of the way, arriving in Taksim. How many miles did he travel totally?

(A) 1.7   (B) 2   (C) 2.3   (D) 2.8   (E) 3.0

8. If $|3 - x| = 2x + 1$, then which of the following could be the value of x?

(A) -4   (B) $\dfrac{1}{3}$ (C) $\dfrac{2}{3}$ (D) 1   (E) 4

9. If y varies inversely as x and x = 4 when y = 20, what is the value of x when y = 16?

(A) 0.5   (B) 2.3   (C) 3.2   (D) 5   (E) 1280

10. If $4x + \dfrac{3}{6 - 3x} = 8 - \dfrac{2}{2x - 4}$ then x can be

(A) 2   (B) 3   (C) 4   (D) 8

(E) None of the above

11. If $\sqrt{3x^3 + 2} = 24$, then x could equal

(A) 0.99   (B) 5.76   (C) 63.78   (D) 191.33   (E) 576

12. What is the maximum area that a rectangle can gave if its perimeter is 120?

(A) 30   (B) 90   (C) 270   (D) 900

(E) It cannot be determined from the information given.

13. There are 60 books on a shelf of which 44 are hardcover and 28 are calculus books. Which of the following cannot be the number of hardcover calculus books?

(A) 10   (B) 12   (C) 16   (D) 18   (E) 28

14. In which quadrants are the points (x, y) that satisfy the relation given by y < |x|?

(A) All four quadrants   (B) 1st and 2nd quadrants

(C) 1st and 4th quadrants   (D) 2nd and 3rd quadrants

(E) 1st , 2nd, and 3rd quadrants

15. What is the total number of positive odd integers x for which $x^4 < 1000$?

(A) One   (B) Two   (C) Three   (D) Four   (E) Five

16. If $\dfrac{2x^2 + x - 1}{x + 1} = 2x - 1$ then x can be

(A) 0.5 only   (B) All real numbers except for 1

(C) 0.5 or -1 only   (D) All real numbers except for -1

(E) All real numbers

17. The function g, where g(x) = x² – 1, is defined for – 1 < x < 2. What is the range of g(x)?

(A) 0 < g(x) < 3   (B) -1 < g(x) <3   (C) 1 < g(x) < 3   (D) 0 < g(x) < 4   (E) 1 < g(x) < 4

18. If 0° < θ < 90°, then (sinθ – 2)(sinθ + 2) + cos²θ =

(A) – 3   (B) – 4   (C) – 5   (D) 4

(E) It cannot be determined from the information given.

19. From a group of 5 experts and 10 trainees, a team will be made so as to include experts only. How many such teams are possible?

(A) 5   (B) 24   (C) 31   (D) 32   (E) 1023

20. If i² = – 1 and if iᵐ = – i, then which of the following can be the value of m?

(A) 42   (B) 43   (C) 44   (D) 45   (E) 46

21. What is the remainder when the polynomial x⁴ – 2x³ + 3x² – 4x + 5 is divided by the binomial x – 1?

(A) – 3   (B) 2   (C) 3   (D) 4   (E) 15

22. Which of the following lines is perpendicular to the line 2x + 3y = 26?

(A) 2x + 3y = 4   (B) 4x – 6y = 26   (C) 6x – 4y = 3   (D) 2x – 3y = 26   (E) 6x + 4y = 32

23. If in ΔABC, AB = BC then which of the following must be correct?

    I. tan A = tan C   II. sin A – cos C = 0   III. cos(A – C) = 1

(A) I only   (B) II only   (C) III only   (D) I and III only   (E) I, II, and III

24. If x(x + 1)(x + 2)(x + 3) = 6,359.0625, then x =

(A) 4.5   (B) 5.5   (C) 6.5   (D) 7.5   (E) 8.5

25. The sum of the two roots of a quadratic equation is – 4 and their product is 5. Which of the following-could be the equation?

(A) $x^2 – 4x + 5 = 0$ (B) $x^2 + 4x + 5 = 0$ (C) $x^2 – 4x – 5 = 0$

(D) $x^2 + 5x + 4 = 0$ (E) $x^2 – 5x + 4 = 0$

26. If each of the three small circles in figure has a radius of 4 inches, what is the outer perimeter of the given figure 22?

(A) 12 + 4π

(B) 24 + 4π

(C) 12 + 8π

(D) 24 + 8π

(E) It cannot be determined from the information given.

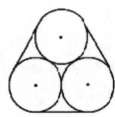

Figure 22

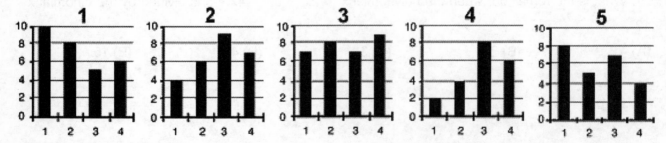

27. Each of the five different sets represented by the graphs given above contains four data. Mean is the greatest for the data set given by which of the above graphs? (Courtesy ÖSYM Turkey)

(A) 1   (B) 2   (C) 3   (D) 4   (E) 5

28. What is the area of the shaded region given in figure 23 in square inches if A and C are the corresponding centers of two congruent quarter circles with radius 4 inches each, and have their centers at the opposite corners of the square ABCD?

(A) 3.41   (B) 3.42   (C) 3.43   (D) 3.44   (E) 3.45

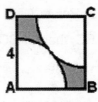

Figure 23

29. In figure 24, B and C are both right angles and AD ∥ BC. Which of the following does not equal BC?

(A) BD·sinθ   (C) AB·tanθ·sinθ

(B) AD·sin²θ   (D) AB·tanθ·cosθ

(E) AD·− AD·cos²θ

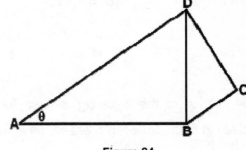

Figure 24

30. The function h(x) is defined for all real numbers except for 2. Which of the following can be f(x)?

I. $\dfrac{1}{\sqrt[3]{x-2}}$ II. $\dfrac{1}{\sqrt{x-2}}$ III. $\dfrac{1}{x-2}$

(A) I only   (B) II only   (C) III only   (D) I and III only   (E) I, II and III

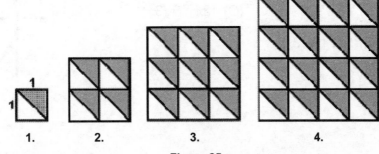

Figure 25

31. What is the perimeter of all shaded triangles in the nth pattern given in figure 25 above?

(A) $\dfrac{n^2}{2}$ (B) $n^2\sqrt{2}$ (C) $n\cdot(2+\sqrt{2})$ (D) $n^2\cdot(2+\sqrt{2})$ (E) $n^2\cdot(1+\sqrt{2})$

32. Points A, B, and C lie on a circle. If the center of that circle lies in the exterior region of triangle ABC, then △ABC must be

(A) acute   (B) obtuse   (C) right   (D) equilateral   (E) isosceles

33. If $3 + \sqrt{2}$ is one root of a quadratic equation with rational coefficients then the other root is

(A) $2 - \sqrt{3}$ (B) $3 - \sqrt{2}$ (C) $3 + \sqrt{2}$ (D) $-3 + \sqrt{2}$ (E) $-3 - \sqrt{2}$

34. Which of the following is false for the parallelogram ABCD given in figure 26 if α represents an acute angle?

(A) Altitude to side x equals $y \cdot \sin\alpha$.

(B) Altitude to side y equals $y \cdot \sin\alpha$.

(C) Area of parallelogram ABCD is $x \cdot y \cdot \sin\alpha$.

(D) Perimeter of parallelogram ABCD is $2x + 2y$.

(E) Area of parallelogram ABCD is never less than xy.

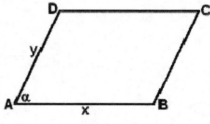

Figure 26

35. The circle with center P is given by $(x - 6)^2 + y^2 = 36$ and it is intersected by the line x = 9 as is given in figure 27. What is the area of the shaded region?

(A) $12 - 9\sqrt{3}$ (B) $12 + 9\sqrt{3}$ (C) $12\pi - 9\sqrt{3}$

(D) $9\pi - 12\sqrt{3}$ (E) $12\pi + 9\sqrt{3}$

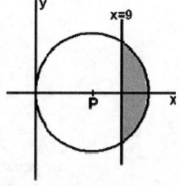

Figure 27

36. The quadratic function f(x) is given by $f(x) = ax^2 + bx + c$ where a, b, and c are all nonzero real numbers. Which of the following gives all possibilities for the number of points that f(x) and -f(x) can intersect at?

(A) 1, 2, or more than 2

(B) 0 or 1

(C) 0, 1, or more than 2

(D) 0, 1, or 2

(E) 0, 1, 2, or more than 2

37. Line *l* given by 2x + 3y = 12 intersects the x and y axes at B and C respectively as is given in figure 28. What is the equation of the perpendicular bisector of segment BC?

(A) $y - 2 = \dfrac{3}{2}(x - 3)$

(B) $y - 3 = -\dfrac{3}{2}(x - 2)$

(C) $y = \dfrac{3x}{2}$

(D) $y - 3 = \dfrac{3}{2}(x - 2)$

(E) $y + 2 = -\dfrac{2}{3}(x + 3)$

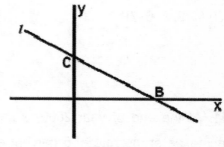

Figure 28

Figure not drawn to scale

x	f(x)	g(x)
1	3	5
2	2	4
3	5	5
4	1	2
5	2	1

38. Which of the following is not correct regarding f(x) and g(x) defined in the table above?

(A) Range of f(x) is {1, 2, 3, 5}.

(B) Range of g(x) is {1, 2, 4, 5}.

(C) Range of f(g(x)) is {1, 4, 5}.

(D) Domain of both functions is {1, 2, 3, 4, 5}.

(E) The equation g(f(x)) = 5 has exactly one solution.

39. If a rectangle with sides of 3 and 5 is rotated around one of its longer sides, what will be the volume of the solid generated?

(A) 9π (B) 15π (C) 25π (D) 45π (E) 75π

40. The symmetric difference is defined as $A \triangle B = (A - B) \cup (B - A)$ for any two sets A and B. If A = {1, 2, 3, 4} and B = {3, 4, 5, 6, 7}, then $A \triangle B$ = ?

(A) {1, 2, 3, 4, 5, 6, 7}   (B) {1, 2}   (C) {5, 6, 7}

(D) {1, 2, 5, 6, 7}   (E) {3, 4}

41. At the end of year 2000, a certain classical car was worth $145,000. If the value of the car increases at the rate of 5 percent each year, approximately how much will the car be worth at the beginning of 2010?

(A) $225,000   (B) $236,000   (C) $242,000   (D) $248,000   (E) $252,000

42.   20, 23, 26, 29, 32, 35, 38,…

Sum of the first n terms of the sequence above exceeds 2400. What is the minimum value of n?

(A) 34   (B) 35   (C) 36   (D) 794   (E) 795

43. Which of the following is the locus of points 5 inches from a horizontal plane and 7 inches from a point located 1 inch above that plane?

(A) A sphere

(B) Portion of a cone

(C) Two parallel planes

(D) Two circles of equal radii

(E) Two circles of unequal radii

44. If $(2x - 3)(3x - 4) = px^2 + qx + r$, then $-p - q + r =$?

(A) -11 (B) 1   (C) 23   (D) 35

(E) None of the above

45. If $f(x)$ is a function, which of the following must be false?

   I. $f(1) = f(2) = 3$

   II. $f^{-1}(4) = f^{-1}(5) = 6$

   III. the graph of $f(x)$ intersects the line $x = 2$ at two points

   IV. the graph of $f(x)$ intersects the line $y = 2$ at two points

(A) I and II only   (B) I and IV only   (C) I, II, III and IV

(D) II and III only   (E) III and IV only

46. A cannon ball is projected to hit a horizontal target and its trajectory looks like figure 29. If the coordinates of the position of the cannon ball at any time t during its flight is given by $x = 60t$ and $y = 80t - 5t^2$ then at $t = 9$ where will the cannon ball most likely be?

 (A) at point A   (B) at point B   (C) at point C

 (D) at point D   (E) at point E

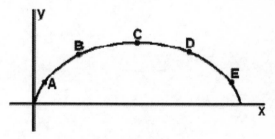

Figure 29

Figure not drawn to scale

47. Quadrilateral ABCD has vertices the of A(-3,1), B(2,4), C(5,1) and D(-1, -3). What is the area of ABCD?

(A) 20   (B) 25   (C) 27   (D) 28   (E) 32

48. The solution set for the system of equations $\begin{cases} 2x + 5y = 3 \\ ax - 3y = 4 \end{cases}$ is empty when a equals

(A) -1.5   (B) -1.2   (C) 0.8   (D) 1.2   (E) 2.6

49. If $\left(\dfrac{x}{x+1}\right)^2 - \left(\dfrac{3x+3}{x}\right) + 2 = 0$ then x can be?

(A) -2   (B) -1   (C) 0   (D) 1   (E) 2

50. If $g(x) = x^2$ and $h(x) = x^2 - 2x + 3$, relative to the graph of g, the graph of h is

(A) 2 units to the left and 3 units up.   (B) 1 unit to the right and 2 units up.

(C) 2 units to the right and 1 unit up.   (D) 1 unit to the left and 2 units down.

(E) 2 units to the right and 3 units down.

S T O P

END OF TEST

Test Duration: 60 Minutes

Directions: For each of the following problems, decide which is the best of the choices given. If the exact numerical value is not one of the choices, select the choice that best approximates this value. Then fill in the corresponding oval on the answer sheet.

Notes:

- A calculator will be necessary for answering some (but not all) of the questions in this test. For each question you will have to decide whether or not you should use a calculator. The calculator you use must be at least a scientific calculator; programmable calculators and calculators that can display graphs are permitted.

- The only angle measure used on this test is degree measure. Make sure your calculator is in the degree mode.

- Figures that accompany problems in this test are intended to provide information useful in solving the problems. They are drawn as accurately as possible except when it is stated in a specific problem that its figure is not drawn to scale.

- All figures lie in a plane unless otherwise indicated.

- Unless otherwise specified, the domain of any function f is assumed to be the set of all real numbers x for which f(x) is a real number.

Reference Information: The following information is for your reference in answering some of the questions in this test.

- Volume of a right circular cone with radius r and height h: $V = \frac{1}{3}\pi r^2 h$

- Lateral area of a right circular cone with circumference of the base c and slant height l: $S = \frac{1}{2}cl$

- Volume of a sphere with radius r: $V = \frac{4}{3}\pi r^3$

- Surface area of sphere with radius r: $S = 4\pi r^2$

- Volume of a pyramid with base area B and height h: $V = \frac{1}{3}Bh$

1. $\frac{A}{B} = \frac{3}{5}$, $\frac{B}{C} = \frac{4}{7}$. If B=40, then A+2C?

(A) 94　　　　(B) 120　　　　(C) 140　　　　(D) 164　　　　(E) 168

2. A mixture of 165 grams is made by mixing a, b and c grams of substances A, B and C respectively.

If $\dfrac{a}{0.4} = 2b$ and $1.5b = c$ then what is the value of a in grams?

(A) 40   (B) 50   (C) 60   (D) 75   (E) 80

3. Ebru travels a distance of 15 mi to and from work with respective speeds of 30 mph and 40 mph respectively. What is the difference between the times taken between the journeys?

(A) 7.5 minutes   (B) 22.5 minutes   (C) 30 minutes   (D) 40 minutes   (E) 52.5 minutes

4. If $-4 < x^2 < 7$, then x cannot be

(A) $-\sqrt{3}$ (B) 1   (C) $\sqrt{2}$ (D) 2   (E) $2\sqrt{2}$

5. For the equations given by $\sqrt{2}x + 2y = 1$ and $x - \sqrt{2}\,y = \sqrt{2}$, $\dfrac{x}{y} = ?$

(A) $-\dfrac{1}{4}$ (B) $\dfrac{\sqrt{2}}{2}$ (C) $-3\sqrt{2}$ (D) $\dfrac{3\sqrt{2}}{4}$ (E) $\dfrac{3\sqrt{2}}{2}$

6. If x is an integer between the interval $-2 < x < 4$ and y is an integer between the interval $-3 \le y < 0$ find the minimum value of $(x-y)^2 = ?$

(A) -1   (B) 0   (C) 1   (D) 4   (E) 9

7. In a right triangle, the lengths of the sides are a, b and 4 where a>4>b. If the smallest angle is θ, then what is the relation between b and a?

(A) $\sin\theta = \dfrac{b}{a}$ (B) $\tan\theta = \dfrac{b}{a}$ (C) $a = b\cdot\sin\theta$ (D) $\cot\theta = \dfrac{b}{a}$ (E) $a = b\cdot\cos\theta$

8. What are all values of x for which $x^3 < x < x^2$?

(A) $x < 1$ (B) $x \geq 1$ (C) $0 < x < 1$ (D) $-1 < x < 1$ (E) $-1 < x < 0$

9. For a function given by $y = f(x)$ which of the following is false?

(A) $f(x - 1)$ Shifts it rightward for 1 unit

(B) $f(-x)$ Reflects it with respect to the y-axis

(C) $f(2x)$ Stretches it horizontally by a factor of 2

(D) $-f(x)$ Reflects it with respect to the y-axis

(E) $g(x) + 1$ Shifts it upward for 1 unit.

10. What is the degree measure of the smallest angle of the triangle given in figure 30?

(A) 30°   (B) 31.04°   (C) 32.26°   (D) 35°   (E) 37.04°

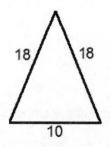

Figure 30

Figure not drawn to scale

11. If $a^2 - b^2 = 54$, $a + b = 9$, then $b - a$?

(A) -27   (B) -9   (C) -6   (D) 6   (E) 27

12. If $e^{2x+1} = 7$, then x=?

(A) 0.47   (B) 0.95   (C) 1.47   (D) 2.95   (E) 3

13. It is given that y varies inversely as x. If y = 3 when x = 20, then what is y when x = 3?

(A) -14   (B) $\frac{9}{20}$ (C) $\frac{20}{9}$ (D) 20   (E) 60

14. If $1 - 2\cos^2 x = 2\sin^2 x - 1$, then x can be

I. 0° or 360°

II. 45° or 135°

III. any angle measure

(A) None   (B) I only   (C) II only   (D) I and II only   (E) III

point label	x-coordinate	y-coordinate
A	1	3
B	- 4	7
C	3	5
D	4	- 4

15. What is the slope of the line BD?

(A) $\frac{3}{8}$ (B) $-\frac{8}{11}$ (C) $-\frac{3}{8}$ (D) $-\frac{11}{8}$ (E) $-\frac{8}{3}$

16. If $y = \dfrac{x+1}{|x|}$ then what is the domain of the function?

(A) All real numbers

(B) All real numbers except 0

(C) All real numbers except -1

(D) All natural numbers except 0

(E) All natural numbers except -1

$$a = \frac{5}{x} + kx - 4x^2$$

$$4x^3 - 2x^2 + ax - 5 = 0$$

17. When $x \neq 0$ nonzero, the above equations give the same solution for a; k = ?

(A) – 4   (B) – 2   (C) 2   (D) 4

(E) None of the above

18. If $\log_x 5 = 3$, then x=?

(A) 1.67   (B) 1.71   (C) 15   (D) 125   (E) 243

$$\frac{2}{x^2} + \frac{2}{y^2} = 4 \text{ and } \frac{1}{x^2} - \frac{1}{y^2} = 2$$

19. How many elements does the solution set of the above system of equations have?

(A) 0   (B) 1   (C) 2   (D) 3   (E) 4

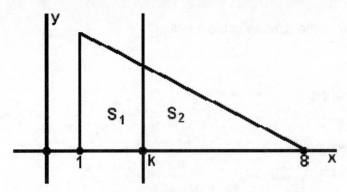

Figure 31

Figure not drawn to scale

20. The right triangle given in figure 31 is partitioned into two regions equal in area by a line given by $x = k$; $k = ?$

(A) 3.05   (B) 3.5   (C) 4.05   (D) 4.12   (E) 4.5

21. The point A(-4, -6) is kept fixed while the origin is translated to the point (1, -2). What are the new coordinates of A?

(A) (-3, -4)   (B) (-3, -8)   (C) (-5, -4)   (D) (-5, -8)   (E) (-6, -4)

22. In figure 32, the length of AC is 49 inches and the curved portion corresponds to a circle of radius 25 inches centered at B. What is the area of the shaded region?

(A) 549.78   (B) 573   (C) 763.39   (D) 977

(E) It cannot be determined from the information given.

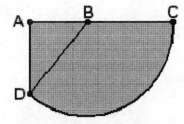

Figure 32

Figure not drawn to scale

23. If it is given that f(x) is a linear function such that f(f(x)) = 4x+3 then f(x) can be

(A) -2x + 3   (B) –2x + 1   (C) 2x – 1   (D) 2x + 1   (E) 2x – 3

24. According to the data given in figure 33, x = ?

(A) 8

(B) $7\sqrt{2}$

(C) $7\sqrt{3}$

(D) $\sqrt{85}$

(E) 9

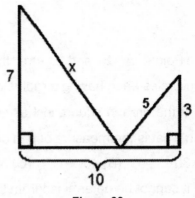

Figure 33

Figure not drawn to scale

25. $x \geq 0$ and $\sqrt[n]{x} \geq 0$, then n can be

    I. 0   II. 2   III. 3

(A) I only   (B) II only   (C) III only   (D) I and III only   (E) II and III only

26. Given in the table to the right are the distances covered by a traveler with the corresponding speeds. What is the average speed of the traveler in mph?

(A) 30   (B) 32.97   (C) 36.67

(D) 38   (E) 41.13

Speed (mph)	Distance (mi)
20	26
40	34
50	32

27. A deadly virus population initially having a single inhabitant grows by 10% every hour and causes the death of an animal when its population reaches 70,000. If at 3:00 PM it contains 30,000 inhabitants, at what time will the animal be dead?

(A) 1:53 AM   (B) 11:35 AM   (C) 11:53 AM   (D) 11:53 PM   (E) 11:35 PM

28. Points A, B and C are the centers of the three semicircles each having a radius of 9 inches given in figure 34. If the area in square inches of the shaded region is 9π then what is the measure of β in degrees?

(A) 30   (B) 40   (C) 50   (D) 60

(E) It cannot be determined from the information given.

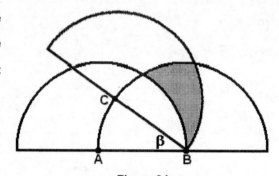

Figure 34

Figure not drawn to scale

29. If the radius of the circle given in figure 35 is 5 inches, what is the equation of the circle?

(A) $(x - 5)^2 + (y - 5)^2 = 25$

(B) $(x + 5)^2 + (y - 5)^2 = 25$

(C) $(x - 5)^2 + (y + 5)^2 = 25$

(D) $(x + 5)^2 + (y - 5)^2 = 5$

(E) $(x - 5)^2 + (y + 5)^2 = 5$

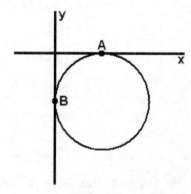

Figure 35

Figure not drawn to scale

30. Which of the following are not sufficient to determine the equation of the parabola given in figure 36?

(A) A and C

(B) B and C

(C) B and D

(D) A, D and E

(E) A, B and D

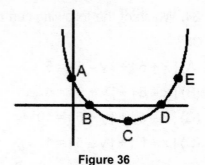

Figure 36

Figure not drawn to scale

31. If a road has a slope of 8%, what is the minimum distance a car must travel on this road in order to raise 100 ft?

(A) 800 ft   (B) 1000 ft   (C) 1250 ft   (D) 1500 ft   (E) 1750 ft

32. Figure 37 shows two concentric squares such that the each diagonal of one square is parallel to two sides of the other. What is the degree measure of the angle given by β?

(A) 30°   (B) 32°   (C) 36°   (D) 45°   (E) 48°

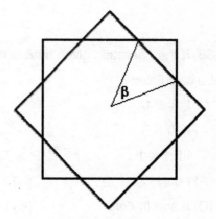

Figure 37

Figure not drawn to scale

33. If 6 + 2i is one root of a quadratic equation with real coefficients then the other root is

(A) 2i – 6   (B) – 2i + 6   (C) – 2i – 6   (D) 6 + 2i   (E) 2 + 6i

34. Which of the following can be the equation of the curve given in figure 38?

(A) $|x + 5| + |y - 5| = 5$

(B) $|x - 5| + |y + 5| = 5$

(C) $|x - 5| + |y + 5| = 10$

(D) $|x + 5| + |y - 5| = 10$

(E) $|x - 5| + |y + 5| + 10 = 0$

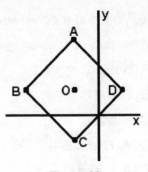

Figure 38

Figure not drawn to scale

35. If $f(x) = x^2 - 1$ and $x \geq 0$ then $f^{-1}(x) = ?$

(A) $f(x) = \sqrt{x+1}$　　　　(B) $f(x) = (x+1)^2$　　　　(C) $f(x) = \pm\sqrt{x+1}$

(D) $f(x) = -\sqrt{x+1}$　　　　(E) $f(x) = -(x+1)^2$

36. If the operation given by & is defined as $x \,\&\, y = 3x + 4y + 2(y \,\&\, x)$ then which of the following can be calculated?

　　I. 3 & 4

　　II. 0 & 0

　　III. 1 & 1

(A) I only　　　　　　　(B) II only　　　　　　　(C) III only

(D) II and III only　　　(E) I, II and III

37. If $f = \begin{pmatrix} 1 & 2 & 3 & 4 & 5 \\ 3 & 4 & 2 & 1 & 5 \end{pmatrix}$ and $g = \begin{pmatrix} 1 & 2 & 3 & 4 & 5 \\ 2 & 3 & 5 & 1 & 4 \end{pmatrix}$, then find $f\left(g^{-1}(3)\right) = ?$

(A) 1　　　　　　(B) 2　　　　　　(C) 3　　　　　　(D) 4　　　　　　(E) 5

38. Which of the following is an example of vertical stretch?

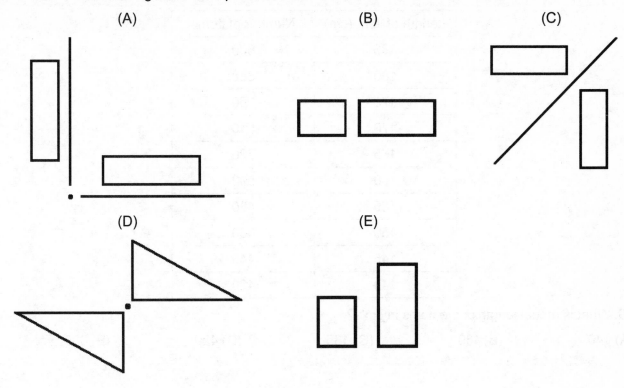

39. Figure 39 shows the base and lateral surface of a cone that is opened and

flattened. If R = 4r then what is α in degrees?

(A) 45°

(B) 60°

(C) 90°

(D) 120°

(E) 180°

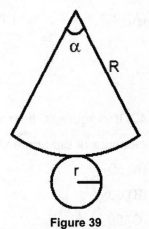

Figure 39

Figure not drawn to

scale

For questions 40 and 41 please refer to the data given in the following table

Length of item (cm)	Number of items
185	600
180	580
175	560
170	540
165	520
160	500
155	480
150	460
145	440
140	420

40. What is modal length of the items in cm's?

(A) 140   (B) 180   (C) 185   (D) 420   (E) 600

41. Assuming that there is a linear relation between the length of an item and the number of such items, then what is the number of items produced when the length is 156.5 cm?

(A) 482   (B) 484   (C) 486   (D) 488   (E) 490

42. If in figure 40 the rays with arrows are parallel, find the degree measure of the angle x?

(A) 50

(B) 60

(C) 80

(D) 120

(E) It cannot be determined from the information given.

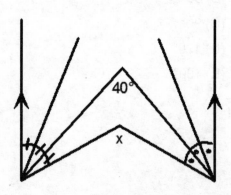

Figure 40

Figure not drawn to scale

43. If two opposite vertices of the rhombus coincide with those of the square in figure 41 then what is the area of the square indicated by the shaded region?

(A) 17.86　　　(B) 35.72　　　(C) 40.88

(D) 50　　　(E) 76.60

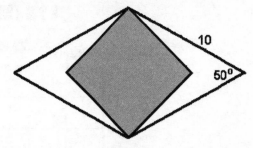

Figure 41

Figure not drawn to scale

44. All points outside the rectangular field in figure 42 at a distance of 2 meters from the field are joined to from a closed curve. What is the length of this curve rounded to the nearest meter?

(A) $120 + 2\pi$　　　(B) $120 + 4\pi$　　　(C) $150 + 2\pi$

(D) $150 + 4\pi$　　　(E) $300 + 4\pi$

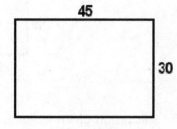

Figure 42

Figure not drawn to scale

45. If the arc AB is 2π inches and r is 6 inches then what is the shaded area in square inches in figure 43?

(A) 2.63　　　(B) 2.36　　　(C) 3.26

(D) 3.46　　　(E) 3.62

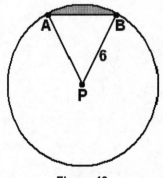

Figure 43

Figure not drawn to scale

46. How many distinct positive divisors does the number n = $2^3 \cdot 3^4 \cdot 4^5$ have?

(A) 60　　　(B) 80　　　(C) 100　　　(D) 120　　　(E) 240

$$$ IMPORTS EXPORTS

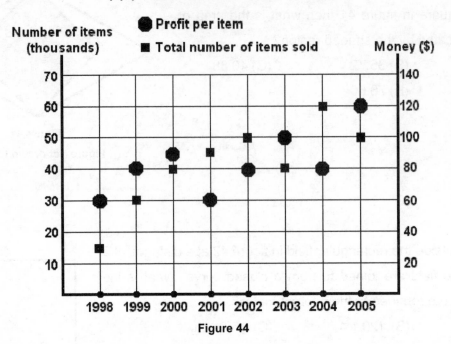

Figure 44

47. The graph given in figure 44 above shows the number of items processed and the profit per item made by the $$$ Imports Exports Company between 1998 and 2005 inclusive. What is the total profit made by this company in this interval?

(A) $14,200   (B) $28,400   (C) $1.42 Million   (D) $2.84 Million   (E) $28.4 Million

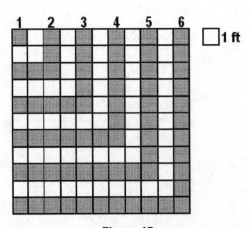

Figure 45

48. How many shaded squares each having a side of length 1ft are there in the n'th pattern given in figure 45 above?

(A) 3n – 4   (B) 3n + 4   (C) 4n – 3   (D) 4n + 3   (E) 4n + 4

49. In figure 46, the origin O is the center of the semicircle. A is a point on OB, K is the shaded area, L is the un-shaded area, r is the radius of the semicircle and d is parallel to x-axis. Which of the following must be correct?

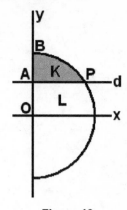

I. If $\angle$ AOP measures $60°$ then AB = AO.

II. If $K = r^2 \left(\dfrac{\pi}{3} - \dfrac{\sqrt{3}}{8} \right)$ .then AB < AO.

III. If K = L then AB > AO.

(A) I only

(B) I and III only

(C) I, II and III

(D) II only

(E) I and II only

Figure 46

Figure not drawn to scale

50. Sixty four identical cubes each having six self adhesive faces are joined together to make one big cube as shown in figure 47. Totally how many faces of the smaller cubes are in contact?

(A) 64

(B) 128

(C) 192

(D) 288

(E) 384

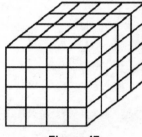

Figure 47

S T O P

END OF TEST

Level 1 – Model Test 4

Test Duration: 60 Minutes

Directions: For each of the following problems, decide which is the best of the choices given. If the exact numerical value is not one of the choices, select the choice that best approximates this value. Then fill in the corresponding oval on the answer sheet.

Notes:

- A calculator will be necessary for answering some (but not all) of the questions in this test. For each question you will have to decide whether or not you should use a calculator. The calculator you use must be at least a scientific calculator; programmable calculators and calculators that can display graphs are permitted.

- The only angle measure used on this test is degree measure. Make sure your calculator is in the degree mode.

- Figures that accompany problems in this test are intended to provide information useful in solving the problems. They are drawn as accurately as possible except when it is stated in a specific problem that its figure is not drawn to scale.

- All figures lie in a plane unless otherwise indicated.

- Unless otherwise specified, the domain of any function f is assumed to be the set of all real numbers x for which f(x) is a real number.

Reference Information: The following information is for your reference in answering some of the questions in this test.

- Volume of a right circular cone with radius r and height h: $V = \frac{1}{3}\pi r^2 h$

- Lateral area of a right circular cone with circumference of the base c and slant height l: $S = \frac{1}{2}cl$

- Volume of a sphere with radius r: $V = \frac{4}{3}\pi r^3$

- Surface area of sphere with radius r: $S = 4\pi r^2$

- Volume of a pyramid with base area B and height h: $V = \frac{1}{3}Bh$

1. If a = 20, ab = 240 and c = 1 − a + b, then c=?

(A) − 7   (B) 7   (C) − 8   (D) 12   (E) − 12

2. Which of the following is not a rational number?

(A) A negative fraction

(B) A recurring decimal

(C) A terminating decimal

(D) Square root of the 6'th power of an integer

(E) Ratio of the perimeter of a circle to its radius

3. If the straight line given by $2x - 3 = ky$ passes through the point $(-6, 3)$ then k=?

(A) -3   (B) 3   (C) -5   (D) 5

(E) None of the above

4. A group of 8 integers are multiplied out and their result is positive. Which of the following cannot be correct about this group?

(A) all of them are negative

(B) all of them are positive

(C) half of them are negative and the remaining half are positive

(D) 2 of them are positive and the remaining numbers are negative

(E) 5 of them are positive and the remaining numbers are negative

5. If $1 + x^4 - 81 = 82 - x^4$ then which of the following is a list of all possible real values of x?

(A) 3 only   (B) 0 only   (C) – 3 only   (D) – 3 and 3 only   (E) – 3, 0 or 3

6. If $f(x) = x^2 - 1$ and $g(x) = (x - 1)^3$, then what is the value of f(g(-2))?

(A) – 27   (B) – 3   (C) 8   (D) 728

(E) None of the above

7. Which of the following is not always true of a set of 10 consecutive even integers?

(A) Median is an odd number.

(B) Mean and median are equal.

(C) The least number in this set is 9 less than the median.

(D) 10 times the median gives the sum of the numbers in this set.

(E) The difference between the greatest and the least number in this set is 20.

8. The set of odd integers is closed under

    I. subtraction

    II. multiplication

    III. division

(A) I only   (B) II only   (C) III only

(D) I and II only   (E) none of these

9. If a and b are positive even integers, which one(s) of the following must also be even?

    I. $a^2 + b^3 - 12$

    II. $2(a + b)$

    III. $a + 2b$

(A) I only   (B) II only   (C) I and II only

(D) II and III only   (E) I, II and III.

10. The average height of 7 people is 72 inches. If the tallest and the shortest are 75 and 64 inches respectively, the average height of the remaining 5 people is

(A) 60.7   (B) 69.5   (C) 72   (D) 73

(E) None of the above

11. If $a^x = b^x$ then which of the following statements are correct?

    I. If $x = 0$ then a and b can be any real numbers.

    II. If x is a nonzero even integer then $|a| = |b|$.

    III. If x is an odd integer then $a = b$.

(A) I only   (B) II only   (C) III only

(D) II and III only   (E) I, II and III

12. $ax + by = 10$

       $ax - by = 4$

If (1, 2) is a solution of the above system of equations, then (a, b) = ?

(A) (3, 3.5)   (B) (3.5, 3)   (C) (7, 1.5)   (D) (1.5, 7)

(E) None of the above.

13. In a production plant the total cost of operation is calculated by adding fixed cost to the variable cost that is directly proportional with the number of units produced. Given that the total cost of producing 500 and 1000 items are $1500 and $2500 respectively, what will be the total cost of producing 1500 items?

(A) $3000   (B) Less than $3000

(C) $3500   (D) More than $4000

(E) $4000

14. If $ab = 2$ and $4 < a < 10$ then which of the following is correct?

(A) $2 < b < 5$ (B) $0.1 < b < 0.5$ (C) $0.1 < b < 0.25$

(D) $0.2 < b < 0.25$ (E) $0.2 < b < 0.5$

15. Which of the following is not a solution of -3y + 5x < 15 ?

(A) (4, 2)   (B) (-2, 2)   (C) (0, -3)   (D) (5, 5)   (E) (2, -2)

16. Given in figure 48 are two congruent circles whose centers are at A and at B and a smaller circle whose diameter is the segment AB. How many of the following quantities can be determined if the length of segment CD is also known?

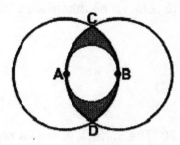

Figure 48

   I.   Measure of arc $\overset{\frown}{DAC}$

   II. Measure of angle ∠DAC

   III. Length of segment AB

   IV. Perimeter of the shaded region

   V. Area of the shaded region

(A) 1   (B) 2   (C) 3   (D) 4   (E) 5

17. An isosceles right triangle ABC, 90° at the vertex B is rotated 180° about its side AB. If the hypotenuse of the triangle is $6\sqrt{2}$ inches then volume of the resulting solid will be

(A) 36π cubic inches.   (B) 72π cubic inches.   (C) 108π cubic inches.

(D) 216π cubic inches.   (E) none of the above.

18. How many pairs of parallel edges are there in a right regular pentagonal prism?

(A) 8   (B) 10   (C) 12   (D) 14

(E) More than 14

19. The parallel chords AB and CD of the circle given in figure 49 measure 24

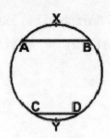

and 10 inches respectively. If it is given that m$\overset{\frown}{AXB}$ + m$\overset{\frown}{CYD}$ = 180° then

area of the circle

(A) is 25π square inches.   (B) is 144π square inches.

(C) is 169π square inches.   (D) is 289π square inches.

(E) cannot be determined from the given information.

20. The surface area of a right circular cylinder is 150π square inches while the radius of the base and altitude sum up to 15 inches. What is the volume of the cylinder in cubic inches?

(A) 125π   (B) 150π   (C) 250π   (D) 300π

(E) The given information is not enough to find the volume of the cylinder.

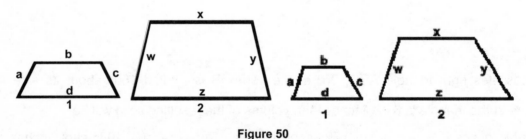

Figure 50

Figure not drawn to scale

21. For the trapezoids 1 and 2 given in figure 50, a || w, c || y, b || d || x || z.

If $\dfrac{\text{length of side a}}{\text{length of side w}} = k_1$ and $\dfrac{\text{length of side b}}{\text{length of side x}} = k_2$ then which of the following will always be correct?

  I.   Measure of each interior angle of trapezoid 1 is equal to the measure of an interior angle of trapezoid 2.

  II. In each trapezoid there are at least two pairs of supplementary angles.

  III. The trapezoids are similar therefore $k_1 = k_2$.

(A) I only   (B) II only   (C) I and II only   (D) I and III only   (E) I, II and III

22. If in figure 51, BA = BC and DC = DE then which of the following are correct?

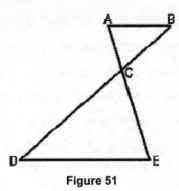

Figure 51

    I. Triangles ACB and ECD are similar.

    II. Triangles ACB and ECD are congruent.

    III. $\dfrac{BC}{DC} = \dfrac{AB}{ED}$

(A) I only

(B) II only

(C) I and III only

(D) II and III only

(E) I, II and III

23. If the straight lines given by $\begin{cases} -3x + y = 6 \\ 2x - ky = 3 \end{cases}$ are parallel, then k=?

(A) -6   (B) 6   (C) $\dfrac{2}{3}$ (D) $-\dfrac{2}{3}$

(E) None of the above

24. If f(x)= x – 9 and g(x)= $\dfrac{x^2 - 81}{x + 9}$, how are the graphs of f and g related?

(A) They are exactly the same.   (B) They are the same except x = – 9.

(C) They are the same except x = 9.   (D) They have no points in common.

(E) They have the same shape but only a finite number of points in common.

25. The function f(x) = x^2 is given for all x. $f^{-1}(x)$ = ?

(A) $\sqrt{x}$ (B) $-\sqrt{x}$ (C) $\pm\sqrt{x}$ (D) 2x   (E) x/2

26. A square A is folded along its horizontal axis of symmetry to give rectangle B. The resulting rectangle B is folded along its vertical axis of symmetry to give square C. The square C is then folded along its horizontal axis of symmetry to give rectangle D and finally the resulting rectangle D is folded along its vertical axis of symmetry to give square E which is shaded as in figure 52. Shaded region in square E is what part of the original square A?

Figure 52

(A) $\dfrac{1}{4}$ (B) $\dfrac{1}{8}$ (C) $\dfrac{1}{16}$ (D) $\dfrac{1}{32}$ (E) $\dfrac{1}{64}$

27. As shown in figure 53, POQ is an isosceles triangle where side PQ is tangent to the circle O at the point C. If length of OC is x and POQ measures θ degrees, then what is the length of PQ in terms of x and θ?

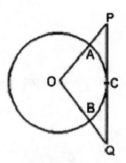

(A) $x \cdot \tan\theta$ (B) $2x \cdot \tan\theta$ (C) $x \cdot \tan\dfrac{\theta}{2}$ (D) $2x \cdot \tan\dfrac{\theta}{2}$

(E) None of the above

Figure 53

28. Two planes P_1 and P_2 intersect at right angles. What is the locus of points that are at a distance of 27 inches from P_1 and 32 inches from P_2?

(A) 4 planes (B) 4 points (C) 1 line (D) 2 lines (E) 4 lines

29. A line has parametric equations $x = 2 - t$ and $y = t + 2$, where t is the parameter. The x – intercept of the line is

(A) -2 (B) 0 (C) t (D) 2 (E) 4

30. A theorem states that if perpendicular segments are drawn to each of the three sides of an equilateral triangle ABC from any point P inside the triangle, as in figure 54, then the sum of the lengths of the perpendicular segments will be a constant. This constant is equal to

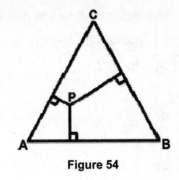

Figure 54

(A) half the perimeter of ABC

(B) the perimeter of ABC

(C) the altitude of ABC

(D) $\sqrt{3}$ times the length of a side of ABC

(E) the length of a side of ABC

31. The following instructions are carried out:

   1. P = 1 and N = 1

   2. If N $\leq$ 5 go to step 3 otherwise go to step 6

   3. Multiply P by N

   4. Increase N by 1

   5. Go to step 2

   6. Print P

What number is printed?

(A) 2   (B) 6   (C) 24   (D) 120   (E) 720

32. What is the range of the relation given in figure 55?

(A) [0,3]

(B) [-3,3]

(C) (-3,3)

(D) {0, 1, 2, 3}

(E) {-3, -2, -1, 0, 1, 2, 3}

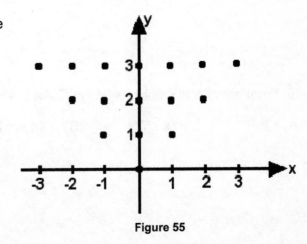

Figure 55

33. The block of cubes in figure 56 consists of 90 small cubes. If the block is painted blue, then how many smaller cubes will have exactly two blue faces?

(A) 8

(B) 12

(C) 32

(D) 38

(E) None of the above

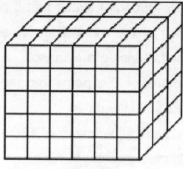

Figure 56

34. What is the equation of the line that passes through the point $\left(3, -\dfrac{1}{2}\right)$ and is perpendicular to the line $2y = 3x - 2$?

(A) $2y - 3x = -2$ (B) $2y + 10 = 3x$ (C) $6y = -4x + 9$

(D) $6y + 4x = -9$ (E) $3y - 2x = 10$

35. What is the domain of the function given in figure 57?

(A) $-2 \le x < 3$

(B) $-2 \le x \le 3$

(C) $\{-2, -1, 0, 1, 2\}$

(D) $\{-2, -1, 0, 1, 2, 3\}$

(E) None of the above

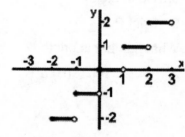

Figure 57

36. What are all values of x for which $|3 - x| \ge 4$?

(A) $x \ge -1$ (B) $x \le 7$ (C) $-1 \le x \le 7$ (D) $x = -1$ or $x = 7$ (E) $x \le -1$ or $x \ge 7$

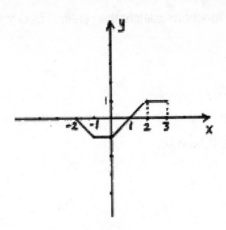

Figure 58

37. If y=f(x) is represented by the graph shown in figure 58 above, then what would be the graph of y=f(-|x|)

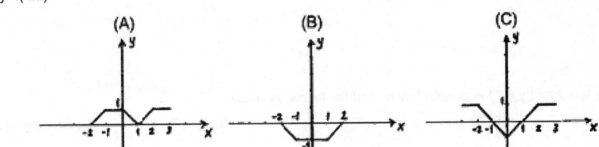

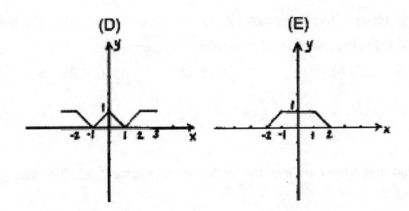

38. If $g(x) = 2x - 3$ for all x, then the y-intercept of the line given by $y = g\left(\dfrac{x+1}{2}\right)$ is

(A) -3   (B) -2   (C) 0   (D) 1   (E) 2

39. Which one(s) of the following functions satisfy the relation f(-x) = f(x)?

   I. $f(x) = x^6 - x$

   II. $f(x) = x^2 + 2$

   III. $f(x) = x^3 \cdot (x + x^5) + 1$

(A) I only   (B) II only   (C) III only

(D) II and III only   (E) I, II, and III.

40. Which of the following is the converse of the statement given by "If x=3, then x²=9"?

(A) x≠3 or x²=9.   (B) If x² = 9, then x=3.   (C) If x ≠ 3, then x²≠9.   (D) If x²≠9, then x≠3.

(E) None of the above

41. The line 2x – 3y = 11 is parallel to which of the following lines?

(A) 4x = 6y + 7   (B) 3x + 2y = 8   (C) 4x + 6y = 9   (D) 2y = 3x + 10   (E) 2x + y = 11

42. A function f(x) has the property that f(-x) = -f(x) for all real values of x. Given that (5, - 25) is a point on the graph of f(x), then which of the following points must also be on the graph?

(A) (- 5, 25)   (B) (- 5, - 25)   (C) (0, 25)   (D) (5, 25)   (E) (25, - 5)

43. If points A, B and C lie on a circle and if the center of the circle lies on segment AB, then triangle ABC can be

(A) an acute triangle.   (B) an equiangular triangle.   (C) an obtuse triangle.   (D) an isosceles triangle.

(E) a right triangle where the right angle is either at A or B.

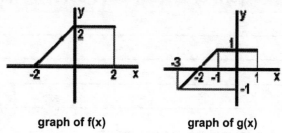

graph of f(x)   graph of g(x)

Figure 59

44. Graph of f(x) and g(x) are given in figure 59 above. Which of the following is the relation between f(x) and g(x)?

(A) g(x) = f(x + 1) – 1   (B) g(x) = f(x – 1) + 1   (C) g(x) = f(x – 1) – 1

(D) f(x) = g(x + 1) – 1   (E) f(x) = g(x + 1) + 1

45. How many of the following can be obtained by the intersection of a cone with a plane?

I. a line   II. an angle   III. a triangle   IV. a circle   V. an ellipse

(A) 1   (B) 2   (C) 3   (D) 4   (E) 5

46. If f is a linear function and f(-5) < f(-1), which of the following cannot be correct?

(A) f(1) < f(3)   (B) f(4) > f(-2)   (C) f(-2) < f(6)   (D) f(-1) > f(2)   (E) f(1) < f(2)

47. Given the graph of the circle whose equation is $(x+2)^2+(y-1)^2=4$, which of the following is an endpoint of the diameter with slope -1?

(A) (-2, 1)   (B) (-2+$\sqrt{2}$, 1-$\sqrt{2}$)   (C) (-2-$\sqrt{2}$, 1-$\sqrt{2}$)

(D) (-4, 3)   (E) (-2+$\sqrt{2}$, 1+$\sqrt{2}$)

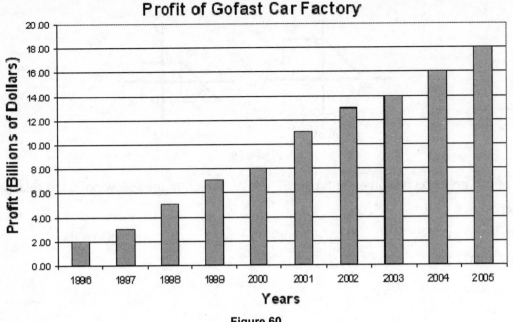

Figure 60

48. The graph given in figure 60 above shows the annual profit of Gofast Car Factory in the period 1996 – 2005. Which of the following is not a correct conclusion?

(A) The difference between the greatest three and the lowest three annual profits was $38 Billions of Dollars.

(B) The greatest increase in profit over the previous year took place in 2001.

(C) The greatest percentage increase in profit over the previous year took place in 1998.

(D) Between 1996 and 2005, the mean annual profit was slightly less than the median value.

(E) If the percentage increase in profit over the previous year in 2006 is projected to be twice as much as the percentage increase in profit over the previous year in 2005, then the profit in 2006 would be around $23 Billions of Dollars.

49. An equation for the circle with its center at (2, 5) and passing through the origin is

(A) $x^2 - y^2 = \sqrt{29}$ (B) $(x + 2)^2 + (y + 5)^2 = 29$

(C) $x^2 + y^2 = \sqrt{29}$ (D) $(x - 2)^2 + (y - 5)^2 = 29$

(E) $x^2 + y^2 = 29$

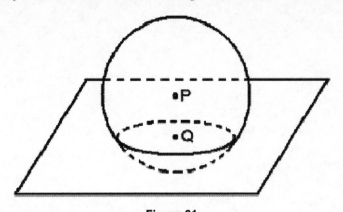

Figure 61

Figure not drawn to scale

50. Given in figure 61 above is a sphere whose radius is 10 inches and whose center is at P. The sphere is intersected by a plane so that the minimum distance from point P to the plane is 8 inches. If the intersection is the circle whose center is at Q, what is the area of this circle?

(A) 12π (B) 16π (C) 36π (D) 64π (E) 100π

S T O P

END OF TEST

Level 1 – Model Test 5

Test Duration: 60 Minutes

Directions: For each of the following problems, decide which is the best of the choices given. If the exact numerical value is not one of the choices, select the choice that best approximates this value. Then fill in the corresponding oval on the answer sheet.

Notes:

- A calculator will be necessary for answering some (but not all) of the questions in this test. For each question you will have to decide whether or not you should use a calculator. The calculator you use must be at least a scientific calculator; programmable calculators and calculators that can display graphs are permitted.

- The only angle measure used on this test is degree measure. Make sure your calculator is in the degree mode.

- Figures that accompany problems in this test are intended to provide information useful in solving the problems. They are drawn as accurately as possible except when it is stated in a specific problem that its figure is not drawn to scale.

- All figures lie in a plane unless otherwise indicated.

- Unless otherwise specified, the domain of any function f is assumed to be the set of all real numbers x for which f(x) is a real number.

Reference Information: The following information is for your reference in answering some of the questions in this test.

- Volume of a right circular cone with radius r and height h: $V = \frac{1}{3}\pi r^2 h$

- Lateral area of a right circular cone with circumference of the base c and slant height l: $S = \frac{1}{2}cl$

- Volume of a sphere with radius r: $V = \frac{4}{3}\pi r^3$

- Surface area of sphere with radius r: $S = 4\pi r^2$

- Volume of a pyramid with base area B and height h: $V = \frac{1}{3}Bh$

1. If 9m = 10.98 then 6m = ?

(A) 1.22　　　　(B) 3.66　　　　(C) 4.88　　　　(D) 7.23　　　　(E) 7.32

2. If $\dfrac{x}{3} - \dfrac{5-x}{5} = \dfrac{x}{5} - \dfrac{9-x}{3} + 2x$, x = ?

(A) -1   (B) $-\dfrac{1}{2}$ (C) 0   (D) $\dfrac{1}{2}$ (E) 1

3. If $t \neq \pm 2$, $\dfrac{\dfrac{t^2 + 2t - 8}{3}}{\dfrac{4}{t^2 - 4t + 4}}$ =?

(A) $\dfrac{4(t+2)}{3(t-4)}$ (B) $\dfrac{4(t-2)}{3(t+4)}$ (C) $\dfrac{3(t+2)}{4(t-4)}$ (D) $\dfrac{3(t-2)}{4(t+4)}$ (E) $\dfrac{4(t+2)}{3(t+4)}$

4. If $3^{x-2y+1} = 5^{y+3}$ then x=?

(A) -7   (B) 3   (C) 5   (D) 7

(E) The given information is not enough to find x.

5. Let $\triangle ABC$ be an isosceles triangle. If the coordinates of A, B and C are (3, t),

(-2, -1) and (8, -1) respectively, which of the following can not be the value of t?

(A) -3   (B) -1   (C) 0   (D) 1   (E) 3

6. $(x^2 - 4x + 4)(x^2 + 4x + 4)$ = ?

(A) $\left(x^2 - 4\right)^2$ (B) $\left(x^2 + 4\right)^2$ (C) $(x-2)^2 + 4x$ (D) $(x-2)^2 - 4x$

(E) None of the above

7. What is the y-intercept of the line given by 3x – 4y + 12 = 0 ?

(A) -4   (B) -3   (C) 0   (D) 3   (E) 4

8. The following are given for figure 62. line m || line n; x = 20º; y = 110º; z = 30º; v = 140º; then w = ?

(A) 60º

(B) 40º

(C) 80º

(D) 100º

(E) 120º

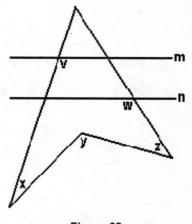

Figure 62

Figure not drawn to scale

9. If $\dfrac{1}{2} = y^2$, then $\dfrac{1}{y^4}$ = ?

(A) $\dfrac{1}{4}$ (B) $\dfrac{1}{2}$ (C) 2   (D) 4   (E) 16

10. If 2x+y = A and x – 3y = -B, then $\dfrac{x}{y}$ = ?

(A) $3 - \dfrac{B}{A}$ (B) $\dfrac{9A - 7B}{2B + A}$ (C) $\dfrac{3A - B}{2B + A}$ (D) $\dfrac{2B + A}{9A - 7B}$ (E) $\dfrac{2B + A}{3A - B}$

11. If the cube root of the square of a number is 4, what is the number?

(A) 4   (B) 8   (C) 16   (D) 64   (E) 128

12. Selami's age is two-fifths that of Can's whose age is three-fourths that of Burak's. If their ages sum up to 82 now, how old was Selami two years ago?

(A) 10   (B) 12   (C) 14   (D) 28   (E) 38

13. What is the measure of the angle α between the hour and minute hands of a clock at 10:30 pm?

(A) 120°   (B) 125°   (C) 130°   (D) 135°   (E) 145°

14. If $a + 1 = \dfrac{3b - 10}{5b}$, then b = ?

(A) $\dfrac{-10}{2 - 5a}$ (B) $\dfrac{-10}{5a - 2}$ (C) $\dfrac{10}{5a + 2}$ (D) $\dfrac{-10}{5a + 2}$ (E) $-\dfrac{a}{2} - \dfrac{1}{5}$

15. If $f(x) = (x+1)^2 - 2x$ and $g(x) = x - 2$, which of the following must be added to $f(g(x))$ in order to get $f(x)$?

(A) $-4 \cdot x$ (B) $4 \cdot x$ (C) $-4 \cdot x + 4$ (D) $4x - 4$ (E) $-4(x+1)$

16. If $\left(4^2\right)^4 = 2^{x+1}$, then which of the following is a factor of x = ?

(A) 2   (B) 3   (C) 4   (D) 6   (E) 8

17. 6 years ago, Murat was 2/3 as old as Selin was and 9 years later, Murat will be 7/8 as old as Selin will be. If they are both under older than ten years old, what are their ages now?

(A) Murat is 15 and Selin is 12.   (B) Murat is 14 and Selin is 12.

(C) Murat is 12 and Selin is 15.   (D) Murat is 12 and Selin is 14.

(E) It cannot be determined from the given information.

18. Which of the following gives all values of x for which $|x - 2| + |2x - 4| < 12$?

(A) 14 < x < 10   (B) 10 < x < 14   (C) -6 < x < -2   (D) -6 < x < 2   (E) -2 < x < 6

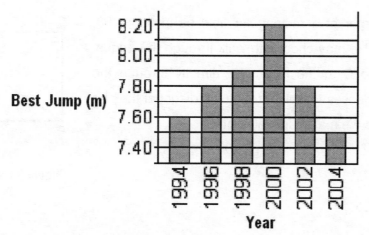

19 The graph above shows the best jumps in meters that a long jumper made in the years 1994 through 2004. Between which of the following years, was the percentage change made by the sportsman a maximum?

(A) 1994 – 1996   (B) 1996 – 1998   (C) 1998 – 2000   (D) 2000 – 2002   (E) 2002 – 2004

20. The ID cards in a firm are coded by LLDDD, where LL represents the sequence of letters that always start with A, and DDD represents the digits that follow. If all letters and numerals used in a code are distinct, then how many unique codes can be generated?

(A) 486.720   (B) 468.000   (C) 25.000   (D) 18.720   (E) 18.000

21. Each of the four wheels of a car has a radius of r inches and while the car is traveling with a speed of v miles per hour, each wheel revolves at the rate of 6000 revolutions per minute. What is v?

(A) 0.19r (B) 0.19πr (C) 11.36r (D) 11.36πr (E) 113.6πr

22 For i = $\sqrt{-1}$, what is the value of $(1+i^3)(1-i^3)$?

(A) -2i (B) –i (C) i (D) 1 (E) 2

23. Eser, who is on the corner of a rectangular field as in figure 63, wishes to walk from A to C. He may choose to walk through the edges; from A to D then from D to C; or he may walk directly through the diagonal from A to C. If he chooses to walk through the diagonal then he saves x% of the way. What is the maximum value of x?

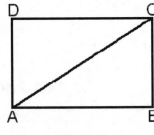

(A) 17.6 (B) 22.4 (C) 23.9
(D) 29.3 (E) 32.1

Figure 63
Figure not drawn to scale

24. For the parallelogram ABCD given in figure 64, AE=EF=FB and DI=IH=HG=GC. What is the ratio of the area of the parallelogram to the shaded area?

(A) $\dfrac{12}{5}$ (B) $\dfrac{6}{5}$ (C) $\dfrac{4}{3}$ (D) 2 (E) 3

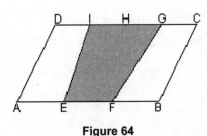

Figure 64

25. The two circles in figure 65 with their centers at M_1 and M_2 have radii in the ratio of 3:2 and each of them moves towards right covering exactly the same distance. If point P on circle M_1 goes through a clockwise angle of $\alpha = 120°$ coinciding with point P' then what is the degree measure of the angle that point T on circle M_2 goes through?

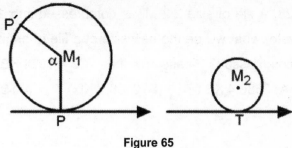

Figure 65

Figure not drawn to scale

(A) 145º   (B) 150º   (C) 180º

(D) 200º   (E) 240º

26. For the right triangle ABC given in figure 66, if $m \angle CAB = 30°$ and DB=BC, then what is the ratio AC/DC?

(A) $2\sqrt{3}$ (B) $2\sqrt{2}$ (C) $\sqrt{3}$

(D) $\sqrt{2}$ (E) 1

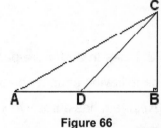

Figure 66

Figure not drawn to scale

27. Given that $f(x) = ax^2 + bx + c$. If $f(x)$ and $|f(x)|$ intersect at no points then which of the following statements must be correct?

(A) $\dfrac{b}{2a} > 0$ and $a < 0$ (B) $b^2 - 4ac < 0$ and $a < 0$ (E) $b^2 - 4ac < 0$

(C) $\dfrac{c}{a} < 0$ and $\dfrac{b}{a} > 0$ (D) $b^2 - 4ac < 0$ and $a > 0$

28. A file of size 2.2 MB is compressed into 1.8 MB by a special file compression algorithm. At this rate, what will be the new size of a file of original size 3.6 MB to the nearest tenth of a KB, when it is compressed? Please note that 1MB = 1024 KB.

(A) 3686.4 KB   (B) 3106.2 KB   (C) 3276.8 KB   (D) 3016.2 KB   (E) 1126.4 KB

29. If the xy – plane is translated 2 units up and 3 units left without any rotation, then what will be the new coordinates of the point (4, -5) ?

(A) (6, -8)   (B) (7, -7)   (C) (4, -5)   (D) (2, -2)   (E) (1, -3)

30. Lines m and n are parallel. If line m has a positive x intercept and a negative y intercept, which of the following cannot be true of line n?

(A) Line n has a positive x intercept and a negative y intercept.

(B) Line n has a negative x intercept and a positive y intercept.

(C) Line n passes through the origin.

(D) Line n can pass through the 1st, 2nd, and the 3rd quadrants of the xy plane at the same time.

(E) Line n can pass from the 1st, 2nd and the 4th quadrants of the xy plane at the same time.

31. In a math contest each student is scored in two categories A and B where in each category the highest score is 200. Nazmi's scores are 160 and 120 in categories A and B respectively. If the weights given to the scores in categories A and B are in the ratio of 3:2 respectively, what is the cumulative grade point average of Nazmi in the contest?

(A) 128   (B) 130   (C) 132   (D) 136   (E) 144

32. If b varies inversely as the square of c, and b = 25 when c = 5, then what is the value of b when c = 25?

(A) 1   (B) 5   (C) 25   (D) 125   (E) 625

33. Find the real roots of the given equation $x^4 - x^3 - 2x^2 - 4x - 24 = 0$?

(A) -2 and -3   (B) -1 and 2   (C) -1 and 1   (D) -2 and 1   (E) -2 and 3

34. In the given figure 67, m $\angle$ ACD = m $\angle$ ABC, AD = x and AC = 3x. What is the value of y in terms of x?

(A) 3x   (B) 4x   (C) 6x

(D) 8x   (E) 9x

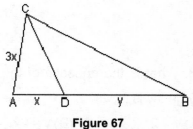

Figure 67

Figure not drawn to scale

35. $\sin^2 \theta - (1 - \cos \theta)(1 + \cos \theta)$ = ?

(A) -2   (B) -1   (C) 0   (D) 1   (E) 2

36. Lines p and q intersect at point A whose coordinates are (1, 4). If the equation of line p is y = 2x – k, which of the following points cannot be on line q?

(A) (-2, -1)   (B) (3, 8)   (C) (2, 5)   (D) (-1, 1)   (E) (4, 8)

37. The two parallelograms given in figure 68 are congruent. Point E and F are given by (-1,1) and (-4,5) and length of segment EH is 6. If the coordinates of point D are given by (1,-3.5) then what are the coordinates of point B?

(A) (5, -0.5)

(B) (6.5, -5)

(C) (4, -4.5)

(D) (5, -6.5)

(E) (4, -5.5)

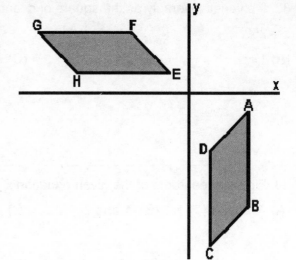

Figure 68

38. What is the equation of the line tangent to the circle $(x - 1)^2 + (y + 1)^2 = 9$ where the point of tangency is (1, 2)?

(A) y = 2   (B) y = 2x   (C) x = 1   (D) x = 2   (E) y = x + 2

39. $\log(x^2 - y^2) =$

(A) $\log(x + y) + \log(x - y)$ (B) $(\log x)^2 - (\log y)^2$ (C) $2\log\left(\dfrac{x}{y}\right)$

(D) $\log(x + y) - \log(x - y)$ (E) $\log\dfrac{x + y}{x - y}$

40. If in figure 69, EF = 3GF = 6 inches and AB = 15 inches then what is the shaded area in square inches?

(A) 10

(B) 20

(C) 30

(D) 40

(E) 40

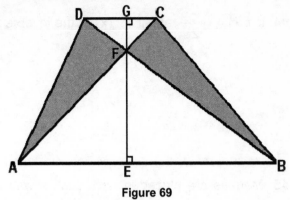

Figure 69

Figure not drawn to scale

41. In figure 70, if m∠ACO = 4·m∠BCO, what is the measure of ∠AOC?

(A) 18º

(B) 36º

(C) 48º

(D) 54º

(E) 72º

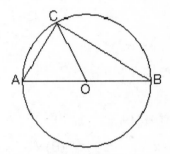

Figure 70

Figure not drawn to scale

42. If $f(x) = \dfrac{x-1}{\sqrt{x-1}}$, which of the following represents the domain of f(x)?

(A) 0 < x < 1   (B) x > 1   (C) x > 0 and x ≠ 1   (D) 0 ≤ x ≤ 1   (E) x ≥ 1

43. If a hemisphere and a cone have equal volumes of V cubic inches and radii of r inches, what is the height of the cone in terms of r?

(A) $\dfrac{3}{4}$r   (B) $\dfrac{4}{3}$r   (C) 2r   (D) 4r   (E) r^2

44. If $f(x) = \dfrac{x-6}{2}$ and if $f^{-1}(x)$ is the inverse function of f, what is $f^{-1}(4)$?

(A) -1   (B) 2   (C) 8   (D) 10   (E) 14

45. Marbles are placed in rows such a way that there is 1 marble in the first row, 2 marbles in the second, 4 marbles in the third, 8 marbles in the fourth, etc.; in each row, twice the number of marbles in the previous row are placed. If there are n such rows, what is the total number of marbles placed in all rows?

(A) 2^{n-1} (B) $2^n - 1$ (C) $1 - 2^n$ (D) $1 - 2^{n-1}$ (E) 2^n

46. If $f(x) = -x + 1$, $f(f(f(x))) = ?$

(A) $-x$ (B) x (C) $x - 1$ (D) $-x - 1$ (E) $-x + 1$

47. If the polynomials given by $P(x) = x^2 + 2x - 3$ and $Q(x) = x^3 + x^2 - 9x + k$ have a common factor other than $(x - 1)$, what is the value of k?

(A) -9   (B) -3   (C) -2   (D) 3   (E) 9

48. A circular pool with a radius of 24 meters is surrounded by a uniform walk of width 2 meters. What is the area of the walk to the nearest square meters?

(A) 312   (B) 313   (C) 314   (D) 315   (E) 316

For questions 49 – 50 please refer to the data given in the following graph:

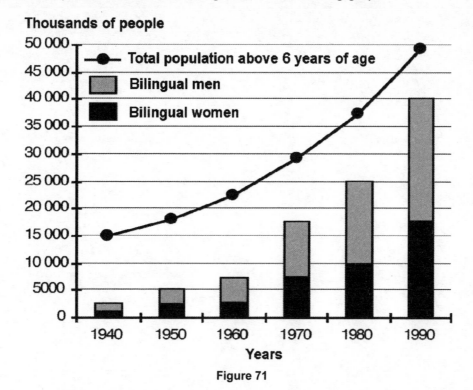

Figure 71

49. In 1980 what percent of the total population above 71 years of age consisted of bilingual men?

(A) 25 (B) 27 (C) 33 (D) 40 (E) 45

50. Which of the following cannot be inferred from the data given in the graph in figure 71?

(A) Bilingual women never exceeded 50% of the total bilingual population.

(B) In 1970 the number of bilingual women was 200% more than that in 1960.

(C) In 1990 the ratio of the female bilingual population to the male bilingual population was about 7/9.

(D) In the year when the bilingual population was around 18,000 approximately one fourth of all population consisted of bilingual men.

(E) In 1960 there were as many bilingual females as there were in 1950.

S T O P

END OF TEST

Level 2 – Model Test 1

Test Duration: 60 Minutes

Directions: For each of the following problems, decide which is the best of the choices given. If the exact numerical value is not one of the choices, select the choice that best approximates this value. Then fill in the corresponding oval on the answer sheet.

Notes:

- A calculator will be necessary for answering some (but not all) of the questions in this test. For each question you will have to decide whether or not you should use a calculator. The calculator you use must be at least a scientific calculator; programmable calculators and calculators that can display graphs are permitted.

- For some questions in this test you may have to decide whether your calculator should be in the radian mode or the degree mode.

- Figures that accompany problems in this test are intended to provide information useful in solving the problems. They are drawn as accurately as possible except when it is stated in a specific problem that its figure is not drawn to scale.

- All figures lie in a plane unless otherwise indicated.

- Unless otherwise specified, the domain of any function f is assumed to be the set of all real numbers x for which f(x) is a real number.

Reference Information: The following information is for your reference in answering some of the questions in this test.

- Volume of a right circular cone with radius r and height h: $V=\dfrac{1}{3}\pi r^2 h$

- Lateral area of a right circular cone with circumference of the base c and slant height l: $S=\dfrac{1}{2}cl$

- Volume of a sphere with radius r: $V = \dfrac{4}{3}\pi r^3$

- Surface area of sphere with radius r: $S=4\pi r^2$

- Volume of a pyramid with base area B and height h: $V=\dfrac{1}{3}Bh$

1. If x-3= y, what is the value of |x-y+|y-x||=?

(A) 0   (B) 3   (C) 6   (D) -3   (E) -6

2. One more than the sum of twice a number and its square is 441. The number is

(A) 18   (B) 19   (C) 20   (D) 21   (E) 22

3. If n is a positive integer, then which of the following quantities are always even?

     I. $(n+3)!$

     II. $2^n + 3n$

     III. $n^{n+1} + (n+1)^n$

(A) I only   (B) II only   (C) I and II only   (D) I and III only   (E) I, II and III

4. How many numbers in the set of integers satisfy the conditions $|n+4|<2$ and $|n-1| \leq 5$?

(A) 1   (B) 2   (C) 3   (D) 4   (E) 5

5. The lines $2x - 3y + 5 = 0$ and $2y = -3x + 6$ intersect at point A. One angle formed at point A is

(A) 30º   (B) 45º   (C) 60º   (D) 90º

(E) Point A doesn't exist because the lines are parallel.

6. The sum of the roots of the equation $2 \cdot (x-\sqrt{3})^2 \cdot (x+\sqrt{2}) \cdot (x^2-2) = 0$ is

(A) 0.32   (B) 2.05   (C) 2.32   (D) 2.52   (E) 4.05

7. If $f(r,\theta) = r \cdot \sin(-\theta)$, then $f(3, \dfrac{3\pi}{4}) =$

(A) -2.12   (B) 0   (C) 0.71   (D) 2.12   (E) 7.06

8. If $f(x)=e^x$, where x is a real number, and if the inverse function of f is denoted by f^{-1}, then $f^{-1}(ab)$ where a>1 and b>1?

(A) e^{ab}
(B) $\dfrac{1}{e^{ab}}$
(C) lna·lnb
(D) lna + lnb
(E) ln(a+b)

9. The probability that Damla hits the dartboard is $\dfrac{4}{7}$ and, independently, the probability Fuat misses it is $\dfrac{1}{3}$. What is the probability that Damla misses the dartboard and Fuat hits it?

(A) 1/7
(B) 4/21
(C) 2/7
(D) 13/21
(E) 5/7

10. As x becomes infinitely large the value of $\dfrac{6x^2 - 3x - 5}{4x^3 + 2x - 5}$ becomes

(A) 0
(B) 1
(C) 3/2
(D) ¾
(E) ∞

11. The number of terms in the expansion $(3x^2 - 2y)^6$ is
(A) 2
(B) 6
(C) 7
(D) 12
(E) 15

12. A mixture is made by mixing alcohol with water in such a way that 40% of the mixture is alcohol by weight. If one fifth of the mixture is taken and replaced by pure water, then what percent of the final mixture will be water?
(A) 22
(B) 32
(C) 40
(D) 68
(E) 78

13. If $5^x=7$, then $7^x=$
(A) 2
(B) 5
(C) 8.5
(D) 10.5
(E) 12

14. The norm of vector $-\sqrt{3}\,i + \sqrt{2}\,j$ is

(A) 1   (B) 2.41   (C) 2.24   (D) 2.64   (E) 3.60

15. What is the smallest positive x-intercept of the graph of $y = 2 \cdot \sin\left[3\left(x + \dfrac{3\pi}{4}\right)\right]$?

(A) 0.26   (B) 0.52   (C) 0.79   (D) 1.04   (E) 2.36

16. If $x - k$ is a factor if $x^2 - 3x + k$, then k=

(A) 1   (B) 2   (C) 3   (D) 4   (E) 5

17. In the triangle given in figure 72, $\theta = 80°$ and $\beta = 60°$. What is the length of side AC?

(A) 4.61

(B) 5.46

(C) 6.01

(D) 9.21

(E) 10.91

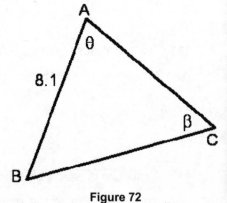

Figure 72

Figure not drawn to scale

18. If $f(x) = \sqrt[3]{x^3 - 4}$, what is $f^{-1}(4) =$

(A) -4   (B) -1.58   (C) 3.91   (D) 4.08   (E) 8.25

19. In figure 73, A is the midpoint of one of the edges of the cube. If the length of each edge of the cube is a, what is the volume of the pyramid ABCD?

(A) $a^3/12$ (B) $a^3/6$ (C) $a^3/4$

(D) $a^3/2$ (E) a^3

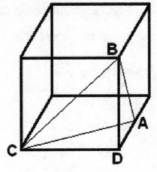

Figure 73

20. If the solution set of f(x)=0 is {-2,3} then what is the solution set of $f(x^2-1)=0$?

(A) {-2, 2}   (B) {-1, 4}   (C) {3, 8}   (D) {-5, 8}   (E) {-3, 2}

21. The set of points (x,y) that satisfy $x \cdot (y-4) < 0$ lies in which quadrants?

(A) Only IV   (B) Only I and IV   (C) Only II and IV

(D) Only I, II and IV   (E) I, II, III and IV

22. In figure 74, O is the center of the circle and POQ is an isosceles triangle such that PQ is tangent to the circle at point C. If the measure of the angle $\angle OPC$ is 20° and length of PQ is 20 inches, then what is the length of AB (not shown)?

(A) 1.24

(B) 2.49

(C) 3.42

(D) 3.64

(E) 6.84

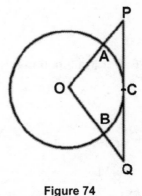

Figure 74

Figure not drawn to scale

23. Figure 75 shows a chord of length x in a circle of radius r. Determine the inscribed angle θ in terms of x and r.

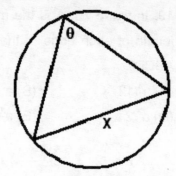

(A) $\theta = \arctan\left(\dfrac{x}{r}\right)$

(B) $\theta = \arcsin\left(\dfrac{x}{r}\right)$

(C) $\theta = \arccos\left(\dfrac{x}{r}\right)$

(D) $\theta = \arcsin\left(\dfrac{x}{2r}\right)$

(E) $\theta = 2\cdot\arcsin\left(\dfrac{x}{r}\right)$

Figure 75

24. If $y=ax^2+12x+10=0$ has its minimum value at y=1, then what is the value of a?

(A) 5   (B) 4   (C) 3   (D) 2   (E) 1

25. What is the range of the function given by $f(x)=3\sin(kx)-4\cos(kx)+2$ where k is an integer greater than 50?

(A) $3 \le y \le 7$ (B) $-3 \le y \le 7$ (C) $-7 \le y \le 3$ (D) $-7 \le y \le -3$

(E) Cannot be determined from the information given

26. For the function $f(x) = \dfrac{1}{1+\dfrac{1}{x-1}}$, for which of the following numbers is there no image?

I. -1

II. 0

III. 1

(A) I only   (B) II only   (C) III only   (D) I and II only   (E) II and III only

27. $(3\cdot cis45^\circ)^2$ written in rectangular form is

(A) 9   (B) 9i   (C) 9+9i   (D) 9-9i   (E) -9+9i

28. If cosθ=0.25, then cos(π+θ)=

(A) -9.7   (B) -0.25   (C) 0.25   (D) 0.75   (E) 9.7

29. What is the length of the radius of the sphere given by $x^2+y^2+z^2- 4x+6y-2z=11$?

(A) 5   (B) 10   (C) 11   (D) 25

(E) None of the above.

30. $\dfrac{1}{n!} - \dfrac{1}{(n+1)!} =$

(A) $\dfrac{1}{n(n+1)!}$ (B) $\dfrac{n}{n+1}$ (C) $\dfrac{n}{(n+1)!}$ (D) $\dfrac{2n+1}{(n+1)!}$ (E) $\dfrac{2n+1}{n.(n+1)!}$

31. If a right triangle with legs 4 and 6 is rotated 360° about its longer leg, it generates a solid of volume

(A) 24π (B) 32π (C) 48π (D) 96π (E) 144π

32. What is the least positive n such that the sum $\displaystyle\sum_{k=1}^{n}(x+k)$ is odd for every integer x?

(A) 1   (B) 2   (C) 3   (D) 4   (E) 5

33. If y varies inversely as –x, which of the following could be the graph of y as a function of x?

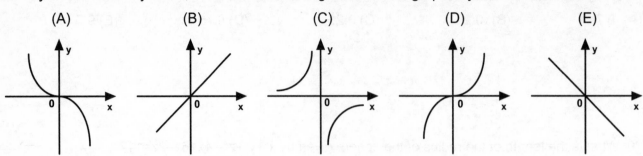

(A)   (B)   (C)   (D)   (E)

34. If the first three terms of an arithmetic sequence are given by $\frac{x}{3}$, x-3, and 2x-7 for some real number x, then what is the numerical value of the fourth term?

(A) 1   (B) -1   (C) 0   (D) 2   (E) -2

35. If f is a linear function and f(-3)=0, f(-1)=6, and f(x-1)=3.6 then x=?

(A) -2.8   (B) -1.47   (C) -0.8   (D) 0.8   (E) 1.13

36. The set of points (x, y) that satisfy the equation $(x - 1) + iy = \dfrac{4}{(x - 1) - iy}$ where $i = \sqrt{-1}$ represent which of the following?

(A) circle with center at (0, -1) and radius of length 2

(B) circle with center at (-1, 0) and radius of length 4

(C) circle with center at (1, 0) and radius of length 2

(D) ellipse with center at (1,0) and mean radius of length 2

(E) ellipse with center at (-1,0) and mean radius of length 2

37. It is given that $f(x) = a^{x+b}$ where f(2)=250 and f(-1)=2; b = ?

(A) -5   (B) 5   (C) 0   (D) -1.43   (E) 1.43

38. Given that $f(x) = -x^2 + 3x + 1$ and $x_1 < x_2$. $f(x_1) < f(x_2)$ if and only if

(A) $x_k < 1.5$ where $k \in \{1,2\}$

(B) x_k is any real number where $k \in \{1,2\}$

(C) $0 < x_k < 3.3$ where $k \in \{1,2\}$

(D) $-0.3 < x_k < 3.3$ where $k \in \{1,2\}$

(E) $0 < x_k < 3.3$ where $k \in \{1,2\}$

39. The vertical asymptotes of $y = \dfrac{2x}{9 - x^2}$ are

(A) $x = 3$

(B) $x = -3$ and $x = 3$

(C) $y = -2$ and $x = 3$

(D) $y = 0$ and $x = 3$

(E) $x = 9$ and $y = 2/9$

40. What is the area of a right triangle with an angle of $62°$ and the shorter leg of length 8?

(A) 40

(B) 50

(C) 60

(D) 80

(E) 120

41. If $f(x) = |x-1| + [x+1]$ and brackets denote the greatest integer function, the value of $f(-1.8) + f(1.8)$?

(A) -1

(B) 3.6

(C) 4.6

(D) 5

(E) 5.6

42. All distinct 6 letter words are written on separate cards using capital letters only and one card is picked at random. What is the probability that the word written on this card does not contain adjacent letters that are the same?

(A) $\dfrac{1}{26^6}$

(B) $\dfrac{1}{26 \cdot 25^5}$

(C) $\left(\dfrac{25}{26}\right)^5$

(D) $\dfrac{25 \cdot 24 \cdot 23 \cdot 22 \cdot 21}{26^5}$

(E) None of the above

43. In figure 76, the shaded sector OPR belongs to a circle O with a radius of length 5. If the major arc PR measures $\frac{6\pi}{5}$ radians and the shaded sector is bent to form a cone with vertex at O, then what will be the height of the resulting cone?

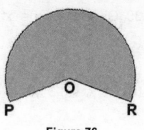

Figure 76

(A) 4   (B) 5   (C) 6   (D) 12   (E) 16

44. The graph of $\begin{cases} x = 2t + 3 \\ y = 4t^2 \end{cases}$ in the x-y plane is

(A) a circle.   (B) an ellipse.   (C) a hyperbola.   (D) a parabola.   (E) a straight line.

45. If A(x, $x\sqrt{2}$) is 4 units from line 3x+4y-5=0, then x can equal

(A) 1.73 only   (B) 2.89 only   (C) -1.73 only   (D) -1.73 or 2.89   (E) -1.73 or 2.89

46. If f(x) = $\frac{x^2 - 36}{x - 6}$, what value does f(x) approach as x approaches 6?

(A) 0   (B) 3   (C) 6   (D) 12   (E) undefined

47. If f(x)=$2x^2$+tx–2, what must the value of t equal so that both of the points (-5, A) and (5, A) lie on the graph of f(x)?

(A) -5   (B) -1   (C) 0   (D) 1   (E) 5

48. $\dfrac{1}{i} + \dfrac{i}{1+i} = ?$

(A) $\dfrac{1}{2}$ (B) $\dfrac{1-i}{2}$ (C) $\dfrac{1-3i}{2}$ (D) $\dfrac{-1-3i}{2}$ (E) $\dfrac{-1+3i}{2}$

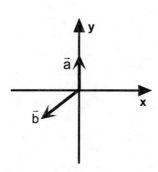

Figure 77

49. Vectors $\vec{a}$ and $\vec{b}$ are as given in the figure 77 above. Which of the following can be the graph of $2\vec{a} + \vec{b}$?

(A) (B) (C) (D) (E)

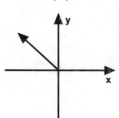 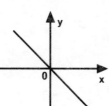 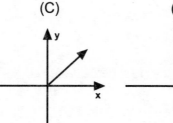 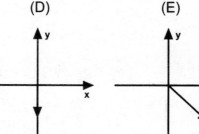

50. If f(x) = sin(x) and g(x) = 2x, which of the following are even functions?

I. f(x)·g(x)

II. f(x)+g(x)

III. (fog)(x)

(A) I only (B) II only (C) I and II only (D) I and III only (E) I, II and III

S T O P

END OF TEST

Test Duration: 60 Minutes

Directions: For each of the following problems, decide which is the best of the choices given. If the exact numerical value is not one of the choices, select the choice that best approximates this value. Then fill in the corresponding oval on the answer sheet.

Notes:

- A calculator will be necessary for answering some (but not all) of the questions in this test. For each question you will have to decide whether or not you should use a calculator. The calculator you use must be at least a scientific calculator; programmable calculators and calculators that can display graphs are permitted.

- For some questions in this test you may have to decide whether your calculator should be in the radian mode or the degree mode.

- Figures that accompany problems in this test are intended to provide information useful in solving the problems. They are drawn as accurately as possible except when it is stated in a specific problem that its figure is not drawn to scale.

- All figures lie in a plane unless otherwise indicated.

- Unless otherwise specified, the domain of any function f is assumed to be the set of all real numbers x for which f(x) is a real number.

Reference Information: The following information is for your reference in answering some of the questions in this test.

- Volume of a right circular cone with radius r and height h: $V = \dfrac{1}{3}\pi r^2 h$

- Lateral area of a right circular cone with circumference of the base c and slant height l: $S = \dfrac{1}{2} cl$

- Volume of a sphere with radius r: $V = \dfrac{4}{3}\pi r^3$

- Surface area of sphere with radius r: $S = 4\pi r^2$

- Volume of a pyramid with base area B and height h: $V = \dfrac{1}{3} Bh$

1. If $g(x) = \dfrac{1}{\sqrt[5]{x^3 - 6}}$, what is the value of $g(-1.2)$?

(A) -1.98   (B) -1.73   (C) -.66   (D) -.51   (E) 0

2. $\dfrac{1}{a} \cdot \left(\dfrac{b}{a} + \dfrac{a}{c} \right) =$

(A) $\dfrac{b}{a^2} + \dfrac{a}{c}$
(B) $\dfrac{b}{a^2} + \dfrac{1}{c}$
(C) $\dfrac{bc + a^2}{ac}$
(D) $\dfrac{b}{ac}$
(E) $\dfrac{b}{a}$

3. What is the perimeter of a right triangle with an angle of 27° and with shorter leg of 11?

(A) 21.59
(B) 21.82
(C) 32.59
(D) 40.05
(E) 56.82

4. If $\sqrt[3]{5x+1} = 2.7$, then x=

(A) .98
(B) 2.50
(C) 3.74
(D) 3.94
(E) 18.68

5. Figure 78 shows a portion of the graph of the function y = f(x). Which of the following is the period of f(x)?

(A) -1
(B) $\dfrac{\pi}{4}$
(C) $\dfrac{\pi}{2}$
(D) π
(E) 1

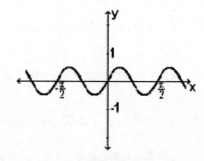

Figure 78

6. If $x - 5$ is a factor of $x^3 - 4x^2 + \dfrac{3a}{2}x + 10$, then a=

(A) -5
(B) $-\dfrac{14}{3}$
(C) $-\dfrac{3}{14}$
(D) $\dfrac{3}{14}$
(E) $\dfrac{14}{3}$

7. Given a point C in the plane, the set of all points in the plane that are the same distance r from C is described by

(A) A hyperbola with major axis r and centered at C

(B) A square with side r and centered at C

(C) A circle with radius 2r, centered at C

(D) A circle with radius r, centered at C

(E) An ellipse with center C

8. In figure 79, which of the following equals $\sin\theta$?

I. $\dfrac{b}{2r}$ II. $\dfrac{b}{c}$ III. $\dfrac{2r-a}{b}$

(A) I only   (B) I and II only   (C) I and III only

(D) II and III only   (E) I, II and III

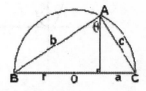

Figure 79

9. If $\dfrac{\frac{3}{x}}{\frac{7}{5}} = x$, then x could equal which of the following?

(A) -1.46   (B) .47   (C) .68   (D) 2.14   (E) 3.02

10. If $\csc\theta \cdot \cos\theta = -3$, what is the value of $\tan\theta = ?$

(A) - 3   (B) $-\dfrac{1}{3}$ (C) 0   (D) $\dfrac{1}{3}$ (E) 3

11. The area between the lines y = -0.5x + 1, x = - 6, x = - 2, and x-axis is

(A) 8   (B) 10   (C) 11   (D) 12   (E) 14

12. If $f(x) = \dfrac{4x-1}{x+1}$ and $g(x) = \sqrt[3]{x^2-1}$, then $g(f(4)) =$

(A) 1   (B) 1.15   (C) 2   (D) 2.55   (E) 3

13. If x varies inversely with y, then which of the following graphs could represent the relation between x and y?

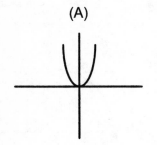
(A)

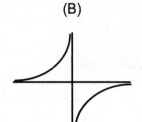
(B)

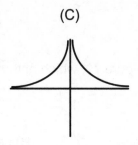
(C)

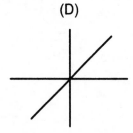
(D)

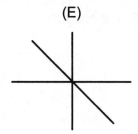
(E)

14. $\dfrac{3}{x} = \dfrac{7}{2x+1} + \dfrac{2x}{4x^2-1}$

Which of the following values can be a solution of the above equation?

(A) -0.75   (B) -0.5   (C) 0   (D) 0.5   (E) 1

15. Line d is defined by the equation Bx = Ay + C. Which of the following lines is perpendicular to the line d?

(A) Ay – Bx + C = 0   (B) Bx = Ay + C   (C) By + Ax + C = 0

(D) By = Ax + C   (E) Bx - Ay + C = 0

16. The graph of $y = |f(x)|$ is shown in figure 80. Which of the

following could be the graph of $y = f(x)$?

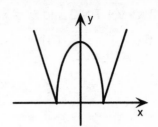

Figure 80

(A) 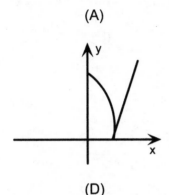   (B) 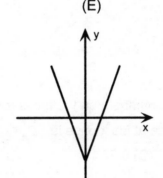   (C)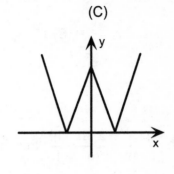

(D) 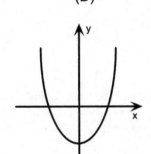   (E)

17. If f(g(x)) = 2x + 1 and g(x) = ax + b where a and b are both nonzero real numbers then f(x) cannot
be equal to

    I. $\dfrac{x-b}{a}$ II. x   III. 3

(A) I only   (B) II only   (C) III only   (D) I and III only   (E) I, II and III

18. The arithmetic mean of 7 numbers is 52. When a new number is added, the new average will be
48. What was the value of the number that was added?

(A) 15   (B) 20   (C) 28   (D) 48   (E) 55

19. If $3 \cdot x - y + 7 = 0$ and $x^2 = y$ for $x \geq 0$, then x=

(A) -1.54　　　　(B) 0　　　　(C) 2.27　　　　(D) 3　　　　(E) 4.54

20. For $-180° \leq x \leq 180°$, how many times do the graphs of $f(x) = \dfrac{-1}{120} x$ and $f(x) = \cos x$ intersect?

(A) 0　　　　(B) 1　　　　(C) 2　　　　(D) 3　　　　(E) 4

21. If $\dfrac{n!}{(n-1)!} = \dfrac{2 \cdot (n-1)!}{(n-2)!}$, then n could be which of the following?

(A) 1　　　　(B) 2　　　　(C) 3　　　　(D) 4　　　　(E) 5

22. A six-sided die with the first six prime numbers on the faces is rolled 4 times. The probability that an even number comes up on the top face at least once is

(A) 0.16　　　　(B) 0.52　　　　(C) 0.62　　　　(D) 0.65　　　　(E) 0.75

23. In a senior class of 95 students, 48 play basketball, 35 play football and 32 play neither basketball nor football. What percent of the students in the senior class plays only football?

(A) 16%　　　　(B) 21%　　　　(C) 29%　　　　(D) 37%　　　　(E) 51%

24. A geometric sequence has a second term equal to 16 and a fifth term equal to 6.75. What is the sixth term in the sequence?

(A) 6.25　　　　(B) 5.86　　　　(C) 5.06　　　　(D) 4.12　　　　(E) 4.01

25. If the lengths of the sides of a triangle are in a ratio of 6:8:11, what is the degree measure of the greatest angle?

(A) 102.64°　　　　(B) 77.26°　　　　(C) 68.11°　　　　(D) 65.11°　　　　(E) 62.41°

26. The domain of $g(x) = \sqrt{x^2 + x - 6}$ is given in which of the following answer choices?

(A) $-2 \le x \le 3$　　　　　(B) $-3 \le x \le 2$　　　　　(C) $0 \le x \le 2$

(D) $x < -3$ or $x > 2$　　　　(E) $x \le -3$ or $x \ge 2$

27. The quadratic function $f(x)$ is given by $f(x) = ax^2 + bx + c$ where a, b, and c are all real numbers. If $f(x)$ and $-f(x)$ intersect at two distinct points then which of the following must be correct?

(A) $b^2 + 4ac > 0$　　　　(B) $b^2 < 4ac$　　　　(C) $b^2 > 4ac$

(D) $b^2 + 4ac < 0$　　　　(E) $b^2 = 4ac$

28. What is the range of the function $f(x) = 2 - \dfrac{1}{x-1}$?

(A) All real numbers except 1　　　　(B) All real numbers except 2

(C) All negative real numbers　　　　(D) All positive real numbers

(E) All real numbers

29. The height of a right circular cylinder is twice its radius. If the volume of the cylinder is 12, what is the base area of the cylinder?

(A) 4.84　　　　(B) 6.21　　　　(C) 8.62　　　　(D) 9.50　　　　(E) 9.53

30. If $\dfrac{tx+t}{x+t} = 2$ then which of the following sets contains all values of t for which the equation cannot be solved for x?

(A) {-2, -1, 0}   (B) {-1, 0, 1}   (C) {0, 1}   (D) {1, 2}   (E) {0, 1, 2}

31. A line has parametric equations x = t - 1 and y = 2t + 2, where t is the parameter. What is the x-intercept of the line?

(A) – 2   (B) -1   (C) 1   (D) 2   (E) 4

32. At 08:00 AM the population of a bacteria colony was 1,200. If the population can be calculated using the function $P(t) = 1{,}200 \cdot (1.18)^{t/4}$, and the population becomes approximately 1,972 at 11:00 AM, then t denotes

(A) the number of hours passed since 08:00 AM

(B) the number of half hours passed since 08:00 AM

(C) the number of quarter hours passed since 08:00 AM

(D) the number of minutes passed since 08:00 AM

(E) none of the above

33. Which of the following could be the equation of an ellipse centered at (-5, -3) and tangent to both the x-axis and the y-axis?

(A) $\dfrac{(x+5)^2}{5} + \dfrac{(y+3)^2}{3} = 1$ (B) $\dfrac{(x+5)^2}{25} - \dfrac{(y+3)^2}{9} = 1$ (C) $\dfrac{(x+5)^2}{25} + \dfrac{(y+3)^2}{9} = 1$

(D) $\dfrac{(x+5)^2}{5} - \dfrac{(y+3)^2}{3} = 1$ (E) $\dfrac{(x-5)^2}{25} + \dfrac{(y-3)^2}{9} = 1$

34. If $f(x) = 3^x - 5$, then $f^{-1}(x) =$

(A) $\log_3 x - 5$ (B) $\log_3(x+5)$ (C) $\log_3(x-5)$ (D) $\log_5(x-3)$ (E) $\log_5(x+3)$

35. If $x_1 = 1$ and $x_{n+1} = x_n \cdot (x_n + 1)$, then $x_5 =$

(A) 42   (B) 43   (C) 1800   (D) 1806   (E) 1809

36. In figure 81, what is the area of $\triangle SAT$ in terms of θ?

(A) $\dfrac{9}{2}\tan\theta$ (B) $\dfrac{9}{2}\cot\theta$ (C) $\dfrac{2}{9}\cot\theta$

(D) $\dfrac{2}{9}\tan\theta$ (E) $\dfrac{1}{2}\tan\theta$

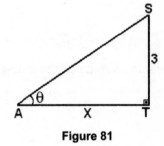

Figure 81

37. a + bi and c + di are two complex numbers. If (a + bi)·(c + di) = i, then which of the following must be true?

(A) ac – bd = 0 and ad + bc = 1   (B) ac – bd = 1 and ad + bc = 0   (C) ac – bd = 1 and ad + bc = 1

(D) ac – bd = 0 and ad + bc = 0   (E) ac – bd = 0 and ad + bc = i

38. If a card is drawn at random from a standard deck of 52 cards, what is the probability that it is a black card or an ace?

(A) 7/12   (B) 7/13   (C) 3/17   (D) 6/13   (E) 1/2

39. If $8^n = 2^{n^2 - n - 5}$, then n could be which of the following?

(A) -1   (B) 0   (C) 1   (D) 2   (E) 3

40. If vector $\vec{u} = (2,3)$ and vector $\vec{v} = (-4,5)$, then which of the following is equal to $4\vec{u} - \vec{v}$?

(A) (12, 7)   (B) (6, -2)   (C) (-6, -2)   (D) (-18, 17)   (E) (4, 7)

41. If $\cos^{-1}(\sin\theta) = \dfrac{\pi}{4}$ for $0 \leq \theta \leq \dfrac{\pi}{2}$, then θ could equal

(A) $\dfrac{\pi}{3}$ (B) $\dfrac{\pi}{4}$ (C) $\dfrac{\pi}{5}$ (D) $\dfrac{2\pi}{5}$ (E) $\dfrac{\pi}{2}$

42. $x - 4$, $x - 2$, and $2x - 1$ (where x is a real number) form the first three terms of a geometric sequence. Which of the following could be the value of x?

(A) 3   (B) 2   (C) 1   (D) 0   (E) -1

43. Which of the following could not be formed by the intersection of a cube and a cylinder?

(A) A point   (B) A circle   (C) A line segment   (D) An ellipse   (E) A parabola

44. What is the value of $\displaystyle\lim_{x\to\infty} \dfrac{3x^2 - 2x + 1}{7x - 4}$?

(A) $-\infty$ (B) -3/7   (C) 0   (D) 3/7   (E) $+\infty$

45. If $f(x) = \sqrt[5]{2x^3 - 1}$ what is the value of $f^{-1}(2) = ?$

(A) 1.72   (B) 2.55   (C) 1.55   (D) 1.48   (E) 0.48

46. In how many different ways can 10 letters be mailed through 8 mailboxes?

(A) 10^8 (B) $\dfrac{10!}{2!}$ (C) 8^{10} (D) $\dfrac{10!}{2!\,8!}$ (E) 1440

47. If $\cos^2\theta + 3\sin\theta - 3 = 0$ for $0 \le x \le \dfrac{\pi}{2}$, then θ is

(A) $\dfrac{\pi}{3}$ (B) $\dfrac{\pi}{4}$ (C) $\dfrac{\pi}{5}$ (D) $\dfrac{2\pi}{5}$ (E) $\dfrac{\pi}{2}$

48. The converse of the statement "If a triangle is equilateral, then it is equiangular."

(A) If a triangle is equiangular, then it is equilateral.

(B) If a triangle is not equilateral, then it is not equiangular.

(C) If a triangle is not equiangular, then it is not equilateral.

(D) A triangle is equilateral or it is not equiangular.

(E) A triangle is both equilateral and equiangular.

49. What is the solution set to $\dfrac{-2}{x^2 - 5x + 4} > 0$

(A) x < 1 or x > 4   (B) x < -1 or x > 4   (C) -1 < x < 4

(D) 1 < x < 4   (E) x ≥ 0

50. Which of the following is the center of the conic section defined by the equation
$16x^2 - 9y^2 - 96x + 18y - 9 = 0$?

(A) (-3, -1)   (B) (-3, 1)   (C) (1, 3)   (D) (-1, 3)   (E) (3, 1)

S T O P

END OF TEST

Test Duration: 60 Minutes

Directions: For each of the following problems, decide which is the best of the choices given. If the exact numerical value is not one of the choices, select the choice that best approximates this value. Then fill in the corresponding oval on the answer sheet.

Notes:

- A calculator will be necessary for answering some (but not all) of the questions in this test. For each question you will have to decide whether or not you should use a calculator. The calculator you use must be at least a scientific calculator; programmable calculators and calculators that can display graphs are permitted.

- For some questions in this test you may have to decide whether your calculator should be in the radian mode or the degree mode.

- Figures that accompany problems in this test are intended to provide information useful in solving the problems. They are drawn as accurately as possible except when it is stated in a specific problem that its figure is not drawn to scale.

- All figures lie in a plane unless otherwise indicated.

- Unless otherwise specified, the domain of any function f is assumed to be the set of all real numbers x for which f(x) is a real number.

Reference Information: The following information is for your reference in answering some of the questions in this test.

- Volume of a right circular cone with radius r and height h: $V = \dfrac{1}{3}\pi r^2 h$

- Lateral area of a right circular cone with circumference of the base c and slant height l: $S = \dfrac{1}{2}cl$

- Volume of a sphere with radius r: $V = \dfrac{4}{3}\pi r^3$

- Surface area of sphere with radius r: $S = 4\pi r^2$

- Volume of a pyramid with base area B and height h: $V = \dfrac{1}{3}Bh$

1. If $\dfrac{5}{\sqrt[3]{x^2 - 1}} = 6$, then x could be

(A) -1.58　　　　(B) -0.58　　　　(C) 0.58　　　　(D) 1.26　　　　(E) 1.58

2. $\dfrac{11!}{10!+9!}=?$

(A) .58   (B) 1   (C) 1.1   (D) 1.22   (E) 10

3. If $F(x,y,z)=\dfrac{x+y+z}{xyz}$, then which of the following is equal to $F(1,3,4)$?

(A) F(1,2,4)   (B) F(1,2,3)   (C) F(1,4,3)   (D) F(2,3,4)   (E) F(2,3,5)

4. In figure 82, AB is the diameter and O is the center of the circle. If C is an arbitrarily selected point on the semicircular arc AB and $\sin\theta=\dfrac{12}{13}$, then $\tan\alpha=?$

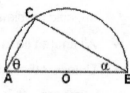

Figure 82

(A) $\dfrac{5}{12}$ (B) $\dfrac{5}{13}$ (C) $\dfrac{12}{5}$ (D) $\dfrac{13}{5}$ (E) $\dfrac{13}{12}$

5. If $f(x)=\dfrac{1}{\sqrt{x}+1}$, then what is the value of $f(f(3))$?

(A) 0.50   (B) 0.80   (C) 0.82   (D) 0.89   (E) 1.22

6. If $-|x+4|=(y-3)^2$ then $x+y=?$

(A) – 4   (B) – 1   (C) 1   (D) 3   (E) 7

7. The graph of which of the following is perpendicular to the graph of $y = -\dfrac{2}{3}x + \dfrac{5}{7}$?

(A) $y = -\dfrac{3}{2}x - \dfrac{7}{5}$ (B) $y = -\dfrac{3}{2}x + \dfrac{7}{5}$ (C) $y = -\dfrac{3}{2}x$ (D) $y = \dfrac{3}{2}x + \dfrac{5}{7}$ (E) $y = \dfrac{1}{2}x - \dfrac{7}{5}$

8. If $x \notin \{-2, -1\}$ then $\dfrac{1}{1 + \dfrac{1}{1 + x}} =$

(A) $\dfrac{1}{x+1}$ (B) $\dfrac{x}{x+1}$ (C) $\dfrac{x}{x+2}$ (D) $\dfrac{x+1}{x+2}$ (E) $\dfrac{x+2}{x+1}$

9. The graph of $y = ax^2 + bx + c$ cannot have points in the first or second quadrants if

(A) $b^2 - 4ac < 0$ and $b < 0$ (B) $b^2 - 4ac > 0$ and $b < 0$ (C) $b^2 - 4ac \le 0$ and $a > 0$

(D) $b^2 - 4ac \le 0$ and $a < 0$ (E) $b^2 - 4ac > 0$ and $a < 0$

10. If $\cot^2 \theta + 1 = 5$, then $\csc^2 \theta =$

(A) $1/5$ (B) $1/4$ (C) 1 (D) 4 (E) 5

11. $\dfrac{\dfrac{1}{a^2} - \dfrac{1}{b^2}}{\dfrac{1}{a} + \dfrac{1}{b}} =$

(A) $\dfrac{a+b}{ab}$ (B) $1 + \dfrac{a}{b}$ (C) $\dfrac{1}{ab}$ (D) $\dfrac{b-a}{ab}$ (E) $\dfrac{a-b}{ab}$

12. Three items are drawn at random from a box containing 7 pencils and 5 pens. What is the probability that the items selected are 2 pencils and 1 pen?

(A) 0   (B) 0.123   (C) 0.477   (D) 0.523   (E) 1

13. What is the product of the zeros of the polynomial given by $P(x) = x^4 - 1$?

(A) -2   (B) -1   (C) 1   (D) 2   (E) 4

14. According to the data given in figure 83, what is the radius of the circle passing through the vertices of the shaded triangle?

(A) 2.63

(B) 4.95

(C) 5.26

(D) 10.53

(E) It cannot be determined from the information given.

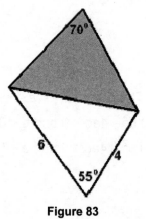

Figure 83
Figure not drawn to scale

15. If Melis makes $20 per hour for the first 24 hours she works, $30 per hour for each additional hour of work up to 48 hours, and $40 per hour for each hour of work over 48 hours, then how many hours must she work in order to make $1600?

(A) 24   (B) 40   (C) 48   (D) 58   (E) 64

16. Which of the following is the least of the zeros of $f(x) = x^2 - 7x + 5$?

(A) 0.81   (B) 6.19   (C) -9.16   (D) -0.81   (E) -6.19

17. If $\log_6(\log_4(\log_2(x))) = 0$, then x=

(A) 2 (B) 4 (C) 6 (D) 16 (E) 32

18. An operation is defined on two pairs of real numbers by $(a,b)*(c,d) = \dfrac{a \cdot b}{c+d}$, where c + d is nonzero. If $(2,6)*(1,5) = (3,8)*(7,x)$, then x is

(A) 3 (B) 4 (C) 5 (D) 6 (E) 7

19. A sequence is recursively defined as $x_{n+1} = x_n{}^2 + x_n - 2$ where $x_1 = -2$. What is the value of x_{555}?

(A) -2 (B) 0 (C) 2 (D) 4 (E) 6

20. If $\begin{vmatrix} x-2 & 3 & 5 \\ 0 & x-3 & -2 \\ 0 & 0 & x+1 \end{vmatrix} = 2$ then x can be

(A) -3.343 (B) -1.147 (C) -0.813 (D) -0.814 (E) 0.813

21. The remainder when $2x^4 - 5x^2 + x - 3$ is divided by x + 1 is

(A) -7 (B) -5 (C) 0 (D) 1 (E) 5

22. The distance between the points (2, -3, 4) and (-1, 3, 5) is approximately

(A) 4.02 (B) 4.12 (C) 6.16 (D) 6.78 (E) 9.06

23. Which of the following are the x-coordinates of the points at which the ellipse $\dfrac{x^2}{16} + \dfrac{y^2}{9} = 1$ intersects the line y = 2?

(A) -1.02 and 1.02   (B) -2.98 and 2.98   (C) -3 and 3   (D) -4 and 4   (E) -5 and 3

24. In figure 84, cos θ =

(A) $\sqrt{x^2 - y^2}$ (B) $\sqrt{x^2 + y^2}$ (C) $\dfrac{x}{\sqrt{x^2 - y^2}}$

(D) $\dfrac{x}{\sqrt{x^2 + y^2}}$ (E) $\dfrac{y}{\sqrt{x^2 + y^2}}$

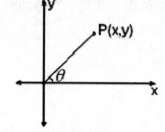

Figure 84

25. What is the semi-perimeter of a parallelogram that has the vertices at
(-5, -2), (1, -2), (-3, 3) and (3, 3)?

(A) 11   (B) $6 + \sqrt{29}$ (C) 22   (D) $12 + 2\sqrt{29}$ (E) 24

26. What is the minimum value of the function f(x) = 2x² – 16x + 30 over the interval $\dfrac{3}{2} \le x \le \dfrac{9}{2}$?

(A) -2   (B) -1.5   (C) 1.5   (D) 4   (E) 4.5

27. If a = b² – 2b – 2 and c = b – 1, what is a in terms of c?
(A) c – 3   (B) c + 3   (C) 2c – 2   (D) c² – 3   (E) c² – 2c

28. A tiger population grows at a rate of 1% per year. If there were 1500 tigers in 1971, approximately how many tigers will there be in 2003?

(A) 2,041   (B) 2,062   (C) 2,083   (D) 3,167   (E) 3,240

29. The second term of a geometric sequence is 3 and the fifth term is 243. Which of the following could be the sum of the first seven terms?

(A) 364   (B) 1012   (C) 1084   (D) 1092   (E) 1093

30. If $2\sin^2\theta - 7\sin\theta + 3 = 0$, then θ could be which of the following?

(A) 30°   (B) 45°   (C) 60°   (D) 120°   (E) 135°

31. If $\sin\theta = x \cdot \cos\theta$ and $\tan\theta = 0.25$, then x = ?

(A) 4   (B) 1   (C) $\dfrac{1}{2}$ (D) $\dfrac{1}{3}$ (E) $\dfrac{1}{4}$

32. What is the tangent of the acute angle whose cosine is 0.02?

(A) 40   (B) 45   (C) 50   (D) 55   (E) 60

33. An ellipse centered at (2, -1) has a major axis of length 16 and a minor axis of length 6. Which of the following could be the equation of such an ellipse?

(A) $\dfrac{(x-2)^2}{16} + \dfrac{(y+1)^2}{6} = 1$ (B) $\dfrac{(x-2)^2}{16} - \dfrac{(y+1)^2}{6} = 1$ (C) $\dfrac{(x+2)^2}{64} + \dfrac{(y-1)^2}{9} = 1$

(D) $\dfrac{(x-2)^2}{64} + \dfrac{(y+1)^2}{9} = 1$ (E) $\dfrac{(x-2)^2}{64} - \dfrac{(y+1)^2}{9} = 1$

34. A right circular cone has a slant height of 13 and a base diameter of 10. What is its volume?

(A) 170.17   (B) 314.16   (C) 340.34   (D) 942.48   (E) 1256.64

35. If x+1 is a positive odd integer, which of the following must also be a positive odd integer?

(A) x^2 (B) x(x -1)   (C) 2(x+1)   (D) $2+(x-1)^2$ (E) (x -1)(x+1)

36. The circle $(x - 2)^2 + y^2 = 9$ is tangent to the circle $(x - 2)^2 + (y + 5)^2 = 4$. What are the coordinates of the point of tangency?

(A) (-2, 5)   (B) (2, -5)   (C) (2, 0)   (D) (2, -3)   (E) (-2, -3)

37. If figure 85 represents the graph of $f(x) = ax^3 + bx^2 + cx + d$ with zeros at -3, 0 and 2, then which of the following must be correct?

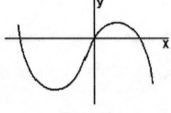

Figure 85

  I. a > 0

  II. d = 0

  III. b = 0

(A) I. only   (B) II. only

(C) I. and II. only   (D) II. and III. only

(E) I., II. and III.

38. ΔKLM has side k = 7, side l = 10, and side m = 8. What is the measure of ∠L?

(A) 30°   (B) 44.05°   (C) 52.62°   (D) 60°   (E) 83.33°

39. Which of the following could be the graph of $f(x) = 2^x + \dfrac{1}{2^x}$?

(A)

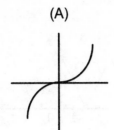

(B)

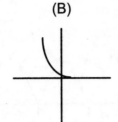

(C)

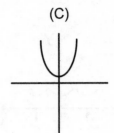

(D)

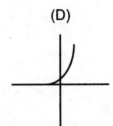

(E)

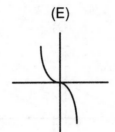

40. $\displaystyle \lim_{x \to \infty} \frac{4x^2 + x - 6}{5x^2 - x + 2} = ?$

(A) $-\infty$ (B) -3   (C) $-\dfrac{4}{5}$ (D) $\dfrac{4}{5}$ (E) $+\infty$

41. The axis of symmetry of the circle given by $(x - 1)^2 + y^2 = 12$ can be

I. the line given by x=1

II. the line given by y = 2x – 2

III. the x - axis

(A) I only   (B) II only   (C) I and II only

(D) II and III only   (E) I, II and III

42. A function *f* has the property that $f(x + 3) = f(x)$ for all x in the domain. Which could be a portion of the graph of *f*?

(A)

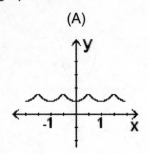

(B)

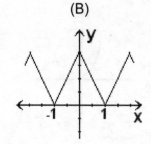

(C)

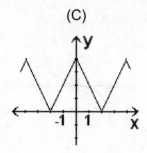

(D)

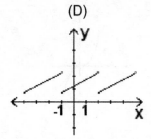

(E)

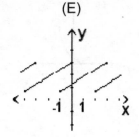

43. In figure 86, cos(A – B) is equal to which of the following?

(A) $\dfrac{c^2}{a^2 - b^2}$

(B) $\dfrac{a - b}{2c}$

(C) 0

(D) $\dfrac{a^2 - b^2}{c^2}$

(E) $\dfrac{2ab}{c^2}$

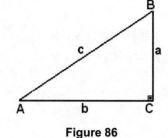

Figure 86

44. The solution to $\begin{cases} y \le 3x + 6 \\ y \ge 0 \\ x \le 0 \end{cases}$ is represented graphically by

(A)

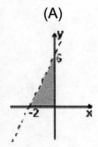

(B)

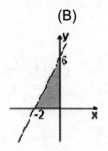

(C)

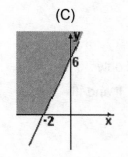

(D)

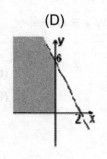

(E)

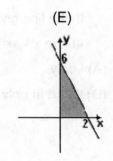

45. Let △f(x) be defined as the y-intercept of the graph of y = f(x). If f(x) = 3x − 1, then △f(x) = -1. Suppose that f(x) and g(x) represent distinct lines, and that △f(x) = △g(x), then which of the following must be correct?

I. f(x) = g(x) + k for any real number k.

II. f(x) − g(x) = 0 when x=0.

III. The line given by f(x) is perpendicular to the line given by g(x).

(A) I only   (B) II only   (C) I and II only   (D) II and III only   (E) I, II, and III

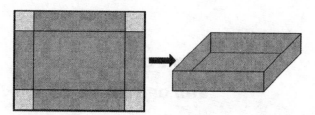

Figure 87

46. From the corners of a rectangular cardboard with dimensions a and b feet, identical squares each having a side of length x are cut and an open top box is made by bending the remaining cardboard along the thin lines as is given in figure 87 above. If the volume of the open top box is nonzero, then which of the following gives all possible values of x?

(A) $0 \le x \le \min\left(\dfrac{a}{2}, \dfrac{b}{2}\right)$ (B) $0 < x < \max\left(\dfrac{a}{2}, \dfrac{b}{2}\right)$ (C) $0 < x < \min\left(\dfrac{a}{2}, \dfrac{b}{2}\right)$

(D) $0 \le x \le \min(a, b)$ (E) $0 < x < \min(a, b)$

47. A regular hexagon is inscribed within a circle of radius r = 2. What is the area of the hexagon?

(A) 1.73   (B) 2.60   (C) 5.20   (D) 8.66   (E) 10.39

48. What is the radius of the sphere that has a surface area numerically 30% less than its volume?

(A) 2.10   (B) 2.31   (C) 3.90   (D) 4.29   (E) 7.00

49. If $g(x) = \ln(x^3 - 1)$ for $x > 1$, then $g^{-1}(x) =$

(A) $\sqrt[3]{2e^x - 1}$ (B) $\sqrt[3]{2e^x + 1}$ (C) $\sqrt{e^{2x} + 1}$ (D) $\sqrt{3^{ex} - 1}$ (E) $\sqrt[3]{e^x + 1}$

50. There are 4 bananas, 5 apples and 6 oranges in a box. In how many ways can 4 fruits be selected so that there will be at least one of each kind of fruit in the selection?

(A) 15   (B) 120   (C) 720   (D) 2880

(E) None of the above.

S T O P

END OF TEST

Level 2 – Model Test 4

Test Duration: 60 Minutes

Directions: For each of the following problems, decide which is the best of the choices given. If the exact numerical value is not one of the choices, select the choice that best approximates this value. Then fill in the corresponding oval on the answer sheet.

Notes:

- A calculator will be necessary for answering some (but not all) of the questions in this test. For each question you will have to decide whether or not you should use a calculator. The calculator you use must be at least a scientific calculator; programmable calculators and calculators that can display graphs are permitted.

- For some questions in this test you may have to decide whether your calculator should be in the radian mode or the degree mode.

- Figures that accompany problems in this test are intended to provide information useful in solving the problems. They are drawn as accurately as possible except when it is stated in a specific problem that its figure is not drawn to scale.

- All figures lie in a plane unless otherwise indicated.

- Unless otherwise specified, the domain of any function f is assumed to be the set of all real numbers x for which f(x) is a real number.

Reference Information: The following information is for your reference in answering some of the questions in this test.

- Volume of a right circular cone with radius r and height h: $V = \frac{1}{3}\pi r^2 h$

- Lateral area of a right circular cone with circumference of the base c and slant height l: $S = \frac{1}{2}cl$

- Volume of a sphere with radius r: $V = \frac{4}{3}\pi r^3$

- Surface area of sphere with radius r: $S = 4\pi r^2$

- Volume of a pyramid with base area B and height h: $V = \frac{1}{3}Bh$

1. If $a^2 < a$ and $b > 1$, then

(A) $a \cdot b < a$ (B) $a \cdot b < b$ (C) $a \cdot b > b$ (D) $a + b < 2 \cdot a$ (E) $a + b > 2 \cdot b$

2. β is a relation defined in the set of positive integers as follows:

β={(x,y): x varies directly as the square of y}.

Two elements of the relation given by β cannot be

(A) (1, 1) and (4, 2)   (B) (2, 1) and (8, 2)   (C) (2, 2) and (8, 4)

(D) (4, 1) and (16, 2)   (E) (2, 2) and (3, 3)

3. What is the amplitude of the function given by $f(x) = 3 \cdot \sin^2(2x) + 1$?

(A) -3   (B) -1.5   (C) 1.5   (D) 3

(E) None of the above

4. The line given by $\frac{2}{3}x + \frac{4}{5}y = 12$ is parallel to which of the following lines?

(A) $y = \frac{5}{6}x + 1$ (B) $y = -\frac{5}{6}x + 3$ (C) $y = \frac{6}{5}x + 2$ (D) $y = -\frac{6}{5}x$ (E) $y = -\frac{2}{3}x + 1$

5. If $f(x) = \frac{1}{x^2 - 1}$ and g(f(5)) = 10, then g(x) can be

(A) $x^2 - 1$ (B) $\frac{1-4x}{2x}$ (C) 2x   (D) $\frac{1-2x}{4x}$ (E) $\frac{1}{2x}$

6. If n is divisible by 6, 7, and 9, then which of the following cannot be the value of n?

(A) 252   (B) 1260   (C) 1512   (D) 1572   (E) 3780

7. If a line d is perpendicular to a line given by y = - 2, the slope of line d will be

(A) -2 (B) 0 (C) 1 (D) 1/2

(E) an undefined quantity

8. For $x \neq 0$ or $x \neq 1$, $\dfrac{x^2 - 1}{1 - \dfrac{1}{x}} =$

(A) $\dfrac{x^2}{1 - x}$ (B) $\dfrac{x - 1}{x + 1}$ (C) $\dfrac{x + 1}{x - 1}$ (D) $1 + \dfrac{1}{x}$ (E) $x^2 + x$

9. If $\tan\theta$ = -15/8 and θ is an obtuse angle, then $\sin\theta + \cos\theta$ = ?

(A) -8/15 (B) -7/17 (C) 7/17 (D) 15/17 (E) 23/17

10. If $x^4 - 52x^2 = 81x$, then x cannot be

(A) -6.25 (B) -1.64 (C) 0 (D) 6.25 (E) 7.89

11. If the point (-5, -2) is on the graph of y=f(x), then which of the following points must also be on the graph of $y = f(-|x|)$?

(A) (-2, -5) (B) (-2, 5) (C) (5, 2) (D) (-5, 2) (E) (5, -2)

12. If $\sin\theta$ = 0.82, then $\cos(\pi - \theta)$=

(A) -0.57 (B) -0.18 (C) 0.18 (D) 0.57 (E) 0.70

13. If θ is an obtuse angle in figure 88, then which of the following cannot be the value of x?

(A) 15   (B) 16   (C) 17   (D) 18   (E) 19

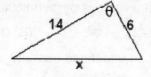

Figure 88

14. f(x) = The remainder when [x] is divided by 5, where [x] represents the greatest integer less than or equal to x. What is the period of f(x)?

(A) 1   (B) 2   (C) 2.5   (D) 5

(E) The function is not periodic.

15. If $y = \sqrt{x} - 1$ and $x = t^2$, what is y in terms of t?

(A) t + 1   (B) t – 1   (C) | t | + 1   (D) | t | – 1   (E) $y = \sqrt{t} - 1$

16. What is the locus of points in the three dimensional space that is at a distance of 6 inches from a plane P and at a distance of 10 inches from a given line in plane P?

(A) Two parallel line segments   (B) Four parallel line segments

(C) Four coplanar lines   (D) Two coplanar points

(E) Four parallel lines

17. Sebla's average on her quizzes is 88%. If she gets 100% on the next 2 quizzes, her average will increase by 4%. How many quizzes has Sebla taken so far?

(A) 1   (B) 2   (C) 3   (D) 4   (E) 5

18. In figure 89, what is the slope of the line d?

(A) -sinθ

(B) -cosθ

(C) -tanθ

(D) -cotθ

(E) -cscθ

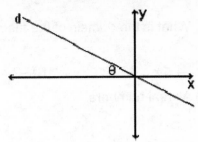

Figure 89

19. $8000 is invested in an account that pays 4% interest being compounded semiannually. To the nearest dollar what will be the account balance after 4 years?

(A) $9,280   (B) $9,358   (C) $9,600   (D) $9,373   (E) $10,122

20. If P(x) is a polynomial given by $P(x)=6x^6-ax^5+bx^4+cx^3-15$ where a, b, and c are all integers, then which of the following cannot be a zero of P(x)?

(A) $\dfrac{-3}{2}$ (B) $\dfrac{3}{4}$ (C) $\dfrac{1}{6}$ (D) $\dfrac{5}{3}$ (E) -15

21. The first term in a geometric sequence is 4, and the second term is 2. What is the sum of the first 4 terms?

(A) 4   (B) 6   (C) 7   (D) 7.5   (E) 15

22. If $P(x) = ax^3 + bx^2 + cx + d$ such that P(0)=5, P(1)=8, and P(-1)=6, then the value of b is

(A) 0   (B) 1   (C) 2   (D) 5

(E) The information given is not enough to solve this problem.

23. What is the domain of the function given by $f(x) = \dfrac{x-2}{\sqrt[4]{16 - x^2}}$?

(A) $-4 \leq x \leq 4$ (B) $-2 < x < 2$ (C) $-2 \leq x \leq 2$ (D) $-4 < x < 4$

(E) All real numbers

24. In figure 90, the area of the semicircle is 8π and the length of the arc ACB is 6. What is the value of $\angle AOB$?

(A) 36°   (B) 75°   (C) 83°

(D) 86°   (E) 90°

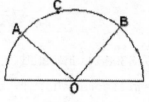

Figure 90

25. If $\csc^2 \theta \neq 0$, then $\cos^2 \theta + \dfrac{1}{\csc^2 \theta} =$

(A) 0   (B) 1   (C) $2\sin^2 \theta$ (D) $\tan^2 \theta$ (E) $\cot^2 \theta$

26. If $\sin(2x) = \cos(35°)$ and $0 < x < \dfrac{\pi}{2}$ then the value of x can be

(A) 17.5   (B) 27.5   (C) 0.47   (D) 0.48   (E) 1.48

27. What is the sum of the y-coordinates of the points of intersection of the line x=-5 and the circle with the radius of length 6 inches centered at (-2, 1)?

(A) -2   (B) -1   (C) 0   (D) 1   (E) 2

28. Which of the following choices gives all vertical asymptotes of the function given by $f(x) =$ $\dfrac{x^2 + x - 6}{x^2 - 9}$?

(A) x= -3   (B) x=1   (C) x=3   (D) y= -3   (E) x= -3 and x=3

29. A fast growing plant whose height is 25 inches at the end of 21st of October becomes 26 inches tall at the end of 22nd of October. If the plant grows by the same rate until it becomes 100 inches, how tall will the plant be in inches at the end of the 31st of October?

(A) 35.00   (B) 36.00   (C) 35.58   (D) 37.01   (E) 38.49

30. What is the area of the shaded region in figure 91?

(A) 31.25

(B) 32.15

(C) 51.35

(D) 62.50

(E) 65.20

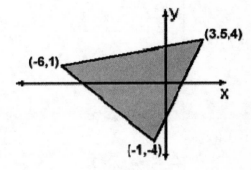

Figure 91

31. If $x_0 = -1$ and $x_{n+1} = (x_n + 1)^3$, what is the value of x_4?

(A) -1   (B) 0   (C) 1   (D) 8   (E) 729

32. If $f(x)$ is defined by the function $f(x)=\sin(\cos(x))$, then $f(250°)=?$

(A) -0.342   (B) -0.335   (C) -0.006   (D) 0.239   (E) 1.000

33. If $x^2 + y^2 = 9$ and $x - y = -2$, then x could be equal to which of the following?

(A) –1.13   (B) -0.87   (C) -2.87   (D) 0.87   (E) 2.87

34. In figure 92, if the length of AB is 12 inches, then area of the shaded region in square inches will be

(A) 18   (B) 20   (C) 39   (D) 57   (E) 95

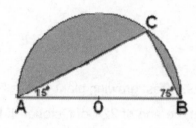

Figure 92

35. The graph given in figure 93 can correspond to which of the following functions?

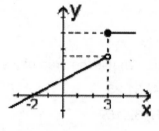

Figure 93

(A) $f(x) = \begin{cases} \dfrac{-x+2}{2} & x < 3 \\ 4 & x \geq 3 \end{cases}$ (B) $f(x) = \begin{cases} \dfrac{x+2}{2} & x < 3 \\ 4 & x \geq 3 \end{cases}$

(C) $f(x) = \begin{cases} 4 & x < 3 \\ \dfrac{x+2}{2} & x \geq 3 \end{cases}$ (D) $f(x) = \begin{cases} 4 & x < 3 \\ \dfrac{x-2}{2} & x \geq 3 \end{cases}$

(E) $f(x) = \begin{cases} 4 & x < 3 \\ \dfrac{1}{2}x + 2 & x \geq 3 \end{cases}$

36. From the set A={0, 1, 2, 3,..,11}, three different numbers are randomly chosen. What is the probability that the product of these three numbers is even?

(A) 0.5   (B) 0.25   (C) 1/8   (D) 1/11   (E) 10/11

37. For what values of x is the equality given by $\dfrac{\log_3(x^{36})}{\log_3(x^{30})} = \dfrac{6}{5}$ valid?

(A) For all values of x except for -1 and 1

(B) For all values of x

(C) For all positive values of x except for 1

(D) For all nonzero values of x

(E) For all nonzero values of x except for -1 and 1

38. If vector v has a magnitude of 6.8 and if vector w has a magnitude of 10.1, then which of the following can not be the magnitude of v + 2w?

(A) 15.3   (B) 16.9   (C) 17.8   (D) 25.2   (E) 27.4

39. The sum of the first 6 terms of an arithmetic sequence is 102 and the first term is 7. What is the second term?

(A) 22   (B) 18   (C) 12   (D) 11   (E) 8

40. $\dfrac{(n+1)!-n!}{n!+(n-1)!} =$

(A) $\dfrac{n^2}{n-1}$ (B) $\dfrac{n^2}{n+1}$ (C) $\dfrac{n-1}{n^2}$ (D) $\dfrac{n}{n+1}$ (E) $\dfrac{n}{n-1}$

41. If $\sec^2 x - 3\tan x + 1 = 0$, then x could be which of the following?

(A) $\dfrac{\pi}{3}$ (B) $\dfrac{3\pi}{4}$ (C) $\dfrac{\pi}{6}$ (D) $\dfrac{5\pi}{4}$ (E) $\dfrac{5\pi}{6}$

42. A circle is to be drawn on the surface of a sphere of volume 288π. What is the maximum possible area for this circle?

(A) 6   (B) 12π (C) 36π (D) 52π

(E) There is not enough information to solve this problem.

43. An indirect proof of the statement "If x is a real number between 0 and 1, then x^2 is less than x" could begin with the assumption that

(A) x = -1.   (B) x is not a real number between 0 and 1.

(C) x = 1.   (D) x^2 is greater than or equal to x.

(E) x^2 is greater than x.

44. The area of a convex equilateral polygon can be calculated by the formula given by $4R^2 \sin\left(\dfrac{\pi}{4}\right)$ where R is the radius of the circle that passes through the vertices of this polygon. How many sides does this polygon have?

(A) 3   (B) 4   (C) 5   (D) 6   (E) More than 6

45. If a hemisphere of radius r inches is inscribed in a right circular cylinder that has a radius and height of both r inches, then, what is the ratio of the volume of the hemisphere to the volume outside the hemisphere and inside the cylinder?

(A) 1/2   (B) 1/3   (C) 2   (D) 3   (E) 4

46. In how many ways can 7 identical apples be distributed to 3 people?

(A) $\binom{7}{2}$ (B) $\binom{7}{3}$ (C) $\binom{9}{2}$ (D) $\binom{9}{3}$ (E) $\binom{10}{3}$

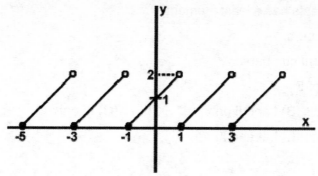

Figure 94

47. Which of the following best describes the periodic function given in figure 94 above?

(A) f(x)=x+1+k where 2k-1 ≤ x < 2k+1; k is an arbitrary integer

(B) f(x)=x+1-k where 2k-1 ≤ x < 2k+1; k is an arbitrary integer

(C) f(x)=x+1-2k where 2k+1 ≤ x < 2k+3; k is an arbitrary integer

(D) f(x)=x+1-k where 2k+1 ≤ x < 2k+3; k is an arbitrary integer

(E) f(x)=x+1-2k where 2k-1 ≤ x < 2k+1; k is an arbitrary integer

48. If $\dfrac{1}{R} = \dfrac{x}{yz} + \dfrac{y}{xz} + \dfrac{z}{xy}$, for x, y, z, R ≠ 0, then R =

(A) $\dfrac{1}{xyz}$

(B) $\dfrac{x+y+z}{xyz}$

(C) $\dfrac{x^2+y^2+z^2}{xyz}$

(D) $\dfrac{xyz}{x^2+y^2+z^2}$

(E) $\dfrac{xy+xz+yz}{xyz}$

49. Which of the following could be the equation of a hyperbola that has its center at (2, -1) and that passes through the point (0, -1)?

(A) $\dfrac{(x+2)^2}{2} - \dfrac{(y+1)^2}{2} = 1$

(B) $\dfrac{(x+2)^2}{2} - \dfrac{(y-1)^2}{2} = 1$

(C) $\dfrac{(x-2)^2}{4} - \dfrac{(y-1)^2}{4} = 1$

(D) $\dfrac{(x-2)^2}{4} - \dfrac{(y+1)^2}{4} = 1$

(E) $\dfrac{(x-2)^2}{2} - \dfrac{(y+1)^2}{2} = 1$

50. Which of the following sets has a least element?

    I. The set of prime numbers

    II. The set of positive real numbers

    III. Negative multiples of 5

(A) I only   (B) I and II only   (C) III only

(D) I and III only   (E) I, II and III

S T O P

END OF TEST

Level 2 – Model Test 5

Test Duration: 60 Minutes

Directions: For each of the following problems, decide which is the best of the choices given. If the exact numerical value is not one of the choices, select the choice that best approximates this value. Then fill in the corresponding oval on the answer sheet.

Notes:

- A calculator will be necessary for answering some (but not all) of the questions in this test. For each question you will have to decide whether or not you should use a calculator. The calculator you use must be at least a scientific calculator; programmable calculators and calculators that can display graphs are permitted.

- For some questions in this test you may have to decide whether your calculator should be in the radian mode or the degree mode.

- Figures that accompany problems in this test are intended to provide information useful in solving the problems. They are drawn as accurately as possible except when it is stated in a specific problem that its figure is not drawn to scale.

- All figures lie in a plane unless otherwise indicated.

- Unless otherwise specified, the domain of any function f is assumed to be the set of all real numbers x for which f(x) is a real number.

Reference Information: The following information is for your reference in answering some of the questions in this test.

- Volume of a right circular cone with radius r and height h: $V = \dfrac{1}{3}\pi r^2 h$

- Lateral area of a right circular cone with circumference of the base c and slant height l: $S = \dfrac{1}{2}cl$

- Volume of a sphere with radius r: $V = \dfrac{4}{3}\pi r^3$

- Surface area of sphere with radius r: $S = 4\pi r^2$

- Volume of a pyramid with base area B and height h: $V = \dfrac{1}{3}Bh$

1. $x^2 - y^2 = 7$

   $x^2 + 2y^2 = 1$

The number of real solutions to the system of equations given above is

(A) 0.   (B) 1.   (C) 2.   (D) 4.   (E) more than 4.

2. Where defined, what is the value of $\dfrac{y + y^{-2}}{1 - y^{-1} + y^{-2}}$?

(A) $2y$ (B) $y + 1$ (C) $y - 1$ (D) $y^2 - 1$ (E) $y^2 + 1$

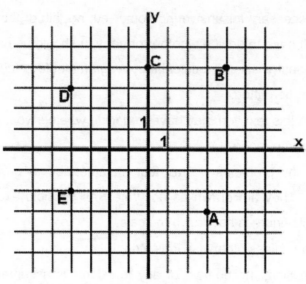

Figure 95

3. Which of the dotted points given in figure 95 above lies on the circle whose equation is given by $x^2 + y^2 = 25$?

(A) A   (B) B   (C) C   (D) D   (E) E

4. A plant uses water at the rates of 0.15 kg/hour and 0.05 kg/hour during day-time and night-time respectively. If the sunrise is at 6 AM and sunset is at 8 PM, then what is the amount of water in kilograms that the plant will use between 8 AM and 10 PM on the same day?

(A) $2 \cdot 0.15 + 2 \cdot 0.05$ (B) $4 \cdot 0.15 + 10 \cdot 0.05$ (C) $18 \cdot 0.15$

(D) $12 \cdot 0.15 + 2 \cdot 0.05$ (E) $14 \cdot 0.15 + 2 \cdot 0.05$

5. If $x = \log_7 777$ then x is between which pair of consecutive integers?

(A) 1 and 2   (B) 2 and 3   (C) 3 and 4   (D) 4 and 5   (E) 5 and 6

6. What is the least positive value of x such that cosx = -1?

(A) -3π (B) $\dfrac{\pi}{2}$ (C) π (D) $\dfrac{3\pi}{2}$ (E) 2π

7. The graph shown in figure 96 corresponds to f(x). f(x) can be

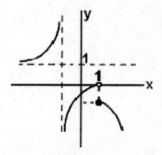

Figure 96

(A) $f(x)= \begin{cases} -x^2 & x \geq 1 \\ \dfrac{x+1}{x-1} & x < 1 \end{cases}$ (B) $f(x)= \begin{cases} -x^2 & x < 1 \\ \dfrac{x-1}{x+1} & x \geq 1 \end{cases}$

(C) $f(x)= \begin{cases} -x^2 & x \geq 1 \\ \dfrac{x-1}{x+1} & x < 1 \end{cases}$ (D) $f(x)= \begin{cases} -x^2 & x \geq 1 \\ \dfrac{1-x}{1+x} & x < 1 \end{cases}$

(E) $f(x)= \begin{cases} -x^2 & x > 1 \\ \dfrac{x-1}{x+1} & x \leq 1 \end{cases}$

8. A point P(x, y) is defined such that the length of segments PA and PB sum up to 10 where coordinates of A and B are (1, -2) and (1, 8) respectively. The locus of all such points P is

(A) a circle.   (B) an ellipse.   (C) a cardioid.   (D) a parabola.   (E) a hyperbola.

9. Which of the following is not valid for all x?

(A) $\log(x^2)=2\log x$ (B) $(e^x)^x = e^{x^2}$ (C) $\sqrt{x^2} = |x|$ (D) $\sqrt[3]{x^3} = x$ (E) $|x|^4 = x^4$

10. If $\sin^2 x + \cos^2 y = 0.234$, what is the value of $\cos^2 x + \sin^2 y$?

(A) 0.383   (B) 0.766   (C) 0.883   (D) 1.383   (E) 1.766

11. Which of the following can be the function represented by the graph shown in figure 97 if the coordinates of points A and B are $(\pi, 2)$ and $(3\pi, -2)$ respectively?

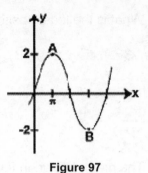

Figure 97

Figure not drawn to scale

(A) $f(x) = 2\cos\left(\dfrac{x}{2} - \dfrac{\pi}{2}\right)$

(B) $f(x) = \sin\left(\dfrac{x}{2}\right) + 1$

(C) $f(x) = -2\sin\left(\dfrac{x}{2} + \dfrac{\pi}{2}\right)$

(D) $f(x) = 2\cos\left(\dfrac{x}{2}\right)$

(E) $f(x) = 2\sin\left(\dfrac{x}{2} + \pi\right)$

12. If $f(x) = f^{-1}(x)$ for all real numbers x, then $f(x)$ can equal

(A) $-x + 3$ (B) $-x^2 + 3$ (C) $x + 3$ (D) $x^2 + 3$ (E) $2x$

13. The quadratic function $f(x)$ is given by $f(x) = ax^2 + bx + c$ where a, b, and c are all real numbers. If $f(x)$ and $|f(x)|$ intersect at a single point then which of the following cannot be correct?

(A) $ac > 0$ (B) $ac = 0$ (C) $ac < 0$ (D) $b=0$ (E) discriminant is zero

14. If a triangle has sides of lengths 82, 82, and 41, what is the measure of the largest angle in this triangle rounded to the nearest degree?

(A) 14°   (B) 15°   (C) 29°   (D) 76°   (E) 151°

15. A function $h(x)$ is said to be one to one if it satisfies the following condition: If x and y are in the domain of h given that $x \neq y$; then for all x and y, $h(x) \neq h(y)$. Which of the following functions is not one to one?

(A) $h(x) = (x-1)^3$ (B) $h(x) = \ln x$ (C) $h(x) = 5-3x$ (D) $h(x) = 2^{3x}$ (E) $h(x) = 2x + x^2$

16. Students in two classes A and B are given the same test. The mean score in class A is greater than that in class B, but the standard deviation of scores in class A is less than that in class B. Which of the following must be correct?

(A) Median score in class A is greater than the median score in class B.

(B) Highest score in class A is greater than the highest score in class B.

(C) Range of scores in class A is equal to the range of scores in class B.

(D) Scores are more closely grouped about the mean in class A than in class B.

(E) Number of students in class A is less than the number of students in class B.

17. $\vec{u}$ has an initial point of (-3, 3) and a terminal point of (3, 5). $\vec{v}$ has an initial point of (2, 3) and a terminal point of (-3, 0). $\vec{u} - \vec{v}$?

(A) (-5, 11)　　　　(B) (-11, -5)　　　　(C) (11, 5)　　　　(D) (5, 11)　　　　(E) (5, -11)

18. What is the length of the longest stick that can fit into the rectangular solid given in figure 98?

(A) 8.60　　　　(B) 10.30　　　　(C) 11.40

(D) 12.45　　　　(E) 17.75

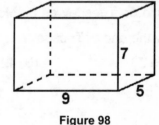

Figure 98
Figure not drawn to scale

19. Since starting his part time job as CD cleaner at E&R music store, Toprak cleans the CD's at regular intervals. If he cleans the CD's at E&R music store for the first time on Day 4 of his service, for the second time on Day 10, and for the third time on Day 16, then on which of the following days of his service will Toprak clean the CD's at E&R music store?

(A) Day 216　　　　(B) Day 217　　　　(C) Day 218　　　　(D) Day 219　　　　(E) Day 220

20. The system of equations given by –12x + 2my = –20 and 3x + 4y = 5 has infinitely many solutions. m = ?

(A) – 16   (B) 4   (C) – 8   (D) 8   (E) – 4

21. Which of the following points lies on the circle given by $x^2 + y^2 = 24$?

(A) (4, 2)   (B) ($\sqrt{18}$, 4)   (C) ($\sqrt{8}$, -4)   (D) ($\sqrt{8}$, $\sqrt{6}$)

(E) None of the above

Voted for Pemra	35%
Voted for Semra	25%
Undecided	40%

22. The table above shows the votes of the 300 high school juniors on a Monday who voted for either of the twin sisters Semra and Pemra that were nominated for class president. If all students who were undecided on Monday voted again on the next day and the new votes were distributed in the same ratio on Tuesday as on Monday leaving no one undecided, how many more people voted for Pemra by the end of Tuesday?

(A) 30   (B) 42   (C) 50   (D) 70   (E) 105

23. A polynomial P(x) is defined for all real values of x as P(x) = px^2 + qx + r and it is given that P(–1) = 0; what is r in terms of p and q?

(A) q – p   (B) p – q   (C) p + q   (D) p·q

(E) There is insufficient information.

24. f(x) = ln(x); g(x) = 3x – 2; $f\left(g\left(\sqrt{3}\right)\right)$=?

(A) -0.352   (B) -1.284   (C) 0.505   (D) 1.162   (E) 1.974

25. A polynomial function P(x) is given by P(x) = 4x^3 – 2x^2 + ax – 5. If 3 ≤ |a| ≤ 7, then which of the following cannot be a zero of P(x)?

(A) 0.82   (B) 0.91   (C) 1.50   (D) 1.68   (E) 1.76

26. If A is a point on the parabola given by y = x^2 + x and B is the point (2, 6) what is the slope of segment AB?

(A) x + 3   (B) – x – 3   (C) $\dfrac{1}{x+3}$ (D) $\dfrac{-1}{x+3}$

(E) None of the above

27. If x is an acute angle for which cos(x) = 0.32 then tan(x)=?

(A) -2.96   (B) 0.0175   (C) 0.175   (D) 0.952   (E) 2.96

28. Given in figure 99 is the graph of f(x) = ax^2 – b. Which of the following expresses all possible values of a and b?

(A) a < 0 and b < 0

(B) a < 0 and b ≤ 0

(C) a > 0 and b = 0

(D) a > 0 and b < 0

(E) a > 0 and b > 0

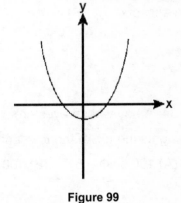

Figure 99

Figure not drawn to scale

29. A rectangular box with open top is to be constructed by cutting identical squares each having a side of length x inches from the corners of a 6 inch by 8 inch piece of cardboard and folding up the sides. In terms of x, what is the volume of the box in cubic inches?

(A) (6–x)·(8–x)·x   (B) (6–2x)·(8–2x)   (C) 48x   (D) (6–2x)·(8–2x)·x   (E) (6+2x)·(8+2x)·x

30. If $5^{xy} > 15$, which of the following must be true?

(A) x > 1.2 and y > 1.4   (B) xy < -1.68   (C) – 1.68 < xy < 1.68

(D) x < -1.2 and y > 1.4   (E) xy > 1.68

31. What is the center of the circle defined by $x^2 + 4x = -y^2 + 6y$

(A) (4, 6)   (B) (- 4, 6)   (C) (2, 3)   (D) (2, -3)   (E) (-2, 3)

32. A point given by (a, a^2-1) is revolved about the x axis. What is the area of the circle?

(A) πa^2 (B) $\pi(a^2-1)^2$ (C) $\pi (a^3-(A)^2$ (D) $\pi a(a^2-1)$

(E) It cannot be determined from the information given.

33. $1+\dfrac{\cos^2 x}{\sin^2 x} = ?$

(A) $\sec^2 x$ (B) $\csc^2 x$ (C) $\cot^2 x$ (D) $\tan^2 x$ (E) None of the above

34. A boy whose eyes are 5 ft above the ground stands 100 feet away from the base of a building and sights the top of the tower at an angle of elevation of Φ. What is the height of the building?

(A) 100·sinΦ – 5   (B) 100·tanΦ – 5   (C) 100·sinΦ + 5   (D) 100·tanΦ + 5   (E) 100·cosΦ – 5

35. A function f(x) is given by $f(x) = \dfrac{3}{2-x}$. Which of the following is correct regarding the asymptotes of f(x)?

(A) The vertical asymptote of f(x) is x = 2 and it has no horizontal asymptotes.

(B) The vertical asymptote of f(x) is x = 0 and its horizontal asymptote is y = 2.

(C) The vertical asymptote of f(x) is x = 2 and its horizontal asymptote is y = 0.

(D) The vertical asymptote of f(x) is x = -2 and its horizontal asymptote is y = 0.

(E) The vertical asymptote of f(x) is x = 2 and its horizontal asymptote is y = 1.5.

36. If both of the points (-1, 3) and (3, b) are on the graph of $f(x)=e^{cx}$ then b = ?

(A) $\dfrac{1}{27}$ 　　　　(B) $\dfrac{1}{3}$ 　　　　(C) 3 　　　　(D) 27

(E) None of the above

37. If the surface area of a sphere is 144π, what is its volume?

(A) 288π 　　　(B) 576π 　　　(C) 1152π 　　　(D) 1728π 　　　(E) 2304π

38. What are all values of x in the interval $0 \le x \le 2\pi$ for which $\cos(x)=c$ and $\sin(x)=\sqrt{1-c^2}$?

(A) $0 \le x \le \dfrac{\pi}{2}$ or $\dfrac{3\pi}{2} \le x \le 2\pi$ 　　　(B) $0 \le x \le \dfrac{\pi}{2}$ 　　　(C) $0 \le x \le 2\pi$

(D) $0 \le x \le \dfrac{\pi}{2}$ or $\pi \le x \le \dfrac{3\pi}{2}$ 　　　(E) $0 \le x \le \pi$

39. What are all values of tanx for which $\tan(2x) < 0$?

(A) -1 < tanx < 0 or tanx > 1 　　　(B) tanx > 1 　　　(C) -1 < tanx < 0

(D) tanx < -1 or 0 < tanx < 1 　　　(E) tanx < 0

40. A number is selected at random from the set {1, 2, 3, ..., 49, 50}. What is the probability that the number selected is divisible by 4 or 5?

(A) 0.04 　　　(B) 0.20 　　　(C) 0.24 　　　(D) 0.40 　　　(E) 0.44

41. If (x + 3) − (y − 4)i = -3 + 2i then x − 2y=?

(A) -10 　　　(B) -6 　　　(C) 2 　　　(D) 6 　　　(E) 10

42. If $a_{n+1} = a_n^2 - 1$, and $a_k = 3$, then $a_{k-2} = ?$

(A) 1.65　　　　(B) 1.73　　　　(C) 2　　　　(D) 8　　　　(E) 63

43. In how many ways can a committee of 2 sophomores and 3 juniors be selected from 8 sophomores and 7 juniors?

(A) 28　　　　(B) 35　　　　(C) 63　　　　(D) 980　　　　(E) 1176

44. If it is given that $\begin{vmatrix} 2a & 4b & 6c \\ 2p & 4q & 6r \\ 2x & 4y & 6z \end{vmatrix} = e \cdot \begin{vmatrix} a & b & c \\ p & q & r \\ x & y & z \end{vmatrix}$ then e = ?

(A) 2　　　　(B) 4　　　　(C) 6　　　　(D) 12　　　　(E) 48

45. The counterclockwise angle from the positive x – axis to the line given in figure 100 is α, where $90° < \alpha < 180°$. If the slope of the line equals $\cos\alpha$, which of the following is correct?

(A) $90° < \alpha < 108°$

(B) $108° < \alpha < 126°$

(C) $126° < \alpha < 144°$

(D) $144° < \alpha < 162°$

(E) $162° < \alpha < 180°$

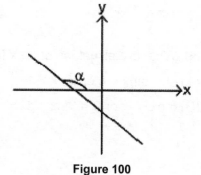

Figure 100
Figure not drawn to scale

46. The rat population in a laboratory increases by 15 percent every month and at the end of each month 1000 of the rats are exported to a research plant. If there were 5000 rats when the laboratory was newly established in the beginning of January, how many rats will there be at the end of April after the last export rounded to the nearest 10 rats?

(A) 5050　　　　(B) 4750　　　　(C) 4460　　　　(D) 3750　　　　(E) 3310

47. A cylindrical block of wood with a diameter of 5 inches and a height of 8 inches is cut into two identical pieces as shown in figure 101. What is the total surface area of one of the pieces in square inches?

(A) 19.64   (B) 62.83   (C) 82.47

(D) 122.47   (E) 164.93

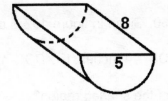

Figure 101
Figure not drawn to scale

48. What is the equation of the ellipse that is tangent to both axes and that has its center at (2, -5)?

(A) $\dfrac{(x+2)^2}{4}+\dfrac{(y-5)^2}{25}=1$

(B) $\dfrac{(x+2)^2}{2}+\dfrac{(y-5)^2}{5}=1$

(C) $\dfrac{(x-2)^2}{4}+\dfrac{(y+5)^2}{25}=1$

(D) $\dfrac{(x-2)^2}{2}+\dfrac{(y+5)^2}{5}=1$

(E) $\dfrac{(x-2)^2}{4}+\dfrac{(y-5)^2}{25}=1$

49. On a recent math competition, the rankings of Yaprak and Yasemin were 55th and 77th percentiles respectively. If Yonca's ranking was lower than Yasemin's, which of the following cannot be correct?

(A) Yonca's ranking was 44th percentile.

(B) Yonca's ranking was 66th percentile.

(C) Yonca's ranking was 88th percentile.

(D) Both Yasemin and Yaprak did better than Yonca.

(E) Yasemin did the best and Yaprak did the worst in the competition.

50. Given in figure 102 is a semicircle where AB is the diameter and AO =

OB = 4 inches. If ∠DOC measures $\dfrac{4\pi}{5}$ radians then what is the perimeter

of the shaded region?

(A) 7.61

(B) 10.05

(C) 13.86

(D) 15.40

(E) 17.66

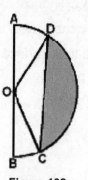

Figure 102

Figure not drawn to scale

S T O P

END OF TEST

Answer to Level 1 – Model Tests

Model Test 1		Model Test 2		Model Test 3		Model Test 4		Model Test 5	
1.	D	1.	A	1.	D	1.	A	1.	E
2.	E	2.	A	2.	A	2.	E	2.	E
3.	E	3.	B	3.	A	3.	C	3.	B
4.	E	4.	C	4.	E	4.	E	4.	A
5.	D	5.	D	5.	C	5.	D	5.	B
6.	A	6.	D	6.	B	6.	D	6.	A
7.	C	7.	E	7.	A	7.	E	7.	D
8.	C	8.	C	8.	E	8.	B	8.	D
9.	D	9.	D	9.	D	9.	E	9.	D
10.	E	10.	E	10.	C	10.	D	10.	C
11.	A	11.	B	11.	C	11.	D	11.	B
12.	E	12.	D	12.	A	12.	C	12.	A
13.	B	13.	A	13.	D	13.	C	13.	D
14.	D	14.	A	14.	E	14.	E	14.	D
15.	B	15.	C	15.	D	15.	E	15.	D
16.	C	16.	D	16.	B	16.	E	16.	B
17.	C	17.	B	17.	C	17.	A	17.	C
18.	A	18.	A	18.	B	18.	E	18.	E
19.	B	19.	C	19.	A	19.	C	19.	D
20.	A	20.	B	20.	A	20.	C	20.	E
21.	D	21.	C	21.	C	21.	C	21.	D
22.	A	22.	C	22.	D	22.	C	22.	E
23.	A	23.	D	23.	D	23.	C	23.	D
24.	D	24.	D	24.	D	24.	B	24.	A
25.	C	25.	B	25.	E	25.	C	25.	C
26.	D	26.	D	26.	B	26.	D	26.	D
27.	C	27.	C	27.	D	27.	D	27.	B
28.	C	28.	C	28.	B	28.	E	28.	D
29.	B	29.	D	29.	C	29.	E	29.	B
30.	B	30.	D	30.	C	30.	C	30.	E
31.	E	31.	D	31.	C	31.	D	31.	E
32.	A	32.	B	32.	D	32.	D	32.	A
33.	C	33.	B	33.	B	33.	C	33.	E
34.	D	34.	E	34.	D	34.	C	34.	D
35.	B	35.	C	35.	A	35.	A	35.	C
36.	D	36.	D	36.	E	36.	E	36.	B
37.	E	37.	A	37.	D	37.	B	37.	D
38.	B	38.	E	38.	E	38.	B	38.	A
39.	C	39.	D	39.	C	39.	D	39.	A
40.	C	40.	D	40.	C	40.	B	40.	C
41.	D	41.	A	41.	C	41.	A	41.	B
42.	D	42.	B	42.	B	42.	A	42.	B
43.	A	43.	E	43.	B	43.	D	43.	C
44.	A	44.	C	44.	D	44.	A	44.	E
45.	B	45.	D	45.	C	45.	E	45.	B
46.	D	46.	D	46.	D	46.	D	46.	E
47.	D	47.	D	47.	E	47.	B	47.	A
48.	A	48.	B	48.	C	48.	D	48.	C
49.	C	49.	A	49.	B	49.	D	49.	D
50.	E	50.	B	50.	D	50.	C	50.	D

Answer to Level 2 – Model Tests

Model Test 1		Model Test 2		Model Test 3		Model Test 4		Model Test 5	
1.	C	1.	C	1.	D	1.	B	1.	A
2.	C	2.	B	2.	E	2.	E	2.	B
3.	A	3.	E	3.	C	3.	C	3.	D
4.	B	4.	C	4.	A	4.	B	4.	D
5.	D	5.	C	5.	C	5.	B	5.	C
6.	B	6.	B	6.	B	6.	D	6.	C
7.	A	7.	D	7.	D	7.	E	7.	C
8.	D	8.	C	8.	D	8.	E	8.	B
9.	C	9.	A	9.	D	9.	C	9.	A
10.	A	10.	B	10.	E	10.	D	10.	E
11.	C	11.	D	11.	D	11.	E	11.	A
12.	D	12.	C	12.	C	12.	A	12.	A
13.	D	13.	B	13.	B	13.	A	13.	C
14.	C	14.	E	14.	A	14.	D	14.	D
15.	C	15.	C	15.	D	15.	D	15.	E
16.	B	16.	D	16.	A	16.	E	16.	D
17.	C	17.	D	17.	D	17.	D	17.	C
18.	D	18.	B	18.	C	18.	C	18.	D
19.	A	19.	E	19.	A	19.	D	19.	E
20.	A	20.	C	20.	D	20.	B	20.	C
21.	D	21.	B	21.	A	21.	D	21.	C
22.	E	22.	B	22.	D	22.	C	22.	D
23.	D	23.	A	23.	B	23.	D	23.	A
24.	B	24.	C	24.	D	24.	D	24.	D
25.	B	25.	A	25.	B	25.	B	25.	C
26.	E	26.	E	26.	A	26.	D	26.	A
27.	D	27.	C	27.	D	27.	E	27.	E
28.	B	28.	B	28.	B	28.	C	28.	E
29.	A	29.	A	29.	E	29.	D	29.	D
30.	C	30.	E	30.	A	30.	A	30.	E
31.	B	31.	A	31.	E	31.	E	31.	E
32.	B	32.	C	32.	C	32.	B	32.	B
33.	C	33.	C	33.	D	33.	D	33.	B
34.	E	34.	B	34.	B	34.	C	34.	D
35.	C	35.	D	35.	D	35.	B	35.	C
36.	C	36.	B	36.	D	36.	E	36.	A
37.	E	37.	A	37.	B	37.	E	37.	A
38.	A	38.	B	38.	E	38.	E	38.	E
39.	B	39.	A	39.	C	39.	D	39.	A
40.	C	40.	A	40.	D	40.	B	40.	D
41.	C	41.	B	41.	E	41.	D	41.	A
42.	C	42.	D	42.	D	42.	C	42.	B
43.	B	43.	E	43.	E	43.	D	43.	D
44.	D	44.	E	44.	B	44.	E	44.	E
45.	D	45.	B	45.	B	45.	C	45.	C
46.	D	46.	C	46.	C	46.	C	46.	D
47.	C	47.	E	47.	E	47.	E	47.	D
48.	B	48.	A	48.	D	48.	D	48.	C
49.	A	49.	D	49.	E	49.	D	49.	C
50.	A	50.	E	50.	C	50.	A	50.	E

Level 1 – Model Test 1 Solutions

1. (D)
$$\frac{25-1}{4} + \frac{36-1}{5} + \frac{49-1}{6} = \frac{24}{4} + \frac{35}{5} + \frac{48}{6}$$
$$= 6 + 7 + 8 = 21$$

2. (E)
$$9x^2 = 16y^2 \Rightarrow \frac{x^2}{y^2} = \frac{16}{9}$$
$$\frac{x}{y} = \mp\frac{4}{3} \qquad \frac{x}{y} = \frac{-4}{3}$$

3. (E)
$\frac{e}{r}$ is an integer therefore $\frac{e^2}{r^2} = \left(\frac{e}{r}\right)^2$ is also an integer.

4. (E)
$E = x \cdot (y + 1)$
$E = 3 \cdot 3 = 9$
$x = 3$
$y = 2$
Positive divisors= {1,3,9}
E cannot have 4 distinct positive divisors.

5. (D)
$$M_{AB} = \frac{-1-(-4)}{1-0} = 3, \quad M_{BC} = \frac{2-(-1)}{2-1} = 3$$
$$M_{AC} = \frac{2-(-4)}{2-0} = 3, \quad M_{CD} = \frac{6-2}{3-2} = \frac{4}{1}$$
So $D \notin$ line

6. (A)
$a^2 = 3^{46} \Rightarrow a = 3^{2b}$
$$\frac{a}{27} = \frac{3^{2b}}{27} = \frac{3^{2b}}{3^3} = 3^{2b-3}$$

7. (C)
$\frac{1}{e} < \frac{1}{r} < 0 \Rightarrow e < 0$ and $r < 0 \Rightarrow \frac{e}{r} > 0$ and
$\frac{e}{r} < 1$. So $\frac{e}{r}$ can be $\frac{3}{7}$

8. (C)
I) $\left. \begin{array}{l} -3 < x < 0 \\ 0 < y < 3 \\ |x| < |y| \end{array} \right\}$ So, $x + y < y$

II) For $y = 2$ and $x = \frac{-1}{2}$, we get
$y - \frac{x}{2} = 2 - \left(\frac{-1}{2}\right) = \frac{5}{2} \Rightarrow y < \frac{5}{2} < 3$. So it is true.

III) For $y = 2$ and $x = -1$, we get
$-1 - \frac{2}{2} = -2 \Rightarrow -2 < x$. So, it is false.

9. (D)
$\underline{3} \cdot \underline{3} \cdot \underline{3} \cdot \underline{3} \cdot \underline{3} \Rightarrow 3^5 = 243$

10. (E)
$AB = \frac{2a+4}{2} = a + 2$
$AC = AB + BC = 2a + 4 + a + 2 = 3a + 6$

11. (A)
Inclination will be increased, so the line will be steeper.

12. (E)

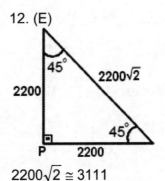

$2200\sqrt{2} \cong 3111$

13. (B)
slope $= \frac{4}{3}$
If lines are parallel, their slopes are equal. The slope of the line that is parallel to m can be 4/3.

14. (D)

$$A\left(\overset{\triangle}{ABC}\right) = \frac{[3-(-4)]\cdot 3}{2} = \frac{21}{2} = 10,5$$

$$A\left(\overset{\triangle}{DAC}\right) = \frac{[3-(-4)]\cdot 2}{2} = 7$$

Area $= 10,5 + 7 = 17,5$

15. (B)

$m(\overparen{AC}) = 72° \cdot 2 = 144°$

$144° + 7x + 5x = 360°$

$12x = 360° - 144° = 216°$

$x = 18°$

16. (C)

$$x = 7^{1/7} \Rightarrow \log_{1/7} 77 = \frac{\log 77}{\log(1/7)} = 15.6$$

17. (C)

$$\frac{1}{x} = \cos\alpha \Rightarrow x = \frac{1}{\cos\alpha}$$

$$\frac{y}{1} = \tan\alpha \Rightarrow y = \tan\alpha$$

$$x + y = \frac{1}{\cos\alpha} + \tan\alpha = \frac{1}{\cos\alpha} + \frac{\sin\alpha}{\cos\alpha}$$

$$= \frac{1+\sin\alpha}{\cos\alpha}$$

18. (A)

For $x = 1$ the minimum value is $15 - \dfrac{3}{1} = 12$.

19. (B)

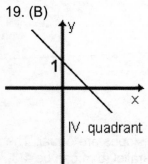

Y intercept is 1; in order to have points in the 4th quadrant, slope = m must be negative.

20. (A)

Let $m(A\hat{P}B) = x, m(B\hat{P}C) = y,$ and $m(C\hat{P}D) = z.$

$\underbrace{x + y}_{40°} + z = 90°$

$40° + z = 90° \Rightarrow z = 50°$

$x + \underbrace{y + z}_{70°} = 90°$

$x + 70° = 90° \Rightarrow x = 20°$ and $y = 20°$

$\dfrac{m(B\hat{P}C)}{2} = \dfrac{20°}{2} = 10°$

21. (D)

$z = 3y$ and $x = 9y$

$V = x \cdot y \cdot z = 9y \cdot y \cdot 3y = 27y^3$

22. (A)

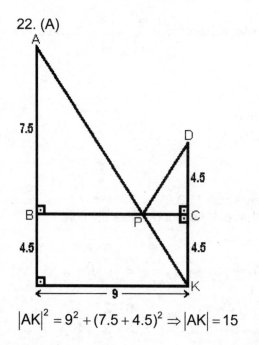

$|AK|^2 = 9^2 + (7.5 + 4.5)^2 \Rightarrow |AK| = 15$

23. (A)

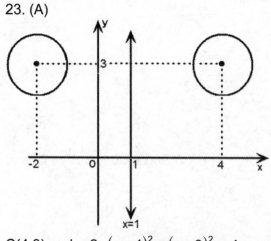

$C(4,3)$ and $r=2$; $(x-4)^2 + (y-3)^2 = 4$

24. (D)

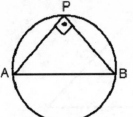

AB: diameter

25. (C)

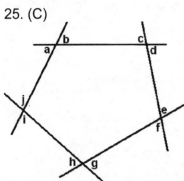

Sum of the measures of one set of exterior angles of a convex polygon is 360°; we have two sets therefore sum of the measures of the marked angles is 720°.

26. (D)

From A to K distance is constant therefore B and E cannot be correct. From M to K distance increases but not linearly therefore C cannot be correct. From M to B distance changes as shown in D.

27. (C)

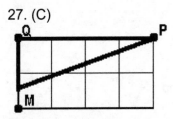

Distance $= t \cdot 1 = t$

$QM = 1$ feet

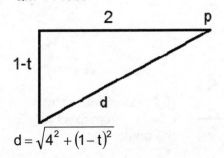

$d = \sqrt{4^2 + (1-t)^2}$

28. (C)

Volume is half of the resulting cone and it equals $\dfrac{\pi \cdot 3^2 \cdot 7}{3} \cdot \dfrac{1}{2} = 32.98 \approx 33.0$

29. (B)

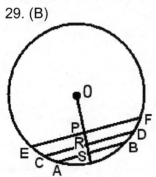

AB<CD<EF; therefore OS>OR>OP. The list of these chords in the order of decreasing distance from the center of the circle is c, a, b.

30. (B)

Let a be the length of one side of the regular octagon. So,

$$x = a + 2 \cdot \frac{a}{\sqrt{2}} = a\left(1 + \frac{2}{\sqrt{2}}\right) = a\left(\frac{\sqrt{2}+2}{\sqrt{2}}\right)$$

Then, $a = \dfrac{\sqrt{2}x}{2+\sqrt{2}} = \dfrac{\sqrt{2}x}{\sqrt{2}(\sqrt{2}+1)} = \dfrac{x}{\sqrt{2}+1}$

31. (E)

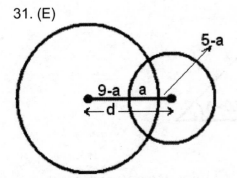

$6 < d < 12 \Rightarrow 6 < (9-a) + a + (5-a) < 12$

$\Rightarrow 6 < 14 - a < 12$

$\Rightarrow 2 < a < 8$

$\Rightarrow 2 < 5 < a < 8 < 9$

32. (A)
(3,6), (4,5), (4,6), (5,5), (5,6), (6,6), (6,3), (5,4), (6,4), (6,5)
Probability that Emel wins in a trial is:
$\dfrac{10}{6^2} = \dfrac{10}{36} = \dfrac{5}{18}$; probability that she loses in a

trial is : $1 - \dfrac{5}{18} = \dfrac{13}{18}$

First trial is a lose: $\dfrac{13}{18}$

Second trial is a win: $\dfrac{5}{18}$

$\Rightarrow \dfrac{13}{18} \cdot \dfrac{5}{18}$

33. (C)
For a = 1, b = 2, c = 3, and d = 9, we get
a − b − c + d = 1 − 2 − 3 + 9 = 5.

34. (D)
A) $i^4 + i^6 = 1 + i^2 = 0$
B) $i^6 + i^8 = i^2 + 1 = 0$
C) $i^9 + i^{11} = i + i^3 = i - i = 0$
D) -8
E) 0

35. (B)

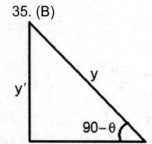

$c'(-x', y')$

$\dfrac{x'}{y} = \cos(90° - \theta) \Rightarrow x' = y \cdot \sin\theta,$ and

$\dfrac{y'}{y} = \sin(90° - \theta) \Rightarrow y' = y \cdot \cos\theta$

$c'(-y \cdot \sin\theta, y \cdot \cos\theta)$

36. (D)

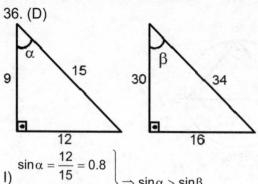

I)
$\left. \begin{aligned} \sin\alpha = \dfrac{12}{15} = 0.8 \\ \sin\beta = \dfrac{16}{34} = 0.47 \end{aligned} \right\} \Rightarrow \sin\alpha > \sin\beta$

II)
$\left. \begin{aligned} \cos\alpha = \dfrac{9}{15} = 0.6 \\ \cos\beta = \dfrac{30}{34} = 0.88 \end{aligned} \right\} \Rightarrow \cos\alpha < \cos\beta$

III)
$\left. \begin{aligned} \tan\alpha = \dfrac{12}{9} = 1.33 \\ \tan\beta = \dfrac{16}{30} = 0.53 \end{aligned} \right\} \Rightarrow \tan\alpha > \tan\beta$

37. (E)
$f\left(\sqrt{x-1}\right) = \dfrac{1}{\left(\sqrt{x-1}\right)^2 - 1} = \dfrac{1}{x - 1 - 1}$

$= \dfrac{1}{x - 2}, \ (x \neq 2)$

$x - 1 \geq 0 \Rightarrow x \geq 1$
So, $x \geq 1$ and $x \neq 2$

38. (B)
Let $f(x) = mx + n$
$f(1) = m + n = 2$
$f(4) = 4m + n = 6$
$\left. \begin{aligned} m + n = 2 \\ 4m + n = 6 \end{aligned} \right\} \Rightarrow m = \dfrac{4}{3}$ and $n = \dfrac{2}{3}$

So, $f(x) = \dfrac{4}{3}x + \dfrac{2}{3} = \dfrac{4x + 2}{3}$

$f^{-1}(x) = \dfrac{3x - 2}{4}$

39. (C)

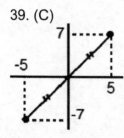

(5,7) is symmetric to (-5,-7) with respect to the origin.

40. (C)

$$\frac{\sin x \cdot \cos x}{\frac{\sin x}{\cos x}} = \sin x \cdot \cos x \cdot \frac{\cos x}{\sin x} = \cos^2 x$$

41. (D)

$$f(g(6)) = \frac{2}{g(6) - 2} = 2 \Rightarrow 2g(6) - 4 = 2$$

$$\Rightarrow 2g(6) = 6 \Rightarrow g(6) = 3$$

Since, $\frac{2 \cdot 6}{6 - 2} = \frac{12}{4} = 3$, $g(x)$ can be $\frac{2x}{x - 2}$

42. (D)

$$\left.\begin{array}{l} f(x_2) \geq f(x_1) \\ x_2 < x_1 \end{array}\right\} \Rightarrow \text{non-increasing function}$$

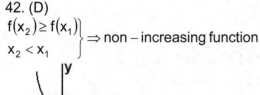

43. (A)

n	1	2	3	4	5
Number of shaded squares	3	6	10	15	21

$$\Rightarrow \frac{n^2 + 3n + 2}{2}$$

44. (A)

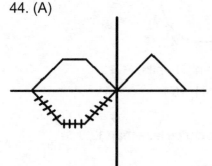

45. (B)

$$u = \frac{9 + 10 + 17}{2} = \frac{36}{2} = 18$$

$$A\left(A\overset{\Delta}{D}B\right) = \sqrt{18 \cdot 1 \cdot 9 \cdot 8} = 9 \cdot 4 = 36$$

$$\frac{9 \cdot x}{2} = 36 \Rightarrow x = 8 \quad \text{where x is the length of CD}$$

46. (D)

Let x be the price in 1994.

$$120,000 = x \cdot (1 + 0.05)^{10} \Rightarrow x = \frac{120,000}{(1.05)^{10}} = 74,000$$

47. (D)

$$f(x) = y = x^2 - 1$$

$$x = y^2 - 1 \Rightarrow y^2 = x + 1$$

$$\Rightarrow y = \mp\sqrt{x + 1}$$

but since $x \leq 0$, $f^{-1}(x) = -\sqrt{x + 1}$

48. (A)

$$f(g(x)) = f(x^2) = \sqrt{x^2 - 1}$$

The graph of $y = \sqrt{x^2 - 1}$ looks like A.

49. (C)

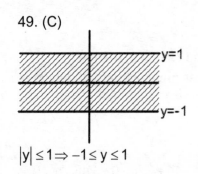

$$|y| \leq 1 \Rightarrow -1 \leq y \leq 1$$

50. (E)

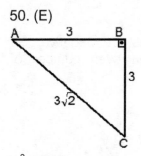

$$a^3 = 216 \Rightarrow a = 6$$

$$\text{Perimeter} = 4 \cdot |AC| = 4 \cdot 3\sqrt{2} = 12\sqrt{2}$$

Level 1 – Model Test 2 Solutions

1. (A)
$$\frac{12a+36}{12}=\frac{b}{12} \Rightarrow \frac{12(a+3)}{12}=\frac{b}{12} \Rightarrow a+3=\frac{b}{12}$$

2. (A)
$300-50=250$

$250 \cdot 0.84 = 210$ delegates support Mr.Leadit

$250-210=40$ delegates do not support Mr.Leadit

3. (B)

3	9	8	2
3	9	4	2
3	9	2	2
3	9	1	3
1	3	1	3
L	1	1	

$LCM(3,9,8)=72$ and $72 \cdot 3 = 216$ is the least positive integer greater than 200 which is divisible by 3, 9, and 8.

4. (C)
$$3^{11}=3^n \cdot 3^{11+n} \Rightarrow 3^{11}=3^{11+2n}$$
$$\Rightarrow 11=11+2n \Rightarrow 0=2n \Rightarrow n=0$$

5. (D)
At least one integer must be negative. So definitely there is not an even number of positive integers in set X.

6. (D)
$$x^2=\frac{11}{3} \Rightarrow x=\sqrt{\frac{11}{3}} \Rightarrow x^3=7.02$$

7. (E)
$$\frac{2}{5}+\frac{1}{6}=\frac{12+5}{30}=\frac{17}{30}$$
Let x be the total way
$$x-\frac{17}{30} \cdot x=\frac{13}{30} \cdot x=1.3 \Rightarrow x=3$$

8. (C)
For $3-x>0 \Rightarrow 3>x$
$$3-x=2x+1 \Rightarrow 2=3x \Rightarrow x=\frac{2}{3}$$

9. (D)
$x_1 \cdot y_1 = x_2 \cdot y_2$
$4 \cdot 20 = x \cdot 16 \Rightarrow x=5$

10. (E)
$$4x+\frac{3}{3 \cdot (2-x)}=8-\frac{2}{2(x-2)}$$
$$\Rightarrow 4x+\frac{1}{2-x}=8+\frac{1}{2-x}$$
$$\Rightarrow 4x=8 \text{ and } x=2$$
but for $x=2$, the denominator will be 0
So, $x \neq 2$

11. (B)
$$3x^3+2=24^2 \Rightarrow 3x^3=24^2-2$$
$$\Rightarrow x^3=\frac{24^2-2}{3} \Rightarrow x=\left(\frac{24^2-2}{3}\right)^{\frac{1}{3}} \Rightarrow x=5.76$$

12. (D)
$2(x+y)=120 \Rightarrow x+y=60$
For $x=y$ the rectangular area can be max.
So, for $x=30$, the area is $30 \cdot 30 = 900$

13. (A)

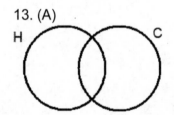

$n(H \cup C)=n(H)+n(C)-n(H \cap C)$
$60=44+28-n(H \cap C)$
$n(H \cap C)=12$,
So, $n(H \cap C)$ can not be less than 12.

14. (A)

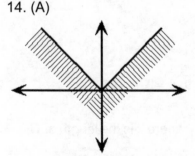

$y < |x|$, all four quadrants

15. (C)

$x^4 < 1000$

for $x = 1$, $\ 1^4 = 1 < 1000$

for $x = 3$, $\ 3^4 = 81 < 1000$

for $x = 5$, $\ 5^4 = 625 < 1000$

$\{1, 3, 5\}$

16. (D)

$\dfrac{2x^2 + x - 1}{x + 1} = \dfrac{(2x - 1)(x + 1)}{(x + 1)} = 2x - 1$

but $x + 1 \neq 0$, so, $x \neq -1$

17. (B)

$x^2 = g(x) + 1 \Rightarrow x = \sqrt{g(x) + 1}$

$\Rightarrow -1 < \sqrt{g(x) + 1} < 2$

$\Rightarrow 0 < g(x) + 1 < 4$

$\Rightarrow -1 < g(x) < 3$

18. (A)

$\sin^2 - 4 + \cos^2 \theta = \underbrace{\sin^2 \theta + \cos^2 \theta}_{1} - 4 = 1 - 4 = -3$

19. (C)

$\dbinom{5}{1} + \dbinom{5}{2} + \dbinom{5}{3} + \dbinom{5}{4} + \dbinom{5}{5} = 2^5 - 1 = 31$

20. (B)

$i^{42} = (i^4)^{10} \cdot i^2 = -1$

$i^{43} = (i^4)^{10} \cdot i^3 = -i$

21. (C)

$P(x) = x^4 - 2x^3 + 3x^2 - 4x + 5$

$P(1) = 1 - 2 \cdot 1 + 3 \cdot 1 - 4 \cdot 1 + 5$

$\quad = 1 - 2 + 3 - 4 + 5$

$\quad = -2 + 5 = 3$

22. (C)

The slope of $2x + 3y = 26$ is $m = \dfrac{-2}{3}$

$\dfrac{-2}{3} \cdot m_x = -1 \Rightarrow m_x = \dfrac{3}{2}$

For $6x - 4y = 32$, slope is $\dfrac{6}{4} = \dfrac{3}{2}$

23. (D)

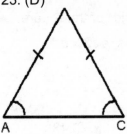

$m(\hat{A}) = m(\hat{C}) \Rightarrow \tan A = \tan C$

$m(\hat{A}) = m(\hat{C}) \Rightarrow m(\hat{A}) - m(\hat{C}) = 0$

$\cos 0° = 1 \Rightarrow \cos(A - C) = 1$

24. (D)

$x(x + 1)(x + 2)(x + 3) - 6{,}359.0625 = 0$

$y = x(x + 1)(x + 2)(x + 3) - 6{,}359.0625$

Graph the function given above to see that it has a zero at x=7.5.

25. (B)

$ax^2 + bx + c = 0$

$\left. \begin{aligned} x_1 + x_2 &= \dfrac{-b}{a} = -4 \\[2mm] x_1 + x_2 &= \dfrac{c}{a} = 5 \end{aligned} \right\} \begin{aligned} &\Rightarrow x^2 - (-4)x + 5 = 0 \\ &\Rightarrow x^2 + 4x + 5 = 0 \end{aligned}$

26. (D)

$8 \cdot 3 + 2\pi \cdot 4 = 24 + 8\pi$

27. (C)

$1 \rightarrow \dfrac{10 + 8 + 4.5 + 6}{4} = 7.125$

$2 \rightarrow \dfrac{4 + 8 + 8.5 + 6.5}{4} = 6.75$

$3 \rightarrow \dfrac{6.5 + 8 + 6.5 + 8.5}{4} = 7.375$

$4 \rightarrow \dfrac{2 + 4 + 8 + 6}{4} = 5$

$5 \rightarrow \dfrac{8 + 4.5 + 6.5 + 4}{4} = 5.75$

28. (C)

Let a be the length of each side of the square.

The diagonal of the square is : $a\sqrt{2} = 8$.

So, $a = 4\sqrt{2}$

$A(ABCD) = \left(4\sqrt{2}\right)^2 = 32$

Shaded area : $32 - \dfrac{16\pi}{2} = 32 - 8\pi = 3.43$

29. (D)

A) $\dfrac{BC}{BD} = \sin\theta \Rightarrow BC = BD \cdot \sin\theta$

B) $\dfrac{BD}{AD} = \sin\theta \Rightarrow BD = AD \cdot \sin\theta$

$BC = AD \cdot \sin\theta \cdot \sin\theta = AD \cdot \sin^2\theta\,0$

C) $\dfrac{BD}{AD} = \tan\theta \Rightarrow BD = AB \cdot \tan\theta$

$BC = AB \cdot \tan\theta \cdot \sin\theta$

D) $BC \neq AB \cdot \tan\theta \cdot \cos\theta$

30. (D)

I) $x - 2 \neq 0 \Rightarrow \Re - \{2\}$

II) $x - 2 > 0 \Rightarrow x > 0$

III) $x - 2 \neq 0 \Rightarrow x \neq 2 \Rightarrow \Re - \{2\}$

31. (D)

There are n2 right triangles in each pattern and each right triangle has a perimeter of $1 + 1 + \sqrt{2} = 2 + \sqrt{2}$. So the answer is $n^2 \cdot \left(2 + \sqrt{2}\right)$.

32. (B)

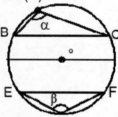

$\alpha > 90°$ and $\beta > 90°$

$A\overset{\Delta}{B}C$, $D\overset{\Delta}{E}F$ must be obsute

33. (B)

The other root must be the conjugate of $3 + \sqrt{2}$ so it is $3 - \sqrt{2}$.

34. (E)

$A(ABCD) = x \cdot y \sin\alpha$

$\qquad\qquad = x \cdot y \sin\alpha < x \cdot y$

$0° < \alpha < 90° \Rightarrow 0 < \sin\alpha < 1$

35. (C)

$P(6,0), r = 6$

For $x = 9, y = 3\sqrt{3}$

Shaded Area $= 36\pi \cdot \dfrac{120°}{360°} - \dfrac{6\sqrt{3} \cdot 3}{2}$

$\qquad\qquad = 12\pi - 9\sqrt{3}$

36. (D)

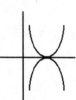

0 points   1 point   2 points

Only one of the above cases are possible.

37. (A)

$y = 0 \Rightarrow 2x = 12 \Rightarrow x = 6$

$x = 0 \Rightarrow 3y = 12 \Rightarrow y = 4$

$k\left(\dfrac{6+0}{2}, \dfrac{0+4}{2}\right) = (3, 2)$

The slope of the line with equation $2x + 3y = 12$ is $\dfrac{-2}{3}$. The slope of the perpendicular bisector is $m \cdot \dfrac{-2}{3} = -1 \Rightarrow m = \dfrac{3}{2}$. So, the equation of the perpendicular bisector is: $y - 2 = \dfrac{3}{2}(x - 3)$.

38. (E)

For $f(1) = 3$ and $g(1) = 5$, $g(f(1)) = 5$

For $f(2) = 2$ and $g(2) = 4$, $g(f(2)) = 4$

For $f(3) = 5$ and $g(3) = 5$, $g(f(3)) = 5$

So, $g(f(x)) = 5$ has two solutions

39. (D)

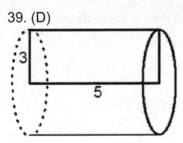

$$\text{Volume} = \pi \cdot 3^2 \cdot 5$$
$$= \pi \cdot 9 \cdot 5 = 45\pi$$

40. (D)

$$A - B = \{1, 2\}$$
$$B - A = \{5, 6, 7\}$$
$$(A - B) \cup (B - A) = \{1, 2, 5, 6, 7\}$$

41. (A)

$$145,000.(1 + 0.05)^{10} = 225,000$$

42. (B)

$$S_n = \left(\frac{a_1 + a_n}{2}\right) \cdot n$$

$$S_n = \left(\frac{20 + (n-1) \cdot 3 + 20}{2}\right) \cdot n > 240$$

$$n = 35$$

43. (E)

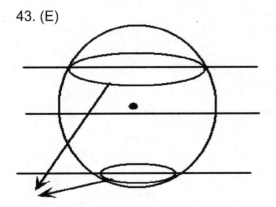

44. (C)

$$6x^2 - 8x - 9x + 12 = px^2 + qx + r$$
$$p = 6, \ q = -17, \ r = 12$$
$$-p - q + r = -6 + 17 + 12 = 23$$

45. (D)

II) $f^{-1}(4) = 6 \Rightarrow f(6) = 4$
     $f^{-1}(5) = 6 \Rightarrow f(6) = 5$

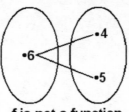

f is not a function

III)

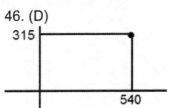

f(x) can not intersect x=2 at two points

46. (D)

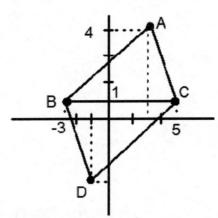

For $t = 9$, $x = 540$ and

$$y = 80 \cdot 9 - 5 \cdot 9^2 = 720 - 405 = 315$$

47. (D)

$$A(\overset{\Delta}{ABC}) = \frac{8 \cdot 3}{2} = 12 \left.\right\}$$
$$A(\overset{\Delta}{ADC}) = \frac{8 \cdot 4}{2} = 16 \left.\right\} \Rightarrow A(ABCD) = 12 + 16 = 28$$

48. (B)

$$\frac{2}{a} \neq \frac{5}{-3} \Rightarrow 5a \neq -6 \Rightarrow a \neq -1.2$$

49. (A)

$$f(x) = \left(\frac{x}{x+1}\right)^2 - \frac{3x+3}{x} + 2 = 0$$

Graph the function and find its x – intercept; the zero is at x = – 2.

50. (B)

$$x^2 - 2x + 3 = (x-1)^2 + 2$$

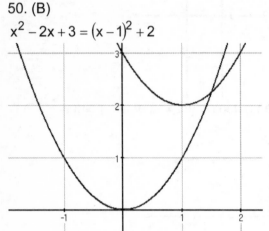

Shift 1 unit right and 2 units up.

Level 1 – Model Test 3 Solutions

1. (D)

$$\left.\begin{array}{l} \dfrac{A}{B} = \dfrac{3}{5} = \dfrac{3 \cdot 4}{5 \cdot 4} = \dfrac{12}{20} \\[2mm] \dfrac{B}{C} = \dfrac{4}{7} = \dfrac{4 \cdot 5}{7 \cdot 5} = \dfrac{20}{35} \end{array}\right\} \Rightarrow \begin{array}{l} A = 12k \\ B = 20k \\ C = 35k \end{array}$$

$$B = 20k = 40 \Rightarrow k = 2$$

$$\left.\begin{array}{l} A = 12k = 24 \\ C = 35k = 70 \end{array}\right\} \Rightarrow A + 2C = 24 + 140 = 164$$

2. (A)

$$\frac{a}{0.4} = 2b \Rightarrow a = 0.8b$$

$$c = 1.5b$$

$$a + b + c = 0.8b + b + 1.5b = 165$$

$$b = 50$$

$$a = 0.8 \cdot b = 0.8 \cdot 50 = 40$$

3. (A)

$$\left.\begin{array}{l} t_1 = \dfrac{15\,m}{30\,mph} = \dfrac{1}{2} = 0.5\,m \\[3mm] t_2 = \dfrac{15\,m}{40\,mph} = \dfrac{3}{8} = 0.375\,h \end{array}\right\} \Rightarrow t_1 - t_2 = 0.125\,h$$

$$1h = 60\,min$$

$$0.125\,h = 0.125 \cdot 60\,min = 7.5\,min$$

4. (E)

$$-4 < x^2 < 7 \Rightarrow 0 \le x^2 < 7 \Rightarrow -\sqrt{7} < x < \sqrt{7}$$

$$x \neq 2\sqrt{2} \text{ because } 2\sqrt{2} > \sqrt{7}$$

5. (C)

$$\sqrt{2}x + 2y = 1 \Rightarrow x + \sqrt{2}y = \frac{1}{\sqrt{2}}$$

$$\left.\begin{array}{l} x + \sqrt{2}y = \dfrac{1}{\sqrt{2}} \\[3mm] x - \sqrt{2}y = \sqrt{2} \end{array}\right\} \Rightarrow \begin{array}{l} 2x = \dfrac{1}{\sqrt{2}} + \sqrt{2} = \dfrac{3}{\sqrt{2}} \\[3mm] x = \dfrac{3}{2\sqrt{2}} \end{array}$$

$$x - \sqrt{2}y = \sqrt{2} \Rightarrow \frac{3}{2\sqrt{2}} - \sqrt{2} = \sqrt{2}y \Rightarrow y = -\frac{1}{4}$$

$$\frac{x}{y} = \frac{\dfrac{3}{2\sqrt{2}}}{-\dfrac{1}{4}} = \frac{3}{2\sqrt{2}} \cdot (-4) = -3\sqrt{2}$$

6. (B)

$-2 < x < 4 \Rightarrow x = \{-1, 0, 1, 2, 3\}$

$-3 \le y < 0 \Rightarrow y = \{-3, -2, -1\}$

$x - y = \{0, 1, 2, ..., 6\}$

min value of $(x - y)^2$ is $0^2 = 0$

7. (A)

$\sin\theta = \dfrac{b}{a}$

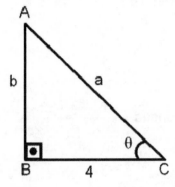

8. (E)

$x^3 < x < x^2 \Rightarrow x < -1$

For $x = -2$, $x^2 = 4 \Rightarrow x^3 = -8$

9. (D)

$-f(x)$: reflects $y = f(x)$ with respect to the x-axis

10. (C)

$\dfrac{5}{18} = \sin\theta \Rightarrow \theta = \sin^{-1}\left(\dfrac{5}{18}\right) \Rightarrow 2\theta \cong 32.26°$

11. (C)

$a^2 - b^2 = (a - b)\underbrace{(a + b)}_{9} = 54$

$a - b = \dfrac{54}{9} = 6 \Rightarrow b - a = -6$

12. (A)

$e^{2x+1} = 7 \Rightarrow \log_e 7 = 2x + 1$

$\dfrac{-1 + \ln 7}{2} = x \Rightarrow x \cong 0.47$

13. (D)

$x_1 \cdot y_1 = x_2 \cdot y_2 \Rightarrow 20 \cdot 3 = 3 \cdot y \Rightarrow y = 20$

14. (E)

$1 - 2\cos^2 x = \sin^2 x - 1$

$2 = 2\sin^2 x + 2\cos^2 x$

$2 = 2\left(\sin^2 x + \cos^2 x\right)$

$2 = 2 \cdot 1$

$2 = 2$

x can be any angle mesure

15. (D)

For $B(-4, 7)$ and $D(4, -4)$, $m_{BD} = \dfrac{-4 - 7}{4 - (-4)} = -\dfrac{11}{8}$

16. (B)

$|x| \ne 0 \Rightarrow x \ne 0$, so the domain is : $\Re - \{0\}$

17. (C)

$4x^3 - 2x^2 + (\dfrac{5}{x} + kx - 4x^2) \cdot x - 5 = 0$

$4x^3 - 2x^2 + 5 + kx^2 - 4x^3 - 5 = 0$

$-2x^2 + kx^2 = 0 \Rightarrow x^2(-2 + k) = 0$

Since $x^2 \ne 0$, $-2 + k = 0 \Rightarrow k = 2$

18. (B)

$\log_x 5 = 3 \Rightarrow x^3 = 5 \Rightarrow \sqrt[3]{x^3} = \sqrt[3]{5} \Rightarrow x = \sqrt[3]{5} \cong 1.71$

19. (A)

$\left(\dfrac{2}{x^2} + \dfrac{2}{y^2}\right) + 2 \cdot \left(\dfrac{1}{x^2} - \dfrac{1}{y^2}\right) = 4 + 2 \cdot 2$

$\dfrac{2}{x^2} + \dfrac{2}{y^2} + \dfrac{2}{x^2} - \dfrac{2}{y^2} = 8$

$\dfrac{4}{x^2} = 8 \Rightarrow x^2 = \dfrac{1}{2}$

$\Rightarrow \dfrac{2}{y^2} = 0$; so the solution set is empty

20. (A)

$$\left(\frac{8-k}{8-1}\right)^2 = \frac{S_2}{S_2 + S_1} = \frac{1}{2}$$

$$\Rightarrow \frac{8-k}{7} = \frac{1}{\sqrt{2}}$$

$$\Rightarrow 8\sqrt{2} - \sqrt{2}k = 7$$

$$\Rightarrow k = \frac{8\sqrt{2} - 7}{\sqrt{2}} \cong 3.05$$

21. (C)

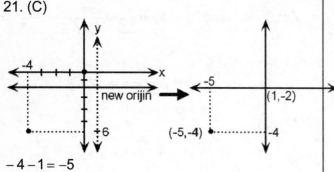

$$-4 - 1 = -5$$
$$-6 + 2 = -4$$

22. (D)

$$AB = 49 - 25 = 24$$

$$AD = \sqrt{25^2 - 24^2} = 7$$

$$A(ABD) = \frac{1}{2} \cdot 7 \cdot 24 = 84$$

$$\text{Area (portion of circle)} = \pi \cdot 25^2 \cdot \frac{\tan^{-1}\left(\frac{7}{24}\right)}{360°}$$

23. (D)

$$f(x) = mx + n$$
$$f(f(x)) = m \cdot (mx + n) + n$$
$$\qquad = m^2x + mn + n$$
$$m^2x + mn + n = 4x + 3$$
$$\Rightarrow m^2 = 4 \text{ and } mn + n = 3$$
$$\Rightarrow m_1 = +2, \ n_1 = 1 \ \left.\right] f(x) = 2x + 1$$
$$\Rightarrow m_2 = -2, \ n_2 = -3 \left.\right] f(x) = -2x - 3$$

24. (D)

$$x^2 = 6^2 + 7^2 \Rightarrow x = \sqrt{36 + 49} = \sqrt{85}$$

25. (E)

$$x \geq 0 \Rightarrow x^{\frac{1}{n}} \geq 0$$

$$n \neq 0 \text{ because } \frac{1}{0} \text{ is undefined}$$

So, n can be 2 or 3

26. (B)

$$\text{Average speed} = \frac{\text{total distance}}{\text{total time}} = \frac{d_1 + d_2 + d_3}{t_1 + t_2 + t_3}$$

$$t = \frac{\text{distance}}{\text{speed}}$$

$$\left.\begin{array}{l} t_1 = \dfrac{26}{20} \\[2mm] t_2 = \dfrac{34}{40} \\[2mm] t_3 = \dfrac{32}{50} \end{array}\right\} \Rightarrow \text{Average speed} = \frac{26 + 34 + 32}{\dfrac{26}{20} + \dfrac{34}{40} + \dfrac{32}{50}} \cong 32.97$$

27. (D)

$$30{,}000 \cdot (1 + \text{rate})^n = 70{,}000$$

$$(1.1)^n = \frac{7}{3} \Rightarrow n = \log_{1.1}(7 \div 3) \cong 8.89 \text{ hours}$$

8.89 hours means 8 hours and $(8.89 - 8) \cdot 60 = 53$ min.

$$03:00\,\text{PM} + 08:53 = 11:53\,\text{PM}$$

28. (B)

Since the semicircle with center at C is the rotated semicircle with center at A, β degrees clockwise around the point B, the area of the shaded region is the same as the area of the sector ABC of the semicircle with center at B. So,

Area of the semicircle $ABO = \pi \cdot 9^2 \cdot \dfrac{\beta}{360°}$

Area of the shaded region: 9π

$$\Rightarrow \pi \cdot 9^2 \cdot \frac{\beta}{360°} = 9\pi$$

$$\Rightarrow \beta = \frac{360°}{9} = 40°$$

29. (C)

$$C(5, -5), \ r = 5$$

$$(x - 5)^2 + (y + 5)^2 = 25$$

30. (C)
In order to find the equation of the parabola, we need at least the vertex and a point other than the vertex or three distinct points none of which is the vertex. Therefore B and D are not sufficient.

31. (C)

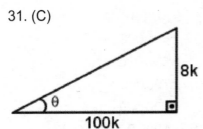

$$\tan\theta = \frac{8}{100} = \frac{100}{x} \Rightarrow x = \frac{10000}{8} = 1250 \text{ feet}$$

32. (D)

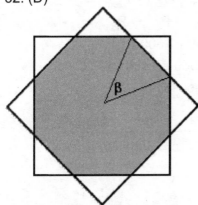

The shaded polygon is a regular octagon (having 8 sides); therefore the angle β measures 360/8=45°.

33. (B)
If 6+2i is one root of a quadratic equation then other root must be the conjugate of 6+2i: 6-2i

34. (D)

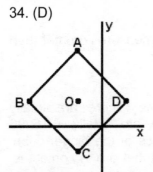

A rhombus is defined by the equation given by $|x - a| + |y - b| = c$ where (a, b) is the center O. Therefore (a, b) can be (-5, 5) so the rhombus

has the equation $|x + 5| + |y - 5| = c$. Since it must pass through the origin, $|0 + 5| + |0 - 5| = c = 10$. Therefore the rhombus is given by $|x + 5| + |y - 5| = 10$.

35. (A)
$$x = y^2 - 1$$
$$y^2 = x + 1 \Rightarrow f^{-1}(x) = \begin{cases} \sqrt{x+1}, & x \geq 0 \\ -\sqrt{x+1}, & x < 0 \end{cases}$$
So, $f^{-1}(x) = \sqrt{x+1}$

36. (E)
x & y = 3x + 4y + 2(y & x)
y & x = 3y + 4x + 2(x & y)
Let x & y = A and y & x = B.
Then A = 3x + 4y + 2B and B = 3y + 4x + 2A.
There is sufficient information to determine both A and B therefore all of the requested operations can be carried out.

37. (D)
$$g = \begin{pmatrix} 1 & 2 & 3 & 4 & 5 \\ 2 & 3 & 5 & 1 & 4 \end{pmatrix} \Rightarrow g^{-1} = \begin{pmatrix} 1 & 2 & 3 & 4 & 5 \\ 4 & 1 & 2 & 5 & 3 \end{pmatrix}$$
So, $g^{-1}(3) = 2$ and $f(g^{-1}(3)) = f(2) = 4$

38. (E)

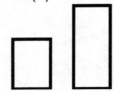

The figure above represents vertical stretch.

39. (C)
$$2\pi r = 2\pi \cdot 4r \frac{\alpha}{360°} \Rightarrow \alpha = \frac{360°}{4} = 90°$$

40. (C)
There are 5100 items.
$$\underbrace{140, 140, ..., 520,}_{\text{first 2549 items}} \underbrace{520, 520}_{\substack{2550^{\text{th}} \text{ and} \\ 2551^{\text{th}} \text{items}}}, \underbrace{520, ..., 600}_{\text{last 2549 items}}$$

So, the modal length of the items is 520 cm's.

41. (C)

$y = mx + n$

$m = \dfrac{600 - 580}{185 - 180} = 4$

$f(180) = 4 \cdot 180 + n = 580 \Rightarrow n = -140$

$f(156.5) = 4 \cdot 156.5 - 140 = 486$

42. (B)

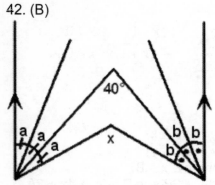

$2a + 2b = 40° \Rightarrow a + b = 20°$

$x = 3a + 3b = 3 \cdot (a + b) = 3 \cdot 20° = 60°$

43. (B)

$\sin 25° = \dfrac{x}{10} \Rightarrow x = 10 \cdot \sin 25° = 4.23 \Rightarrow 2x \cong 8.45$

The length of the diagonal of the square is 8.45,
So, the length of one side of the square is :

$a\sqrt{2} = 8.45 \Rightarrow a = \dfrac{8.45}{\sqrt{2}}$

$\text{Area} = \left(\dfrac{8.45}{\sqrt{2}}\right)^2 \cong 35.72$

44. (D)

$2 \cdot (45 + 30) + 2\pi \cdot 2 = 150 + 4\pi$

45. (C)

$2\pi = 2\pi \cdot 6 \cdot \dfrac{\theta}{360°} \Rightarrow \theta = 60°$

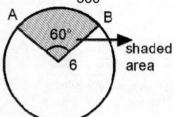

$\text{Shaded area} = \pi \cdot 6^2 \cdot \dfrac{60°}{360°} - \dfrac{1}{2} \cdot 6 \cdot 6 \cdot \sin 60°$

$= 6\pi - 9\sqrt{3} = 26$

46. (D)

$n = 2^3 \cdot 3^4 (2^2)^5 = 2^3 \cdot 2^{10} \cdot 3^4 = 2^{13} \cdot 3^4$

the number of distinct positive divisors :

$(13 + 1) \cdot (4 + 1) = 14 \cdot 5 = 70$

47. (E)

$P_{1998} = 15,000 \cdot 60 = 900,000$

$P_{1999} = 30,000 \cdot 80 = 2,400,000$

$P_{2000} = 40,000 \cdot 90 = 3,600,000$

$P_{2001} = 45,000 \cdot 60 = 2,700,000$

$P_{2002} = 50,000 \cdot 80 = 4,000,000$

$P_{2003} = 40,000 \cdot 100 = 4,000,000$

$P_{2004} = 60,000 \cdot 80 = 4,800,000$

$P_{2005} = 50,000 \cdot 120 = 6,000,000$

$P_{total} = P_{1998} + P_{1999} + P_{2000} + P_{2001}$

$+ P_{2002} + P_{2003} + P_{2004} + P_{2005}$

$= 900 + 2,400 + 3,600 + 2,700$

$+ 4,000 + 4,000 + 4,800 + 6,000$

$= \$28,400 \text{ thousands}$

48. (C)

n	Number of shaded squares
1	1
2	5
3	9
4	13
n	[1+(n − 1)·4]=4n − 3

49. (B)

I. If $\angle AOP$ measures 60° then Cos60° = 1/2 implies that AB = AO = R/2 (Correct).

II. If $K = r^2\left(\dfrac{\pi}{3} - \dfrac{\sqrt{3}}{8}\right)$ .then $\angle AOP$ measures

60° and AB = AO (False).

III. If K = L then $\angle AOP$ measures greater than 60° and AB > AO.

50. (D)

Each cube has 6 faces. There are totally 6·64=384 faces. There are totally 6·16=96 faces on the outer surface of the bigger cube. So, the number of faces that are in contact is: 6·64−6·4·4=288

Level 1 – Model Test 4 Solutions

1. (A)
$20 \cdot b = 240 \Rightarrow b = 12$
$c = 1 - 20 + 12 = -7$

2. (E)
$\dfrac{2\pi r}{r} = 2\pi$

since π is not a rational number, 2π is not either.

3. (C)
We insert the coordinates of the point $(-6, 3)$ in the equation of the line $2x - 3 = ky$
$2 \cdot (-6) - 3 = k \cdot 3 \Rightarrow -12 - 3 = 3k$
$\Rightarrow 3k = -15 \Rightarrow k = -5$

4. (E)
If we multiply an odd number of negative numbers with any number of positive numbers, we get a negative number.
If we multiply an even number of negative numbers with any number of positive numbers, we get a positive number.
$(+) \cdot (+) \cdot (+) \cdot (+) \cdot (+) \cdot (-) \cdot (-) \cdot (-) = (-)$

5. (D)
$1 + x^4 - 81 = 82 - x^4 \Rightarrow 2x^4 = 82 + 81 - 1$
$\Rightarrow 2x^4 = 162 \Rightarrow x^4 = 81 \Rightarrow x = \mp 3$

6. (D)
$f(g(-2)) = f\left((-2-1)^3\right) = f(-27) = (-27)^2 - 1 = 728$

7. (E)
Let n be an even integer. A list of 10 consecutive even integer will be: n, n + 2, n + 4, n + 6, n + 8, n + 10, n + 12, n + 14, n + 16, n + 18

A) Median=$\dfrac{n+8+n+10}{2} = n+9$. Since n is an even number, n+9 will be always an odd number.
B) Since the given numbers are consecutive, the mean and the median are equal.
C) $(n + 9) - n = 9$
D) $10 \cdot (n + 9) = n + n + 2 + n + 4 + n + 6 + n + 8 + n + 10 + n + 12 + n + 14 + n + 16 + n + 18$
E) $(n + 18) - n = 18 \neq 20$

8. (B)
Let $2n - 1$ and $2m - 1$ are two odd integers for $m, n \in Z$
I) $(2n-1)-(2m-1) = 2(n-m)$ which is an even number. So, the set of odd integers is not closed under subtraction.
II) $(2n-1)\cdot(2m-1) = 4nm - 2(n+m) + 1$ which is an odd integer. So, the set of odd integers is closed under multiplication.
III) The dvision of odd integers may not be an integer.

9. (E)
Let $a = 2n$ and $b = 2m$
I) $(2n)^2 + (2m)^3 - 12 = 4n^2 + 8n^3 - 12$ is an even number
II) $2 \cdot (2n + 2m) = 4 \cdot (n+m)$ is an even number
III) $2n + 2 \cdot 2m = 2n + 4m$ is an even number

10. (D)
$\dfrac{\text{sum of the heights of the 7 people}}{7} = 72$
$\Rightarrow$ sum of the heights of the 7 people $= 504$
The average height of the remaining 5 people :
$\dfrac{504 - (75 + 64)}{5} = 73$

11. (D)
$0^0 = 0^0 \to$ undefined
II) $x \neq 0$ is even $\sqrt{a^2} = \sqrt{b^2} \Rightarrow |a| = |b|$
III) x is odd, let $x = 3 \Rightarrow a^3 = b^3 \Rightarrow a = b$

12. (C)
$\left.\begin{array}{l} a \cdot 1 + b \cdot 2 = 10 \\ a \cdot 1 - b \cdot 2 = 4 \end{array}\right\}$
$\Rightarrow 2a = 14$ and $a = 7$
$\Rightarrow 2b = 3$ and $b = 1.5$
$\Rightarrow (a, b) = (7, 1.5)$

13. (C)

fixed cost $\rightarrow f$

number of units $\rightarrow n$

price $\rightarrow p$

$c = f + n \cdot p$

$1500 = f + 500p$ and $2500 = f + 1000p$

Therefore p =2 and f = 500 and the new total cost is $500 + 2 \cdot 1500 = 3500$

14. (E)

$a = \dfrac{2}{b}$

Since $a = \dfrac{2}{b}$

$4 < \dfrac{2}{b} < 10 \Rightarrow 2 < \dfrac{1}{b} < 5 \Rightarrow 0.2 < b < 0.5$

15. (E)

$-3 \cdot (-2) + 5 \cdot 2 = 16 > 15$

16. (E)

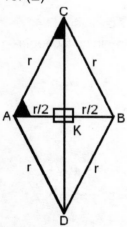

DACB rhoumbus

$\angle ACK = 30°$

$\angle CAK = 60°$

$\angle DAC = 120°$

There is sufficient information to determine all quantities.

17. (A)

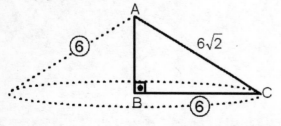

Requested volume corresponds to half of a cone for which r=6 and h=6.

Volume= $\dfrac{1}{2} \cdot \left(\pi \cdot 6^2 \cdot 6 \cdot \dfrac{1}{3} \right) = 36\pi$

18. (E)

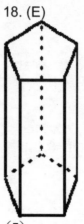

$\dbinom{5}{2} + 5 = 10 + 5 = 15$

19. (C)

Move CD so that AB and CD have a common point where they have to be perpendicular.

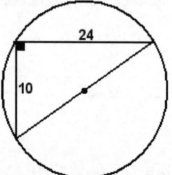

Therefore diameter =26 and area is $\pi \cdot 13^2$.

20. (C)

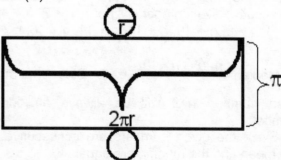

$A = 2\pi rh + 2 \cdot \pi r^2 = 2\pi r \cdot (h + r)$

$A = 2\pi r \cdot 15 = 150\pi \Rightarrow r = 5 \text{ and } h = 10$

$V = \pi r^2 \cdot h = \pi \cdot 5^2 \cdot 10 = 250\pi$

21. (C)
I) a // w, c // y, b // d, x // z
So measure of each interior angle of the trapezoid 1 is equal to the measure of an interior angle of trapezoid 2.
II.

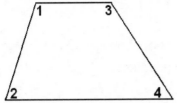

1+2=180° and 3+4=180°
III) Since the ratio of b to x is not the same as the ratio of d to z, the given trapezoids may not be similar.

22. (C)
I) $\overset{\Delta}{ABC} \sim \overset{\Delta}{EDC}$ or $\overset{\Delta}{ABC} \sim \overset{\Delta}{CDE}$
II. We don't know that |AB|=|DE| or |BC|=|DC| or
|AC|=|CE|. So, we don't know whether triangles ABC and EDC are congruent or not.
III. $\overset{\Delta}{ACB} \sim \overset{\Delta}{ECD} \Rightarrow \dfrac{BC}{DC} = \dfrac{AB}{ED}$

23. (C)
If lines are parallel slopes are equal.
$-\dfrac{-3}{1} = -\dfrac{2}{-k} \Rightarrow k = \dfrac{2}{3}$

24. (B)
$\dfrac{(x^2 - 81)}{(x + 9)} = \dfrac{(x-9)(x+9)}{(x+9)} = x - 9$
where $x + 9 \neq 0$, or $x \neq -9$

25. (C)
$f(x) = y = x^2$
$\Rightarrow x = y^2 \Rightarrow f^{-1}(x) = y = \pm\sqrt{x}$

26. (D)

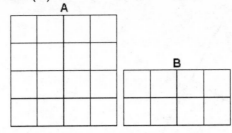

shaded region: 1 right triangle.
Original square A: 16 small squares = 32 right triangles.

27. (D)
$\tan\dfrac{\theta}{2} = \dfrac{|PC|}{x} \Rightarrow |PC| = x \cdot \tan\dfrac{\theta}{2}$

$|PQ| = 2 \cdot |PC| = 2 \cdot x \cdot \tan\dfrac{\theta}{2}$

28. (E)

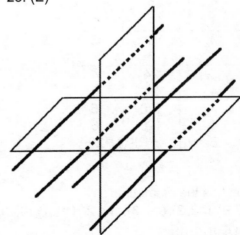

four lines.

29. (E)
$t = 2 - x \Rightarrow y = 2 - x + 2 = 4 - x$
for $y = 0, 0 = 4 - x \Rightarrow x = 4$

30. (C)

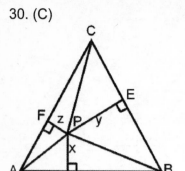

$A(ABC) = A(APB) + A(BPC) + A(CPA)$

$A(ABC) = \dfrac{a \cdot x}{2} + \dfrac{a \cdot y}{2} + \dfrac{a \cdot z}{2} = \dfrac{a \cdot h}{2}$

$\Rightarrow \dfrac{a}{2} \cdot (x + y + z) = \dfrac{a \cdot h}{2}$

$\Rightarrow x + y + z = h$

31. (D)

Step No	P	N
1.	1	1
3.	1	1
4.	1	2
3.	2	2
4.	2	3
3.	6	3
4.	6	4
3.	24	4
4.	24	5
3.	120	5
4.	120	6
6.	PRINT 120	

32. (D)
The relation has the elements:
$(\mp 3, 3), (\mp 2, 3), (\mp 2, 2), (\mp 1, 3), (\mp 1, 2), (\mp 1, 1), (0, 3),$
$(0, 2), (0, 1)$ and $(0, 0)$

So the range of the relation is the second components of the elements of the relation, namely, $\{0, 1, 2, 3\}$

33. (C)
$4 \cdot (4+3+1) = 32$

34. (C)
The slope of the line $2y = 3x - 2$ is : $m_1 = \dfrac{3}{2}$

Since the lines are perpendicular, the new line has a slope of $m_2 = -\dfrac{1}{\frac{3}{2}} = -\dfrac{2}{3}$.

With the slope - point equation formula the new line has the equation :

$y - (-\dfrac{1}{2}) = m_2 \cdot (x - 3)$

$y + \dfrac{1}{2} = -\dfrac{2}{3} \cdot (x - 3)$

$6y = -4x + 9$

35. (A)
Domain of a function are the x values:
$-2 \le x < 3$

36. (E)
$3 - x \ge 4 \Rightarrow 3 - 4 \ge x \Rightarrow -1 \ge x$ or
$3 - x \le -4 \Rightarrow 3 + 4 \le x \Rightarrow 7 \le x$

37. (B)
$f = (-|x|) = \begin{cases} f(-x), & x \ge 0 \\ f(x), & x < 0 \end{cases}$

So, first delete the right hand side of the graph, take the left hand side and reflect it with respect to the y axis.

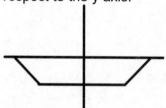

38. (B)
$9\left(\dfrac{x+1}{2}\right) = 2 \cdot \left(\dfrac{x+1}{2}\right) - 3 = x + 1 - 3 = x - 2$

For $x = 0$, we find y – intercept as : $y = -2$

39. (D)
If f(-x)=f(x), then it is an even function which is symmetric with respect to the y-axis
Graph I, II, and III.
II and III symmetric with y-axis.

40. (B)
The converse of the statement "If p then q" is: "if q then p". So the converse is "If $x^2 = 9$ then $x = 3$".

41. (A)
If lines are parallel then slopes are equal.

slope of $2x - 3y = 11$ is $: m = \dfrac{2}{3}$

A) slope $= \dfrac{4}{6} = \dfrac{2}{3}$

42. (A)
If f(-x) = f(x), then it is an odd function which is symmetric with respect to the origin. So, the point (-5, 25) is symmetric with (5, -25) in the origin.

43. (D)

△ABC can be an isosceles triangle

44. (A)
Shift 1 unit left: f(x+1), then shift 1 unit down: f(x+1)-1

45. (E)

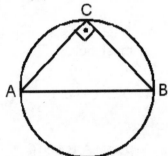

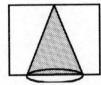
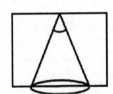
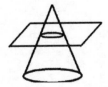

ellipse

46. (D)
If $f(-1) > f(-5)$, then $f(x)$ is an increasing function so $f(-1) \ge f(2)$ cannot be correct.

47. (B)
The center of the circle with an equation $(x+2)^2+(y-1)^2 = 4$ is (-2, 1). If the slope of the diameter of this circle is -1, then the diameter is on the line with the equation:

$y - 1 = -1 \cdot (x - (-2)) \Rightarrow y = -x - 2 + 1 = -x - 1$.

If we substitute the line equation $y = -x - 1$ within the circle equation, we will get the abscissa of the intersection of the line and the circle, namely the abscissa of the endpoints of the diameter with a slope of -1. So,

$(x + 2)^2 + (-x - 1 - 1)^2 - 4 = 0$

$\Rightarrow (x^2 + 4x + 4) + (x^2 + 4x + 4 - 4) = 0$

$\Rightarrow 2x^2 + 8x + 4 = 0$

$\Rightarrow x^2 + 4x + 2 = 0$

$\Delta = 16 - 4 \cdot 1 \cdot 2 = 8$

$x_1 = \dfrac{-4 + \sqrt{8}}{2} = -2 + \sqrt{2} \Rightarrow y_1 = 1 - \sqrt{2}$

$x_2 = \dfrac{-4 - \sqrt{8}}{2} = -2 - \sqrt{2} \Rightarrow y_2 = 1 + \sqrt{2}$

So, the endpoints are $\left(-2 + \sqrt{2}, 1 - \sqrt{2}\right)$ and $\left(-2 - \sqrt{2}, 1 + \sqrt{2}\right)$

48. (D)
A) $(18 + 16 + 14) - (2 + 2,5 + 4,5) = 48 - 9 = 38$

B) greatest increase 2000-2001: $10.5 - 8 = 2.5$

C) $\dfrac{500}{300} = 1\dfrac{2}{3} \Rightarrow 67\%$ increase

D)

$M = \dfrac{2 + 2,5 + 4,5 + 6,5 + 8 + 10,5 + 12,5 + 14 + 16 + 18}{2}$

$= 9.45$

Median $= \dfrac{8 + 1.5}{2} = 9.25$

Mean is not less than the median

49. (D)

$(x-2)^2 + (y-5)^2 = r^2$.

For $(0,0) \Rightarrow (-2)^2 + (-5)^2 = r^2$

$\Rightarrow r^2 = 4 + 25$

$\Rightarrow r^2 = 29$

50. (C)

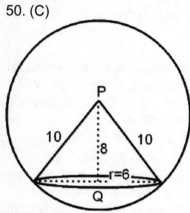

r=6 and Area= $\pi \cdot 6^2 = 36\pi$

Level 1 – Model Test 5 Solutions

1. (E)

$m = \dfrac{10.98}{9} = 1.22 \Rightarrow 6m = 6.1.22 = 7.23$

2. (E)

$\dfrac{x}{3} - \dfrac{5}{5} + \dfrac{x}{5} = \dfrac{x}{5} - \dfrac{9}{3} + \dfrac{x}{3} + 2x$

$\Rightarrow \underbrace{\dfrac{x}{3} - \dfrac{x}{3}}_{0} - 1 = \underbrace{\dfrac{x}{5} - \dfrac{x}{5}}_{0} - 3 + 2x \Rightarrow -1 + 3 = 2x$

$\Rightarrow 2x = 2 \Rightarrow x = 1$

3. (B)

$\dfrac{4}{t^2 + 2t - 8} \cdot \dfrac{t^2 - 4t + 4}{3} \Rightarrow \dfrac{4}{(t+4)(t-2)} \cdot \dfrac{(t-2)^2}{3}$

$\Rightarrow \dfrac{4 \cdot (t-2)}{3 \cdot (t+4)}$

4. (A)

$x - 2y + 1 = 0$ and $y + 3 = 0$ must hold.

$y + 3 = 0 \Rightarrow y = -3$

For $y = -3$, $x - 2 \cdot (-3) + 1 = 0 \Rightarrow x = -7$.

5. (B)

$t \neq -1$ because if $t = -1$, the points A, B, and C will be collinear

6. (A)

$(x^2 - 4x + 4) \cdot (x^2 + 4x + 4) = (x - 2)^2 \cdot (x + 2)^2$

$= [(x-2) \cdot (x+2)]^2 = (x^2 - 4)^2$

7. (D)

For x = 0, $3 \cdot 0 - 4y + 12 = 0 \Rightarrow 4y = 12 \Rightarrow y = 3$

8. (D)

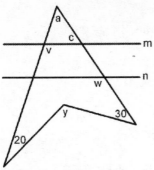

$a + 20° + 30° = 110° \Rightarrow a = 60°$

$v = a + c = 140° \Rightarrow c = 80° \Rightarrow w = 100°$

9. (D)

$$y^2 = \frac{1}{2} \Rightarrow \frac{1}{y^2} = 2 \Rightarrow \left(\frac{1}{y^2}\right)^2 = 2^2 \Rightarrow \frac{1}{y^4} = 4$$

10. (C)

$x - 3y = -B \Rightarrow x = 3y - B$

For $x = 3y - B$,

$2 \cdot (3y - B) + y = A$

$\Rightarrow 6y - 2B + y = A$

$\Rightarrow 7y = A + 2B$

$\Rightarrow y = \dfrac{A + 2B}{7}$

$x = 3y - B \Rightarrow x = 3 \cdot \left(\dfrac{A + 2B}{7}\right) - B = \dfrac{3A - B}{7}$

$\dfrac{x}{y} = \dfrac{\dfrac{3A - B}{7}}{\dfrac{A + 2B}{7}} = \dfrac{3A - B}{A + 2B}$

11. (B)

$\sqrt[3]{a^2} = 4 \Rightarrow a^2 = 4^3 \Rightarrow a = \left(4^3\right)^{\frac{1}{2}} = (2^2)^{\frac{3}{2}} = 8$

12. (A)

$S = \dfrac{2}{5} \cdot C$ and $C = \dfrac{3}{4} \cdot B$

$\left. \begin{array}{l} \dfrac{S}{C} = \dfrac{2}{5} = \dfrac{6}{15} \\ \dfrac{C}{B} = \dfrac{3}{4} = \dfrac{15}{20} \end{array} \right\} \begin{array}{l} S = 6x \\ \Rightarrow C = 15x \\ B = 20x \end{array}$

$S + C + B = 6x + 15x + 20x = 41x = 82$

$\Rightarrow x = 2$

$S - 2 = 6x - 2 = 6 \cdot 2 - 2 = 10$

13. (D)

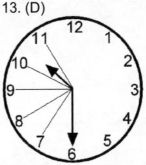

The angle between the hour hand and the minute hand is $4 \cdot 30° + 15° = 135°$.

14. (D)

$a + 1 = \dfrac{3b}{5b} - \dfrac{10}{5b} \Rightarrow a + 1 = \dfrac{3}{5} - \dfrac{2}{b}$

$\dfrac{2}{b} = \dfrac{3}{5} - a - 1 \Rightarrow \dfrac{2}{b} = \dfrac{-5a - 2}{5}$

$b = \dfrac{-10}{5a + 2}$

15. (D)

$f(g(x)) = f(x - 2) = (x - 2 + 1)^2 - 2(x - 2)$

$= (x - 1)^2 - 2x + 4$

$= x^2 - 2x + 1 - 2x + 4$

$= x^2 - 4x + 5$

$f(x) = x^2 + 2x + 1 - 2x = x^2 + 1$

So, $x^2 + 1 - \left(x^2 - 4x + 5\right) = 4x - 4$ must be added

16. (B)

$\left(4^2\right)^4 = 4^8 = \left(2^2\right)^8 = 2^{16} = 2^{x+1}$

$\Rightarrow x + 1 = 16$

$\Rightarrow x = 15$

So, 3 is a factor of 15.

17. (C)

$M - 6 = \dfrac{2}{3} \cdot (S - 6)$ and

$M + 9 = \dfrac{7}{8} \cdot (S + 9)$

$\dfrac{M - 6}{S - 6} = \dfrac{2}{3} \Rightarrow 2S - 12 = 3M - 18 \Rightarrow 2S - 3M = -6$

$\dfrac{M + 9}{S + 9} = \dfrac{7}{8} \Rightarrow 8M + 72 = 7S + 63 \Rightarrow 8M - 7S = -9$

$\left. \begin{array}{l} 2S - 3M = -6 \\ 8M - 7S = -9 \end{array} \right\} \Rightarrow \begin{array}{l} S = 15 \\ M = 12 \end{array}$

18. (E)

$|x - 2| + |2x - 4| - 12 < 0$

$|x - 2| + 2|x - 2| - 12 < 0$

$3|x - 2| < 12$

$|x - 2| < 4$

$-4 < x - 2 < 4$

$-2 < x < 6$

19. (D)

$1994 - 1996 \rightarrow \dfrac{0.2}{7.6} = 0.026 \Rightarrow 2.6\%$

$1996 - 1998 \rightarrow \dfrac{0.1}{7.8} = 0.013 \Rightarrow 1.3\%$

$1998 - 2000 \rightarrow \dfrac{0.3}{7.9} = 0.038 \Rightarrow 3.8\%$

$2000 - 2002 \rightarrow \dfrac{0.4}{8.2} = 0.049 \Rightarrow 4.9\%\ (max)$

$2002 - 2004 \rightarrow \dfrac{0.3}{7.8} = 0.038 \Rightarrow 3.8\%$

20. (E)

L		L		D		D		D
↓		↓		↓		↓		↓
1	·	25	·	10	·	9	·	8

$1 \cdot 25 \cdot 10 \cdot 9 \cdot 8 = 18{,}000$

21. (D)

1mi = 1760 yd; 1yd = 3 ft; 1ft = 12 in and

$\dfrac{2\pi R \cdot 6000 \cdot 60}{12 \cdot 3 \cdot 1760} = v$. Therefore v = 11.36π.

22. (E)

$i^3 = -i$

$(1 + i^3) \cdot (1 - i^3) \Rightarrow$

$1^2 - (i^3)^2 = 1 - (-i)^2 = 1 - i^2 = 1 + 1 = 2$

23. (D)

If ABCD is a square, AC = AB · $\sqrt{2}$

Then he saves 2 · AB − AC = 2 · AB − AB · $\sqrt{2}$

$= AB \cdot (2 - \sqrt{2})$

$\dfrac{AB \cdot (2 - \sqrt{2})}{2 \cdot AB} = \dfrac{(2 - \sqrt{2})}{2} = \dfrac{x}{100} \Rightarrow x \cong 0.2928$

The maximum gain is : 29.3%

24. (A)

Let AE = x and DI = y, then, 3x = 4y

$\Rightarrow$ x = 4k and y = 3k

$A(EFGI) = \dfrac{4k + 6k}{2} \cdot h = 5k \cdot h$

$A(ABCD) = 12k \cdot h$

$\dfrac{A(ABCD)}{A(EFGI)} = \dfrac{12k \cdot h}{5k \cdot h} = \dfrac{12}{5}$

25. (C)

$r_1 = 3k$ and $r_2 = 2k$

$2\pi r_1 \cdot \dfrac{120°}{360°} = 2\pi \cdot 3k \cdot \dfrac{1}{3} = 2\pi \cdot k$

$2\pi \cdot k = 2\pi r_2 \cdot \dfrac{\alpha_2}{360°} \Rightarrow k = 2k \cdot \dfrac{\alpha_2}{360°}$

$\Rightarrow \dfrac{360°}{2} = \alpha_2 \Rightarrow \alpha_2 = 180°$

26. (D)

Let DB = BC = x, then,

$|AC| = 2x$ and $|DC| = x\sqrt{2}$. So,

$\dfrac{AC}{DC} = \dfrac{2x}{x\sqrt{2}} = \dfrac{2\sqrt{2}}{2} = \sqrt{2}$

27. (B)

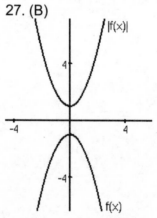

f(x) doesn't intersect x axis so $b^2 - 4ac < 0$ and convex down: a<0

28. (D)

$\dfrac{2.2}{1.8} = \dfrac{3.6}{x} \Rightarrow x = 29.45 \cdot 1024 = 3016.2\,KB$

29. (B)

new coordinates: (4 − (-3), -5 − 2) = (7,-7)

30. (E)

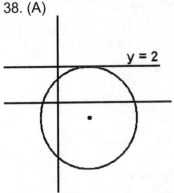

$\alpha < 90°$ Line n can not pass from 1st, 2nd and the 4th quadrants of the xy plane at the same time.

31. (E)
$$160 \cdot \frac{3}{5} + 120 \cdot \frac{2}{5} = 96 + 48 = 144$$

32. (A)
$$b_1 \cdot c_1^2 = b_2 \cdot c_2^2 \Rightarrow 25 \cdot 5^2 = b \cdot 25^2 \Rightarrow b = 1$$

33. (E)
Graph $f(x) = x^4 - x^3 - 2x^2 - 4x - 24$
find zeros as 2 and 3

34. (D)
$$C\overset{\Delta}{B}A \sim D\overset{\Delta}{C}A \Rightarrow \frac{BA}{CA} = \frac{CA}{DA}$$
$$\Rightarrow \frac{x+y}{3x} = \frac{3x}{x} \Rightarrow 9x^2 = x^2 + yx$$
$$\Rightarrow 8x^2 = yx \Rightarrow y = 8x$$

35. (C)
$$\sin^2 \theta - (1 - \cos^2 \theta) = \sin^2 \theta - \sin^2 \theta = 0$$

36. (B)
$$4 = 2 \cdot 1 - k \Rightarrow k = -2$$
$$\Rightarrow y = 2x - (-2) = 2x + 2$$
For $(3, 8) \Rightarrow 8 = 2 \cdot 3 + 2$, that is the point $(3, 8)$ is a point on the line p. So, it can not be on the line q.

37. (D)
To go from point F to point E, first go 3 units in the direction of G to F, then turn right, move for 4 units. By the same procedure, the coordinates of the point A will be (5, -0.5).

Since point B is 6 units to the south of point A, the coordinates of point B will be (5, -6.5).

38. (A)

The radius at the intersection point is perpendicular to the x-axis. So, the tangent is paralel to the x-axis. Since it passes through (1,2), its equation is y=2.

39. (A)
$$\log(x^2 - y^2) = \log[(x - y) \cdot (x + y)]$$
$$= \log(x - y) + \log(x + y)$$

40. (C)
$$B\overset{\Delta}{F}A \sim D\overset{\Delta}{F}C \Rightarrow \frac{DC}{AB} = \frac{1}{3} \Rightarrow DC = 5 \text{ inches}$$
shaded area $= A(ABCD) - A(ABF) - A(CDF)$
$$= \frac{15 + 5}{2} \cdot (6 + 2) - 15 \cdot 6 \cdot \frac{1}{2} - 5 \cdot 2 \cdot \frac{1}{2}$$
$$= 10 \cdot 8 - 45 - 5 = 30$$

41. (B)
Let $m(B\hat{C}O) = x$ and Let $m(A\hat{O}C) = y$, then,
$$5x = 90° \Rightarrow x = 18°$$
$$8x + y = 180° \Rightarrow y = 36°$$

42. (B)
$$x - 1 > 0 \Rightarrow x > 1$$

43. (C)
$$V_{hemisphere} = V_{cone}$$
$$\Rightarrow \left(\frac{4}{3} \cdot \pi r^3\right) \cdot \frac{1}{2} = \pi r^2 \cdot h \cdot \frac{1}{3}$$
$$\Rightarrow h = 2r$$

44. (E)
$$\frac{x - 6}{2} = 4 \Rightarrow x = 14$$

Complete Prep for the SAT Math Subject Tests – Level 1 and Level 2

45. (B)

$1, 2, 4, 8, \ldots$

$S_n = 1 + 2 + 4 + 8 + \ldots + 2^{n-1}$

$= a_1 \cdot \dfrac{1-r^n}{1-r} = 1 \cdot \dfrac{1-2^n}{1-2} = \dfrac{1-2^n}{-1} = 2^n - 1$

46. (E)

$f^{-1}(x) = f(x) \Rightarrow f(f(x)) = f(f^{-1}(x)) = x$

$f(f(f(x))) = f(x) = -x + 1$

47. (A)

$P(x) = x^2 + 2x - 3 = (x-1) \cdot (x+3)$

So, the next common factor other

than $(x-1)$ is : $(x+3)$

Since $(x+3)$ is a common factor of $Q(x)$,

$Q(-3)$ must be zero.

Then, $(-3)^3 + (-3)^2 - 9(-3) + k = 0 \Rightarrow k = -9$

48. (C)

$\pi \cdot 26^2 - \pi \cdot 24^2 = \pi \cdot (26^2 - 24^2) \cong 314$

49. (D)

$\dfrac{\text{number of bilingual men in 1980}}{\text{total population in 1980}}$

$= \dfrac{25,000 - 10,000}{37,500} = \dfrac{15,000}{37,500} = 0.4 \to 40\%$

50. (D)

In the year when the bilingual population was around 18,000 (in 1970); the population that consisted of bilingual men was approximately 10,000 and the total population was 30,000. So, not one fourth but one third of all population consisted of bilingual men.

Level 2 – Model Test 1 Solutions

1. (C)

$x - 3 = y \Rightarrow x - y = 3$ and $y - x = -3$

$|x - y + |y - x|| = |3 + |-3|| = |3 + 3| = 6$

2. (C)

let x be the number.

Than $x^2 + 2x + 1 = 441$

$(x+1)^2 = 21^2 \Rightarrow x + 1 = 21 \Rightarrow x = 20$

3. (A)

I. for n>0,(n+3)! Is always even.

For example if $n=1 \Rightarrow n!=24$ even

if $n=2 \Rightarrow 5!=120$ even etc.

II. 2^n is always even

3n is even when n is even

3n is odd when n is odd

So, $2^n + 3n$ is not always even

III. i) if n is even, than, n+1 is odd

$n^{n+1} + (n+1)^n \to$ even+odd=odd

ii) if n is odd, then, n+1 is even.

$n^{n+1} + (n+1)^n \to$ odd+even=odd

4. (B)

i) $|n+4| < 2 \Rightarrow -2 < n+4 < 2 \Rightarrow -6 < n < -2$

ii) $|n-1| \le 5 \Rightarrow -5 \le n-1 \le 5 \Rightarrow -4 \le n \le 6$

for -6<n<-2 and $-4 \le n \le 6$, we get $-4 \le n < -2$,

So n can be -4 or -3.

5. (D)

for the line with equation 2x-3y+5=0, the slope is:2/3

for the line with equation 2y=-3+6,0, the slope is:-3/2. So the two lines are perpendicular.

6. (B)

If $2 \cdot (x - \sqrt{3})^2 \cdot (x + \sqrt{2}) \cdot (x^2 - 2) = 0$ then,

$(x - \sqrt{3})^2 = 0$ or $x + \sqrt{2} = 0$ or $x^2 - 2 = 0$

$(x - \sqrt{3}) \cdot (x - \sqrt{3}) = 0 \Rightarrow x_1 = x_2 = \sqrt{3}$

or $x = -\sqrt{2}$ or $x^2 = 2 \Rightarrow x = \mp\sqrt{2}$

The roots are, $\sqrt{3}, \sqrt{3}, -\sqrt{2}, -\sqrt{2}, \sqrt{2}$

The sum of the roots is

$\sqrt{3} + \sqrt{3} - \sqrt{2} - \sqrt{2} + \sqrt{2} = 2\sqrt{3} - \sqrt{2} \cong 2.05$

7. (A)

$$f\left(3, \frac{3\pi}{4}\right) = 3 \cdot \sin\left(-\frac{3\pi}{4}\right) = 3 \cdot \sin\left(\frac{5\pi}{4}\right)$$

$$= 3 \cdot \left(-\frac{1}{\sqrt{2}}\right) = \frac{-3}{\sqrt{2}} \cong -2.12$$

8. (D)

$f(x) = e^x \Rightarrow f^{-1}(x) = \ln x$ and

$f^{-1}(a \cdot b) = \ln(a \cdot b) = \ln a + \ln b$

9. (C)

D: event that Damla hits the dartboard

F: event that Fuat hits the dartboard

So, $P(D) = \frac{4}{7} \Rightarrow P(D') = 1 - \frac{4}{7} = \frac{3}{7}$ and

$P(F') = \frac{1}{3} \Rightarrow P(F) = 1 - \frac{1}{3} = \frac{2}{3}$.

The probability that Damla misses the dartboard and Fuat hits it is:

$P(D' \cap F) = P(D') \cdot P(F) = \frac{3}{7} \cdot \frac{2}{3} = \frac{2}{7}$

10. (A)

$\lim$

$x \to \infty$

$$\lim_{x \to \infty} \frac{6x^2 - 3x - 5}{4x^3 + 2x - 5} = \lim_{x \to \infty} \frac{x^3 \cdot \left(\frac{6}{x} - \frac{3}{x^2} - \frac{5}{x^3}\right)}{x^3 \cdot \left(4 + \frac{2}{x^2} - \frac{5}{x^3}\right)}$$

$$= \frac{0 - 0 - 0}{4 + 0 - 0} = 0$$

11. (C)

The number of terms in the expansion of a binomial $(a + b)^n$ is n+1 provided that n is a positive integer.

12. (D)

Let the initial weight of the mixture be 100 quarts. So, when one fifth of the micture is taken, $80 \cdot \frac{40}{100} = 32$ quarts of the mixture will be alcohol, 80 – 32=48 quarts of the mixture will be water and the amount of pure water which is added to the mixture is

$\frac{1}{5} \cdot 100 = 20$ quarts. So,

$$\frac{\text{total pure water}}{\text{total mixture}} = \frac{48 + 20}{100} = \frac{68}{100}.$$

Namely, 68% of the final mixture is pure water.

13. (D)

$5^x = 7 \Rightarrow x = \log_5 7$

$7^x = 7^{\log_5 7} \cong 10.51$

14. (C)

$$\sqrt{\left(\sqrt{2}\right)^2 + \left(-\sqrt{3}\right)^2} = \sqrt{2 + 3} = \sqrt{5} \cong 2.24$$

15. (C)

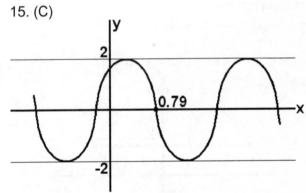

The graph of $y = 2 \cdot \sin\left[3\left(x + \frac{3\pi}{4}\right)\right]$ is given above. So, the least positive zero is approximately 0.79

16. (B)

If x-k is a factor, then, $x^2 - 3x + k$ must be zero for x = k.

$k^2 - 3k + k = 0$

$k^2 - 2k = 0 \Rightarrow k(k - 2) = 0$ So, $k_1 = 0$ or $k_2 = 2$

17. (C)

i) $m(\hat{B}) = 180° - (80° + 60°) = 40°$

ii) $\frac{AC}{\sin 40°} = \frac{8.1}{\sin 60°} \Rightarrow AC \cong 6.01$

18. (D)

$\sqrt[3]{x^3 - 4} = 4 \Rightarrow x^3 - 4 = 64 \Rightarrow x^3 = 68$

$\Rightarrow x = \sqrt[3]{68} \cong 4.081$

19.(A)

$|AD| = \dfrac{a}{2} \Rightarrow A(A\overset{\Delta}{C}D) = a \cdot \dfrac{a}{2} \cdot \dfrac{1}{2} = \dfrac{a^2}{4}$

$V(ABCD) = |BD| \cdot A(A\overset{\Delta}{C}D) \cdot \dfrac{1}{3} = a \cdot \dfrac{a^2}{4} \cdot \dfrac{1}{3} = \dfrac{a^3}{12}$

20. (A)

If the solution set of f(x)=0 is {-2, 3}, then, f(x)=a·(x+2)·(x-3) for some $a \in R$.

$f(x^2 - 1) = a \cdot (x^2 - 1 + 2)(x^2 - 1 - 3)$

$\qquad = a(x^2 + 1)(x^2 - 4) = 0$

i) $x^2 + 1 = 0$ has no real solution

ii) $x^2 - 4 = 0$ has $x_1 = 2$ and $x_2 = -2$ as real solutions.

21. (D)

If x(y-4)<0, then

i)x<0 and y-4>0$\Rightarrow$y>4 or

ii)x>0 and y-4<0$\Rightarrow$y<4

The graph of the solution set will be

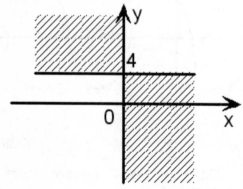

22. (E)

$PC = \dfrac{1}{2} \cdot PQ = \dfrac{1}{2} \cdot 20 = 10$

Let $OC = OA = OB = r = 10 \cdot \tan 20° \cong 3.64$

$m(O\hat{P}C) = m(O\hat{Q}P) = 20° \Rightarrow m(P\hat{O}Q) = 140°$

$AB^2 = r^2 + r^2 - 2 \cdot r \cdot r \cdot \cos 140°$

$AB^2 = 26.4948 + 20.2961 = 46.79 \Rightarrow AB = 6.84$

23. (D)

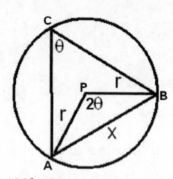

$m(P\hat{A}B) = \dfrac{180° - 2\theta}{2} = 90° - \theta$

$\dfrac{x}{\sin 2\theta} = \dfrac{r}{\sin(90° - \theta)}$

$\Rightarrow x = \dfrac{r \cdot \sin 2\theta}{\cos \theta} = \dfrac{r \cdot 2 \cdot \sin \theta \cdot \cos \theta}{\cos \theta}$

$\Rightarrow \sin \theta = \dfrac{x}{2r} \Rightarrow \theta = \arcsin\left(\dfrac{x}{2r}\right)$

24. (B)

$1 = \dfrac{4ac - b^2}{4a}$ where b is the coefficient of x and c is the constant term 10.

So, $1 = \dfrac{4a \cdot 10 - 12^2}{4a} \Rightarrow 40a - 4a = 144 \Rightarrow a = 4$

25. (B)

Since $-\sqrt{a^2 + b^2} \le a \cdot \sin x \mp b \cdot \cos x \le \sqrt{a^2 + b^2}$

for k>50, we'll get

$-\underbrace{\sqrt{3^2 + 4^2}}_{5} + 2 \le f(x) \le \underbrace{\sqrt{3^2 + 4^2}}_{5} + 2$

$\Rightarrow -3 \le f(x) \le 7$

26. (E)

$f(x) = \dfrac{1}{1 + \dfrac{1}{x - 1}} = \dfrac{x - 1}{x}$

i) $x - 1 \ne 0 \Rightarrow x \ne 1$ and ii) $x \ne 0$

27. (D)

$[3 \cdot (\cos 45° + i \cdot \sin 45°)]^2$

$= 9 \cdot [\cos(2 \cdot 45°) + i \cdot \sin(2 \cdot 45°)]$

$= 9 \cdot (\cos 90° + i \cdot \sin 90°)$

$= 9 \cdot (0 + i \cdot 1) = 9i$

28. (B)
$\cos(\pi + \theta) = -\cos\theta = -0.25$

29. (A)
$r = \sqrt{\left(\dfrac{-4}{2}\right)^2 + \left(\dfrac{6}{2}\right)^2 + \left(\dfrac{-2}{2}\right)^2 - (-11)}$

$\quad = \sqrt{4 + 9 + 1 + 11} = 5$

30. (C)
$\dfrac{1}{n!} - \dfrac{1}{(n+1)!} = \dfrac{(n+1)!-n!}{n!\cdot(n+1)!} = \dfrac{(n+1)\cdot n!-n!}{n!\cdot(n+1)!}$

$\qquad\qquad = \dfrac{n!(n+1-1)}{n!\cdot(n+1)!} = \dfrac{n}{(n+1)!}$

31. (B)

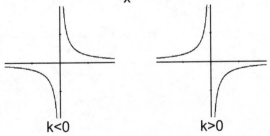

$r = 4$ and $h = 6$, $V = \dfrac{1}{3}\pi r^2 \cdot h = \dfrac{1}{3}\cdot\pi\cdot 4^2\cdot 6 = 32\pi$

32. (B)

For n=1 $\Rightarrow \displaystyle\sum_{k=1}^{1}(x+k) = x+1$ is odd when x is even, and it is even when x is odd. For n=2 $\Rightarrow$ $\displaystyle\sum_{k=1}^{2}(x+k) = (x+1)+(x+2) = 2x+3$ is always odd.
So, least positive n is 2.

33. (C)
y varies inversely as –x means $y\cdot(-x) = k$ for some $k \in R$. So, $y = \dfrac{-k}{x}$ has the graph of

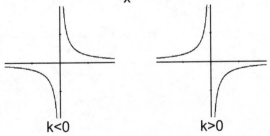

$k<0$ $\qquad\qquad$ $k>0$

34. (E)
$\left.\begin{array}{l} 2x - 7 + \dfrac{x}{3} = 2\cdot(x-3) \\ \Rightarrow 6x - 21 + x = 6x - 18 \\ \Rightarrow x = 3 \end{array}\right\}$ $\begin{array}{l} \dfrac{x}{3} = 1 \\ \Rightarrow x - 3 = 0 \\ 2x - 7 = -1 \end{array}$

So, the fourth term is -2

35. (C)
$f(x) = ax + b$
$f(-3) = -3a + b = 0 \Rightarrow b = 3a$
$f(-1) = -a + b = 6 \Rightarrow -a + 3a = 6$
$2a = 6 \Rightarrow a = 3$ and $b = 9$
So, $f(x) = 3x + 9$ and $f(x-1) = 3\cdot(x-1) + 9 = 3.6$
$\qquad\qquad \Rightarrow x - 1 + 3 = 1.2$
$\qquad\qquad \Rightarrow x = -0.8$

36. (C)
$[(x-1)+iy]\cdot[(x-1)-iy] = 4$
$\Rightarrow (x-1)^2 - i^2 y^2 = 4$
$\Rightarrow (x-1)^2 + y^2 = 4$

37. (E)
$\left.\begin{array}{l} f(2) = a^{2+b} = 250 \\ f(-1) = a^{-1+b} = 2 \end{array}\right\}$
$\left.\dfrac{f(2)}{f(-1)} = a^{2+b-(-1+b)} = a^3 = 125 = 5^3 \Rightarrow a = 5\right\}$
$5^{2+b} = 250$
$\Rightarrow \log_5 250 = 2 + b$
$\Rightarrow b = -2 + \log_5 250 \cong 1.43$

38. (A)
$x_1 < x_2 \Rightarrow f(x_1) < f(x_2)$ means $f(x)$ is an increasing function. Since the coefficient of x^2 is negative the increasing portion of the function in the part left to $-\dfrac{b}{2a}$. So,
$x_k < -\dfrac{3}{2\cdot(-1)} \Rightarrow x_k < \dfrac{3}{2}$

39. (B)

The vertical asymptotes of $y = \dfrac{2x}{9 - x^2}$ are the zeros of the denominator $9 - x^2$. So, $9 - x^2 = 0 \Rightarrow (3 - x)(3 + x) = 0 \Rightarrow x_1 = -3$ and $x_2 = 3$

40. (C)

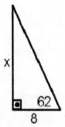

$\text{Area} = \dfrac{1}{2} \cdot 8 \cdot x = \dfrac{1}{2} \cdot 8 \cdot (8 \cdot \tan 62°) \cong 60.18$

41. (C)

$\left. \begin{aligned} f(-1.8) &= \left| -1.8 - 1 \right| + \left[-1.8 + 1 \right] \\ &= \left| -2.8 \right| + \left[-0.8 \right] = 2.8 + (-1) = 1.8 \\ f(1.8) &= \left| 1.8 - 1 \right| + \left[1.8 + 1 \right] \\ &= \left| 0.8 \right| + \left[2.8 \right] = 0.8 + 2 = 2.8 \end{aligned} \right\}$

$f(-1.8) + f(1.8) = 4.6$

42. (C)

$\dfrac{26 \cdot 25^5}{26^6} = \dfrac{25^5}{26^5} = \left(\dfrac{25}{26} \right)^5$

43. (B)

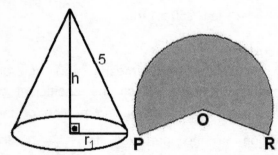

$2\pi \cdot r_1 = \dfrac{6\pi}{5} \Rightarrow r_1 = \dfrac{3}{5}$ (r_1 is the radius of the cone). The radius of the shaded circle is the slant height of the cone;

$h = \sqrt{5^2 - \left(\dfrac{3}{5} \right)^2} \cong 4.96$.

44. (D)

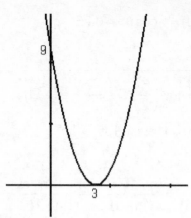

$x = 2t + 3 \Rightarrow 2t = x - 3$
$y = 4t^2 = (2t)^2 = (x - 3)^2$

45. (D)

$4 = \dfrac{\left| 3x + 4 \cdot x\sqrt{2} - 5 \right|}{\sqrt{3^2 + 4^2}} \Rightarrow 20 = \left| 3x + 4\sqrt{2}x - 5 \right|$

i) $x(3 + 4\sqrt{2}) = 25 \Rightarrow x_1 = \dfrac{25}{3 + 4\sqrt{2}} \cong 2.89$

ii) $x(3 + 4\sqrt{2}) = -15 \Rightarrow x_2 = \dfrac{-15}{3 + 4\sqrt{2}} \cong -1.73$

46. (D)

$\displaystyle \lim_{x \to 6} \dfrac{x^2 - 36}{x - 6} = \lim_{x \to 6} \dfrac{(x - 6)(x + 6)}{x - 6} = 6 + 6 = 12$

47. (C)

The function must be an even function. So, the coefficient of the x must be zero, namely, there must not exist any odd powered term.

48. (B)

$\dfrac{1}{i} + \dfrac{i}{1 + i} = \dfrac{1 + i + i^2}{i + i^2} = \dfrac{1 + i - 1}{i - 1} = \dfrac{i}{i - 1}$

$= \dfrac{i \cdot (i + 1)}{(i - 1) \cdot (i + 1)} = \dfrac{i^2 + i}{-1 - 1} = \dfrac{1 - i}{2}$

49. (A)

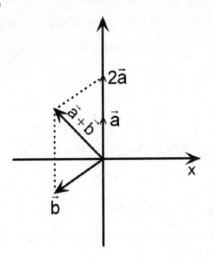

50. (A)

I. $f(x) \cdot g(x) = 2x \cdot \sin x$ is an even function.

II. $f(-x) + g(-x) = 2(-x) + \sin(-x)$
$= -(2x + \sin x) = -[f(x) + g(x)]$
it's an odd function.

III. $(f \circ g)(-x) = f(g(-x)) = \sin(-2x)$
$= -\sin 2x = -(f \circ g)(x)$; it's an odd function.

Level 2 – Model Test 2 Solutions

1. (C)
$$g(-1.2) = \frac{1}{\sqrt[5]{(-1.2)^3 - 6}} = -0.664$$

2. (B)
$$\frac{1}{a} \cdot \left(\frac{b}{a} + \frac{a}{c}\right) = \frac{1}{a} \cdot \frac{b}{a} + \frac{1}{a} \cdot \frac{a}{c} = \frac{b}{a^2} + \frac{1}{c}$$

3. (E)

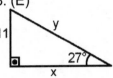

$$\tan 27° = \frac{11}{x} \Rightarrow x = \frac{11}{\tan 27°} = 21.56$$
$$\sin 27° = \frac{11}{y} \Rightarrow y = \frac{11}{\sin 27°} = 24.23$$
Perimeter=21.56+24.23+11=56,82

4. (C)
$$5x + 1 = (2.7)^3 \Rightarrow x = \frac{(2.7)^3 - 1}{5} \cong 3.74$$

5. (C)
From $-\dfrac{\pi}{2}$ to 0, period is : $\dfrac{\pi}{2}$

6. (B)
$P(x) = x^3 - 4x^2 + \dfrac{3a}{2}x + 10$
$P(5) = 0$
$$5^3 - 4.5^2 + \frac{3a}{2} \cdot 5 + 10 = 0 \Rightarrow a = \frac{-14}{3}$$

7. (D)

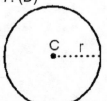

8. (C)

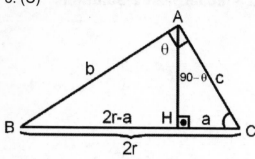

From the $\triangle ABC$: $\sin\theta = \dfrac{b}{2r}$

From the $\triangle AHB$: $\sin\theta = \dfrac{2r-a}{b}$

9. (A)

$\dfrac{3}{x} \cdot \dfrac{5}{7} = x \Rightarrow 15 = 7x^2 \Rightarrow x^2 = \dfrac{15}{7} \Rightarrow x = \mp 1.46$

10. (B)

$\csc\theta \cdot \cos\theta = -3$

$\Rightarrow \dfrac{1}{\sin\theta} \cdot \cos\theta = -3$

$\Rightarrow \cot\theta = -3 \Rightarrow \tan\theta = \dfrac{1}{-3}$

11. (D)

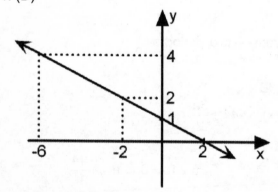

For x=-6, y=-0.5·(-6)+1=4
For x=-2, y=-0.5·(-2)+1=2

$\left(\dfrac{4+2}{2}\right) \cdot \left[-2-(-6)\right] = 3 \cdot 4 = 12$

12. (C)

$f(4) = \dfrac{4\cdot 4 - 1}{4+1} = \dfrac{15}{5} = 3$

$\Rightarrow g(f(4)) = g(3) = \sqrt[3]{3^2 - 1} = \sqrt[3]{8} = 2$

13. (B)

If x varies inversely as y, then, the graph of

$x \cdot y = k \Rightarrow y = \dfrac{k}{x}$ looks like B if k is negative.

14. (E)

$\dfrac{3}{x} - \dfrac{7}{2x+1} - \dfrac{2x}{4x^2 - 1} = 0$

Graph the function and get the zero as 1.

15. (C)

The slope of the line Bx = Ay + C is: $\dfrac{B}{A}$

Since the lines are perpendicular, the product of the slopes is: - 1

$\dfrac{B}{A} \cdot m = -1 \Rightarrow m = -\dfrac{A}{B}$

16. (D)

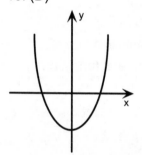

$y = |f(x)|$ means reflecting the portion of the graph that is below the x-axis with respect to the x-axis. So, we get the graph below.

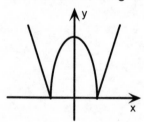

17. (D)
If f(x) = 3 so is f(g(x)).

If $f(x) = \dfrac{x-b}{a}$ then $f(g(x)) = \dfrac{ax+b-b}{a} = x$.

So f(x) cannot equal I and III.

18. (B)
Let $a_1, ..., a_7$ be the 7 numbers.

$\dfrac{a_1 + ... + a_7}{7} = 52 \Rightarrow a_1 + ... + a_7 = 7 \cdot 52 = 364$

Let a_8 be the new number.

$\dfrac{a_1 + ... + a_7 + a_8}{8} = 48 \Rightarrow a_1 + ... + a_8 = 8 \cdot 48 = 384$

$a_8 = 384 - 364 = 20$

19. (E)
Both equations can be combined to give the equation $3x - x^2 + 7 = 0$; what we do is to graph $y = 3x - x^2 + 7$ then, find the x intercept that is 4.54.

20. (C)

We grapy $y = \dfrac{-1}{120} \cdot x$ and $y = \cos x$ in the radian mode and we see that the curves intersect at two points only. Please note that if you have to sketch a non – trigonometric function and a trigonometric on the same set of axes then you must be in the radian mode.

21. (B)

$\dfrac{n \cdot (n-1)!}{(n-1)!} = \dfrac{2 \cdot (n-1) \cdot (n-2)!}{(n-2)!} \Rightarrow n = 2n - 2 \Rightarrow n = 2$

22. (B)
{2, 3, 5, 7, 11, 13}

Since the sample space has 6^4 elements,

$1 - \left(\dfrac{5}{6}\right)^4 = 0.52$

23. (A)

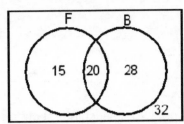

$s(F \cup B) = 95 - 32 = 63$

$s(F \cup B) = s(F) + s(B) - s(F \cap B)$

$63 = 35 + 48 - s(F \cap B)$

$\Rightarrow s(F \cap B) = 20$

$s(F \setminus B) = s(F) - s(F \cap B) = 35 - 20 = 15$

$\dfrac{15}{95} = 0.1578 \approx 16\%$

24. (C)

$a_n = a_1 \cdot r^{n-1}$

$a_2 = 16, \ a_5 = 6{,}75, \ a_6 = ?$

$\dfrac{a_5}{a_2} = \dfrac{a_1 \cdot r^{5-1}}{a_1 \cdot r^{2-1}} = \dfrac{6.75}{16} \Rightarrow r^3 = \dfrac{6.75}{16} \Rightarrow r = 0.75$

$16 = a_1 \cdot 0.75 \Rightarrow a_1 = 21.33$

$a_6 = 21.33 \cdot (0.75)^{6-1} = 5.06$

25. (A)

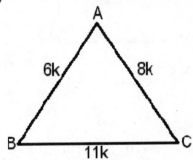

$(11k)^2 = (6k)^2 + (8k)^2 - 2 \cdot 6k \cdot 8k \cdot \cos \hat{A}$

$\cos \hat{A} = -0.51 \Rightarrow m(\hat{A}) = 102.64°$

26. (E)

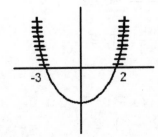

$x^2 + x - 6 \geq 0 \Rightarrow x \geq 2 \ \text{ or } \ x \leq -3$

27. (C)

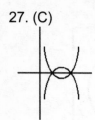

In order to get two distinct intersection points, $\Delta = b^2 - 4ac$ for the function $f(x) = ax^2 + bx + c$ must be greater than zero. Thus:

$b^2 - 4ac > 0 \Rightarrow b^2 > 4ac$.

28. (B)

$f(x) = 2 - \dfrac{1}{x-1} = \dfrac{2x-3}{x-1}$

Domain : $\Re - \{1\}$

Range : $\Re - \{2\}$

Please note that f(x) never equals 2 since the limit as x becomes infinetly large is 2.

29. (A)

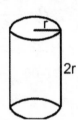

$\pi r^2 \cdot 2r = 2\pi r^3 = 12 \Rightarrow \pi r^3 = 6 \Rightarrow r^3 = \dfrac{6}{\pi}$

$\pi \cdot r^2 = \pi \cdot \left(\dfrac{6}{\pi}\right)^{2/3} = 4.84$

30. (E)

$tx + t = 2x + 2t \Rightarrow x \cdot (t-2) = 2t - t$

$\Rightarrow x = \dfrac{t}{t-2}$

$\Rightarrow t - 2 \neq 0 \Rightarrow t \neq 2$

For $t = 0$, $\dfrac{0 \cdot x + 0}{x + 0} = 0 \neq 2$

For $t = 1$, $\dfrac{1 \cdot x + 1}{x + 1} = 1 \neq 2$

31. (A)

$x = t - 1 \Rightarrow t = x + 1$

$y = 2t + 2 = 2(x+1) + 2$

For $y = 0 \Rightarrow 0 = 2 \cdot (x+1) + 2 \Rightarrow 2x = -4 \Rightarrow x = -2$

32. (C)

$1972 = 1200 \cdot (1.18)^{t/4} \Rightarrow \dfrac{1972}{1200} = (1.18)^{t/4}$

$\Rightarrow 1.64 = (1.18)^{t/4} \Rightarrow \dfrac{\log(1.64)}{\log(1.18)} = \dfrac{t}{4}$

$\Rightarrow t = 12$

11:00 AM – 8:00 =3 hours = 12 quarter hours. Since t = 12, t means the number of quarter hours passed.

33. (C)

The equation of the elipse with center at (a,b) and is tangent to both axes is: $\dfrac{(x-a)^2}{a^2} + \dfrac{(y-b)^2}{b^2} = 1$. So, the equation of the elipse with center at (-5,-3) tangent to both axes is: $\dfrac{(x+5)^2}{25} + \dfrac{(y+3)^2}{9} = 1$

34. (B)

$3^y - 5 = x \Rightarrow x + 5 = 3^y \Rightarrow f^{-1}(x) = y = \log_3(x+5)$

35. (D)

$x_2 = x_1 \cdot (x_1 + 1) = 1 \cdot 2 = 2$

$x_3 = x_2 \cdot (x_2 + 1) = 2 \cdot 3 = 6$

$x_4 = x_3 \cdot (x_3 + 1) = 6 \cdot 7 = 42$

$x_5 = x_4 \cdot (x_4 + 1) = 42 \cdot 43 = 1806$

36. (B)

$\tan\theta = \dfrac{3}{x} \Rightarrow x = \dfrac{3}{\tan\theta} = 3\cot\theta$

$\text{Area} = \dfrac{1}{2} \cdot |ST| \cdot |AT| = \dfrac{1}{2} \cdot 3 \cdot 3\cot\theta = \dfrac{9}{2} \cdot \cot\theta$

37. (A)

(a+bi)(c+di)=ac+adi+bci+bdi^2

=ac-bd+(ad+bc)i =1+0i, then,

ac-bd=0 and ad+bc=1

38. (B)

Let P(A): probability of drawing black card, P(B): probability of drawing ace, and $P(A \cap B)$: probability of drawing black and ace. Then,

$P(B \cup A) = P(A) + P(B) - P(A \cap B)$

$= \dfrac{26}{52} + \dfrac{4}{52} - \dfrac{2}{52} = \dfrac{7}{13}$

39. (A)

$2^{3n} = 2^{n^2-n-5} \Rightarrow 3n = n^2 - n - 5$

$\Rightarrow n^2 - 4n - 5 = 0 \Rightarrow (n-5)\cdot(n+1) = 0$

So, $n = 5$ or $n = -1$

40. (A)

$4\vec{u} = (8,12)$. So, $4\vec{u} - \vec{v} = (8,12) - (-4,5) = (12,7)$

41. (B)

$\cos^{-1}(\sin\theta) = \dfrac{\pi}{4} \Rightarrow \cos\left(\dfrac{\pi}{4}\right) = \sin\theta$

$\Rightarrow \sin\left(\dfrac{\pi}{2} - \dfrac{\pi}{4}\right) = \sin\theta \Rightarrow \theta = \dfrac{\pi}{4}$

42. (D)

$\dfrac{x-2}{x-4} = \dfrac{2x-1}{x-2} \Rightarrow (x-2)^2 = (x-4)\cdot(2x-1)$

$\Rightarrow x^2 - 4x + 4 = 2x^2 - x - 8x + 4$

$\Rightarrow x^2 - 5x = 0$

$\Rightarrow x(x-5) = 0$

$x = 0$ or $x = 5$

For $x = 0$, the sequence starts with the terms

$-4, -2, -1$

43. (E)

A)

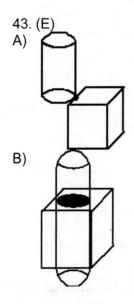

B)

C)

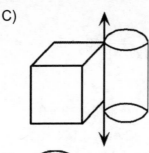

D)

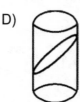

44. (E)

$\lim\limits_{x\to\infty} \dfrac{1}{x} = 0$

$\lim\limits_{x\to\infty} \dfrac{x^2 \cdot \left(3 - \dfrac{2}{x} + \dfrac{1}{x^2}\right)}{x \cdot \left(7 - \dfrac{4}{x}\right)} = \dfrac{x \cdot (3 - 0 + 0)}{(7 - 0)} = \infty \cdot \dfrac{3}{7} = \infty$

45. (B)

$\sqrt[5]{2x^3 - 1} = 2 \Rightarrow 2x^3 - 1 = 2^5 \Rightarrow 2x^3 = 33$

$\Rightarrow x = \left(\dfrac{33}{2}\right)^{\frac{1}{3}} = 2.55$

46. (C)

$\underline{8\cdot 8\cdot 8\cdot 8\cdot 8\cdot 8\cdot 8\cdot 8\cdot 8\cdot 8} = 8^{10}$

47. (E)

$\sin^2\theta + \cos^2\theta = 1 \Rightarrow \cos^2\theta = 1 - \sin^2\theta$

$1 - \sin^2\theta + 3\sin\theta - 3 = 0$

$\sin^2\theta - 3\sin\theta + 2 = 0 \Rightarrow (\sin\theta - 2)\cdot(\sin\theta - 1) = 0$

i) $\sin\theta - 2 = 0 \Rightarrow \sin\theta = 2$, no solution

ii) $\sin\theta - 1 = 0 \Rightarrow \sin\theta = 1 \Rightarrow \theta = \dfrac{\pi}{2}$

48. (A)

$q \Rightarrow p$ is the converse of the statement $p \Rightarrow q$.
Let p: "a triangle is equilateral" and q: "it is equiangular". Then, $q \Rightarrow p$ will be as "If a triangle is equiangular, then it is equilateral"

49. (D)

$$\frac{-2}{x^2-5x+4} > 0 \Rightarrow \frac{2}{(x-1)(x-4)} < 0 \Rightarrow 1 < x < 4$$

50. (E)

$$16x^2 - 96x + 144 - 144 - 9y^2 + 18y - 9 = 0$$

$$\Rightarrow 16(x^2 - 6x + 9) - 9(y^2 - 2y + 1) = 144$$

$$\Rightarrow \frac{(x-3)^2}{9} - \frac{(y-1)^2}{16} = 144$$

So, the center has the coordinates $(3, 1)$

Level 2 – Model Test 3 Solutions

1. (D)

$$\frac{5}{\sqrt[3]{x^2-1}} = 6 \Rightarrow \frac{5}{6} = \sqrt[3]{x^2-1} \Rightarrow x^2 - 1 = \left(\frac{5}{6}\right)^3$$

$$\Rightarrow x = \sqrt{\left(\frac{5}{6}\right)^3 + 1} = 1.26$$

2. (E)

$$\frac{11!}{10!+9!} = \frac{11\cdot10\cdot9!}{10\cdot9!+9!} = \frac{11\cdot10\cdot9!}{9!\cdot(10+1)} = \frac{110}{11} = 10$$

3. (C)

$$\left. \begin{array}{l} f(1,4,3) = \dfrac{1+4+3}{1\cdot4\cdot3} = \dfrac{8}{12} \\[2mm] f(1,3,4) = \dfrac{1+3+4}{1\cdot3\cdot4} = \dfrac{8}{12} \end{array} \right\} \Rightarrow f(1,4,3) = f(1,3,4)$$

4. (A)

$$\sin\theta = \frac{BC}{AB} = \frac{12}{13} \Rightarrow BC = 12k \text{ and } AB = 13k.$$

So, $AC = 5k$. Then, $\tan\alpha = \dfrac{AC}{BC} = \dfrac{5k}{12k} = \dfrac{5}{12}$

5. (C)

$$f(f(3)) = f\left(\frac{1}{\sqrt{3+1}}\right) = f\left(\frac{1}{\sqrt{4}}\right) = f\left(\frac{1}{2}\right) =$$

$$\frac{1}{\sqrt{\dfrac{1}{2}+1}} = 0.82$$

6. (B)

$$x + 4 = 0 \Rightarrow x = -4$$
$$y - 3 = 0 \Rightarrow y = 3$$
$$x + y = -4 + 3 = -1$$

7. (D)

$$\ell : y = -\frac{2}{3}x + \frac{5}{7} \Rightarrow \text{slope} = \frac{-2}{3}$$

A line perpendicular to line ℓ has a slope that equals $\dfrac{-1}{\dfrac{-2}{3}} = \dfrac{3}{2}$. So, the answer is (D).

8. (D)

$$\frac{1}{1+\dfrac{1}{1+x}} = \frac{1}{\dfrac{x+1+1}{x+1}} = \frac{x+1}{x+2}$$

9. (D)
The graph should open downwards so a<0 and the graph should not intersect the x-axis more than once so b²-4ac ≤ 0.

10. (E)

$$\cot^2\theta + 1 = 5 \Rightarrow \frac{\cos^2\theta}{\sin^2\theta} + \frac{\sin^2\theta}{\sin^2\theta} = 5$$

$$\Rightarrow \frac{\cos^2\theta + \sin^2\theta}{\sin^2\theta} = \frac{1}{\sin^2\theta} = \csc^2\theta = 5$$

11. (D)

$$\frac{\dfrac{1}{a^2} - \dfrac{1}{b^2}}{\dfrac{1}{a} + \dfrac{1}{b}} = \frac{\left(\dfrac{1}{a} - \dfrac{1}{b}\right)\left(\dfrac{1}{a} + \dfrac{1}{b}\right)}{\dfrac{1}{a} + \dfrac{1}{b}} = \frac{1}{a} - \frac{1}{b} = \frac{b-a}{a \cdot b}$$

12. (C)

$$\text{Probability} = \frac{\dbinom{7}{2} \cdot \dbinom{5}{1}}{\dbinom{12}{3}} = \frac{21 \cdot 5}{220} = 0.477$$

13. (B)
x⁴-1=(x²-1)(x²+1)=(x-1)(x+1)(x-i)(x+i)
Product on the zeros is 1·(-1)·i·(-i)=-1·(-i²)
=-1·1=-1

14. (A)

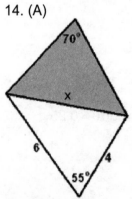

By cosine rule,
$$x^2 = 6^2 + 4^2 - 2 \cdot 6 \cdot 4 \cdot \cos 55° \Rightarrow x = 4.95$$
by sine rule,
$$\frac{x}{\sin 70°} = 2R \Rightarrow \frac{4.95}{\sin 70°} = 2R \Rightarrow R = 2.63$$

15. (D)
24·$20+24·$30+x·$40=·$1600 ⇒ x=10
Number of hours is 24+24+10=58

16. (A)

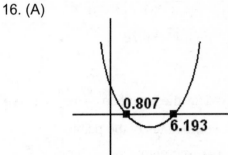

Graph the function f(x) = x² – 7x + 5. The zeros are 0.807 and 6.193. The least one is: 0.807

17. (D)
$$\log_6(\log_4(\log_2 x)) = 0$$
$$\Rightarrow \log_4(\log_2 x) = 6^0 = 1$$
$$\Rightarrow \log_2 x = 4^1 = 4$$
$$\Rightarrow x = 2^4 = 16$$

18. (C)
$$\frac{2 \cdot 6}{1+5} = \frac{3 \cdot 8}{7+x} \Rightarrow \frac{12}{6} = \frac{24}{7+x} \Rightarrow 7 + x = 12 \Rightarrow x = 5$$

19. (A)
$x_{n+1} = x_n^2 + x_n - 2$.
For n=1, $x_2 = x_1^2 + x_1 - 2 = (-2)^2 + (-2) - 2 = 0$
For n=2, $x_3 = x_2^2 + x_2 - 2 = 0^2 + 0 - 2 = -2$
For n=3, $x_4 = x_3^2 + x_3 - 2 = (-2)^2 + (-2) - 2 = 0$,
and so on. So, For n:odd, $x_{even}= 0$ and for n:odd, $x_{odd}= -2$. And, $x_{555} = -2$.

20. (D)
Determinant: (x-2)(x-3)(x+1)=2
⇒ Graph of y=(x-2)(x-3)(x+1)-2 looks like

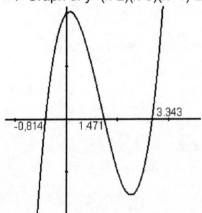

21. (A)
By remainder theorem, P(-1)=2-5-1-3=-3-4=-7

22. (D)
$$d = \sqrt{(2-(-1))^2 + (-3-3)^2 + (4-5)^2}$$
$$= \sqrt{9+36+1} = \sqrt{46} = 6.78$$

23. (B)

If we write y=2 in the equation $\dfrac{x^2}{16} + \dfrac{4}{9} = 1$, we

will get the x coordinates of the points.

$$\Rightarrow \dfrac{x^2}{16} + \dfrac{4}{9} = 1 \Rightarrow x^2 = 8.89 \Rightarrow x = \mp 2.98$$

24. (D)

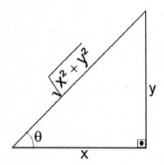

$$\text{Cos}\theta = \dfrac{x}{\sqrt{x^2+y^2}}$$

25. (B)

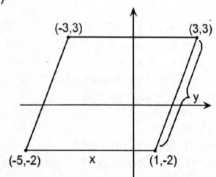

x=1-(-5)=6
$$y = \sqrt{(3-1)^2 + (3-(-2))^2} = \sqrt{4+25} = \sqrt{29}$$
$$\Rightarrow x + y = 6 + \sqrt{29}$$

26. (A)
$$\text{min.value} = f(-\dfrac{-16}{2 \cdot 2})$$
$$= f(4) = 2 \cdot 4^2 - 16 \cdot 4 + 30 = -2$$

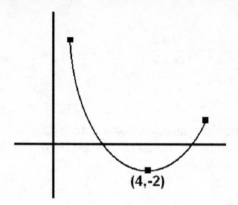

(4,-2)

27. (D)
c=b-1 $\Rightarrow$ b=c+1
a=(c+1)²-2(c+1)-2=c²+2c+1-2c-2-2=c²-3

28. (B)
t=2003—1971=32

$$\text{Number of tigers} = 1500 \cdot \left(1 + \dfrac{1}{100}\right)^{32}$$

$$= 1500 \cdot (1.01)^{32} = 2{,}062$$

29. (E)
$$a_2 = a \cdot r \text{ and } a_5 = a \cdot r^5$$

$$\dfrac{a \cdot r^5}{a \cdot r} = \dfrac{243}{3} \Rightarrow r^4 = 81 \Rightarrow r = 3$$

$$a_2 = a \cdot 3 = 3 \Rightarrow a = 1$$

$$a_1 + a_2 + ... + a_7 =$$
$$1 + 3 + 9 + 27 + 81 + 243 + 729 = 1093$$

30. (A)
$$(2\sin\theta - 1) \cdot (\sin\theta - 3) = 0$$

i) $\sin\theta = \dfrac{1}{2} \Rightarrow \theta = 30° \text{ or } 150°$

ii) $\sin\theta = 3 \Rightarrow \text{no solition}$

31. (E)
$$\sin\theta = x \cdot \cos\theta \Rightarrow \dfrac{\sin\theta}{\cos\theta} = x = \tan\theta = 0.25$$

32. (C)
tan(cos⁻¹(0.02))=49.99°≈50°

33. (D)

$a = \dfrac{16}{2} = 8$
$b = \dfrac{6}{2} = 3$ $\Rightarrow$
$\dfrac{(x-2)^2}{8^2} + \dfrac{(y-(-1))^2}{3^2} = 1$, or
$\dfrac{(x-2)^2}{3^2} + \dfrac{(y-(-1))^2}{8^2} = 1$

34..(B)

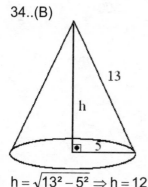

$h = \sqrt{13^2 - 5^2} \Rightarrow h = 12$

$V = \dfrac{1}{3} \cdot \pi r^2 \cdot h = \dfrac{1}{3} \pi \cdot 5^2 \cdot 12 = 100\pi = 314.16$

35. (D)
If x+1 is an odd integer, then x is an even integer. Therefore 2+(x-1)² is positive and odd.

36. (D)

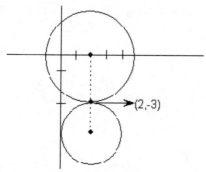

(x-2)²+y²=9 $\Rightarrow$ center at (2,0), r=3
(x-2)²+(y+5)²=4 $\Rightarrow$ center at (2,-5), r=2
or, algebraically,
(x-2)²+y²-9=(x-2)²+(y+5)²-4
y²-9= y²+10y+25-4
-30=10y, then, y=-3 and x=2.

37. (B)
f(x)=-1·(x-(-3))·(x-0)·(x-2)
=-1·(x+3)·x·(x-2)
=-x(x²+x-6)=-x³-x²+6x $\Rightarrow$ d=0
a<0, since, the graph end in the IV.th quadrant of the xy-plane.

38. (E)

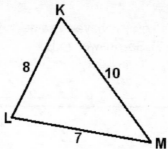

Cosine rule:
10²=8²+7²-2·8·7·Cos L $\Rightarrow$ m(L)=83.33°

39. (C)
Draw the graph of f(x). It will look like (C).

40. (D)

$\lim_{x\to\infty} \dfrac{4x^2 + x - 6}{5x^2 - x + 2} =$

$\lim_{x\to\infty} \dfrac{x^2 \cdot \left(4 + \dfrac{1}{x} - \dfrac{6}{x^2}\right)}{x^2 \cdot \left(5 - \dfrac{1}{x} + \dfrac{2}{x^2}\right)} = \lim_{x\to\infty} \dfrac{4+0-0}{5-0+0} = \dfrac{4}{5}$

41. (E)
Axis of symmetry must pass through the center (1,0). Therefore all three can be the axis of symmetry.

42. (D)
f(x + 3) = f(x) means that the period of the function is 3. So the answer is D.

43. (E)
cos(A - B) = cosA · cosB + sinA · sinB
$= \dfrac{b}{c} \cdot \dfrac{a}{c} + \dfrac{a}{c} \cdot \dfrac{b}{c} = \dfrac{2ab}{c^2}$

44. (B)

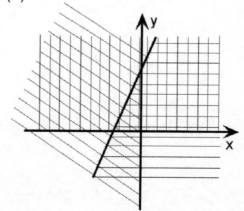

45. (B)

f(x) and g(x) have same y-intercept $\Rightarrow$ f(0) = g(0). So, answer is B.

46. (C)

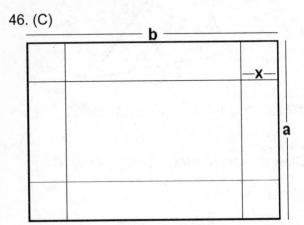

x>0, since the volume is nonzero.

$2x < b \Rightarrow x < \dfrac{b}{2}$

$2x < a \Rightarrow x < \dfrac{a}{2}$

x must be less than both $\dfrac{a}{2}$ and $\dfrac{b}{2}$ (if a and b are equal), or, less than the least of $\dfrac{a}{2}$ and $\dfrac{b}{2}$ (if a and b are not equal).

47. (E)

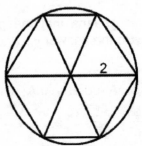

$\text{Area} = 6 \cdot \dfrac{2^2\sqrt{3}}{4} = 6\sqrt{3} = 10.39$

48. (D)

$4 \cdot \pi r^2 = \dfrac{70}{100} \cdot \dfrac{4}{3} \cdot \pi r^3 \Rightarrow r = \dfrac{300}{70} = 4.29$

49. (E)

g(x)=y=ln(x³-1)

i) x=ln(y³-1)

ii) $y^3 - 1 = e^x \Rightarrow y^3 = 1 + e^x \Rightarrow y = \sqrt[3]{1 + e^x}$

50. (C)

2 B, 1 A, 1 Or : $\dbinom{4}{2} \cdot \dbinom{5}{1} \cdot \dbinom{6}{1} = 180$

1 B, 1 A, 2 Or : $\dbinom{4}{1} \cdot \dbinom{5}{2} \cdot \dbinom{6}{1} = 240$

1 B, 1 A, 2 O : $\dbinom{4}{1} \cdot \dbinom{5}{1} \cdot \dbinom{6}{2} = 300$

180+240+300=720

Level 2 – Model Test 4 Solutions

1. (B)

$$\left.\begin{array}{l} a^2 < a \Rightarrow 0 < a < 1 \\ b > 1 \end{array}\right\} \Rightarrow ab < b$$

2. (E)

$$\frac{x}{y^2} = k$$

A) $\dfrac{1}{1^2} = \dfrac{4}{2^2} = 1$

B) $\dfrac{2}{1^2} = \dfrac{8}{2^2} = 2$

C) $\dfrac{2}{2^2} = \dfrac{8}{4^2} = \dfrac{1}{2}$

D) $\dfrac{4}{1^2} = \dfrac{16}{2^2} = 4$

E) $\dfrac{2}{2^2} \neq \dfrac{3}{3^2}$

3. (C)

$f(x) = 3 \cdot \sin^2(2x) + 1$

$\Rightarrow y_{max.} = 3 + 1 = 4$

$\Rightarrow y_{min.} = 0 + 1 = 1$

$$\text{Amplitude} = \frac{y_{max.} - y_{min.}}{2} = \frac{4 - 1}{2} = \frac{3}{2}$$

4. (B)

$$\frac{2}{3}x + \frac{4}{5}y = 12 \Rightarrow \text{slope} = -\frac{\frac{2}{3}}{\frac{4}{5}} = -\frac{2}{3} \cdot \frac{5}{4} = -\frac{5}{6}$$

B) $y = y = -\dfrac{5}{6}x + 3 \Rightarrow \text{slope} = -\dfrac{5}{6}$

5. (B)

$$f(5) = \frac{1}{5^2 - 1} = \frac{1}{25 - 1} = \frac{1}{24}$$

$$g(f(5)) = g\left(\frac{1}{24}\right) = 10$$

B) $\dfrac{1 - 4 \cdot \dfrac{1}{24}}{2 \cdot \dfrac{1}{24}} = \dfrac{1 - \dfrac{1}{6}}{\dfrac{1}{12}} = \dfrac{\dfrac{5}{6}}{\dfrac{1}{12}} = \dfrac{5}{6} \cdot 12 = 5 \cdot 2 = 10$

6. (D)

	252	1260	1512	1572	3780
6	yes	yes	yes	yes	yes
7	yes	yes	yes	no	yes
9	yes	yes	yes	no	yes

7. (E)

The slope of the line y= - 2 is zero.

If a line is perpendicular to line d, then slope is undefined.

8. (E)

$$\frac{x^2 - 1}{1 - \dfrac{1}{x}} = \frac{x^2 - 1}{\dfrac{x - 1}{x}} = x^2 - 1 \cdot \frac{x}{x - 1}$$

$$= (x + 1)(x - 1) \cdot \frac{x}{x - 1} = x^2 + x$$

9. (C)

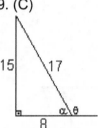

$\theta = 180° - \alpha$

$$\tan\theta = \tan(180° - \alpha) = -\frac{15}{8} \Rightarrow \tan\alpha = \frac{15}{8}$$

$$\Rightarrow \sin\alpha = \frac{15}{17} \Rightarrow \sin\theta = \frac{15}{17}$$

$$\Rightarrow \cos\alpha = \frac{8}{17} \Rightarrow \cos\theta = -\frac{8}{17}$$

$$\Rightarrow \sin\alpha + \cos\alpha = \frac{15}{17} - \frac{8}{17} = \frac{7}{17}$$

10. (D)

$f(x) = x^4 - 52x^2 - 81x$

All possible x values are -6.25,-1.64,0 and 7.89

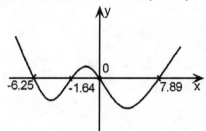

11. (E)

$f(-|5|) = f(-5) = -2$

So, $(5,-2)$ is also on the graph of $y = f(x)$.

12.(A)

$\cos(\pi - \theta) = -\cos\theta = -\sqrt{1-(0.82)^2} = -0.57$

13. (A)

If θ is 90° then $x = \sqrt{14^2 + 6^2} = 15.23$

If $\theta > 90°$ then $x > 15.23$. So, x cannot be less then 15.23.

14. (D)

[x] is an integer and when an integer is divided by 5, the remainder can be 0,1,2,3 or 4. There fore the period is 5.

15. (D)

$y = \sqrt{x} - 1 = \sqrt{t^2} - 1 = |t| - 1$

16. (E)

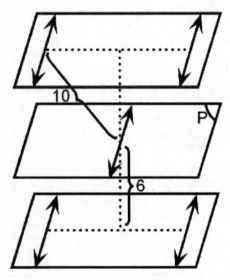

17. (D)

$\dfrac{n \cdot 88 + 2 \cdot 100}{n + 2} = 88 + 4$

$\Rightarrow 88 \cdot n + 200 = 92 \cdot n + 184$

$\Rightarrow 16 = 4n \Rightarrow n = 4$

18. (C)

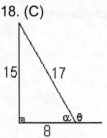

The slope of the line d is: $\tan(180° - \theta) = -\tan\theta$

19.(D)

$8{,}000 \cdot \left(1 + \dfrac{\frac{4}{2}}{100}\right)^{4 \cdot 2} = 8{,}000 \cdot (1.02)^8 = \$9{,}373$

20. (B)

If $\dfrac{m}{n}$ is a rational root of P(x) then m is a factor of -15 and n is a factor of 6. There fore $\dfrac{m}{n}$ cannot be $\dfrac{3}{4}$ because 4 is not a factor of n.

21. (D)

$\left.\begin{array}{l} a = 4 \\ a \cdot r = 2 \end{array}\right\} \Rightarrow r = \dfrac{2}{4} = \dfrac{1}{2}$

$a + a \cdot r + a \cdot r^2 + a \cdot r^3 = 4 + 2 + 1 + \dfrac{1}{2} = 7.5$

22. (C)

$P(0) = 0 + 0 + 0 + d = 5 \Rightarrow d = 5$

$P(1) = a + b + c + d = 8 \Rightarrow a + b + c = 3$

$P(-1) = -a + b - c + d = 6 \Rightarrow -a + b - c = 1$

$\left.\begin{array}{l} a + b + c = 3 \\ -a + b - c = 1 \end{array}\right\} \Rightarrow 2b = 4 \Rightarrow b = 2$

23. (D)

$16 - x^2 > 0 \Rightarrow x^2 < 16$

$\Rightarrow \sqrt{x^2} < \sqrt{14} \Rightarrow |x| < 4 \Rightarrow -4 < x < 4$

24. (D)

$\frac{1}{2} \cdot \pi r^2 = 8\pi \Rightarrow \pi r^2 = 16\pi$

$r^2 = 16 \Rightarrow r = 4$

$2\pi r \cdot \frac{m(A\hat{O}B)}{360°} = 6$

$m(A\hat{O}B) = \frac{6 \cdot 360°}{2 \cdot \pi \cdot 4} \approx 86°$

25. (B)

$\cos^2\theta + \frac{1}{\csc^2\theta} = \cos^2\theta + \sin^2\theta = 1$

26. (D)

$\sin 2x = \cos 35° = 0.819$

$2x = \sin^{-1}(0.819) = 0.96 \Rightarrow x = 0.48$

27. (E)

center(-2,1), radius=6

$(x - (-2))^2 + (y - 1)^2 = 6^2$

$(x+2)^2 + (y - 1)^2 = 36$

For x = -5 $\quad \Rightarrow (-5 + 2)^2 + (y - 1)^2 = 36$

$\Rightarrow (y-1)^2 = 27$

$\Rightarrow y - 1 = \pm\sqrt{27}$

$\Rightarrow y = 1 \pm 3\sqrt{3}$

$y_1 + y_2 = 1 + 3\sqrt{3} + 1 - 3\sqrt{3} = 2$

28.(C)

$f(x) = \frac{(x+3)(x-2)}{(x+3)(x-3)} = \frac{x-2}{x-3}$. So, from x – 3 = 0,

x = 3 is the only vertical asymptote.

29. (D)

$25 \cdot r = 26 \Rightarrow r = \frac{26}{25} = 1.04$

Final height=$25 \cdot 1.04^{10} = 37.006 \approx 37.01$

30. (A)

$\text{Area} = \frac{1}{2} \cdot \begin{vmatrix} -6 & 1 \\ -1 & -4 \\ 3.5 & 4 \\ -6 & 1 \end{vmatrix}$

$= \frac{1}{2} \cdot (1 + 14 + 24 + 24 - 4 + 3.5) = \frac{1}{2} \cdot 62.5 = 31.25$

31. (E)

$x_1 = (x_0 + 1)^3 = (-1+1)^3 = 0$

$x_2 = (x_1 + 1)^3 = (0+1)^3 = 1$

$x_3 = (x_2 + 1)^3 = (1+1)^3 = 8$

$x_4 = (x_3 + 1)^3 = (8+1)^3 = 729$

32. (B)

cos250° = - 0.342 (Calculator in degree mode)

sin(-0.342) = -0.335 (Calculator in radian mode)

33. (D)

$x - y = -2 \Rightarrow y = x+2$

$x^2 + (x + 2)^2 = 9$

$x^2 + x^2 + 4x + 4 - 9 = 0$

$2x^2 + 4x - 5 = 0$

Graph the function f(x) = 2x² + 4x – 5 and find the zeros as -2.871 and 0.871

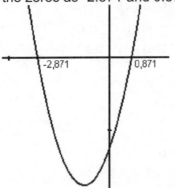

34. (C)

m(C)=90°

AC=12·cos15° and BC=12·sin15°

Shade area=

$\pi \cdot 6^2 \cdot \frac{1}{2} - \frac{12 \cdot \cos 15 \cdot 12 \cdot \sin 15}{2} = 38.5 \approx 39$

35. (B)

Correct answer is B.

36. (E)

Probability that the product is even =

Probability that as least one of them is even =

1 – Probability that all are odd =

$1 - \frac{6}{12} \cdot \frac{5}{11} \cdot \frac{4}{10} = \frac{10}{11}$

37. (E)

x^{30} cannot be 0 or 1. So, x cannot be 0,1 or -1

38. (E)

Magnitude of $\vec{v}$ = 6.8

Magnitude of $2\vec{w}$ =2·10.1=20.2

$20.2 - 6.8 < |\vec{v} + 2\vec{w}| < 20.2 + 6.8$

$13.4 < |v + 2w| < 27$

39. (D)

$$S_n = \frac{n}{2} \cdot (2a + (n-1) \cdot d)$$

$$S_6 = \frac{6}{2} \cdot (2 \cdot 7 + (6-1) \cdot d) = 102$$

$$\Rightarrow 5d = 34 - 14 = 20 \Rightarrow d = 4$$

$$\Rightarrow a_2 = a + d = 7 + 4 = 11$$

40. (B)

$$\frac{(n+1)! - n!}{n! + (n-1)!} = \frac{(n+1) \cdot n! - n!}{n \cdot (n-1)! + (n-1)!}$$

$$= \frac{n! \cdot (n+1-1)}{(n-1)! \cdot (n+1)} = \frac{n \cdot (n-1)! \cdot n}{(n-1)! \cdot (n+1)} = \frac{n^2}{n+1}$$

41. (D)

$\sec^2 x = 1 + \tan^2 x$

$\sec^2 x - 3\tan x + 1 = 0$

$1 + \tan^2 x - 3\tan x + 1 = 0$

$\Rightarrow \tan^2 x - 3\tan x + 2 = 0$

$\Rightarrow (\tan x - 2)(\tan x - 1) = 0$

$\Rightarrow \tan x = 2$ or $\tan x = 1$

If $\tan x = 1$ then x can be $\frac{5\pi}{4}$

42. (C)

$$\frac{4}{3}\pi r^3 = 288\pi \Rightarrow r^3 = 288 \cdot \frac{3}{4} = 216 \Rightarrow r = 6$$

$$\text{maximum area} = \pi \cdot 6^2 = 36\pi$$

43. (D)

Statement: $0 < x < 1 \Rightarrow x^2 < x$

Any statement is equivalent to its

contrapositive: $x^2 \geq x \Rightarrow$ x is not between 0 and 1. Therefore we make the assumption that $x^2 \geq x$

44. (E)

number of side of this polygon is: $\dfrac{2\pi}{\frac{\pi}{4}} = 8$

45. (C)

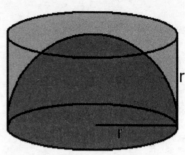

$$\frac{\frac{1}{2} \cdot \frac{4}{3}\pi r^3}{\pi r^2 \cdot r - \frac{1}{2} \cdot \frac{4}{3}\pi r^3} = \frac{\frac{2}{3}\pi r^3}{\frac{1}{3}\pi r^3} = 2$$

46. (C)

AA | AAAA | A

1st person gets 2 apples

2nd person gets 4 apples

3rd person gets 1 apple

We need 7A's and 2S's. (A represents an apple and S represents a separator)

AASAAAASA $\Rightarrow$ Number of distributions is

$$\frac{9!}{7! \cdot 2!} = \binom{9}{2}$$

47. (E)

Correct answer is given in E.

48. (D)

$$\frac{1}{R} = \frac{x}{yz} + \frac{y}{xz} + \frac{z}{xy} = \frac{x^2 + y^2 + z^2}{xyz} \Rightarrow R = \frac{xyz}{x^2 + y^2 + z^2}$$

$\quad$ (x) $\quad$ (y) $\quad$ (z)

49. (D)

$$\frac{(x-2)^2}{A^2} - \frac{(y+1)^2}{B^2} = 1.$$

This equation must be satisfied by x=0 and y= - 1

50. (A)

Smallest prime number is 2.

Smallest positive real number cannot be located.

Smallest negative multiple of 5 does not exist.

Level 2 – Model Test 5 Solutions

1. (A)

$$\left. \begin{array}{l} x^2 - y^2 = 7 \\ x^2 + 2y^2 = 1 \end{array} \right\} \Rightarrow -3y^2 = 6 \Rightarrow y^2 = -2$$

So, no real solution.

2. (B)

$$a^3 + b^3 = (a+b)(a^2 - ab + b^2)$$

$$\frac{y + \dfrac{1}{y^2}}{1 - \dfrac{1}{y} + \dfrac{1}{y^2}} = \frac{\dfrac{y^3+1}{y^2}}{\dfrac{y^2 - y + 1}{y^2}}$$

$$= \frac{y^3 + 1}{y^2 - y + 1} = \frac{(y+1)(y^2 - y + 1)}{(y^2 - y + 1)} = y + 1$$

3. (D)

$$x^2 + y^2 = 25 \Rightarrow r^2 = 25 \Rightarrow r = 5$$

in (D), the distance between the point (4,3) and the origin is the same as the radius of the circle: $\sqrt{(-4)^2 + 3^2} = 5$

4. (D)

day time →0,15 kg/h
Night time →0.05 kg/h
From 8 AM to 8 PM 12 hours day time
From 8 PM to 10 PM 2 hours night time
12·0.15+2·0.05

5. (C)

$$x = \log_7 777 = \frac{\log 777}{\log 7} = 3.42 .$$

So, x is between 3 and 4.

6. (C)

$$x = \cos^{-1}(-1) = \pi$$

7. (C)

For $x \ge 1, y = -x^2$

$\dfrac{x-1}{x+1}$; $x + 1 = 0 \Rightarrow x = -1$ is the vertical asymptote

$y = \lim_{x \to \infty} f(x) = 1$ is the horizontal asymptote

8. (B)
From the definition of ellipse

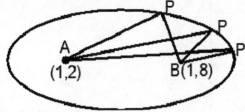

|PA|+|PB|=10 (fixed)
A and B are the foci of the elipse.

9. (A)

$\log(x^2) = 2 \cdot \log x$ is valid for $x > 0$ only

10. (E)

$$\cos^2 x + \sin^2 y = 1 - \sin^2 x + 1 - \cos^2 y$$
$$= 2 - \left(\sin^2 x + \cos^2 y\right) = 2 - 0.234 = 1.766$$

11. (A)
Amplitute = 2
Period = 4π
For x = 0, f(x) = 0
For $x = \pi$, f(x) = 2
For x=3π, f(x) = -2
(A) satisfies all these conditions.

12. (A)

$$f(x) = f^{-1}(x) \Rightarrow f\left(f^{-1}(x)\right) = x$$

For (A),

$$f(-x + 3) = -(-x + 3) + 3 = x - 3 + 3 = x$$

13. (C)
If f(x) intersects |f(x)| at a single point, then, f(x) has open downwards and is tangent to the x axis; therefore

$$\Delta = b^2 - 4ac = 0 \Rightarrow b^2 = 4ac = 0 .$$

$b^2 \ge 0 \Rightarrow 4ac \ge 0 \Rightarrow ac \ge 0$. Thus, ac cannot be negative.

14. (D)

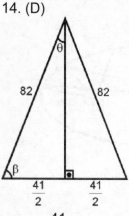

$$\tan\theta = \dfrac{\dfrac{41}{2}}{82} = \dfrac{41}{164} \Rightarrow \theta = 14°$$

$$\beta = \dfrac{180° - 2\cdot 14°}{2} = 76°$$

15. (E)
For h(x) = 2x + x²
$h(0) = 2\cdot 0 + 0^2 = 0$
$h(-2) = 2\cdot(-2) + (-2)^2 = 0$. Since h(0) = h(-2), the function h(x) = 2x + x² is not a one-to-one function.

16. (D)
If the standard deviation of class A is less than class B, then scores of A are distributed closely around the mean. This comes from the definition of standard deviation.

17. (C)
$\vec{u} = (3,5) - (-3,3) = (3-(-3), 5-3) = (6,2)$
$\vec{v} = (-3,0) - (2,3) = (-3-2, 0-3) = (-5,-3)$
$\vec{u} - \vec{v} = (6,2) - (-5,-3) = (11,5)$

18. (D)
Longest diagonal $= \sqrt{7^2 + 5^2 + 9^2} = 12.45$

19. (E)
$\overset{1^{st}}{4} \to \overset{2^{nd}}{10} \to \overset{3^{rd}}{16} \to \overset{4^{th}}{22}$
$a_k = 4 + 6k$
for k=36, $a_{36} = 4 + 6\cdot 36 = 4 + 216 = 220$

20. (C)
$\dfrac{-12}{3} = \dfrac{2m}{4} = \dfrac{-20}{5} \Rightarrow \dfrac{m}{2} = -4$

21. (C)
For a, b any point on the circle, $a^2 + b^2 = r^2$.
In (C), $\left(\sqrt{8}\right)^2 + (-4)^2 = 8 + 16 = 24$

22. (D)
undecided $= 300 \cdot \dfrac{40}{100} = 120$ people

For Pemra $120 \cdot \dfrac{35}{60} = 70$ more people will vote on Tuesday.

23. (A)
p(-1) = p – q + r = 0, then, r = q – p.

24. (D)
$g\left(\sqrt{3}\right) = 3 \cdot \left(\sqrt{3}\right) - 2 = 3.2$
f(3.2) = ln(3.2) = 1.162

25. (C)
$4x^3 - 2x^2 + ax - 5 = 0$
$\dfrac{ax}{x} = \dfrac{5 + 2x^2 - 4x^3}{x} \Rightarrow a = \dfrac{5 + 2x^2 - 4x^3}{x}$
For a= -2.66, x can not be 1.5

26. (A)
The slope of the linet hat passes through the points $(x, x^2 + x)$ and $(2,6)$ is:
$$\dfrac{x^2 + x - 6}{x - 2} = \dfrac{(x+3)(x-2)}{(x-2)} = x + 3$$

27. (E)
$\cos^{-1}(0.32) = x \Rightarrow x = 71.34$
$\tan(71.34) = 2.96$

28. (E)
The parabola is concave up; therefore a>0. It has a negative y – intercept therefore -b<0. So, b>0.

29. (D)

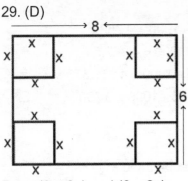

Base $(8 - 2x)$ and $(6 - 2x)$
Height: x,
Volume = $(8 - 2x) \cdot (6 - 2x) \cdot x$

30. (E)
$5^{xy} > 15 \Rightarrow \log 5^{xy} > \log 15$

$xy \cdot \log 5 > \log 15 \Rightarrow xy > \dfrac{\log 15}{\log 5} = 1.68$

$\Rightarrow xy > 1.68$

31. (E)
$x^2 + y^2 + 4x - 6y = 0 \Rightarrow (x+2)^2 + (y-3)^2 - 4 - 9 = 0$

$\Rightarrow (x+2)^2 + (y-3)^2 = 13$

$\therefore C(-2, 3)$

32. (B)

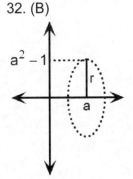

$r = a^2 - 1 \Rightarrow \text{Area} = \pi \cdot \left(a^2 - 1\right)^2$

33. (B)
$1 + \dfrac{\cos^2 x}{\sin^2 x} = \dfrac{\sin^2 x}{\sin^2 x} + \dfrac{\cos^2 x}{\sin^2 x}$

$= \dfrac{\sin^2 x + \cos^2 x}{\sin^2 x} = \dfrac{1}{\sin^2 x} = \csc^2 x$

34. (D)

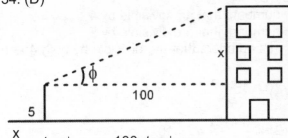

$\dfrac{x}{100} = \tan\phi \Rightarrow x = 100 \cdot \tan\phi$

Height of the building $= 5 + 100 \cdot \tan\phi$

35. (C)
i) $y = \lim\limits_{x \to \infty} \dfrac{3}{2 - x} = 0$ is the horizontal asymptote.

ii) For $2 - x = 0 \Rightarrow x = 2$, the function is undefined. So, $x = 2$ is the vertical asymptote.

36. (A)
$e^{c \cdot (-1)} = 3 \Rightarrow e^{-c} = 3 \Rightarrow \log_e 3 = -c \Rightarrow c = -\ln 3$

$b = e^{(-\ln 3) \cdot 3} = e^{\ln(27^{-1})} = \dfrac{1}{27}$

37. (A)
$4\pi r^2 = 144\pi \Rightarrow r^2 = 36 \Rightarrow r = 6$

$V = \dfrac{4}{3} \cdot \pi r^3 = \dfrac{4}{3} \cdot \pi \cdot 6^3 = 288\pi$

38. (E)
$\sin(x) = \sqrt{1 - c^2} \geq 0 \Rightarrow 0 \leq x \leq \pi$

$1 - c^2 \geq 0 \Rightarrow c^2 \leq 1 \Rightarrow -1 \leq c \leq 1$

So all values of x are in the I. and II. Quadrant, or in the interval $0 \leq x \leq \pi$.

39. (A)
$\tan 2x = \dfrac{2\tan x}{1 - \tan^2 x}$

Let $\tan x = x$. Then graph $f(x) = \dfrac{2x}{1 - x^2} < 0$

Solution set : $-1 < x < 0$ or $x > 1$

So, $-1 < \tan x < 0$ or $\tan x > 1$

40. (D)
A: numbers that are divisible by 4
B: numbers that are divisible by 5
A∩B: numbers that are divisible by both 4 and 5

$S(A) = \dfrac{48 - 4}{4} + 1 = 12$

$S(B) = \dfrac{50 - 5}{5} + 1 = 10$

$S(A \cap B) = 2$

$P(A \cup B) = P(A) + (B) - P(A \cap B)$

$\quad = \dfrac{12}{50} + \dfrac{10}{50} - \dfrac{2}{50}$

$\quad = \dfrac{20}{50} = 0.4$

41. (A)
$x + 3 = -3 \Rightarrow x = -6$
$-y + 4 = 2 \Rightarrow y = 2$
$x - 2y = -6 - 2 \cdot 2 = -10$

42. (B)
$a_{k+1} = a_k^2 - 1$

$a_k = a_{k-1}^2 - 1 \Rightarrow 3 = a_{k-1}^2 - 1 \Rightarrow a_{k-1} = 2$

$a_{k-1} = a_{k-2}^2 - 1 \Rightarrow 2 = a_{k-2}^2 - 1 \Rightarrow a_{k-2} = \sqrt{3} = 1.73$

43. (D)
$_8C_2 \cdot _7C_3 = 28 \cdot 35 = 980$

44. (E)

$2 \cdot \begin{vmatrix} a & 4b & 6c \\ p & 4q & 6r \\ x & 4y & 6z \end{vmatrix} = 2 \cdot 4 \cdot \begin{vmatrix} a & b & 6c \\ p & q & 6r \\ x & y & 6z \end{vmatrix} = 2 \cdot 4 \cdot 6 \cdot \begin{vmatrix} a & b & c \\ p & q & r \\ x & y & z \end{vmatrix}$

$= 48 \cdot \begin{vmatrix} a & b & c \\ p & q & r \\ x & y & z \end{vmatrix} = e \cdot \begin{vmatrix} a & b & c \\ p & q & r \\ x & y & z \end{vmatrix} \Rightarrow e = 48$

45. (C)
slope=$\tan\alpha \Rightarrow \cos\alpha = \tan\alpha$
graph the function of $f(x) = \cos\alpha - \tan\alpha = 0$
$\alpha = 141.82°$
α is in the 2nd quadrant, $126° < \alpha < 144°$

46. (D)
$a_1 = (1.15) \cdot 5,000 - 1000 = 4,750$

$a_2 = 4,750 \cdot 1.15 - 1000 = 4,462.5$

$a_3 = 4,462.5 \cdot 1.15 - 1000 = 4,131.875$

$a_4 = 4,131.875 \cdot 1.15 - 1000 \approx 3,750$

47. (D)

one of the semicircular base $= \dfrac{1}{2} \cdot \pi \cdot \left(\dfrac{5}{2}\right)^2$

Lateral Area $= 2\pi rh \cdot \dfrac{1}{2} = \pi \cdot \dfrac{5}{2} \cdot 8 = 20\pi$

Surface Area=

$20\pi + 2 \cdot \dfrac{1}{2} \cdot \pi \cdot (2.5)^2 = 40 + 82.47 = 122.47$

48. (C)
The given ellipse looks as shown below and its

equation is given by $\dfrac{(x-2)^2}{2^2} + \dfrac{(y+5)^2}{5^2} = 1$.

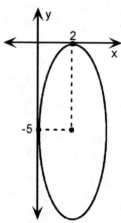

49. (C)
Yaprak → 55th
Yasemin → 77th
Yonca's ranking < Yasemin's ranking
So Yonca's ranking can not be 88th percentile.

50. (E)
$|DC| = \sqrt{4^2 + 4^2 - 2 \cdot 4 \cdot 4 \cdot \cos 144°}$

$|DC| = \sqrt{32 - 32 \cdot \cos 144°} = 7.608$

length of arc DC $= 2 \cdot \pi \cdot 4 \cdot \dfrac{144°}{360°} = 10.053$

perimeter $= 7.608 + 10.053 = 17.661$

ANSWERS TO EXERCISES

FUNCTIONS

Answers to Exercises P. 8-12

1. a) x=y b) x, y none zero positive c) x=y **2.** a and b **3.** a=b=c and all have the same sign

4. a) a=-7 b=12 b) a=-10 b=9 c) a=-21 b=35 d) a= $-\frac{5}{4}$ b= $\frac{3}{4}$ **5.** a) a=-1 b= $\frac{5}{3}$ b) a=-1 b= $\frac{7}{5}$ **6.** a) (1, 7)

b) (3, 4) c) (- $\frac{1}{2}$, 1.84) d) (-2, 0) and (1, 3) e) (2, ∞) and (-1, 0) f) [2, ∞) or (-∞ , -1]

g) ($\frac{2}{3}$, ∞) or (-∞ , 0) h) (- $\frac{3}{4}$, 1) i) (0, ∞) j) (3, 4) **7.** empty set **8.** -2 **9.** 4 **10.** (-∞ , 12) or (3, ∞) **11.** 2

12. 9 **13.** a, d, e **14.** $\frac{cx-a}{dx+b}$ **15.** a) (3, ∞) b) (-∞ , 0) c) (0, ∞) d) (-∞ , -1) or (1 ∞) e) (-1, 0) or (0, 1)

16. a) 3.64 b) 1.18 c) 4.11 d) -0.406 e) 9.98 **17.** (-1, 3) **18.** infinitely many **19.** 3 **20.** 2 **21.** 4 **22.** -0.71

23. {2, -1.33} **24.** {0.33, 3} **25.** Empty set **26.** 0.6 **27.** (-∞ , 0) or (0.5, ∞) **28.** [-1, ∞) or (-∞ , -4]

29. [1, 3] **30.** a) (-1, 1) b) Empty set c) (-2, 2) d) (1, ∞) or (-∞ , -1) e) empty set f) (-∞ , -2) or (2, ∞)

g) (-∞ , -3) or (1, ∞) h) empty set i) all real numbers j) empty set **31.** (1.9, 2.1) **32.** a) (3, ∞) b) (1, ∞)

c) (-∞ , 1) d) {x=1 y=-3} e) empty set **34.** (0.8, 1.2) **35.** a) 3 b) 1 c) 2

Answers to Exercises P. 20-21

1. A-1 B-7 C-6 D-2 E- 5 F-3 G-4 **2.** A, D, E **3.** All Real numbers – { 2} **4.** All real numbers **5.**a

Answers to Exercises P. 23-25

1. (-∞ , 5] **2.** [0, 25] **3.** c=0 **4.** (-3, 5) **5.** ($-\frac{1}{2},-\frac{1}{6}$) **6.** Domain: all real numbers, Range: (-∞ , 2.57]

7. 2.08 **8.** (-∞ , -2.74) and (2.74, ∞) **9.** Domain: all real numbers- {0}, Range: (0, ∞)

10. Domain: [2, ∞), Range: (-∞ , 4] **11.** ± 1 **12.** Domain: (-∞ , -3] and [3, ∞) Range: [0, ∞)

13. Domain: [-3, 3] Range: [0, 3] **14.** a) All real numbers-{ -2, 2} b) [-4, 3) and (3, ∞) c) (3, 9) – {4}

15. b, c, f **16.**a, c, e, h, k

Answers to Exercises P. 26-27

1. 0.57 **2.** $-\frac{13}{4}$ **3.** {-9, 10} **4.** $\frac{x+5}{3}$ **5.** 0, 17 **6.** $\frac{11}{32}$ **7.** a, b, c **8.** 14 **9.** 124 **10.** 3a^2 +5a+2 **11.** -1.26

12. 1.71 **13.** d

Answers to Exercises P. 30-31

1. 6x-1 **2.** i, ii **3.** 3x-5 **4.** $-\frac{1}{3}$ **5.** $-\frac{x}{4}$ **6.** x-4 **7.** -0.73

Answers to Exercises P. 36-44

1. Domain: All real numbers Range: [0, 1] Period: 3 Frequency: $\frac{1}{3}$ **2.** Domain: All real numbers

Range: [0, 1] Period: 2 Frequency: $\frac{1}{2}$ Amplitude: 0.5 Offset: 0.5 Axis of wave y=0.5 **3.** $\frac{\log x}{\log n}$ **4.** log$_n$ m

5. 2^x **6.** 10^x **7.** e^x **8.**x$\geq$ 0 **9.** c **10.** a=-1 b= 2 **11.**All Real Numbers except {3} **12.** a, c, e **13.** ±1 **14.** 1

15. 0 **16.** a) c^x b) 1 **17.** a) log$_c$x b) 0 **18.** -12 **19.** -2b-1 **20.** 1, 3, 5 **21.** a) Domain: [-2, 2] Range: [-6, 6]

b) no **22.** B, C, D, G **23.** 0 **24.** y$\geq$ 6 or y=1 or y ≤ -6 **25.** Domain: All real numbers except {0}

Range: y>3 or y<-3 **26.** 3, - 1, 2, (1/2) **27.** {-3} **28.** for f(x) Domain: x$\leq$ 9 Range: y<0;

for g(x) Domain: All real numbers Range: y$\geq$ 0 ; for (fog) (x) Domain: [-3, 3] Range[0, 3];

for (gof) (x) Domain: $x \le 9$ Range: $y \ge 0$ **29.** All real numbers – {0, 1, -1} **30.** Range: [-1, 1] **31.** a) x b) 2 **32.** 2 **33.** 5.41 **34.** Domain: $x \ge -4$ Range: $y \ge 0$ **35.** ii, iii, iv **36.** A, H **37.** a) 12 b) -12 c) (1/2) d) 4 e) 4 **38.** 0.852 **39.** a) f^{-1} = {(4, 3), (1, 2), (3, 2), (-1, 0), (0, 0) } b) $\sqrt{x-1}$ c) $-\sqrt{x-1}$ d) x^2-3, $x \ge 0$ e) $-x^{(1/3)}$ f) $\dfrac{-3x+2}{x}$ **40.** a) $y=a^x$ b) $y=a^x$ c) $\log_a x$ d) $\log_a x$ e) $y=x^a$ f) x^e **41.** 5^{23} **42.** 22.36 **43.** 5.39 **44.** 0.427 **45.** 2.14 **46.** -13.16 **47.** -1.12 **48.** 19762.27 **49.** -3.28 **50.** a) x<2 or x>3 b) 0, 2 **51.** 1.59 **52.** a) All real numbers except {0} b) All real numbers except {3} c) $x \ge 3$ d) $x \ge 3$ or $x \le -3$ e) All real numbers except {2} **53.** Domain: $x \ge 1$ or x<-3 Range: y<-4 or y=3 **54.** a) 2 b) 4 c) 3 d) π e) π f) 2 g) π h) 3 **56.** i. max: (-2, 4), (2, 4) min: (0, 0) ii. max: (2, 8) min: (-2, -8) iii. max: (4, 2) min: (0, 0) iv. max: (8, 2) min: (-8, -2)

Answers to Exercises P. 46-51
1. a) odd b) even c) even d) odd e) both f) neither g) even h) odd i) neither j) even k) even l) odd m) neither n) even o) even p) even q) odd r) odd s) neither t) odd u) even v) even w) neither x) even **2.** a) neither b) even c) odd d) odd e) even f) even g) even h) odd i) neither j) even k) odd l) odd m) even n) even o) even p) neither q) neither r) odd s) neither t) both u) odd v) even **3.** A=0 **4.** A=0 **5.** a=b **6.** i) neither ii) neither iii) even **7.** i. neither ii. neither iii. even iv even v. even vi. even vii. odd vii. even **8.** A-3, B-1, C-2 **9.** i. b; ii. a; iii. a, d, e; iv. a, b, c, d, e; v. f; vi. a, b, c; vii. a, b, c; viii. a, d, e; ix. a, d, e **10.** a) even b) even c) neither d) odd e) neither f) neither g) even h) even i) even j) even k) even l) odd **11.** a) even b) one to one $\sqrt[3]{x+1}$ c) one to one $9-x^2$ d) even **12.** a, b **13.** a-3, b-1, c-1, d-1, e-2 **14.** 1, 4

Answers to Exercises P. 62
1. x=0 **2.** a) area=7, inverse transformation (x-1, y+2) b) area=7, inverse transformation (x, -y) c) area=7, inverse transformation (-x, y) d) area=7, inverse transformation (-x, -y) e) area=7, inverse transformation (y, x) f) area=14, inverse transformation (x, y/2) g) area=28, inverse transformation (-x/2, -y/2)

Answers to Exercises P. 67
1. (-2, 2) **2.** a) A'(13, 1) B'(9, 1) C'(11, 3) b) A'(-13, 1) B'(-11, 1) C'(-9, 3) c) A'(-3, 3) B'(1, 7) C'(-1, 5) d) A'(-3, -9) B'(1, -9) C'(-1, -11) e) A'(7, 1) B'(3, -3) C'(5, -5) **3.** y=x-5 **4.** y= $-x^2$-4 **5.** A'(0, -1) B'(6, -1) C'(6, 2) D'(0, 2)

Answers to Exercises P. 76-77
1.
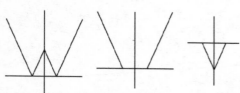
i ii ii

2. {5, 0} **3.** -26.04 **4.** 1) $y=-x^2$ 2) $(x-1)^2$ 3) $3.(x-1)^2$ 4) $3.(x-1)^2+4$ **5.** 6

6.
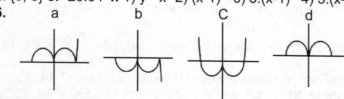
a b C d

7. (1, 2)

Answers to Exercises P. 78
f(x-2): Amplitude: 10 Offset: -1 Range: $-11 \le y \le 9$ Period: 10 Frequency: 0.1

f(x+2): Amplitude: 10 Offset: -1 Range: $-11 \le y \le 9$ Period: 10 Frequency: 0.1

f(2x): Amplitude: 10 Offset: -1 Range: $-11 \le y \le 9$ Period: 5 Frequency: 0.2

$f(\frac{x}{2})$: Amplitude: 10 Offset: -1 Range: $-11 \le y \le 9$ Period: 20 Frequency: 0.05

f(-x): Amplitude: 10 Offset: -1 Range: $-11 \le y \le 9$ Period: 10 Frequency: 0.1

f(x) -2: Amplitude: 10 Offset: -3 Range: $-13 \le y \le 7$ Period: 10 Frequency: 0.1

f(x) +2: Amplitude: 10 Offset: 1 Range: $-9 \le y \le 11$ Period: 10 Frequency: 0.1

2f(x): Amplitude: 20 Offset: -2 Range: $-22 \le y \le 18$ Period: 10 Frequency: 0.1

$\frac{f(x)}{2}$: Amplitude: 5 Offset: $\frac{-1}{2}$ Range: $-5.5 \le y \le 4.5$ Period: 10 Frequency: 0.1

-f(x): Amplitude: 10 Offset: 1 Range: $-9 \le y \le 11$ Period: 10 Frequency: 0.1

f(2x $\pm$ 6): Amplitude: 10 Offset: -1 Range: $-11 \le y \le 9$ Period: 5 Frequency: 0.2

Answers to Exercises P. 80
1. AB=AC **2.** 17 **3.** iv **4.** i, ii **5.** (-1, 6)

Answers to Exercises P. 83
1. x=1.16, y= -0.33 **2.** a=-0.2, b= 0.8 **3.** 4 **4.** -12

Answers to Exercises P. 89-92
1. 3.65 **2.** 4.85 **3.** a-(x=-4), b-(x=4), c- (x-y=4), d- (y=x), e- (y=4) **4.** i, iii, iv **5.** -3 **6.** y=x+10
7. the x intercept of l is positive, x intercept of m is negative **8.** 2y+x+14=0 **9.** y=x-4, slope=1
10. a) (4, 3) b) (-4, -3) c) (-3, 4) d) (3, -4) e) (-4, 3) f) (10, -7) g) (-2, -3) h) (4, 5) **11.** (1, 11) **12.** 7.14
13. (5, 11) **14.** slope= -2/5 y intercept= -7/5 **15.** infinite **16.** y=-4, x=2 **17.** i) y=3x-5 ii) y=-x-5 iii) y=2x
iv) 2x+3y=-6 v) x+2y-10=0 vi) 3x+5y=-15 **18.** minimum: 3.9 maximum: 21.9 **19.** m= -4/3 **20.** 105^0
21. b=3 **22.** 3x-y-7= 0 **23.** 4 **24.** 25.5 **25.** 0.83 **26.** 1/2 **27.** 14 **28.** a) y=-2x+8 b) 2y-3x+1=0 c) y=3x-5
d) y=3x+4 e) y=2x-6 f) 2x+y=4 **29.** a) 3y-2x-1=0 b) 3y-2x-1=0 **30.** y=3x+1 **31.** 3y+x-13=0 **32.** y+3x-4=0
33. 3y-x-12=0 **34.** -13/2 **35.** (9, 0), (-7, 3), (5, -7) **36.** (3.7, 4) **37.** 18.68

Answers to Exercises P. 96-97
1. x^2-5x-6 **2.** {1.14, -2.64} **3.** vertex= (3, 9), x intercept= (6, 0), (0, 0), y intercept= (0, 0),
axis of symmetry: x=3, Domain: all real numbers, Range: $(-\infty, 9]$ **4.** x^2+x-6 **5.** 2 **6.** a-i, b-iii, c-ii, d-iii, e-ii,
f-i

Answers to Exercises P. 99-101
1. 2.22 **2.** y= $-x^2$+4x-5, (1, -2), (5, -10) **3.** b(-0.9, 0.4), (3.9, 7.6) **4.** 2 **5.** a=1, b=-6 **6.** p=3.16 **7.** (2, 5)
8. (3, 0), (2, -1) **9.** a) y=$(-x^2/2)$ +(x/2) +1 b) y= 3/4[(x-2) ^{2}+1] c) y= 3/2(x^2-3x+2) d) y= -8/9[(x-3) ^{2}+7]
10. y= $-5x^2$+50x-18 **11.** 1 **12.** k=3 **13.** y=1/6 **14.** 2 **15.** have a maximum at (1, -5), axis of symmetry: x=1
16. (-8, 9] **17.** a) -12 b) -4.75 **18.** a) b^2-4ac$\ge$0 b) b^2-4ac=0 c) b^2-4ac>0 d) b^2-4ac<0
e) b^2-4ac is a perfect square **19.** ii **20.** [-6.25, ∞) **21.** a) -1 b) 4 c) -0.25 d) -7 **22.** a) [1.75, 14] b) [0, 8]
c) [3, 7] d) [3, -1] **23.** P(n) =(1/2) n^2+(1/2) n+1

Answers to Exercises P. 108-114
1. (x-1) ^{2} **2.** a) 2 b) 4 **3.**) { -2/3, 0, 2} 10, 5 **4.** 10, 5 **5.** i, iv **6.** (0, 1) **7.** 2, 12 **8.** No **9.** {-1, 2}
10. 1 **11.** 2 **12.** no real roots **13.** a) -9 b) 21 c) -5 d) 1 e) 149 f) 21 g) -59 h) -5 i) -23 j) 1 k) 67
l) -9 m) -5 n) 21 o) -23 **14.** x=2, 5 **15.** 4, 12 **16.** q={0.35, -2.35} **17.** -1, 33 **18.** a={1.14, -2.64} **19.** 5.44
20. A=3/4, B=5/4 **21.** A=3/16, B= 5/4, C= -3/16 **22.** {1, 2} **23.** Two real roots **24.** no **25.** 1 **26.** 32 **27.** 4
28. -18 **29.** y decreases without bound **30.** y increases without bound **31.** A-5 B-6 C-3 D-3 E-4 **32.** -x-1
33. i) 2^{12} ii) 1 **34.** A-3 B-4 C-5 **35.** 24+5i **36.** sum: 3 product: 0 **37.** 13 **38.** 1, 2, 3, 7 **38.** 1, 2, 3 **40.** 1, 2, 4
41. a) (x-1) (x+1) (x^2+x-1) (x^2-x+1) b) (x-y) (x^6+x^5y+x^6y^2+x^5y^3+x^4y^4+x^3y^5+x^2y^6+y^7)

c) $(x-4y^2)$ $(x^2+4xy^2+16y^4)$ d) $(x+1)$ $(x^4-x^3+x^2-x+1)$ **42**. a, c, f **43**. $\frac{\mp 6}{1}$, $\frac{\mp 6}{4}$, $\frac{\mp 3}{1}$, $\frac{\mp 3}{4}$, $\frac{\mp 1}{2}$, $\frac{\mp 1}{1}$, $\frac{\mp 1}{4}$,

$\frac{\mp 2}{1}$ **44**. v **45**. b **46**. a, b, c, d **47**. a) $x^3+2x^2+9x+18$ b) x^3-x^2+x+-1 c) $x^3-5x^2+4x+10$ **48**. a, c **49**. 2

50. ii.0.75 **51**. a=b=1/2 c=1 **52**.-1.5 **53**. 3 **54**. i) 5.67 ii) a and b are integers **55**. a) 3 b) 2.67 **56**. x^2+4x-1
57. $x^2+4x+13$ **58**. 1.16 **59**. (x+8) /3 **60**. 3x+(5/3)

Answers to Exercises P. 117-120

1. 16.91 **2**. sinx=$\dfrac{a}{\sqrt{16+a^2}}$ cosx=$\dfrac{4}{\sqrt{16+a^2}}$ **3**. cosx=$\dfrac{\sqrt{16-a^2}}{4}$ tanx=$\dfrac{a}{\sqrt{16-a^2}}$ **4**. 1/$\sqrt{3}$ **5**. $\dfrac{\sqrt{b^2-a^2}}{b}$

6. -$\dfrac{\sqrt{b^2-a^2}}{b}$ **7**. 184.95 **8**. 1 53.21 **9**. 1.13 **10**. 0.8 **11**. 9.63 **12**. y=14.62 x=13.74 **13**. BC=16 AB=20

14. sin(2ϕ) **15**. a) i.ii b) i-b ii-a iii- .(a^2/b) **16**. 0.6 **17**. B(1.76, 3.8) C(5, 6.15) D(8.24, 3.8)

18. d=$\dfrac{x.\cos\beta}{\sin(\beta-\alpha)}$ y=$\dfrac{x.\sin\beta}{\sin(\beta-\alpha)}$ **19**. 367.22 **20**. 29.81 **21**. 20.57, **22**. 964.42 **23**. 160.59 **24**. 34831.27

25. i) 231 cm ii) 31 cm **26**.186.6 **27**. 33.56 **28**. 20.55 **29**.4.3 **30**.347.3

Answers to Exercises P. 126
1. i. (fog)(x) =$\cos^2 x$ (gof)(x) = cos(x^2) ii. 1 **2**. 90^0, 60^0, 45^0, 30^0, 180^0, 120^0, 270^0, 150^0, 360^0, 57.3^0, 90^0

3. $\dfrac{5\pi}{6}$, $\dfrac{\pi}{10}$, $\dfrac{\pi}{6}$, $\dfrac{\pi}{5}$, $\dfrac{\pi}{4}$, $\dfrac{\pi}{3}$, $\dfrac{\pi}{2}$, $\dfrac{2\pi}{3}$, $\dfrac{3\pi}{4}$, $\dfrac{5\pi}{6}$, π, $\dfrac{5\pi}{4}$, $\dfrac{3\pi}{2}$, $\dfrac{7\pi}{4}$, 2π **4**. 120^0 **5**. a) 81 b) 3 c) tanx d) 1

e) 1 f) 2 g) 2 h) 2 **6** 0.58, 0, 0.5, 1, -1, 6.48 **7**.270^0

Answers to Exercises P. 130-131
1. 3 **2**.39.99 **3**.0.32 **4**. 50^0 **5**. 0.786 **6**.111.5^0 - 248.5^0 **7**. (0, 2π) **8**. 59.31^0 **9**. 80.54^0 **10**.234^0 **11**. (62.23^0)
12.1.57, 3.68 **13**.22, 98^0 **14**. 240^0 **15**.15^0, 75^0 **16**. 15^0, 75^0, 195^0, 255^0 **17**.11.25^0 **18**. 10^0 **19**. 0.52
20. 4.52 **21**. 135^0 **22**. 1.05, 4.19 **23**. 2.13

Answers to Exercises P. 134-135
1. 0.7 **2**. 2cosθ **3**. 165^0 **4**. 0.37 **5**. 2.36 **6**. 4.71 **7**. 0 **8**. i. 14.9 ii. 289.25 **9**. c **10**. 9 **11**. 3.14 **12**. 269.9^0

13. 100^0 **14**. 0.33 **15**. $\dfrac{\sqrt{3}}{2}$

Answers to Exercises P. 138-139
1. 240 **2**. 5.66 **3**. 77.32 **4**. xysinθ **5**. 81.97 **6**. 15.04

Answers to Exercises P. 140-141
1.(4.71, -2) **2**. 1-3 **3**. 1-3 **4**. 4

Answers to Exercises P. 143-144
1. increases **2**. Amplitude=13 offset=-2 Axis of wave y=-2 **3**. 2.24 **4**. 2.45 **5**. 0.25 **6**. 3.142 **7**. 1.57 **8**. 1.5
9. 5 **10**. 0.26 **11**. 2 **13**. 0.79 **14**. 88.95^0 **15**.1 **16**. i. period=2 frequency=1/2 Amplitude =2 ii. period=4π
frequency=1/(4π) Amplitude =3/4 iii.(180^0, 1)

Answers to Exercises P. 148-165

1. i. π/2 ii.210^0, 330^0 iii.7/24 **2**. ia=2 b=1/2 ii. a=1/2 iii. perimeter=αR + x Area=$\dfrac{\alpha R^2}{2}$

3. 0 **4.** y=x **5**. Area=15π/4 Perimeter=(3π/2) +10 **6**. -0.96 **7**. 0.96 **8**. i. 45^0, 135^0 ii.60^0, 120^0, 240^0, 300^0
iii. π/6, π/2, 5π/6, 3π/2 iv.0, 3.14 6.28 **9**. i.A=12.5 B=3 ii.1.20 AM iii.1.38 AM-2.22AM
5.38AM-6.22AM 9.38AM-10.22AM 1.38PM-2.22PM 5.38PM-6.22PM 9.38PM-10.22PM **10**. 105.63
11. 86.41^0 **12**. 1.27 **13**. x=97.63 **14**. 2 **15**. x=45^0 y=45^0 **16**. 20^0 **17**. x= 1/2 **18**. 310^0 **19**. 71.57^0
20. x= 40^0 y= 50^0 **21**. (-8/15) **22**.(-5/12) **23**. A(2.01, 2.23) B(1.93, -2.3) C(-1.17, -2.76) **24**. x= 7.9

y= 4.24 z=2.31 k=3.56 **25**. -0.478 **26**. 90^0 **27**. 720 **28**. x=270^0 **29**. 54.74^0 **30**. 0.26 **31**. 54.74^0 32. $\dfrac{2x}{1-x^2}$

33. 2cosx **34**. Amplitude= 2 Period=π Frequency=(1/π) Phase shift=(-π/6) y intercept =-1.73

x intercept 2.09, -1.05, -2.62, **35**. 0.96 **36**. a) 30^0, $\dfrac{\pi}{6}$ b) -60^0, $-\dfrac{\pi}{3}$ c) 30^0, $\dfrac{\pi}{6}$ d) 150^0, $\dfrac{5\pi}{6}$ e) 45^0, $\dfrac{\pi}{4}$

f) -45^0, $-\dfrac{\pi}{4}$ g) 60^0, $\dfrac{\pi}{3}$ h) 120^0, $\dfrac{2\pi}{3}$ i) 45^0, $\dfrac{\pi}{4}$ j) 135^0, $\dfrac{3\pi}{4}$ k) 135^0, $\dfrac{3\pi}{4}$ l) -30^0, $-\dfrac{\pi}{6}$ **37**. 3/5 **38**. -0.51

39. $\dfrac{\sqrt{3}}{2}$ **40**. 0.74 **41**. -0.83 **42**. -1.33 **43**. 2.62 **44**. 45^0, $\dfrac{\pi}{4}$ **45**. 45^0, $\dfrac{\pi}{4}$ **46**. 0.65 **47**. 68.2 **48**. 17.88

49. 54.46 **50**. 9 **51**. a) 56.44 b) 9 c) 16.37 d) 2 **52**. 1 **53**. 0 **54**. $\dfrac{-a^2+1}{a^2+1}$ **55**. a **56**. a **57**. (2, 2)

58. $\sqrt{1-a^2}$ **59**. b+$\sqrt{1-b^2}$ **60**. 1-2x^2 **61**. $\dfrac{3\pi}{2}$ **62**. $\dfrac{8\pi}{3}$ **63**. $\dfrac{\pi}{2}$ **64**. 142.62 **65**. 0.22 **66**. a) $\sqrt{1-a^2}$

b) $\dfrac{a}{\sqrt{1-a^2}}$ **67**. a) $\dfrac{a}{\sqrt{1+a^2}}$ b) $\dfrac{1}{\sqrt{1+a^2}}$ **68**. a) $\sqrt{1-a^2}$ b) $\dfrac{\sqrt{1-a^2}}{a}$ **69**. a) -$\sqrt{1-a^2}$ b) - $\dfrac{a}{\sqrt{1-a^2}}$

70. a) $\dfrac{a}{\sqrt{1+a^2}}$ b) -$\dfrac{1}{\sqrt{1+a^2}}$ **71**. a) $\sqrt{1-a^2}$ b) -$\dfrac{\sqrt{1-a^2}}{a}$ **72**. a) 2a^2-1 b) 2a $\sqrt{1-a^2}$ **73**. a) 1-2a^2

b) 2a-$\sqrt{1-a^2}$ **74**. a) -12/13 b) -5/13 c) 12/5 **75**. 2.25 **76**. 63.43 **77**. 1714.1 **78**. cos^{-1} (2/$\sqrt{6}$)

79. cos^{-1} (2/$\sqrt{6}$) **80. a**) 60.07 b) 2.1 **81**. a) 2.5 b) 1 c) $\dfrac{\pi}{6}$ d) 1.5 **82**. a) -2 b) $\dfrac{\pi}{2}$ c) -$\dfrac{\pi}{2}$ d) +2 **83**. 2

84. 1 **85**. 107.46 **86**. 56.57 **87**. h$=\dfrac{x\cdot\sin\alpha\cdot\sin\beta}{\sin(\alpha-\beta)}$, y$=\dfrac{x\cdot\cos\alpha\cdot\sin\beta}{\sin(\alpha-\beta)}$ **88**. a) 35.66 b) 71.79 **89**. 15.56

90. $\dfrac{\pi}{4}$ **91**. 64.28 **92**. All three **93**. -30° **94**. 1.87 **95**. 120^0 **96**. a) cos90^0<cos60^0<cos30^0<cos0^0
b) sin0^0<sin30^0<sin60^0<sin90^0 c) tan1^0<tan29^0< tan60^0<tan89^0 d) sin169^0<sin143^0<sin120^0<sin91^0
e) cos169^0<cos143^0<cos120^0<cos91^0 f) tan91^0<tan120^0<tan143^0<tan163^0 **97**. a, b **98**. 198.4 **99**. 0.58

100. $\dfrac{20+12\sqrt{65}}{117}$ **101**. sinx = 1 / b, cosx = -a / b **102**. (1.047, -1) **103**. a) sec x+ csc x b) 1 c) tan^2 x-1

d) 0 e) -1+2tan x **104**. 0.69 **105**. 10.89 **106**. $\dfrac{\sqrt{6}}{2}$ **107**. $\dfrac{\sqrt{6}}{2}$ **108**. 13.39 **109**. -0.468 **110**. 311.5° **112**. 0.7

113. a) 0.97 b) 0.97 c) 0.27 d) -0.97 e) 0.97 f) -1 **114**. 90^0 **115**. 175.73 **116**. 1.69 **117**. III quadrant

118. 1 **119**. 1.1 **120**. 0.95 **121**. -0.61 **122**. -$\dfrac{\sqrt{7}}{3}$ **123**. 0.64 **124**. -0.5 **125**. 3.41 **126**. 240^0 **127**. -1.37

128. 1 **129** 4th quadrant **130**. 0.32 **131**. -0.99 **132**. sin(2θ) = 0.96, tan(2θ) = 3.43 **133**. -1 **134**. 0.75

135. 0.77 **136**. -3.42 **137**. a) $\dfrac{1-y^2}{1+y^2}$ b) $\dfrac{2y}{1+y^2}$ **138**. a) Amplitude= 3, Period= 6.28, Frequency= 0.16,

Phase-shift= 0 b) Amplitude= 4, Period= 6.28, Frequency= 0.16, Phase-shift= 0 c) Amplitude= 2,
Period= 2.09, Frequency= 0.48, Phase-shift= 0 d) Amplitude= 4, Period= 3.14, Frequency= 0.32,

Phase-shift= 0 e) Amplitude= 3, Period= 1.57, Frequency= 1.64, Phase-shift= 0 f) Amplitude= 2,

Period= 6.28, Frequency= 0.16, Phase-shift= $-\frac{\pi}{6}$ g) Amplitude= 2, Period= 6.28, Frequency= 0.16,

Phase-shift= $\frac{\pi}{6}$ h) Amplitude= 3, Period= 3.14, Frequency= 0.32, Phase-shift= $-\frac{\pi}{2}$ I) Amplitude=3,

Period= 3.14, Frequency= 0.32, Phase-shift= $\frac{\pi}{2}$ j) Amplitude= 2, Period= 1.57, Frequency= 0.64,

Phase-shift= $-\frac{\pi}{4}$ k) Amplitude= 2, Period= 1.05, Frequency= 0.96, Phase-shift= $\frac{\pi}{6}$ l) Amplitude= 3,

Period= 1.05, Frequency= 0.96, Phase-shift= $\frac{\pi}{6}$ **140.** $\cos\theta = \sqrt{1-x^2}$, $\tan\theta = \dfrac{x}{\sqrt{1-x^2}}$,

$\cot\theta = \dfrac{\sqrt{1-x^2}}{x}$, $\sec\theta = \dfrac{1}{\sqrt{1-x^2}}$, $\csc\theta = \dfrac{1}{x}$ **141.** a) $2\cos\theta$ b) $3\tan\theta$ c) $2/\sec\theta$ **142.** a) 120^0 b) 60^0

c) 120^0, -60^0 d) 120^0 e) 135^0 f) -45^0 g) 150^0 h) 240^0, -60^0 I) 120^0 m) 210^0 n) 150^0 o) 150^0 **144.** $\sin x = t$,

$\cos x = \sqrt{1-t^2}$, $\tan x = \dfrac{t}{\sqrt{1-t^2}}$, $\cot x = \dfrac{\sqrt{1-t^2}}{t}$, $\sec x = \dfrac{1}{\sqrt{1-t^2}}$, $\csc x = \dfrac{1}{t}$ **145.** $\cos x = t$, $\sin x = \sqrt{1-t^2}$,

$\cot x = \dfrac{t}{\sqrt{1-t^2}}$, $\tan x = \dfrac{\sqrt{1-t^2}}{t}$, $\csc x = \dfrac{1}{\sqrt{1-t^2}}$, $\sec x = \dfrac{1}{t}$ **146.** $\tan x = t$, $\sin x = \dfrac{t}{\sqrt{t^2+1}}$, $\cos x = \dfrac{1}{\sqrt{t^2+1}}$,

$\cot x = \dfrac{1}{t}$, $\sec x = \sqrt{t^2+1}$, $\csc x = \dfrac{\sqrt{t^2+1}}{t}$ **147.** $\cot x = t$, $\cos x = \dfrac{t}{\sqrt{t^2+1}}$, $\sin x = \dfrac{1}{\sqrt{t^2+1}}$, $\tan x = \dfrac{1}{t}$, $\csc x =$

$\sqrt{t^2+1}$, $\sec x = \dfrac{\sqrt{t^2+1}}{t}$ **148.** $\sec x = t$, $\cos x = \dfrac{1}{t}$, $\sin x = \dfrac{\sqrt{t^2-1}}{t}$, $\tan x = \sqrt{t^2-1}$, $\cot x = \dfrac{1}{\sqrt{t^2-1}}$,

$\csc x = \dfrac{t}{\sqrt{t^2-1}}$ **149.** $\sin x = \dfrac{1}{t}$, $\cos x = \dfrac{\sqrt{t^2-1}}{t}$, $\cot x = \sqrt{t^2-1}$, $\tan x = \dfrac{1}{\sqrt{t^2-1}}$, $\csc x = t$, $\sec x = \dfrac{t}{\sqrt{t^2-1}}$

150. $\dfrac{4}{3}(\csc x)^2$ **151.** $\dfrac{4}{3}(\sec x)^2$ **152.** a) Amplitude: 2, Period: 2.09 Frequency: 0.48 Phase shift: $\dfrac{\pi}{3}$

b) Amplitude: 2, Period: 3.14 Frequency: 0.32 Phase shift: 1/2 c) Amplitude: 5, Period: 3.14
Frequency: 0.32 Phase shift: -0.464 assuming a sine function d) Amplitude: 13, Period: 3.14

Frequency: 0.32 Phase shift: 0.588 assuming a sine function **153.** a) $\dfrac{5\pi}{6}$ b) $\dfrac{\pi}{3}$ c) $\dfrac{\pi}{3}$ **154.** 70.53^0

155. c **156.** a **157.** a.i b.iv c.ii d. iii **158.** a) Amplitude: 0.96, Period: 3.14 Frequency: 0.32
Domain: All Real Numbers Range: [-0.96, 0.96] Offset: 0 max value: 0.96 min value: -0.96
b) Amplitude: 2, Period: 3.14 Frequency: 0.32 Domain: All Real Numbers Range: [-2, 2] offset: 0 max
value: 2 min value: -2 c) Amplitude: 0.5, Period: 1.57 Frequency: 0.28 Domain: All Real N umbers
Range: [-0.5, 0.5] offset: 0 max value: 0.5 min value: -0.5 **159.** a) [-0.94, 0.96] b) [-0.5, 0.5] c) [-2, 2]
d) [0.199, 0.998]

Answers to Exercises P. 168-169
1. 4 **2.** iii is the greatest and v is the least **3.** 2 **4.** 1/3 **5.** 3^{36a} **6.** empty set **7.** 546 **8.** 1 **9.** 3787.43
10. i) -0.67 ii) 7.33 iii) -2/3 **11.** Jan 2000= 22.28 billion, Jan 2001= 100.66 billion, growth= 77.86
12. i) 49.12 ii) 6 years **13.** 22.36 **14.** 3.3 years

Answers to Exercises P. 172-179

1. empty set **2.** i. 2s+r ii. 2r+2s iii. r-2s iv. –r-s **3.**-5/3 **4.** 1.2 **5.** i. (0, ∞) ii. (0, ∞) iii.31/6 **6.** a^c=b

7. 4< $\log_3$ 100 <5 **8.** 2.76 **9.** 4logA-4logB-logC **10.** $\log_3 5$ = y/x $\log_a 75$ = 2y+x **11.** $\log_b a$ **12.** 6104

13. 1.73 **14.** 8.08 **15.**4.5 **16** 0.702 **17.** 3.726 **18.** 0.683 **19.** 1 **20.** ii..ii **21.** i.ii.iii.iv **22.** i.-3<x<1 ii. x< -3

23. for all values of x that make sinx>0 24. 3.41 **25.** -8.79 **26.** -0.774 **27.** 9.383 **28.** 1.86 **29.** 0.44

30. 14.48^0 **31.** 0.852 **32.** A<B<C<D<E **33.**i.y+2x ii.2x-y **34.** i.3logA+3 logB ii.logA-3logB

iii.$\frac{1}{5}$[logA-logB] iv. logA+$\frac{1}{3}$logB **35.** i. 2.47 ii. 4.98 iii. 1.92 iv. 1.92 v. 5.35 vi. 3.33 vii. 2.53 viii. 8.497

ix. 1.46 x. 1.26 xi. ln3, ln 4 xii. {0, 0.57} **36.** i.1 ii.3 iii.1/2 iv.1 v.2 vi.2 **37.** i. 109.1 ii. 3 iii.11/3 iv.e^8, e^5

vi. 25/4 **38.** i. $\log_2(\frac{4 \cdot 12}{36})$ = 0.42 ii. $\log_3(\frac{x.x^2}{(\sqrt{x})^{1.5}}$ = -0.25 $\log_3 x$ **39.** Domain (-∞,0)

inverse function: ln $\frac{(\frac{x}{4})-3}{2}$ ii. Domain(2.33, ∞) inverse function: $\frac{10^x+7}{3}$ **40.** i. x=28.4 y=1.69 ii. x=3

y=-1 iii. x= $e^{(8/5)}$ y= $e^{(3/5)}$ **41.** 2 **42.** 2.335 **43.** $\frac{e^{-2}+4}{3}$ **44.**(2, 3) **45.**0.25 **46.** i. 113/12 ii.3 iii.41/6 iv. 4

v.1.33 vi.-9, 98 **47.** i. x>0 or x<1 ii. Empty set iii. x>1 or x<-1 **48.** i. 20 ii. 9 iii. $\log_x$ y-$\log_x$z iv. 1+ $\log_y$z

v.1+ $\log_y$ x **49.** i. $\log_2 x$ ii. lnx iii. logx iv.3^x v.e^x vi.10^x vii. ln ($\frac{x+1}{2}$) viii. $\frac{(\log x)-4}{2}$ ix. 4- $e^{(x/2)}$ **50.** i.5 ii.1

ii. Empty Set iv.-1 v. 2.58 **51.** a) 3^{-x} b) y>0 **52.** y>0 **53.**(2, 3) **54.** 250 **55.** 0.08 **56.**Empty Set

57.{ -0.77, 2, 4} **58.** Domain: All Real Numbers except zero Range: All real numbers **59.** x=y^2 x>0 y>0

60. i, ii, iv, vi **61.**logy= 3.log(x+1) +$\frac{3}{4}$log(2x − 3) − $\frac{1}{3}$log(1+ 7x) − $\frac{3}{2}$log(2x + 3) **62.** i.-3 ii. -6 iii.0.001

iv.-$\frac{2}{15}$ v.e^{-2} **63.** $3^{(5/6)}$ **64.**ln ($\frac{1}{2}$) **65.** a) ???b) 3B-4A c) A+B+3 d) 32A+12B+20 **66.** i. Empty set ii.11

iii.{1, 100} iv. {0, ln5} v.{ ln ($\frac{1}{2}$), ln($\frac{1}{3}$)} **67.** 1-a 2-b 3-c 4-d 68. 1-a-f 2-b-e 3-c 4-d

Answers to Exercises P. 183-187

1. L **2.** L **3.** x=3 vertical asymptote **4.** x=4 vertical asymptote, y=1 horizontal asymptote, (0, 0) intercept
5. ∞ **6.** x=±4 **7.** 8 **8.** 3/2 **9.** y=1 horizontal asymptote, x=0 (y axis) vertical asymptote **10.** x=4 **11.** a) 0
b) 0 c) 1/4 d) 1 e) no limit f) 0 g) 1 h) -∞ l) 2 j) -1 k) ½ l) 1 m) 0 n) 1 o) - ∞ p) ∞ q) 2/3 r) +∞ s) -∞ t)
1/4 u) 1 v) -1 w) no limit x) 6 y) 0 z) 1/4 aa) ¼ bb) 1/18 cc) ∞ **12.** 8/3 **13.** 12 **14.** a) vertical asymptote
x=2, x=-2 hole, y=0 (x axis) horizontal asymptote, Domain: all real numbers except {+2, -2}, Range: all
real numbers except {0} b) vertical asymptote x=1, x=-1 hole, y=1 (x axis) horizontal asymptote,
Domain: all real numbers except {+1, -1}, Range: all real numbers except {1} c) vertical asymptote
x=3, x=-3 hole, y=0 (x axis) horizontal asymptote, Domain: all real numbers except {+3, -3}, Range: all
real numbers except {0} **15.** Domain: all real numbers except {-2}, Range: all real numbers except {3}
16. Domain: all real numbers except {1}, Range: all real numbers except {1/2} **17.** Domain: all real
numbers except {0, 2}, Range: all real numbers except {1} **18.** a) 5 b) 4 **19.** a) -∞ b) +∞ c) +∞ d) 0
e) it is asymptotic **20.** a) ∞ b) ∞ c) ∞ d) no e) 0 f) undefined g) no it is asymptotic **21.** 2 **22.** a) 2 b) 1
c) No; removable **23.** a) 4 b) 2 c) 6 d) no jump **24.** Domain: all real numbers except {3}, Range: (0, ∞),
horizontal asymptote y=0 **25.** a) X=2 vertical asymptote, y=1 horizontal asymptote
b) x=2 vertical asymptote, x=1 hole, y=1 horizontal asymptote c) X=1 vertical asymptote, y=0
horizontal asymptote d) y=2 horizontal asymptote e) X=±1/2 vertical asymptote,
y=3/4 horizontal asymptote

Answers to Exercises P. 189

1. 5.83 **2.** 1 **3.** not periodic **4.** all nonnegative integers **5.** a and c **6.** a) 2, 3, 1, 0, -6, -1, 0
b) 3, 4, 2, 1, -5, 0, 1 c) all nonnegative integers d) all non positive integers **7.** 3

COMBINATORICS

Answers to Exercises P. 202-208

1. 200 **2.** (1/n) +n+1 **3.** (1/n^2) **4.** 58 **5.** 499.83 6. a) 9 b) 6 **7.** $\binom{15}{5}$ **8.** $2 \cdot \binom{15}{5}$

9. 26^4. 10^2-26^3. 10^3 **10.** a) $\binom{5}{2} \cdot 3 + 5.$ $\binom{3}{2}$ b) $\binom{8}{2} - \binom{5}{2} - \binom{3}{2} + 2$ **11.** 680 **12.** a) 15!

b) 3!. 4!. 5!.6! **13.** a) 14! b) 2!.4!.5!.6! **14.** a) 14! b) 12!.3! c) 13!.2! d) 14!-13!.2! e) 8!.7!

f) 7!.7!.2 **15.** a) 13! b) 3!.11! c) 2!.12! d) 13!-2!.12! e) 7!.7! f) 6!.7! **16.** a) $\binom{6}{2} \cdot \binom{7}{3}$

b) $\binom{6}{3} \cdot \binom{7}{2}$ c) $\binom{7}{3} \cdot \binom{6}{2} + \binom{7}{4} \cdot \binom{6}{1} + \binom{7}{5}$ d) $\binom{6}{2} \cdot \binom{7}{3} + \binom{7}{2} \cdot \binom{6}{3} + \binom{7}{1} \cdot \binom{6}{4} + \binom{7}{0}$

e) $\binom{11}{3}$ f) $\binom{11}{5}$ **17.** $\binom{8}{3} \cdot \binom{10}{6}$ **18.** a) 18.17.16 b) 10.8.16 c) 18.17.16. $\binom{15}{3}$ **19.** a) $\binom{15}{10}$

b) $\binom{7}{5} \cdot \binom{8}{5}$ c) $\binom{7}{5} \cdot \binom{8}{5} + \binom{7}{6} \cdot \binom{8}{4} + \binom{7}{7} \cdot \binom{8}{5}$ **20.** a) 2^8 b) $\binom{8}{5}$ c) $\binom{8}{5} + \binom{8}{6} + \binom{8}{7} + \binom{8}{8}$

d) $\binom{8}{5} + \binom{8}{4} + \binom{8}{3} + \binom{8}{2} + \binom{8}{1}$ e) 2^7 f) 2^6 g) 2^5 h) $\binom{6}{4}$ i) $\binom{6}{3}$ j) $\binom{5}{3}$ k) $\binom{6}{5}$

21. a) $\binom{3}{2} \cdot \binom{4}{2} \cdot 4!$ b) $\binom{3}{2} \cdot \binom{4}{2} \cdot 3!.2!$ c) $\binom{3}{2} \cdot \binom{4}{2} \cdot 2!.2!.2!$ d) $\binom{3}{2} \cdot \binom{4}{2} \cdot 2!.2!.2!$

22. 11!/(5!.2!.2!) **23.** 12!/(10!.2!) **24.** 4000 **25.** 3200 **26.** 3200 **27.** 4000 **28.** a) 5832
b) 2592 c) 3240 d) 2688 e) 1176 f) 1512 g) 630 **29.** a) 900 b) 450 c) 450 d) 648 e) 320 f) 328 g) 136

30. a) 120 b) $\binom{120}{2}$ c) 3500 d) $\binom{50}{2} \cdot \binom{70}{3}$ **31.** 31 **32.** a) 9 b) 90 c) 90

d) 900 **33.** $\binom{8}{3}$ **34.** a) 10! b) 6!.5! c) 2!.5!. 5! d) 5!. (2!)^5 e) 9! f) 5!.5! g) 5!.5! h) 4!.(2!)^5

35. 496 **36.** a) 42 b) 2^{42} c) 7^6 d) 5040 e) 7 **37.** 36 **38.** a) 12 b) 144 c) 72 **39.** $\binom{n}{2} - n$

40. a) 6840 b) 6840. $\binom{17}{3}$ **41.** 6! **42.** 5!.2! **43.** 5! **44.** 4!.2! **45.** 8^5 **46.** 6720 **47.** 870. $\binom{28}{4}$

48. $\binom{10}{2} \cdot \binom{20}{4}$ **49.** 12!/(3!.4!.5!) **50.** 4!.10! **51.** 5!/(2!.2!) **52.** 3! **53.** 4!/2! **54.** 11 **55.** 80

56. a) 16 b) 4 **57.** a) 504 b) $\binom{9}{3}$ **58.** a) $\binom{12}{3} - \binom{5}{3} - \binom{7}{3}$ b) 35 c) $\binom{12}{2} - \binom{5}{2} - \binom{7}{2} + 2$

Answers to Exercises P. 211-212
1. 2 **2.** -960 **3.** x^{20}-30.x^{18}.y+405.x^{16}.y^2-3240.x^{14}.y^3 **4.** a={4, 2} **5.** a) 1312500 b) 78750 c) 900x^{12} **6.** -61236/x^5 **7.** 50936x^6.y^6 **8.** 9 !/ (2 !.3 !.4 !) .x^2. (-2y)^3. (3z)^4

Answers to Exercises P. 222-228

1. a) 3/8 b) 3/8 c) 1/8 d) 7/8 e) ½ **2.** a) (1/32) . $\binom{5}{3}$ b) 0, 81 **3.** 1/3 **4.** a) 4/52 b) 13/52

c) 26/52 d) 12/52 e) 6/52 f) 3/52 g) 11/26 h) 8/52 I) 16/52 **5.** a) 2/42 b) 20/49 c) 20/42 **6.** a) (1/169) b) 144/169 c) 24/169 **7.** a) 1/221 b) 188/221 c) 32/221 **8.** a) 4/52 b) 16/221 c) 384/5525 d) 1201/5525 **9.** a) 63/125 **b)** 729/1000 5 **10.** 1/9 **11.** 2/9 **12.** a) 1/2 b) 1/2 c) 1/6 **13.** a) 2/3 b) 1/6 **14.** 11/36 **15.** a) 2/9 b) 1/3 c) 1/6 d) 1/15 **16.** 3/5 **18.** a) 1/22 b) 1/11 c) 5/33 d) 7/22 e) 47/66 **19.** a) 5/33 b) 5/18 c) 2/11 d) 3/11 **20.** a) 8/65 b) 1/13 c) 1/5 d) 8/65 e) 24/65 **21.** a) 8/65 b) 1/13 c) 1/5 d) 8/65 e) 24/65 **22.** a) $(8/15)^3$ b) $(7/15)^3$ c) $(8/15)^3 + (7/15)^3$ d) $(8/15) \cdot (7/15)^2$ e) $(8/15) \cdot (7/15)^2 \cdot 3$ **23.** n=25

24. a) 1/9 b) 4/9 c) 4/9 **25.** a) $C(7, 3) \cdot C(11, 3) / C(18, 6)$ b) $\dfrac{7}{18} \cdot \dfrac{6}{17} \cdot \dfrac{6}{16} \cdot \dfrac{5}{15} \cdot \dfrac{4}{14} \cdot \dfrac{5}{13}$

c) $C(7, 2) \cdot C(6, 3) \cdot C(5, 1) / C(18, 6)$ **26.** $1 - \dfrac{280}{300} \cdot \dfrac{279}{299} \cdot \dfrac{278}{298} \cdot \dfrac{277}{297} \cdot \dfrac{276}{296}$ **27.** a) 28/57 b) 8/19 c) 8/95

d) 29/57 **28.** a) $(4/5)^3$ b) $3(1/5)(4/5)^2$ c) $(1/5)^2 \cdot (12/5)$ d) 61/125 **29.** a) 7/15 b) 4/9 c) 7/9 d)) 3/5 **30.** a) 42/69 b) 39/69 c) 15/69 **31.** a) i.16/80 ii. 28/80 iii. 4/80 iv. 1/2 v. 4/28 vi.4/16 b) no c) no **32.** 5/9 **33.** a) 1/9 b) 28/100 c) 72/100 d) 1/5 **34.** a) 0.4 b) 49/125 **c)** 40/49 d) 0.8 **35.** 1/3 **36.** 2/3

Answers to Exercises P. 233-234

1. a) mode=6 median =7 mean = 7.625 std dev= 4.58 b) mode: 27 median =27.5 mean = 28.4 std dev= 2.87 **2.** mode: 25 median =25 mean = 25.83 std dev= 12.01 Range;=50 L=15 U=35 IQR= 20 **3.** a) mode, median, mean will be increased by a and range, standard deviation and variance stay the same b) mode, median, mean will be decreased by a and range, standard deviation and variance stay the same c) all quantities will be multiplied by a and variance by a^2 d) all quantities will be divided by a and variance by a^2 **4.** 0 **5.** 1 **6.** subtract mean from each term and divide the result by standard deviation **7.** a) mode=63 median =63.5 mean = 67.3 b) mode=56 median =56.5 mean = 60.3 **8.** a) mode=21 median =27.5 mean = 29 Range= 22 standard deviation=7.41 b) no change **9.** mode=1 median =2 mean = 2 Range= 4 standard deviation=1.37 **10.** least-d greatest-e

GEOMETRY

Answers to Exercises P. 279-283

1. c, d **2.** 15079 **3.** 3.52 **4.** 27.27 **5.** w=50, l=70 **6.** a) 3, 4, 5 b) 6, 8, 10 c) 12, 16, 20 d) 15, 20, 25 **7.** 91.16 **8.** 900 **9.** 9/2 **10.** 5 **11.** R= x/(1+2$\sqrt{3}$) **12.** 607830, 18

13. $\dfrac{R \cdot (1 - Sin(\alpha/2))}{Sin(\alpha/2)}$ **14.** 8059.25 **15.** h= $R \cdot Sin2\alpha$ **16.** 10.44 **17.** 1.16 **18.** R= x/(2$\sqrt{3}$ -2)

19. $R^2 \cdot (\dfrac{\pi}{2} - 1)$ **20.** 31.52 **21.** 100 **22.** 100

Answers to Exercises P. 286-287

1. 109.7 **2.** a) 2110.86 b) 36π **3.** $R\sqrt{3}$ **4.** a) h/3 b) $4x^2/9$ **5.** a) 125 b) 54 c) 36 d) 8 e) 27 f) 12 g) volume: 117, surface area: 54 h) 4/51 **6.** a) 18 b) 28 c) 29 **7.** a) increased by 17.4% **10.** a, b **11.** 9 **12.** 0.89 **13.** a, b, c, d, e **14.** 216$ **15.** 26 **16.** volume: 570, surface area: 414 **17.** 1/6 **18.** volume: 400, area: 360 **19.** 1/$\sqrt{3}$ **20.** a) 0.13 b) 5763.78 **21.** 6

Answers to Exercises P. 296-297

1. 1/2 **2.** 25π **3.** 13/30 **4.** 7.042 **5.** 216.86 **6.** 8 **7.** 4678.88 **8.** 34 **9.** 16π **10.** 6

11. 1/6 **12.** $\dfrac{\pi R^3 \cdot (16 - 3\sqrt{3})}{12}$ **13.** 1/$\sqrt{3}$ **14.** a circle and a point

Answers to Exercises P. 300-302

1. $\dfrac{500\pi}{3}$ **2.** 125π **3.** 1/2 **4.** a) 96π b) 108π c) 24π d) 36π **5.** $\dfrac{16\pi}{3}$ **6.** 1.89π **7.** a) $32\pi/3$ b) $16\pi/3$

c) $16\pi/3$ **8.** a) $4\pi/3$ b) $8\pi/3$ **9.** a) 480π b) 240π c) 120π d) 100π **10.** a) $\dfrac{2\sqrt{3}\pi}{3}$ b) 2π **11.** a) 64π

b) 84π

MISCELLANEOUS

Answers to Exercises P. 310-312

1. 0..7-3.9i -2+13i **2.** -2+13i **3.** 0 **4.** 0 **5.** $\dfrac{3-4i}{25}$ **6.** $\dfrac{i+7}{50}$ **7.** 10.33+24.95i **8.** a) $(2, 60^0)$ b) $(\sqrt{2}, 135^0)$

c) $(4, 150^0)$ d) $(2, 240^0)$ **9.** (Cis 300^0) **10.** 12i **11.** 1-A, 2-C, 3-B **12.** 1-A, 2-B, 3-C **13.** a) $x^2+y^2=3x$

b) $x^2+y^2=-2y$ **15.** (3.86, -2.57) **16.** $(4, 60^0)$ **17.** $(2, 330^0)$ **18.** a) $x^2-y^2=1$ b) 2xy=1 c) $(x^2+y^2)^2-2xy=0$

d) $(x^2+y^2)^2=x^2-y^2$ **19.** a) symmetric in x axis b) symmetric in y axis c) symmetric in origin

20. a) $(x^2+y^2)=y$ b) $(x^2+y^2)=4$ c) $(x^2+y^2)=-x$ d) $y=\sqrt{3}x$ e) y=1 f) x=1 g) $(x^2+y^2)=2.\sqrt{x^2+y^2}+3y$

h) $(x^2+y^2)=2.\sqrt{x^2+y^2}-3y$ **21.** a) circle b) line c) spiral d) two leaved rose e) two leaved rose

22. a) $\theta=\pi/4$ b) $\theta=-\pi/4$ c) $\theta=-5\pi/6$ d) r=1 **23.** r=1/2

Answers to Exercises P. 319-320

1. 6<x<22 **2.** x=2-3t, y=-3+4t **3.** 67.17 **4.** $\begin{pmatrix} x \\ y \end{pmatrix}=\begin{pmatrix} 2+4t \\ -3+3t \end{pmatrix}$, $\dfrac{x-2}{4}=\dfrac{y+3}{3}$ **5.** a) 4.84 b) 2.04

c) 2x-0.4y=6.4 **6.** a) vector: $\begin{pmatrix} 3 \\ -2 \end{pmatrix}+t\begin{pmatrix} 1 \\ 2 \end{pmatrix}$, parm: x=3+t, y=-2+2t, cart: y=2x-8 b) vector: $\begin{pmatrix} 1 \\ 3 \end{pmatrix}+t\begin{pmatrix} 1 \\ 1 \end{pmatrix}$,

parm: x=1+t, y=-3+t, cart: y=x+2 c) vector: $\begin{pmatrix} 1 \\ 3 \\ -3 \end{pmatrix}+t\begin{pmatrix} 3 \\ -1 \\ 4 \end{pmatrix}$, parm: x= 1+3t, y=2-t, z=-3+4t,

cart: $\dfrac{x-1}{3}=\dfrac{y-2}{-1}=\dfrac{z+3}{4}$ d) vector: $\begin{pmatrix} 1 \\ 3 \\ 4 \end{pmatrix}+t\begin{pmatrix} 3 \\ -9 \\ 1 \end{pmatrix}$, x= 1+t, y=3-9t, z=t+4, cart: $x-1=\dfrac{y-3}{-9}=z-4$

7. a) 10 b) 5 c) $\begin{pmatrix} 1 \\ 2 \end{pmatrix}$ **8.** (-2, 3, 0) **9.** (8.34;18.34) **10.** 2.11 **11.** 1 and 3 **12.** 13.49 **13.** 7.69 **14.** 2000

Answers to Exercises P. 322-323

1. line - function- Domain: All Real Numbers Range: All Real Numbers **2.** line - function- Domain: All Real Numbers Range: All Real Numbers **3.** function Domain: $x \geq 0$ Range (3, ∞) **4.** function Domain: x >0   Range [1,, ∞), **5.** parabola function Domain: (-∞,∞)   Range [0, ∞) **6** ellipse Domain: (-3, 3) Range (-4, 4) .**7.** ellipse Domain: (-2, 4)   Range (-6, 2) **8.** hyperbole Domain: (-∞,0) (0, ∞) Range: All Real Numbers except zero) **9.** function(0, ∞) Range={1} **10.** line - function- Domain: All Real Numbers Range: All Real Numbers **11.** parabola function Domain: All Real Numbers Range (0, ∞) **12.** Not function Domain={1} Range: All real numbers**13.** not function Domain={2} Range: (0, ∞)**14.** . Not function Domain={-4} Range: All real numbers **15.**function Domain(-1, ∞) Range {1}

Answers to Exercises P. 337-342

1. a) $\dfrac{(x-3)^2}{9} + \dfrac{(y-3)^2}{25} = 1$ b) $\dfrac{(y-3)^2}{16} - \dfrac{(x-3)^2}{9} = 1$ c) $(x-3)^2 + (y+1)^2 = 100$

d) $(y+1)^2 = 20(x+2)$ **2.** $9\pi - 18$ **3.** $\dfrac{-3}{4}(x+2)^2 = y$ **4.**(0.76, 5.24) **5.**$x^2 + y^2 = 169$ **6.** b **7.** c **8.** d

9. $y = -(x-2)^2 - 4$ **10.** $2\sqrt{5}$ **11.**3 **12.** $(x-1)^2 = 8.(y+2)$ **13.** a) circle C(2, -3) r= 4 b) point (2, -3) c) empty set

14. $\dfrac{9\pi}{2}$ **15.**8π **16.** a) Vertex(-2, 1) Focus(-2, $\dfrac{3}{2}$) directrix: $y = \dfrac{1}{2}$ b) Vertex(-1, -2) Focus($\dfrac{-1}{2}$,-2)

directrix: $y = \dfrac{-3}{2}$ c) Vertex(-1, 0) Focus(-2, 0) directrix: y axis d) Vertex(0, 1) Focus(0, 2)

directrix: x axis **17.**a) major axis length: 10 minor axis length: 6 e= 0.8 C(0, 0) Focus($\pm$4,0)

directrices: x= $\pm\dfrac{5}{0.8}$ L = 15/8 A=15π b) major axis length: 10 minor axis length: 8 e= 0.6 C(0, 0)

Focus(0, ± 3) directrices: $y = \pm\dfrac{5}{0.6}$ L = 6.4 A=20π c) major axis length: 4 minor axis length: 2 e= 0.8

C(1, -2) Focus(-3, -2) (5, -2) directrices: x= 7.25 x= -5.25 L = 3.6 A=15π d) (1, -2) point e) Empty Set
f) major axis length: 10 minor axis length: 8 e= 0.6 C(-3, 1) Focus(-3, 4) (-3, -3) directrices: y= 9.33

y= -7.33 L = 6.4 A=20π **18.** C(1, -2) F(1, -2) F(1, -7) e=(5/3) asymptotes: y-5 = $\dfrac{-7}{4}(x+3)$,

y-1= $\dfrac{-3}{4}(x+3)$ directrices: y= -0.2 y= -3.8 transverse axis length: 6 conjugate axis length: 8

LR: (32/3) b) C(0, 0) V(4, 0) v(-4, 0) F(5, 0) F(-5, 0) e: 1.25 asymptotes: y= $\dfrac{3x}{4}$ y= $\dfrac{-3x}{4}$

directrices: x=$\pm$3.2 transverse axis length: 8 conjugate axis length: 6 c) C(0, 0) V(0, 5) v(0, -5) F(0, 13)

F(0, -13) e: 2.6 asymptotes: y= $\dfrac{\pm 5}{12}x$ directrices: y=$\pm$1.92 transverse axis length: 10

conjugate axis length: 24 **20.** a-i b-ii c-iii d- iv **21.** a, b, c, f, g **22.** a, b, c, d, e, f, g, h **23.** a) y= $\mp\dfrac{3x}{4}$

b) y= $\pm$x c) y= $\pm$x d) x=-1, y=1 e) x=0, y= -1 f) x=1, y=-2 **25.** $(x-5)^2 = 12(y+1)$
26. a) $(x-2)^2 + (y+2)^2 = 4$ b) $x^2 + y^2 = 169$ c) $(x+5)^2 + (y-2)^2 = 25$ d) $(x-3)^2 + (y-4)^2 = 25$

Answers to Exercises P. 346-352
1. 5 **2.** 2.98 **3.** 14.33 **4.** 33, **5.** 1.75: **6.** 11 sum=88573 **7.**161, sum=30751 **8.** 0.2 **9.** a) 132 b) 5
10. 14000 **11.** 14693.28 **12.** a) 41 b) 246 **13.** 65.98 **14.** . a) 3.702 b) 3.702 c) 3.702**15.**39 **16.** 5610
17. a) arithmetic b) a_1= -1 d=6 c) 6n-7 d) 53 **18.** f(2n) - f(n) **19.** -1 **20.** 1 **21.** 2^{64} -1 **22.** 1/16 **23.** 1/26

Answers to Exercises P. 350

1. A, B **2.** C, E **3.** C **4.** increases 16 times **5.** a) 5/32 b) $\dfrac{5\sqrt{3}}{2}$

Answers to Exercises P. 351-352

1. 0.15 **2.** 0.71 **3.** a) 0 b) -12/5 c) -25/3 **4.**13, **5.**-1/3: **6.** a) 4 b) $\dfrac{-4}{3x+4}$ c) -4/9 d) -4/3 e) yes f) yes .**7.** { 2.29, 3.23}

Answers to Exercises P. 353-354
1. 60 **2.** 14 **3.**126

Answers to Exercises P. 357

1. Inverse: If x= 6 then x^2=36, Converse: If $x^2 \neq$ =36 then x≠6   Contrapositive: If x^2=36 then x= 6
Negation: x ≠ 6 and x^2=36 **2.** All always use umbrella. b) Some numbers are not real.
c) x= -2 and $x^2 \neq 4$ d) Some people will not die one day. e) All people are not brunettes
f) for all x, $x^2 \neq 1$ g) Every lady is not a blonde . **3.** any negative number **4.** If $x^2 \neq 4$ then x ≠ 2
5. Let the roots of x^2=5 be rational.

Answers to Exercises P. 363

1. -5.26, 2.121, 3.138 **2.** a) 5, -2 b) 1, 2 and -1 **3.** a) $\begin{bmatrix} 4 & -5 & -5 \\ -8 & 5 & 13 \end{bmatrix}$ b) not possible c) $\begin{bmatrix} -9 & 20 & 6 \\ -1 & 15 & -7 \\ -4 & -5 & 11 \end{bmatrix}$

d) $\begin{bmatrix} -6 & 7 & -11 \\ 10 & -27 & 35 \end{bmatrix}$ e) $\begin{bmatrix} 30 & 4 \\ 4 & 5 \end{bmatrix}$ f) not possible g) $\begin{bmatrix} 9 & 58 \\ -29 & -194 \end{bmatrix}$

h) $\begin{bmatrix} 1.5 & 0.5 \\ -0.25 & -0.25 \end{bmatrix}$

Answers to Exercises P. 367-374

Rate Problems 1. plane: 675 wind: 75 **2.** 36mph, 45 mph **3.** 200 mile, 220 miles **4.** 2 hrs **5.** 8.75,
13.75 mph **6.** 20 miles **7.** 2 mph **8.** 70 kmph **9.** 12h **10.** 8hr **11.** 60mph **12.** 25 and 30 min

Mixture Problems 1. 290 **2.** 50 **3.** 30lt **4.**260 adults 740 children **5.**50lt **6.** 200 pounds of each **7.** 1lt
8.3 **9.** $\dfrac{x.(c-b)}{a-b}$ **10.** $\dfrac{10}{3}$ quarts **11.** $\dfrac{40}{3}$

Work-Pool Problems 1. Ekin: 9days Emine: 4.5days **2.** 1.85 hr **3.** 3.93 hr **4.**6 hr **5.**3 days **6.** 9 days
7. 6.75 days **8.**8 hours **9.** 6 and 3 hours **10.** 10. 8 hr **11.** 75 hr **12.** 10.6 **13.** 1 **14.** 2.963

Age Problems 1.2 **2.** 30 **3.** N: 7 M: 15

Investment Problems 1. 1520: 9% 24080: 6% **2.** 9000$: 6 %, 12000$: 11% **3.** 16800: 4% 19800: 6%
4.13200$: 5% 8700 $: 6%

Fraction Word Problems 1. a) 30 b) 900million gallons of gas **2.** 280$ **3.** 60 **4.**12

Miscellaneous Word Problems 1. 3n+7 **2.** 5x-20 **3.** $\dfrac{13}{14}$ **4.** 8 **5.** 192 more than Ferhan and 128 more

than Gizem **6.** $\dfrac{100.(9-a^2)}{a^2}$% **7.** a) 6 b) 128 sec c) $2(\sqrt{k}-1)$ **8.** (2k-1) . (x/k) **9.** 114 **10.** 30$ **11.** 8, 3,
3 **12.** 4 **13.** 1000x/12 **14.** 20 **15.** 30 **16.** c(a+b(x-1)) =a+b(y-1) **17.** 33.3% **18.** 102.4$ **19.** 280.175 **20.**
10, 20 **21.** 12$ **22.** a, b **23.** a) 100 b) 39 **24.** 22, 28 **25.** 4 quarters and 4 dimes **26.** 800, 600 **27.** 270
pounds each **28.** 63 **29.** 1, 2, 3, 4 or 5 **30** . 10 **31.**53 **32.** a) 110 b) 100 **33.**91 **34.** 111 **35.**7

Absolute value function	52
Absolute values	5
Absolute value transformations on functions	71
Additional trigonometric functions with TI	147
Advanced graphing of transformations on functions	68
Age problems	370
Algebra and basics	3
All powers of tangent and cotangent	141
Amplitude in a trigonometric model	142
Angle between two lines	83
Angle in standard position	115
Angle of elevation and angle of depression	116
Angles	248
Arc length and area of a sector	124
Arc length and area of a sector when central angle is given in degrees	124
Arc length and area of a sector when central angle is given in radians	124
Area of a closed convex figure	84
Area of a triangle	136
Area of the ellipse	326 – 327
Arithmetic mean	8
Arithmetic sequences and series	343
Associative property	351
Asymptotes of the hyperbola	330
Axis of symmetry of the parabola	335
Axis of wave in a trigonometric model	142
Basic functions	52
Basis vectors	315
Binary operations	351
Binomial	102
Binomial probabilities	221
Binomial theorem	209
Built in trigonometric functions in TI	147
Cartesian (rectangular) form of a line	317
Chimney function	53
Circle	324
Circle equation	115
Circle inscribed in a quadrilateral	291
Circle inscribed in a square	291
Circle inscribed in a triangle	292
Circle inscribed in an equilateral triangle	293
Circle inscribed in an isosceles triangle	293
Circles	273
Closure property	351
Coefficients of a polynomial function	102
Combined events	215
Common rotations	298
Common transformations on trigonometric functions	127
Commonly used formulas in sigma notation	346
Commutative property	351
Complement of a set	214
Completing the square	33 – 97
Complex numbers, polar coordinates and graphing	307
Composition of transformations	60

Computer programs	353
Conditional probability	216
Cone inscribed in a sphere	295
Congruence	263
Conic sections in two dimensions	246 – 321
Conjugate axis of the hyperbola	330
Conjunction	355
Constant function	20
Constant polynomial	102
Constant term of a polynomial function	102
Continuity	180
Contradiction	355
Contrapositive of a logical statement	355
Converse of a logical statement	355
Coordinates of the center of the ellipse	326 – 327
Coordinates of the center of the hyperbola	330
Cos^{-1}x	144
Cosine function	54
Cosine rule	136
Cosx	140
Cot^{-1}x	144
Cotx	140
Counting by multiplication	195
Cramer's rule for 2 unknowns	362
Cramer's rule for 3 unknowns	362
Csc^{-1}x	144
Cscx	140
Cube – root function	52
Cube function	52
Cube inscribed in a sphere	294
Cubic polynomial	102
Cubic term of a polynomial function	102
Cylinder inscribed in a cone	296
Cylinder inscribed in a sphere	295
De Moivre's identities	307
Definition of a function	16
Definition of an angle	115
Definition of combination	195
Definition of permutation	195
Degree of the polynomial function	102
Descartes' rule of signs	106
Determinants	361
Diagonal matrix	360
Difference between permutation and combination	198
Difference between two sets	213
Direct variation	349
Direction cosines of a line	317
Direction vector of a line	317
Directrices of the ellipse	326 – 327
Directrices of the hyperbola	330
Directrix of the parabola	335
Discrete data	229
Disjunction	355
Distance between two points in three dimensions	319
Distance between two points in two dimensions	79
Distance from a point to a line	83

Distance from a point to a plane	318
Domain of a hyperbolic rational function	334
Domain of logarithms	170
Domains and ranges inverse trigonometric functions	145
Domains and ranges of trigonometric functions	139
Domains of specific functions	22
Double angle formulas	134
Double implication	355
Easy Trigonometric identities	125
Eccentricity of the ellipse	326 – 327
Eccentricity of the hyperbola	330
Eccentricity of the parabola	335
Eccentricity of the parabola	335
Ellipse	326
Ellipses in standard position (x – ellipse and y – ellipse)	326 – 327
Equilateral triangle inscribed in a circle	292
Equivalent of a logical statement	355
Euler's identity	307
Even and odd trigonometric functions	139
Even powers of sine and cosine	141
Evenness and oddness	45
Evenness and oddness explored algebraically	45
Evenness and oddness explored graphically	45
Evenness and oddness in polynomial functions	45
Evenness and oddness in relations given algebraically	45
Evenness and oddness in relations given as sets	45
Event	214
Existence of limit	180
Explicit definition of a geometric sequence	343
Explicit definition of an arithmetic sequence	343
Exploring limits with TI	182
Exponential and logarithmic functions	166
Exponential decay	166
Exponential decay function	54
Exponential growth	166
Exponential growth function	54
Exponents	166
Factor theorem	104
Factorial notation	195
Finding a trigonometric model	142
Finding other function when the composition and one function are given	28
Finding the equation of a line using regression	88
Finite sequence	343
Finite series	343
Foci of the ellipse	326 – 327
Foci of the hyperbola	330
Focus of the parabola	335
Fraction word problems	371
Fractions	4
Frequency	229
Frequency in a trigonometric model	142
Function compositions and inverses	28
Functions	16
Functions and cofunctions in trigonometry	125
General form of a line	81
Geometric mean	8

Geometric sequences and series	343
Geometric transformations	56
Geometry basics	239
Given the roots, construct the equation	94
Graphs of trigonometric functions	140
Greatest integer function	53 - 188
Hard Trigonometric identities	125
Harmonic mean	8
Hole of a Rational function	180
Horizontal asymptote of a hyperbolic rational function	334
Horizontal asymptote of a Rational function	180
Horizontal line test	17
Horizontal shifts on functions	68
Horizontal shrink – stretch on functions	69
How to find the inverse of a function	27
Hyperbola	330
Hyperbolas in standard position (x – hyperbola and y – hyperbola)	330
Hyperbolas in the form xy = k	334
Hyperbolic rational function (decreasing)	55
Hyperbolic rational function (increasing)	55
Hyperbolic rational functions	180 – 334
Identity element	351
Identity function	20 – 52
Identity matrix	360
Implication	355
Independent events	215
Indirect proof	355
Inequalities	4
Infinite geometric series	344
Infinite sequence	343
Infinite series	343
Inscribed figures in three dimensions	294
Inscribed figures in two dimensions	291
Integral polynomial	102
Intersectionof two sets	213
Interval notation	3
Into function	19
Inverse element	351
Inverse of a function on functions	72
Inverse of a logical statement	355
Inverse of a matrix	360
Inverse transformations	59
Inverse trigonometric functions	144
Inverse variation	349
Inverses of specific functions	31
Investment problems	370
Isometry in transformations	56
Isosceles triangle inscribed in a circle	293
Leading coefficient of a polynomial function	102
Leading term of a polynomial function	102
Length of latus rectum of the ellipse	326 – 327
Length of latus rectum of the hyperbola	330
Length of major axis of the ellipse	326 – 327
Length of minor axis of the ellipse	326 – 327
Length of the latus rectum of the parabola	335
Letters in the English alphabet	4

Limits at infinity	180
Line equations	85
Line passing through the origin	52
Line symmetry	63
Linear combination of two vectors	314
Linear functions	79
Linear interpolation	88
Linear models	88
Linear polynomial	102
Linear term of a polynomial function	102
Lists and charts in probability	217
Lists in probability	217
Locus	245
Logarithmic function (decreasing)	54
Logarithmic function (increasing)	54
Logarithmic inequalities	170
Logarithms	169
Logic	355
Logical statement	355
Magnitude of a vector	313
Many to one function	19
Matrices	358
Matrices and determinants	358
Matrix arithmetic	358
Matrix multiplication	358
Matrix transposition	361
Mean	229
Means	8
Median	229
Midpoint of a line segment	79
Miscellaneous word problems	371
Mixture problems	368
Mode	229
Monomial	102
Most common graphing calculator techniques	13
Multivariable function	20
Mutually exclusive events	215
Necessary condition in an implication	355
Necklace – bracelet problem	196
Negation of a logical statement	355
Negation of conjunction	355
Negation of disjunction	355
Negations in logic	355
Negative and fractional powers of binomials	211
Negative of a vector	313
Number sets	3
Odd powers of sine and cosine	141
Odds against an event	215
Odds in favor of an event	215
Offset in a trigonometric model	142
One to one function	19
Onto function	19
Operations on functions	26
Parabola	335
Parabola and a line	97
Parabolas in standard position	335

Parallelogram in the cartesian plane	80
Parametric equations and parametric graphing	319
Parametric form of a line	317
Pascal's triangle	210
Period in a trigonometric model	142
Periodic functions	36
Periodicity	141
Permutations and combinations	195
Perpendicular bisector of a line segment	87
Phase shift in a trigonometric model	142
Plane equation	316
Point symmetry	64
Polar coordinates	307
Polar graphing with TI	309
Polar to rectangular conversion	307
Polygons	252
Polynomial functions	20 – 102
Polynomial identities	103
Population	229
Position vector	313
Possibility space charts in probability	217
Probability	213
Probability of an event	214
Properties of combinations	199
Properties of complex numbers	308
Properties of determinants	361
Properties of higher degree polynomial functions	103
Properties of the real numbers	3
Quadratic functions	93
Quadratic models	98
Quadratic polynomial	102
Quadratic term of a polynomial function	102
Quadrilateral inscribed in a circle	291
Quadrilaterals	269
Quartic polynomial	102
Quartic term of a polynomial function	102
Quartiles	229
Quintic polynomial	102
Quintic term of a polynomial function	102
Radian and degree	123
Range	229
Range in a trigonometric model	144
Range of a hyperbolic rational function	334
Rate problems	367
Rational functions	180
Rational polynomial	102
Rational root theorem	105
Real polynomial	102
Reciprocal function	53
Reciprocal of a function	73
Rectangle inscribed in a circle	292
Rectangular box inscribed in a sphere	294
Rectangular coordinates	307
Rectangular to polar conversion	307
Recursive definition of a geometric sequence	344
Recursive definition of an arithmetic sequence	343

Reference angle	125
Reflections in the x – axis on functions	71
Reflections in the y – axis on functions	69
Reflections in three dimensions	319
Reflections of functions	35
Reflections of points in the cartesian plane	87
Relation between zeros and coefficients	106
Remainder theorem	104
Repeated permutations	197
Resultant vector	313
Roots of a quadratic equation	93
Round table problem	196
Rules of divisibility	5
Sample	229
Sample space	214
Scalar	313
Scalar product, dot product or inner product	315
Sec^{-1}x	144
Secx	140
Semicircles centered at the origin	325
Sequences	343
Sequences and series	343
Series	343
Set theory in brief	213
Sigma notation	346
Signs of trigonometric functions	121
Similarity	265
Sin^{-1}x	144
Sine function	54
Sine rule	135
Sinx	140
Slope – intercept form of a line	81
Slope of a line segment	81
Solving equations with TI 83 – 84	13
Solving inequalities with TI 83 – 84	13
Solving inverse trigonometric equations with TI	145
Solving trigonometric equations with the TI	128
Solving trigonometric inequalities with TI	131
Special angles	121
Special angles in trigonometry: 0°, 90°, 180°, 270°, 360°	122
Special angles in trigonometry: 30°, 60°	122
Special angles in trigonometry: 45°	121
Sphere equation	319
Sphere inscribed in a cone	295
Sphere inscribed in a cube	294
Square function	52
Square inscribed in a circle	292
Square root function	52
Statistics	229
Sufficient condition in an implication	355
Sum and difference formulas	134
Sum and product of the roots of a quadratic equation	94
Sum of the first n terms of a geometric series	344
Sum of the first n terms of an arithmetic series	343
Symmetry and rotations	63
Synthetic division	107

Table of transformations on functions	74
Tables of outcomes in probability	218
Tan⁻¹x	144
Tanx	140
Tautology	355
Tests for symmetry of functions	46
The unit circle	325
The universal set	213
Three by three determinant	361
Three dimensional loci	246
Three Dimensişonal line equation	317
Three-dimensional geometry	284
TI calculator usage in statistics	230
TI usage for complex numbers	308
TI usage for the Greatest integer function	188
Transformations – enlargement	58
Transformations – reflection	57
Transformations – rotation	56
Transformations – shear	58
Transformations – stretch	57
Transformations – translation	58
Transverse axis of the hyperbola	330
Tree diagrams in probability	220
Triangle inscribed in a circle	292
Triangles	254
Triangular matrices	360
Trigonometric equations	128
Trigonometric identities	125
Trigonometric ratios in the right triangle	116
Trinomial	102
Truth table for And	356
Truth table for Implication	356
Truth table for Or	356
Truth tables in logic	356
Two by two determinant	361
Two by two matrices	360
Two dimensional loci	245
Two lines (general form)	82
Two lines (slope – intercept form)	82
Two vectors being parallel	315
Two vectors being perpendicular	315
Types of functions	19
Types of symmetry	63
Types of transformations	56
Union of two sets	213
Unit circle	121
Unit conversions	4
Unit vector	315
Variance and standard deviation	229
Variation	349
Vector	313
Vector form of a line	317
Vectors and three dimensional coordinate geometry	313
Venn diagrams	216
Vertex of the parabola	335
Vertical asymptote of a hyperbolic rational function	334

Vertical asymptote of a Rational function	180
Vertical line test	17
Vertical shifts on functions	70
Vertical shrink – stretch on functions	70
Vertices of the ellipse	326 – 327
Vertices of the hyperbola	330
When coordinates of center is (h,k) in a hyperbola	331
When coordinates of center is (h,k) in an ellipse	327
When coordinates of the vertex is (h,k) in a parabola	336
Word problems	364
Work – pool problems	369
x, y, z intercepts	316
xy, xz, yz traces	316
Zero matrix	360
Zero of a Rational function	180
Zero polynomial	102

THE LEGENDARY PREP MATERIAL FOR SAT MATH LEVEL 2

(FORMERLY KNOWN AS 2C)

15 Realistic Tests for the SAT Math Level 2 Subject Test

This book contains 15 full length model practice tests that simulate the SAT Math Level 2 subject test. Each test is up to date and true to life reflecting the latest question types. The tests come with answers and solutions along with two additional chapters, one on the description of the real test and the other on the most effective graphing calculator techniques to make a student's life easier on the real test. The model tests have been produced in a course of 5 years by a perfect scorer team; therefore they are very useful for diagnosing weaknesses and getting more questions right; therefore this book promises a higher score for the ones who use it.

"Shorten 40 hours of college preparatory precalculus study to an easy 4 hours…"

- The usage of the TI 83 – TI 84 family of graphing calculators particularly in the context of Algebra, Pre-Calculus and SAT and IB Mathematics with over 400 questions carefully designed and fully solved questions;
- A detailed additional chapter on TI 89 with a special focus on the algebra menu and the graphing facilities of this device;
- 10 original and fully solved sample tests 5 or Level 1 and 5 for Level 2.

This book is intended to help high school students who are bound to take either or both of the SAT Math Level 1 and Level 2 tests. Being one of a kind, this book is devoted to the usage of the TI 83 – TI 84 family of graphing calculators particularly in the context of Algebra, Pre-Calculus and SAT and IB Mathematics with over 400 questions carefully designed and fully solved questions. The method proposed in this book has been developed through 5 years' experience; has been proven to work and has created a success story each and every time, having helped hundreds of students who are currently attending the top 50 universities in the USA including many Ivy League schools.

The main advantage of the approach suggested in this book is that, one can solve, any equation or inequality with the TI, whether it is algebraic, trigonometric, exponential, logarithmic, polynomial or one that involves absolute values, without needing to know the related topic in depth and having to perform tedious steps One can solve all types of equations and inequalities very easily and in a very similar way just needing to learn a few very easy to remember techniques.

However there are still more to what can be done with the TI; find period, frequency, amplitude, offset, axis of wave of a periodic function, find the maxima minima and zeros as well as the domains and ranges of all types of functions; perform any operations on complex numbers, carry out any computation involving sequences and series, perform matrix algebra, solve a system of equations for any number of unknowns and even write small programs to ease your life. More than 20 of the 50 questions in the SAT Mathematics Subject Tests are based on the topics given above and this is why this book upgrades the SAT Mathematics subject test scores by at least 200 points.

Topics covered are:

- **EQUATIONS:** Polynomial, Algebraic, Absolute Value, Exponential and Logarithmic, Trigonometric, Inverse Trigonometric
- **INEQUALITIES:** Polynomial, Algebraic and Absolute Value, Trigonometric
- **FUNCTIONS:** Maxima and Minima, Domains and Ranges, Evenness and Oddness, Graphs of Trigonometric Functions, the Greatest Integer Function
- **BASIC CALCULUS:** Zeros, Holes, Limits, Continuity, Horizontal and Vertical Asymptotes
- **CONIC SECTIONS:** Circle, Ellipse, Parabola and Hyperbola
- **LINEAR ALGEBRA:** System of Linear Equations, Matrices and Determinants
- **MISCELLANEOUS:** Parametric and Polar Graphing; Complex Numbers; Permutations and Combinations, Computer Programs, Sequences and Series, Statistics, and more…

THE LEGENDARY

10 Realistic SAT II Math IC Test Booklets

available at

www.amazon.com

- 10 full length practice tests in one volume one for the SAT II Math Level 1 Subject Test.
- Each test comes with answers and a score conversion table.
- Each model test is on a separate booklet, for easier & more efficient use.
- Ideal for diagnosing the weaknesses and getting more questions right on the actual tests.,
- Learn to pace oneself.
- Although SAT II tests are not released by the College Board, our team members have taken each and every SAT II Math test that has been administered in the past 6 years; therefore the tests prepared by our team are "up-to-date" and "true-to-life".
- We have more than %90 match on the SAT II Math question types.
- Therefore the real test will not be a surprise any more for a college bound student and higher score is guaranteed.
- The motivation behind writing these this book was to provide enough study materials as there was a gap in this area.
- Solutions on site: w w w . r u s h s o c i e t y . c o m

About the Author

Ruşen* Meylani is the co – founder of **RUSH** Publications and Educational Consultancy, LLC. Born on the 2nd of August, 1972 he shows all the leadership characteristics of a Leo. He was awarded many times in mathematics since the age of 14 and he holds a Master of Science degree in Electrical and Electronics Engineering having written tens of papers in this field. When he was a graduate student (between 1995 and 1997), he invented three methods that are currently being used with sophisticated printing devices, the last generation white goods, and, the state of the art quality control systems. He worked in the field of Information Technology where he was the leader of a team that built the wide area network of a major supermarket chain in Europe.

In 1998 he decided to build a career in education listening to the sound of his heart and that was it. He created a method that shortens 40 hours of mathematics to 4 hours gaining the attraction of Eisenhower National Clearinghouse funded by the US Department of Education. In 2004 and 2005 he gave several conferences in the United States on this particular method. In the mean time he published three SAT II Mathematics books that became bestselling among their peers in Amazon just in a few months. He has 15 other books that will have all been published by mid 2007. He is a researcher, educator and academician having taught at several distinguished institutions at the K9 – 12, undergraduate and graduate levels, all in Europe. He has dedicated his life to creating easy to teach and easy to learn methods in mathematics. He considers himself as a "gifted loony" as he claims that one day it will be possible to shorten the learning time to less than one tenth of the usual. When people ask him about how it will be done, he borrows Albert Einstein's words: "If at first the idea is not absurd then there is no hope for it."

However, he is not an "all work, no play" type of person. He is a guitar player, poet and story writer being awarded several times in the United States for his poems. He is also a great movie watcher. He is happily married to the sweetest genius lady who is crazy enough to marry him. The couple has created their own language which is the funniest way of communication that has ever existed in the world.

Ruşen Meylani's motto is somewhat similar to Robert Kennedy's: "Some men see things as they are and say 'Why?' I see the things that never were and say 'Why not!' "

www.rusenmeylani.com

---

*ş is pronounced as "sh" like in "Ash Wednesday" (a poem by T.S. Elliot)

collegeboard.com

SAT Registration & Scores

SAT Registration

RUSEN MEYLANI

Update SAT Personal Info

Date	Test	Score	Percentile*	Status
10/2002	**SAT II**			Test Completed
	Math Level 1 w/Calculator	800	99	
	Physics	800	93	
05/2002	**SAT II**			Test Completed
	Math Level 1 w/Calculator	800	99	
	Math Level 2 w/Calculator	800	90	
	Physics	800	93	
06/2000	**SAT II**			Test Completed
	Math Level 1 w/Calculator	800	99	
	Math Level 2 w/Calculator	800	90	
	Physics	800	93	
05/2000	**SAT II**			Test Completed
	Math Level 1 w/Calculator	800	99	
	Math Level 2 w/Calculator	800	90	